Robert J. Mason and Mark T. Mattson
ATLAS OF UNITED STATES ENVIRONMENTAL ISSUES

CORRIGENDA

page 9   legend next to gray box, lower right corner,
            should read "Dry Domain and Prairies" instead of
            "Grass and Shrubland"

page 45   colors in lower two boxes of key are incorrect.
            "Probably ineffective" should be orange instead of
            yellow; "Ineffective" should be red instead of light
            green

page 87   table in upper right corner should be
            accompanied by note: ANC = Acid Neutralizing
            Capacity. Lakes with ANC less than or equal to
            $0 \mu eq L^{-1}$ have no capacity to neutralize acid.

page 90   Bar key in lower right corner should carry legend:
            "Million Gallons per Day"

page 93   light green, north central area of map currently
            labeled "Great Basin" should be labeled "Missouri
            Basin"

page 154   bars in chart designating South Atlantic: 1986
            Natural Gas consumption = 1,095 trillion BTUs;
            1986 Petroleum consumption = 4,275 trillion
            BTUs

Atlas of
United States Environmental Issues

Atlas of
United States Environmental Issues

Robert J. Mason and Mark T. Mattson

Macmillan Publishing Company
New York

Collier Macmillan Canada
Toronto

Maxwell Macmillan International
New York Oxford Singapore Sydney

Macmillan Publishing Company
A Division of Macmillan, Inc.
866 Third Avenue, New York, N.Y. 10022

Collier Macmillan Canada, Inc.
1200 Eglinton Avenue East, Suite 200
Don Mills, Ontario M3C 3N1

Library of Congress Catalog Card Number: 90-43707

Printed in the United States of America

printing number
1 2 3 4 5 6 7 8 9 10

Library of Congress Cataloging-in-Publication Data

Mason, Robert J.
       Atlas of United States environmental issues

       Includes bibliographical references and index.
       1. Nature conservation—United States—Maps.
       2. Pollution—Environmental aspects—United
       States—Maps.   3. Natural resources—United
       States—Maps.
       I. Mattson, Mark T.   II. Title.
       III. Title: United States environmental issues.
G1201.G3M3   1990   363.7'00973   90-43707
ISBN   0-02-897261-9

Contents

Figures

viii

Tables

Foreword

Where is America headed as we prepare to enter the twenty-first century? Have we irrevocably laid waste to once pristine natural resources? Are clean air, pure water, and open space relics of the past?

Today our cities are plagued with smog and blighted by neighborhoods too dangerous to enter. Highways are congested and noisy, public transportation systems inadequate and expensive, and water and sewage facilities often antiquated. The air we breathe is laden with a wide variety of toxic and hazardous chemicals: so much so that tens of thousands of sick and elderly people must stay inside many days of the year. Solutions are slow in coming, and those that have emerged fall far short of the mark.

The widespread use of chlorofluorocarbons has damaged, perhaps irreparably, the ozone layer. As a result, our vulnerability to skin cancers is expected to increase substantially in coming decades. During the long hot summers of the 1980s, the "greenhouse effect" became a topic of national and indeed international concern. Carbon dioxide and other trace gases from factories, power plants, and vehicles are altering global climate in ways that we are just beginning to understand. Toxic wastes have infiltrated our groundwater and streams, poisoned our drinking water, and fouled our beaches. Radon gas in many areas is a menace to homeowners and schoolchildren and is now the second leading cause of lung cancer.

One of our primary energy sources, oil, is in the headlines almost daily. One accident after another contaminates precious coastal waters with oil and devastates marine and terrestrial ecosystems. Nuclear power and its accompanying wastes present us with the task of separating what is essential for our energy needs and what is safe for those who live and work near nuclear plants.

Even the food we eat is a matter of renewed concern as people become more alarmed about the pesticides used in its production. Indeed, the widely publicized health risks posed by specific chemicals—such as the pesticide alar—are prompting us to examine more generally the hazards associated with what we eat.

Our natural environment itself may not survive as we know it. Unless our landscapes are preserved and protected, our children may never experience the vast open spaces on which America has built her history. Nor may they enjoy the smaller, accessible spaces in and near our major urban areas. Farmland and open space are vanishing at the rate of 5,500 acres every day. And many of the wild animals that once roamed the land, if not already extinct or close to it, are seriously endangered.

So, we ask ourselves, "Where do we go from here? How are we to protect America's natural beauty—her spacious skies, her amber waves of grain, her shining seas?" How do we satisfy our basic needs and wants in humane, just ways—while at the same time respecting the "rights of nature"?

There is much to be done. But if we are to find answers, we need to understand the state of the American environment today and especially the ways that we are altering it. The *Atlas of United States Environmental Issues* seeks to do this: It provides a graphic representation of the major environmental concerns facing the nation, accompanied by substantive text, tables, charts, and photographs.

Robert J. Mason and Mark T. Mattson of the Department of Geography and Urban Studies at Temple University have assembled an essential research book. Concerned Americans need just such a tool as we set out to solve the environmental problems of the present—and preserve the beauty of America for ourselves and generations to come.

Peter Kostmayer
Representative, 8th District

Acknowledgments

This atlas, created entirely on the Macintosh, stands as a tribute to Apple's ingenuity. Their generous contribution of several Macintosh workstations helped turn tedious tasks into engaging experiments. For his early work on computer systems design and map preparation, we owe a special debt to Iden Rosenthal. It was he who introduced us to the Macintosh and its mapmaking capabilities. We wish him our best in his current career with the National Oceanic and Atmospheric Administration.

Yvonne Keck Holman of *Alternative Productions* deserves special recognition for time and care spent on editing, design, and copyfitting. Her effort has resulted in a better atlas.

Evan McGinley's dedication and research skills were invaluable. He has an extraordinary capacity to find his way through hard-to-decipher publications and complex bureaucratic channels. Moreover, it is truly a pleasure to work with him.

We also had research assistance from Mark Duffy, Gayle Glover, Yu Wu, and Alberto Zerpa. Scott Fort, John Graybill, Dennis Hayes, Steve Karp, Jennifer Rahn, and Steve Shore provided cartographic assistance. Map librarian Ida Ginsburgs, government documents librarian Martha Henderson, business librarian Barbara Wright, and Mark Jacobs, head of Reference and Information Services at Temple's Paley Library, were especially helpful.

Our work has benefitted from the advice of Sue Lawson of the New Jersey Department of Environmental Protection and David Cuff of Temple University's Department of Geography. Marvin Baker, Associate Professor of Geography at the University of Oklahoma, provided thoughtful criticism throughout.

We also wish to thank our department secretaries, Connie Coates and Brenda Harris. Our department chair, Carolyn Adams, has been exceedingly supportive throughout, as was her predecessor David Bartelt. Lloyd Chilton, Executive Editor at Macmillan, has been with us from the start, offering encouragement and helping us find our way through a long, difficult, seemingly endless process.

Among the many persons in government and the private sector who generously and patiently offered information and advice, we wish to single out the following: Jim Ayer, State Resource Conservationist for Iowa; Dave Barnhold of the Minerals Management Service; Tom Birch and Lloyd Casey of the U.S. Forest Service, Radnor, PA; Margi Böhm of the Western Conifers Research Cooperative; James Bones of the U.S. Forest Service; Earl Brabb and Al Rogers of USGS (Geologic Risk Assessment); Jane Bullock of the Federal Emergency Management Agency; David Crawford of Kitts Peak National Observatory; Nancy Bushwick of Resources for the Future; Sandy Crystal of EPA's Office of Emergency and Remedial Response; Carroll Curtis of the Virginia Institute of Marine Science; Tom Dahl and Ralph Tiner of the U.S. Fish and Wildlife Service; Shelly Dresser of the Council of State Governments; Dana Duxbury of Dana Duxbury and Associates; Bill Fecke and Gerald Root of the Soil Conservation Service; Sharon Edmonds, former hydrologic information assistant with USGS; Len Gianessi of Resources for the Future; Sharon Green of the Conservation Foundation; Ralph Heimlich and Roger Hexam of USDA (Economic Research Service); Gerry Hertel, Forest Response Program, national manager; Susan Husband of the University of Arizona's Center for Creative Photography; Dorothy Leonard of NOAA's Strategic Assessment Branch; Dave Lewis of the Bureau of the Census in Philadelphia; Pat Lockeridge of the National Geophysical Data Center; Ann Mattheis of *Waste Age* magazine; Larry Mirandi of the National Conference of State Legislatures; David Morton of the Natural Hazards Research and Applications Information Center; Volker Mohnen of the Atmospheric Sciences Research Center (SUNY Albany); John Papp of the U.S. Bureau of Mines; Frances Sussman of the Congressional Budget Office, Chris Rice of EPA's Office of Public Affairs; Jim Riggs of the Association of State Park Directors; Mike Rogers of the National Park Service; Richard Smith of the USGS (Water Resources Division); Dave Stonefields of EPA's Office of Air Quality Planning and Standards; and Jack Wittmann of USGS (National Mapping Division).

To all, our thanks. And of course reprieve from any responsibility for errors or omissions.

Introduction 1

The United States leads the world in consumption of natural resources. It ranks fourth in land area, fourth in population, and third in per capita income. As a result, it faces a set of environmental issues quite different from those confronting other industrialized nations. Paradoxically, the United States both leads and lags in its efforts to come to terms with these problems.

The American experience has been shaped by an exceptional combination of physical, cultural, and historical circumstances. While this country is blessed with an abundance of natural resources—including vast areas of wilderness—it also possesses a national mentality that has traditionally regarded those resources as limitless. The cultural geographer Wilbur Zelinsky (1973) identifies four "culture themes":

1. an intense, almost anarchistic individualism
2. a high valuation placed upon mobility and change
3. a mechanistic vision of the world
4. a messianic perfectionism

In the broadest sense, these themes portray a population that is always on the move; the persistence of rural values in an urbanized society; a general antagonism toward planning; a mechanistic, utilitarian view of natural resources and their exploitation; and a moralistic national vision. These generalizations obviously cannot fully explain our complicated and seemingly contradictory attitudes toward nature and environment, but they can take us a long way in understanding the contexts that have nurtured them. Each of these culture themes is interwoven with the issues taken up below. This volume deals mainly with recent environmental issues and our responses to them, with only occasional references to their historical contexts. It is useful at the outset, therefore, to make brief mention of the history of environmentalism in the United States.

Three major eras can be identified. The first is the Progressive Era of the late 1800s and early 1900s (roughly 1890 to 1920). It

Half Dome, Yosemite National Park.
R. Mason.

was, in fact, just prior to this era that the United States began to establish national parks, starting with Yellowstone in 1872. The early parks, including those designated during the Progressive Era, conformed to a congressional imperative that only "worthless" lands be set aside in perpetuity: that is, lands with little to no apparent mineral, timber, or other economic value.

Succinctly stated, the Progressive idea of conservation is this: The greatest long-term good should accrue to the greatest numbers of people. Resources should be managed wisely and scientifically, above and beyond the fray of day-to-day politics. Prior to 1905, however, such was not the case for most of the federal estate. In that year, management of the national forest reserves (established under the Forest Reserve Act of 1891) was transferred from the General Land Office to the newly created Forest Service. At that time the service was under the then-visionary leadership of Gifford Pinchot, the preeminent spokesman for conservationist thinking. Pinchot had headed the former Division of Forestry (Department of Agriculture) since 1898 and had already made great headway in promoting the "multiple use" concept. This policy—which provides for a combination of grazing, lumbering, power generation, and water-quality protection—guides national forest management to this day.

Although Pinchot's scientific brand of stewardship was fully and officially exercised over only a portion of the federal domain, its influence spread much further. Indeed, President Theodore Roosevelt in large part subscribed to the conservationist ideals that Pinchot held so dear. Roosevelt, Pinchot, and Secretary of the Interior James R. Garfield were instrumental in setting up a leasing system for grazing lands outside the national forest system (although the era of the "free range" did not fully come to an end until the Taylor Grazing Act—described in chapter 5—was passed in 1934). The multiple-use concept that had been applied to national forests was also promoted by the Bureau of Reclamation in its western water-development projects. Dams were to be used not only to provide irrigation water but also for electric power generation, flood control, and provision of recreation.

The mechanistic world view of the Progressive conservationists stood in counterpoint to that of the emerging preservation movement. It was in the late 1800s that the Sierra Club was founded by John Muir, one of the most prominent and revered preservationists in U.S. history. The preservationists saw great value in setting aside lands for the sole purpose of preservation. Conservationists, by contrast, saw ecological or landscape preservation not as an end in itself but rather as a means for providing for future resource needs. Indeed, the conflicts that developed during the Progressive Era set the stage for many of the environmental debates of succeeding decades.

The second major period of environmental concern and action accompanied the economic recovery following the Great Depression. Franklin Delano Roosevelt's New Deal policies, programs, and projects were marked by an unprecedented degree of government intervention in the market economy and concern about economic equity and social welfare. Resource policies sought not only to conserve natural resources but also to promote individual and collective human welfare. The activities of the Civilian Conservation Corps, the Works Progress Administration, the Tennessee Valley Authority, and the Soil Conservation Service are exemplary of this period. Many of the initiatives stemming from the emphasis on coordinated planning and multiple use of resources have persisted until the present day.

After 1940, energies were directed first toward the war effort and later toward reaping the benefits of postwar economic growth. Environmental concerns were not to reemerge forcefully until the 1960s. The "environmental movement," the beginnings of which may be traced to the early and mid-1960s, blended traditional interests of the earlier phases with new concerns about human and ecosystem health. The environmental movement fostered a level of popular concern, scientific interest, legislation, and adjudication that was without precedent. The National Environmental Policy Act of 1969, the Clean Air Act Amendments of 1970, the Federal Water Pollution Control Act Amendments of 1972, the Wilderness Act of 1964, the Land and Water Conservation Fund Act of 1964, the Coastal Zone Management Act of 1972, and the Forest and Rangeland Renewable Resources Planning Act of 1974 are but a few of the more significant pieces of legislation enacted in the 1960s and 1970s (see appendix 2).

The activism of this era sets the context for this atlas. The environmental initiatives of the 1960s and 1970s are now permanent features of our political and administrative landscapes and undoubtedly shall remain so at least through the remainder of the century. The vigor and effectiveness of these initiatives were diminished somewhat in the Reagan years, but if the administrative intent was to weaken the nation's fundamental commitment to environmental protection, clearly it has not succeeded.

Nonetheless, the Reagan strategy of devolving fiscal and administrative functions from the federal government to states and localities has had its long-term effects. At the same time, important new environmental concerns have emerged at all levels of government. One of the purposes of this atlas is to portray the changing spatial nature of environmental policy administration. The maps and text that follow are meant not to pass judgment on these policies; indeed, they are not sufficient instruments for doing so. They can, however, serve as an overview, a reference source for specific details, and a basis for drawing some general inferences about the changing nature of environmental issues and policy administration in the United States.

Several of the "focus maps"—which deal with specific issues in specific places—help chronicle this country's recent resurgence of environmentalism. East Coast beach pollution, the Alaskan oil spill, wandering cargoes of trash, the 1988 drought, the Yellowstone fires, high urban ozone levels, and revelations about nuclear fuel and weapons plants all drew enormous media attention, and all played important roles in fostering the renewed concern. As we began to develop the atlas, the special importance of this "era" (1988–1990) was of course not immediately evident. But as its importance became increasingly apparent, we tried to interpret recent events in ways that would be useful to scholars interested in this period and to make clear this era's implications for environmental policies of the 1990s and beyond. While myopia is inevitable in a project of such limited duration as this one, we still believe our efforts offer an important perspective on a critical period in the nation's environmental history.

Again, the primary motivation for creating the atlas was to provide an informative, thought-provoking reference work. There are already countless maps, as well as masses of other data, that deal with environmental matters. In this volume, we try to weave together appropriate parts of this vast data base— using existing representations of environmental information and adding many of our own. What emerges is an analysis of the spatial "texture" of the country's environmental condition. The regional, state, and local patterns that present themselves may then be interpreted with reference to variations in the physical environment, settlement patterns, historical trends, political cultures, and fiscal policies in the public and private sectors. The atlas raises questions about the patterns it displays—perhaps attempting to answer a few of them—but more important, it provides its users with information and provokes them to think about these questions. It offers them tools and insights to assist in this endeavor.

How is "environment" defined for these purposes? It is always tempting to subscribe to the broadest possible definition; the result is to exclude nothing. In the interest of producing a coherent, concise atlas, therefore, our definition must to some degree be constrained. The choice of topics and specific issues is guided by the criterion that they link human activity with familiar and valued physical environments. Thus, the "sensible" aspects of environment—air, water, and land—and the activities that most directly affect or are affected by these aspects of the environment are of concern here. The "psychological environment" and environments that are quite thoroughly controlled (e.g., the urban and indoor environments) are not explicitly treated here. This is not in any way to deny their importance to the subject at hand; indeed, they deserve their own treatment in the form of separate books and atlases.

Clearly, there is a rich diversity of material in the chapters of this atlas. One of the greatest difficulties in organizing a volume about environmental matters is that of sorting it into discrete chapters. They all overlap one another. The "focus features" tend especially to cross chapter lines, and this has made their placement in several cases very difficult. Within the limits of practicability, we have sought to cross-reference all our material. But perhaps the reader's best strategy for dealing with overlapping issues is always to bear in mind the complex interrelationships among environmental resources, pollution, and the physical and political contexts within which they occur.

OVERVIEW OF CHAPTERS

The atlas's early chapters provide an introduction and set the context for much of the rest of the book. Chapter 2 illustrates the physical diversity of the country, the extent of urbanization, the transportation network, and population characteristics and trends. Chapter 3 presents a general picture of land use, with particular emphasis on the federal lands and on state and federal land-use planning.

Chapters 4 through 7 offer a more detailed assessment of specific types of land and associated resource uses: farmlands, grazing lands, forests, wetlands, and the coastal zone. A variety of indicators is used to portray present conditions, and trends and prospects are briefly discussed. There are a great many interesting local and regional problems; we have tried to choose those that best illuminate the general discussion and those that highlight spatial diversities.

Chapters 8 and 9 deal with the "conventional" environmental topics of air and water. To the extent that existing data allow, national assessments of these resources, and our management of them, are provided. The sources and transmission of pollutants are emphasized, with particular attention to acid precipitation, groundwater depletion, and drinking-water quality. Chapter 10 considers the important but somewhat neglected questions of noise and light pollution. The production, use, and disposal of toxic and nontoxic materials are taken up in the next two chapters. The distinction, of course, is not so clear as the titles of the two chapters might imply. Nonetheless, it is useful first to consider solid waste (chapter 11) because it raises concerns about landfill capacity, recycling programs, and resource recovery projects. These are very controversial issues, but those raised in the next chapter sometimes provoke greater hostility and even fiercer battles. Chapter 12 examines hazardous-waste-management programs and facility siting, the status of the Superfund program, and radon, asbestos, and pesticide-related questions.

Chapter 13 deals with energy resources—a vast topic that can be treated only in summary fashion here. The maps and accompanying text offer a broad inventory of "conventional" energy resources (fossil fuels, nuclear) and several "alternative" energy sources (wind, solar, geothermal). Given the controversial nature of such assessments and the associated policy dilemmas, this chapter can be little more than a provocative introduction to the topic.

Mineral resources are covered in chapter 14, and again there is the difficulty of providing an accurate assessment of the situation. We highlight key issues by focusing on U.S. dependence on mineral imports and the controversies surrounding the practice of strip mining.

Chapter 15 deals with parks, recreation, and wildlife. It examines recreational lands and waters administered by the National Park Service, the United States Forest Service, the Fish and Wildlife Service, and a host of state agencies. "Recreation" is defined broadly here—it ranges from preservation (with minimal human presence) to less environmentally benign activities such as the use of snowmobiles and other off-road vehicles.

The characteristics and occurrences of a wide range of natural hazards—floods, hurricanes, tornadoes, landslides and mudslides, earthquakes, and volcanic activity—are illustrated in chapter 16. Special emphasis is given to the eruptions of Mount St. Helens and to the widespread drought conditions of 1988.

The final chapters raise more explicitly "human" environmental questions. Chapter 17 looks at environmental economics and politics. State-to-state differences in political cultures, environmental voting records of legislators, spending for environmental protection, and participation in environmental organizations are represented. Chapter 18 is the most speculative. It portrays possible consequences for the United States of global warming and nuclear war. To counter the somber finality of those scenarios, we conclude with an illustration and comment on David Callenbach's "Ecotopia."

Physical and Political Overview 2

A nation's physical geography not only offers its inhabitants opportunities; it also sets constraints. But the physical realm is more than merely a backdrop for human activities. Indeed, it is as much defined by economic and political systems, cultural practices, and technological capabilities as it is by climate, landforms, soils, and biota. A resource is not a resource unless we have some use for it. Petroleum reserves were of little value before we had kerosene lamps and internal combustion engines. Nor was wilderness considered a resource to be preserved—until we learned to appreciate it.

We possess an enormous capability for modifying our physical surroundings to suit our needs—and this presents an analytical dilemma. Do we seek first to understand humankind's abilities to alter those environments (thus enabling us to learn about their "baseline" characteristics before human modification)—or do we begin simply by studying those environments as altered? Ideally, geographers and other environmental analysts strive for an interactive approach that views human-environment systems in all their complexity. But unfortunately, we often must segment our thinking—in the case of this atlas, into discrete chapters. This chapter presents a physical and political overview that is best interpreted in the context of the nation's historical development as well as its current (and of course always-changing) political-economic circumstances.

The physical mass that we recognize as North America has been distinguishable only for perhaps 200 million years—not very long in geologic terms. Even as recently as 12,000 years ago, ice sheets covered Alaska and the northern tier of the forty-eight conterminous states—and their climatic and vegetational influences extended much further. But we need not look back that far. During just the past several centuries, humans have radically altered the physical landscape of the United States. Most of the country—excluding Alaska—has had its forests cut or its wildlands converted to agricultural use. Drainage patterns have been rearranged at both the macro- and micro-scales.

Climate has been changed at the local level and very likely is also being modified at the national—and global—levels.

Whatever the significance of our landscape modifications, there is a basic and enduring diversity to America's physical environment. Within the United States' 3.6 million square miles (9.3 million square kilometers) are represented all but two (tropical monsoon, ice cap) of the major world climate types defined by the Köppen classification system. All the major biomes (ecosystem associations) can be found, though subtropical and tropical biomes occupy small areas. The Mississippi River Basin (1.25 million square miles) is the third largest in the world; there are also extensive mountain ranges, plains, and plateaus. In Alaska and in the forty-eight conterminous states are found large, sparsely populated areas. Given its size and relatively low average-population density, most of the United States is remarkably accessible via an extensive network of interstate and other major highways, railroads, and telecommunications systems.

By providing rapid and convenient access to center cities, the Interstate Highway System has helped foster the decentralization of America's metropoli. On an even larger scale, the past several decades have seen significant shifts of population toward the southern and western "Sunbelt" states.

The maps that follow provide only an overview. That overview can be enriched by reference to detailed physical geography, geology, climate, population, and related atlases and texts. It can also be brought into much deeper perspective by considering it in light of subsequent chapters in this atlas. Climatic factors, for example, are important determinants of water availability, dispersal of air pollutants, and certain classes of natural hazards; hydrology influences the fate of toxic materials leached from landfills; the Interstate Highway System has facilitated dramatic alterations of physical landscapes; and rapid population growth and industrialization bring with them a host of air-quality, water-quality, and land-use management problems.

Mount Hood, Oregon, from Lost Lake. R. Mason.

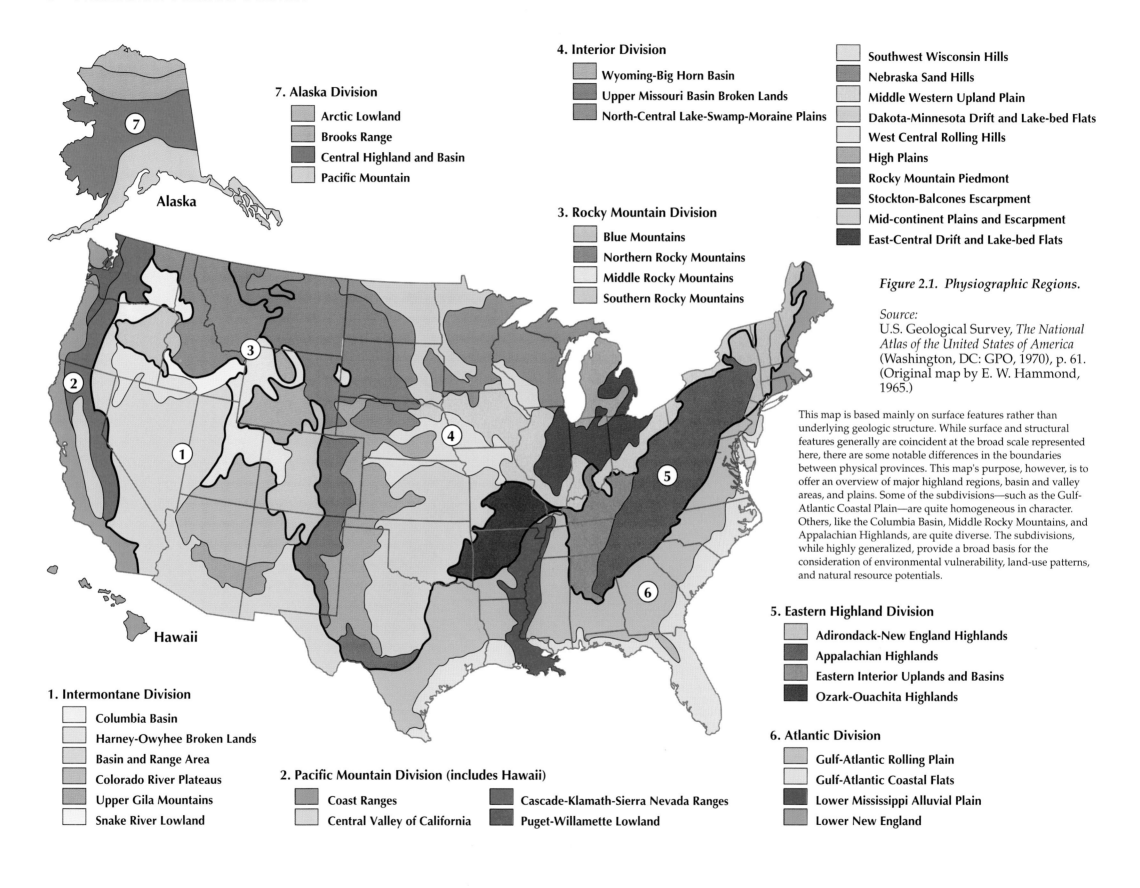

7. Alaska Division

- Arctic Lowland
- Brooks Range
- Central Highland and Basin
- Pacific Mountain

4. Interior Division

- Wyoming-Big Horn Basin
- Upper Missouri Basin Broken Lands
- North-Central Lake-Swamp-Moraine Plains
- Southwest Wisconsin Hills
- Nebraska Sand Hills
- Middle Western Upland Plain
- Dakota-Minnesota Drift and Lake-bed Flats
- West Central Rolling Hills
- High Plains
- Rocky Mountain Piedmont
- Stockton-Balcones Escarpment
- Mid-continent Plains and Escarpment
- East-Central Drift and Lake-bed Flats

3. Rocky Mountain Division

- Blue Mountains
- Northern Rocky Mountains
- Middle Rocky Mountains
- Southern Rocky Mountains

Figure 2.1. Physiographic Regions.

Source:
U.S. Geological Survey, *The National Atlas of the United States of America* (Washington, DC: GPO, 1970), p. 61. (Original map by E. W. Hammond, 1965.)

This map is based mainly on surface features rather than underlying geologic structure. While surface and structural features generally are coincident at the broad scale represented here, there are some notable differences in the boundaries between physical provinces. This map's purpose, however, is to offer an overview of major highland regions, basin and valley areas, and plains. Some of the subdivisions—such as the Gulf-Atlantic Coastal Plain—are quite homogeneous in character. Others, like the Columbia Basin, Middle Rocky Mountains, and Appalachian Highlands, are quite diverse. The subdivisions, while highly generalized, provide a broad basis for the consideration of environmental vulnerability, land-use patterns, and natural resource potentials.

5. Eastern Highland Division

- Adirondack-New England Highlands
- Appalachian Highlands
- Eastern Interior Uplands and Basins
- Ozark-Ouachita Highlands

6. Atlantic Division

- Gulf-Atlantic Rolling Plain
- Gulf-Atlantic Coastal Flats
- Lower Mississippi Alluvial Plain
- Lower New England

1. Intermontane Division

- Columbia Basin
- Harney-Owyhee Broken Lands
- Basin and Range Area
- Colorado River Plateaus
- Upper Gila Mountains
- Snake River Lowland

2. Pacific Mountain Division (includes Hawaii)

- Coast Ranges
- Central Valley of California
- Cascade-Klamath-Sierra Nevada Ranges
- Puget-Willamette Lowland

Alaska

Hawaii

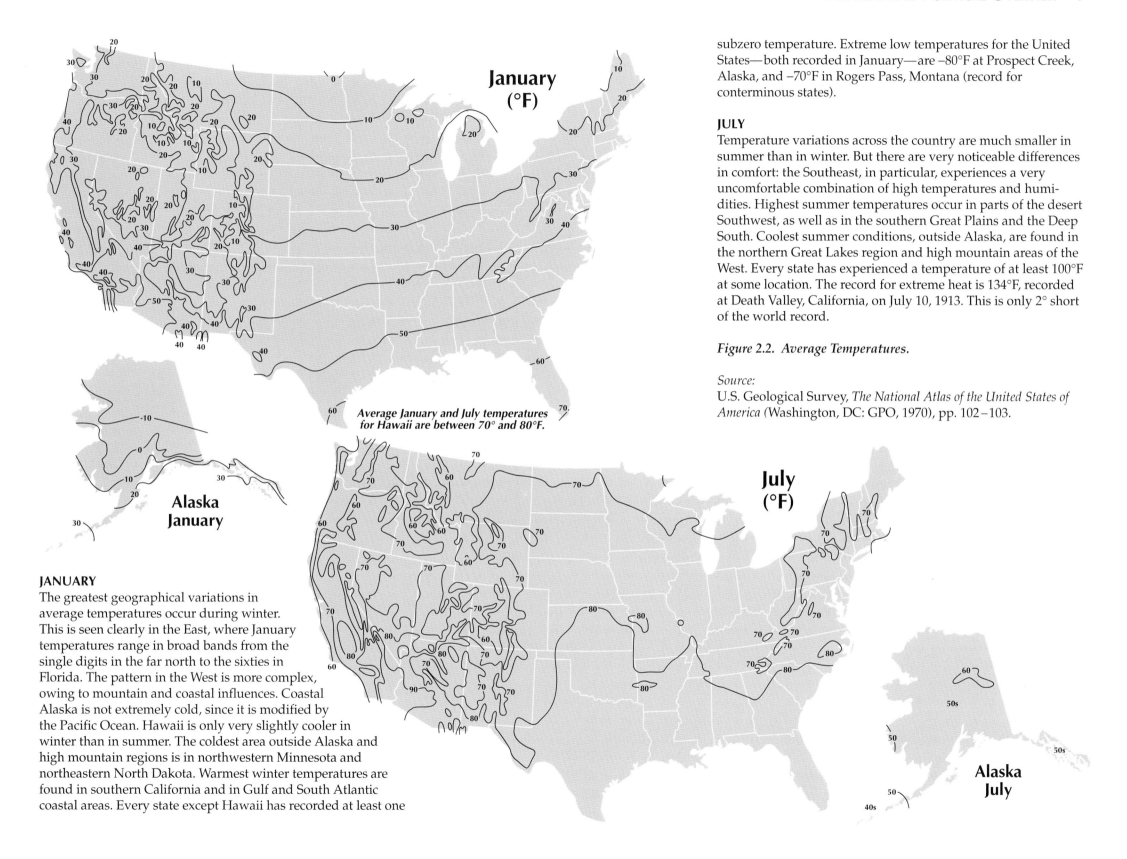

January (°F)

Average January and July temperatures for Hawaii are between 70° and 80°F.

Alaska January

July (°F)

Alaska July

subzero temperature. Extreme low temperatures for the United States—both recorded in January—are –80°F at Prospect Creek, Alaska, and –70°F in Rogers Pass, Montana (record for conterminous states).

JULY

Temperature variations across the country are much smaller in summer than in winter. But there are very noticeable differences in comfort: the Southeast, in particular, experiences a very uncomfortable combination of high temperatures and humidities. Highest summer temperatures occur in parts of the desert Southwest, as well as in the southern Great Plains and the Deep South. Coolest summer conditions, outside Alaska, are found in the northern Great Lakes region and high mountain areas of the West. Every state has experienced a temperature of at least 100°F at some location. The record for extreme heat is 134°F, recorded at Death Valley, California, on July 10, 1913. This is only 2° short of the world record.

Figure 2.2. Average Temperatures.

Source:
U.S. Geological Survey, *The National Atlas of the United States of America* (Washington, DC: GPO, 1970), pp. 102–103.

JANUARY

The greatest geographical variations in average temperatures occur during winter. This is seen clearly in the East, where January temperatures range in broad bands from the single digits in the far north to the sixties in Florida. The pattern in the West is more complex, owing to mountain and coastal influences. Coastal Alaska is not extremely cold, since it is modified by the Pacific Ocean. Hawaii is only very slightly cooler in winter than in summer. The coldest area outside Alaska and high mountain regions is in northwestern Minnesota and northeastern North Dakota. Warmest winter temperatures are found in southern California and in Gulf and South Atlantic coastal areas. Every state except Hawaii has recorded at least one

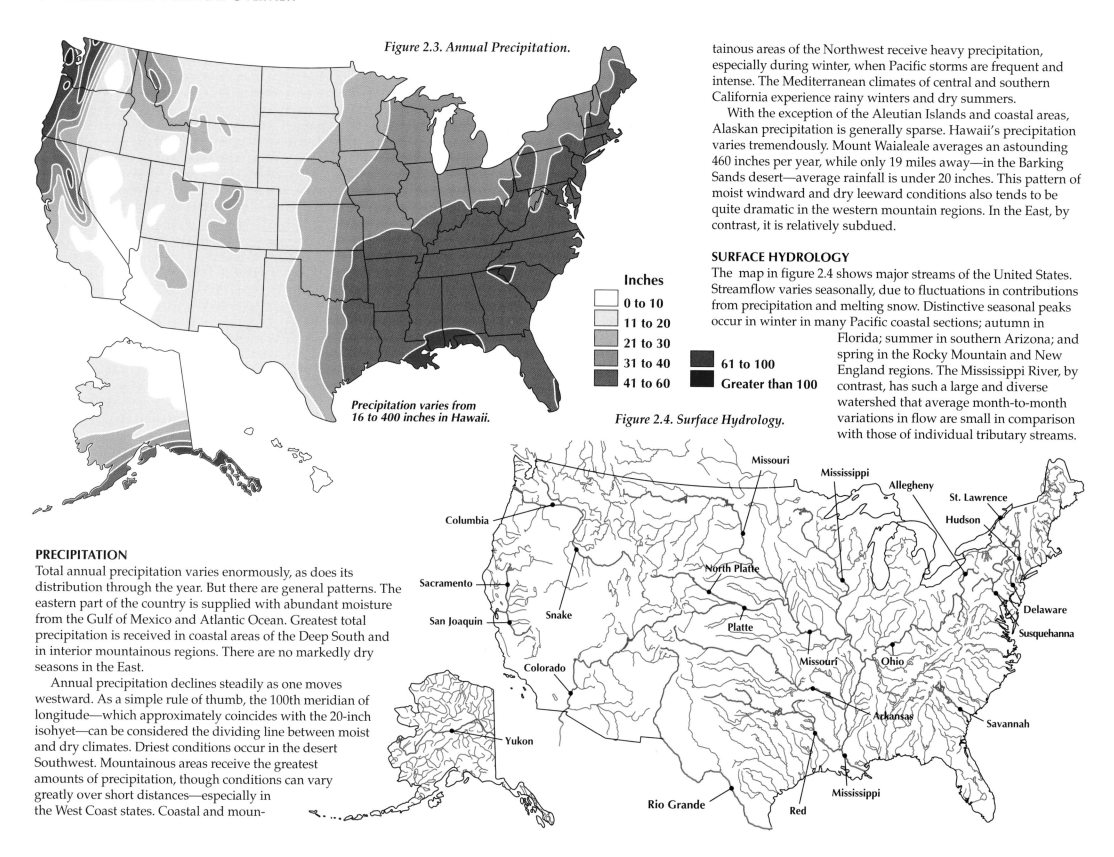

Figure 2.3. Annual Precipitation.

Inches

☐	0 to 10
☐	11 to 20
☐	21 to 30
☐	31 to 40
■	41 to 60

■	61 to 100
■	Greater than 100

Precipitation varies from 16 to 400 inches in Hawaii.

Figure 2.4. Surface Hydrology.

tainous areas of the Northwest receive heavy precipitation, especially during winter, when Pacific storms are frequent and intense. The Mediterranean climates of central and southern California experience rainy winters and dry summers.

With the exception of the Aleutian Islands and coastal areas, Alaskan precipitation is generally sparse. Hawaii's precipitation varies tremendously. Mount Waialeale averages an astounding 460 inches per year, while only 19 miles away—in the Barking Sands desert—average rainfall is under 20 inches. This pattern of moist windward and dry leeward conditions also tends to be quite dramatic in the western mountain regions. In the East, by contrast, it is relatively subdued.

SURFACE HYDROLOGY

The map in figure 2.4 shows major streams of the United States. Streamflow varies seasonally, due to fluctuations in contributions from precipitation and melting snow. Distinctive seasonal peaks occur in winter in many Pacific coastal sections; autumn in Florida; summer in southern Arizona; and spring in the Rocky Mountain and New England regions. The Mississippi River, by contrast, has such a large and diverse watershed that average month-to-month variations in flow are small in comparison with those of individual tributary streams.

PRECIPITATION

Total annual precipitation varies enormously, as does its distribution through the year. But there are general patterns. The eastern part of the country is supplied with abundant moisture from the Gulf of Mexico and Atlantic Ocean. Greatest total precipitation is received in coastal areas of the Deep South and in interior mountainous regions. There are no markedly dry seasons in the East.

Annual precipitation declines steadily as one moves westward. As a simple rule of thumb, the 100th meridian of longitude—which approximately coincides with the 20-inch isohyet—can be considered the dividing line between moist and dry climates. Driest conditions occur in the desert Southwest. Mountainous areas receive the greatest amounts of precipitation, though conditions can vary greatly over short distances—especially in the West Coast states. Coastal and moun-

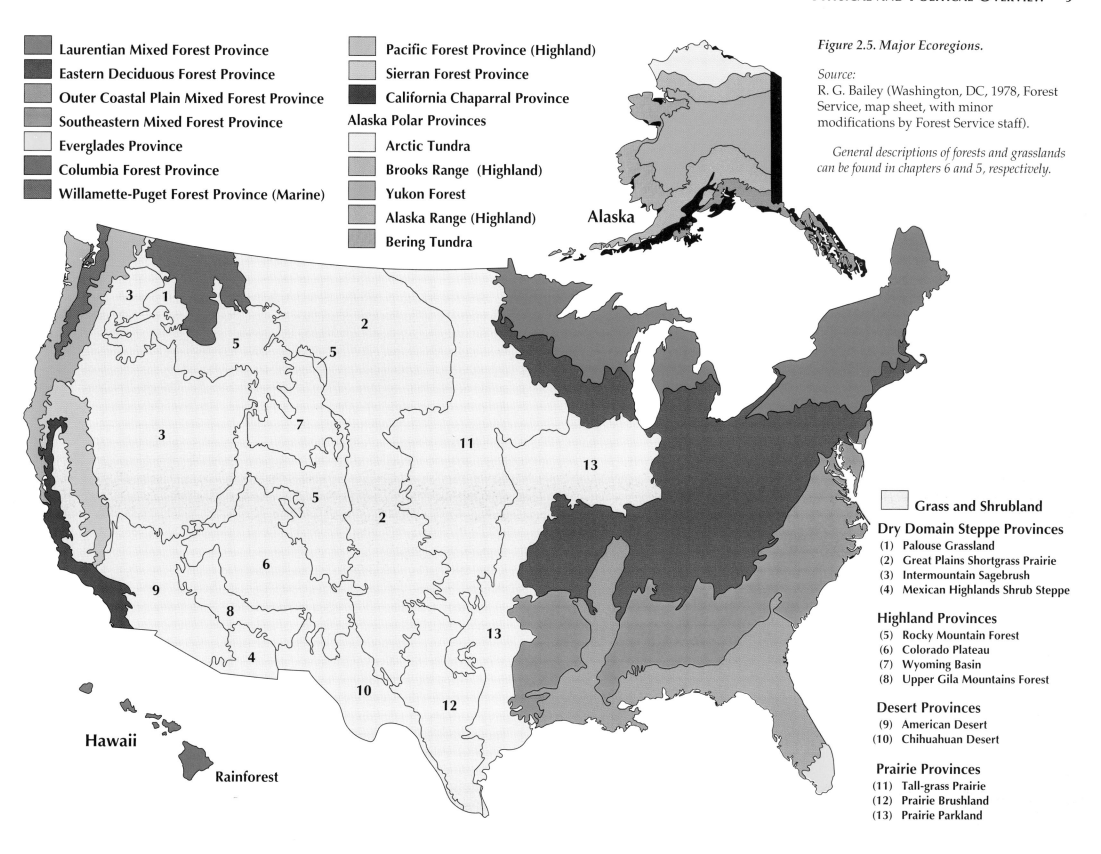

Laurentian Mixed Forest Province

Eastern Deciduous Forest Province

Outer Coastal Plain Mixed Forest Province

Southeastern Mixed Forest Province

Everglades Province

Columbia Forest Province

Willamette-Puget Forest Province (Marine)

Pacific Forest Province (Highland)

Sierran Forest Province

California Chaparral Province

Alaska Polar Provinces

Arctic Tundra

Brooks Range (Highland)

Yukon Forest

Alaska Range (Highland)

Bering Tundra

Alaska

Figure 2.5. Major Ecoregions.

Source:
R. G. Bailey (Washington, DC, 1978, Forest Service, map sheet, with minor modifications by Forest Service staff).

General descriptions of forests and grasslands can be found in chapters 6 and 5, respectively.

Hawaii

Rainforest

Grass and Shrubland

Dry Domain Steppe Provinces
(1) Palouse Grassland
(2) Great Plains Shortgrass Prairie
(3) Intermountain Sagebrush
(4) Mexican Highlands Shrub Steppe

Highland Provinces
(5) Rocky Mountain Forest
(6) Colorado Plateau
(7) Wyoming Basin
(8) Upper Gila Mountains Forest

Desert Provinces
(9) American Desert
(10) Chihuahuan Desert

Prairie Provinces
(11) Tall-grass Prairie
(12) Prairie Brushland
(13) Prairie Parkland

Table 2.1. Physical and Political Facts

	Area in Sq. Mi.	1988 Population	Per Sq. Mi.	High Elevation	Low Elevation	Mean Elevation	Interstate Miles	Total H'Way Miles	H'Way Density
Alabama	51,705	4,127,000	80	2,407	0	500	880	88,166	1.71
Alaska	591,004	513,000	1	20,320	0	1,900	1,089	12,082	0.02
Arizona	114,000	3,466,000	30	12,633	70	4,100	1,161	77,723	0.68
Arkansas	53,187	2,422,000	46	2,753	55	650	542	77,087	1.45
California	158,706	28,168,000	177	14,494	-282	2,900	2,389	158,932	1.00
Colorado	104,091	3,290,000	32	14,433	3,350	6,800	942	76,730	0.74
Connecticut	5,018	3,241,000	646	2,380	0	500	342	19,721	3.93
Delaware	2,045	660,000	323	442	0	60	41	5,341	2.61
Dist. of Columbia	69	620,000	8,986	410	1	150	12	1,102	15.97
Florida	59,664	12,377,000	207	345	0	100	1,354	100,423	1.68
Georgia	58,910	6,401,000	109	4,784	0	600	1,243	106,767	1.81
Hawaii	6,471	1,093,000	169	13,796	0	3,030	39	4,070	0.63
Idaho	83,564	999,000	12	12,662	710	5,000	605	71,639	0.86
Illinois	56,345	11,544,000	205	1,235	279	600	1,934	135,310	2.40
Indiana	36,185	5,575,000	154	1,257	320	700	1,117	91,535	2.53
Iowa	56,275	2,834,000	50	1,670	480	1,100	784	112,472	2.00
Kansas	82,277	2,487,000	30	4,039	680	2,000	870	132,931	1.62
Kentucky	40,410	3,721,000	92	4,145	257	750	752	69,629	1.72
Louisiana	47,752	4,420,000	93	535	-5	100	709	58,272	1.22
Maine	33,265	1,206,000	36	5,268	0	600	366	21,964	0.66
Maryland	10,460	4,644,000	444	3,360	0	350	394	27,965	2.67
Massachusetts	8,284	5,871,000	709	3,491	0	500	563	33,807	4.08
Michigan	58,527	9,300,000	159	1,979	572	900	1,210	117,803	2.01
Minnesota	84,402	4,306,000	51	2,301	602	1,200	900	132,843	1.57
Mississippi	47,689	2,627,000	55	806	0	300	686	72,065	1.51
Missouri	69,697	5,139,000	74	1,772	230	800	1,177	119,682	1.72
Montana	147,046	804,000	5	12,799	1,800	3,400	1,181	71,811	0.49
Nebraska	77,355	1,601,000	21	5,426	840	2,600	481	92,401	1.19
Nevada	110,561	1,060,000	10	13,143	470	5,500	545	44,754	0.40
New Hampshire	9,279	1,097,000	118	6,288	0	1,000	222	14,611	1.57
New Jersey	7,787	7,720,000	991	1,803	0	250	393	34,041	4.37
New Mexico	121,593	1,510,000	12	13,161	2,817	5,700	998	53,749	0.44
New York	49,108	17,898,000	364	5,344	0	1,000	1,499	110,321	2.25
North Carolina	52,669	6,526,000	124	6,684	0	700	805	93,234	1.77
North Dakota	70,702	663,000	9	3,506	750	1,900	571	86,243	1.22
Ohio	41,330	10,872,000	263	1,550	433	850	1,565	112,154	2.71
Oklahoma	69,956	3,263,000	47	4,973	287	1,300	927	111,082	1.59
Oregon	97,073	2,741,000	28	11,239	0	3,300	716	93,915	0.97
Pennsylvania	45,308	12,027,000	265	3,213	0	1,100	1,523	115,908	2.56
Rhode Island	1,212	995,000	821	812	0	200	70	5,852	4.83
South Carolina	31,113	3,493,000	112	3,560	0	350	790	63,420	2.04
South Dakota	77,116	715,000	9	7,242	962	2,200	678	73,469	0.95
Tennessee	42,144	4,919,000	117	6,643	182	900	1,062	83,691	1.99
Texas	266,807	16,780,000	63	8,749	0	1,700	3,208	293,530	1.10
Utah	84,899	1,691,000	20	13,528	2,000	6,100	889	49,901	0.59
Vermont	9,614	556,000	58	4,393	95	1,000	320	14,071	1.46
Virginia	40,767	5,996,000	147	5,729	0	950	1,059	66,125	1.62
Washington	68,139	4,619,000	68	14,410	0	1,700	754	79,509	1.17
West Virginia	24,232	1,884,000	78	4,863	240	1,500	479	35,173	1.45
Wisconsin	56,153	4,858,000	87	1,951	581	1,050	578	108,925	1.94
Wyoming	97,809	471,000	5	13,804	3,100	6,700	914	40,075	0.41

THE INTERSTATE HIGHWAY SYSTEM

America's Interstate Highway System is the most extensive in the world—a fact that has helped make Americans more mobile than citizens of any other industrialized nation. The Interstate Highway Act, passed in 1956, initially provided for a 41,000-mile system (later expanded to 42,500 miles) of limited-access, toll-free expressways. Ninety percent of the cost is paid by the federal government's Highway Trust Fund, which receives revenues from gasoline taxes. A chief rationale for the system was defense-related: A decentralized population would be better able to withstand a nuclear attack, and the highways would allow for efficient transport of men and matériel. The concept also enjoyed the support of a powerful coalition of interest groups, ostensibly concerned with reducing highway congestion and promoting commerce. Its members included auto, steel, oil, asphalt, and rubber manufacturers; construction concerns; labor unions; car dealers; trucking and busing enterprises; and banks. As the Interstate Highway System took shape, the quality and availability of mass transportation declined markedly. In the Los Angeles region—where the automobile seemed to reach its apotheosis in the 1960s—residents must contend with clogged freeways, air pollution, and hopelessly inadequate public transportation. Only the broadest outlines of the intense highway development in and around major metropolitan areas are apparent on the map in figure 2.6; but reference to more detailed road atlases reveals just how intricate and complex those networks are. The resultant settlement and personal transport patterns presented formidable barriers to mass-transit programs of the 1960s and 1970s.

In short, the Interstate Highway System fostered rapid interurban transport as well as suburbanization. To be sure, highways alone are not responsible for the massive postwar suburbanization of the United States; rising personal incomes, the ideal of the detached home, racial prejudice, Federal Housing Administration and Veterans Home Administration subsidies, the tax deductibility of mortgage interest and property taxes, and inexpensive construction techniques all can be cited as contributing factors. But the highway system was the facilitator; it allowed rapid movement between city and suburbs. At the regional and national scales, the truck has become the chief mode of intercity transport of goods, and rural areas have become much more accessible to everyone.

Only in the late 1960s did the interstate vision begin to meet with serious challenges. Many urban, suburban, and rural segments were delayed by court challenges and in some cases entirely abandoned. Still, even as we face today's urban air-quality problems and the prospect of global warming (vehicle emissions contribute heavily to both), the private automobile continues to reign supreme.

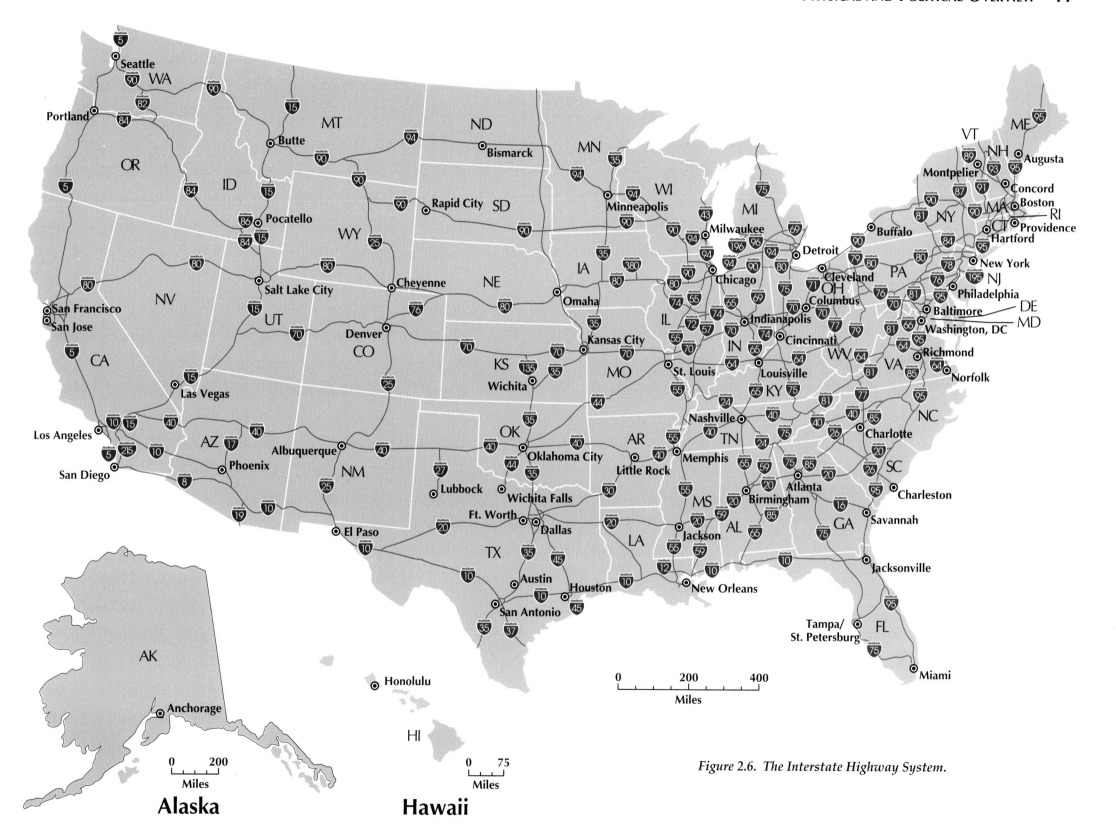

Figure 2.6. The Interstate Highway System.

Alaska

Hawaii

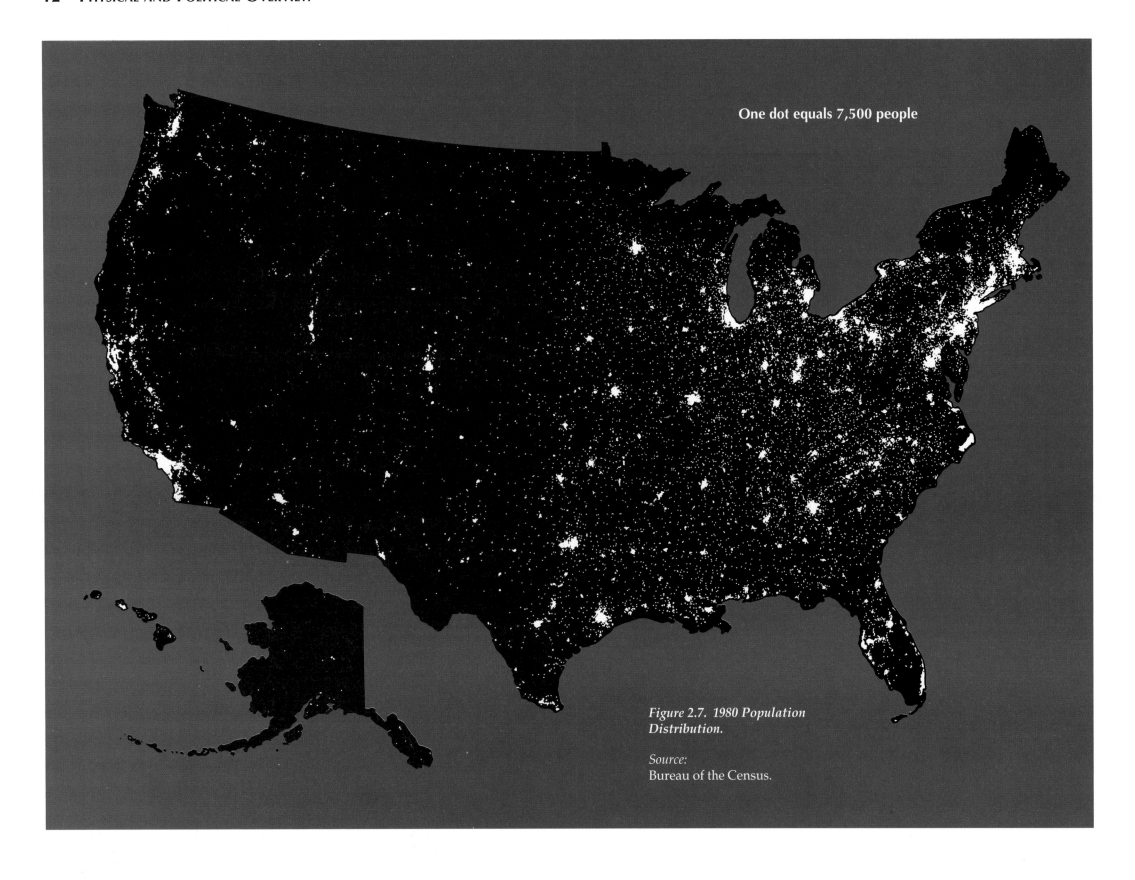

One dot equals 7,500 people

Figure 2.7. 1980 Population Distribution.

Source:
Bureau of the Census.

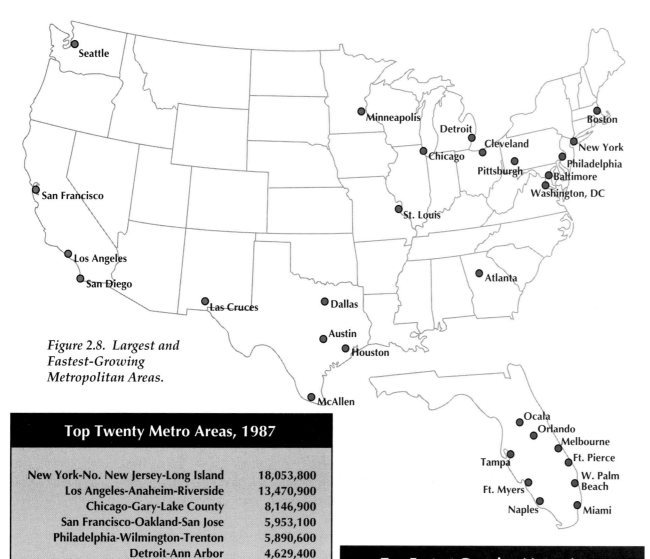

Figure 2.8. Largest and Fastest-Growing Metropolitan Areas.

Top Twenty Metro Areas, 1987

New York-No. New Jersey-Long Island	18,053,800
Los Angeles-Anaheim-Riverside	13,470,900
Chicago-Gary-Lake County	8,146,900
San Francisco-Oakland-San Jose	5,953,100
Philadelphia-Wilmington-Trenton	5,890,600
Detroit-Ann Arbor	4,629,400
Boston-Lawrence-Salem	4,092,900
Dallas-Fort Worth	3,724,900
Washington, DC	3,646,000
Houston-Galveston-Brazoria	3,626,300
Miami-Fort Lauderdale	2,954,100
Cleveland-Akron-Lorain	2,766,900
Atlanta	2,656,800
St. Louis	2,458,100
Seattle-Tacoma	2,340,600
Minneapolis-St. Paul	2,335,600
Baltimore	2,302,900
Pittsburgh-Beaver Valley	2,296,400
San Diego	2,285,900
Tampa-St. Petersburg-Clearwater	1,985,100

Ten Fastest Growing Metro Areas

Metro Area	Population	% Increase 1980 to 1987
Naples, FL	127,900	49
Ocala, FL	181,300	48
Fort Myers, FL	294,600	44
Fort Pierce, FL	215,400	43
Austin, TX	738,000	38
Melbourne, FL	374,900	37
West Palm Beach, FL	790,100	37
Las Cruces, NM	128,800	34
McAllen, TX	378,600	34
Orlando, FL	934,700	34

POPULATION

In 1961, Jean Gottmann described the densely populated northeastern corridor—extending approximately from Boston to Washington—as "Megalopolis": a region where one city's suburbs blend into the next to form a continuous chain of human settlement. Other areas have since been similarly characterized—among them these urban corridors: Sacramento-Los Angeles-San Diego; Milwaukee-Chicago-Detroit; Dallas-Fort Worth-San Antonio-Houston; and Jacksonville-Tampa-Miami. Figure 2.7, an enhanced "nighttime" view of the urban population of the United States, highlights these and other megalopoli.

Approximately three-quarters of America's 246 million people live in its 282 metropolitan areas. At each metropolitan area's core is at least one large city—usually with a population of 50,000 or more—and the county in which it is located. Surrounding counties with strong social and economic links to the core county also are considered part of the metropolitan area—even though in some cases they are physically quite remote. Almost half the U.S. population lives in the thirty-seven metropolitan areas that have at least one million population.

Figure 2.8 shows populations of the largest metropolitan areas, as well as those that are growing fastest. All fastest-growing areas are in the South, reflecting the general north-to-south population shift of recent decades (figure 2.9). But these top twenty areas also have relatively low base populations, which in part explains the impressive percentage gains. Still, even the *large* southern metropolitan areas are gaining more population than their northern counterparts. Although the New York-northern New Jersey-Long Island region dominates decisively, its lead continues to erode. Indeed, between 1980 and 1987 the New York metropolitan region grew by 2.9 percent, while the second-ranked Los Angeles region grew by 17.2 percent. Of all the metropolitan areas with a million or more population, Phoenix gained the most (30 percent); while Dallas-Fort Worth came in second at 27 percent. Several large metropolitan areas actually lost population: Buffalo (–5.5 percent), Pittsburgh (–5.2 percent), Detroit (–2.6 percent), Cleveland (–2.4 percent), and Milwaukee (–0.5 percent).

It should be evident from the above definition that metropolitan areas do not contain uniformly dense concentrations of people, homes, and businesses. Before World War II, immigrants to metropolitan areas did settle principally in or very near to the built-up urban cores. But with the enormous postwar growth of the suburbs, metropolitan populations— new as well as old—expanded spatially, thus becoming less dense. While most of today's metropolitan areas still contain densely populated urban cores, they also have their share of vacant urban areas, vast suburban sprawl, medium-size cities and towns, and even small towns and rural regions. Indeed, as Gottmann (1961) observed, even Megalopolis has its "wild-lands," its places where high-priced rural lands are fastidiously maintained by gentleman farmers. New Jersey, for example—though entirely classified as metropolitan—has areas in its northwestern and southern sections that are fairly sparsely populated (see figure 15.8). What this means, then, is that each metropolitan area is faced with a diverse array of transportation, infrastructure, land-use, park and recreation, and other planning and policy concerns. In most places, they are dealt with by tens or even hundreds of local governments that treat regional issues more competitively than cooperatively.

Figure 2.9 shows state population trends over the past several decades. Between the mid-1940s and early 1960s, the postwar baby boom brought relatively rapid population growth to most parts of the country—with *greatest* growth in the Great Lakes, South Atlantic, Rocky Mountain, and Pacific Coast regions. By the 1970s and 1980s, however, a dramatic interregional trend had become apparent. Popularly referred to as the "Frostbelt-Sunbelt" shift, it involves migration from the Northeast and Midwest to the southern and western states. While Frostbelt growth rates approached zero—with declines in some states—the Sunbelt experienced large gains in the 1970s and 1980s. During the 1970s, as well as between 1980 and 1987, the southern and western states accounted for a remarkable 90 percent of all national growth in population. Two-thirds of the nation's 1980–1987 population growth took place in the Sunbelt (Starsinic and Forstall 1989). Sunbelt definition is a matter of some controversy; in this instance, it includes North and South Carolina, Georgia, Florida, Tennessee, Alabama, Mississippi, Arkansas, Louisiana, Oklahoma, Texas, Arizona, New Mexico, Hawaii, and southern Nevada and California.

Largest state increases have been in California, Florida, and Texas. Much of the increase, though, has occurred in metropolitan areas—especially in the Southeast, where the rural decline of earlier decades continues unabated in many areas. Moreover, the general trend has been counterbalanced, especially in the 1980s, by strong resurgences in some parts of the Frostbelt—such as the high-tech corridor connecting Boston and southern New Hampshire. Indeed, the precise spatial characterization—as well as economic, social, and political rationales for the Frostbelt-Sunbelt shift—are the subject of much debate. Among the reasons cited are the lessened need for industry to be close to natural resources; aging northern industrial and urban infrastructures; the South's more congenial climate; government investments that have stimulated Sunbelt economies; less stringent state government regulations in the Sunbelt; and lower land, building, energy (though air conditioning can be costly), and labor costs in the South.

Postwar suburbanization trends are described above. But during the 1970s, population deconcentration seemed to extend well beyond metropolitan area boundaries. The terms "population turnaround," "rural renaissance," and "counter-urbanization" all refer to the phenomenon of proportionally greater growth in the nation's nonmetropolitan areas than in its metropolitan areas. This was a reversal of previous trends—albeit a short-lived one, because in the 1980s the previous pattern was reestablished.

Nonmetropolitan areas consist of all counties not included in metropolitan areas. About two-thirds of all counties are non-metropolitan, but they contain only 23 percent of the country's population. "Nonmetropolitan" is frequently used as a surrogate for "rural," though technically the two terms are not synonymous. Urban areas—which include any place with 2,500 or more people—are common in nonmetropolitan areas, while rural areas are found in metropolitan counties. Nonetheless, because of intercensal data availability, the metro-nonmetro dichotomy is widely used for analytical purposes.

Between 1970 and 1980, nonmetropolitan population grew by 15.8 percent, while metropolitan population growth was 9.8 percent (although the absolute increases in metropolitan areas were greater, because of their much larger base populations). In the first half of the 1980s, however, nonmetro growth was 0.7 percent, compared with metro growth of 1.2 percent. During the 1970s, nonmetro areas experienced a net in-migration of about 350,000 people per year; by the mid-1980s, they were losing almost one million people per year (O'Hare 1988). The 1980s' out-migration trends are believed to stem from declines in rural, resource-based industries; the failure of many rural areas to attract new forms of economic development; scarce public assistance (welfare and other programs) in many rural regions; and substantially increased rural poverty.

One view of the 1970s' turnaround is that it was a temporary part of a regional restructuring of the population, with people and jobs moving from the old metropolitan regions of the Northeast and Midwest to smaller nonmetro and metro areas in the South and West. In contrast—according to the rural renaissance hypothesis—individuals were (and in some parts of the country still are) taking advantage of new technological, transport, and other opportunities to act out their desires to live in rural locales. This is seen as the harbinger of a population spread increasingly thin. Although generally contradicted by the reversal of the 1980s, the rural renaissance still seems to be under way in particular parts of the country—especially nonmetro areas proximate to large urban concentrations in the New England, Middle Atlantic, and West Coast states. The economic, land-use, and other policy questions raised by rural repopulation should continue to spur lively debates in these places.

Table 2.2. Metropolitan Population, 1987

	Percent
Alabama	67.2
Alaska	42.4
Arizona	76.2
Arkansas	39.5
California	95.7
Colorado	81.7
Connecticut	92.6
Delaware	66.0
Florida	90.8
Georgia	64.6
Hawaii	76.7
Idaho	19.6
Illinois	82.5
Indiana	68.0
Iowa	43.1
Kansas	52.8
Kentucky	45.8
Louisiana	69.0
Maine	36.1
Maryland	92.9
Massachusetts	90.7
Michigan	80.2
Minnesota	66.2
Mississippi	30.3
Missouri	66.0
Montana	24.2
Nebraska	47.2
Nevada	82.6
New Hampshire	56.3
New Jersey	100.0
New Mexico	48.4
New York	90.5
North Carolina	55.3
North Dakota	38.0
Ohio	78.9
Oklahoma	58.8
Oregon	67.6
Pennsylvania	84.7
Rhode Island	92.6
South Carolina	60.4
South Dakota	28.7
Tennessee	67.0
Texas	81.0
Utah	77.2
Vermont	23.1
Virginia	71.7
Washington	81.2
West Virginia	36.3
Wisconsin	66.5
Wyoming	29.0
United States	**76.9**

Source: D. E. Starsinic and R. L. Forstall, *Patterns of Metropolitan Area and County Population Growth: 1980 to 1987* (Washington, DC: GPO, 1989).

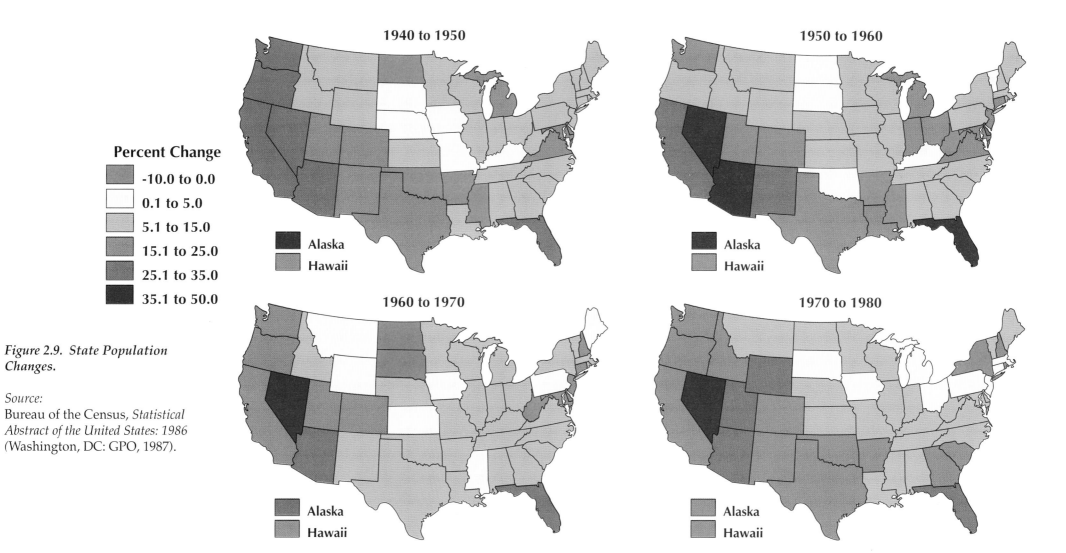

Figure 2.9. State Population Changes.

Source:
Bureau of the Census, *Statistical Abstract of the United States: 1986* (Washington, DC: GPO, 1987).

Table 2.3. Population Change, 1980–1988.

Source:
Bureau of the Census, *County Population Estimates: July 1, 1988, 1987, and 1986,* Current Population Reports, series P-26, no. 88-A. (Washington, DC: GPO, 1989).

Table 2.3. Population Change, 1980–1988

	Percent		Percent		Percent		Percent
Alabama	5.4	Indiana	1.2	Nebraska	2.1	South Carolina	11.2
Alaska	30.5	Iowa	−2.7	Nevada	31.7	South Dakota	3.2
Arizona	28.4	Kansas	5.6	New Hampshire	17.9	Tennessee	6.6
Arkansas	4.7	Kentucky	1.8	New Jersey	4.8	Texas	18.4
California	19.6	Louisiana	4.8	New Mexico	15.6	Utah	15.7
Colorado	14.2	Maine	7.2	New York	2.0	Vermont	9.0
Connecticut	4.0	Maryland	9.6	North Carolina	10.3	Virginia	12.5
Delaware	11.1	Massachusetts	2.7	North Dakota	2.2	Washington	12.5
Florida	26.6	Michigan	−0.2	Ohio	0.5	West Virginia	−3.8
Georgia	16.1	Minnesota	5.7	Oklahoma	7.2	Wisconsin	3.2
Hawaii	13.8	Mississippi	3.9	Oregon	5.1	Wyoming	2.1
Idaho	6.2	Missouri	4.6	Pennsylvania	1.2		
Illinois	1.6	Montana	2.3	Rhode Island	4.8	**United States**	**8.5**

Land is immensely important in the United States. It is physically, spiritually, and financially nurturing; in turn, it has been both shepherded and abused. Our contradictory views of the land are reflected in the "land as resource" versus "land as commodity" debate—a debate that has surfaced repeatedly through this country's history.

European settlers, unlike the native populations they displaced, saw before them a virtually limitless land base. It had only to be subdued. The notion of the American frontier, the reverence for private property rights, and fierce resistance to anything larger than local control have persisted through our history. Paradoxically, the federal government has played—and continues to play—a leading role in land-use planning and land development. It currently owns about 32 percent of the nation's land—most of it in the West and Alaska. But the government has—at one time or another—owned approximately four-fifths of the present land base.

The Land Ordinance of 1785 provided for the survey and appropriation of the large federal domain. As the government acquired vast landholdings in the West, it simultaneously devised ways to distribute those lands. By the 1930s, the government had sold or given away about 60 percent of its holdings to the states, homesteaders, railroad corporations, mining and timber interests, and various other corporate and individual concerns. Through much of this period, ecological or preservation-oriented land-use planning was virtually nonexistent. Only in the late 1800s were the first national parks and forest reserves designated. During the 1920s, there was some movement toward state land-use controls, while the 1930s witnessed broader sentiment for regional land-use planning. The Tennessee Valley Authority, created in 1933, is still the outstanding single example of a major government land-use and regional development scheme.

But the general advent of more widespread and significant land-planning activities would have to await the environmental era of the 1960s and 1970s. Fred Bosselman and David Callies (1971) described this emerging period as the "quiet revolution in land-use control." In response to rapid suburban growth, large leisure home developments, intrusive facilities such as power plants and jetports, the loss of agricultural land and other countryside amenities, and the perceived inadequacy of local planning and zoning controls, states and communities began to enact more stringent land-use controls. Between 1965 and 1977, state legislatures alone adopted ninety-four statutes promulgating minimum development-control standards for sensitive areas. Federal land-use controls also were proposed. In 1974, the National Land Use Policy Act passed in the Senate but fell short of House approval by seven votes. By the mid- to late 1970s, the quiet revolution seemed to lose much of its fire, but this has not prevented communities and state legislatures from enacting more specialized, local-level laws and regulations (see figure 3.3).

Despite the recent proliferation of land-use controls, and despite the federal government's continued key role as a landlord (see figure 3.2), the notions of private property rights and local control are still revered across America. If anything, these sentiments are being reasserted—in the form of opposition to such intrusive facilities as landfills and transmission lines. This leads to another basic question: Who owns and controls how much land? Unfortunately, data on land ownership are rather limited. A 1978 survey by the U.S. Department of Agriculture revealed that approximately 90 percent of nonpublic landowners are individuals or couples (Lewis 1980). Most hold small parcels: three-quarters of the landowning population owns only about 3 percent of the land, while 38 percent of the American land is held by less than 0.5 percent of landowners. Even though the small landowner may be rather rigidly constrained by political and economic circumstances, the illusion of full and absolute control over one's land remains a vital part of the American dream.

Satellite Image, Manhattan, Kansas.
U.S. Geological Survey.

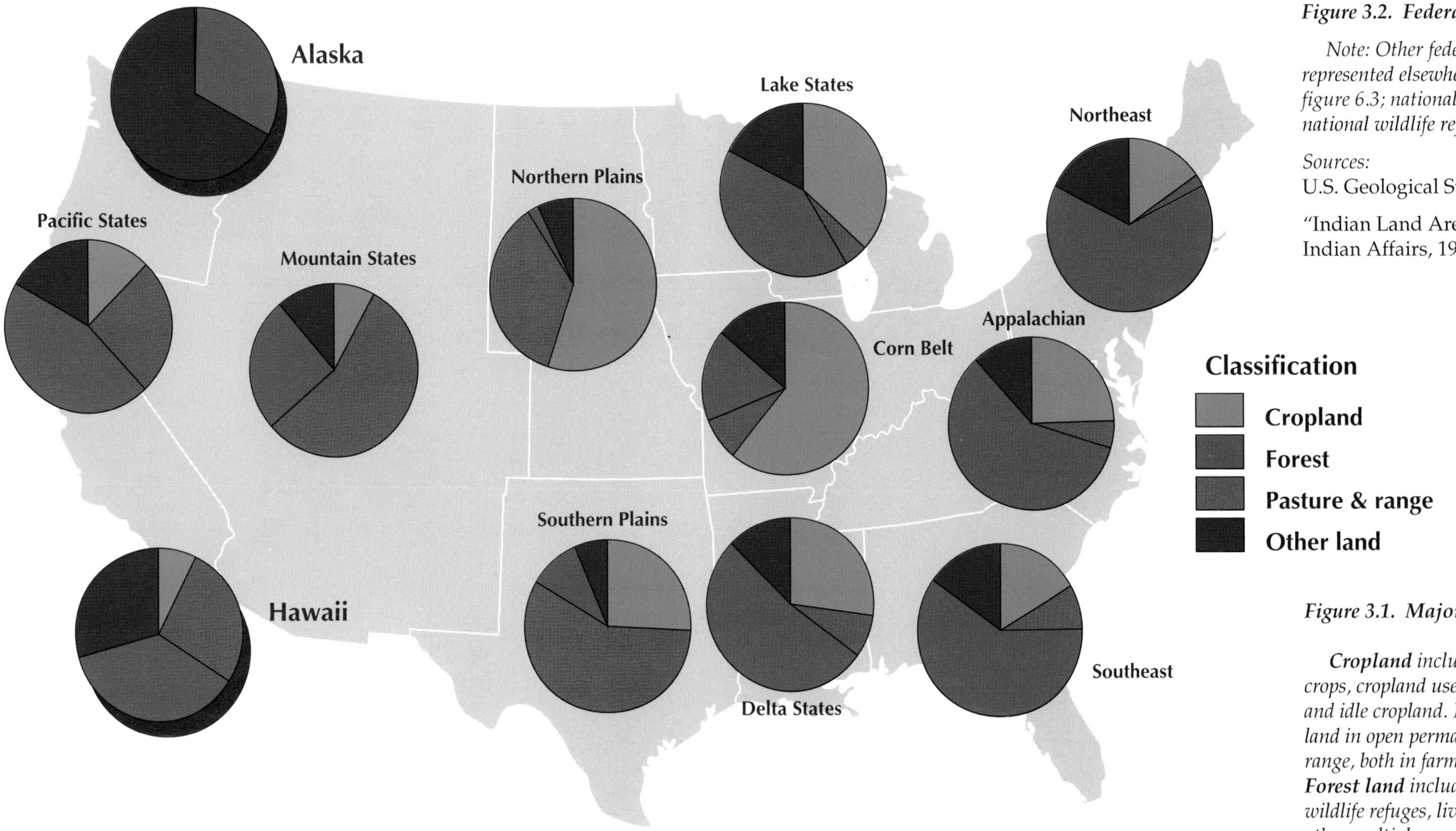

Alaska

Lake States

Northeast

Pacific States

Northern Plains

Mountain States

Corn Belt

Appalachian

Hawaii

Southern Plains

Delta States

Southeast

Classification

- Cropland
- Forest
- Pasture & range
- Other land

Figure 3.2. Federal Lands.

Note: Other federal lands are represented elsewhere: national forests, figure 6.3; national parks, figure 15.1; national wildlife refuges, figure 15.10.

Sources:
U.S. Geological Survey (map).

"Indian Land Areas" (Bureau of Indian Affairs, 1987, map).

Figure 3.1. Major Land Uses, 1982.

Cropland includes cropland used for crops, cropland used only for pasture, and idle cropland. Pasture and range is land in open permanent pasture and range, both in farms and not in farms. Forest land includes that used for parks, wildlife refuges, livestock grazing, and other multiple purposes. Other land includes land used for transportation, defense, and energy purposes. It also includes large areas of marsh, swamp, desert, and tundra—mainly in Alaska, the West, and parts of the Gulf and Atlantic coasts.

Note: Total U.S. land area is 2,265 million acres.

Source:
H. T. Frey and R. W. Hexam, Major Uses of Land in the United States: 1982, USDA, Agricultural Economic Report, no. 535 (Washington, DC: GPO, 1982), p. 4.

MAJOR LAND USES

America's largest forested acreages are found in the East and Alaska. Cropland dominates in the Corn Belt and Northern Great Plains, while pasture and range is the most significant land use in the Southern Great Plains and Mountain states. For the nation as a whole, approximately 21 percent of the land area in 1982 was cropland; 26 percent grassland pasture and range; 32 percent forest (including lands used for parks and similar purposes); and 21 percent fell into the "special purposes" and unclassified categories. These categories are not mutually exclusive. Livestock grazing, for example, occurs not only on pasture and rangeland but also on forest and cropland. In 1982, grazing took place on some 36 percent of U.S. land.

Cropland—which had declined markedly between 1950 and 1974—increased about 6 percent between 1974 and 1982.

However, the 1985 Food Security Act (chapter 4) has resulted in subsequent reductions of cropland acreage. The amount of land in pasture and range has declined continually since 1950 but especially between 1969 and 1978, when pasture land—including high-quality pasture—was being converted to crops. Total forest land declined from the colonial period through about 1920, increased between 1920 and 1960, and again declined during the 1960s and 1970s. Land classified as urban increased substantially during the 1970s. The decline after 1960 is attributed to both land reclassification and accelerated forest clearing for agriculture, reservoirs, highways, and urban and residential development. Still, urban areas account for only 2 percent of the nation's land base. Even in the densely populated Northeast, they compose about 8.5 percent of the land. These statistics are from Frey and Hexam (1982) and references therein.

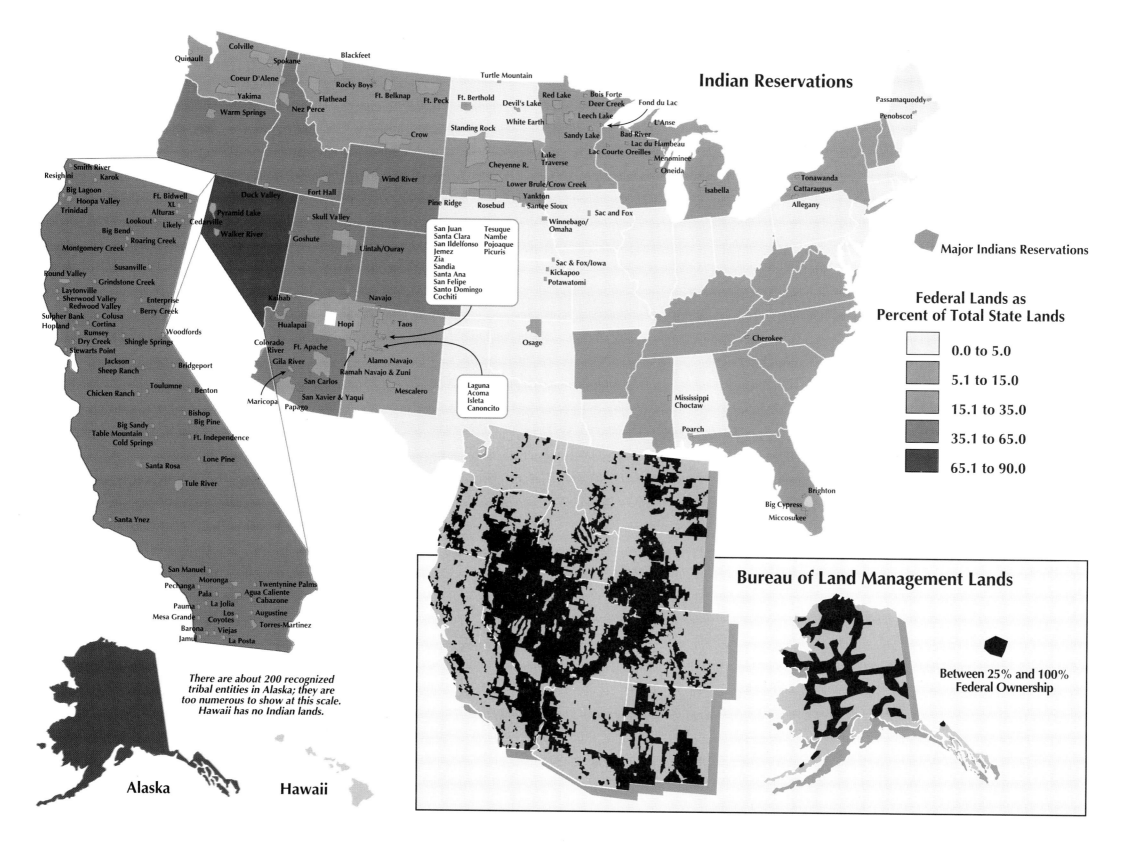

Indian Reservations

Colville
Quinault
Spokane
Blackfeet
Turtle Mountain
Coeur D'Alene
Rocky Boys
Red Lake
Bois Forte
Deer Creek
Fond du Lac
Passamaquoddy
Yakima
Flathead
Ft. Belknap
Ft. Peck
Ft. Berthold
Devil's Lake
Leech Lake
L'Anse
Penobscot
Warm Springs
Nez Perce
Ft. Peck
Standing Rock
White Earth
Sandy Lake
Bad River
Lac du Flambeau
Crow
Lac Courte Oreilles
Menominee
Oneida
Cheyenne R.
Lake Traverse
Smith River
Resighini
Karok
Wind River
Fort Hall
Lower Brule/Crow Creek
Tonawanda
Cattaraugus
Big Lagoon
Hoopa Valley
Ft. Bidwell
XL
Duck Valley
Pine Ridge
Yankton
Santee Sioux
Isabella
Allegany
Trinidad
Alturas
Pyramid Lake
Skull Valley
Rosebud
Sac and Fox
Lookout
Likely
Cedarville
Winnebago/Omaha
Big Bend
Roaring Creek
Walker River
Goshute
Uintah/Ouray
San Juan   Tesuque
Santa Clara   Nambe
San Ildelfonso   Pojoaque
Jemez   Picuris
Zia
Sandia
Santa Ana
San Felipe
Santo Domingo
Cochiti
Sac & Fox/Iowa
Kickapoo
Potawatomi
Montgomery Creek
Susanville
Round Valley
Grindstone Creek
Kaibab
Navajo
Laytonville
Enterprise
Taos
Sherwood Valley
Berry Creek
Hualapai
Hopi
Redwood Valley
Osage
Cherokee
Sulpher Bank
Cortina
Woodfords
Colorado River
Ft. Apache
Hopland
Rumsey
Shingle Springs
Dry Creek
Alamo Navajo
Stewarts Point
Gila River
Ramah Navajo & Zuni
Laguna
Acoma
Isleta
Canoncito
Jackson
Sheep Ranch
Bridgeport
San Carlos
Mescalero
Chicken Ranch
Toulumne
Benton
Maricopa
San Xavier & Yaqui
Mississippi
Choctaw
Bishop
Papago
Big Sandy
Big Pine
Poarch
Table Mountain
Ft. Independence
Cold Springs
Santa Rosa
Lone Pine
Tule River
Santa Ynez
Brighton
San Manuel
Moronga
Big Cypress
Pechanga
Pala
Twentynine Palms
Miccosukee
Pauma
La Jolia
Agua Caliente
Cabazone
Mesa Grande
Los Coyotes
Augustine
Barona
Viejas
Torres-Martinez
Jamul
La Posta

Colusa
Cotati

Major Indians Reservations

Federal Lands as Percent of Total State Lands

	0.0 to 5.0
	5.1 to 15.0
	15.1 to 35.0
	35.1 to 65.0
	65.1 to 90.0

There are about 200 recognized tribal entities in Alaska; they are too numerous to show at this scale. Hawaii has no Indian lands.

Alaska   **Hawaii**

Bureau of Land Management Lands

Between 25% and 100% Federal Ownership

FEDERAL LANDS

About one-third of the United States is owned by the federal government. But at one time or another, about four-fifths of the current land base has been in federal hands. This is because the United States expanded by leaps and bounds in its first century of nationhood—and all the new lands went to the federal government. Among the largest acquisitions were the Louisiana Purchase (1803), the Mexican Cession (1848), and the Alaska Purchase (1867).

At the same time as it was acquiring all this land, the federal government was "disposing" of other parts of its estate. Of a total of 1.14 billion acres of lands disposed, 330 million were granted to the states. Nearly 290 million acres went to homesteaders. The Homestead Act of 1862 granted a 160-acre "quarter section" to settlers who stayed on the homestead and made modest improvements over a five-year period. Other major beneficiaries included railroads (94 million acres) and veterans (61 million acres). Most of the remaining acres were dispensed through cash sales. Through the late 1800s, disposal was frenetic, and the process was fraught with abuses and corruption.

In 1872, however, Yellowstone was set aside as the first national park. The first *systematic* reservation of federal land came in the form of the forest reserves (now national forests), created by the Forest Reserve Act of 1891. And perhaps the crowning preservation achievement came in 1978 with passage of the Alaska National Interest Lands Conservation Act. It designated 56 million acres as wilderness and transferred over 100 million acres from Bureau of Land Management (BLM) jurisdiction into the National Park and National Wildlife Refuge systems. Nationwide, the BLM currently has exclusive jurisdiction over 37 percent (270 million acres) of the federal estate. The National Forest System comprises 230 million acres, the National Park System 76 million acres, and the National Wildlife Refuge System about 90 million acres.

The federal lands are valued for their energy resources, minerals, timber, forage, recreation, and simply as part of the national heritage. As a result, the debate over retention (and acquisition of new land) versus disposal has raged for many decades. In 1976, the Federal Land Policy and Management Act (FLPMA) established retention as public policy. This undoubtedly helped set off the latest "sagebrush rebellion." Several western states, with the support of Ronald Reagan and Interior Secretary James Watt, claimed that federal lands should be transferred into state and private hands. But much of the state protestation amounts to little more than posturing. Most of the prime farms and grazing lands are already in private hands, and it soon became apparent to the states that they are better off leaving most of the administrative and fiscal burdens of land management with Uncle Sam.

Figure 3.2 shows Indian and BLM lands. The BLM was created in 1946 through merger of the General Land Office and the National Grazing Service. It manages the "unappropriated" federal land, much of it in the form of scattered parcels. Prior to the 1976 passage of the FLPMA, the BLM operated with little formal policy guidance. Indeed, even though the Wilderness Act was passed in 1964 (figure 15.4), the BLM was not granted authority to study and designate wilderness areas until 1976. Besides wilderness study, the FLPMA calls for comprehensive land-use planning and designation of "areas of critical environmental concern." Resource Management Plans for BLM lands are to be completed by 1991.

As of 1988, 5.3 million of the BLM's 270 million acres were designated as areas of critical environmental concern. Also, about 465,000 acres were in wilderness designation; an additional 100,000 were recommended for designation; and over 25 million were under study, as required by litigation (*Sierra Club v. Watt*). Environmentalists charge the BLM with mismanagement of many critical areas. Mining, overgrazing, and off-road vehicles are among the key issues. One special area designated by the FLPMA—the 12-million-acre California Desert Conservation Area—has been singled out. Environmentalists are calling for new wilderness designations and transfer of part of this area to the National Park Service.

Indian lands also are marked by intense resource conflicts. Over the course of 200 years the U.S. government has steadily, and often through abusive and deceptive means, expropriated Indian lands. What remains are 53 million acres mostly held in trust by the government. Yet these lands hold about 60 percent of known uranium reserves, one-third of low-sulfur coal, one-quarter of the nation's oil, and perhaps 15 percent of its natural gas (Churchill 1986). But Indians receive payments far below market value for many of the resources extracted. The federal government, as trustee of Indian lands, has frequently subsumed Indian interests to corporate economic interests.

Only in recent years have Indians begun to strongly assert their own interests in lands and natural resources. The Alaska Native Claims Settlement Act of 1971 ceded 44 million acres (12 percent of Alaska's land) to 70,000 native Aleuts, Eskimos, and Indians. The federal government paid reparations of nearly a billion dollars, allocated principally for the creation of a number of profit-making native corporations.

But despite some progress, resource conflicts abound. Water rights controversies are common in the West, as are land claim disputes in South Carolina, Wisconsin, and Arizona. Tribal recognition is critical in many places. Only with formal federal recognition can tribes become eligible for certain federal benefits. Moreover, recognition increases the ability of tribes to self-govern and thus manage their own affairs and resources.

Table 3.1. Federal Lands

	Percent
Alabama	3.3
Alaska	87.1
Arizona	43.1
Arkansas	9.9
California	46.4
Colorado	36.2
Connecticut	0.4
Delaware	2.4
Florida	12.4
Georgia	5.4
Hawaii	16.4
Idaho	63.7
Illinois	1.4
Indiana	1.9
Iowa	0.5
Kansas	1.1
Kentucky	5.5
Louisiana	4.0
Maine	0.8
Maryland	3.1
Massachusetts	1.6
Michigan	9.7
Minnesota	6.8
Mississippi	5.5
Missouri	4.7
Montana	30.5
Nebraska	1.5
Nevada	85.1
New Hampshire	12.8
New Jersey	3.3
New Mexico	31.3
New York	5.1
North Carolina	7.0
North Dakota	4.4
Ohio	1.2
Oklahoma	1.9
Oregon	48.7
Pennsylvania	2.2
Rhode Island	0.7
South Carolina	6.0
South Dakota	5.6
Tennessee	7.0
Texas	1.9
Utah	63.6
Vermont	5.4
Virginia	9.7
Washington	29.2
West Virginia	7.6
Wisconsin	5.2
Wyoming	49.5
U.S. Total	**31.9**

Source: Bureau of Land Management, *Public Land Statistics 1988*, vol.173 (Washington, DC: GPO, 1989), p. 5.

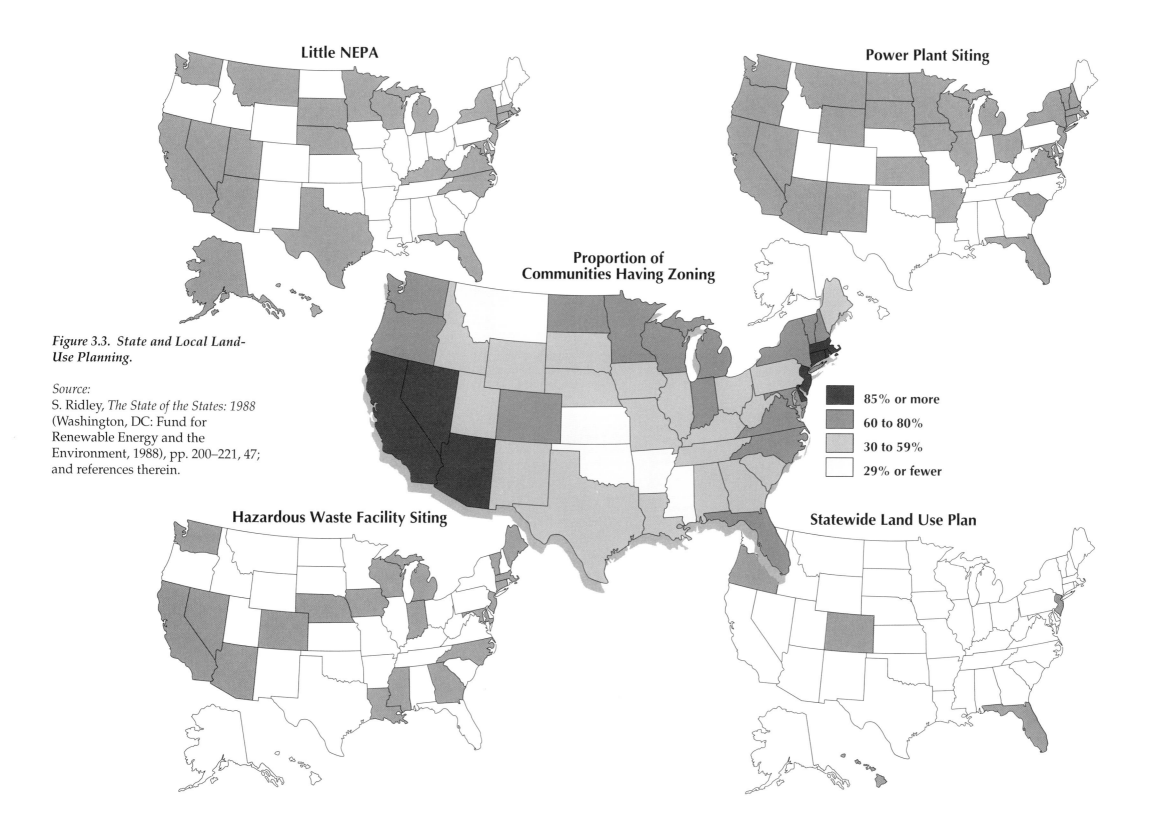

Little NEPA

Power Plant Siting

Proportion of Communities Having Zoning

Figure 3.3. State and Local Land-Use Planning.

Source:
S. Ridley, *The State of the States: 1988* (Washington, DC: Fund for Renewable Energy and the Environment, 1988), pp. 200–221, 47; and references therein.

85% or more
60 to 80%
30 to 59%
29% or fewer

Hazardous Waste Facility Siting

Statewide Land Use Plan

STATE AND LOCAL LAND-USE PLANNING

While the 1970s "quiet revolution in land-use control" may have faltered, reports of the death of federal and state land-use planning clearly are premature. Perhaps more significant than the volume of land-use controls is their changing scale. The 1970s' trend toward increased centralization has been replaced by rather vigorous planning and regulatory activities that are more specialized—geographically as well as administratively—in what they control. To a degree, we are witnessing a reaffirmation of powerful, enduring traditions of local control—but with more teeth than earlier controls. The notion of comprehensive land-use planning (i.e., regulation of virtually all land use) is less fashionable than it was during the 1970s, but the perceived need to regulate specific threats probably has increased during the late 1970s and 1980s. In part, this may be a response to perceived weakening of federal will to deal with environmental problems.

It is difficult to back these contentions with precise data—especially regarding community-level activities. At the state level, we see that several states have land-use plans. These tend to be comprehensive in nature and were either enacted during the Quiet Revolution or have developed through processes initiated during that period. Hawaii was a pioneer in formulating a state land-use plan; it did so in 1961. Vermont passed its Environmental Control Act (Act 250) in 1970. The act created a state environmental review board along with eight district review boards. The district boards issue permits, taking into consideration impacts on the natural environment, scenery, historic sites, and transportation and other public services. Decisions may be appealed to the state board.

Florida's Land and Water Management Act of 1972 focuses on "developments of regional impact" and "areas of critical concern." In 1985 Florida adopted a comprehensive land-use plan along with other measures that strengthened its regulatory system. Oregon's Land Use Law, passed in 1973, requires states and cities to adopt comprehensive land-use plans that conform with statewide goals. The statewide Land Conservation and Development Commission exercises review and approval authority over the plans.

Some important initiatives are not represented on the map. Vermont, for example, has a comprehensive land-use law, but has not developed a statewide plan or map to guide it. California has a comprehensive planning program—but only for its coastal zone. In 1971, New York State created the Adirondack Park Agency. In 1973, the agency unveiled its comprehensive regional plan for the Adirondacks. It divides the Adirondacks into five classifications: hamlet, moderate-intensity development, low-intensity development, rural use, and resource management. Resource management areas have the most strin-

gent restrictions. A similar plan for the New Jersey Pinelands came on line in 1980 (figure 15.8). While there is general agreement that the 1970s land-use programs have improved the quality of development, it is also worth noting that many of them have been substantially reshaped through bargaining and negotiation.

Nearly every state has legislative provisions for protection of certain critical areas—such as coastal zones, wetlands, and/or wellheads. Many states also have developed oversight programs for hazardous waste facility siting. Most try to lessen the intrusiveness of such regulations by providing for local participation, funding for communities to retain their own technical experts, and/or local veto power over higher-level decisions. A majority of states also oversees the siting of power plants, while about half the states have "little NEPAs." Fashioned after the National Environmental Policy Act (NEPA), these laws require state review of the environmental impacts of certain classes of projects or activities. State and local land-use planning are not necessarily in harmony with one another. Power plant and hazardous waste facility siting are typical of the activities that provoke state-local confrontations. Nor are states and localities equal partners under the law. It is the state government—through enabling legislation—that authorizes local planning and zoning. As is evident from figure 3.3, however, most states do not mandate local zoning.

Although a community's destiny may apparently be guided by benevolent zoning and planning controls, it is perhaps just as likely to be influenced by less-structured forms of economic and political influence—including outright graft, corruption, or racial and ethnic prejudice. Still, the presence of zoning regulations usually indicates some desire to control the rate and character of local growth and protect aspects of the physical environment. Other legal controls include subdivision regulations that establish standards for streets, open space, and other public amenities. In order to reduce capital and energy costs—and leave more land as open space—communities may promote clustering of housing units. Various restrictions may be placed on critical areas or applied to particular land uses. Some communities have instituted moratoria on development while others exact environmental concessions from developers.

Communities may also acquire lands—through outright purchase, or by securing easements that impose restrictions on the owner's use of the land. Moreover, development may be directed to certain areas through selective provision of public facilities and granting of building permits. Various tax and fee systems may be used to promote or discourage development in particular areas. While we cannot offer a comprehensive national assessment of such programs, suffice it to say that there are a great many of them, and their numbers seem to be increasing.

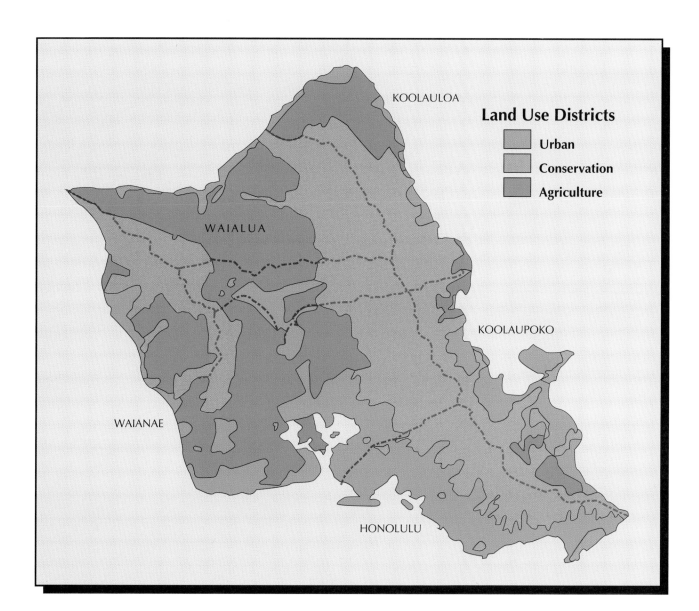

Land Use Districts

Urban

Conservation

Agriculture

KOOLAULOA

WAIALUA

KOOLAUPOKO

WAIANAE

HONOLULU

Figure 3.4. FOCUS: Hawaii's Land-Use Plan: An Example from Oahu.

Source:
R. W. Armstrong, ed., *Atlas of Hawaii*, 2d ed. (Honolulu: University of Hawaii Press, 1983), p. 150.

Hawaii's 1961 Land-Use Law, and subsequent amendments passed in 1963 and 1965, divide the islands into four major districts. These are depicted in generalized form on the accompanying map of the island of Oahu.

Urban Districts *include existing urban land, and provide reserve areas for projected growth.*

Rural Districts, *not shown on the map, seek to maintain rural character by requiring a minimum lot size of one-half acre per residence. Public facilities can be constructed in rural districts.*

Agriculture Districts *contain lands with high potential for intensive cultivation. Minimum lot size is one acre.*

Conservation Districts *include existing parks and reserves, marine waters and offshore islands, and areas with slopes greater than 20 percent.*

FOCUS: LAND-USE PLANNING IN HAWAII

Hawaii, as already noted, was a forerunner of the Quiet Revolution. Several factors conspired to make land-use planning a reality in 1961. But the key one was a desire to protect agricultural lands. Hawaii was experiencing a tourism boom even before it became a state in 1959, and its farmers—including several large and powerful ones— supported state land-use planning. Moreover, Hawaiians were accustomed to strong centralized government, because Hawaii had been ruled that way as a territory; indeed, Hawaii had only four local governments when it became a state. Moreover, land ownership was already concentrated in public and a limited number of private hands. And the obvious: Hawaii's land base is very limited.

All these factors set the stage for Hawaiian acceptance of the comprehensive zoning plan represented on the accompanying map. But the principal concerns of the time were orderly land development, efficient and economical delivery of public services and utilities, and minimal encroachment on prime agricultural land—*not* environmental preservation as such. Not until later in the 1960s and 1970s were the specific concerns of a developing environmental movement incorporated into Hawaii's land-use planning program. Indeed, the conservation districts (see map caption) at first consisted only of state-owned Forest and Water Reserve Zones. Private land was later added to the conservation districts, much of it in areas with slopes greater than 20 percent. A 1970 law authorized the inclusion of a 40-foot band of shoreline extending along the entire coastline.

Hawaii's program is administered by the state Land-Use Commission along with the state departments of Planning and Economic Development, Land and Natural Resources, Agriculture, and Taxation, the counties of Kauai, Maui, and Hawaii; and the City and County of Honolulu. The four land-use zones are briefly described in the map caption. In urban districts, land use is administered solely by the counties, while in agriculture and rural districts, the commission makes the rules and the counties administer them. Conservation districts are the sole province of the state Department of Land and Natural Resources.

In 1978, Hawaii's legislature adopted a broadly-based "guide plan" that deals not only with immediate land-use issues, but also health, education, culture, and public safety. Localities must conform with the state plan—and this has created intergovernmental tension. Moreover, there have been problems with "rural sprawl" in the form of agricultural subdivisions, as well as questionable reclassifications of land from agricultural to urban (DeGrove 1984)—even though since 1975 all boundary changes have been made through a quasi-judicial process and all changes are to conform with the state guide plan.

Agricultural Lands 4

Industrialized as it is, the United States still ranks as one of the world's leading agricultural nations. It is a major producer, consumer, and exporter of agricultural goods. The combination of fertile soils, favorable temperatures, and adequate moisture that allows such bountiful harvests is found in several parts of the country—but especially through the Great Plains, Mississippi Delta, and "Corn Belt" regions (indicated in figure 4.6).

This chapter treats agricultural lands as a resource. We look at the location and condition of the resource, threats to the resource base (specifically erosion and irrigation), and programs and policies that seek to deal with those threats. Other agricultural issues—among them pesticide toxicity and groundwater contamination—are more fully treated in other chapters (chapters 12 and 9 respectively).

Not until relatively recently in America's history did agricultural conservation become a collective concern. Early European settlers viewed agricultural resources in much the same way they regarded land in general: When soils were exhausted, it was always possible to move on. As settlement gradually progressed westward during the nineteenth century, the fertile lands of the plains and prairies were opened up to farming. Since that time, much of the inferior land of the East has been abandoned and left to revert to forest.

Major environmental modification accompanied the westward spread of agriculture. Not only were forests cleared and grasslands converted to croplands; wetlands were drained and drylands irrigated. Prior to the twentieth century, little heed was given to the few concerns that were expressed about future land scarcity, soil depletion, or water shortages.

Surplus production reached an all-time high following World War I. During the 1920s came calls for a national land policy that, among other things, would have eliminated farming on submarginal lands. No federal legislation emerged, though several states did develop land-use programs. In 1933, the Soil Erosion Service was established within the Department of the Interior. Conservation was promoted through provision of technical assistance and informational materials to farmers.

But it took the Dust Bowl of the 1930s to jolt the nation into a real sense of urgency about soil conservation. Severe drought—added to a history of exploitative agricultural practices—took a tremendous toll on Great Plains topsoil. Indeed, some of that soil traveled all the way across the country and out over the Atlantic. The accompanying social and economic distress—greatly worsened by the national depression—forced the exodus of many thousands of farmers from the southern Great Plains.

In response to the crisis, the Soil Conservation Act was passed in 1935. It set up new conservation grant and loan programs and replaced the Soil Erosion Service with a new USDA agency: the Soil Conservation Service (SCS). Over the next thirty years, 3,000 soil conservation districts were established, creating a decentralized system that reaches nearly all private rural landowners in the United States. The SCS cannot force farmers to conserve soil—but it does provide them with information on soil capabilities, assistance in developing conservation plans, and other technical advice.

Clearly, agricultural conservation has become more institutionalized since the depression era. But the administration of these programs is no simple matter. They are woven into a complex fabric of loans, payments, and production controls that have sometimes promoted and at other times inhibited conservation goals. For example, the Soil Bank program of the 1950s provided for establishment of conservation reserves, while the lifting of price supports in the 1970s was accompanied by a call for fencerow-to-fencerow planting. The excesses of the 1970s became the crises of the 1980s, as national attention focused on debt foreclosures, the plight of the family farmer, and soil erosion problems. The 1985 Food Security Act, discussed below, contains several important conservation initiatives—initiatives that in all likelihood will be extended by future legislation.

Center-Pivot Irrigation. United States Department of Agriculture.

Figure 4.1. Total Cropland, 1982.

One dot =50,000 *acres.*

Source:
Bureau of the Census, *Graphic Summary of the 1982 Census of Agriculture* (Washington, DC: GPO, 1985), p. 55.

Figure 4.2. Changes in Cropland Acreage, 1949–1982.

Source:
USDA, *Cropland Use and Supply: Outlook and Situation Report*, CUS-2 (Washington, DC: USDA, 1982), pp. 15, 17.

TOTAL CROPLAND, 1982

The United States is exceptionally well endowed with high-quality farmland. A great deal of additional land, even though it is only of marginal or submarginal agricultural value, can be viewed as *potentially* arable. The principal reasons are poor soils, steep slopes, and/or inadequate moisture. This does not mean that all "inferior" lands stay out of production. Indeed, extensive dryland areas have been made highly productive though irrigation—though sometimes at high environmental cost (figures 4.9, 4.10).

In 1988 there were approximately 406 million acres of cropland (excluding pasture), 328 million of which were actually planted. The remaining 78 million acres were idled through both short- and long-term government programs. The acreage actually harvested totaled 284 million; the rest was either in fallow or experienced crop failures (USDA 1988). Although a great variety of crops is grown, the ones that by far account for the largest share of production are wheat, corn, hay, and soybeans.

Figure 4.1 represents cropland acreage in 1982. Particularly striking is the intensity of farming in the Corn Belt and Great Plains states. The map provides a rather vivid illustration of why agriculture is so important to the economies of Illinois, Iowa, Indiana, Kansas, Nebraska, the Dakotas, and Texas.

Subregions also stand out: east Texas, the lower Mississippi Valley, California's irrigated Central Valley, the Palouse region of the Northwest, and even such less-intensively cultivated (or at least smaller) regions as the southeastern Piedmont, Pennsylvania's Lancaster County, and the interior plateaus of Tennessee and Kentucky.

Cropland acreage (total acreage, as well as that actually planted and harvested) declined between 1981 and 1988, reaching a low in 1988. The decline reflects lowered export demand for crops and significant increases in idled croplands in recent years. The increase in idled acreage has been especially notable since 1984 in the northern Great Plains. In 1988, total acreage idled under federal programs reached a record high. The other key factor in explaining 1988's relatively low harvested-acreage figure is the high rate of crop failure. This is in large part due to the widespread summer drought conditions (see figure 16.4). Indeed, planted and harvested acreage was up in 1989—despite continued successes with federal acreage-reduction programs.

Changes in Cropland Acreage

1949 to 1969

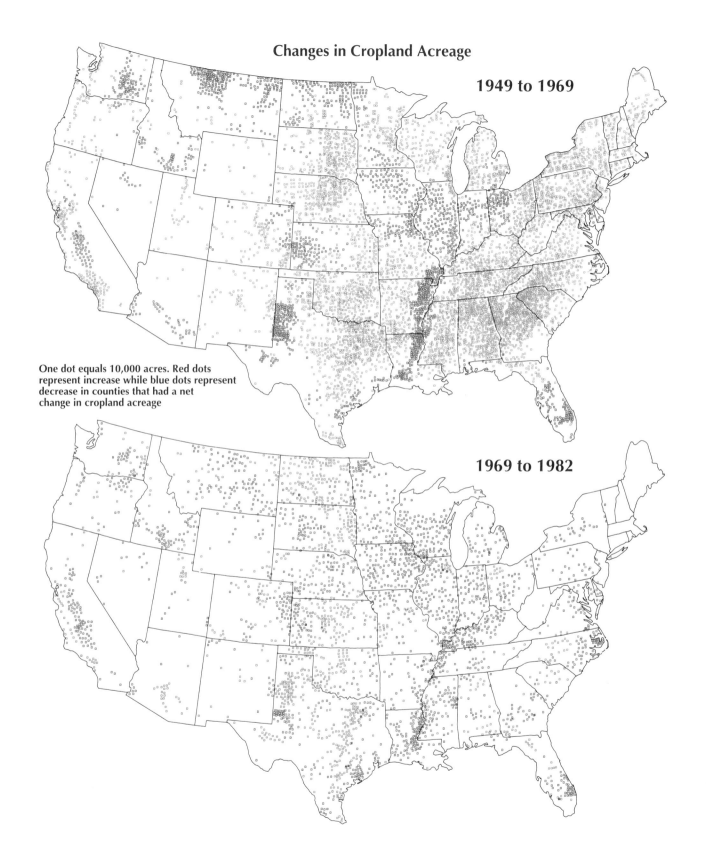

One dot equals 10,000 acres. Red dots represent increase while blue dots represent decrease in counties that had a net change in cropland acreage

1969 to 1982

CHANGES IN CROPLAND ACREAGE, 1949–1982

Changes in cropland acreages over the past several decades reflect changing technologies, economies of scale, and farmers' responses to government programs. The 1949–1969 period witnessed a significant decrease in cropland area; indeed, acreage declined or remained the same in about three-fourths of U.S. counties. Total cropland acres (excluding pasture) had peaked at 409 million in 1949; the 1969 figure was 370 million (USDA 1985b). The largest declines occurred in the Northeast, Southeast, Appalachian, and Great Plains regions (these and other regions are indicated in figure 4.6). In the Northeast and Appalachian areas, there were significant shifts to urban and forest uses; while in the Southeast, Great Plains, and also Appalachian areas, large acreages shifted to pasture. Much of the cropland-turned-pastureland had been only temporarily planted in crops, in response to federal farm programs of the time.

The only net increases in cropland acreage between 1949 and 1969 occurred in the Corn Belt and Mountain regions. The Mississippi Delta states (Mississippi, Louisiana, and Arkansas) also had large increases—but they were balanced by significant decreases. Many of the new acres became available as the result of clearing of forests, drainage of wetlands, and improved irrigation of dry lands. The loss of wetlands is especially notable in the lower Mississippi Valley, while significant irrigation occurred in Idaho, Montana, and California's Central Valley.

The 1969–1982 period contrasts sharply with the previous two decades: most of the country—the Great Plains the main exception—saw net cropland increases between these two years. In 1982, cropland acreage (excluding cropland used for pasture) totaled 380 million acres, up about 3 percent from 1969 (USDA 1985b). The peak year was 1981 (387 million crop acres)—a year during which *no* cropland was idled under federal programs. The greatest net increases were in the Corn Belt, Great Lakes states, and Mississippi Delta regions. The overall spatial pattern of increases is quite similar to that of the 1949–1969 period. Most of the converted land was formerly pasture or forest land, though drainage of wetlands and irrigation of dry lands also were significant. The greatest decreases in cropland acreages occurred in the Great Plains. In other regions, there were conversions to urban, forest, and other uses—but these changes, especially in the East, were much smaller than during the 1949–1969 period. The overall downward trend is likely to continue, at least in the near term, as a result of federal efforts to retire current cropland and restrict cultivation of new lands.

Over the long term, major cropland shifts may be induced by a changing climate. Indeed, various climate change scenarios show the Great Plains becoming too hot and dry to support today's high levels of agricultural productivity (figure 18.1).

Table 4.1. Prime Cropland

	Prime Cropland (acres)	All Prime Land (acres)	Percent Prime	Total Cropland (acres)	Percent Prime
Alabama	2,889.8	7,270	40	4,510	64
Arizona	1,059.8	1,090	97	1,206	88
Arkansas	6,641.4	11,624	57	8,102	82
California	5,544.7	5,891	94	10,518	53
Colorado	1,596.7	1,686	95	10,603	15
Connecticut	141.0	355	40	245	58
Delaware	327.4	430	76	519	63
Florida	419.7	1,104	38	3,557	12
Georgia	3,883.6	7,728	50	6,568	59
Hawaii	243.4	296	82	333	73
Idaho	3,036.6	3,413	89	6,390	48
Illinois	19,089.0	21,253	90	24,727	77
Indiana	11,190.6	13,510	83	13,781	81
Iowa	16,683.9	18,683	89	26,441	63
Kansas	19,007.0	25,602	74	29,118	65
Kentucky	3,757.0	6,050	62	5,934	63
Louisiana	5,653.6	12,975	44	6,409	88
Maine	388.5	1,273	31	953	41
Maryland	839.1	1,249	67	1,794	47
Massachusetts	138.8	381	36	297	47
Michigan	5,707.5	7,798	73	9,443	60
Minnesota	16,051.1	20,838	77	23,024	70
Mississippi	5,354.7	10,340	52	7,415	72
Missouri	9,863.3	15,000	66	14,998	66
Montana	857.9	1,014	85	17,19	5
Nebraska	10,600.2	12,243	87	20,277	52
Nevada	285.1	313	91	860	33
New Hampshire	43.5	144	30	158	28
New Jersey	448.6	863	52	809	55
New Mexico	573.9	615	93	2,413	24
New York	2,732.8	5,138	53	5,912	46
North Carolina	2,808.0	5,679	49	6,695	42
North Dakota	12,682.7	13,912	91	27,039	47
Ohio	9,764.2	12,248	80	12,447	78
Oklahoma	7,908.9	15,049	53	11,56	68
Oregon	1,340.5	1,935	69	4,356	31
Pennsylvania	2,181.5	4,285	51	5,896	37
Rhode Island	23.0	78	29	27	85
South Carolina	1,660.7	3,428	48	3,579	46
South Dakota	5,348.9	6,426	83	16,947	32
Tennessee	3,415.6	6,317	54	5,592	61
Texas	19,229.8	37,621	51	33,320	58
Utah	732.6	787	93	2,039	36
Vermont	171.4	336	51	648	26
Virginia	1,757.4	5,032	35	3,397	52
Washington	1,418.5	2,308	61	7,793	18
West Virginia	319.4	539	59	1,093	29
Wisconsin	6,288.2	9,414	67	11,457	55
Wyoming	293.4	349	84	2,587	11

PRIME CROPLAND

Most of America's crops are produced on prime farmlands—lands that are inherently suited to crop production because of low erosiveness, good drainage, lack of stones, and favorable climate conditions. The 1982 total of 343 million acres of prime farmland represents a decline of about 2 million acres from 1977. Between 1967 and 1975, 8 million acres of prime farmland were converted to nonagricultural (primarily urban-related) uses (USDA et al. 1981).

Most of the prime land is found in the Corn Belt, Mississippi Delta, and Great Plains regions (indicated in figure 4.6). These are the areas where the greatest percentages of prime farmlands are used for crop production (as opposed to other uses) and where the highest percentages of all croplands are *prime* croplands. Prime land is in relatively short supply in the Mountain states, though Arizona grows a very high proportion of crops on prime land because of extensive irrigation. A substantial proportion of the Southeast's prime land is held by forest companies; whereas in the Northeast, many small parcels are found in or adjacent to metropolitan areas.

Table 4.1. Prime Cropland and Figure 4.3. Prime Cropland as Percent of Total Cropland, 1982.

*Prime cropland (or prime farmland) has the best combination of physical and chemical characteristics for producing crops. While pastureland, rangeland, and forest land may be classified as prime land, urban land is excluded from the definition. Irrigated lands are included—but **not** included are those lands that would qualify as prime **only** after irrigation is provided.*

Source:
Soil Conservation Service, *Basic Statistics: 1982 National Resources Inventory*, Statistical Bulletin no. 756 (Ames, IA: Iowa State University Statistical Laboratory, 1987), pp. 62, 137–138.

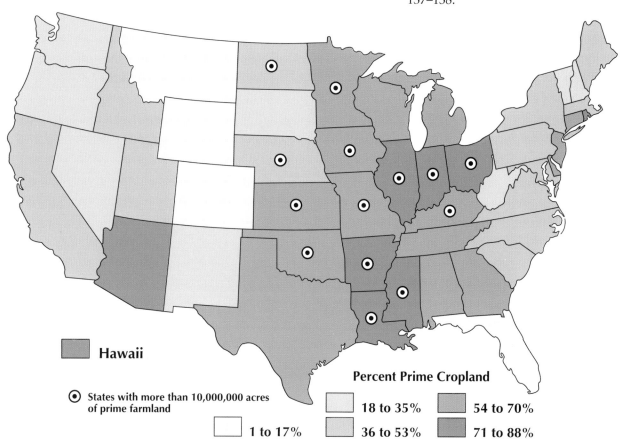

Hawaii

⊙ **States with more than 10,000,000 acres of prime farmland**

Percent Prime Cropland

1 to 17%
18 to 35%
36 to 53%
54 to 70%
71 to 88%

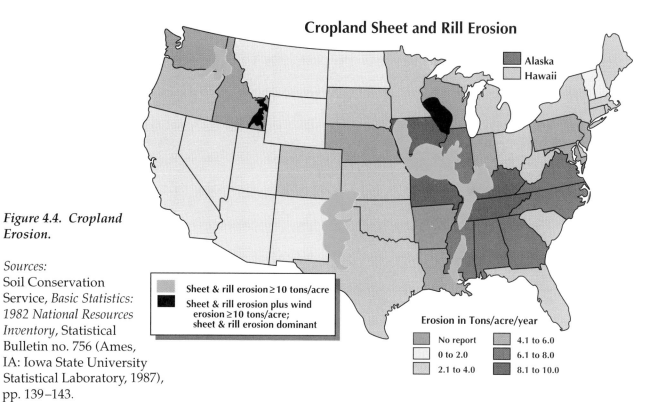

Cropland Sheet and Rill Erosion

Alaska
Hawaii

Sheet & rill erosion ≥10 tons/acre
Sheet & rill erosion plus wind erosion ≥10 tons/acre; sheet & rill erosion dominant

Erosion in Tons/acre/year

No report
0 to 2.0
2.1 to 4.0
4.1 to 6.0
6.1 to 8.0
8.1 to 10.0

Figure 4.4. Cropland Erosion.

Sources:
Soil Conservation Service, *Basic Statistics: 1982 National Resources Inventory*, Statistical Bulletin no. 756 (Ames, IA: Iowa State University Statistical Laboratory, 1987), pp. 139–143.

L. K. Lee, "Land Use and Soil Loss: A 1982 Update," *Journal of Soil and Water Conservation* 39 (1984): 227–228.

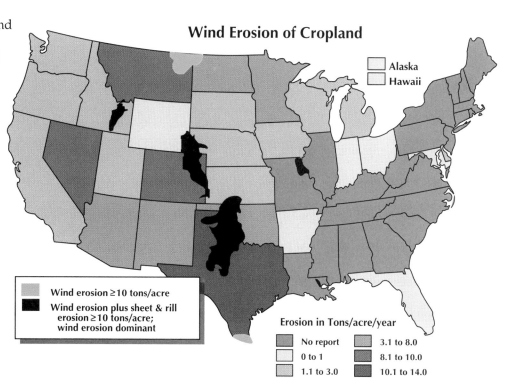

Wind Erosion of Cropland

Alaska
Hawaii

Wind erosion ≥10 tons/acre
Wind erosion plus sheet & rill erosion ≥10 tons/acre; wind erosion dominant

Erosion in Tons/acre/year

No report
0 to 1
1.1 to 3.0
3.1 to 8.0
8.1 to 10.0
10.1 to 14.0

CROPLAND EROSION

Erosion is the wearing away of soil by wind, water, ice, or other geologic means. Soil erosion creates problems both on and off the farm. The major off-farm impact is the addition of sediment to water bodies. The sediment reduces the value (and/or increases the cost of treatment) of the water for recreation and drinking purposes. It also carries pollutants and settles behind dams, shortening the life of reservoirs.

Of greatest concern here, however, are the on-farm impacts. Depletion of soil translates into reduced agricultural productivity; in cases of severe erosion, land may be rendered useless for crop production.

Sheet and rill erosion and wind erosion are the major types of cropland erosion. Sheet erosion is the removal of thin, fairly uniform layers of soil by rain falling on and water running over the soil. Rill erosion removes soil through the formation of small channels (rills). Channels deeper than 1 foot are termed gullies. Wind erosion is a particular problem in areas with low rainfall and high wind velocities. One such area is the Great Plains.

The intensity of soil erosion is a function of both inherent erosiveness of the soil and management practices. There is considerable debate about how to gauge the severity of soil erosion, especially at the aggregated levels of the region, state, and nation. The National Resources Inventory provides assessments in relation to the T-value—the maximum amount of soil loss that can be sustained without a loss of soil productivity. T-values provide a rough indication of erodibility of cropland. If we define as "highly erodible" those lands with erosion rates greater than "3-T," then it is clear that the most severe problems are in the Corn Belt and Great Plains regions.

The maps show average erosion rates by state, without reference to T-values. As a very rough rule of thumb, a loss of 5 tons per acre per year (from wind and/or water erosion) may be equated with soil depletion. This rate results in a loss of about one-thirtieth of an inch of soil per acre. In 1982, approximately 24 percent of cropland had sheet- and rill-erosion rates equal to or greater than 5 tons/acre/year, while 16 percent had wind erosion rates of 5 tons or greater (National Research Council 1986). In addition to average state rates of erosion, figure 4.4 shows areas with severe problems (rates greater than or equal to 10 tons/acre/year). The most severe erosion is found in parts of the Corn Belt and Great Plains regions and in the Snake River Plains, Eastern Idaho Plateaus, and Palouse and Nez Perce Prairies.

One reason for high erosion rates is the intensity of American agriculture. Indeed, even as additional cropland is retired under federal programs (figure 4.7), new concerns are raised about more intense use of acreages that remain in production. This may mean *more* soil erosion per acre as well as pollution from fertilizers and pesticides.

FARMLAND PRESERVATION

Soil-conservation and income-support programs for farmers have been with us since the 1920s. Some of them seek to reduce planted acreages, in many cases to retire lands permanently. These efforts remain firmly in place today; indeed, a major new conservation initiative was launched in 1985 (figure 4.7). But we have also witnessed, over the past two decades, a proliferation of new laws and policies aimed at keeping farmers farming. In contrast to conservation and income-support programs, their principal objective is to keep farmland from being converted to other uses. Yet the two types of programs rarely are in direct conflict: farmland preservation programs are directed toward specific land-use conflicts usually quite distinct—spatially as well as politically—from those addressed by acreage reduction programs. Furthermore, most preservation activities are administered at the state rather than national level.

The impetus for many preservation programs is a presumed current or future shortage of agricultural land. Indeed, the National Agricultural Lands Study—released in 1980—portrayed the situation in rather urgent terms, calling for efforts to slow the conversion of agricultural lands to nonagricultural uses. But if we consider the land availability question at the gross national level, there appears to be no shortage of farmland. According to the 1982 National Resources Inventory, 153 million acres of land—now in pasture, range, forest, and other uses—have high or medium potential for conversion to cropland. This represents a potential expansion of the 1982 cropland base by 36 percent. If we consider only the conversion potential of Class I and II lands—those that have few or only moderate limitations for agriculture—we find that the total is 52 million acres (12 percent of the 1982 cropland base).

About 110 million acres of prime farmland (32 percent of total prime farmland acres) were in noncrop uses in 1982 (table 4.1). While prime lands are particularly well suited to crop production, they are valued for other uses as well. Because use as forest, pasture, or range does not preclude future conversion to cropland, these activities often find wide acceptance. And indeed, the primary stated concern of farmland preservation advocates is *future* cropland availability. Even though it does appear that potential cropland is adequate to meet projected needs, this assumption must be tempered in light of uncertainty about future export markets; our ability to maintain high levels of productivity through increased use of chemical fertilizers, pesticides, and herbicides; possible effects of soil erosion; and potential large-scale climate changes that could affect agriculture.

Despite these lofty national concerns, it appears that local and regional issues are the *main* motivating factors for farmland preservation activities. Especially in the more urbanized parts of the country, there is deep concern over loss of prime cropland to

suburban development. The desire to maintain pleasing, productive rural landscapes within driving distance of urban areas is intertwined with preferences for locally grown food and fears about irretrievable losses of land that may be needed for future food production. The result, in many cases, is conflict between farmers who do not want their economic options restricted and urban dwellers concerned about amenity and land-scarcity issues.

Much of the farmland protection activity has occurred at the state level. A variety of tools and techniques are employed; key among them are the ones shown on these maps:

1. *Right-to-farm laws* are state or local statutes that protect farmers from specified legal actions against such farm-related nuisances as noise, odors, and pesticide drift.
2. *Tax-relief incentives* seek to reduce the tax burden on farmers. Differential and preferential assessment laws permit agricultural lands to be assessed at their current agricultural use values rather than (generally higher) market values. Various restrictions may be placed upon the farmer; in some cases the taxes are deferred rather than eliminated.
3. *Purchase of development rights* programs allow state or local governments to buy from farmers the rights to develop land. The farmer retains all other rights of ownership.
4. *Transfer of development rights* programs entail designation of "sending" and "receiving" areas for the rights to develop land. Development is restricted or prohibited in the sending areas; while in the receiving areas development credits may be used to build at higher densities than otherwise permitted. The objective is to create a market that sets the price for development credits and fosters their private transfer. In practice, a variety of factors impede the smooth operation of such markets, and they often must be primed—sometimes unsuccessfully—through the establishment of government-operated "development credit banks."
5. *Agricultural districting* is a voluntary process whereby one farmer or a group organizes into geographic entities where farming is to be the only activity for a specified period of years. Government incentives generally are offered to the farmers.
6. *Agricultural zone ordinances* prescribe land uses within the zoned areas. Nonexclusive ordinances permit nonagricultural uses, while exclusive ordinances allow only farm-related uses.

All states have enacted *some* form of farmland preservation legislation, and many have developed highly specialized programs using multiple techniques. The heavily urbanized northeastern states have been most active in farmland protection; southern states the least.

Figure 4.5. Farmland Preservation Activities.

Source:
National Association of State Departments of Agriculture, "Current State Farmland Protection Activities," *Farmland Notes* 7 (January 1988).

Right to Farm Law

Alaska
Hawaii

Transfer of Development Rights

Alaska
Hawaii

Participating states

Tax Relief- Preferential/Differential

Alaska
Hawaii

Agricultural Districting

Alaska
Hawaii

Purchase of Development Rights

Alaska
Hawaii

Agricultural Zoning

Alaska
Hawaii

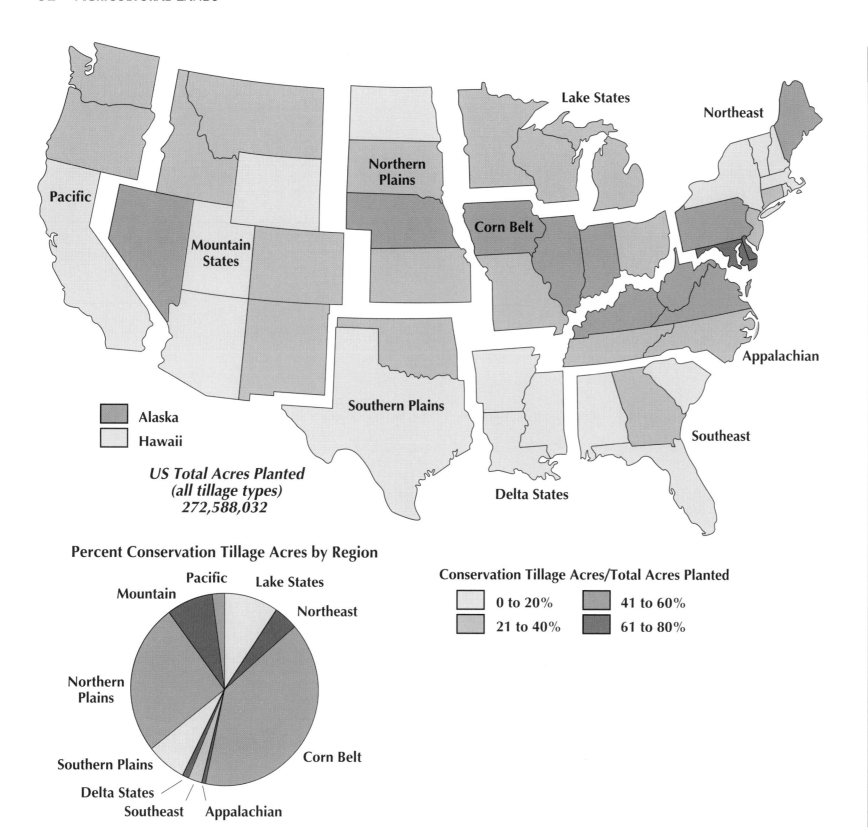

Lake States

Northeast

Pacific

Northern Plains

Corn Belt

Mountain States

Appalachian

Alaska

Hawaii

Southern Plains

Southeast

*US Total Acres Planted
(all tillage types)
272,588,032*

Delta States

Percent Conservation Tillage Acres by Region

Mountain

Pacific

Lake States

Northeast

Northern Plains

Corn Belt

Southern Plains

Delta States

Southeast

Appalachian

Conservation Tillage Acres/Total Acres Planted

| | 0 to 20% | | 41 to 60% |
| | 21 to 40% | | 61 to 80% |

Total Acres Planted, 1987	
Alabama	2,259,298
Alaska	12,875
Arizona	830,300
Arkansas	6,378,941
California	7,243,045
Colorado	5,505,953
Connecticut	51,759
Delaware	518,200
Florida	1,716,288
Georgia	3,823,847
Hawaii	300,000
Idaho	4,538,804
Illinois	20,812,329
Indiana	11,044,166
Iowa	20,378,346
Kansas	18,819,606
Kentucky	3,586,167
Louisiana	3,768,699
Maine	264,327
Maryland	1,479,810
Massachusetts	77,144
Michigan	5,831,353
Minnesota	17,340,911
Mississippi	4,378,645
Missouri	9,828,524
Montana	7,773,559
Nebraska	14,426,509
Nevada	97,329
New Hampshire	22,129
New Jersey	346,565
New Mexico	1,189,195
New York	2,289,948
North Carolina	4,226,644
North Dakota	17,041,296
Ohio	9,086,349
Oklahoma	8,567,852
Oregon	1,884,316
Pennsylvania	2,926,085
Rhode Island	8,846
South Carolina	1,856,018
South Dakota	11,749,980
Tennessee	3,645,056
Texas	19,867,702
Utah	651,496
Vermont	111,875
Virginia	3,813,888
Washington	149,151
West Virginia	7,172,526
Wisconsin	895,283
Wyoming	47,687

Figure 4.6. Adoption of Conservation Tillage, 1987.

Source:
Conservation Technology Information Center, *1987 National Survey: Conservation Tillage Practices* (West Lafayette, IN: CTIC, 1988).

CONSERVATION TILLAGE

Conservation tillage is a very effective means for reducing soil erosion—and its adoption by farmers has increased rapidly in recent years. It offers an alternative to the traditional practice of deep plowing, a practice that loosens and exposes soil particles, making the soil more vulnerable to erosion. The Conservation Technology Information Center (1988) defines conservation tillage as those practices that maintain coverage of at least 30 percent of the soil surface with crop residue in areas where erosion by water is the main concern. Where wind erosion is the primary concern, the criterion is maintenance of at least 1,000 pounds of "flat small-grain residue equivalent." The addition of crop residue to the soil reduces the rate of soil depletion by slowing the runoff of water and reducing vulnerability to wind erosion. It also replenishes the organic fraction of the soil.

The Conservation Technology Information Center also defines specific types of conservation tillage as follows:

1. *No-till.* The soil is left undisturbed prior to planting. Planting is completed in a narrow seedbed or slot. Weed control is usually accomplished with herbicides.
2. *Ridge-till.* The soil is left undisturbed prior to planting. Approximately one-third of the soil surface is filled at planting time. Planting is completed in the seedbed prepared on ridges, generally 4 to 6 inches higher than the row middles. Weed control is accomplished with a combination of herbicides and cultivation.
3. *Strip-till.* The soil is left undisturbed prior to planting. Approximately one-third of the soil is tilled at planting time. Tillage in the row may consist of a rototiller, in-row chisel, row cleaners, and so forth. Weed control is accomplished with a combination of herbicides and cultivation.
4. *Mulch-till.* The total soil surface is disturbed by tillage prior to planting. Tillage tools such as chisels, field cultivators, discs, sweeps, or blades are used. Weed control is accomplished with a combination of herbicides and cultivation.
5. *Reduced-till.* Any other tillage and planting system not covered above that meets the 30 percent residue requirement.

Mulch-till accounted for about two-thirds of all conservation tillage in 1987. Ridge-till is favored in parts of the Midwest where drainage is poor and soils are slow to warm up in the spring. Strip-till methods are increasing in popularity in parts of the South and Great Plains. In addition, a variety of more specific methods and equipment have been developed to meet a variety of needs. Generally, farmers are finding conservation tillage advantageous because it saves time, cuts fuel and equipment costs, and reduces erosion. It also reduces—but does not eliminate—the problem of soil compaction. Crop yields are usually comparable to—sometimes better than—those obtained with conventional tillage. Why, then, has it taken so long for the practice to begin to catch on? The best answers seem simply to be lack of knowledge and inertia: Spring plowing is a cultural ritual that has been with us for centuries.

Conservation tillage offers clear environmental benefits: It reduces rates of soil erosion, reduces the rate of runoff of agricultural chemicals, and over the long term may reduce the need for chemical fertilizers. But it is not without environmental cost. More herbicides are necessary to control the weeds that sprout from the undisturbed or minimally disturbed soils. More pesticides may also be needed to control increased insect, rodent, and other problems. Despite some successes with nonchemical methods of weed and pest control, as well as with less toxic chemicals, most farmers still favor increased use of hazardous chemicals as the most expedient way to deal with the weed and pest problems associated with conservation tillage. This has caused some environmental organizations, including the Audubon Society, to express deep reservations about conservation tillage.

In 1987, 32 percent of the nation's farms had adopted conservation tillage in some form (Conservation Technology Information Center 1988)—and recent trends suggest that the adoption rate will continue to rise. But in the absence of a comprehensive farm-by-farm assessment, it is difficult to gauge the overall effectiveness of conservation tillage in reducing soil erosion. Concern has been expressed that many of the areas adopting conservation tillage are those where soils are not inherently erosive. At the same time—as is evident from the map in figure 4.6—conservation tillage has gained wide acceptance in at least some of the regions with severe erosion problems—in particular parts of the Corn Belt, Northern Great Plains, and Appalachian regions.

Conservation tillage is promoted through a variety of channels. The National Association of Conservation Districts works with the Conservation Technology Information Center to provide information. To varying degrees, conservation tillage is also researched and/or promoted nationally by the Agricultural Research Service (a division of the USDA), the Soil Conservation Society of America (private), the Rodale Institute and Institute for Alternative Agriculture (both promote "alternative"—including organic—farming), the Agricultural Stabilization and Conservation Service (ASCS), and the Soil Conservation Service (SCS). The latter two are part of the USDA. The ASCS administers government payment and support programs, while the SCS provides technical assistance to farmers. In addition, state agronomists and extension representatives are available to work with farmers.

THE CONSERVATION RESERVE PROGRAM

Passage of the 1985 Food Security Act marked the beginning of a new era in agricultural conservation. Among other things, the act seeks to remove highly erodible lands from production and to promote better management of those erodible lands that stay in production. It also attempts to stem the conversion of wetlands and highly erodible lands to cropland. The major components of the act are: the Conservation Reserve program, the Conservation Compliance Policy, conservation easement provisions, the sodbuster policy, and the swampbuster policy (see figure 5.6). These programs complement and expand considerably upon earlier federal cost-share and technical assistance activities. Most significantly, the new programs are long-term rather than annual in nature.

The purpose of the Conservation Reserve Program (CRP) is the long-term removal of highly erodible croplands from production. They are to be put into grass and tree cover for a period of at least ten years. The goal for the reserve is 40 to 45 million acres by 1990. Participating farmers enter into contracts with the Agricultural Stabilization and Conservation Service (ASCS), which makes annual rental payments to the farmers. In addition, up to half the cost of establishing permanent vegetative cover may be provided by the Commodity Credit Corporation. In times of national emergency, crop production may be allowed on CRP lands. Indeed, emergency haying and grazing were permitted during the summer of 1988 (figure 16.4).

As of late 1988, the Agricultural Stabilization and Conservation Service (had conducted seven signups for the CRP. Early results were rather disappointing, but enrollments picked up in subsequent signups. Activity was relatively slow in the seventh signup (July 18 through August 31, 1988), probably the result of the summer drought. However, significant acreage increases were recorded in Iowa, Illinois, Indiana, Ohio, New York, California, and New Mexico. The U.S. Department of Agriculture reports that total contracted acreage was approximately 27 million. Average erosion rates on contracted acres declined from 22 to 1.6 tons/acre/year. In short, this represents significant progress toward the program's goals. Future progress will depend upon commodity prices, export demand, and modifications to the legislation and regulations. Already, the regulations have been altered—with some success—to promote more tree planting and to encourage filter strips, which act as a buffer between cropland and water.

The map in figure 4.7 represents CRP enrollment through 1988. Highest participation has been in the West and Southeast; participation rates in the Northeast and Corn Belt are relatively low. Highest per-acre rental payments have been made in the Corn Belt. But with the exception of the Corn Belt, there is no apparent association between rental payments and participation rates.

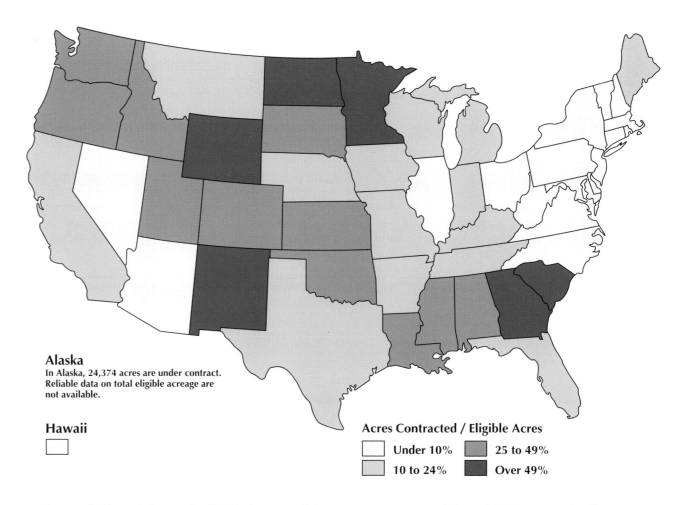

Alaska
In Alaska, 24,374 acres are under contract. Reliable data on total eligible acreage are not available.

Hawaii

Acres Contracted / Eligible Acres

- Under 10%
- 10 to 24%
- 25 to 49%
- Over 49%

As was indicated above, the CRP is just one of the conservation provisions of the 1985 bill. The Conservation Compliance Policy requires farmers to adopt an approved conservation plan for their highly erodible lands. If they fail to do so by 1990, they become ineligible for federal loan, insurance, and price-support programs. This use of disincentives rather than incentives marks a departure from earlier programs. Of the 118 million acres of cropland that the 1982 National Resources Inventory classified as highly erodible, 35 million currently meet compliance specifications, 28 million are enrolled in the CRP, and at least 55 million still require conservation treatment. Approximately one-quarter of those 55 million acres are in the Corn Belt, with substantial acreages also in the Great Plains and Mountain regions (USDA 1988).

Under the sodbuster provisions, farmers who bring highly erodible lands into production without a conservation plan lose their eligibility for federal benefits. As of mid-1988, approximately $1.9 billion in benefits had been forgone by 105 farmers. About half this loss occurred in the Southwest (USDA 1988).

Figure 4.7. Conservation Reserve Program Participation (through mid-1988).

Source:
USDA, *1989 Agriculture Chartbook* (Rockville, MD: USDA, 1989), p. 45.

Total eligible acres for the Conservation Reserve Program (CRP) at the time of the sixth signup (1988) were approximately 101.5 million. CRP enrollment is limited, however, to a maximum of 25 percent of a county's cropland. As of late summer 1988, fifty-five of 2,326 counties with land enrolled in the CRP had reached the 25 percent limit. Exemptions from the limit had been granted to 47 percent of those counties.

Polk County, Iowa

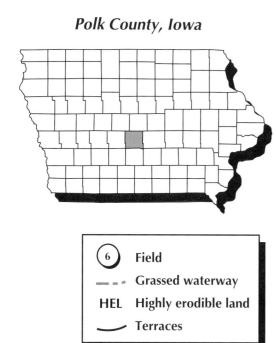

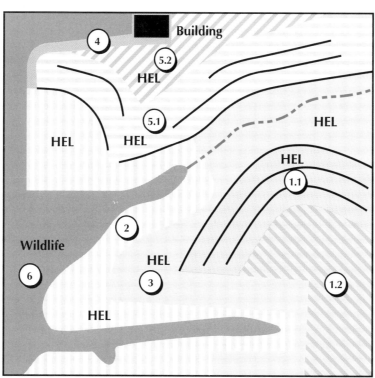

Legend:
- ⑥ Field
- – · – Grassed waterway
- HEL Highly erodible land
- ⌒ Terraces

Fields	Total Acres	Conservation Tillage	Contour Farming	Terraces	Underground Outlet	Conservation Cover	Grassed Waterway	Livestock Exclusion	Filter Strip	Wildlife Upland Habitat Management
Management Practices										
1.1	16.5	■	■	■	■					
1.2	15.8	■								
2	31.6					■	■	■		
3	29.8					■	■			
4	1.8							■	■	
5.1	18.4	■	■	■						
5.2	12.0	■								
6	18.9							■		■

Figure 4.8. FOCUS: A Farm Conservation Plan in Polk County, Iowa.

Source:
Soil Conservation Service, *Record of Decisions and Application: Conservation Plan for the Food Security Act* (Ankeny, IA: Soil Conservation Service, 1989).

FOCUS: A FARM CONSERVATION PLAN IN POLK COUNTY, IOWA

The Soil Conservation Service (SCS) works with individual farmers in pursuit of a wide variety of objectives. They include long-term soil productivity, water-quality maintenance, fish and wildlife habitat protection, and environmental conservation generally. The SCS provides farmers with data on soils, land use, wildlife and vegetation, and environmental impacts of various activities; helps farmers interpret this information; and assists them in making and evaluating decisions.

Under the Food Security Act of 1985 (figures 4.7, 5.6), farmers are required—or at least given powerful incentives—to adopt certain environmental protection measures. Figure 4.8 represents a conservation plan for a farm in Polk County, Iowa—a plan that meets the Food Security Act's conservation requirements, and thus keeps the farmer eligible for various U.S. Department of Agriculture subsidy programs. While the farmer is not bound by the plan, it may well be in his best interests (short- as well as long-term) to abide by at least certain of its provisions.

Fields 1.1, 1.2, 5.1, and 5.2 are planted in corn. Sheet and rill erosion is reduced through contour planting and tilling (which slow the downhill flow of water) and construction of terraces. The terraces, made of tile, collect surface water and convey it to an underground outlet. Soil erosion also is reduced through conservation tillage (figure 4.8). In the fall, corn stalks are incorporated into the soil; the objective is to have at least 30 percent of crop residue in place at planting time.

Fields 2, 3, and 4 are enrolled in the ten-year Conservation Reserve Program (figure 4.8). Perennial vegetative cover (conservation cover) is established to control erosion and provide wildlife habitat. Filter strips (strips or areas of vegetation) are strategically situated to remove sediment and other pollutants from runoff and wastewater. They do this through filtration, deposition, infiltration, absorption, adsorption (adhesion to soil particles), bacterial decomposition, and volatilization (conversion to gaseous state). Grassed waterways, by controlling runoff, assist in pollutant removal and prevention of gullying. Soil and vegetation also are protected through exclusion of livestock from conservation-reserve and wildlife-management lands. The highly erodible lands, shown on map, are targeted for special protection; in fact, much of this land is included in the conservation reserve.

IRRIGATED ACREAGE

Approximately 13 percent of U.S. cropland is irrigated, and these lands account for about 30 percent of the value of crop production. Irrigated acreage increased quite steadily between 1900 and the late 1970s, then declined somewhat between 1978 and 1982. Most of the decline was in the southern Great Plains and Mountain regions. Between 1983 and 1988, the upward trend resumed (USDA1988).

The crops that account for the largest shares of these acreages are corn, hay, wheat, cotton, fruit, and rice. As the map indicates, the greatest proportions of irrigated croplands are found in the arid west. Irrigation, especially in dry regions, consumes vast amounts of water (chapter 9). Federal water-resource projects—most administered by the Bureau of Reclamation—have provided western farmers with water at subsidized rates. Since 1976, however, no new federal irrigation projects have been authorized. It seems unlikely that much new capacity will be added—except that provided by completion of previously authorized projects. Perhaps of even greater urgency than surface-water issues, though, are those associated with groundwater: In parts of the West—especially sections of the Great Plains—groundwater supplies are being rapidly depleted by heavy agricultural use (chapter 9).

The map shows relatively small ratios of irrigated land to total cropland in the eastern regions. However, irrigated acreage has been growing rapidly over the past thirty years as farmers seek protection against periodic drought conditions. In contrast to the West, eastern surface and groundwater supplies seem sufficient to allow for continued expansion of irrigation. Currently, most of the eastern irrigation takes place in the Southeast and Mississippi Delta regions, with the most rapid growth occurring in the Great Lakes states and Corn Belt.

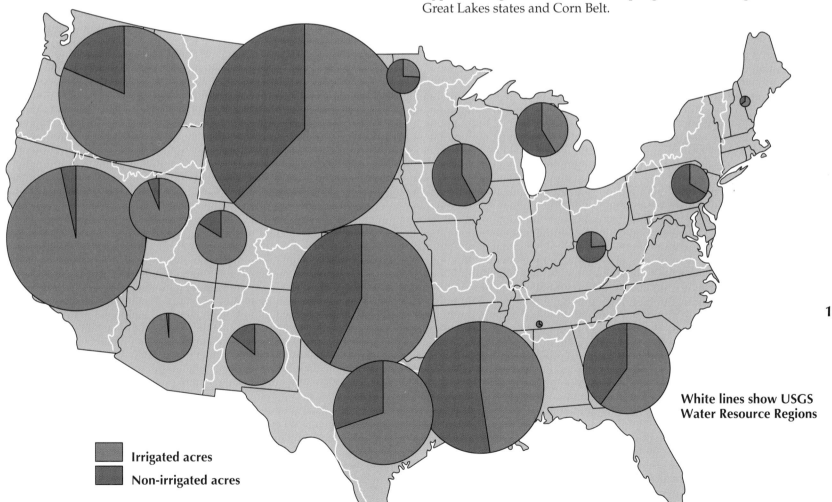

White lines show USGS
Water Resource Regions

Irrigated acres

Non-irrigated acres

Figure 4.9. Irrigated Cropland, 1984.

Source:
Bureau of the Census, *1984 Farm and Ranch Irrigation Survey* (Washington, DC: Bureau of the Census, 1986), p. 4.

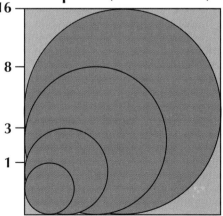

Cropland (million acres)

16
8
3
1

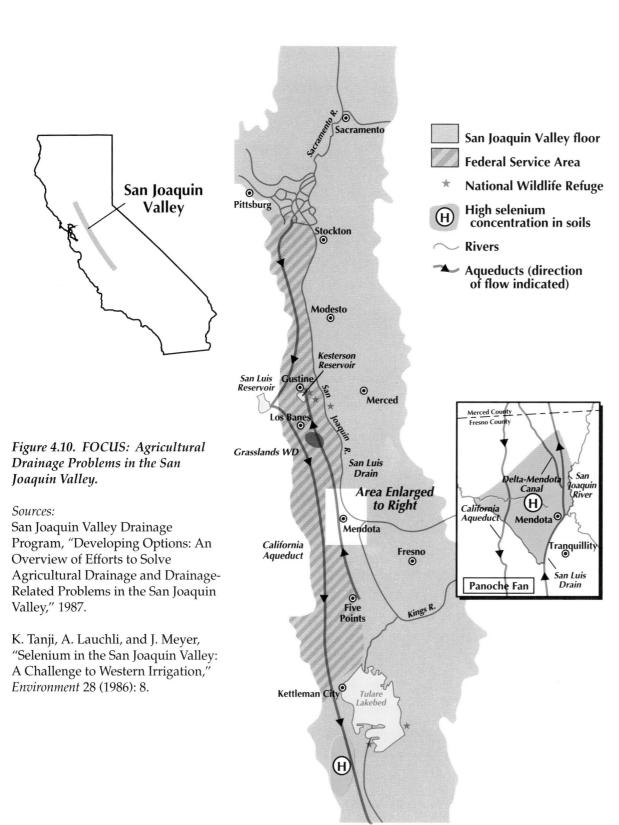

Figure 4.10. FOCUS: Agricultural Drainage Problems in the San Joaquin Valley.

Sources:
San Joaquin Valley Drainage Program, "Developing Options: An Overview of Efforts to Solve Agricultural Drainage and Drainage-Related Problems in the San Joaquin Valley," 1987.

K. Tanji, A. Lauchli, and J. Meyer, "Selenium in the San Joaquin Valley: A Challenge to Western Irrigation," *Environment* 28 (1986): 8.

FOCUS: SAN JOAQUIN VALLEY

Thanks to irrigation, California's Central Valley is one of the world's most productive agricultural regions. But it also experiences some of irrigation's worst problems: high concentrations of salt and toxic chemicals in drainage waters. In July 1982, selenium concentrations in fish from Kesterson Reservoir were found to be 100 times greater than those in fish from nearby noncontaminated waters. Selenium, a naturally occurring element essential in animal diets, is toxic at high levels. A 1983 survey of waterfowl nests revealed that 20 percent contained at least one deformed embryo or hatchling and 40 percent had at least one dead embryo (Tanji et al. 1986).

The selenium is believed to originate in the sedimentary rocks of the California Coast Range, which have been eroded to form deposits along the western side of the San Joaquin Valley. The Panoche Fan, shown on the map, is an area of extensive sediment deposits and high selenium concentrations. It is also a major contributor of drainage water to the San Luis Drain.

Between 10 and 40 feet beneath the San Joaquin Valley's soils is a shallow but impermeable layer of clay that restricts downward drainage of irrigation water. Because this "perched water" is not far beneath the surface, water levels do not have to rise very much for the root zone to become saturated. Salts then accumulate near the surface and may inhibit plant growth.

In order to remove the drainage water, the Bureau of Reclamation began building the San Luis Drain in 1968. Ultimately, it was to carry the water to an outlet in the Sacramento-San Joaquin Delta. But because of federal budget restrictions and concerns about environmental and health impacts of discharging drainage water into San Francisco Bay, the Kesterson Reservoir was created in 1971 as a temporary terminus for the drain. In 1970, the reservoir and 4,700 acres of adjacent marshland were designated a national wildlife refuge.

Although concerns about pollution had been articulated before, the 1982 and 1983 revelations led to an urgent new round of government studies. Water deliveries to the 42,000-acre Westlands District, which contains the Panoche Fan, were restricted. The San Joaquin Valley Interagency Drainage Program, established in 1984, is evaluating an array of future management options. They include fish and wildlife habitat restoration and protection, groundwater management in high water-table areas, use of salt-tolerant and/or low-water-use crops, idling of croplands or conversion to wildlife habitat or open space, and treatment of drainage water to remove selenium and other substances. Drainage water reuse and disposal options—including evaporation ponds, deep-well injection, and discharge to the San Joaquin River—are under study. Also being considered are legal and institutional changes that would promote water conservation. A final report is due in late 1990.

Rangelands are mainly dry-weather, western phenomena. Wetlands, by contrast, encompass a wide variety of physical landscapes, ranging from coastal grasslands to isolated inland swamps and bogs. There is, however, some definitional overlap; indeed, coastal marshes and wet meadows are sometimes classified as rangelands.

The U.S. Department of Agriculture (USDA 1981: 119) defines rangeland as "land on which the potential natural vegetation is predominantly grasses, grass-like plants, forbs, or shrubs; including land revegetated naturally or artificially that is managed like native vegetation. Rangeland includes natural grasslands, savannas, shrublands, most deserts, tundra, alpine communities, coastal marshes, and wet meadows, that are less than 10 percent stocked with forest trees of any size."

Pastureland is distinct from rangeland in that it is more intensively managed by such means as cultivation, drainage, irrigation, or mechanical harvesting (pastureland acreage information is included in chapter 3). Rangeland management is by most definitions limited to the regulation of grazing and protection of plant cover.

The era of the "free range"—characterized by virtually unrestricted use of the vast federal rangelands—came to an official close with the 1934 passage of the Taylor Grazing Act. Under it, grazing districts were established on lands considered most suitable for grazing. The act's larger purposes were to restrict overgrazing and associated soil depletion, to end the large-scale disposal of federal lands, and to elevate the government's role as steward of the land.

Conflicts among environmentalists, ranchers, miners, recreationists, and other range users are intense. Resultant concerns about overgrazing and ecological damage have led to the creation of a system of national grasslands (with proposals for major additions to that system) and passage of the Federal Land Policy and Management Act of 1976 (the Organic Act) and the Public Rangelands Improvement Act of 1978. The former act requires multiple-use and sustained-yield management of publicly owned grazing lands. The latter, among other things, provides incentives for ranchers to improve the conditions of their lands. However, the implementation of the Rangelands Improvement Act has been criticized by environmentalists because the public's control over federal lands has been diminished. Indeed, state and private interests have periodically challenged the federal government to transfer lands to state governments and individuals. The most recent of these "sagebrush rebellions" enjoyed the support of former President Ronald Reagan and then Secretary of the Interior James Watt. None of the rebellions, however, has achieved more than limited success.

While wetlands are not nearly so extensive in area as rangelands, they present a wider set of management issues. Wetlands are situated between aquatic and terrestrial environments and generally are covered with water for at least a part of the year. While wetlands classification schemes differ considerably, most include wetlands associated with marine tidal zones, estuarine environments, rivers and streams, lakes, topographic depressions, and various other environments conducive to wet conditions.

Wetlands are highly valued for several reasons. They are very productive ecologically. They provide nursery and spawning grounds for perhaps two-thirds or more of America's commercial fisheries; crucial breeding and wintering grounds for waterfowl; and habitat for almost one-third of the nation's threatened and endangered species. They are valued for recreational, aesthetic, and economic reasons. Specifically, they support the fish, timber, and peat industries. Wetlands also reduce erosion, reduce the amount and extent of flooding, increase the rate of recharge of groundwater, and filter significant quantities of pollutants. Only rather recently, though, has this full range of physical and cultural values even begun to be widely appreciated.

Florida Everglades.
Florida Department of Commerce,
Division of Tourism.

RANGELANDS IN THE WESTERN UNITED STATES

Rangeland is found primarily in the western states, though as indicated in the caption for figure 5.1, there are a few significant areas of rangeland in the East. Much of this eastern rangeland consists of coastal marshes. While rangeland consists primarily of grasslands, some definitions include forested land that is used for grazing—especially pinyon-juniper and chaparral-mountain shrub forests.

The U.S. Forest Service (1984) determined that in 1982 there were 770.4 million acres of rangeland in the United States, 43 percent of which (328.9 million acres) were in federal ownership. These numbers are somewhat deceptive in that much of the federally owned land is in interior Alaska and the desert and semiarid Southwest. The more productive rangelands of the Great Plains and central and northern Rocky Mountain areas are largely in private ownership. In recent decades, total rangeland area has declined. The Forest Service anticipates that continuing conversions to crop, pasture, and urban lands will cause a further decline of 7 percent by 2030.

RANGELAND CONDITION

Range condition, as described in the map caption for figure 5.2, is a measure of the extent to which vegetation cover resembles potential natural climax vegetation. This is not necessarily indicative of range value for food and fiber production nor for any other particular use. However, the association between better range conditions and greater food and fiber productivity is fairly consistent.

The best quality rangelands are found in the central and northern Great Plains and Rocky Mountain regions. Indeed, in parts of these areas, grazing might be viewed as an ecologically efficient land use. In comparison with grain-fed animals, the upkeep of range-fed stock requires smaller amounts of fuel and agricultural chemicals, results in less pollution, and creates less disruption of the physical landscape. If kept within the limits of the land's ecological carrying capacity, rangeland grazing need not impair the ecological well-being of the land.

Unfortunately, ecologically responsible grazing has not been the norm—on public or privately owned lands. The poorest quality rangelands are concentrated in, though by no means limited to, Texas and the desert Southwest. These areas are characterized by soil and vegetation depletion, and the main culprit is usually overgrazing.

Little information is available regarding long-term trends in the health of private rangelands. Much more data are available for public lands, but they are difficult to compare, due to continual changes in the ways information is reported. It is quite clear, however, that rangeland depletion was a very major problem in the early part of this century. This was officially recognized in the enactment of the Taylor Grazing Act in 1934.

The Bureau of Land Management, along with a majority of range-management professionals outside the bureau, concludes that the condition of the public rangelands has improved substantially since the 1930s. This is attributed to reduced numbers of livestock and improved management practices. But the bureau's interpretation is far from universally shared; such critics as the General Accounting Office (GAO) and environmental organizations point to the large gaps in the data, as well as the changing classification systems, and question the "professional" judgments exercised in reaching these conclusions. Indeed it may be argued that overgrazing has contributed to desertification problems not unlike those of Sahelian Africa. Areas of particular concern are Navajo Indian lands and the regions surrounding El Paso.

Despite the initiatives described above, federal management of rangelands is impaired by a tradition of low federal leasing fees, difficulties in adequately monitoring rangeland conditions, and strong political opposition to grazing restrictions.

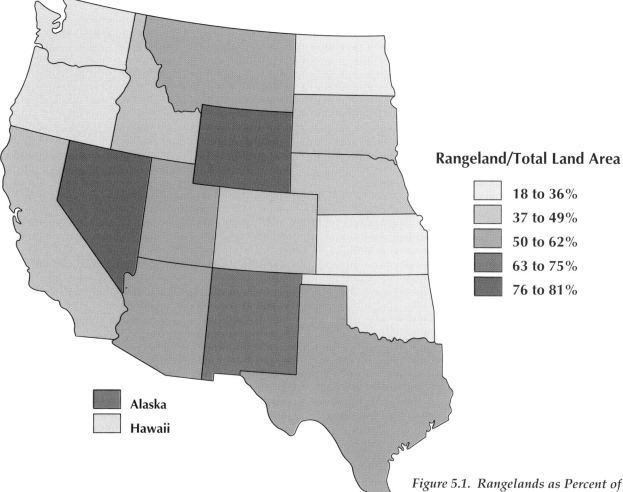

Rangeland/Total Land Area

- 18 to 36%
- 37 to 49%
- 50 to 62%
- 63 to 75%
- 76 to 81%

Alaska

Hawaii

Figure 5.1. Rangelands as Percent of Total Lands—Western U.S.

Source:
U.S. Forest Service, *An Assessment of the Forest and Range Land Situation in the United States* (Washington, DC: GPO, 1981), pp. 12–13.

Rangelands are present but account for less than 0.5 percent of total land in New York, Virginia, South Carolina, Alabama, Mississippi, Indiana, Illinois, Wisconsin, Iowa, and Minnesota. In New Jersey and Maryland, rangelands represent about 1 percent of total land; in Tennessee and Louisiana the figure is 2 percent; in Missouri it is 3 percent; and in Florida it is 6 percent.

Condition of Nonfederal Rangeland (thousand acres)

	Excellent	Good	Fair	Poor	Other
Arizona	517.7	4,923.6	16,574.1	8,831.9	100.9
California	29.3	472.9	613.2	434.0	16,575.2
Colorado	33.2	5,802.6	14,012.2	4,033.2	41.3
Idaho	322.6	2,187.3	2,565.9	1,255.3	401.8
Kansas	965.5	8,091.9	6,121.9	1,666.2	63.4
Montana	5,027.5	17,272.1	12,605.1	2,747.2	185.1
Nebraska	2,188.5	12,636.1	7,110.2	1,069.0	91.9
Nevada	239.2	2,674.4	4,027.0	658.8	308.4
New Mexico	658.7	12,262.5	22,617.4	5,421.5	21.8
North Dakota	1,524.2	6,295.3	2,760.7	368.2	0.0
Oklahoma	906.8	3,601.6	7,638.6	2,903.9	8.7
Oregon	226.4	1,813.2	3,485.5	3,731.1	135.8
South Dakota	1,876.7	13,715.9	6,486.0	704.0	1.0
Texas	479.9	13,546.3	53,542.8	25,680.6	2,103.5
Utah	154.9	1,724.5	4,027.0	2,451.3	131.6
Washington	629.0	1,168.5	1,816.1	1,933.0	90.4
Wyoming	331.0	11,609.6	13,988.1	976.4	10.0

Condition of Federal Rangeland

	Percent by Range Condition				Unclassified or Unsuitable
	Excellent	Good	Fair	Poor	
Arizona	3	23	44	21	9
California	1	47	39	9	4
Colorado	3	16	43	28	10
Idaho	1	24	32	38	5
Montana	8	59	23	1	9
Nevada	3	24	37	23	13
New Mexico	1	25	50	23	1
Oregon	4	26	49	17	4
Utah	4	30	39	13	14
Wyoming	4	45	35	7	9

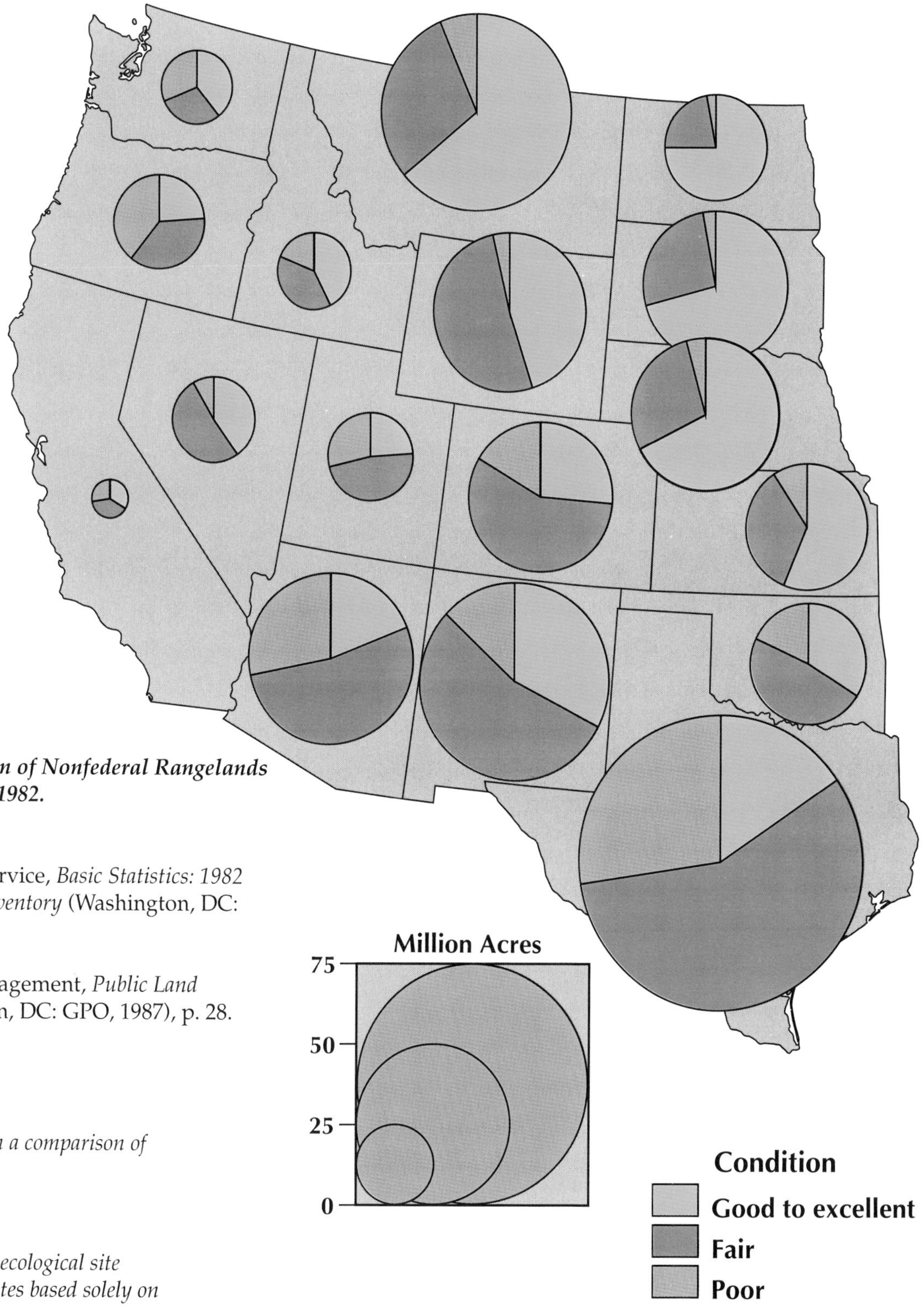

Figure 5.2. Condition of Nonfederal Rangelands in the Western U.S., 1982.

Sources:
Soil Conservation Service, *Basic Statistics: 1982 National Resources Inventory* (Washington, DC: USDA, 1987), p. 64.

Bureau of Land Management, *Public Land Statistics* (Washington, DC: GPO, 1987), p. 28.

Million Acres
75
50
25
0

Condition
Good to excellent
Fair
Poor

The classification schemes for both federal and nonfederal rangelands are based on a comparison of actual vegetation with the potential natural, or climax, plant community:

Excellent—76–100% similarity   *Fair—26–50% similarity*
Good—51–75% similarity   *Poor—0–25% similarity*

The data on federal rangelands are for 1987 and are merged from several sources: ecological site inventories (50% of lands), estimates based on earlier inventories (30%), and estimates based solely on professional judgment (20% of lands).

RELATIVE ABUNDANCE OF WETLANDS

A comprehensive appraisal of the wetlands situation in the United States must await completion of the National Wetlands Inventory. A general assessment of the occurrence of wetlands is, however, provided by the inventory and is represented on the accompanying map. The gaps and sometimes high margins of error notwithstanding, wetlands are relatively abundant in the lower Mississippi Valley, the North Central states, and the Atlantic Coast region (especially the southeastern states).

A number of previous attempts have been made to determine total acreage and location of wetlands in the United States. Comparisons among the results must at best be crude, because there are significant differences in the definitions and classifications of wetlands as well as the means for identifying them (various combinations of ground identification, aerial photographs, and satellite imagery). Further, different surveys are undertaken for different purposes. For example, early surveys sought to identify lands that could be drained for agriculture; later inventories were concerned with wildlife habitat; and only the most recent have adopted more holistic ecosystem perspectives.

The total of the state wetlands acreages reported by the National Wetlands Inventory at the time of this writing is approximately 88 million acres (nearly 220 million hectares). This number excludes those states that lack reliable data (see map), and also contains some fairly large margins of error for individual states. The following acreage estimates for the forty-eight conterminous states, drawn from various sources, were reported by William Mitsch and James Gosselink (1986).

	Million Hectares
Pre-European Settlement	60.0 – 87.0
1906	32.0
1922	37.0
1940	39.4
1954	30.1
1954	43.8
1974	40.1
1982	17.9 – 19.0 (based on mail survey)
	70.0 – 140.0 (including Alaska)

Although the various assessments do not lend themselves to direct comparison, most individual studies agree that wetlands were being lost rapidly before the mid-1970s. One estimate, by Shaw and Fredine (1956), indicates that perhaps 35 percent of wetlands were lost between "primitive times" and the 1950s. A recent study by the National Wetlands Inventory demonstrates that there have been major net losses of wetlands between the 1950s and the 1970s. The lower Mississippi states of Louisiana,

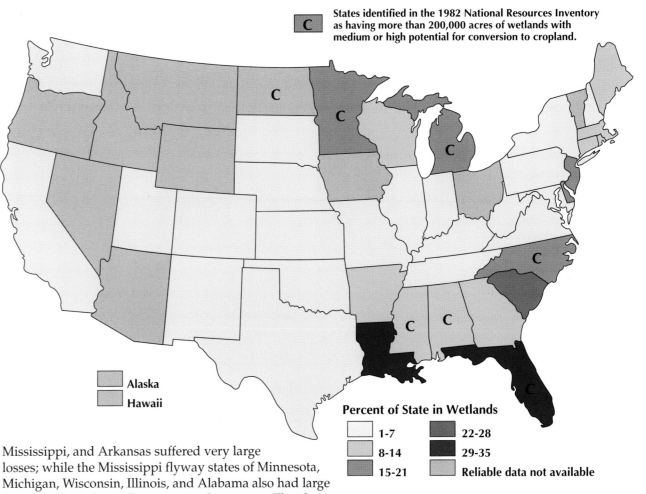

States identified in the 1982 National Resources Inventory as having more than 200,000 acres of wetlands with medium or high potential for conversion to cropland.

Alaska
Hawaii

Percent of State in Wetlands

1-7	22-28
8-14	29-35
15-21	Reliable data not available

Figure 5.3. Relative Abundance of Wetlands.

Sources:

Agricultural Stabilization and Conservation Service (USDA, 1988, mimeographed table).

National Wetlands Inventory, "Wetland Areas in Thousands of Acres and Percent of the Land Area of the State Covered by Wetlands" (Fish and Wildlife Service, 1988, mimeographed table).

Note: Wetlands areas were measured from a complete wetlands inventory at the scale of 1:24,000.

Mississippi, and Arkansas suffered very large losses; while the Mississippi flyway states of Minnesota, Michigan, Wisconsin, Illinois, and Alabama also had large losses. In the Atlantic flyway, major losers were Florida and North Carolina; while Georgia, South Carolina, Maryland, New Jersey, and Delaware also saw large losses. In the Central flyway, significant losses took place in the Dakotas, Nebraska, and Texas. California, with its relatively low initial wetland acreages, suffered the greatest percentage loss in the Pacific flyway. For the nation as a whole, most of the inland losses were the result of conversion to agriculture; while significant coastal losses resulted from urbanization. It should be noted that despite the large net loss of wetlands, significant creation of specific types of wetland habitat occurred in some areas—the result of construction of lakes, reservoirs, and ponds; and shifts in estuarine ecosystem composition.

Specific habitat areas are discussed in greater detail below. States that have the highest potentials for additional loss of wetlands to agriculture are highlighted on this map. This is only a general indication of cause for concern. It considers neither the actual probability of conversion nor the relative value of the threatened wetlands.

WATERFOWL HABITAT AREAS OF NATIONAL CONCERN

This map displays, in order of the priority assigned by the Fish and Wildlife Service, major waterfowl habitat areas. The Prairie Potholes region, with its many glacially formed lakes and marshes, is an extremely important area for the breeding and feeding of migratory waterfowl. It is estimated that a minimum of 50 percent of annual North American waterfowl "production" occurs there. The drought of 1988 (figure 16.4), which severely reduced waterfowl numbers, is expected to add urgency to the efforts of the the Fish and Wildlife Service, the Nature Conservancy, Ducks Unlimited, and other private organizations to protect the remaining Prairie Potholes wetlands.

Much of the formerly extensive wetland area of California's Central Valley has been converted to agriculture, and the wetlands that remain suffer from agricultural chemical pollution. The central and northern portions of the Atlantic coastline contain a variety of wetland types. Among the areas of outstanding concern—and threatened to varying degrees—are the Great Dismal Swamp of Virginia and North Carolina, the Pocosins (evergreen shrub bogs) that predominate in North Carolina, the submerged aquatic beds of the Chesapeake Bay, and the Hackensack Meadowlands in the heart of heavily-urbanized northern New Jersey.

The lower Mississippi River Valley is also exceptionally important—particularly as wintering ground for ducks. It is a complex region of fresh and salt water swamps, marshes, lakes, and levees, extensively modified by dredging, channelization, and oil and gas production. The lower Mississippi has experienced a tremendous loss of wetlands in this century—particularly in its heavily-modified delta.

Alaska's wetland regions, while not immune to threats, are much less vulnerable to pollution or conversion than are the major wetlands of the lower forty-eight. Other notable wetlands can be found in the upper Mississippi Valley and Great Lakes regions, the northern Plains, and the intermountain West. These and other wetland areas are threatened not only by conversion (primarily to agriculture, but also to urban uses in coastal regions), but also by impairment from agricultural and urban runoff and changes in ecological composition that affect the wetland functions described above.

Figure 5.4. Waterfowl Habitat Areas of Major National Concern.

Source:
Fish and Wildlife Service, *Wetlands of the United States: Current Status and Recent Trends* (Washington, DC: GPO, 1984), p. 16.

These areas are recognized for their importance as waterfowl habitat areas. Many of them—particularly the coastal and estuarine wetlands—are also important as fish and shellfish habitat. Further, wetlands serve a host of additional functions; these are listed at the beginning of this chapter.

Even though this map focuses on the waterfowl habitat function, the areas identified tend to be coincident with those identified for other values. However, at least two important areas are excluded. One is southern Florida; this is examined in figure 5.8. The Okefenokee Swamp of northeastern Florida and southeastern Georgia, which consists of several types of wetland plant communities, is also an area of major significance. Of course there are numerous smaller wetlands throughout the country. In the aggregate, these also take on major significance; thus state and national wetlands inventories and policies must be concerned with these lands as well (see figure 5.5).

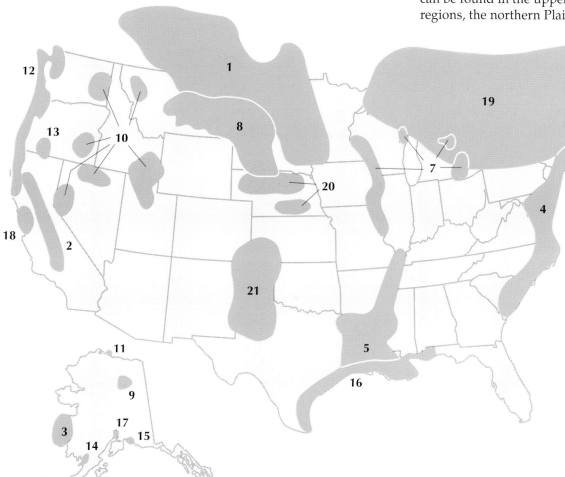

Habitats
1. Prairie Potholes and Parklands
2. Central Valley of California
3. Yukon-Kuskokwim Delta
4. Middle-Upper Atlantic Coast
5. Lower Mississippi River Delta and Red Basin
6. Izembek Lagoon
7. Upper Mississippi River and Northern Lakes
8. Northern Great Plains
9. Yukon Flats
10. Intermountain West (Great Basin)
11. Teshelpuk Lake
12. Middle-Upper Pacific Coast
13. Klamath Basin
14. Upper Alaska Peninsula
15. Copper River Delta
16. West-Central Gulf Coast
17. Upper Cook Inlet
18. San Francisco Bay
19. NE United States/SE Canada
20. Sandhills and Rainwater Basin
21. Playa Lakes

STATUS OF THE NATIONAL WETLANDS INVENTORY

The National Wetlands Inventory (NWI) project was initiated in 1974 by the U.S. Fish and Wildlife Service. The NWI's objectives are to collect and disseminate information about the extent and characteristics of the nation's wetlands. Two major products are to result: (1) detailed wetlands maps and (2) status and trends reports.

The Fish and Wildlife Service's assessments of wetlands status and trends are referred to elsewhere in this chapter. This section reports specifically on the progress of the wetlands mapping program. It is intended that the wetlands maps be used by both public and private decision-makers for a variety of project-specific purposes. In this regard, the Fish and Wildlife Service likens its maps to the Soil Conservation Service's soil survey maps, the National Oceanic and Atmospheric Administration's coastal geodetic survey maps, and the U.S. Geological Survey's topographic sheets.

Much of the data for the NWI maps is compiled from aerial photographs. After the information is field-checked, it is presented on 1:24,000 and 1:100,000 scale maps. When the project is finished, most of the nation's wetlands will be represented at the scale of 1:24,000. Each wetland area is described by means of a classification scheme that usually includes, but is not necessarily limited to, the following categories: system, class, and subclass.

The broad categories of wetlands systems are as follows:

1. *Marine*—includes coastal wetlands as well as the open ocean over the continental shelf
2. *Estuarine*—wetlands located in the zone of mixing between fresh and saltwater; includes deepwater tidal habitats as well as tidal wetlands that are usually partly enclosed by land
3. *Riverine*—wetlands and deepwater habitats contained within a channel, except those that would be classified as estuarine (see above) or palustrine (see below)
4. *Lacustrine*—wetlands and deepwater habitats located in topographic depressions or dammed river channels, except those that would be classified as palustrine (see below)
5. *Palustrine*—nontidal wetlands, as well as tidal wetlands where salinity is low (less than 5 percent), that are dominated by trees, shrubs, emergent (erect, rooted) lichens or mosses, or any other persistent emergents (those emergent plants that remain standing year-round). Also included are small wetlands (less than 20 acres) and shallow wetlands (less than 2 meters at low water).

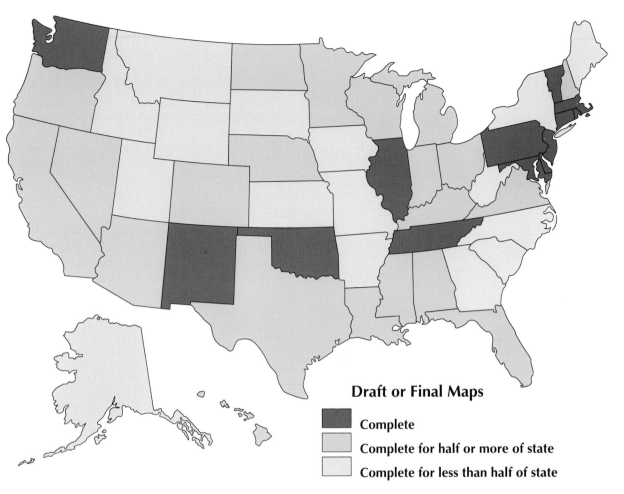

Draft or Final Maps

■ Complete

▨ Complete for half or more of state

☐ Complete for less than half of state

Wetlands subsystems are classified on the basis of tidal characteristics, riverine flow and gradient characteristics, and proximity to lacustrine shorelines. Wetlands classes provide a finer level of detail based on dominant vegetation (when there is at least 30 percent coverage by vegetation) or rock or subsoil characteristics (when there is less than 30 percent coverage). Further subclassification is possible and may be used to describe such characteristics as water regime, pH, salinity, and soil type.

It is apparent from the accompanying map that significant progress has been made in the compilation of wetlands maps. As of mid-1989, draft or final maps were available for many of the critical areas identified in the preceding section of this chapter. However, a large portion of the Prairie Potholes regions remained unmapped—and without contracts arranged for the mapping to be done. Nonetheless, the NWI's goal of complete national coverage—most of it at the scale of 1:24,000—now seems well within reach.

Figure 5.5. Status of the National Wetlands Inventory, 1988.

Source:
"Status of National Wetlands Inventory" (Fish and Wildlife Service, 1988, map).

This map is an approximation based on more detailed maps prepared by the Fish and Wildlife Service. Some of the largest gaps in coverage are found in Montana, Wyoming, Utah, Nevada, Kansas, South Dakota, Wisconsin, Missouri, Arkansas, the Carolinas, and Maine.

SWAMPBUSTER EFFECTIVENESS

"Swampbuster" is the popular name for the wetland conservation provision of the Food Security Act of 1985 (see chapter 4). The swampbuster program seeks to stem the conversion of wetlands to farmlands, by denying government price supports, loans, insurance, and other payments to farm operators who engage in such conversions.

Of the 78 million wetland acres remaining in 1982, 22 percent (17 million acres) are estimated to have some probability of conversion to cropland. However, the swampbuster provision is likely to be effective for only 35 percent of those acres. Greatest success is likely where government payments are large: the Mississippi bottomlands of Arkansas, sections of the southern coastal plain, parts of Nebraska's Sand Hills, and the Klamath Basin of Oregon and northern California. Moderate effectiveness is anticipated for the Prairie Potholes region of Minnesota and North Dakota, central Minnesota, and southern Alabama. Less success is expected in central and eastern Minnesota, the Rainwater Basin of Nebraska, and wheat-growing areas of South Dakota. Swampbuster sanctions are likely to be ineffective in Florida, central Alabama, the Atlantic coastal plain (including the Pocosin region), Wisconsin and upper Michigan, and coastal Massachusetts and Maine, owing to the particular types of crops grown and low dependence on government payments.

These conclusions are tempered by the realization that any shifts in the farm economy are likely to affect participation rates in government programs. Furthermore, farmers do not lose eligibility for government programs simply by converting wetlands; those lands must be shifted into crop production. Even when crops are planted, and eligibility lost, it can be restored in subsequent years by not planting to annual crops. In short, the swampbuster program—along with other federal and state programs—promises at least some reduction in rates of wetland conversion—but no miracles.

Figure 5.6. Swampbuster Effectiveness.

The map, and the statistical analysis from which it is derived, are based on the following precepts:
1. *The swampbuster program can only be effective where wetlands are present.*
2. *There must be some economic and physical possibility for conversion of wetlands to agriculture.*
3. *In order for the swampbuster sanctions to be potentially effective, the farmers in question must be dependent, to at least some degree, on government farm assistance.*

Source:
R. E. Heimlich, "The Swampbuster Provision: Implementation and Impact" (Paper presented at the National Symposium on Protection of Wetlands from Agricultural Impacts, Colorado State University, Fort Collins, CO, April 25–29, 1988).

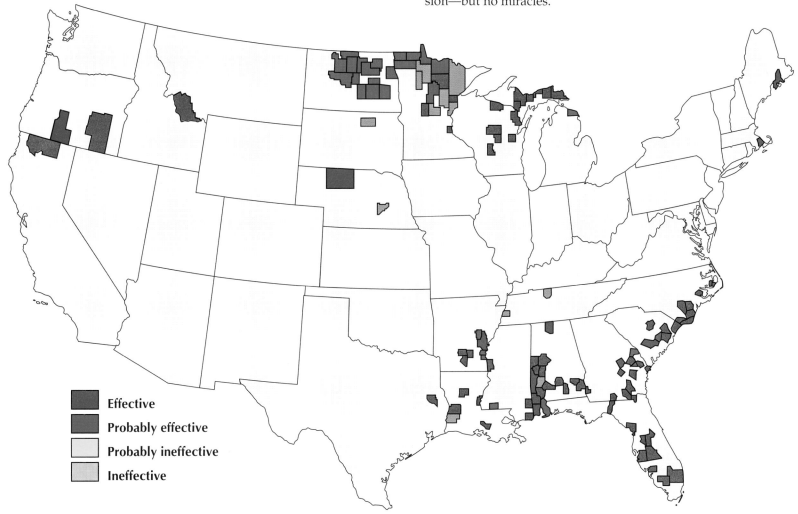

Effective

Probably effective

Probably ineffective

Ineffective

STATE WETLANDS PROTECTION ACTIVITIES

Federal regulatory authority over wetlands derives primarily from a very broad interpretation of Section 404 of Clean Water Act Amendments of 1972. Under this provision, the Army Corps of Engineers issues permits for the discharge of dredge or fill materials into navigable waters and their adjacent wetlands. The courts have supported the U.S. Environmental Protection Agency's (EPA's) right to veto Corps permit decisions. The EPA also has the statutory right to designate wetlands subject to per-mitting, and the Fish and Wildlife Service is required to com-ment on habitat aspects of Corps wetland assessments. How-ever, Section 404 authority does not apply to farming, forestry, and ranching practices, thereby exempting the leading causes of wetlands destruction.

Thus there is an important role for state regulation of wet-lands. While all states have some degree of authority under the Section 401 water-quality certification provisions of the Clean Water Act, effectiveness is limited because this program is not actually designed for wetlands protection. State environmental policy acts (see figure 3.3) are another general instrument for wetlands regulation. Their effectiveness depends on specific legislative provisions, political will, and enforcement capabilities.

A majority of states have developed taxation and/or acquisi-tion programs for wetlands protection. Taxation programs include property tax incentives for maintaining wetlands; income tax credits; and gift and inheritance tax, capital gains tax, and documentary/severance tax programs. Among the problems with tax programs are inconsistencies in funding bases and program administration and concerns over losses to local tax bases (in some cases, payments-in-lieu-of-taxes are offered as compensation). Land acquisition provides secure, long-term protection— but acquisition programs are often costly, difficult to manage, and sometimes lacking in public support. The EPA has identified successful acquisition pro-grams in Illinois, New Jersey, and Florida.

Most states with coastal wetlands have in place some type of protection program, though the majority of them were developed after enactment of the 1972 Coastal Zone Manage-ment Act (see figure 7.4). Inland wetland protection activities, whether alone or in combination with coastal programs, vary widely in regulatory scope and techniques used. In general, small inland wetlands have received the least protection. Strongest efforts have been mainly in the more densely popu-lated states. State efforts are supported to varying degrees by federal laws and programs that provide funds for wetland acquisition and protection. Not only the Coastal Zone Manage-ment Act but also the Land and Water Conservation Fund and Federal Aid to Wildlife Restoration Act are important in this regard.

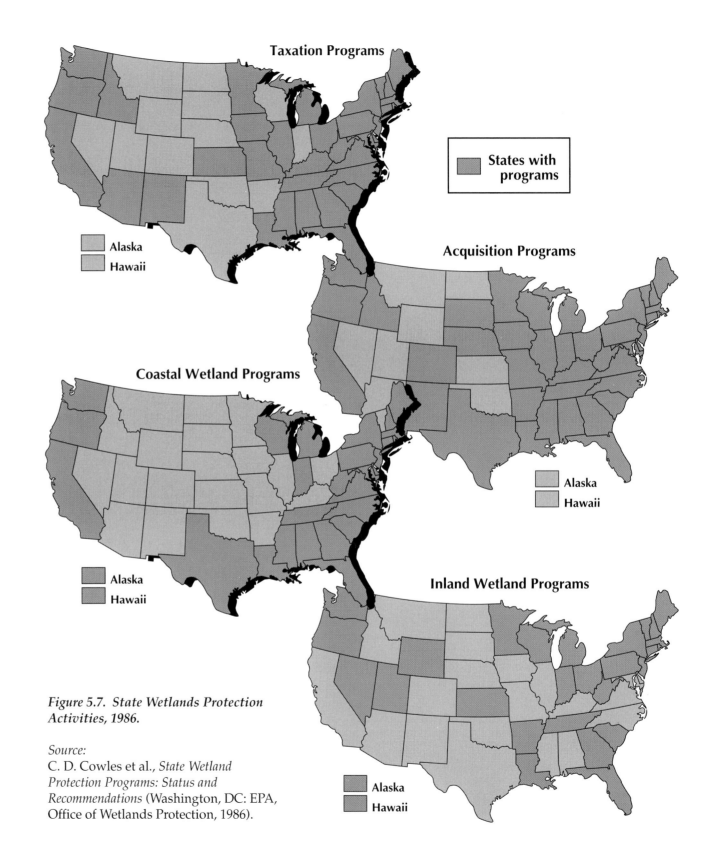

Figure 5.7. State Wetlands Protection Activities, 1986.

Source:
C. D. Cowles et al., *State Wetland Protection Programs: Status and Recommendations* (Washington, DC: EPA, Office of Wetlands Protection, 1986).

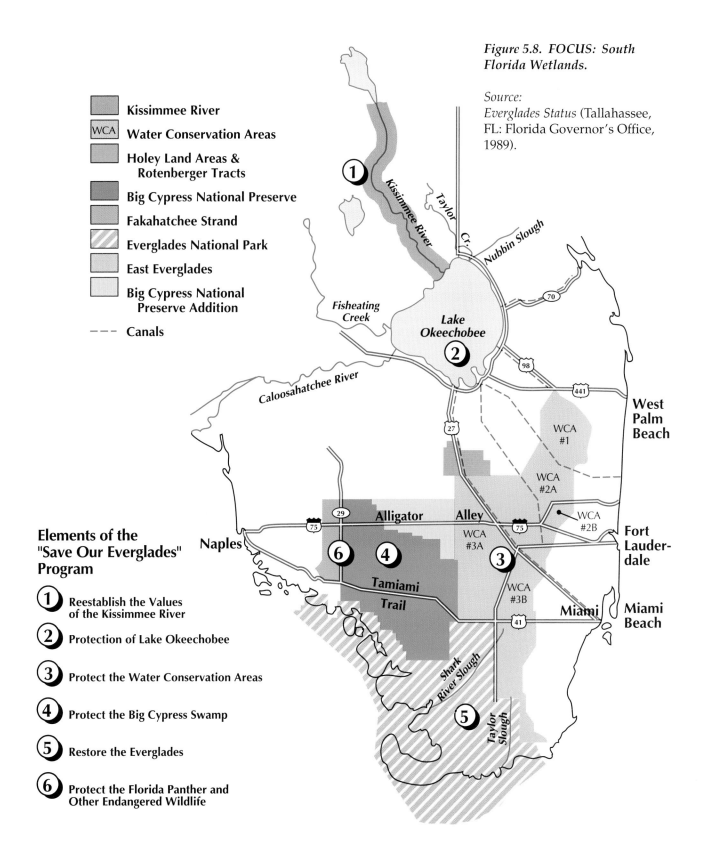

Figure 5.8. FOCUS: South Florida Wetlands.

Source:
Everglades Status (Tallahassee, FL: Florida Governor's Office, 1989).

Legend:

- Kissimmee River
- WCA — Water Conservation Areas
- Holey Land Areas & Rotenberger Tracts
- Big Cypress National Preserve
- Fakahatchee Strand
- Everglades National Park
- East Everglades
- Big Cypress National Preserve Addition
- – – – Canals

Elements of the "Save Our Everglades" Program

1. Reestablish the Values of the Kissimmee River
2. Protection of Lake Okeechobee
3. Protect the Water Conservation Areas
4. Protect the Big Cypress Swamp
5. Restore the Everglades
6. Protect the Florida Panther and Other Endangered Wildlife

FOCUS: SOUTH FLORIDA WETLANDS

Prior to the mid-1800s, most of southern Florida was undisturbed wetland, over which sheets of water flowed gradually from north to south. Since that time, extensive drainage and channelization have been undertaken to support agricultural, commercial, and residential development. During the early 1800s, for example, Governor Napoleon Bonaparte Broward promised to "drain the Everglades." All these activities have negatively affected fish, wildlife, and vegetation and have reduced South Florida's natural ability to buffer against climatic extremes.

Limited recognition of wetlands values came with the 1947 establishment of Everglades National Park and the 1949 creation of a regional Flood Control District. State and federal preservation efforts escalated considerably during the 1970s; among other things, the Big Cypress National Preserve was created. But it was not until 1983 that a truly comprehensive intergovernmental effort got under way. The Save Our Everglades program, guided by the Florida Governor's Office and supported by environmental organizations (collectively, the Everglades Coalition), has as its prime objectives land acquisition and restoration of water quality and flow regimes.

Depicted on this map are the program's six central elements. The Kissimmee River, channelized during the 1960s, is now being restored to a more natural flow regime. Lake Okeechobee, which delivers large quantities of water to the Everglades, is suffering from eutrophication. In order to reduce loadings of nitrogen and phosphorous, "best management practices" are being implemented on dairy farms north of the lake, and backpumping of water from the adjacent Everglades Agricultural Area has been reduced. The Water Conservation Areas, plus the adjacent Holey Land and Rotenberger Tracts, provide half the water for the eastern portion of the Everglades National Park, recharge the Biscayne Aquifer (South Florida's primary source of drinking water), and are valuable fish and wildlife habitat. The Save Our Everglades plan calls for state acquisition and management of these areas to improve water quality and regulate water flow in proportion to actual precipitation. Acquisition plans are also being carried out in the Big Cypress National Preserve (the 83,000-acre "addition" shown on the map occurred in late 1988), the adjoining Fakahatchee Strand, and the Everglades. The Everglades in particular have suffered from excessive floods and prolonged droughts resulting from manipulation of flow regimes on surrounding lands. Protection of the once plentiful Florida panther is to be achieved through land acquisition, highway modification (especially I-75, "Alligator Alley"), and research and breeding programs. By no means are these and other Save Our Everglades projects meeting with universal success—but on balance the program has fostered a remarkable degree of coordination and achieved measurable progress toward its goals.

The United States is generously endowed with forests. Although the nation's woodlands are not as areally extensive as they were before European settlement, the rate of decline has slowed in the twentieth century. Still, there was a 6-percent loss between 1962 and 1987. Our woodland bounty is subject to a diverse, often conflicting array of demands. Among other things, forests provide timber, watershed, recreation, and wildlife habitat.

Much of this chapter is concerned with the use of forests—both public and private—for timber production. This is not to deny the equal or often greater importance of alternative uses; indeed, they are considered more fully in other chapters—especially chapter 15.

The maps in this chapter convey the impression that timber supplies are more than adequate for the immediate future. This is, at face value, an accurate impression. The Forest Service (1984) projects considerably higher demands for most types of timber—and for the hardwoods in particular—through the year 2030. If these projections prove accurate, then it is very likely that forests will have to be managed more intensively for production. And this could, if necessary, be done in most parts of the country—but not without costs. Conflicts with other potential forest uses—especially scenic, wilderness, and other forms of recreational use—could become even more intractable than they are today.

Old-growth timber is relatively abundant on lands administered by the Forest Service (figure 6.3), particularly in the Northwest. Indeed, some critics chide the agency severely for its failure to exploit this valuable resource efficiently. But opponents of harvesting point to the essential nonrenewability of forests that are hundreds of years old, the scientific knowledge forgone, and the loss of wildlife habitat associated with harvesting the old-growth forests.

In the eastern regions, additional harvests and more efficient use of the forest resource would make it possible, if need be, to increase the amount of timber supplied from private lands.

Recent Forest Service projections indicate that the South will become a much larger supplier of softwood by the year 2030, while the importance of the Douglas-fir region of the Northwest will decline somewhat. Overall, the Forest Service (1984) believes that long-term needs can be met through programs to increase net annual growth of timber.

An especially contentious issue is that of how to harvest timber. Large commercial timberlands are usually harvested in one of two ways: selective cutting or clear-cutting. Proponents of clear-cutting argue that it allows better regeneration of the forests, and especially of shade-intolerant species (e.g., Douglas fir); that it allows restocking with genetically superior species; that it is economical; that it can control disease; and that it lessens environmental impacts because the area is disturbed only once and then left to regenerate. Opponents—among them most of the nation's major environmental organizations—point to soil erosion, excessive stream sedimentation, impacts on wildlife, aesthetic damages, and illegality under the Forest Management Act of 1897, which places general restrictions on harvesting of timber.

The Forest Service has responded to the controversy with guidelines that restrict the size and shape of clear cuts and prohibit clear-cutting entirely where physical, environmental, and/or aesthetic impacts are judged to be too great. But the guidelines apply only to the national forests: privately owned forests are regulated only in certain states and through federal water-quality regulations. Some corporate forest owners are very concerned about the long-term health and viability of their investments; others adopt much shorter planning horizons.

The clear-cutting issue, while probably the most notorious, is but one of a whole range of economic, environmental, and social issues that will continue to be debated. Other contentious forest-management questions include wilderness preservation (which prohibits cutting of any kind), road construction, and use of forest lands for grazing and food crops.

Clear-Cut Near Mount St. Helens.
R. Mason.

FOREST LAND

Major forest ecosystems of the United States are represented on the ecoregion map in chapter 2 (figure 2.5). It is evident from that map—as well as the accompanying map —that forests are abundant in the well-watered East, in the humid coastal and mountain areas of the West, and over large areas of Alaska. Hardwood species dominate in the East, while softwoods are predominant in western forests. The hardwoods are chiefly deciduous, or leaf-bearing, trees; while the softwoods are primarily coniferous, or cone-bearing, trees. Principal forest ecosystems in the northeastern states are the commercially valuable spruce-fir and maple-beech-birch associations. Also common are oak-hickory, ash-cottonwood, and white-red-jack pine forests, which vary considerably in commercial value. In the North Central states (figure 6.2 shows exact location of these states) oak-hickory forests are most abundant. Also extensive is aspen-birch, which is important as wildlife habitat, and maple-beech-birch, fir-spruce, and elm-ash-cottonwood.

The subtropical southern states, despite having widespread areas of nutrient-deficient soils, support extensive forests. Oak-hickory forests cover about one-third of the South. The loblolly-shortleaf pine complex predominates over large expanses of the Atlantic and Gulf Coast states; much of this land is managed for timber production. Also in abundance are longleaf-slash pine, oak-pine, and the commercially important oak-gum-cypress and elm-ash-cottonwood ecosystems.

As the result of highly variable temperature and moisture conditions, a considerable diversity of forest associations is found in the Great Plains and Rocky Mountain regions. These range from eastern hardwood systems in the bottomlands and uplands of the Great Plains states to pinyon-juniper, ponderosa pine, Douglas fir, fir-spruce, and lodgepole pine in the Rocky Mountains. All but the pinyon-juniper are significant producers of wood products.

The Pacific Coast states are home to a wide variety of climates and ecosystems. They range from interior deserts to the temperate rainforests of Washington's Olympic Peninsula. Widespread in the region is the Mediterranean climate regime, with its mild, wet winters and very dry summers. In the wetter areas of the Pacific Coast states, we find redwood, Douglas fir, and hemlock-Sitka spruce ecosystems. These forests are major timber producers as well as important wildlife and watershed areas. Fir-spruce associations are the most abundant overall, and they yield significant timber. Ponderosa pine ecosystems, found in drier areas, are valued for recreation, grazing, and lumber. Important as wildlife habitat are the western hardwood systems, which consist of oak, maple, red alder, and Pacific madrone. Lodgepole pine, chaparral, and pinyon-juniper forests are valuable for recreation, wildlife habitat, and watershed protection.

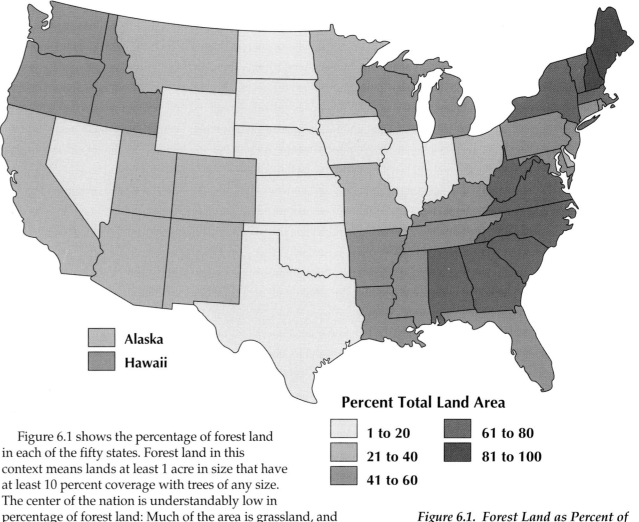

Percent Total Land Area

1 to 20	61 to 80
21 to 40	81 to 100
41 to 60	

Alaska
Hawaii

Figure 6.1 shows the percentage of forest land in each of the fifty states. Forest land in this context means lands at least 1 acre in size that have at least 10 percent coverage with trees of any size. The center of the nation is understandably low in percentage of forest land: Much of the area is grassland, and many of the areas that once were forested have been converted to rangeland and cropland. The Rocky Mountain and southwestern states support forests primarily in the higher, more moist regions. The North Central states, some of which are capable of supporting extensive forests, are largely in agricultural uses. Thus, it is the eastern and Pacific Northwest states in which we find the highest percentages of forest lands. These statewide statistics can, however, be deceptive: in the Pacific Northwest, for example, we find densely forested areas in the western, humid parts of Washington and Oregon and much less extensively forested areas, as well as shrub and grasslands, in the eastern portions. In the heavily urbanized Northeast, we find large urban agglomerations with relatively little forest land (though some suburban areas contain considerable forest) as well as large areas of several states that are remote from population pressures and/or have been set aside as forest preserves.

Figure 6.1. Forest Land as Percent of Total Land.

Source:
U.S. Forest Service, *An Assessment of the Forest and Range Land Situation in the United States*, Forest Resource Report no. 22 (Washington, DC: GPO, 1981), p. 15.

Figure 6.2. Ownership of Commercial Timberland.

Source:
"Area of Timberland Area of the United States, by Ownership and State, 1987" (U.S. Forest Service, 1988, preliminary).

Table 6.1. Ownership of Commercial Timberland

	National Forest (%)	Other Public (%)	Forest Industry (%)	Farmer & Other Private (%)
Northeast	2.8	9.4	15.7	72.1
North Central	9.7	18.7	5.7	65.8
Great Plains	26.7	8.0	0.6	64.7
Southeast	5.8	4.6	19.9	69.8
South Central	6.2	3.6	19.3	70.8
Pacific Northwest	35.8	22.3	17.8	24.0
Pacific Southwest	50.2	4.9	15.8	29.1
Rocky Mountains	60.4	14.0	5.1	20.4

Source: "Area of Timberland Area of the United States, by Ownership and State" (U.S. Forest Service, 1988, preliminary).

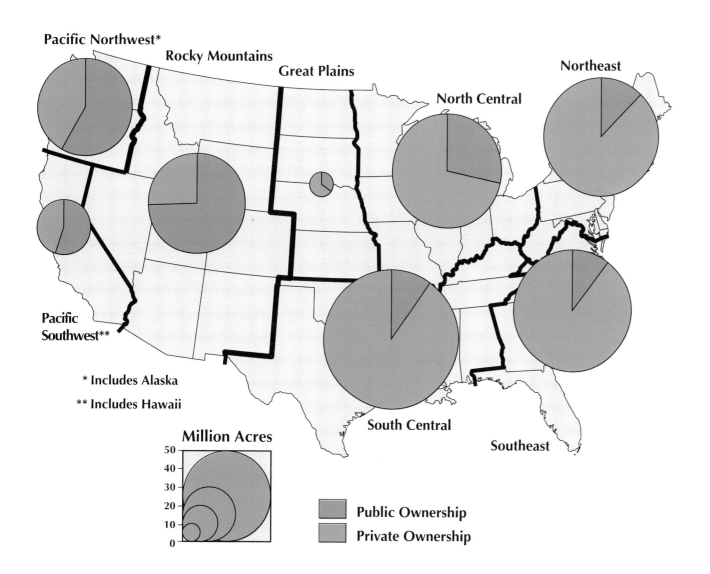

Pacific Northwest*
Rocky Mountains
Great Plains
North Central
Northeast
Pacific Southwest**

* Includes Alaska
** Includes Hawaii

Million Acres
50
40
30
20
10
0

South Central
Southeast

■ Public Ownership
■ Private Ownership

OWNERSHIP OF COMMERCIAL TIMBERLAND

Who owns the forests? Overall, ownership is approximately equally divided between the federal government and other owners (state and private). However, ownership patterns differ drastically between East and West. The bulk of the public land is in the West and Alaska; so too is the bulk of the National Forest System (figure 6.3). But the national forests account for only about 18 percent of commercial timberlands. Commercial timberlands—which compose about two-thirds of all forest lands in the United States—are those forests capable of yielding at least 20 cubic feet of timber per acre per year (figure 6.4). Lands that meet the productivity criterion but where logging is expressly prohibited are not considered commercial. The national forests, because they contain significant amounts of noncommercial timber, account for a somewhat greater portion of the national timber inventory than the above figure suggests. Moreover, many commercial stands remain unharvested because they are of relatively low quality and/or are located in remote, high-elevation areas. Recently, the commercial holdings of the National Forest Service have declined; this is due largely to increased designations during the 1970s of wilderness areas (figure 15.4). Logging is prohibited in wilderness areas.

Forests in the eastern half of the United States are overwhelmingly in private—largely nonindustrial—ownership. Thus, while the bulk of the softwood inventory (found principally in the West) is in the federal estate, approximately 70 percent of the hardwoods (much more common in eastern forests) are in the hands of farmers and other nonindustrial private owners. These distinctions are, of course, important: Corporate forest owners are interested in maximizing profits (though different companies use different time horizons in managing their investments); public forests seek to serve the "public interest" in its many and varying definitions; and small owners have diverse interests and needs that range from commercial to aesthetic and recreational. In this vein, the Focus feature at the end of this chapter explores New England forest owners' intentions to harvest their timber.

Basic ownership patterns have changed little since the 1940s. Industrial ownership of commercial timberland has increased slightly, while the federal share has declined somewhat. This is the result of modest expansions to the federal estate (national forests, parks, wildlife refuges, wilderness areas, and other reserves) and associated withdrawals of these lands from possible timber harvesting. Currently, industrial holdings are greatest in Maine, the East Gulf states, and the Pacific Northwest. Public holdings outside the federal estate may be locally significant but are generally small. Michigan, Minnesota, New York, Pennsylvania, Washington, and Wisconsin—with their extensive state forest systems—are notable exceptions.

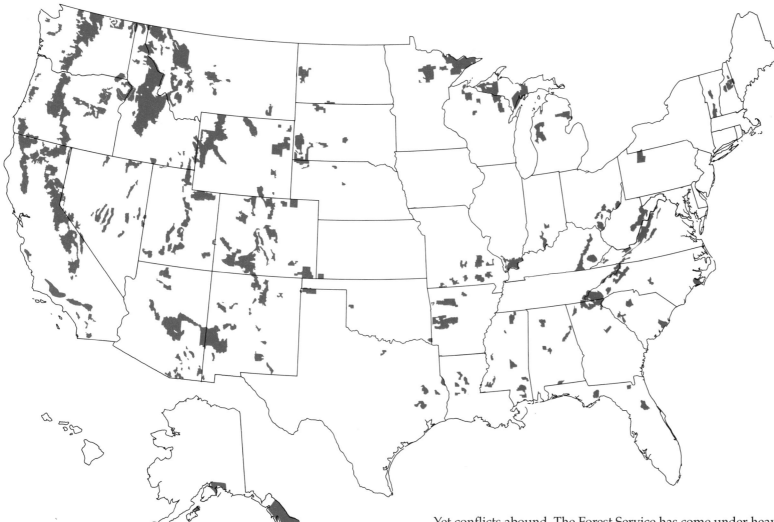

Figure 6.3. The National Forest System.

Source:
The National Forest System (U.S. Forest Service, 1980, map).

THE NATIONAL FOREST SYSTEM

In 1988, the U.S. Forest Service had responsibility for over 190 million acres of lands: mostly forests, but also 3.8 million acres of grasslands. Traditional management philosophy has favored "multiple uses": timber, recreation, flood and erosion control, wildlife management, and other uses. Over the past quarter-century (though to perhaps a lesser degree in the 1980s), the Forest Service has responded to growing environmental concerns. In 1988, 32.5 million national forest acres were in wilderness designations (figure 15.4); many others are managed for recreation and/or ecological protection.

Yet conflicts abound. The Forest Service has come under heavy criticism for its "below-cost timber sales": That is, more is spent on administration, road-building, and other activities than is recovered. Agency officials contend that short-term monetary losses are outweighed by less tangible benefits—including support for local economies, timber-stand improvement, fire protection, and habitat enhancement. Of particular concern is the harvest of old-growth trees—some exceeding 3,000 years in age—in northern California, Washington, Oregon, and Alaska. Much of the harvested timber is exported to Asia as raw logs. Moreover, old-growth forests are habitat for the spotted owl in the Northwest and the bald eagle in Alaska's Tongass National Forest. Presumably because it is cheaper and easier for the timber industry to cut on public lands, many private lands lay fallow. Other major controversies concern clear-cutting versus selective cutting (see page 49) and wilderness protection versus mining (chapter 14).

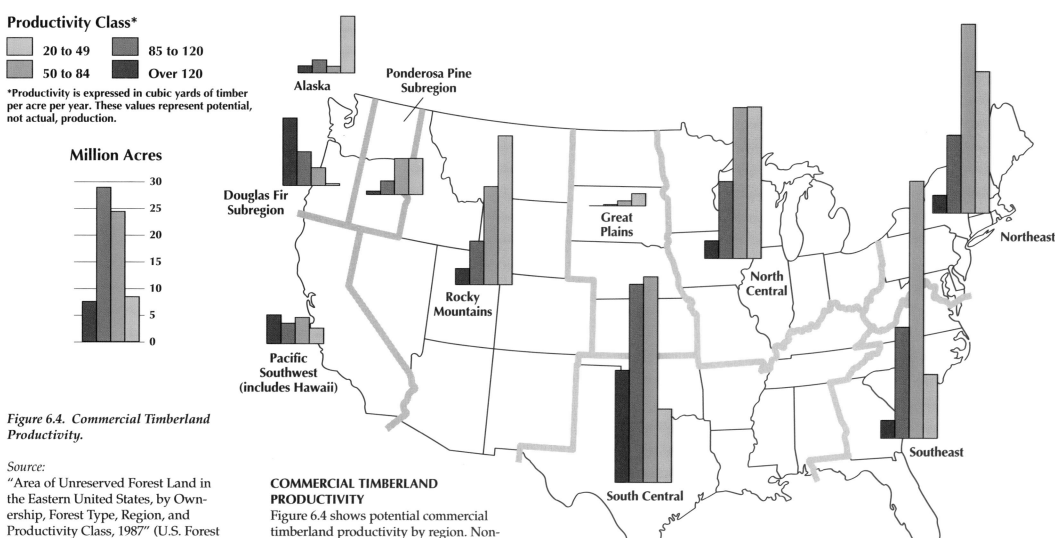

Productivity Class*

20 to 49	85 to 120
50 to 84	Over 120

*Productivity is expressed in cubic yards of timber per acre per year. These values represent potential, not actual, production.

Million Acres

Alaska

Ponderosa Pine Subregion

Douglas Fir Subregion

Great Plains

Northeast

North Central

Rocky Mountains

Pacific Southwest (includes Hawaii)

Southeast

South Central

Figure 6.4. Commercial Timberland Productivity.

Source:
"Area of Unreserved Forest Land in the Eastern United States, by Ownership, Forest Type, Region, and Productivity Class, 1987" (U.S. Forest Service, 1988, preliminary).

COMMERCIAL TIMBERLAND PRODUCTIVITY

Figure 6.4 shows potential commercial timberland productivity by region. Non-commercial lands are not represented. Two-thirds of U.S. forest land—or 482 million acres—is classified as commercial, that is, capable of yielding at least 20 cubic feet of timber per acre per year. Inaccessible areas, which have virtually no chance of actually being harvested, are included within this definition. Lands that meet the productivity criterion, but where harvesting is prohibited by statute or administrative regulation, are considered "reserved timberland." They are not defined as commercial timberland.

Productivity is a measure of potential annual growth in fully stocked natural stands. Thus productivity is principally a function of physical conditions—though it can be affected by historic human modification of the landscape. Greatest productivity occurs where moisture is abundant and growing seasons long. Coastal and low-altitude west slope ecosystems of Alaska, central and northern California, Oregon, and Washington (especially the Olympic Peninsula) are prime examples. Indeed, productive potentials exceed 165 cubic feet per year in some locales. Many of these forests are, of course, highly prized by loggers. By contrast, most—but clearly not all—forest lands in the northern states (outside the Douglas fir subregion) are rather marginal for wood production because of their low productivity. Many southeastern forests consist of young, fast-growing trees, favored by the mild, moist climate. Thus the South is well represented in the middle- and high-productivity classes. Rocky Mountain forests tend to be low in productivity. Although conditions are highly variable, many northern intermontane and southern desert and semiarid regions are very dry, while high-altitude locations have short growing seasons.

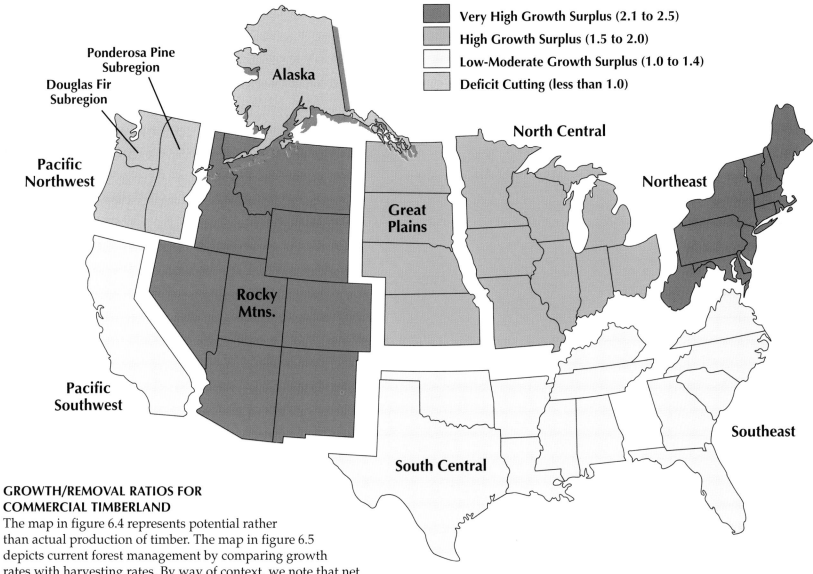

Legend:
- Very High Growth Surplus (2.1 to 2.5)
- High Growth Surplus (1.5 to 2.0)
- Low-Moderate Growth Surplus (1.0 to 1.4)
- Deficit Cutting (less than 1.0)

Ponderosa Pine Subregion

Douglas Fir Subregion

Alaska

North Central

Pacific Northwest

Northeast

Great Plains

Rocky Mtns.

Pacific Southwest

Southeast

South Central

Figure 6.5. Growth/Removal Ratios for Commercial Timberland.

Data are for 1986.

Source:
"Net Annual Growth of Growing Stock on Timberland in the United States, by Ownership, Region, and Species Group, 1952, 1962, 1970, 1976, and 1986" and "Annual Removals of Growing Stock on Timberland in the United States, by Ownership, Region, and Species Group, 1970, 1976, and 1986" (National Forest Service, 1988, preliminary).

Figure 6.6. FOCUS: Small New England Forest Owners' Intentions to Harvest Timber.

Map compares early 1970s' and early 1980s' responses to questions about small forest owners' intentions to harvest timber. Size of circle represents total acreage in hands of small landowners. Wedges show percent of landowners intending to harvest at various future times. "Indefinite" means an intention to harvest, but uncertainty as to when.

Sources:
T. W. Birch, *Forest-land Owners of Maine, 1982*, U.S. Forest Service, Resource Bulletin NE-90 (Broomall, PA: Northeastern Forest Experiment Service, 1986), p. 66.

U.S. Forest Service, "Information on Forest-land Owners of Southern New England"(Broomall, PA: Northeastern Forest Experiment Service, 1988, computer printout).

U.S. Forest Service, "Information on Forest-land Owners of Vermont and New Hampshire" (Broomall, PA: Northeastern Forest Experiment Service, 1988, computer printout).

GROWTH/REMOVAL RATIOS FOR COMMERCIAL TIMBERLAND

The map in figure 6.4 represents potential rather than actual production of timber. The map in figure 6.5 depicts current forest management by comparing growth rates with harvesting rates. By way of context, we note that net annual growth in most parts of the United States has been rising through the twentieth century; this can be attributed to fire protection, tree planting, research, and public forest management programs. Nonetheless, actual growth falls substantially short of potential growth in all regions and under all ownerships. Timber harvests have increased considerably in recent decades, with softwoods composing about 70 percent of total removals (Forest Service 1981).

The ratio of growths to removals provides a crude indication of the general timber situation. In most of the country—but especially the Northeast and Rocky Mountain regions—net growth exceeds removals for most species. Lower ratios in the South are a reflection of the frequency and extent of harvesting.

Softwood removals exceed net growth in the far West, but this "deficit" does not necessarily pose a serious problem in terms of sheer availability of timber. There is still ample availability of old-growth forest in the Pacific Coast section, where most of the deficit cutting is occurring. As noted earlier, however, deficit cutting may be viewed as ecologically and/or aesthetically unwise, in that it may ultimately mean additional cutting of old-growth timber in the Northwest. There are, however, other options for relieving timber deficits. Besides conservation, recycling, and substitution of other materials, the United States can turn increasingly to trade partners—especially Canada—that can help satisfy the nation's timber needs.

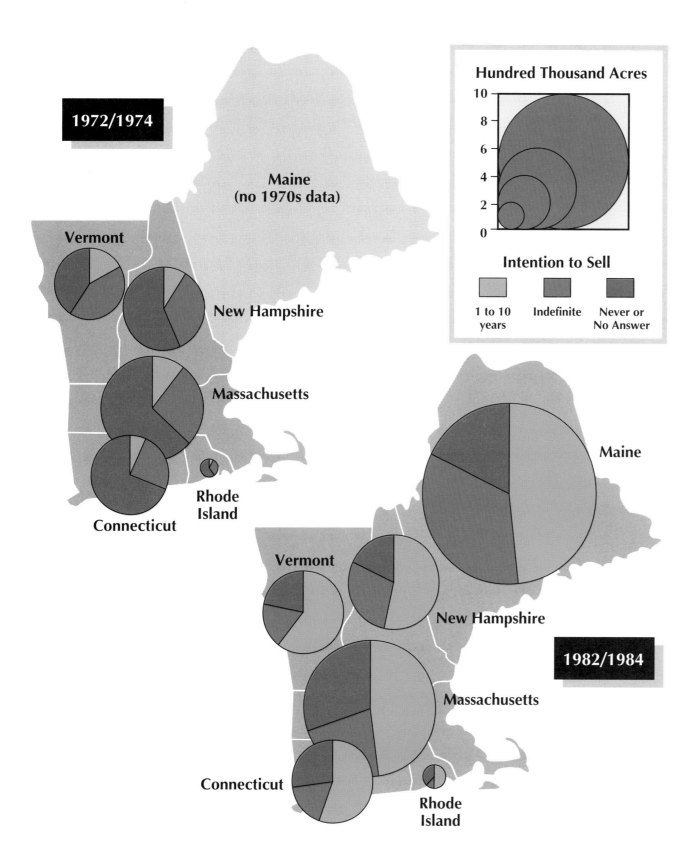

Hundred Thousand Acres

Intention to Sell

| 1 to 10 years | Indefinite | Never or No Answer |

FOCUS: THE SMALL NEW ENGLAND FOREST OWNER

New England can be thought of as having two major forest regions: (1) northern Maine, which is owned and managed largely by the timber industry, and (2) the rest of New England, where the forests are overwhelmingly in small, individual ownerships. While there are scattered state forests, as well as two national forests (Green Mountains in Vermont and White Mountains in New Hampshire and Maine), their principal uses are recreational; little commercial timber is produced. Indeed, most of New England's timber harvesting occurs on small, privately held plots.

Figure 6.6 represents a New England filled with small wooded plots, interspersed with farmlands, towns and cities, lakes and rivers, and various other features. In all states, the percentage of forested land has been increasing at least since the early 1900s. Despite population increases in many sections, the abandonment of agricultural land and its subsequent reversion to forest have brought about a net increase in forested area. Today, timber production is on the rise in much of New England. What can we say about this trend?

Clearly, New England is not destined to become one of the nation's major timber-producing regions. Nor is it a large supplier of agricultural goods. It does, however, contain part of the large megalopolitan population of the Northeast and is readily accessible to a much larger share of that population— for recreation as well as "exurban" year-round living. Thus, rural New England—especially southern New England—is much more intimately woven into the nation's urban fabric than are many other rural regions. New England's forest owners tend to be well educated, are often retired, usually live on or near the forest land, and generally are there by choice. The forests they manage are important both for their amenity value and—perhaps to a more limited (though increasing) extent—timber production.

The energy crises of the 1970s helped propel these changes. Firewood harvesting increased considerably during the 1970s, and—despite preliminary indications of a leveling off in the 1980s—the increased fuelwood harvests are likely to remain a feature of the forest landscape. Interest in harvesting for saw-logs and pulpwood also appears to be rising. Some land-owners refuse to allow harvests on aesthetic grounds or because they distrust the loggers with whom they would contract for timber removal—but these people seem to be in the minority.

The increased intent to allow timber harvesting—depicted on the maps—will not necessarily translate into actual harvests. But if it does, New England's forests will be put to a test: Can increased timber harvests peacefully coexist with the aesthetic, ecological, and recreational values of the forests?

Coastal Zone Management 7

The United States' 95,000 miles of coastline vary widely in character. The Middle Atlantic and Southeast regions have broad, flat inland coastal plains (figure 2.1), wide continental shelves, smooth shorelines, and extensive barrier islands and wetlands. In contrast, northern New England's coastline—where the Appalachian Highlands meet the sea—is jagged and indented. Much of the Pacific Coast is likewise mountainous, with relatively little beach development. With the principal exception of the Yukon Delta, Alaska's western and southern coastlines resemble the Pacific Coast to the south. The Arctic Coastal Plain of northern Alaska is physiographically quite similar to the Gulf and Atlantic Coastal Plain. Hawaii's coastal topography is generally rugged, though there are some significant coastal plains. And in addition to marine coasts, we have the extensive inland shorelines of the Great Lakes. For administrative purposes, the Great Lakes shores are treated as part of the nation's coastal zone.

Coastal waters and adjacent lands are valued for navigation, strategic purposes, sport and commercial fishing, mineral resources, oil and gas, and a wide array of recreational uses. The historic and contemporary importance of coastal regions is demonstrated by the fact that in 1987 approximately 52 percent of the American people lived in counties situated within 50 miles of coastlines, with 22 percent in the Atlantic region alone. About 36 percent of the 1980 population lived in counties that abut an ocean or Great Lake, and additional rapid growth is expected—especially in the Southeast, Gulf, and Pacific regions. Of course, most of these people do not live in condominiums overlooking the beach—but their proximity to the ocean still gives ample cause for concern. Productive coastal ecosystems are threatened; immediate coastal populations are highly vulnerable to storms, tsunamis, and associated coastal erosion; and low-lying urbanized areas may have to cope with a rising sea level that may accompany the global warming predicted for the twenty-first century. Additional threats are posed by offshore oil and gas

development—threats that were deeply impressed upon the entire nation by the 1968 Santa Barbara oil blowout, the huge oil spill in Alaska's Prince William Sound in March 1989 (figure 13.8), and scores of other oil spills and related incidents.

In the early 1970s, concerns about America's coasts culminated in a major piece of legislation: the Coastal Zone Management Act (CZMA) of 1972. The CZMA provides grants to states and guides the development of state coastal zone plans. It does not, however, impose new requirements or regulations upon coastal states. The CZMA is designed as a collaborative state-federal land-use planning enterprise. For want of a few votes in Congress in the early 1970s, that approach might have been enshrined in legislation applying to *all* the nation's lands.

A further expression of federal concern for the coast came in the form of the 1982 Coastal Barrier Resources Act (CBRA). This law seeks to protect barrier islands and sand spits—fragile, shifting, often ephemeral lands highly valued for recreational and commercial development. The main thrust of the CBRA is to deny federal assistance in its various forms—grants, loans, tax incentives, and the like—that in past years have subsidized such development.

The strength and effectiveness of coastal zone programs rely heavily on state initiative. Federal support declined very substantially during the 1980s. Indeed, with the notable exception of the CBRA, most efforts were geared toward resource development—in particular, stepped-up oil and gas leasing on federal offshore lands. Notwithstanding, some important regional initiatives—including the Chesapeake Bay Agreement (figure 9.15) and the Great Lakes Program (figure 9.13)—were initiated during this period. Furthermore, recent concerns about beach pollution have led to a congressional ban on ocean dumping after 1991, delays in oil and gas lease sales, and state programs to deal with medical and other toxic wastes. And it appears that coastal issues will continue to capture public attention, certainly in the near term.

Big Sur, California.
R. Mason.

THE EXCLUSIVE ECONOMIC ZONE

The Law of the Sea Treaty—to which the United States is not signatory—defines the Exclusive Economic Zone (EEZ) as the 200 miles of coastal waters adjacent to nations. Within its EEZ, a country exercises exclusive control over fish, minerals, and other basic resources. The United States in 1946 declared sole jurisdiction over its outer continental shelf (which extends out to approximately the 200-meter depth). This was to ensure control over oil and gas development. In 1976, the United States established a 200-mile Fishery Conservation Zone, laying claim to most of the fish and shellfish within it, and in 1983 unilaterally proclaimed an EEZ that conforms in general principle with Law of the Sea provisions and within which we claim control over ocean dumping. Distinct from the EEZ is the territorial sea, which in 1988 was extended from 3 to 12 miles. Within this zone, all uses are regulated, but the right of "innocent passage" is guaranteed.

The EEZ is valued for petroleum, fish, and nonfuel minerals. Indeed, EEZ resources may in the long term reduce national dependence on foreign sources of critical minerals (figure 14.4). In short, the EEZ's 3.2 billion acres are a very substantial and strategic portion of the nation's 5.3-billion-acre domain.

Figure 7.1. The Exclusive Economic Zone.

Source:
"Map Showing the United States Exclusive Economic Zone Boundaries: 1988" (U.S. Geological Survey, 1988, map).

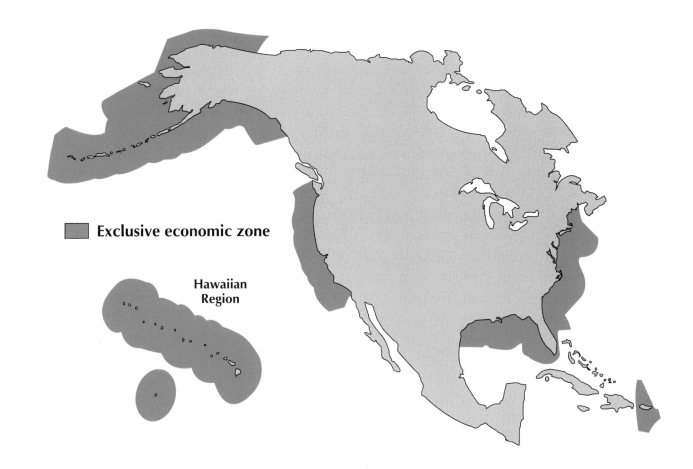

Exclusive economic zone

Hawaiian Region

Regions	Areal Extent of Offshore Submerged Lands		Federal OCS Oil & Gas Leasing Activities			Federal OCS Oil & Gas Resource Estimates [Billion Barrels Oil Equivalent (BBOE)]				State Leases (BBOE)
	State Areas (acres)	Federal OCS Planning Areas (acres)	Total Leases Issued (acres)	Leases Under Department of Interior Supervision 12/31/86 (acres)	Producing Leases (acres)	Original Reserves in New & Developed Fields	Cumulative Production	Remaining Reserves	Undiscovered, Economically Recoverable Oil & Gas Resources	Cumulative Production
Alaska	14,656,000	494,208,000	5,068,818	3,415,222	23,119[1]				4.56	1.10
Atlantic	4,544,000	148,224,000	2,334,885	597,784					2.74	
Gulf of Mexico	8,640,000	131,328,000	31,684,619	20,580,755	6,913,866	32.34	20.31	12.03	16.64	3.87
Pacific	2,880,000	121,920,000	2,540,012	844,486	194,056	2.11[2]	.43[2]	1.68[2]	3.03	2.14

[1] "Producible acreage". Hydrocarbons in paying quantities have been encountered in wells, but no production has taken place.   [2] Southern California only

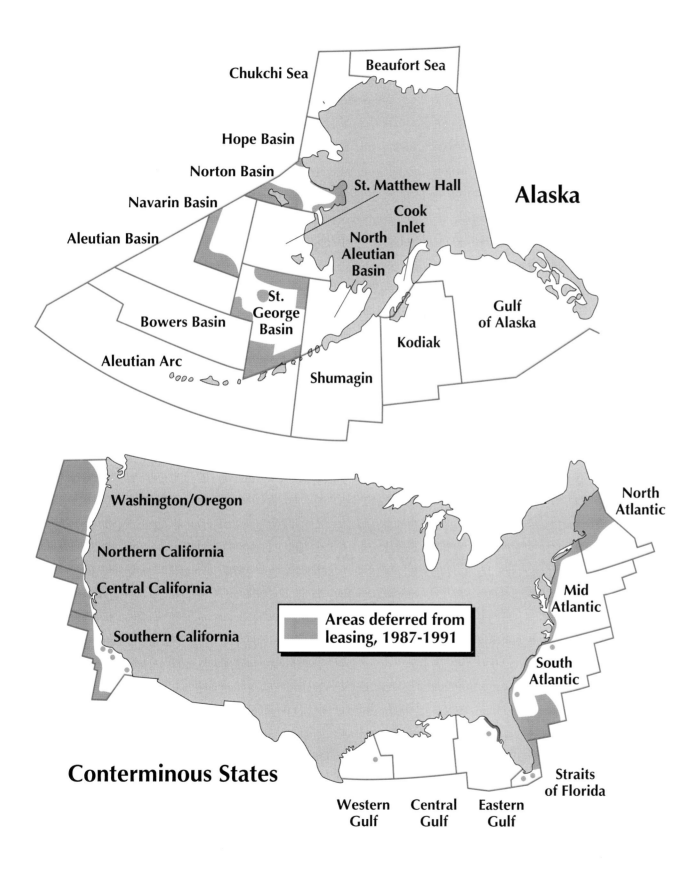

Alaska

Chukchi Sea
Beaufort Sea
Hope Basin
Norton Basin
Navarin Basin
St. Matthew Hall
Aleutian Basin
Cook Inlet
North Aleutian Basin
St. George Basin
Bowers Basin
Gulf of Alaska
Aleutian Arc
Kodiak
Shumagin

Conterminous States

Washington/Oregon
Northern California
Central California
Southern California
North Atlantic
Mid Atlantic
South Atlantic
Straits of Florida
Western Gulf
Central Gulf
Eastern Gulf

Areas deferred from leasing, 1987-1991

OIL AND GAS LEASING

The federal role in coastal zone management is really a dual one, meant to strike a balance between resource protection and resource development. Almost by definition, however, the Outer Continental Shelf Oil and Gas Leasing program—administered by the Department of the Interior—is directed toward resource development. It is also a source of revenue for the federal government, providing land-acquisition monies to state and local governments through the Land and Water Conservation Fund (chapter 15). Moreover, the program does give heed to conservation and preservation interests—through restrictions, bans, and lease-pricing policies.

The areas potentially eligible for leasing are shown in figure 7.2. These planning areas encompass the Outer Continental Shelf (OCS), and their seaward boundary generally parallels, but is not necessarily coincident with, that of the Exclusive Economic Zone (figure 7.1). Boundary questions are further clouded by the fact that the United States has never declared a precise outer limit to the continental shelf over which it claims jurisdiction.

The OCS planning areas total approximately 1.4 million square miles. The states control a further 48,000 square miles. State-controlled lands are those situated 3 nautical miles seaward of each state baseline (except offshore Texas and the Gulf Coast of Florida, where the limit is 3 marine leagues, or roughly 10 statute miles).

Prior to the 1953 passage of the Outer Continental Shelf Lands Act, leasing was confined to state waters—and virtually all of the activity took place offshore Texas and Louisiana. By 1962, federal OCS production had overtaken state production of oil, and federal gas production also pulled far ahead of state production later in the decade. By 1986, federal OCS lands were producing 83 percent of all offshore oil, while OCS gas production represented 90 percent of total offshore gas. State production is significant in Alaska (where there has been no federal production), southern California, and—to a much lesser extent—the Gulf region.

In 1986, OCS production accounted for about one-quarter of the domestic supply of natural gas and one-eighth of domestic oil production. These figures reflect a general upward trend—with some interruptions along the way—in the relative importance of OCS production. Production, however, represents the culmination of a complex set of pre-lease and post-lease activities.

Figure 7.2. Outer Continental Shelf Oil and Gas Lease Areas.

Source:
Minerals Management Service, *Outer Continental Shelf Oil and Gas 5-Year Leasing Program, Mid-1987 to Mid-1992: Proposed Final* (Washington, DC: Department of the Interior, 1987), pp. 27–42.

The process begins with geologic studies, resource studies, and environmental impact statements that lead to identification of areas to be offered for leasing. Further analysis is required before an actual lease sale can take place. Provisions are made throughout this process for public and intergovernmental review and comment.

Through 1986, 478 million acres of federal OCS lands had been offered for lease; 41.6 million acres were actually leased. The Reagan administration's emphasis on federal resource development resulted in an upsurge in lease offerings in 1982 and 1983. Less dramatic were the increases in acreages actually leased, as well as the increases in oil and gas production. By far the most production over the years has taken place in the Gulf of Mexico region, with no production at all on federal OCS lands in the Atlantic and Alaskan regions. (All above statistics are from Minerals Management Service Annual (1988).

Leasing activity is currently guided by a five-year plan that covers the period July 1987 through July 1992. This is the third such plan; the earlier ones were issued in 1980 and 1982. The present plan calls for a total of thirty-eight lease sales in twenty-one of the areas shown on the map. One way in which the current plan differs from the previous ones is in the deferral of specific subregions from leasing. Most of these are situated in or near environmentally sensitive water and/or land areas such as wilderness areas, ecological preserves, and marine sanctuaries. This, of course, does not imply that all the nondeferred areas are equally valued for leasing. Indeed, the lease program attempts to focus on the most promising areas. The study and review processes serve to reduce further—sometimes drastically—the acreages being considered for lease offers.

The expansion of OCS oil and gas development in the 1970s and early 1980s brought with it major environmental concerns. One of the responses to those concerns was the now-defunct Coastal Energy Impact Program (CEIP), enacted as part of the 1976 amendments to the Coastal Zone Management Act. It provided the states with funds to study environmental impacts of offshore energy development. In 1978, a reformed version of the original Outer Continental Shelf Lands Act was enacted. Among other things, it provided grant appropriations to states for implementation of CEIPs, required greater intergovernmental coordination and public consultation, mandated a five-year leasing schedule, and separated the exploration and production processes.

The OCS leasing program has been enormously controversial—especially as regards the location and timing of resource development as well as the basic assumptions about oil and gas needs that guide offshore activity. Among the more contentious coastal and offshore regions are the middle and north Atlantic coastal areas, northern California, and Alaska's Arctic National Wildlife Refuge. In February 1989, President Bush announced a postponement of leasing off California and southwestern Florida. Then, the March 1989 Alaskan oil spill (figure 13.8) cast a long shadow of doubt over *all* offshore activity. Although the president has expressed support for further exploration and development, both he and Congress have thus far responded to public sentiment. New lease activity has come to a virtual standstill.

COASTAL BARRIER RESOURCES ACT

Barrier islands are shifting ribbons of sand, separated from the mainland by lagoons and bays. As sea level has risen in recent millennia, the barriers—along with the lagoons and bays—have gradually migrated in a landward direction. Although some barriers may appear to us to be relatively stable, most are not. Much of their movement occurs in fits and starts, propelled by the energy of violent coastal storms.

In recent decades, the extensive coastal barriers of the Atlantic and Gulf coasts have experienced severe development pressures as well as high levels of property damage from coastal storms. Federal concern over these events culminated in 1982 in the signing of the Coastal Barrier Resources Act (CBRA). In keeping with the prevailing philosophy of the Reagan era, the CBRA relies on negative incentives to restrict development on barrier islands. It prohibits federal subsidies (loans, grants) for construction of infrastructure (roads, bridges, sewers, etc.) on designated, *undeveloped* portions of barrier islands. Federal flood-insurance benefits for new development or major improvements of existing structures are also prohibited, as mandated by the Omnibus Budget Reconciliation Act of 1981 (OBRA). In these ways, CBRA and OBRA seek to shift to the private landowner the full financial burdens and risks associated with development. One of the central objectives of CBRA is to reduce federal spending. At the same time, the preservation of coastal barriers will help protect the mainland from storm waves and surges as well as maintain critical habitat for fish, shellfish, birds, mammals, and other wildlife. The CBRA's success in achieving these objectives will be limited to designated, undeveloped segments of barrier islands. As indicated in figure 7.3, this represents only a fraction of the length of the total barrier system. Even if an additional 1,157 miles of shoreline were added to the system, as was recommended in early 1987, this would still be well under half the length of the total barrier shoreline.

But there is no assurance as to how much—if at all—the Coastal Barrier Resources System (CBRS) will be expanded. Indeed, it is conceivable that large areas may yet be legislatively deleted from the CBRS. At best, CBRA can only partially achieve the broad objectives of barrier island protection, because it offers protection for undeveloped sections only. It is evident from figure 7.3 that the undeveloped barriers represent a small proportion of total barrier length in most states. However, the CBRA still can be effective at the federal level through careful management and new additions to the systems of national seashores (see figure 15.1) and national wildlife refuges (figure 15.10); through wetlands acquisitions pursuant to the Emergency Wetlands Resources Act of 1986 (see chapter 5); and through other regulatory, tax-policy, and legislative means. Furthermore, and perhaps most important, states may implement their own rigorous protection policies as part of their coastal zone management programs.

Figure 7.3. The Coastal Barrier Resources System.

Sources:
U.S. Department of the Interior, *Draft Report to Congress: Coastal Barrier Resources System, Executive Summary* (Washington, DC: Department of the Interior, 1987), p. 10.

Heritage Conservation and Recreation Service, *Report of the Barrier Island Work Group* (Washington, DC: GPO, 1978), p. 7.

J. T. Wells, et al., *Restless Ribbons of Sand: Atlantic and Gulf Coast Barriers* (Baton Rouge, LA: Louisiana Sea Grant College Program, n.d.).

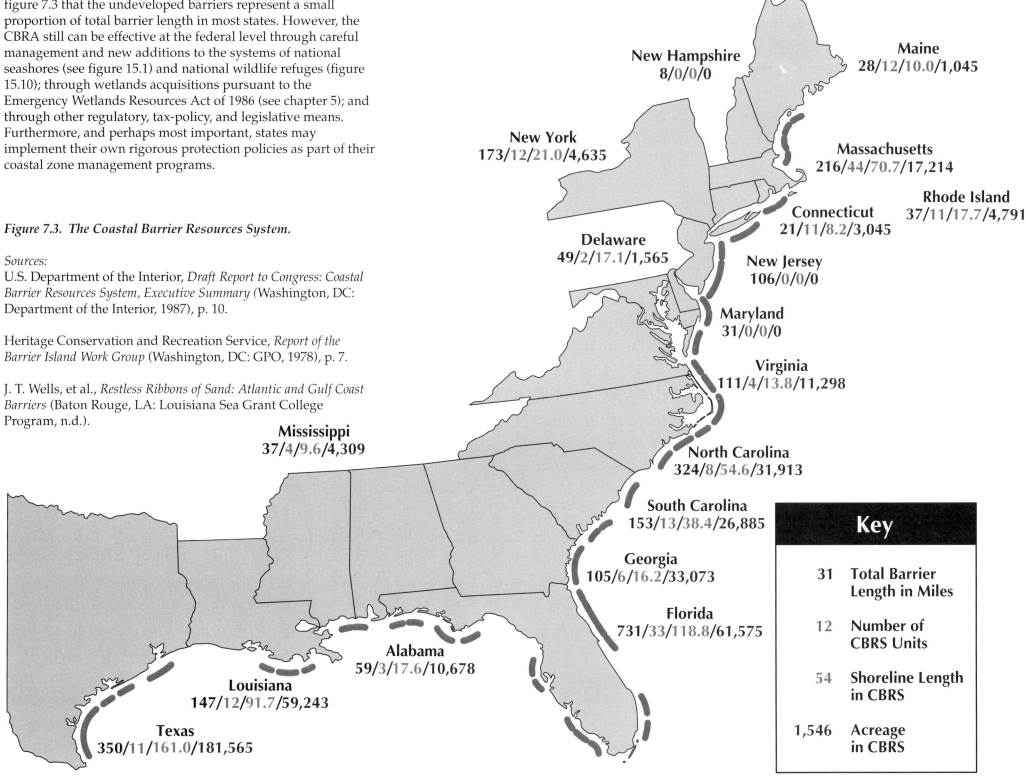

New Hampshire
8/0/0/0

Maine
28/12/10.0/1,045

New York
173/12/21.0/4,635

Massachusetts
216/44/70.7/17,214

Rhode Island
37/11/17.7/4,791

Connecticut
21/11/8.2/3,045

Delaware
49/2/17.1/1,565

New Jersey
106/0/0/0

Maryland
31/0/0/0

Virginia
111/4/13.8/11,298

Mississippi
37/4/9.6/4,309

North Carolina
324/8/54.6/31,913

South Carolina
153/13/38.4/26,885

Georgia
105/6/16.2/33,073

Florida
731/33/118.8/61,575

Alabama
59/3/17.6/10,678

Louisiana
147/12/91.7/59,243

Texas
350/11/161.0/181,565

Key

31	Total Barrier Length in Miles
12	Number of CBRS Units
54	Shoreline Length in CBRS
1,546	Acreage in CBRS

COASTAL ZONE MANAGEMENT

Prior to the 1972 passage of the Coastal Zone Management Act (CZMA), only a handful of state coastal management policies or programs were in place. By 1988, twenty-four coastal states had federally approved programs—most of them having gained approval in the mid- to late-1970s. Only six states do not currently participate in the Coastal Zone Management Program (CZMP).

What does the program entail? Its essential purpose is to strike a balance between environment and development—but it does not uniformly prescribe how the balance is to be struck, nor does it require that states participate. It does set forth a broad policy regarding land and water resource management, specifies general areas of national concern, and provides grants to participating states. The requirements for state plan approval are not particularly rigorous. In general, states are expected to delimit the boundaries of their coastal zones, identify permissible land and water uses therein, specify areas of "particular planning concern," and develop the means to influence local land-use decisions within the coastal zone.

Among the principal means for achieving these objectives are regulatory permit systems, comprehensive planning, "special area management planning," zoning regulations and subdivision controls, land acquisition and restoration, promotion of desirable development, negotiation between proponents and opponents of development, and use of the federal "consistency provision" of the CZMA to reject federal actions that do not conform with the state's program. Application of the consistency provision has, however, been limited by Supreme Court decisions that circumscribe states' rights with respect to Outer Continental Shelf oil and gas leasing.

The National Estuarine Reserve Research System—represented on the map—is an acquisition program that is specifically defined by the CZMA. Initially known as the National Estuarine Sanctuary Program, its name was changed in 1985 to reflect the priority placed on research uses for the reserves. Secondary emphasis is given to public education and ecological protection. The program, in keeping with other provisions of the CZMA, depends on state initiative and commitment; the federal share for acquisition funding is limited to 50 percent. As of late 1988, the system comprised some 262,000 acres. The EPA has a separate program—the National Estuary Program—that seeks to protect estuaries threatened by pollution, development, and overuse. The 1987 Water Quality Act specifies that twelve estuaries be considered for inclusion in the program, with the ultimate objective of developing management plans for each. The EPA's "Near Coastal Water Initiative" is designed to address problems in coastal locations not included in other EPA programs. Yet another effort is represented by the small but expanding system of marine sanctuaries that are owned

and administered by the National Oceanic and Atmospheric Administration (NOAA). They are meant to serve conservation, recreation, ecological, historic, educational, aesthetic, and research needs. As of 1988, seven had been designated; twelve additional sites had either been proposed for designation or were under study.

Overall, though, the federal leadership role in coastal zone management diminished considerably during the 1980s. Federal funding was greatly reduced, innovative programs were eliminated, and staff demoralization was widespread.

In keeping with the "new federalism," coastal zone management now relies heavily on state-level interest and initiative. And indeed, despite weak federal support, some states have managed to craft strong coastal zone programs. They use them to regulate mineral and petroleum development, preserve wetlands, protect endangered species, and provide expanded public access to beaches. Among the states that have developed or maintained strong and effective programs are New Jersey, North Carolina, Washington, Massachusetts, and Virginia. In addition, strong substate and regional programs (with limited federal involvement) have been implemented in some areas—among them the Great Lakes and Chesapeake Bay watersheds.

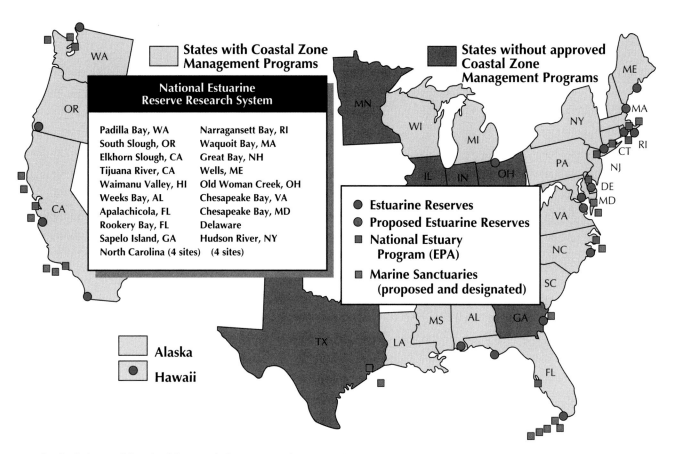

Figure 7.4. State Coastal Zone Management Programs.

Sources:
EPA, *Environmental Progress and Challenges: EPA's Update*, EPA-230-07-88-033 (Washington, DC: GPO, 1988).

NOAA, "State Coastal Zone Management Program, Coastal Energy Impact Program and Outer Continental Shelf Coordination, Heads of Relevant Agencies and Program Managers" (NOAA, 1988, mimeograph).

NOAA, *National Estuarine Research Reserve System: Site Catalogue* (Washington, DC: NOAA, 1989).

NOAA, "National Marine Sanctuary Program" (NOAA, 1989, map).

POLLUTING INCIDENTS IN AND AROUND U.S. COASTAL WATERS

The media and the public take notice of large oil spills and other catastrophic polluting events. Indeed, the 1989 *Exxon Valdez* discharge of 11.2 million gallons of oil into Alaska's Prince William Sound was amply noticed. And the damages to the region's delicate ecosystems and economically important fishing industry were indeed extensive (figure 13.8).

Much less noticed, but in the aggregate perhaps more damaging, are the many smaller leaks and spills that occur with alarming regularity. Offshore oil and gas operations, in particular, are major sources of pollution. On average, between 1,500 and 2,000 tons of drilling muds (used to lubricate drill bits) and cuttings (mud-coated pieces of rock) are discharged annually into coastal waters (NRDC 1989).

The Federal Water Pollution Control Act (Clean Water Act) requires that discharges of "harmful quantities" of oil and hazardous substances be reported to the U.S. Coast Guard and other designated federal agencies. The Coast Guard then compiles and disseminates this information. In both 1983 and 1984, over 40 percent of reported oil spills (by volume) occurred in ports and harbors—as opposed to river channels or other parts of the coastal zone. Regional variability is high from year to year; indeed, a spill like that in Prince William Sound in 1989 can greatly skew the statistics. High also is the variability in reported sources of oil pollution: vessels accounted for 9.4 percent by volume in 1983 and 36.4 percent in 1984. In both years, "miscellaneous/unknown" was the largest source. This seems to imply that there is much more that simply goes unreported—including, perhaps, routine discharges that evade reporting requirements.

As of the early 1980s, over 1,300 major industrial discharges went into marine waters, most of them to estuaries. Moreover, 180 million metric tons of dredged material were being disposed of annually in marine waters (OTA 1987). In addition to the routine, permitted industrial discharges, large amounts of hazardous and other substances enter coastal waters accidentally. In both 1983 and 1984, the largest share entered the territorial sea (figure 7.1). The 1984 data for hazardous and other substances, like that for oil incidents in 1983 and 1984, reveal that 90 percent of the sources of the pollution were either miscellaneous or unknown.

Figure 7.5. Polluting Incidents in and Around U.S. Coastal Waters.

Source:
Department of Transportation and Coast Guard, *Polluting Incidents In and Around U.S. Waters: Calendar Year 1983 and 1984* (Springfield, VA: National Technical Information Service, 1986), pp. 7, 11, 21.

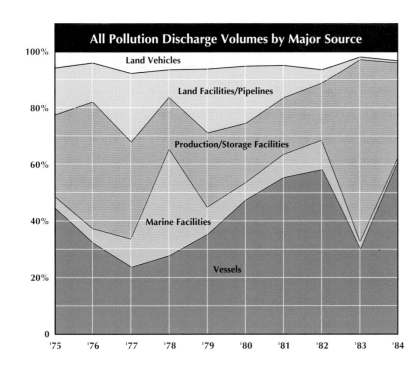

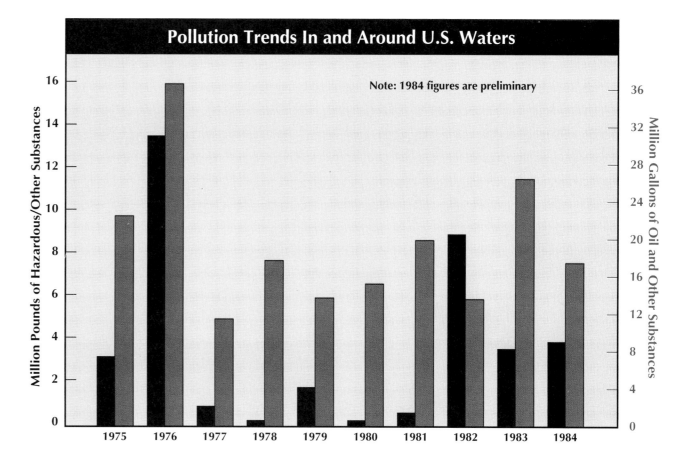

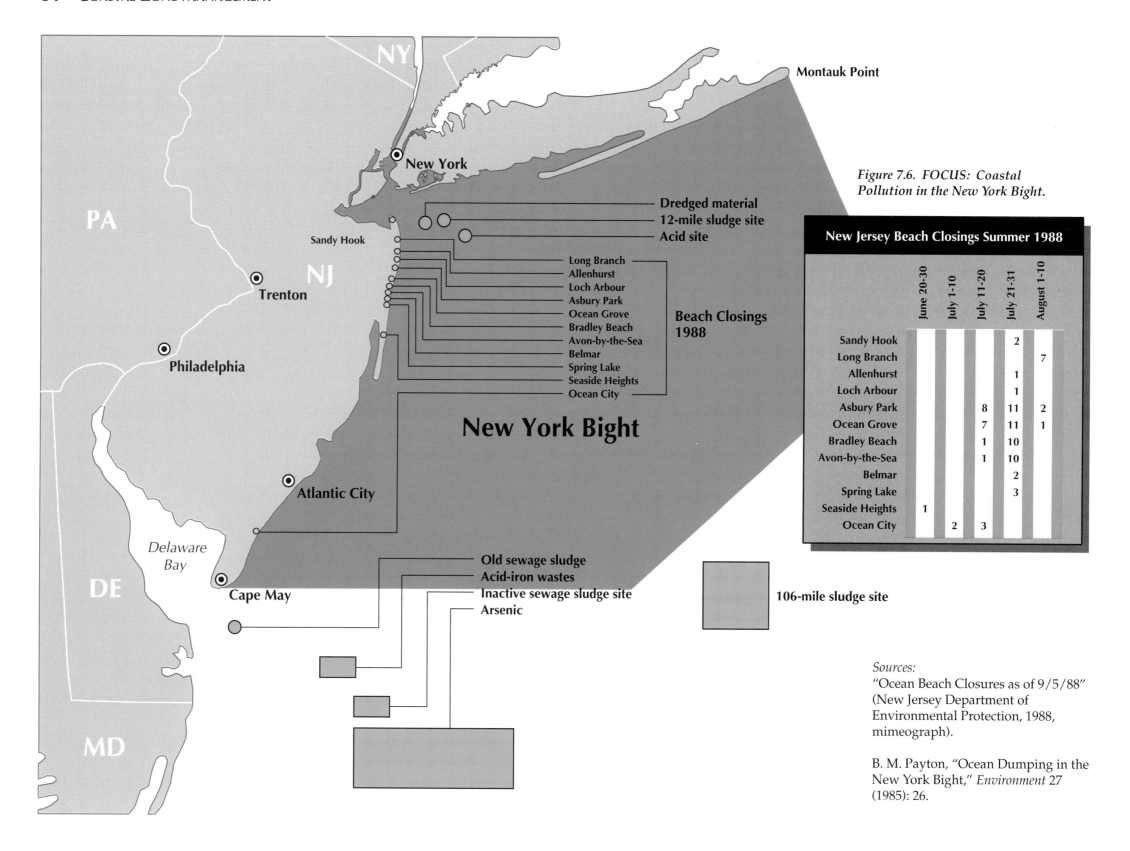

Figure 7.6. FOCUS: Coastal Pollution in the New York Bight.

New York Bight

Dredged material
12-mile sludge site
Acid site

Long Branch
Allenhurst
Loch Arbour
Asbury Park
Ocean Grove
Bradley Beach
Avon-by-the-Sea
Belmar
Spring Lake
Seaside Heights
Ocean City

Beach Closings 1988

Old sewage sludge
Acid-iron wastes
Inactive sewage sludge site
Arsenic

106-mile sludge site

New Jersey Beach Closings Summer 1988					
	June 20-30	July 1-10	July 11-20	July 21-31	August 1-10
Sandy Hook				2	
Long Branch					7
Allenhurst				1	
Loch Arbour				1	
Asbury Park			8	11	2
Ocean Grove			7	11	1
Bradley Beach			1	10	
Avon-by-the-Sea			1	10	
Belmar				2	
Spring Lake				3	
Seaside Heights	1				
Ocean City		2	3		

Sources:
"Ocean Beach Closures as of 9/5/88" (New Jersey Department of Environmental Protection, 1988, mimeograph).

B. M. Payton, "Ocean Dumping in the New York Bight," *Environment* 27 (1985): 26.

COASTAL POLLUTION IN THE NEW YORK BIGHT

The summer of 1988 was filled with news reports about coastal pollution in the New York-New Jersey region. Not only was there the usual bacterial contamination of coastal waters, there were also many cases of medical wastes washing ashore. Alarms were raised about possible transmission of AIDS through syringes that had appeared on several beaches. Matters were only made worse by the fact that the previous summer had had its share of red tides, fish kills, beach closings, and reports of illnesses among swimmers. By the spring of 1988, the New Jersey shore had become a presidential campaign issue. And in 1989, two Wildwood businessmen resorted to chlorination in a vain attempt to forestall closure of the local beaches.

The map in figure 7.6 is not meant to imply that there are direct causal connections between marine waste disposal and specific New Jersey beach closings. Indeed, a variety of explanations may be put forth for the closings. What is significant, though, is the connection between widely publicized beach contamination and public and government reconsideration of coastal waste disposal and other management practices.

The New York Bight, shown on the map, contains the single remaining active sewage-sludge dump site in United States coastal waters. Six municipal sewerage authorities from northern New Jersey and three from New York State (including New York City) use the 106-mile site. Dumping had taken place at the 12-mile site until the EPA prohibited it during the summer of 1987. Federal legislation passed during 1988 prohibits all ocean dumping after 1991.

It may be argued that the pollution contributed by sludge dumping is relatively modest compared with what enters the New York Bight from various other sources. These include raw and treated sewage discharges, combined sewer overflows, dredge spoils, construction debris, and industrial wastes. In 1985, approximately 7 million wet metric tons of sludge and 8 million wet metric tons of dredged material entered the Bight while several billion gallons of raw sewage were introduced (OTA 1987). In addition, the Bight receives large quantities of acid and other industrial waste. Its waters are assaulted with metals, organic chemicals, and PCBs from both "local" and upstream (e.g., Hudson and Raritan rivers) sources.

In 1976, the pollution problem became dramatically visible as bacteria-laden greaseballs washed up on Long Island beaches and oxygen depletion off the New Jersey coast caused the death of most benthic (bottom-dwelling) organisms. That summer's overnourishment has been attributed to unusual weather conditions that created persistent buildups of warm waters. Once again in 1985, parts of the New York Bight experienced unusually low oxygen (anoxic) conditions.

The Bight's plight has drawn public attention for many years. The EPA attempted to prohibit sludge dumping in the late 1970s but was finally rebuffed by a 1981 court decision favorable to New York City. As already noted, the agency did require that the dumpsite be moved to deeper waters; the current 106-mile site is beyond the edge of the continental shelf. But although the questions of long- and short-term effects and deep-water versus shallow-water dumping have prompted considerable debate, clear and simple answers are not forthcoming.

The bill that bans sludge dumping as of 1992 was passed unanimously by both houses of Congress. The act also includes penalties for dumping medical wastes in waterways. A federal pilot program for tracking medical wastes is being instituted, and New York and New Jersey are developing their own separate systems. New Jersey Governor Thomas Kean issued an executive order that prohibits development within 1,000 feet of the shoreline. The intention was to prompt the legislature to create a coastal commission that would comprehensively regulate development in the coastal zone—but as of late 1989 the legislature had not acted. While all these actions should help reduce pollution loadings to the Bight, they may not be sufficient to reduce seriously the region's pollution problems. Major, long-term improvements will most likely depend on vigorous regulation and enforcement—principally under the Clean Water Act—to control urban runoff and discharges of raw and treated sewage.

The 1988 beach closings drew considerable attention to coastal issues, with an inordinate amount of it focused on sludge dumping. Most of the beach closings were in fact attributed to high bacterial levels—but in many cases, the culprit was local discharges (e.g., overflows) of sewage. In a time of declining federal funds for sewage treatment facilities, the role of sewage discharges (as well as the rapid population growth in coastal regions that produce the discharges) becomes all the more prominent. So, too, do the sites where dredged materials are dumped. In this regard, the New York Bight is not alone: Large quantities of dredge spoils are also dumped in the Pacific Ocean and especially the Gulf of Mexico (OTA 1987). Moreover, there are industrial wastes. Dumping has declined markedly in recent years—but previous years' dumping of vast quantities of industrial, military, and radioactive wastes has left its legacy in the form of contaminated bottom sediments. Despite international regulations developed as early as 1970 (the London Dumping Convention) and at subsequent international meetings—and despite all the recent concern about ocean disposal—progress in addressing these various problems has been slow. And the accumulation of knowledge about the long- and short-term effects of marine waste disposal has been even slower.

Table 7.2. Land Use in Estuarine Drainage Basins

| | Percent of Basins[1] | | | |
	Northeast	Southeast	Gulf of Mexico	West Coast
Residential	10.3	3.1	2.7	5.4
Commercial/Services	2.0	0.8	0.6	1.1
Industrial	0.5	0.1	0.5	0.7
Transportation/Communication	0.9	0.4	0.4	0.4
Industrial/Commercial Complex	0.1	0.0	0.0	0.0
Mixed Urban/Built-Up	0.2	0.1	0.1	0.1
Other Urban/Built-Up	1.0	0.1	0.3	0.6
Total Urban	**15.0**	**5.0**	**4.6**	**8.9**
Cropland/Pasture	19.8	24.6	28.3	7.2
Other Agriculture	0.3	1.0	1.0	0.6
Total Agriculture	**20.2**	**25.5**	**29.3**	**8.3**
Herbaceous	0.0	1.9	4.9	2.4
Shrub/Brushland	0.4	0.1	5.4	2.5
Mixed	0.0	0.0	2.4	0.4
Total Range	**0.4**	**2.1**	**12.6**	**6.6**
Deciduous	18.1	6.8	3.0	1.0
Evergreen	12.6	22.5	16.6	30.8
Mixed	25.4	12.1	13.7	8.3
Total Forest	**58.4**	**41.3**	**33.3**	**65.9**
Forested	2.5	18.8	9.0	0.2
Nonforested	2.3	6.3	9.6	0.5
Total Wetland	**5.0**	**25.0**	**18.7**	**0.8**
Dry Salt Flats	0.0	0.0	0.0	0.0
Beaches	0.1	0.1	0.1	0.0
Other Sandy Areas	0.1	0.0	0.2	0.0
Bare Exposed Rock	0.1	0.0	0.0	0.0
Strip Mines/Quarries/Gravel Pits	0.4	0.1	0.3	0.1
Transitional Areas	0.5	0.8	1.1	0.2
Mixed Barren	0.0	0.0	0.0	0.0
Total Barren	**1.1**	**1.0**	**1.6**	**9.1**
All Other	0.0	0.0	0.0	0.5
Regional Total (sq. mi.)	**59,426**	**45,185**	**81,746**	**49,590**

[1]Regional Definitions:
 Northeast : Maine to Virginia
 Southeast: North Carolina to East Florida
 Gulf of Mexico: West Florida to Texas
 West Coast: California to Washington

Source: NOAA, *National Estuarine Inventory: Data Atlas*, vol. 1, *Land Use Characteristics* (Washington, DC: GPO, 1987), pp. 3, 15, 23, 34.

Table 7.3. Commercial Fish Landings, 1987

	Million Pounds	Million Dollars
New England	545.1	512.5
Middle Atlantic	162.8	128.0
Chesapeake	791.3	159.7
South Atlantic	235.1	150.4
Gulf	2,500.1	719.8
Pacific Coast and Alaska	2,492.8	1,360.3
Great Lakes	41.8	16.9
Hawaii	16.1	29.1
Other	110.2	38.0
Total	**6,895.7**	**3,114.7**

Source: NOAA, *Fisheries of the United States, 1987* (Washington, DC: GPO, 1988).

Figure 7.7. Status of Shellfishing Waters.

Source:
NOAA, "A National Atlas: Health and Use of Coastal Waters, United States of America" (Rockville, MD: NOAA, 1988, folio map no. 6).

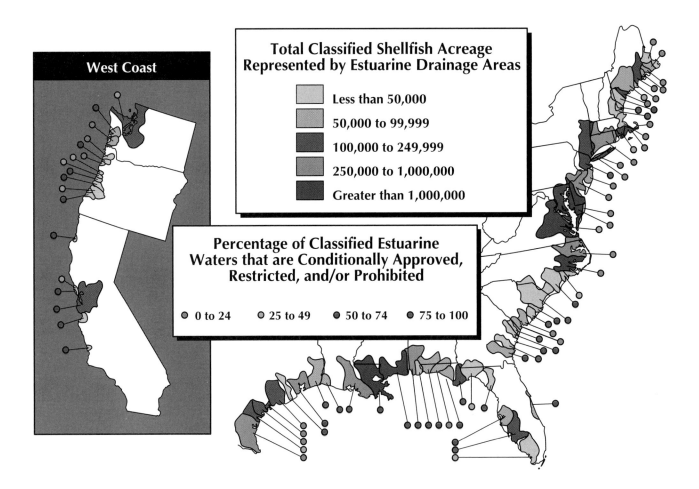

West Coast

Total Classified Shellfish Acreage Represented by Estuarine Drainage Areas

Less than 50,000
50,000 to 99,999
100,000 to 249,999
250,000 to 1,000,000
Greater than 1,000,000

Percentage of Classified Estuarine Waters that are Conditionally Approved, Restricted, and/or Prohibited

0 to 24   25 to 49   50 to 74   75 to 100

STATUS OF SHELLFISH WATERS

Estuarine areas are zones of transition between fresh and salt water, the places where rivers meet the sea. Their salinity is lower than that of the open ocean, and they receive vast quantities of nutrients from the fresh waters flowing into them. In terms of plant biomass per unit area, estuaries are among the most productive ecosystems in the world. They are also very important producers of fish, crustaceans (including crabs and shrimp), and mollusks (including clams and oysters). At the same time, they are often subject to heavy stresses from human activities. Urban, industrial, commercial, and recreational demands on our coastlines tend to be most intense in estuarine areas.

One indicator—albeit an imperfect one—of the ecological and economic health of estuarine waters is their fitness for shellfishing. The National Shellfish Register, first compiled in 1966, is a periodic inventory of the nation's shellfish-growing waters. Those waters are classified as approved (for taking of shellfish), prohibited, conditionally approved, restricted, and nonshellfish/nonproductive. The classification program is conducted by the states, under the coordination of the National Shellfish Sanitation Program—a cooperative venture among states, industry, and the federal Food and Drug Administration. The map in figure 7.7 is based on the 1985 National Shellfish Register, as modified by the National Oceanic and Atmospheric Administration's (NOAA's) Strategic Assessment Program.

This classification is based primarily on measurements of bacterial contamination and provides little direct indication of the presence of toxic chemicals. Furthermore, some waters' classifications may not accurately reflect water-quality characteristics. Louisiana, for example, classifies *all* of its waters as "conditionally approved." Unclassified or unsurveyed areas are in many cases simply classified as "prohibited." Despite these qualifications, the data provide an indication of general estuarine conditions.

The Northeast contains the greatest percentage of productive waters approved for harvesting. While Northeast harvests have been affected in recent years by outbreaks of MX and dermo disease, the water conditions may have stabilized or improved as the result of relatively slow economic growth and improvements in water-pollution control. The Southeast and Gulf States, on the other hand, have had to contend with locally intense growth pressures. These factors may partially explain recent declines in acreages approved for harvesting. Shellfishing is not as important an economic activity on the West Coast as in the other regions. Nonetheless, there have been some significant declines in approved acreages between 1980 and 1985.

Clearly, estuarine health is affected by human activities that contribute fecal coliform bacteria, excessive nitrogen and phosphorous, trace metals, pesticides, and other chemical compounds.

Not only are the contributions from the estuary's immediate drainage area important; so too are those from the larger area that includes all its tributaries. Indeed, NOAA believes that contributions from tributaries account for the greatest pollutant inputs. Data on the relative contributions of various activities in different estuaries are imprecise. However, NOAA's studies of Northeast and Gulf of Mexico estuaries do point to the major significance of nonpoint sources (urban and agricultural runoff) and wastewater treatment plants as contributors of nutrients. Furthermore, the highest levels of toxic chemical contamination of bivalves have been generally—but not exclusively—found in estuarine areas near major coastal cities.

The Office of Technology Assessment (OTA 1987) emphasizes the importance of making policy choices that seek to maintain and improve the quality of our estuarine and coastal waters. The OTA points out that many municipal and industrial wastes are discharged *directly* into these waters. At least 1,300 industrial facilities and 500 municipal sewage treatment plants do so. Industrial discharges are the principal sources of many organic chemicals and some metals, and they account for about 90 percent of the inputs of cadmium, mercury, and chlorinated hydrocarbons. Certain other metals, chromium and lead among them, come more from nonindustrial sources—at least in some parts of the country.

The principal municipal point sources of pollutants are municipal sewage treatment plants. Greatest quantities of waste come from the heavily urbanized parts of the nation. Indeed, over 60 percent of all municipal discharges to marine waters occur in the northern Atlantic region; 20 percent take place in California. Municipal point sources are key contributors of some of the "conventional pollutants." They account for about half of biochemical oxygen demand, total nitrogen, and oil and grease. Interestingly, though, municipal discharges contribute only one-sixth of the total input of fecal coliform bacteria.

Nonpoint runoff is the by far the largest source of fecal coliform bacteria throughout the country. Moreover, it is the predominant source of suspended solids and contributor of at least half of total phosphorous, chromium, copper, lead, iron, and zinc. Nonpoint runoff stands out as a major source of pollutants on the Pacific Coast.

The OTA (1987) concludes that even if current laws were fully implemented and enforced (see chapter 9), we would still be unable to maintain or improve the health of all estuaries and coastal waters. Still, enormous progress could be made with improved enforcement, additional funding for municipal treatment plant construction, expanded regulation of key pollutants and their sources (including toxic and hazardous wastes), and more comprehensive management plans for selected estuaries and coastal waters.

Air Quality and Acid Deposition

What constitutes clean air? The answers to this question depend on individual and collective perceptions of risk, on our evolving knowledge of air pollutants and their transport, and on our ability to detect minute quantities of pollutants. Through the mid-1900s, the concern was mainly with visible pollution, that is, smoke and "smog." During this era, smog was characterized as smoke plus fog (current definitions, by contrast, encompass a wider variety of chemical pollutants and chemical reactions). By the late 1940s and 1950s, localities with severe and visible problems—such as Pittsburgh and Los Angeles County—had started control programs. But it was not until 1963 that a concerted national response would come: the Clean Air Act. In 1970, the act was considerably upgraded and strengthened. The EPA was directed to set standards for what are known as "criteria pollutants": ozone, carbon monoxide, sulfur dioxide, nitrogen oxides, lead, and particulates. There are two types of "ambient air quality standards": primary standards, meant to protect human health, and the stricter secondary standards, which seek to protect "welfare"—crops, livestock, vegetation, buildings, and visibility. The EPA and states were required to reduce pollutants from both stationary sources, such as power plants and industrial facilities, and mobile sources, principally vehicles. Despite implementation delays and enforcement shortcomings, considerable progress has been made under the Clean Air Act.

One of the act's unforeseen consequences was that many industries and utilities began building tall stacks to disperse pollutants from local areas. As it became evident that this practice was contributing to long-range transport and deposition of sulfur oxides, the Clean Air Act Amendments of 1977 attempted to discourage it. Indeed, "acid rain" has gained wide public recognition since the mid-1970s. While research programs have proliferated, very little has been done to control the specific sources of pollutants—especially sulfur dioxide—that are strongly suspected of contributing to the phenomenon.

Besides regulating ambient air quality, the 1970 Clean Air Act called for the EPA to list—and ultimately regulate—hazardous pollutants. These are substances that contribute to increases in mortality and certain types of illnesses. Despite congressional attempts to speed the process, the EPA's progress has been relatively slow. In 1985, however, the agency adopted a comprehensive air toxics strategy; this is further discussed in chapter 12.

In recent years, indoor air pollution has gained recognition as a health threat. Among the household and commercial hazards are gas appliances, wood and kerosene stoves, formaldehyde foam insulation, tobacco smoke, plywood, rugs, furniture, radon gas, asbestos, and such chemicals as chloroform and trichloroethylene that may be transferred from water to air via high-pressure showerheads and faucets. Indoor air pollution may be exacerbated in tightly insulated, energy-efficient houses, since air exchange is reduced. Viruses and molds may be transmitted through ventilating systems of sealed buildings, and gaseous pollutants may also be trapped. Reducing indoor air pollution—at least in the home—implies breaking new regulatory ground, with possible controls on individual behavior and consumer choice. At the same time, this issue conveniently draws attention away from EPA shortcomings in dealing with the "traditional" sources of pollution.

Air quality concerns found renewed urgency during the hot, dry summer of 1988, with its unusual numbers and distribution of smog days. Congress, however, has been at a stalemate since the early 1980s in its attempts to reauthorize the Clean Air Act. A key stumbling block is what to do (or not do) about acid-forming emissions. As we enter the 1990s, though, it finally appears that Congress and the president are ready to resolve the outstanding issues. But in the absence of federal action, several states have themselves adopted strong new measures—most notable among them California, New York, New Jersey, and the New England states.

FOCUS: THE DONORA SMOG EPISODE

Environmental concern is always heightened by a major crisis. And air pollution crises, because of their relatively rapid onset, can capture a great deal of public attention. Over the past several decades, a number of dramatic smog "episodes" have been documented and well publicized. These include the New York episode during the summer of 1965, to which 400 deaths are attributed; the London episodes of 1952 (3,500–4,000 deaths) and 1956 (900 deaths); the Meuse Valley, Belgium, episode of 1930 (sixty deaths); and of course the Donora, Pennsylvania, episode of 1948.

Concerns about air pollution had been present for at least a century before the Donora occurrence. But Donora was instrumental in raising public awareness of air pollution's health effects and in prompting local and federal-level responses to the newly appreciated threats. Indeed, Donora and its consequences helped bring about a fundamental transition in our thinking about the relationships between economic productivity, environmental quality, and public health. Belching smokestacks—once viewed purely as symbols of peacetime prosperity and wartime patriotic effort— were, by the 1950s, being recognized increasingly as conveyors of deadly pollutants.

Donora is situated on the Monongahela River, about 30 miles south of Pittsburgh. Like many Pennsylvania industrial towns, it occupies a small strip of land adjacent to the river, backed by a steep slope and facing a steep slope on the other side of the water. The horseshoe-shaped valley in which Donora is situated tends to retard wind velocity, especially for those winds blowing across the valley. In 1948, the area's population was 14,000, with about three-fifths of the "gainfully employed" working at two large industrial plants: a steel and wire plant and a zinc plant. The region surrounding Donora is home to additional concentrations of heavy industry.

Beginning on October 26, 1948, a high-pressure system established itself for a five-day period over western Pennsylvania. Winds were very light, and the valley fogs that formed at night were not broken up by daytime heating, which was inhibited by the high reflectivity of the fog layer. This was evidenced in four days of high temperatures at Donora (elevation 760 feet) that were lower than those at the Pittsburgh airport (elevation 1,250 feet).

The very stable, stagnant layer of air that persisted in the vicinity of Donora did not allow for the normal dispersal of pollutants (this is sometimes referred to as a "gray air" condition). The result, according to the U.S. Public Health Service (Schrenck 1949), was that 5,910 people (42.7 percent of Donora's population) were affected to some degree by the smog. The Health Service's survey of representative households indicated that 15.5 percent of persons were mildly affected, 16.8 percent

moderately affected, and 10.4 percent severely affected. "Mild" symptoms included eye, nose, and throat ailments, nausea, and headaches; "moderate" symptoms included productive cough (raising mucus, saliva, blood, etc.), chest constriction, vomiting, and diarrhea; while orthopnea (the inability to breathe, except in an upright position) was considered "severe." Twenty deaths occurred in the Donora area during or shortly after the smog episode; seventeen of these were during the third day of the event. Overall, the evidence indicates that those most affected were the aged, the nonwhite population (a small minority of the total population), and those living in the poorer-quality housing. Preexistence of cardiorespiratory disease was a significant factor related to the fatalities.

The U.S. Public Health Service investigation was unprecedented: a team of twenty-five persons spent five weeks in the field. In its recommendations, the agency called for reduced emissions of gaseous and particulate pollutants and development of a weather forecasting system that would alert the public of impending problems. Both these recommendations became important components of subsequent federal policies.

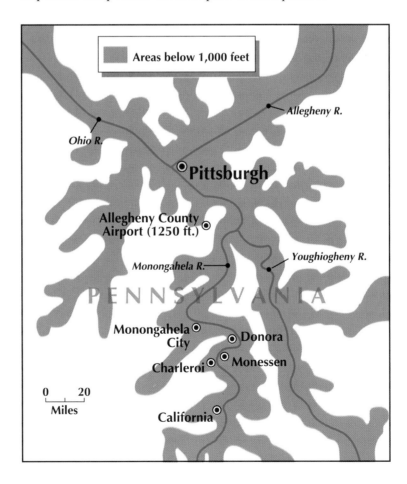

Figure 8.1. FOCUS: The Donora Smog Episode.

Source:
U.S. Public Health Service, *Air Pollution in Donora, PA: Epidemiology of the Unusual Smog Episode of October 1948—Preliminary Report,* Public Health Bulletin no. 306 (Washington, DC: GPO, 1949), p. 141.

Figure 8.2.   Air Quality in Major Metropolitan Areas, 1986.

Source:
Environmental Protection Agency, *National Air Quality and Emissions Trend Report, 1986* (Washington, DC: GPO, 1988).

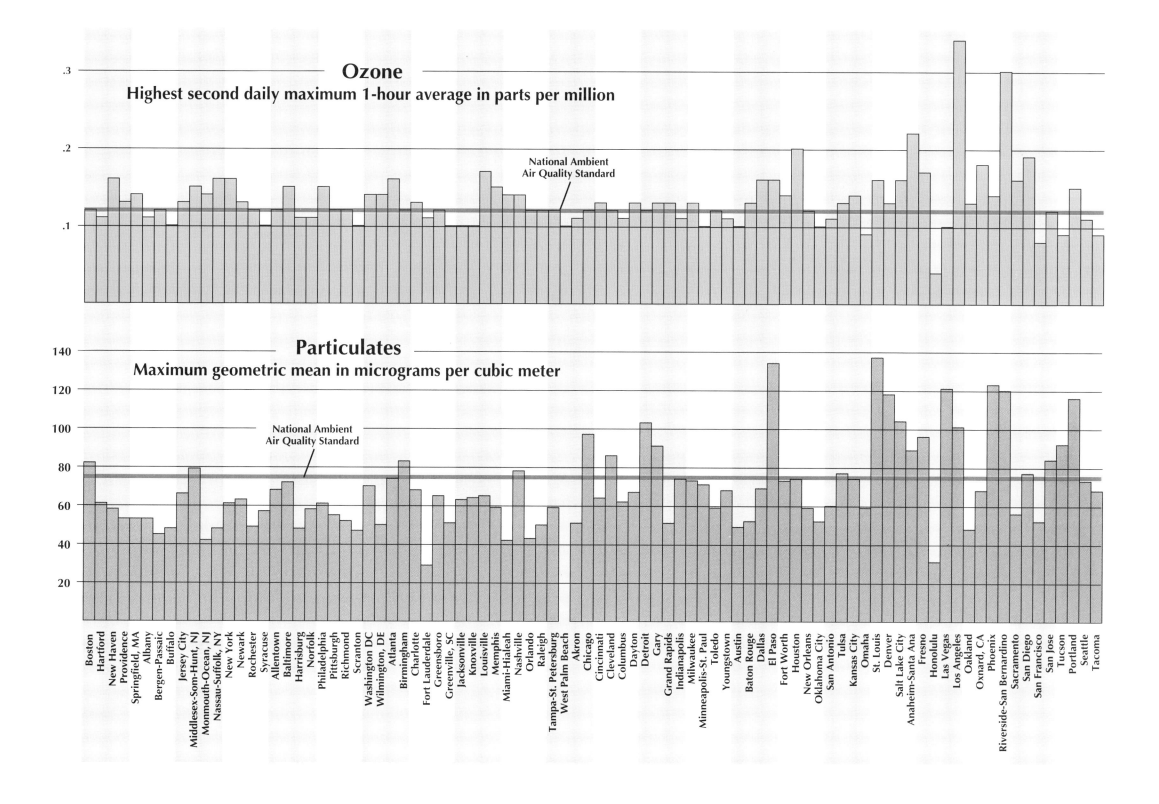

Ozone
Highest second daily maximum 1-hour average in parts per million

National Ambient
Air Quality Standard

Particulates
Maximum geometric mean in micrograms per cubic meter

National Ambient
Air Quality Standard

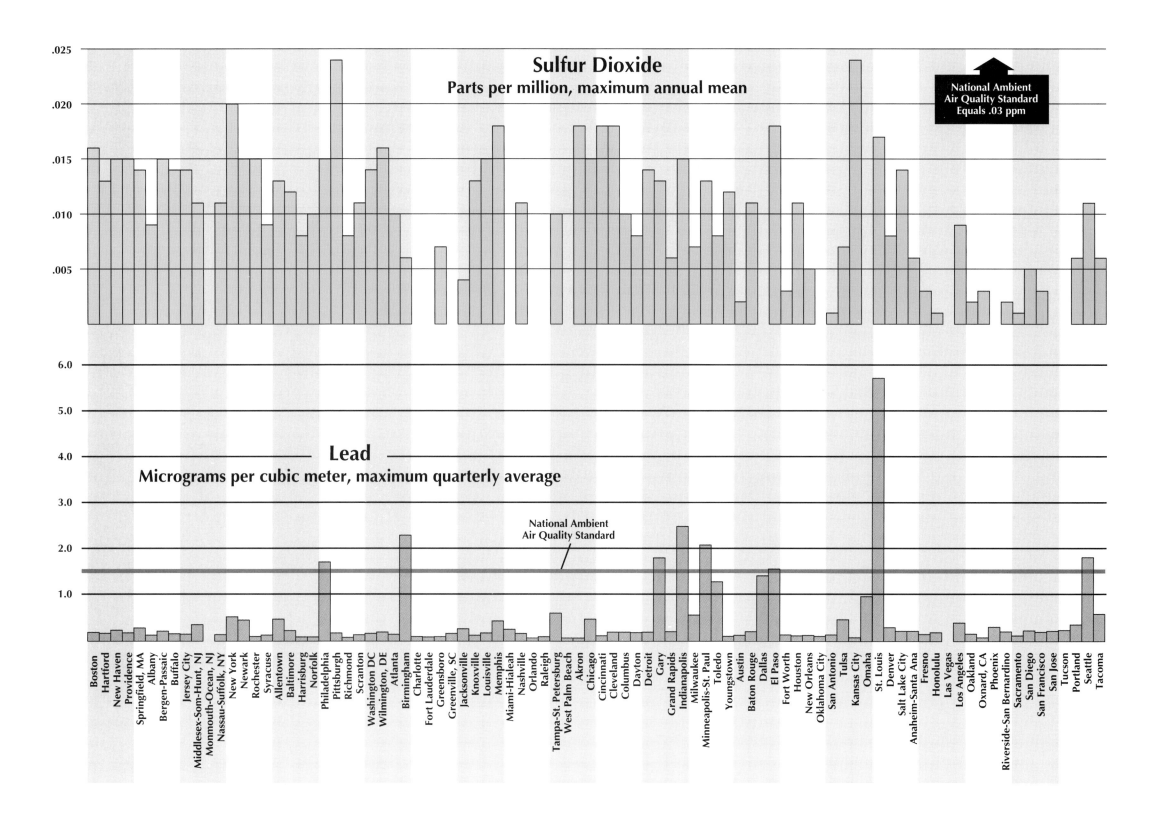

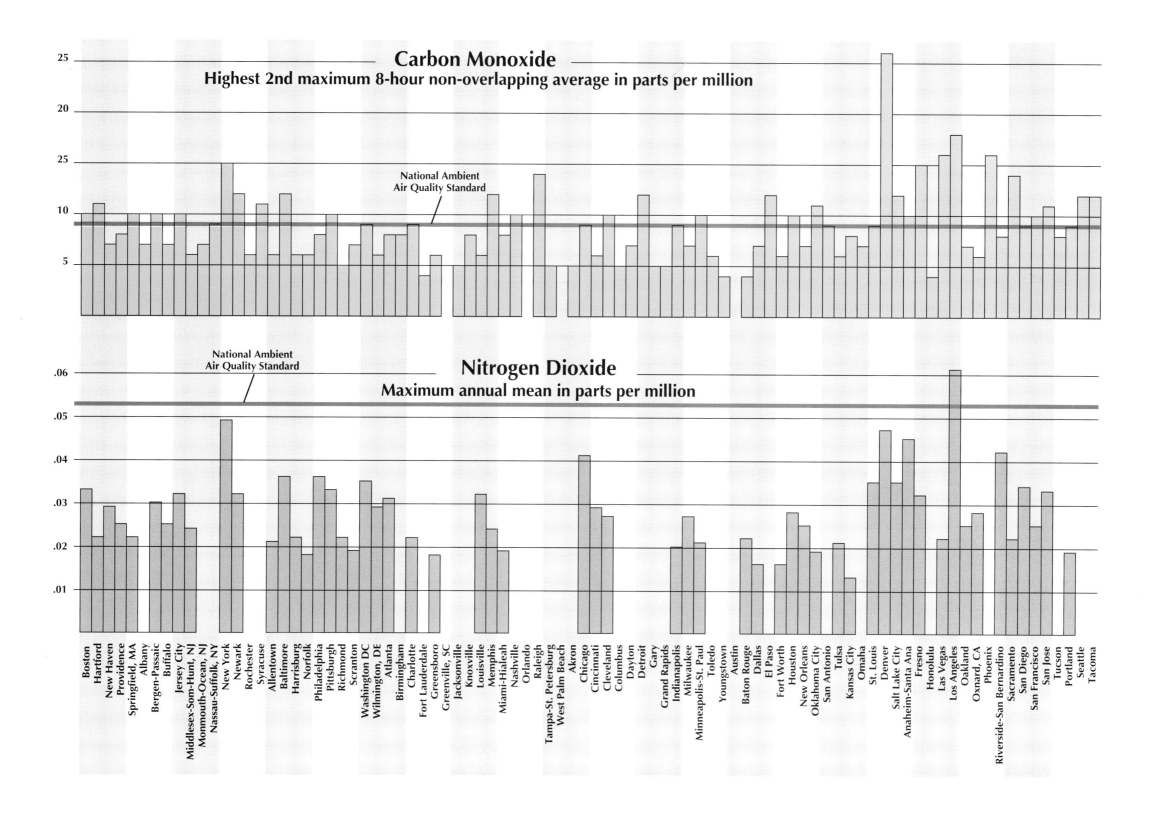

Carbon Monoxide
Highest 2nd maximum 8-hour non-overlapping average in parts per million

National Ambient
Air Quality Standard

National Ambient
Air Quality Standard

Nitrogen Dioxide
Maximum annual mean in parts per million

METROPOLITAN AIR QUALITY

Measuring air quality over large and diverse areas is at best an elusive enterprise. An accurate spatial representation needs to take into account human exposure to pollutants and perhaps vegetation and animal exposure as well. This means incorporating data on such factors as population mobility, transportation patterns, and industrial location. Ideally, data would be collected for every individual and then aggregated to represent spatial patterns. Given the impossibility of doing this, the next best thing is to locate a network of sampling stations and weight the data received from them so as to achieve the best possible representation of human exposure. Unfortunately, this was not the methodology employed by the EPA for collecting most of the data represented in the graphs in figure 8.2. Moreover, these data are plagued by inconsistencies in measurement techniques and incomplete and unvalidated readings. Nonetheless, they provide a broad overview of the "criteria-pollutant" (ozone, carbon monoxide, sulfur dioxide, nitrogen oxide, lead, particulates) situation in major metropolitan areas. Each graph shows 1986 pollutant concentrations—over the averaging times shown—in relation to the primary, or health-based, ambient air quality standard for that pollutant. Metropolitan statistical areas (MSAs) with 500,000 or more residents, which areas contain approximately three-quarters of the United States' population, are represented in figure 8.2.

Ozone is not emitted directly but is formed by the reaction between nitrogen oxides and volatile organic compounds (VOCs) in the presence of sunlight and oxygen. This reaction actually creates a photochemical soup known as smog (sometimes called brown smog), of which ozone is a major component. Sources of VOCs include vehicles and industrial and commercial operations that use solvents. Ozone—so essential in the stratosphere for filtering damaging ultraviolet solar radiation—is harmful at excess concentration in the lower atmosphere: It can hamper breathing; cause eye, nose, and throat irritation; reduce resistance to infection; reduce visibility; and damage vegetation.

Ozone formation—which occurs primarily in warm, sunny, stable-air conditions—is a problem in most metropolitan areas as well as in downwind nonmetropolitan areas in some parts of the country. The summers of 1987 and 1988 witnessed extensive smog development in many metropolitan areas. A recent analysis by the Natural Resources Defense Council contends that the EPA seriously underestimates the number of days the primary standard was exceeded because the agency bases its estimates on readings from only one monitor (the "design value monitor") in each metropolitan area. Some results from that analysis are shown in table 8.1.

Particulate matter—which includes sprays, mists, and dusts as well as solid particles—is introduced into the atmosphere by fire, volcanoes, wind, power plants, factories, vehicles, construction activity, and transformation of such gases as sulfur oxides and VOCs. Particulates in general reduce visibility. The finer particles, in particular, can aggravate or cause respiratory irritation and illness, including lung damage. Total suspended particulate (TSP) counts, represented on the graph in figure 8.2, indicate that there are significant problems. But the standards for TSPs do not distinguish between large and small particles. In 1987, the EPA adopted the PM10 standard, which applies only to particles less than ten microns in diameter. PM10 data will be available in coming years.

The bulk of sulfur-dioxide emissions are from coal-burning power plants, but oil-burning plants and smelters are also major sources. Figure 8.7 shows the concentrated sulfur-dioxide emissions in midwestern states, which are blamed for a large share of the acid deposition that occurs to the east. Locally high concentrations of sulfur dioxide may contribute to respiratory tract damage and cause damage to lung tissue. In 1986, no MSAs exceeded the ambient standard, either for the twenty-four-hour averaging period (see graph) or over the annual averaging period (not represented on graph). Again, however, this in no way indicates an absence of serious localized exposures.

Nitrogen oxides (principally nitric oxide) are produced by fossil-fuel combustion, primarily in motor vehicles and electric power plants. Depending on atmospheric conditions, nitric oxide (NO) may be converted to nitrogen dioxide (NO_2), which may in turn become a component of smog or may be converted to nitric acid. The latter has been implicated in acid deposition, as well as formation of "acid fogs" that occur in southern California. Health effects include respiratory illness and lung damage. Relatively high nitrogen-dioxide levels are observed especially in western MSAs.

Carbon monoxide is produced mainly by the incomplete combustion of gasoline and diesel fuel. It reduces the blood's ability to carry oxygen and affects the cardiovascular, nervous, and pulmonary systems. The effects may be acute—such as headaches—or, in extreme cases, death. Individual exposure within busy urban areas varies enormously with occupation and activity patterns (see Hartwell et al. 1984).

Lead, which may be classified as a toxic substance as well as a "conventional" criteria pollutant, is used in pigments and paints, auto batteries, and as a fuel additive. As indicated below, the use of lead has declined markedly since the 1970s. Still, it causes anemia, convulsions, and brain and kidney damage—especially in children. Furthermore, acid deposition may be responsible for increases in lead exposure, since more acidic water leaches higher quantities of lead from solder and pipes.

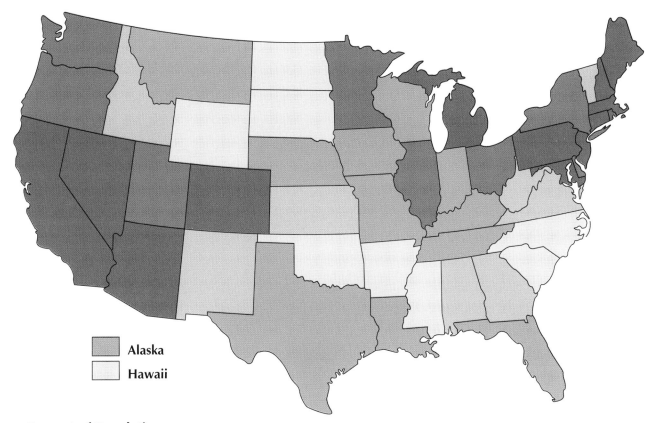

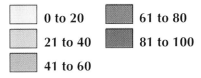

Alaska

Hawaii

Percent of Population

0 to 20	61 to 80
21 to 40	81 to 100
41 to 60	

Figure 8.3. Percentage of Population Living in Clean Air Act Nonattainment Areas.

Source:
Renew America, The State of the States 1989 (Washington, DC: Renew America, 1989), p. 34.

NONATTAINMENT AREAS

In 1977, Congress directed the EPA to draw up lists of "non-attainment areas": areas that had failed to achieve the ambient air quality standards for the criteria pollutants. The 1977 Clean Air Act Amendments prescribed strong measures—to be incorporated into EPA-approved "State Implementation Plans" (SIPs)—for bringing these areas into attainment status by 1982. Among the required SIP revisions were stringent controls on new sources of pollutants, including one-for-one reductions in current emissions to offset any new emissions that would be allowed. Possible sanctions included the withholding of grant monies, which would—in effect—ban most new construction. Areas with severe ozone or carbon-monoxide problems were given an extension until 1987 but in exchange were required to enact auto-emission-control inspection programs and impose new restrictions on stationary pollution sources.

In response to the 1977 amendments, states submitted their lists of nonattainment areas to the EPA, which retained the authority to make changes. With the EPA's approval, states also could make revisions. A subsequent court decision established that the initial list approved by EPA could be revised only after a request had been received from a state. Changing a nonattain-

ment listing to attainment is also administratively cumbersome. As a result, needed status changes have not been made. Another problem has been that of boundary delineation. Inclusion of upwind sources and downwind effects calls for spatially generous definitions of nonattainment areas—especially for ozone, which forms in the atmosphere. The courts, while generally supportive of the EPA's authority to list large geographic areas, have imposed requirements that in practice make such listing difficult. Congress's failure to reauthorize the Clean Air Act has added to the muddle. Moreover, the areawide designations—mostly county-based—do not reflect what are often wide variations within each area. Nor do they tell us anything about the severity of problems within specific non-attainment areas.

Definitional problems notwithstanding, the map makes it clear that a substantial proportion of the population lives in counties that fail to meet Clean Air Act standards. Ozone violations account for most of what appears on the map, with carbon monoxide and particulates vying for second place. Nearly all of the eastern megalopolitan corridor, including the entire states of New Jersey, Massachusetts, Connecticut, and Rhode Island, exceeded the ozone standard as of September 1988. Much of the western shoreline of Lake Michigan and most southern California counties also were in violation. Indeed, most of the major urban and industrial concentrations in the country are—to varying degrees of severity—violating the standards (see table 8.1). Rather similar patterns are in evidence for carbon monoxide and particulates, but the areal coverage is not so extensive. Also, there is relatively strong representation of carbon-monoxide and particulate violations in the Great Plains states and Rocky Mountain regions.

For reasons alluded to above, areas violating national ambient air quality standards are not necessarily classified as non-attainment areas. Congress, via the 1987 "Mitchell-Conte Amendment," required the EPA to identify—and designate as nonattainment areas—those areas violating the standards for ozone and/or carbon monoxide. The agency's subsequent proposals would expand considerably the number of counties in nonattainment status. But they are only proposals. Difficult questions of legislative intent, as well as potential court challenges, await any new designations. These issues probably will not be resolved until the Clean Air Act is reauthorized.

Sulfur-dioxide emissions exceed the standards in areas where there are concentrations of coal-burning power plants, refineries, pulp and paper mills, smelters, steel and chemical plants, and other industrial and energy-related facilities. In the intermountain West, smelters account for violations of the standards in several rural counties, while pulp and paper mills result in violations in northern New England.

The only area in violation of the nitrogen-oxide standard is the Los Angeles region. Indeed, southern California, with its high levels of nitrogen oxides and ozone, is home to the nation's worst smog problems. While the region has led the country in its efforts to control vehicular emissions, much more must be done. In March 1989—at least partially in response to threatened federal sanctions—southern California officials voted to adopt a precedent-setting plan to meet the national air quality standards. Their comprehensive plan includes measures that have only been talked about in many other metropolitan areas. Among the plan's short-term measures are limits on automobile ownership and use; a ban on gasoline-powered lawn mowers; restrictions on charcoal grills; reformulation of paints, solvents, and other substances that release gases that contribute to ozone formation; new diesel emission requirements; and a requirement that new tires be radials, which spew fewer rubber particles into the air. Over the longer term, vehicles would be converted to use methanol and other alternative fuels, with the ultimate and highly speculative goal of no gasoline-powered vehicles by the year 2007.

AIR QUALITY TRENDS

Despite population and economic growth, overall emissions and ambient concentrations of "conventional" air pollutants have generally declined since 1970. Reduced industrial output and improved energy efficiency are partly responsible, but greatest credit probably goes to emission controls.

Most of the long-term reduction in emissions of volatile organic compounds (VOCs)—precursor compounds in the formation of ozone and photochemical smog—can be attributed to vehicular emission controls. Industrial emissions have declined little. The trend for nitrogen oxides—a precursor for acid deposition as well as photochemical smog—has been more mixed. Carbon-monoxide reductions can be attributed primarily to vehicle emission controls, while sulfur-oxide emissions have decreased because of installation of pollution control devices, use of lower-sulfur fuel, energy conservation, and slowed industrial activity. The substantial decreases in particulates can be attributed to energy conservation, reduced industrial activity, and pollution control equipment. Conversion to unleaded gasoline has greatly reduced lead emissions.

Table 8.1. Ozone Violation Days in 48 Non-California Metropolitan Areas.

Source:
Natural Resources Defense Council, "Ozone Violation Days in 48 Non-California Metropolitan Areas" (Washington, DC: EPA, 1989).

Violation days represent numbers of days during which the national ambient air quality standard was exceeded within a metropolitan area. The EPA's "estimated exceedance days" are probabilistic estimates for metropolitan areas. The EPA designates a "design value" monitor for each metropolitan area (which is only one of perhaps many monitoring stations) and uses sampling data from that station to calculate expected exceedances for the entire metropolitan area during its summer smog season. Included in the table are 1987 estimated exceedances in those cases where actual violation days exceeded them by more than 1.5 times (data for 1988 are not available). The estimated exceedances consistently underrepresent violation days—which themselves are only rather crude indicators of degree of population exposure to harmful ozone levels.

Table 8.1. Ozone Violation Days in 48 Non-California Metropolitan Areas

	Violation Days, 1988	Violation Days, 1987	Estimated Exceedance Days, 1987		Violation Days, 1988	Violation Days, 1987	Estimated Exceedance Days, 1987
Houston-Galveston-Brazoria, Texas	54	54	20.8	Richmond-Petersburg, Virginia	12	5	0
New York-N. New Jersey-Long Island	42	32	19.2	Raleigh-Durham, North Carolina	12	4	—
Philadelphia-Wilmington-Trenton	42	31	—	Allentown-Bethlehem, Pennsylvania-New Jersey	12	3	—
Baltimore, Maryland	36	23	11.1	Parkersburg-Marietta, West Virginia-Ohio	12	3	—
Dist. of Columbia-Maryland-Virginia	31	18	10.5	Birmingham, Alabama	12	0	—
Hartford-New Britain-Middletown, Conn.	28	23	11.6	Dallas-Fort Worth, Texas	9	11	5.2
Chicago-Gary-Lake County, Indiana	27	15	—	Grand Rapids, Michigan	8	1	—
Cincinnati-Hamilton, Ohio	27	9	2.1	Providence-Pawtucket-Fall River, Rhode Island	7	8	—
Boston-Lawrence-Salem, Massachusetts	26	9	4.3	Beaumont-Port Arthur, Texas	7	3	—
Milwaukee-Racine, Wisconsin	22	14	—	El Paso, Texas	6	12	—
Atlanta, Georgia	20	24	15.0	Atlantic City, New Jersey	6	5	—
Pittsburgh-Beaver Valley, Pennsylvania	20	6	—	Memphis, Tennessee-Arkansas-Mississippi	6	3	—
St. Louis, Missouri-Illinois	17	13	8.0	Indianapolis, Indiana	5	4	1.1
Springfield, Massachusetts	17	1	—	Miami-Fort Lauderdale, Florida	5		—
Sheboygan, Wisconsin	16	13	—	Lexington-Fayette, Kentucky	5	2	1.1
Louisville, Kentucky-Indiana	16	4	2.0	Salt Lake City-Ogden, Utah	5	1	—
Detroit-Ann Arbor, Michigan	16	3	—	Norfolk-Virginia Beach-Newport News	4	2	—
Portland, Maine	15	4	—	Portland-Vancouver, Oregon-Washington	2	2	1.2
Huntington-Ashland, West Virginia-Kentucky-Ohio	14	8	5.2	Worcester, Massachusetts	2	0	—
Charlotte-Gastonia-Rock Hill, North Carolina-South Carolina	14	8	4.0	Tulsa, Oklahoma	—	2	0
Baton Rouge, Louisiana	13	11	5.1	Montgomery, Alabama	1	4	—
Cleveland-Akron-Lorain, Ohio	13	7	2.2	Phoenix, Arizona	1	2	0
Nashville, Tennessee	13	3	—	Jacksonville, Florida	1	1	—
Muskegon, Michigan	12	8	—	Tampa-St. Petersburg-Clearwater, Florida	0	6	—

Figure 8.4. Air Quality Trends.

Sources:
EPA, *National Air Pollutant Emission Estimates 1940–1984* (Research Triangle Park, NC: EPA, 1986), p. 2.

EPA, *National Air Quality Emissions and Trend Report, 1986* (Washington, DC: GPO, 1988).

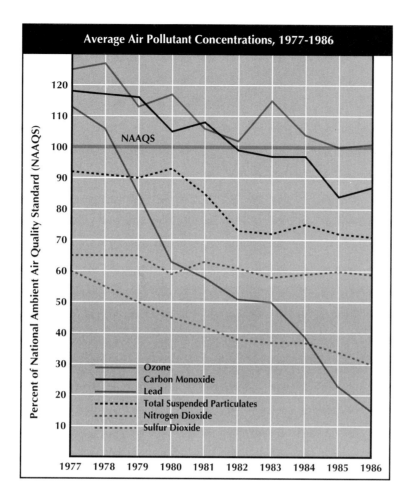

AIR POLLUTANT CONCENTRATIONS

The graph above provides an overview—albeit a rather imprecise one—of recent trends in ambient pollutant concentrations. In general, concentrations have declined—with largest declines occurring before 1982. Pre-1977 data are excluded because they are not readily comparable with later data. Instead, some brief comments are offered below.

The EPA (1978) reports that between 1972 and 1977 the national trend for ozone was rather flat—but downward at California sites (Los Angeles proper has recorded improvement since the early 1960s) and slightly upward at sites outside California. Nitrogen-dioxide concentrations were tentatively reported to be increasing, while general improvement was reported for carbon monoxide. More extensive data were available for sulfur dioxide and total suspended particulates, whose concentrations dropped 17 percent and 8 percent, respectively. Moreover, the EPA reports that between 1972 and 1977 the number of people exposed to particulate levels in violation of the national ambient standard dropped by 29 percent.

AIR POLLUTANT EMISSIONS

Vehicular controls explain much of the reduction in emissions of volatile organic compounds (VOCs). Another ozone precursor—nitrogen oxides—showed similarities in emissions reductions and decreases in ambient concentrations between 1977 and 1986. Unfortunately, the complexity of ozone formation prohibits any simple associations of these trends with those for ambient ozone.

Vehicle emission controls also explain much of the decline in carbon-monoxide emissions—but comparisons with ambient concentrations are compromised by the large proportion of ambient monitors located in congested urban areas. Between 1977 and 1986, measured concentrations of sulfur dioxide declined more than emissions. This is because large rural emitters are greatly underrepresented in the ambient sampling network. The percentage of declines in particulate emissions is about the same (25 percent) as reductions in ambient concentrations—but this is largely coincidental, since ambient levels are affected by natural dust, construction activity, and other factors not included in the EPA's emission estimates.

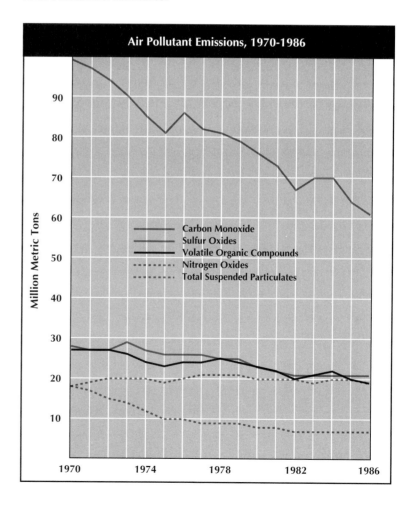

ADMINISTRATIVE SUMMARY

The Clean Air Act Amendments of 1970 and 1977 have had significant effects on land-use, industrial, transportation, and other economic decisions. The 1970 amendments, especially, were a powerful expression of congressional and executive intent to clean up the nation's air. Yet at the time, epidemiological and exposure data on which to base the act's primary (health-based) and secondary (welfare-based) standards were rather scarce. The 1977 amendments provided an opportunity to refine the standards, and they are likely again to be changed when the Clean Air Act is finally reauthorized.

Within the act's current framework, states set standards for existing pollution sources, the EPA develops standards for new sources, and states are responsible for trading off new emissions against existing ones. These emission offsets allow new industry in nonattainment areas (figure 8.3) as long as there is a net reduction in pollutants. The EPA is responsible for controlling interstate pollution, setting emissions standards for hazardous pollutants, and ensuring compliance with congressionally set standards for vehicular emissions of carbon monoxide, nitrogen oxides, and hydrocarbons. Most enforcement actions are administered by the states, but the federal government may impose civil penalties against polluters. As noted above, the EPA may—through what has become a very cumbersome procedure—designate nonattainment areas. In theory at least, federal grant monies may be withheld from those areas.

The basic vehicle for administering the Clean Air Act is the State Implementation Plan (SIP). The SIP lays out in detail the state's plan for achieving the act's ambient air-quality standards. It contains the procedures for approving new pollution sources in "prevention of significant deterioration" (PSD) areas and the administration of "reasonably available control technology" (RACT) in nonattainment areas. Inspection and maintenance programs for vehicle emissions are required in areas that fail to attain ozone and carbon-monoxide standards. SIP procedures are administratively cumbersome, and the EPA's practical ability to force states to develop and implement adequate SIPs often is quite limited. The various statutory deadlines set for ambient standards and vehicle emissions all have been extended and/or only rather weakly enforced.

In the late 1970s, the EPA implemented the "bubble policy," which allows plants in attainment areas to meet specific, plant-wide standards through any mix of controls—even, for example, if it means greater emissions at one point, as long as there are offsetting reductions elsewhere. The EPA also has experimented with other concepts giving polluters greater flexibility, including SIP provisions that permit "clean" firms to store—and possibly sell—pollution rights. The 1990 proposals for a renewed Clean Air Act emphasize economic incentives.

VISUAL RANGE

The Clean Air Act Amendments of 1977 put special emphasis on visibility protection—especially for parks and wilderness areas. Visibility is impaired by the scattering of light by small particles and the absorption of light by gases or particles. Since these factors affect the distribution of incoming solar radiation (see figure 13.4), they also have implications for local, regional, and even global weather and climate.

Figure 8.5 is derived from daytime visual range measurements at 100 suburban and nonurban airports across the country. Under ideally dry, nonpolluted conditions, visual range may approach 260 kilometers (162.5 miles). Visibility is reduced by aerosols (suspended liquid or solid particles), nitrogen oxides, sulfur oxides (which are transformed in the atmosphere into sulfates and particulates), and volatile organic compounds (which contribute to smog formation). Regardless of human activities, areas characterized by high humidities and precipitation are likely to have higher background levels of aerosols than dry areas. Other natural sources of particles include wind-blown soil, volcanic eruptions, forest fires, sea spray, and emissions from vegetation and decomposition processes.

The map clearly indicates that rural and nonurban visibility, on average, is highest in the mountain areas of the Southwest. Although urban measurements are not directly represented, one place where urbanization's effects are especially evident is the southern California coastal region. They are also apparent much further afield—perhaps even contributing to the formation of Arctic haze.

The worst visibilities overall are found in the East. There is also a distinct seasonal pattern: Visibility reaches a minimum during the eastern summers. This, according to Trijonis (1982), is a rather recent phenomenon—evident since the 1950s. High correlations are observed between sulfate concentrations and visibility reduction, particularly in the Ohio Valley. Indeed, up to 70 percent of eastern visibility impairment is attributed to sulfates (OTA 1985). They are a major contributor to the haze that results from vertical mixing of gases and particles and that is sometimes transported over very long distances. In contrast, visibility impairment in interior western areas is more likely to be caused by individual plumes. While these may extend for great distances, the pollution is more discrete and localized than the regional haze of the East.

The 1977 Clean Air Act Amendments divided the nation into three broad air-quality classifications. Class I areas, where visibility is a key concern, consist for the most part of national parks and wilderness areas larger than 6,000 acres (see figures 15.1 and 15.4). Stringent requirements are placed on new pollution sources, and certain existing sources are to be retrofitted to reduce emissions. Progressively greater increments of pollution are allowed in Class II areas (virtually the rest of the nation) and Class III areas, respectively. Because of the complex process required to designate new Class I areas, the original 1977 designations remain almost unchanged—despite important changes in park and wilderness area boundaries.

As noted on page 74, the EPA in 1987 promulgated the PM10 standard, which is for particulates less than 10 microns. It is these fine particulates—especially those less than 2.5 microns in diameter—that commonly form in the atmosphere from sulfates and seem to be the major contributors to urban and regional haze. In order to gauge the urgency and effort necessary to comply with the PM10 standard the agency has divided the country into three categories. Group I areas are those where there is a strong likelihood of violating the PM10 standard and where significant State Implementation Plan (SIP) changes will be needed to attain the new ambient standard. In Group II areas, fewer SIP changes should be necessary. Most Group I and II areas are in or near metropolitan areas. Group III areas, which correspond generally with Class I areas, have a strong likelihood of attaining the standard; SIP adjustments need only address "prevention of significant deterioration/new source review" and monitoring provisions.

Figure 8.5. Visual Range at Suburban/Nonurban Locations.

Source:
J. J. Trijonis and D. Shapland, *Existing Visibility Levels in the U.S.: Isopleth Maps of Visibility in the Suburban/Nonurban Areas During 1974–76* (Research Triangle Park, NC: EPA, 1979).

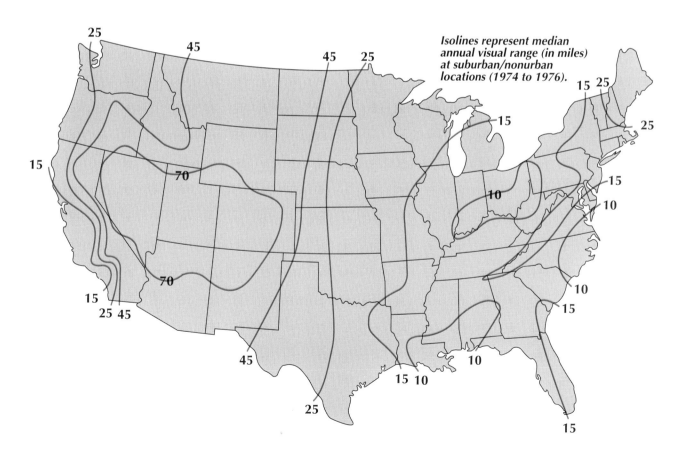

Isolines represent median annual visual range (in miles) at suburban/nonurban locations (1974 to 1976).

FOCUS: THE FOUR CORNERS REGION

The Four Corners region of the Southwest is populated by Navajo, Hopi, Zuni, and many other Indians; possesses rich coal, gas, and uranium resources; and—until relatively recently—had remarkably pure air throughout. Even though the Four Corners does not appear as a problem area in figure 8.5, it dramatically exemplifies certain environmental and social ills unique to the West. Figure 8.6 shows the extent to which energy-related activities have affected the region. Had 1970s designs for large-scale production of synthetic fuels in western states come to fruition, the map would be cluttered with even more operating facilities. For the region's Indians, energy development has yielded some economic benefits—but has also brought forcible relocation, occupational hazards, and environmental contamination. Indian interests have suffered both as a result of tribal conflicts and inadequate legal and political representation by the federal government.

While there is a much longer story to be told about the historic, economic, political, and cultural aspects of regional resource exploitation, the brief account offered here is limited mainly to air pollution—particularly that which comes from coal-burning power plants. The main sources of air pollution in the rural Southwest are copper smelters, power plants, and long-range transport of pollutants from as far away as southern California. Indeed, over 90 percent of southwestern sulfur emissions are from copper smelters (OTA 1985). Eastern and West Coast visibilities often are seriously impaired by large-scale regional haze. In part, this is caused by high humidities—but numerous and diverse sources of pollution also are to blame. In the mountain and intermountain West, widespread visibility impairment does occur—but more common is the localized pollution caused by plumes emanating from power plants and smelters. The resultant "plume blight" often is dramatic, since the contrast between plume and background usually is very sharp. This is exemplified in the photograph that introduces this chapter. Plume pollution does not appear on generalized visibility maps such as figure 8.5.

The concentration of power plants in the Four Corners region makes it a major source area for plume pollution. Outstanding emitters include the huge Four Corners and Navajo power plants, which release vast quantities of sulfur dioxide. In the immediate region of the releases are the Indian reservations shown on the map. Within a 500-mile-diameter circle—centered west of Four Corners and known as the "Golden Circle"—are found several of the crown jewels of the National Park System. Included are Grand Canyon, Glen Canyon, Capitol Reef, Arches, Zion, Bryce Canyon, Mesa Verde, Petrified Forest, and Canyon de Chelly national parks and recreation areas. Thus, this is an area with many Class I visibility regions.

The principal objective in these areas—as defined by the Clean Air Act Amendments of 1977—is to maintain the generally positive ambient air quality. The characteristically clear southwestern air is highly valued by recreationists, among other reasons, for its ambience. But beyond their aesthetic damages, visibility-reducing pollutants can adversely affect fragile desert and alpine ecosystems. Emissions from the Navajo Power Plant—the westernmost plant on the map— have at times filled the Grand Canyon with haze, obscuring the view across the canyon. The National Park Service estimates that the Navajo plant is responsible for between 40 and 70 percent of wintertime pollution at the Grand Canyon. Glen Canyon also has suffered significant visibility reductions over the past fifteen years. During 1990, the EPA is to issue a decision regarding emission reductions at the Navajo plant. But part of the problem—particularly summertime smog—

results from "ultra-long-range transport" from southern California. California not only consumes pollution-producing Four Corners power; it also exports additional pollution to the region.

An air-pollution source in the rural Southwest has a much more dramatic impact than would a similar source in the Los Angeles area or in the urbanized, industrialized Northeast. Addition of 1 microgram per cubic meter of fine particles, spread over one's viewing path, could reduce visual range by about 30 percent in the clear air of the Southwest. In an area that has a lower ambient visual range—for example 20 miles— the same pollution would produce only a 3 percent reduction in visual range (Council on Environmental Quality 1987). It is this extreme sensitivity that makes southwestern visibility such a fragile entity. And as figure 8.5 shows, the resource-rich Four Corners region is almost at the nation's visual epicenter.

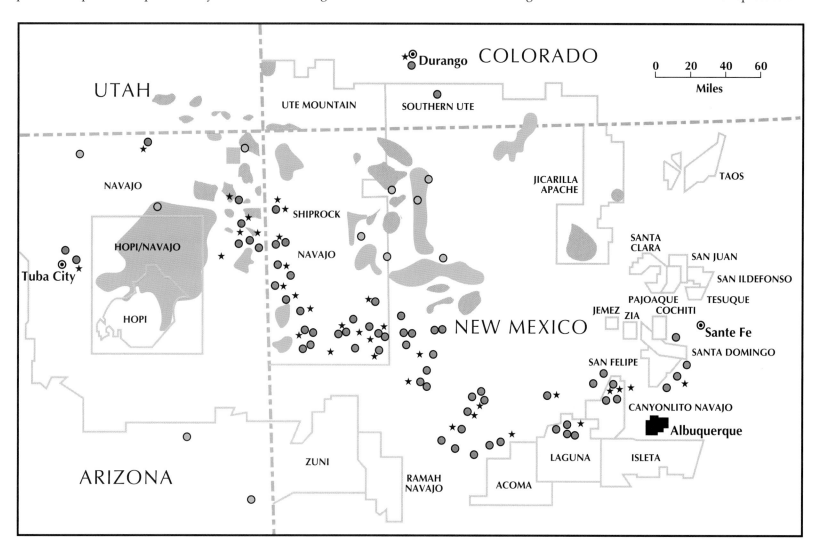

Figure 8.6. FOCUS: The Four Corners Region.

Source:
W. Churchill, "American Indian Lands: The Native Ethic Amid Resource Development," *Environment* 28(6): 28. Modified with permission of the Helen Dwight Reid Educational Foundation. Published by Heldref Publications, 4000 Albemarle St., NW, Washington, DC 20016. Copyright © 1986.

○ **Power plant, present and projected**
★ **Tailing pile**
● **Significant uranium mine**

   Coal lease   **Gas lease**
— **Reservation boundary**

ACID DEPOSITION

Acid rain is difficult to define precisely. Common usages of the term often encompass the entire cycle of emission, transport, and deposition—both wet and dry—of acids and their precursor chemical compounds. On a worldwide basis, acid-forming emissions from natural sources—such as volcanoes, forest fires, and decaying vegetation—exceed those from human activities. But it is human-induced acid deposition that usually creates the greatest problems over relatively small areas.

The first widely received reports linking acid deposition with long-range transport of pollutants came from Europe in the 1960s. Low pH readings in Scandinavian waters were tied to industrial emissions in England. In the United States, similar phenomena came to light in the 1970s. The northeastern states, along with southeastern Canadian provinces, attribute much of their acid deposition to long-range transport of industrial and power plant emissions from the Ohio Valley and Great Lakes regions. Sulfur and nitrogen oxides are converted in the atmosphere to sulfuric and nitric acid, and deposition may occur hundreds, or in some cases even thousands, of miles downwind. More recently, acid deposition has been documented in the mid-Atlantic, southeastern, and western parts of the United States.

Several research efforts were initiated in the 1970s, and in 1978 the National Acid Deposition Program was created to sponsor and coordinate research. In 1980, the governments of the United States and Canada signed a Memorandum of Intent, in which they agreed to reach an agreement on transboundary air pollution. The memorandum also fostered binational research. In 1980, the National Acid Precipitation Assessment Program (NAPAP) was established. This ten-year, interagency effort, with a 1989 budget of about $85 million, looks into atmospheric chemistry, transport, and deposition; aquatic and terrestrial effects; effects on materials; and emissions and controls.

For nearly a decade, regulatory action has been debated—but without congressional result. The Reagan administration argued—virtually until the end—that more research was needed and that no firm evidence linked sulfur and nitrogen emissions with acid deposition. Opposition to emission controls has been strong in the Appalachian and Midwest states—where large quantities of high-sulfur coal are mined. The costs of emissions controls would be high—on the order of several billion dollars per year for a 50 percent annual reduction (OTA 1985)—and the results far from entirely predictable. But in June 1989, President Bush called for a 10-million-ton (50 percent) reduction in sulfur-dioxide emissions, and a 2-million-ton (10 percent) reduction in nitrogen oxide emissions.

SULFUR AND NITROGEN-OXIDE EMISSIONS

Fuel combustion (exclusive of transportation) accounts for 51 percent of nitrogen-oxide emissions; transportation 43 percent. By contrast, fuel combustion and industrial processes are responsible for 96 percent of sulfur-dioxide emissions (EPA Annual (1988)). The bulk of them come from coal-burning power plants.

Emission densities are highest in the East, with greatest recent increases occurring in the rapidly growing Southeast. Combustion of high-sulfur Appalachian coal accounts for high sulfur emissions in the Ohio Valley and Great Lakes area. Just six states—Ohio, Indiana, Illinois, Pennsylvania, Virginia, and Kentucky—are responsible for 40 percent of the nation's emissions. Moreover, that same region's concentrated population and industry are responsible for high nitrogen-oxide emissions.

Figure 8.7. Average Density of Sulfur-Dioxide and Nitrogen-Oxide Emissions.

Source:
EPA, National Emissions Data System, 1987.

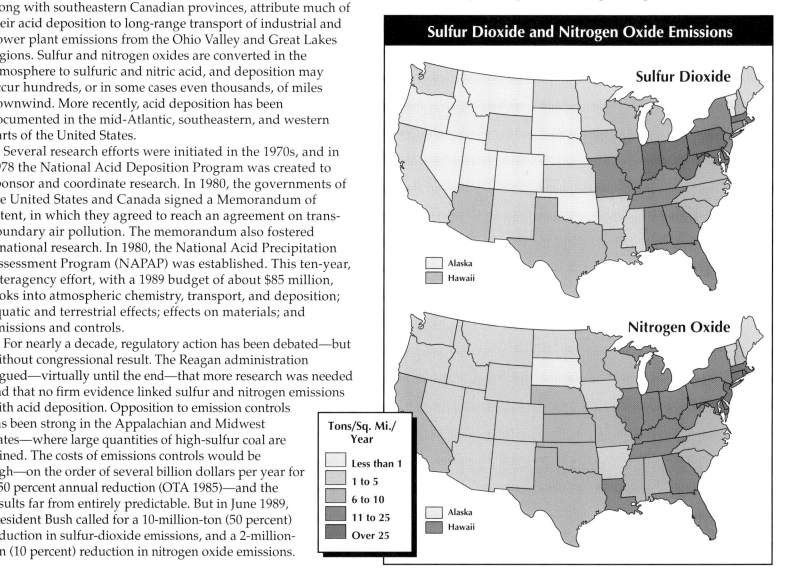

Sulfur Dioxide and Nitrogen Oxide Emissions

Sulfur Dioxide

☐ Alaska
▨ Hawaii

Nitrogen Oxide

☐ Alaska
■ Hawaii

Tons/Sq. Mi./ Year

☐ Less than 1
▨ 1 to 5
▨ 6 to 10
▨ 11 to 25
■ Over 25

THE pH SCALE

pH is shorthand for "potential hydrogen": It is a measure of hydrogen ion concentration. Ions that have a positive electrical charge—for example, hydrogen ions—are known as cations. Negatively charged ions are called anions. Neutral substances have equal concentrations of cations and anions, and a pH of 7. Distilled water is neutral.

A substance with more hydrogen ions than anions is acidic; its pH is less than 7. A substance with more anions than cations is alkaline and has a pH greater than 7. The pH scale is logarithmic, which means that there is a tenfold difference between each whole number on the scale. Thus, precipitation with a pH of 4.2 is ten times as acidic as precipitation of pH 5.2, and precipitation with a pH of 3.2 is 100 times as acidic as that with pH 5.2. This means that Adirondack lakes were on average about 100 times as acidic in the 1970s as they were in the 1930s.

"Normal" precipitation contains low concentrations of carbonic acid and therefore is slightly acidic. The commonly cited pH value of 5.6 for normal precipitation should really be considered an approximation: The boundary line between natural and anthropogenic acidity will vary in different locales and under different conditions. In fact, some analysts use a range of pH values—such as 5.0 to 5.6—to describe normal precipitation. Furthermore, the threshold for concern may be different for streams and lakes than for precipitation. For example, salmon, bass, and trout begin to die at pHs of approximately 5.8; fish eggs die at about 5.4; coatings on metal structures corrode around 5.0; and all fish are likely to die when a water body's pH drops below 3.4.

PRECIPITATION ACIDITY

It is only about thirty years since Scandinavian researchers first became concerned about acid deposition, and some years would pass before American and Canadian scientists became similarly concerned. As a result, there is no systematic historical record of precipitation acidity—even for recent decades—across the United States. Indeed, it was not until 1978—as part of the National Atmospheric Deposition Program (NADP)—that a national monitoring network was established. But despite the paucity of actual pH measurements from earlier years, pH values can be calculated using available data from surveys of sulfate, chloride, potassium, calcium, and magnesium ions present in precipitation. These techniques have been used to create the maps in figure 8.9, and—to a much more limited extent—to make generalizations about precipitation chemistry before the 1950s. Our ability to make historical comparisons is constrained by the following: There were relatively few monitoring stations of any type before the 1970s; only a very few of those have provided continuous data; sampling techniques have become more reliable in recent years; and differing methods have been used to deduce acidity at different times. The series of maps is intended, therefore, for general reference purposes—not for analysis of trends at specific places.

Although there is some dispute about the pH of normal rainfall (see above), there is little question that rainfall in the northeastern states is more acidic than could be expected under natural conditions. If we use a pH of 5.0 or below to indicate acid precipitation, it can be seen that the entire eastern half of the country is affected. The strongest and clearest evidence thus far has come from New York, New England, and Pennsylvania.

Although it appears that current average pH of precipitation in remote parts of the world is relatively close to 5.0 (Irving 1989), analyses of glacial and continental ice indicate that before the Industrial Revolution the pH of most precipitation was above 5.0. Thus it appears as if large increases in acidity had already occurred before the mid-1950s; by that time precipitation was already considerably more acidic than might be expected under natural conditions. This is indicated by the large area on the 1955–1956 map with pH less than 5.6 as well as the substantial region where it was less than 4.52. Although the 1965–1966 map shows lower pH values overall, with the area affected by acidic precipitation expanding toward the northwest and south, much of this may simply be due to the greater detail provided by measurements from more locations. A decade later—in 1975–1976—it appears that the area of low pH values has spread even further. Again, this may largely be an artifact of the number of sampling stations as well as the sampling and analytical techniques. The same might be said of the 1986 data.

These qualifications do not detract from the fact that precipitation tends to be highly acidic in the Northeast and Southeast, in southeastern Canada, in the Midwest, and in parts of the West. In the Northeast, summer precipitation has been

Figure 8.8. The pH Scale.

Source:
EPA, *Research Summary: Acid Rain* (Washington, DC: GPO, 1979), p. 4.

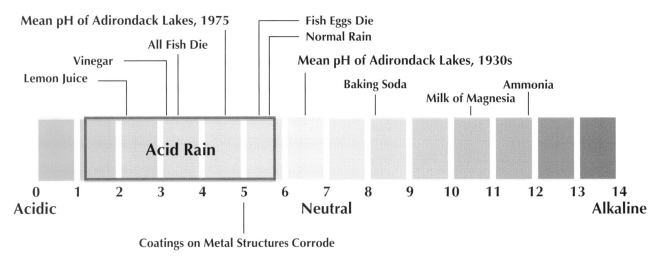

Figure 8.9. Precipitation Acidity.

Sources:
Department of Energy, *Acid Rain Information Book: Final Report*, DOE/EP-0018 (Springfield, VA: National Technical Information Service, 1981), pp. 3–44.

National Atmospheric Deposition Program, *NADP/NTN National Data Summary: Precipitation Chemistry in the United States* (Fort Collins, CO: NADP/NTN, 1986), p. 26.

more acidic than winter precipitation during the past twenty years. The most rapid general increases in acidity have been recorded in the industrializing, urbanizing Southeast. The most research into acid deposition has taken place in the Northeast, although during the past several years, much more attention has begun to focus on other parts of the country.

As to the makeup of acid rain, it is estimated that 65 percent of the acidic content of northeastern precipitation is sulfuric acid, 30 percent nitric acid, and 5 percent other acids. Available evidence indicates that sulfate concentrations have decreased somewhat in recent years (though not to a statistically significant degree) as sulfate emissions have been reduced. However, substantial reductions in precipitation acidity are likely to require much greater reductions. Concentrations of nitrate—

a secondary component of acid precipitation—have increased over the last three decades. This may reflect the general lack of success in reducing emissions. Chloride concentrations also have increased.

Not so well understood is the phenomenon of dry deposition, which may account for as much as half the deposition that occurs in the Northeast. Recent data indicate that dry deposition of sulfur accounts for something between one-third and one-half of total deposition. For nitrogen, dry deposition is between 30 percent and 70 percent of total deposition (Irving 1989). But dry-deposition rates are difficult to measure, and field data remain limited and preliminary. It is conceivable that uncertainties about dry deposition may be an important source of error in models of regional transport and deposition.

As noted earlier, the most recent precipitation acidity data are the most reliable. The National Atmospheric Deposition Program (NADP) was established in 1978, and in 1982 it assumed coordinating responsibility for the National Trends Network and the federally supported National Acid Precipitation Assessment Program (NAPAP). As of July 1988, the network consisted of 202 sites—a nearly tenfold increase over the 1978 network of twenty-two sites. There are stations in all states except Connecticut, Rhode Island, and Delaware; and every state west of the Mississippi River (with the exceptions of Alaska and Hawaii) has at least two sites. On average, about three-quarters of the sites' reports meet the NADP's criteria for inclusion in its annual report.

In order to promote citizen interest in acid-rain issues, the National Audubon Society created a "Citizens' Acid Rain Monitoring Network" in 1987. Volunteer observers use Merk pH paper to test, to an accuracy of + or −0.5, the pH of rain-water samples. The society compiles monthly reports, thus disseminating information much more rapidly than the NADP. Results are verified by a random check of 10 percent of monthly samples by the California Bodega Bay Marine Laboratory. In May 1989, nearly 200 observations were recorded; there were reports from all states except Colorado, South Dakota, and Hawaii.

Audubon's national figures generally tend to confirm those of the NADP. This is not necessarily to be expected, however, since Audubon's sites are biased toward urban locales (where local pollution sources can greatly influence atmospheric chemistry), whereas NADP's are biased toward rural areas. Moreover, according to the Audubon Society, its rain samples—unlike the NADP's—include dry deposition. In short, the citizens' network provides a supplement to—and to a degree a check upon—the NADP's data. It also has captured a good deal of media attention, thus heightening public interest in acid rain and related air-quality issues.

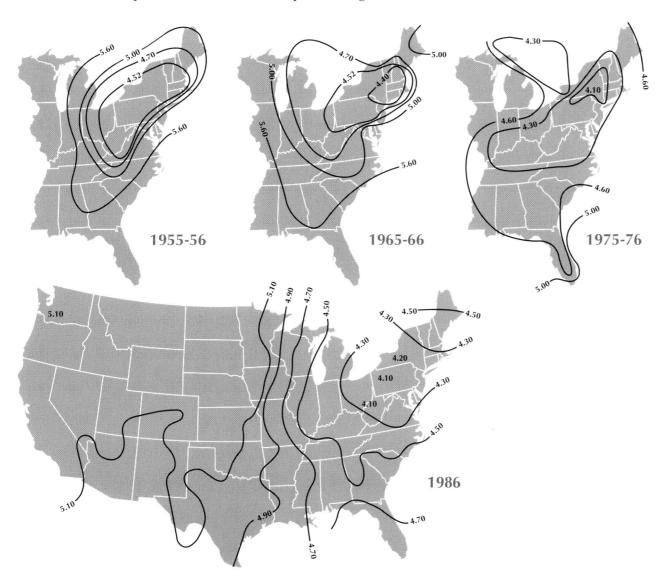

1955-56

1965-66

1975-76

1986

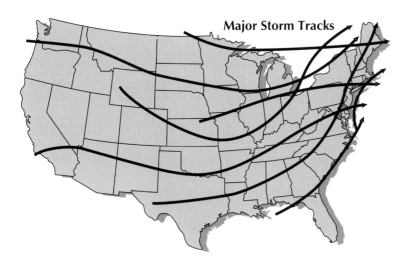

MAJOR STORM TRACKS

The general movement of weather systems across North America is from west to east. Individual storm tracks may be infinite in number; what the map in figure 8.10 shows is a generalization of the most common ones. It is evident that many storms pass over the northeastern states and/or southeastern Canada, often having crossed the Ohio Valley or Great Lakes states enroute.

The removal of pollutants varies considerably from storm to storm, depending on individual storm intensity and duration as well as other atmospheric factors. Furthermore, when air is lifted over mountains—such as the Adirondacks of northern New York State—precipitation is enhanced. This in turn may lead to greater cleansing (removal) of pollutants and thus to more acidic precipitation.

Even in the absence of storm systems, prevailing winds will transport pollutants. In the summer months especially, as stagnant high-pressure systems in the southeastern region direct air from the southwest toward the northeast, pollutant concentrations tend to peak in the Northeast. The sulfuric and nitric acids that form in the atmosphere may be removed either by precipitation or through dry deposition.

SULFUR TRANSPORT

The state of the art of regional transport modeling is such as to provide only a highly generalized overview of sulfur transport and an even less focused picture of nitrogen-oxide transport. The models are unable, therefore, to resolve the contentious questions about causal links between specific emissions sources and specific receiving areas.

It is clear from figure 8.11 that even in the northeastern region, local emissions (i.e., those from within the region) are likely to be predominant. But the model's results also point to the importance of long-range transport of sulfur. Most striking is the contribution of the northwestern quadrant to the Northeast. Significant transport also occurs from south to north. It appears as if dry deposition predominates near the emission source while wet deposition prevails in more distant areas. On an averaged annual basis, it is believed that wet and dry deposition are about equal over the eastern United States.

An analysis by the National Research Council (1986) concludes that there are causal relationships between anthropogenic sources of sulfur dioxide and presence of sulfate aerosol, reduced visibility, wet deposition of sulfate, and sulfate content of streams. The region spanning the midwestern and northeastern states—the same general area referred to in this and preceding illustrations—is found to have the greatest magnitudes of sulfur emissions and sulfur-oxide deposition.

With regard to nitrogen-oxide transport, the case is less clear, the evidence more circumstantial. Some analysts argue that current transport models do not capture the complexity of atmospheric mixing processes and precipitation variability. But despite the many uncertainties regarding both nitrogen and sulfur transport, there is little question as to the overall importance of climatological and meteorological factors.

Figure 8.10. Major Storm Tracks.

Figure 8.11. Sulfur Transport.

Source:
OTA, *Acid Rain and Transported Pollutants: Implications for Public Policy* (New York: UNIPUB, 1985), p. 72.

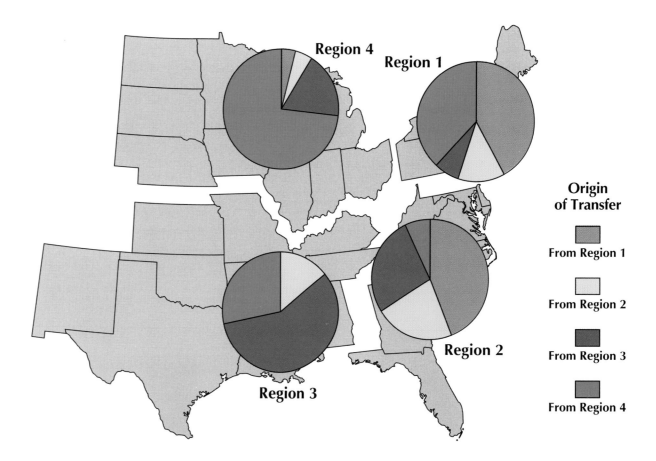

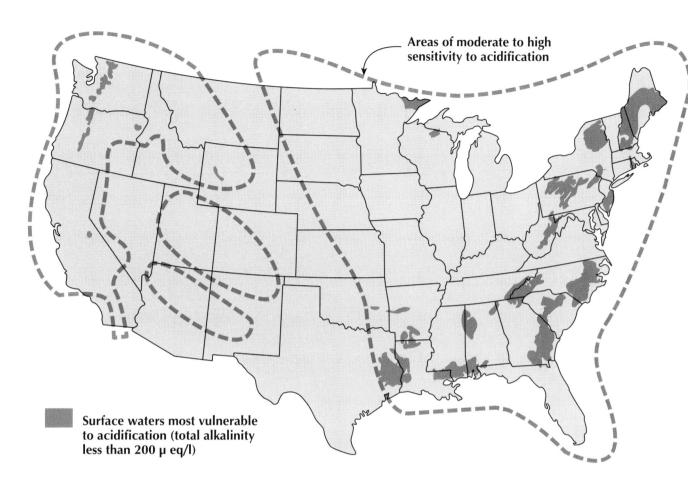

Areas of moderate to high sensitivity to acidification

Surface waters most vulnerable to acidification (total alkalinity less than 200 μ eq/l)

Figure 8.12. Areas of High Surface Sensitivity to Acidification.

Sources:
EPA, *Research Summary: Acid Rain* (Washington, DC: GPO, 1979), p. 5.

J. M. Omernik and C. F. Powers, "Total Alkalinity of Surface Waters: A National Map" *Annals of the Association of American Geographers* 73 (1985): 133–136 and map insert.

AREAS OF HIGH SURFACE SENSITIVITY TO ACIDIFICATION

The small areas highlighted on this map are those judged to be extremely sensitive to acidification. The information initially was derived from alkalinity data for 2,500 streams and lakes in the conterminous states (Omernik and Powers 1985). Alkalinity provides a good approximation of acid-neutralizing capacity, although it does not incorporate all of the biogeochemical and hydrological factors that are relevant. Thus, the authors of the map went on to compare their data with "driving factors" that affect alkalinity—bedrock geology, soils, surface landforms, climate—and "integrating factors," such as land use and potential natural vegetation. The integrating factors reflect regional, or watershed-level, combinations of the driving factors.

There is no universally accepted alkalinity value that defines high sensitivity to acidification. We have highlighted areas with alkalinities less than 200 μeq/l (micro-equivalents per liter); this represents something of a middle ground between various interpretations of what constitutes high sensitivity. Waters in the highlighted areas may be described as having relatively little capacity to absorb additional acidity. In general there is a gradient toward higher alkalinity values in the regions that sur-

round the areas indicated on the map. Low alkalinity values often, but not necessarily, occur in areas where waters are naturally acidic, such as the Cascade and Appalachian mountains, the New Jersey Pine Barrens, and parts of the Gulf-Atlantic Coastal Plain. Despite their natural acidity, waters in these regions may have a limited capacity to absorb additional inputs of acidity—inputs that in most instances would come from anthropogenic sources. In addition to regional-scale acid deposition, these sources might include local inputs, such as acid mine drainage.

In general, Omernik and Powers found low surface-water alkalinities in areas of ungrazed forest and high alkalinities where cropland predominates. In areas of mixed land uses, alkalinity values are generally associated with the degree of agricultural land use. The strongest relationships were found in the West; the weakest in the Southeast. Similar associations did not occur between geological sensitivity—as represented by bedrock or soil types—and surface-water alkalinity. This may be a function of the national scale of the map. The authors are preparing more detailed, regional-level maps that should be much more appropriate for such comparisons. These maps will more accurately depict local alkalinity variations that are lost in the generalization to the national level (see Omernik and Griffith 1986; Omernik and Kinney 1985).

If figure 8.12 is compared with maps of precipitation (figure 2.3) and precipitation acidity (figure 8.9), some valuable observations may be made. The most striking associations are among high sensitivity to acidification, high precipitation, and high acidity of precipitation in parts of the East. The areas of greatest alarm are along the Appalachian Chain and associated mountain groups in Georgia, North Carolina, Tennessee, West Virginia, Maryland, Pennsylvania, New York, New Hampshire, and Maine. These findings are generally comparable with ones reported in figure 8.14 and associated text. Similar concerns can also be raised in parts of the West, particularly in the Sierra Nevada and the Cascades. Mountainous regions tend to be especially vulnerable because precipitation often is high and soils thin and extensively leached.

Of course, these are highly generalized observations, and they require much more detailed assessment at the regional and local levels if they are to be validated for specific places. The small areas highlighted on the map should be viewed as potential hot spots, embedded within much larger areas of deep concern. At some risk of oversimplifying matters, we have included an overlay—based on an EPA map—showing much larger areas of moderate-to-high sensitivity. Undoubtedly there is great variation from place to place within these regions—but the cumulative potential impacts on soils, crops, natural vegetation, buildings, and human health are considerable indeed.

FOREST RESEARCH

Half of West Germany's forests now show signs of damage, ranging from root and needle loss to impaired growth and death (McLaughlin 1985). Forest declines of lesser magnitude have been recorded in the United States, particularly in California's Sierra Nevada and through the Appalachian Mountains in the East. Sulfur and nitrogen oxides, ozone, and trace metals have been implicated as damaging agents. Yet even though much of the forest decline has occurred in areas of acidic precipitation and low buffering capacities, firm causal links have not been established. Air pollution (including acid deposition) is one stress among several, including insects, diseases, drought, frost, and species competition. It may act as a "predisposing stress" by increasing susceptibility to other stresses or as an "inciting stress" by producing a more sudden physiological shock. Gaseous pollutants, such as ozone and sulfur dioxide, may directly damage foliage as well as affect vital biological processes. Acid precipitation can leach plant nutrients from the soil as well as increase the availability of such toxic metals as aluminum. In short, pollution may contribute to forest decline, even in the many cases where it is not the "final cause" of death.

Shown on the map in figure 8.13 are key activities of the Forest Research Program—a component of the National Acid Precipitation Assessment Program (NAPAP). Through its four regional cooperatives and other national efforts, the program studies the extent, causes, and consequences of forest damage in North America. Preliminary general findings are that most North American forests are not affected by decline. The limited declines that have occurred are more likely caused by natural stress or ozone than acid deposition. Acid deposition may, however, be locally detrimental (Irving 1989).

Research results from the Spruce-Fir Cooperative indicate increases in pollutant and acidity levels with elevation, growth declines in recent decades, and greater-than-50-percent red-spruce mortality at elevations above 3,400 feet in the Adirondack and Green mountains. Moreover, there is a significant west-to-east decline across northern New York and New England in percentage of dead red spruce on mountains (55 percent in the west to 8 percent in the east) and in sulfate deposition (11 pounds per acre to 5.3). At the high-elevation sites, which are often shrouded in clouds, more acidification may be caused by cloud deposition than by precipitation. The Mountain Cloud Chemistry Network, consisting of the sites shown on the map, has found that the pH of cloud water averages 3.5 (precipitation is about 4.2), with short-term cloud exposures as acidic as pH 2.7.

Research coordinated by the Eastern Hardwoods Cooperative reveals that many species, including the commercially valued sugar maple (jointly studied with

Canada), have declined over the last century. Yet consistent historical associations with pollutant deposition are not evident. The Ohio Corridor Study (Arkansas to Ohio gradient) shows west-to-east increases in wet-sulfate deposition (three-fold), total sulfur and carbon near the soil surface, and the black-oak mortality rate. A similar association between the sulfate deposition gradient and forest floor and soil sulfur levels was found along the Great Lakes Corridor. In Pennsylvania, sulfate deposition and ozone both decline from west to east. More generally, it is thought that ozone may cause more harm to eastern hardwoods than does acid deposition.

The Southern Commercial Cooperative estimates that growth rates for unmanaged loblolly pine have declined 38 percent between 1949 and 1984. Only 12 percent of the decline is explained by stand dynamics and climate (drought). Laboratory studies have demonstrated impairment of tree growth and development from ozone exposure. Moreover, it is predicted that over the next fifty years, acid deposition will significantly alter soil chemistry in up to 30 percent of the region. In the West, where research has lagged somewhat, studies in the Sierra Nevadas, the Puget Sound area, central Arizona, and the Front Range of Colorado have not shown an association between growth patterns and the ozone gradient.

Figure 8.14. Acidification of Eastern Lakes.

Source:
R. A. Linthurst et al., "Characteristics of Lakes in the Eastern United States," *Population Descriptions and Physico-Chemical Relationships*, vol. 1 (Las Vegas: EPA, 1986).

Figure 8.13. Forest Research.

Source:
Various materials from Forest Response Program.

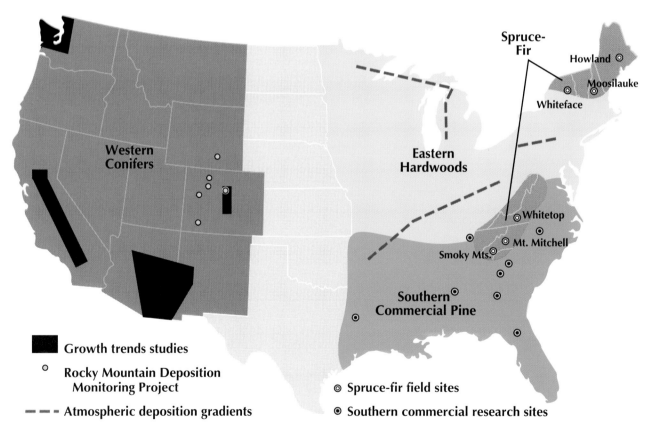

Spruce-Fir
Howland
Moosilauke
Whiteface
Western Conifers
Eastern Hardwoods
Whitetop
Mt. Mitchell
Smoky Mts.
Southern Commercial Pine

■ Growth trends studies

○ Rocky Mountain Deposition Monitoring Project

– – – Atmospheric deposition gradients

◎ Spruce-fir field sites

◉ Southern commercial research sites

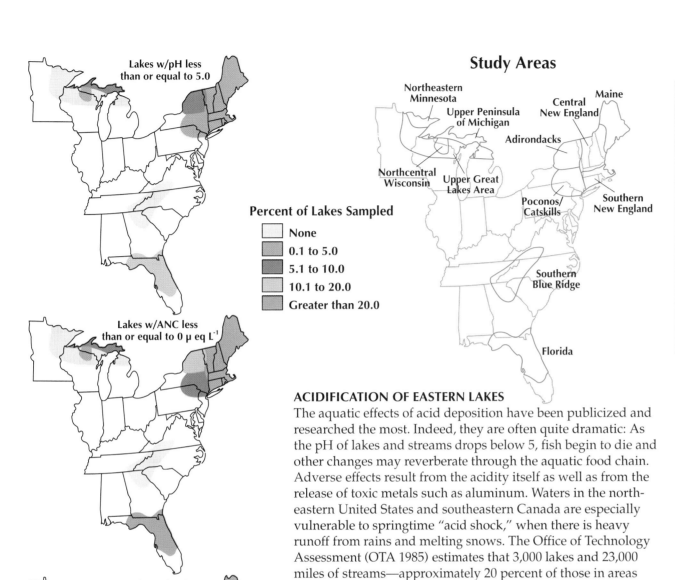

Study Areas

Northeastern Minnesota
Upper Peninsula of Michigan
Central New England
Maine
Adirondacks
Northcentral Wisconsin
Upper Great Lakes Area
Poconos/Catskills
Southern New England
Southern Blue Ridge
Florida

Lakes w/pH less than or equal to 5.0

Percent of Lakes Sampled
- None
- 0.1 to 5.0
- 5.1 to 10.0
- 10.1 to 20.0
- Greater than 20.0

Lakes w/ANC less than or equal to 0 µ eq L⁻¹

Lakes w/pH less than or equal to 6.0

Percent of Lakes w/	Acidity of Eastern Lakes										
	Adirondacks	Poconos/Catskills	Central New England	S New England	Maine	NE Minnesota	U Peninsula of Michigan	NC Wisconsin	Upper Great Lakes	S Blue Ridge	Florida
pH less than or equal to 5.0	10.0	0.8	1.7	5.0	0.5	0.0	9.4	2.1	0.0	0.0	12.4
ANC less than or equal to 0 µ eq L⁻¹	10.7	5.3	2.4	5.0	0.5	0.0	9.8	3.1	0.0	0.0	22.0
pH less than or equal to 6.0	26.6	7.8	12.9	14.6	4.8	1.4	17.7	27.7	4.5	0.4	32.7

ACIDIFICATION OF EASTERN LAKES

The aquatic effects of acid deposition have been publicized and researched the most. Indeed, they are often quite dramatic: As the pH of lakes and streams drops below 5, fish begin to die and other changes may reverberate through the aquatic food chain. Adverse effects result from the acidity itself as well as from the release of toxic metals such as aluminum. Waters in the northeastern United States and southeastern Canada are especially vulnerable to springtime "acid shock," when there is heavy runoff from rains and melting snows. The Office of Technology Assessment (OTA 1985) estimates that 3,000 lakes and 23,000 miles of streams—approximately 20 percent of those in areas defined as sensitive—have already become acidic or are extremely vulnerable to further acid deposition.

The Aquatic Effects Research Program, begun in 1983 as part of the National Acid Precipitation Assessment Program (NAPAP), coordinates research on surface-water sensitivity to acidification. The results of the Eastern Lake Survey are shown in the accompanying maps and table. Acidified lakes may be defined as those with no acid neutralizing capacity (ANC): Their supplies of bicarbonate and other acid-neutralizing ions have been exhausted. In general, these same lakes also have low pHs, relatively high extractable aluminum concentrations, and adversely affected aquatic life. It can be seen that most of the acidified lakes are in the Northeast, parts of northern Michigan and Wisconsin, and Florida. Acid deposition is believed to account for most of the acidification, except in Florida—where organic acids from fertilizer runoff and decaying vegetation may

be responsible. Turk (1983) concludes that most of the acidification of surface waters in the Northeast probably occurred prior to the mid- to late 1960s. Cause-and-effect linkages between atmospheric deposition and sulfate levels in surface waters are made by the National Research Council (1986), the EPA (Annual 1989), and NAPAP (Irving 1989).

The Western Lakes Survey—a companion to the Eastern Lake Survey—found virtually no acidic lakes (by the above definition) in the Sierra Nevada, Cascade, Olympic, or northern, central, or southern Rocky Mountain regions. The National Stream Survey was conducted in the Poconos/Catskills, mid-Atlantic, and southern Blue Ridge regions, as well as parts of Florida and the Interior Southeast (Ozark-Ouachita and Tennessee Valley regions). Of a total of approximately 120,000 stream-miles surveyed, 2.7 percent were found to be acidic; 8.4 percent had pH less than or equal to 5.5. Acidic mine-drainage streams were excluded from this sample. Greatest acidity was found in upstream segments; and in the mid-Appalachian and Poconos/Catskills regions, in small watersheds and at higher elevations. Overall, Florida and the mid-Atlantic region had the highest percentages of stream mileage with no ANC and high acidity.

NAPAP (Irving 1989) identifies six "high-interest" subregions that contain most of the inorganic-dominated acidic systems in the national samples: the southwest Adirondack Mountains, New England, the forested mid-Atlantic Highlands, the Atlantic Coastal Plain, the northern Florida Highlands, and the low silica lakes in the eastern Upper Midwest.

Earth is aptly named the water planet—not only because oceans cover 71 percent of its surface, but also because water can be found everywhere, even in the driest of places. Although oceans account for the vast bulk of the planet's water (over 97 percent by volume), enormous quantities also are found in the form of lakes and streams, groundwater, soil moisture, ice and snow, and atmospheric water vapor. Principal concerns of this chapter are surface water and groundwater availability, uses, and quality.

The average daily precipitation over the forty-eight conterminous states is a generous 4,200 billion gallons. Its nationally averaged fate is as follows:

Evaporation from wet surfaces	66%
Streamflow to Atlantic/Gulf of Mexico	22%
Streamflow to Pacific	7%
Subsurface flows	2%
Consumptive use (not immediately returned to the water cycle)	2%
Streamflow to Canada and Mexico	<1%

While the United States as a whole is quite amply supplied with water, regional availability is highly variable. As indicated by the precipitation map in figure 2.3 and the information presented in this chapter, overall water availability is much greater in the East than in the West. Thus, much of the agriculture, industry, and commercial and residential development of the West depends on our ability to exploit groundwater and manipulate surface flow. Even in the well-watered East, considerable engineering feats are required to provide water in the quantities and condition necessary to serve its huge metropolitan regions.

Much of the West is subject to chronic water scarcity, punctuated by periods of even more severe short-term drought. Not so widely known or accepted—at least until quite recently— is that the eastern half of the United States also suffers from debilitating droughts (see figure 16.4). Traditionally, water scarcity—however defined—has been addressed by building dams and diversions. While the potential savings afforded by water conservation and more efficient water allocation are enormous, progress thus far has been rather limited. The prices charged for western water do not come close to covering the federal investments required to make it available, and only recently has this situation even begun to change. In the East, water conservation becomes a concern mainly during times of drought and usually only in the immediately affected areas. Conservation is hindered by our general reluctance to regulate individual behavior, water laws and pricing policies that encourage maximum use, and the high costs of detecting and controlling leaks and other forms of wastage in public water systems.

Water quality affects water supply, since polluted water often becomes unusable water. "Traditional" water-quality concerns have focused on bacterial and viral contaminants, oxygen-depleting wastes, and increased sediment loads from human activities. But in recent years, much attention also has been directed toward a wide array of toxic substances. They not only affect fish and other aquatic life; they also are linked with cancer, birth defects, and other human health problems. Groundwater, critical in many parts of the country, finally has begun to receive the attention it deserves. Moreover, greater priority is now given to such nonpoint sources of pollution as agricultural and urban runoff.

During the past two decades, laws have been passed and massive investments made in municipal and industrial wastewater treatment. Yet despite marked improvements in individual water bodies such as Lake Erie and the Savannah River, overall surface water quality seems to have changed little. Clearly, much is yet to be learned, and also done, if we are equitably and efficiently to come to terms with water-quality and quantity issues.

Multnomah Falls, Oregon.
R. Mason.

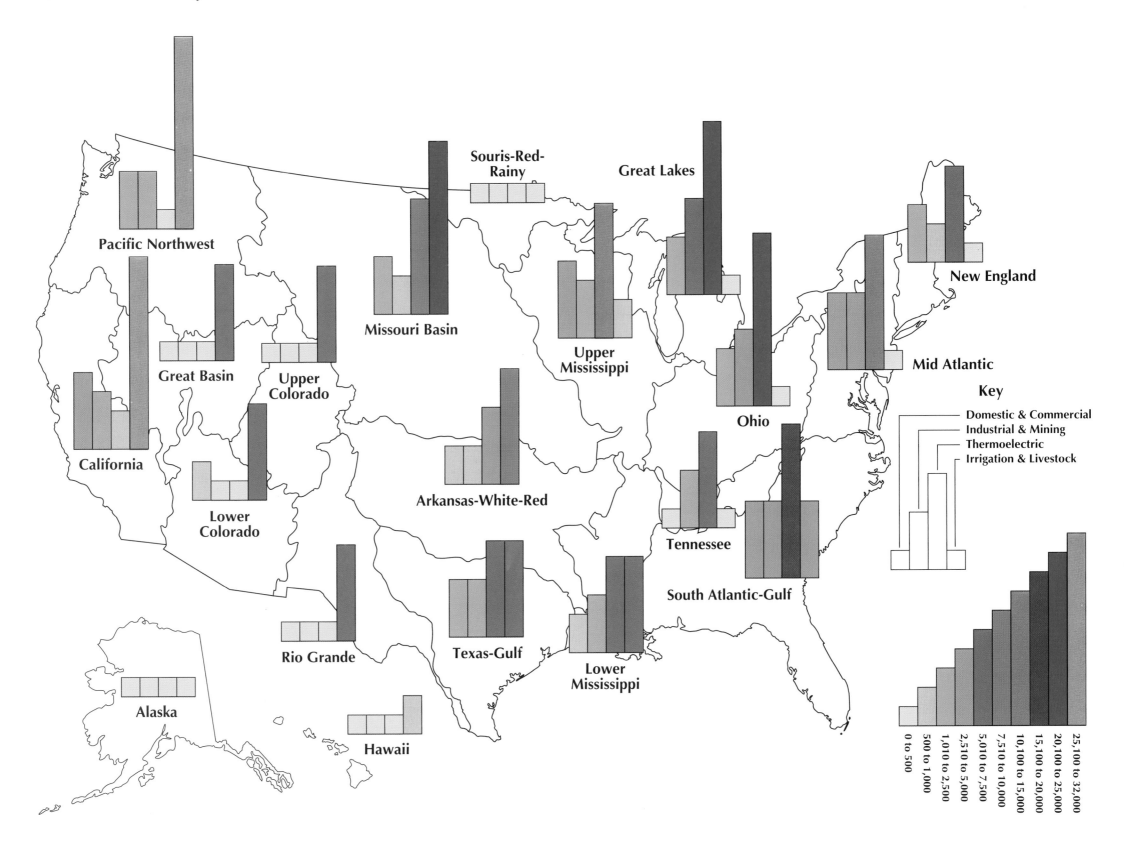

Pacific Northwest

Souris-Red-
Rainy

Great Lakes

New England

Missouri Basin

Upper
Mississippi

Great Basin

Upper
Colorado

Mid Atlantic

California

Ohio

Lower
Colorado

Key

Arkansas-White-Red

Domestic & Commercial
Industrial & Mining
Thermoelectric
Irrigation & Livestock

Tennessee

South Atlantic-Gulf

Rio Grande

Texas-Gulf

Alaska

Lower
Mississippi

Hawaii

0 to 500
500 to 1,000
1,010 to 2,500
2,510 to 5,000
5,010 to 7,500
7,510 to 10,000
10,100 to 15,000
15,100 to 20,000
20,100 to 25,000
25,100 to 32,000

Table 9.1. Offstream Freshwater Use, 1985			
	Per Capita (gal./day)	Percent Groundwater	Percent Surface Water
Alabama	2,140	4	96
Alaska	727	18	82
Arizona	1,960	48	52
Arkansas	2,500	64	36
California	1,420	40	60
Colorado	4,190	17	83
Connecticut	375	12	88
Delaware	222	57	43
Dist. of Columbia	556	0	100
Florida	554	64	36
Georgia	899	19	81
Hawaii	1,100	52	48
Idaho	22,200	22	78
Illinois	1,250	6	94
Indiana	1,470	8	92
Iowa	960	25	75
Kansas	2,310	85	15
Kentucky	1,130	5	95
Louisiana	2,210	15	85
Maine	733	8	92
Maryland	321	16	84
Massachusetts	1,070	5	95
Michigan	1,270	5	95
Minnesota	676	24	76
Mississippi	885	68	32
Missouri	1,210	10	90
Montana	10,500	2	98
Nebraska	6,250	55	45
Nevada	3,860	24	76
New Hampshire	688	12	88
New Jersey	307	29	71
New Mexico	2,320	46	54
New York	508	12	88
North Carolina	1,260	6	94
North Dakota	1,690	10	90
Ohio	1,180	6	94
Oklahoma	386	45	55
Oregon	2,450	10	90
Pennsylvania	1,210	6	94
Rhode Island	152	18	82
South Carolina	2,040	3	97
South Dakota	956	37	63
Tennessee	1,770	5	95
Texas	1,230	36	64
Utah	2,540	19	81
Vermont	235	29	71
Virginia	853	7	93
Washington	1,600	17	83
West Virginia	2,810	4	96
Wisconsin	1,400	8	92
Wyoming	12,200	8	92

OFFSTREAM FRESHWATER USE

The map in figure 9.1 depicts, by category, 1985 offstream uses of freshwater in each of the U.S. Geological Survey's water resource regions. For all offstream uses, an estimated 400 billion gallons of fresh and saline water were withdrawn each day—a 10 percent decline from the Survey's 1980 estimate. Most of that total (87 percent) was freshwater. Of the freshwater, 78 percent (265 billion gallons per day) was surface water and 22 percent (73 billion gallons per day) was groundwater. While groundwater use is not predominant in any of the water resource regions, it does account for over half the freshwater used in the states of Arkansas, Delaware, Florida, Hawaii, Kansas, Mississippi, and Nebraska. In absolute quantity used, California and Texas take the lead. Overall per capita use, as can be seen in table 9.1, generally tends to be higher in the Great Plains and the West.

All of the uses represented here require the withdrawal of water from surface and/or groundwater sources. Instream use, by contrast, takes place within stream channels. It includes such uses as hydroelectric power generation, navigation, fish propagation, and dilution of wastes. With respect to effects on water quantity, offstream uses are of prime concern.

Domestic and commercial needs are supplied mostly (87 percent) by public water suppliers. Major commercial users include business establishments, offices, hotels and motels, and civilian and military institutions. Rural users, both residential and commercial, depend overwhelmingly on private wells. As might be expected, the more heavily populated regions use the greatest quantities of water for domestic and commercial purposes. Nonconsumptive use, whereby water is returned to surface or groundwater soon after it is used, accounts for 80.5 percent of domestic and commercial withdrawals. Consumptive use removes water from the immediate hydrologic environment through evaporation, transpiration by plants, incorporation into products or plants, and ingestion by humans and livestock. Consumptive use accounts for 19.5 percent of domestic and commercial use.

Among the major water-using industries are steel, chemical and allied products, paper and allied products, and petroleum refining. Regions with large concentrations of heavy industry—especially the Great Lakes, Ohio, Mid-Atlantic, and South Atlantic-Gulf—are the biggest industrial users. The largest state users in 1985 were Indiana, Louisiana, New York, and Pennsyl-

Table 9.1 and Figure 9.1. Offstream Freshwater Use, 1985.

Source:
W. B. Solley, C. F. Merk, and R. R. Pierce, *Estimated Use of Water in the United States in 1985,* U.S. Geological Survey Circular 1004 (Washington, DC: GPO, 1988).

vania. In all regions except the Pacific Northwest, much less water is used in mining operations than for industrial purposes. The largest users for mining are the Missouri, Ohio, and south Atlantic regions. But if saline water is included (only freshwater use is shown on the map), then California becomes the largest regional mining user. Texas is also a large user of saline water. For the combined industrial-mining category represented on the map, 16 percent of the use is consumptive; 84 percent nonconsumptive.

Thermoelectric power generation is second only to irrigation in total use of freshwater. By far the largest thermoelectric users are the more industrialized regions: the Great Lakes, Ohio, Mid-Atlantic, and South Atlantic-Gulf regions. Coastal regions are also substantial users of saline water (not shown on the map). The water, nearly all of which comes from surface sources, is used primarily for condenser and reactor cooling. Ninety-seven percent of it is returned; only 3 percent of the use is consumptive. However, the situation varies widely from plant to plant. If the cooling water is reused—especially if it is cycled through ponds or open cooling towers—consumptive use is likely to exceed 60 percent. If the water is used only once and then returned, evaporative loss is much lower, usually under 2 percent. Consumptive use has been increasing, at least in part because of greater use of cooling towers at the nuclear power plants that have recently come on line. The environmental benefit of using cooling towers and ponds is reduced damage to aquatic ecosystems from thermal pollution. This is because the difference in ambient stream temperature and the temperature of the return flow of water is narrowed.

Irrigation, discussed in chapter 4, is the leading user of water. It accounts for the bulk of western water use, and while proportionally still small, its use has also increased in recent years in the East. The livestock category, a much smaller water user than irrigation, includes fish farming as well as feedlots and on-farm uses. Nationally, water withdrawn for livestock uses in 1985 was approximately double that withdrawn in 1980. This is attributed to increases in fish farming—especially in Arkansas, Idaho, and Mississippi—and differences in reporting. Regionally, the Pacific Northwest is the biggest user, accounting for about one-quarter of the total. Groundwater use for the combined irrigation-livestock category is proportionally high in some regions—notably the lower Mississippi, Arkansas-White-Red, and Texas-Gulf drainage areas. Overall, groundwater accounts for about one-third of irrigation-livestock use; surface water two-thirds. Fifty-four percent of the combined use is consumptive and 46 percent is nonconsumptive. These uses present multiple environmental concerns: not only are they highly consumptive; the water that is returned is often highly degraded by salts, nitrates, and pesticide residues.

TRENDS IN WATER WITHDRAWALS

Total water withdrawals in 1985 were 400 billion gallons, down 9 percent from the 440 billion gallons withdrawn in 1980. This is the first drop registered over any five-year span between 1950 and 1985. It should be noted, however, that the rate of increase had already slackened significantly during the 1970s.

These trends are broken out by water-use categories in figure 9.2. But it is difficult to account fully and accurately for these patterns because they are determined by a multitude of factors. These include yearly variations in water availability (ground as well as surface water), changes in water pricing as well as general economic conditions that affect user behavior, and improvements in the reliability of estimates over time. These qualifications notwithstanding, it is possible to draw some broad conclusions about water-use trends.

The U.S. Geological Survey attributes the increases in rural withdrawals primarily to expansion of fish farming operations, especially in Arkansas, Idaho, and Mississippi. The 7-percent increase in public-supply withdrawals corresponds with a 7-percent increase in the population served by public-supply systems. Irrigation and thermoelectric power generation are the largest users of water, and both showed declines between 1980 and 1985. The drop in irrigation usage may in part be the result of slower rates of expansion of irrigated acreage as well as greater irrigation efficiencies—but the evidence is not adequate to isolate these factors. What is clear, however, is that groundwater withdrawals for irrigation decreased during the 1980–1985 period, while surface-water withdrawals increased. This may be attributed to greater availability of surface water during this period.

The substantial decline in industrial withdrawals may be more a reflection of improved estimating techniques than actual declines in use. However, consumptive use of water (i.e., water not immediately returned to the hydrologic cycle) increased 13 percent from 1980 to 1985. This implies improved efficiency and greater reuse of water by plants, which means a reduction in total withdrawals.

Are these trends likely to continue? The now-defunct U.S. Water Resources Council (1978) forecast in the mid-1970s that withdrawals would decline by 9 percent between 1975 and 2000 but that consumptive use would increase by 27 percent. Greater efficiency of use and more recycling would lower withdrawals but lead to greater consumption. In other words, less water would be removed from streams and lakes, but there would be an even greater reduction in the volumes of water returned to those bodies. While this should help to reduce pollution loadings to streams and lakes, it also means less water available for downstream uses (withdrawals, fish, and wildlife) and for recharge of groundwater.

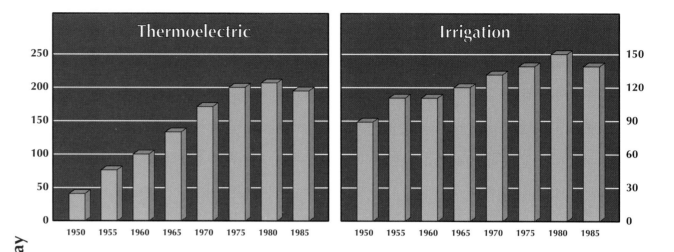

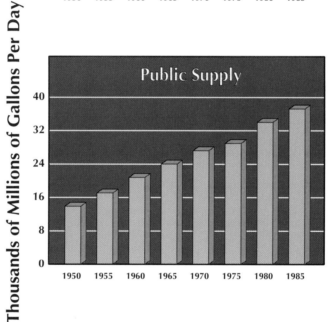

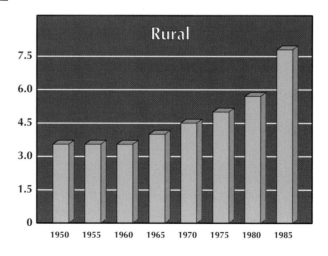

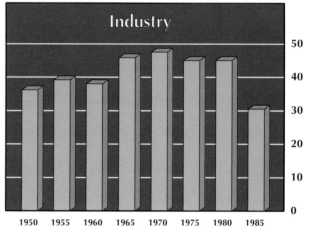

Figure 9.2. Trends in Water Withdrawals.

Source:
W. B. Solley, C. F. Merk, and R. R. Pierce, *Estimated Use of Water in the United States in 1985*, U.S. Geological Survey Circular 1004 (Washington, DC: GPO, 1988), p. 73.

Note: To facilitate historical comparisons, the categories used here are modified from those represented in figure 9.1. The 1985 numbers shown here are not directly comparable with those of figure 9.1.

CONSUMPTIVE USE AND RENEWABLE WATER SUPPLY

Renewable supply—the denominator in figure 9.3's regional ratios—represents the theoretical upper limit on usable water flow. It is derived by adding precipitation to net imports of water from other regions, then subtracting water lost through natural evapotranspiration. Groundwater, which may be available for use, is not included in the calculations because in times of shortage it may become thoroughly depleted. Consumptive-use values represent water withdrawn for offstream uses but not immediately returned to surface or groundwater (see page 91).

Over most of the United States, renewable supply greatly exceeds consumptive use. In the Rio Grande and Great Basin regions, however, consumptive use is between 40 and 60 percent of renewable supply. In the lower Colorado Basin, use actually *exceeds* supply under average conditions. As a result, the Colorado River usually fails to reach its destination in the Gulf of California (see figure 9.4).

The regional ratios sometimes mask significant subregional patterns. In the High Plains, which comprise parts of the relatively well-supplied Missouri, Arkansas-White-Red, and Texas-Gulf regions, there are areas where consumptive use exceeds renewable supply. Conversely, in parts of the supply-scarce Colorado Basin, consumptive use is but a relatively small proportion of renewable supply.

The renewable supply figures should be treated conservatively. For one thing, they may mask wide seasonal or annual variations in supply. Moreover, water is not really available until the appropriate physical, legal, and institutional facilities are in place. Often, its availability for one use is constrained by competition with alternative uses. Finally, water may in theory be available yet too degraded to support specific uses.

Figure 9.3. Consumptive Use in Relation to Renewable Water Supply.

Source:
U.S. Geological Survey, *National Water Summary 1983—Hydrologic Events and Issues,* Water-Supply Paper no. 225 (Washington, DC: GPO, 1984), p. 27.

Explanation (billion gallons per day)

0.6 — Consumptive Use
78.4 — Renewable Supply

Consumptive Use as a Percentage of Renewable Supply

- 0 to 10
- 11 to 40
- 41 to 100
- Greater than 100

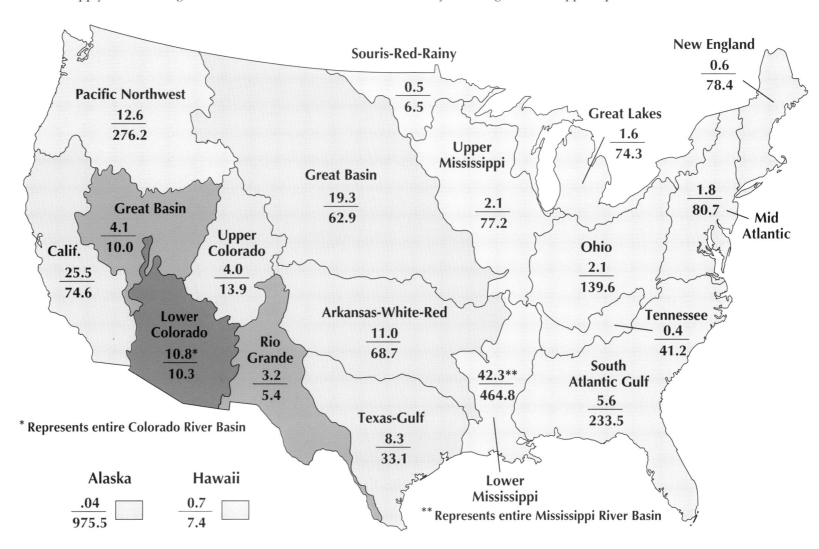

New England
0.6 / 78.4

Souris-Red-Rainy
0.5 / 6.5

Pacific Northwest
12.6 / 276.2

Great Lakes
1.6 / 74.3

Upper Mississippi
2.1 / 77.2

Great Basin
19.3 / 62.9

Mid Atlantic
1.8 / 80.7

Great Basin
4.1 / 10.0

Calif.
25.5 / 74.6

Upper Colorado
4.0 / 13.9

Ohio
2.1 / 139.6

Lower Colorado
10.8* / 10.3

Rio Grande
3.2 / 5.4

Arkansas-White-Red
11.0 / 68.7

Tennessee
0.4 / 41.2

42.3** / 464.8

South Atlantic Gulf
5.6 / 233.5

Texas-Gulf
8.3 / 33.1

Lower Mississippi

* Represents entire Colorado River Basin

** Represents entire Mississippi River Basin

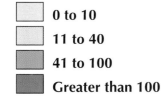

Alaska
.04 / 975.5

Hawaii
0.7 / 7.4

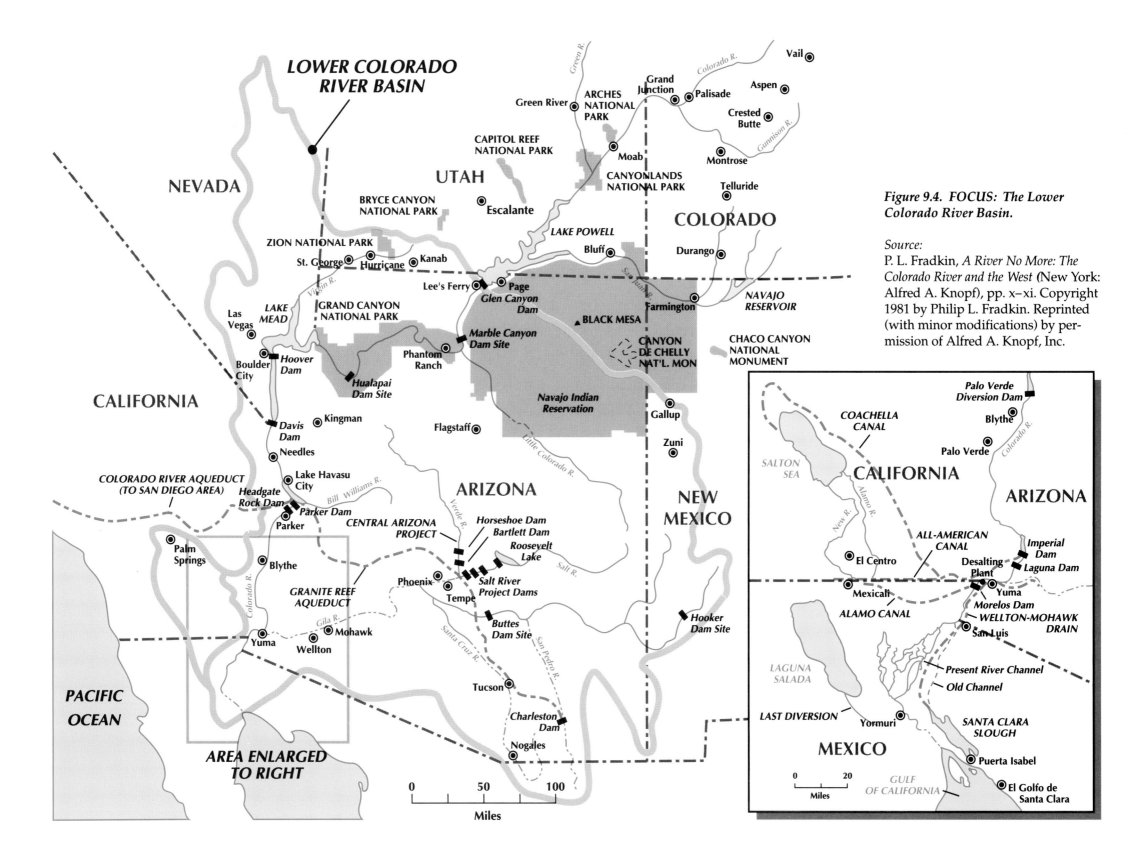

LOWER COLORADO RIVER BASIN

Figure 9.4. FOCUS: The Lower Colorado River Basin.

Source:
P. L. Fradkin, *A River No More: The Colorado River and the West* (New York: Alfred A. Knopf), pp. x–xi. Copyright 1981 by Philip L. Fradkin. Reprinted (with minor modifications) by permission of Alfred A. Knopf, Inc.

Table 9.2. Apportionment of Colorado River Flows

	Average Apportionment (million acre-feet/year)	1978 Consumption (million acre-feet/year)
Lower Basin		
Arizona	2.80	1.11
California	4.40	4.62
Nevada	0.30	0.07
Total	7.50	5.80
Upper Basin		
Arizona	0.05	0.03
Colorado (51.75%)	3.00	1.88
New Mexico (11.25%)	0.65	0.30
Utah (23%)	1.33	0.63
Wyoming (14%)	0.81	0.30
Total	5.84	3.14
Estimated Evaporation Losses		1.89
Subtotal		
U.S.	13.34	10.83
Mexico	1.50	1.74
Total		
U.S. and Mexico	14.84	12.57

Source: T. O. Miller, G. D. Weatherford, and J. E. Thorson, *The Salty Colorado* (Washington, DC, and Napa, CA: The Conservation Foundation and John Muir Institute, 1986), p. 14.

FOCUS: THE LOWER COLORADO RIVER BASIN

The Colorado River, for centuries manipulated on a small-scale basis by Indians, now is so heavily used that it often fails to reach its natural outlet in the Gulf of California. The 1922 Colorado River Compact arbitrarily established an upper and lower basin by dividing the river at Lee's Ferry, Arizona, and rather optimistically allocated to each an annual 7.5 million acre-feet of water. Subject to the compact's general provisions, each basin state controls the appropriation and use of water within its borders. This is in general keeping with the western legal principle of "prior appropriation," whereby the "beneficial use" of water—wherever the user may be located—establishes rights to that water. Legal definitions of "beneficial uses" generally include irrigation and domestic and commercial water supply, but exclude such passive uses as fishing, boating, and protection of wildlife and riparian habitat. The result is fierce competition among both public and private interests and wasteful use of water simply to maintain claims.

Over Arizona's objections, the Hoover Dam was completed in 1935. The Boulder Canyon Project Act—which authorized the dam along with the All-American and Coachella canals—entitles California to 4.4 million acre-feet of water per year. Arizona's entitlement is only 2.8 million acre-feet, and state officials feared they might not receive even that much in dry years. Hoover Dam was succeeded by a series of smaller downstream projects: the Davis, Parker, Headgate Rock, Palo Verde Diversion, and Imperial dams; the Colorado River Aqueduct; the Wellton-Mohawk Drain; and the Morelos Dam in Mexico. Southern California has been the chief beneficiary of the resultant electricity and subsidized irrigation water. In 1934, the frustrated governor of Arizona went so far as to declare martial law and call out the National Guard in a fruitless attempt to stop work on the Parker Dam.

The Colorado River Storage Project, authorized in 1956 and amended in the 1960s, primarily benefits the upper-basin states. Its hydroelectric dams—the Glen Canyon among them—are the project's "cash registers": The power they produce is sold at high rates to help subsidize costly irrigation projects. This is representative of the "river basin accounting" used by the Bureau of Reclamation and Army Corps of Engineers to justify dams and irrigation projects throughout the West.

Meanwhile, Arizona's concerns became much more acute as its population boomed after World War II. By the 1960s, the groundwater on which the state so heavily depends was being seriously drawn down, and the Salt River Project (Gila River) was inadequate to meet the growing needs. A 1964 Supreme Court decision—the culmination of a complex series of court cases dating back to 1952—favored Arizona with a 2.8 million acre-feet-per-year allocation of water. It also validated the reserved rights of the Navajo Indians to a significant entitlement of water.

The setback to California was only temporary; it regained its advantage legislatively. The 1968 Colorado River Basin Project Act guaranteed California its 4.4-million-acre-feet per year allocation in times of shortage. This was the trade-off for California's support of the Central Arizona Project (CAP), which currently accounts for 1.5 million of Arizona's 2.8-million-acre-feet allocation. The upper-basin states also received several new water projects as part of the bargain.

Earlier proposals had called for a dam at each end of the Grand Canyon National Park: cash registers for the Colorado River Basin Project. This ignited a firestorm of opposition, fueled by a major media campaign. In a famous *New York Times* ad, responding to the Bureau of Reclamation's claim that the reservoir would allow better views of the canyon from motorboats, the Sierra Club asked: "Should we also flood the Sistine Chapel so tourists can get nearer the ceiling?" Eventually, CAP went ahead—minus those two dams and minus earlier grandiose thoughts of diverting Columbia River water to the Southwest. Still, it is a very costly subsidy for irrigation of mostly low-value crops that farmers in other parts of the country are paid not to grow. The project was just coming onto line in the late 1980s, and its beneficiaries have yet to settle Indian water-rights questions growing out of the 1964 Supreme Court decision.

Still another obligation that has haunted western water developers is the 1.5 million acre-feet per year of water guaranteed to Mexico by the Mexican Treaty of 1945. By the early 1960s, the Mexican government was protesting that the water's salinity rendered it unusable. The high salinity levels result from: (1) concentrations of salts as water volumes decline and (2) leaching of salts from irrigated lands. Bowing to the threat of international condemnation, the Nixon administration negotiated a salinity accord with Mexico. It is to be fulfilled through a host of projects, among them the world's largest desalination plant in Yuma, Arizona. Critics see this as an incredibly costly alternative to buying out farmers in the Wellton-Mohawk District or forcing them to adopt more efficient irrigation methods.

Fiscal conservatism of the Carter and Reagan years have effectively brought to an end the prospect of huge new water schemes for the Colorado. But the river's future use will be greatly influenced, even determined, for decades to come by the events of the "reclamation era." It will also be guided by short-term and longer-term climatic trends—including the potential effects of global greenhouse warming (figure 18.1)—as well as changing public perceptions of ecological, aesthetic, and non-consumptive recreation values.

INTERBASIN WATER TRANSFERS

One way to augment a river's flow—and not an uncommon practice in parts of the western United States—is to import water from another river basin. The U.S. Geological Survey recently inventoried western interbasin water transfers for the period 1973–1982 (Petsch 1985). The survey's analysis covered all or parts of eleven water-resources regions (the regions are named in figure 9.3) and a total of 111 subregions. Figure 9.5 shows transfers for the water year 1982. Of course, the amount of water transferred in any given year is affected by climate and other conditions for that year. Furthermore, many small transfers may not be shown because they were not reported. Nonetheless, the 1982 figures should at least generally represent the overall movement of water.

The average annual amount of water transferred between 1973 and 1982 was just under 12 million acre-feet—the equivalent of the average annual discharge of the Connecticut River at Thompsonville, Connecticut; the Mississippi River at Prescott, Wisconsin; or the Colorado River near Grand Canyon, Arizona. If transfers only between water-resource regions are considered, then the figure is 5.37 million acre-feet per year. The Lower Colorado region exported by far the most water in 1982. Those exports, mostly to southern California (see figure 9.4), were a little over 4 million acre-feet. The greatest volume of transfers within a region was in California.

Environmentalists argue that river-basin development should be constrained by the amount of available water and its capacity to assimilate waste; that is, the carrying capacity of the basin. Ideally, this means no diversions or impoundments of water—and most certainly excludes interbasin transfers of water. In stark contrast to this is the ethos that has largely guided western water development: Water not used (for agriculture, industry, commerce, or personal consumption) is water wasted. When taken to its extreme—as it has been on more than a few occasions—this means that any water is fair game.

The North American Water and Power Alliance (NAWAPA), conceived in the early 1950s, advocates interbasin transfer of water on a truly monumental scale. NAWAPA envisions massive dams that would reverse the flow of major rivers in western Canada and direct the water to the western United States. Some of the water might make its way into the Great Lakes and the Mississippi River. In the East, water on its way to James Bay would be used to generate hydropower—a process already under way with the Province of Quebec's James Bay Project—and a chief beneficiary would be the United States.

Recent environmental concerns, Canada's sovereign interests, and perhaps just the sheer financial and engineering absurdity of NAWAPA's grand schemes have conspired to make them an improbability. The fortunes of smaller interbasin projects also have been affected by fiscal and environmental concerns. North Dakota's Garrison Diversion has been scaled down, and the diversion of water from the Columbia River Basin to California—at one time a real possibility—now seems highly unlikely. The concept of river-basin carrying capacity hardly has been embraced by the powers that be—but it has gained stature and credibility that would have been inconceivable in the 1950s.

Finally, there is the prospect of climate change. Today's dams and diversions are suited to recent temperature and precipitation patterns—but there is little assurance that these conditions will continue to prevail, even in the near term (figure 18.1).

Figure 9.5. Interbasin Water Transfers, 1982.

Source:
H. E. Petsch, Jr., *Inventory of Interbasin Transfers of Water in the Western Conterminous United States* (Denver, CO: U.S. Geological Survey, 1985), Plate 1.

Acre-feet, 1982
1,500,000 to 3,100,000
750,000 to 1,500,000
250,000 to 750,000
50,000 to 250,000
10,000 to 50,000
Less than 10,000

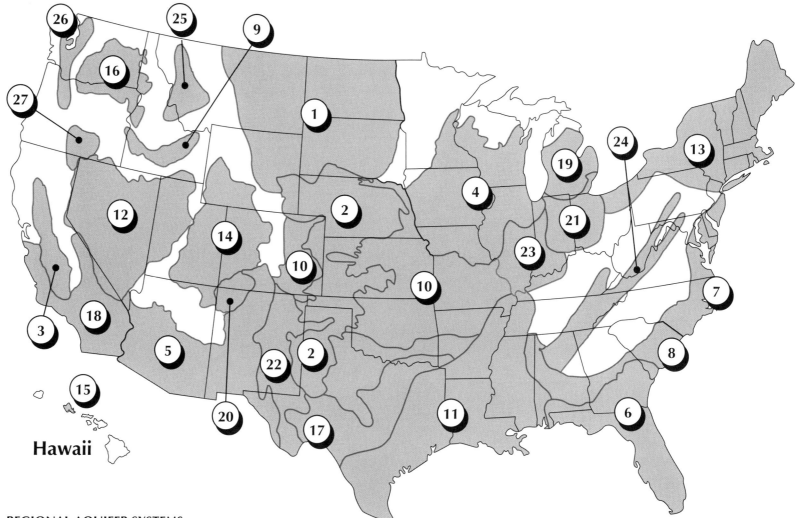

Figure 9.6. Regional Aquifer Systems.

Source:
R. J. Sun, ed., *Regional Aquifer-System Analysis Program of the U.S. Geological Survey: Summary of Projects, 1978–84*, U.S. Geological Survey Circular 1002 (Washington, DC: GPO,1986), p. 4.

Aquifer Systems
1. Northern Great Plains
2. High Plains
3. Central Valley, California
4. Northern Midwest
5. Southwest Alluvial Basins
6. Floridan
7. Northern Atlantic Coastal Plain
8. Southeastern Coastal Plain
9. Snake River Plain
10. Central Midwest
11. Gulf Coastal Plain
12. Great Basin
13. Northeast Glacial
14. Upper Colorado River Basin
15. Oahu Island, Hawaii
16. Columbia Plateau Basalt
17. Edwards-Trinity
18. Southern California Alluvial Basins
19. Michigan Basin
20. San Jaun Basin
21. Ohio-Indiana Glacial Deposits and Carbonates
22. Pecos River Basin
23. Illinois Basin
24. Appalachian Valleys and Piedmont
25. No. Rockies Intermontane Basins
26. Puget-Willamette Trough
27. Alluvial Basins, OR, CA, and NV

REGIONAL AQUIFER SYSTEMS

More than 96 percent of the United States' fresh water is in the form of groundwater; surface waters account for less than 4 percent. Groundwater is found in saturated subsurface rock and soil formations known as aquifers. Loose sand and gravel form unconsolidated aquifers; semiconsolidated aquifers consist of partially cemented materials. Consolidated aquifers are made up of permeable rocks such as limestones, shales, and sandstones. Aquifers vary greatly in beneath-the-surface depth, thickness, and areal extent. Compared with surface water, groundwater movement is extremely slow, averaging between 3 and 3,000 feet per year. About 30 percent of streamflow in the United States is supplied by groundwater.

Much less information is generally available regarding groundwater than surface waters. In an attempt to remedy this, the Regional Aquifer-System Analysis (RASA) Program was initiated by the U.S. Geological Survey in 1978. Its main purpose is to assemble information on aquifer boundaries, water quantity and quality, and recharge characteristics. The RASA Program's twenty-eight aquifer systems, shown on the map, are highly generalized. Some units, including the Northern Great Plains, High Great Plains, and Gulf and Atlantic Coastal Plain, consist of separate aquifers that form interconnected regional systems. Other units, such as the Southwest Alluvial Basins and Northeast Glacial Valleys, consist of virtually independent aquifers that share important hydrogeologic characteristics. Enormous quantities of groundwater are contained in the unconsolidated and semiconsolidated materials that underlie the High Great Plains, California's Central Valley, and the Southeastern Coastal Plain. By contrast, the consolidated rocks of the Appalachian Mountains and the basalt plateau of the Northwest yield relatively small amounts of water.

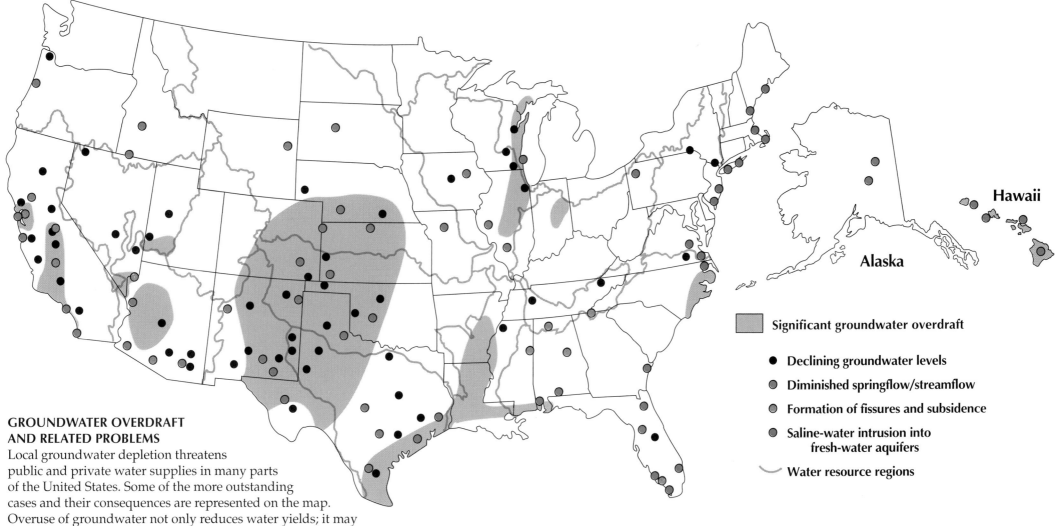

**GROUNDWATER OVERDRAFT
AND RELATED PROBLEMS**

Local groundwater depletion threatens
public and private water supplies in many parts
of the United States. Some of the more outstanding
cases and their consequences are represented on the map.
Overuse of groundwater not only reduces water yields; it may
also result in diminished flows of springs and streams. In some
circumstances—particularly in areas of limestone geology—
excessive removal of groundwater may lead to subsidence of the
land surface. Indeed, subsidence became national news in the
early 1980s when an extraordinary rash of incidents in Florida
caused extensive damage to roads and buildings. A related
phenomenon—development of ground fissures—can allow
polluted surface waters to flow rapidly into aquifers. In coastal
areas, overpumping of fresh water aquifers may allow less dense
salt water to "intrude"; that is, to migrate over the fresh water.
Salt-water intrusion also has occurred in some interior areas as
deep saline waters intrude into depleted upper-level aquifers.

The long-term overuse, or mining, of groundwater over large
areas may lead to regional-scale depletion. Groundwater overdraft is particularly severe in central California, west-central
Arizona, the High Great Plains, the Texas Gulf Coast, the lower

Mississippi Valley, eastern Wisconsin and Illinois, and coastal
North Carolina.

Recently, the plight of the Ogallala Aquifer ("High Plains"
region in figure 9.6) has been widely publicized. The Ogallala
contains as much as 1 quadrillion gallons of water, supports a
$30-billion-per-year agricultural economy, provides irrigation
water for more than 12 million acres of farmland, and helps to
support nearly 500,000 people (Patrick et al. 1987). Intensive
exploitation of the aquifer began after World War II with the
introduction of high-capacity pumps. So much water has been
withdrawn that parts of the water table have declined as much
as 100 feet. The rate at which precipitation recharges much of the
Ogallala formation is slow and is greatly exceeded by the rate of
withdrawal. In coming decades, the southern half of the region is
likely to experience extensive conversion to dryland farming
techniques, a process already well under way in East Texas.

*Figure 9.7. Groundwater Overdraft
and Related Problems.*

*Boundaries represent U.S. Geological
Survey Water Resource Regions, which
are named in figure 9.1.*

Source:
U.S. Water Resources Council, *The
Nation's Water Resources, 1975–2000,*
vol. 1, *Summary* (Washington, DC:
GPO, 1979), p. 59.

GROUNDWATER VULNERABILITY

Figure 9.7 represents cropland areas most hydrogeologically susceptible to pesticide and nitrate pollution. The major potential sources of such pollution are agricultural activities, septic systems, and land application of wastewater and sludge. Non-agricultural as well as agricultural lands also may be susceptible to pollution from landfills, dumps, injection wells, leaking storage tanks and pipelines, and transportation leaks. Various estimates put the number of underground storage tanks (primarily gasoline tanks) in the United States in the neighborhood of 2 million, with anywhere between 15,000 and several hundred thousand of them currently experiencing leaks (Canter et al. 1987). Surface impoundments also are significant sources of contamination: An EPA survey identified a total of 180,973 impoundments (industrial, municipal, agricultural, mining, oil and gas brine pits, and other) at 80,263

sites. Over 98 percent of the sites were located in areas proximate to potential water supplies (EPA 1983c). Additional major sources of groundwater contamination include feedlots, road salting, urban runoff, mining and construction activities, oil production wells, and percolation of atmospheric pollutants.

Many of these activities are concentrated around heavily populated and/or industrialized areas. The Office of Technology Assessment (OTA 1984) has found that septic tanks tend to be concentrated in California and the Northeast, fertilizer and pesticide use is greatest in the West and Midwest, brine-disposal wells are found mainly in the Southwest, and mine drainage is common in the East, Midwest, and Southwest. Unfortunately, detailed site-specific information on the relationships between sources of pollution and hydrogeologic vulnerability is sparse. This much, however, is clear: Many areas face considerable threats of contamination from a wide range of organic and inorganic chemicals, biological substances, and radionuclides.

Figure 9.8. Cropland Vulnerable to Groundwater Contamination from Pesticides and Nitrates.

Source:
Kenneth Algozin (Department of Agriculture, Economic Research Service, Washington, DC, 1988, map).

This map is based solely on hydrogeologic information, and does not reflect actual levels of agricultural chemical use or observed contamination. Twelve crops—those most relevent to federal commodity programs—were used in the determinations: corn, sorghum, soybeans, cotton, wheat, oats, barley, summer fallow, cool and warm season grass hay, and legume/legume-grass hay.

Cropland vulnerability was determined through calculation of DRASTIC scores, a rating scheme that involves seven factors:
D   depth to groundwater
R   recharge rate (net)
A   aquifer media
S   soil media
T   topography (slope)
I   impact of the vadose zone
C   conductivity (hydraulic)
*   of the aquifer*

Each factor is then multiplied by a value that reflects relative pollution potential at the site, and also a more general importance weight for that factor. These figures are summed to give overall site ratings.

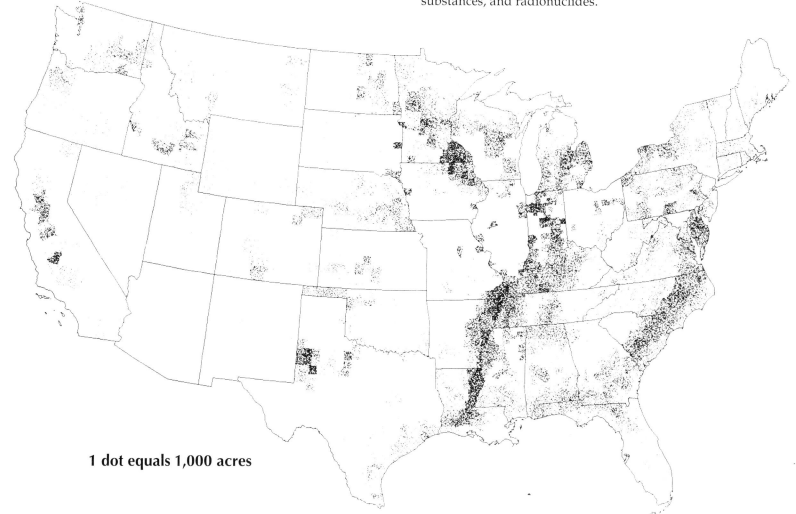

1 dot equals 1,000 acres

GROUNDWATER DEPENDENCE

Several states rely very heavily on groundwater. It is particularly critical as a source of drinking water in coastal towns and cities and in the "sole-source aquifer" areas shown in figure 9.10. Overall, about 97 percent of rural domestic needs are supplied by groundwater. Groundwater also is critical to agriculture and industry in many regions.

Groundwater may be contaminated by a wide array of organic and inorganic chemicals that pose threats not only via direct ingestion by drinking but also through skin absorption, inhalation of volatile contaminants, and ingestion of contaminated food. The potential health effects, acute as well as toxic, are complex and difficult to document. They range all the way from eye and skin irritation to central nervous system damage, cancers, and reproductive effects. But how widespread are these various effects? Several assessments, reviewed by Patrick et al. (1987), conclude that no more than 2 percent of groundwater is likely to be affected by pollution from landfills, surface impoundments, and other sources. However, it is acknowledged that this may understate the significance of the problem in heavily populated and industrialized areas such as the Northeast and Middle Atlantic states. Indeed, such concerns have been dramatically heightened by toxic contamination incidents in Woburn, Massachusetts; Niagara Falls, New York (Love Canal—figure 12.5); and many other localities.

Federal land, water, waste management, mining, energy, and pesticide-related legislation all deal with groundwater management questions; these laws are discussed briefly at the end of this chapter. More specifically, the EPA's "Ground-Water Protection Strategy" seeks to coordinate federal, state, and local groundwater protection activities. The EPA provides support for state programs and institutions, investigates and regulates contamination from underground storage tanks and land disposal facilities, and issues guidelines that promote consistency within its groundwater protection programs.

One of the substantive EPA initiatives is the Sole-Source Aquifer program; this is illustrated in figure 9.10. The Wellhead Protection Program, part of the Safe Drinking Water Act Amendments of 1986, requires states to identify and develop management plans for wellhead areas that supply public water systems. The EPA also has developed regulations regarding design, performance, inspection, and reporting and correction of releases from underground storage tanks. Under the Resource Conservation and Recovery Act (RCRA), a trust fund has been established to assist states in cleaning up leaks at specific sites. The EPA estimates that there are over 500 million tanks in total; that approximately 1.5 million tanks that store petroleum and hazardous substances are regulated; and that about 400,000 tanks leak (EPA 1988).

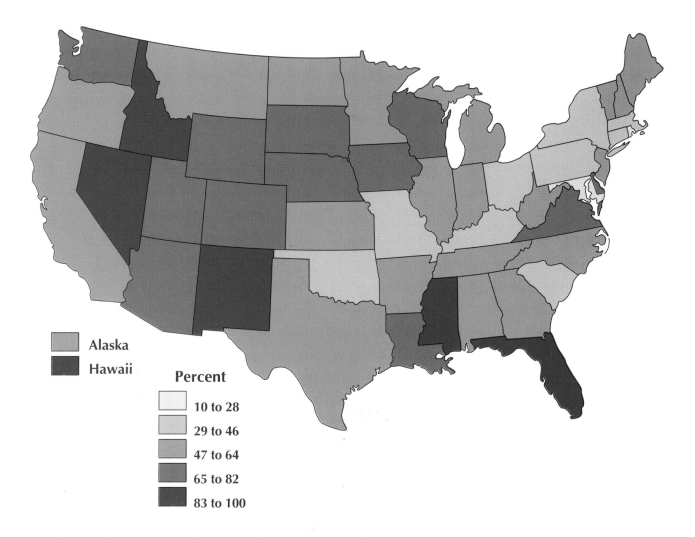

Alaska
Hawaii

Percent

- 10 to 28
- 29 to 46
- 47 to 64
- 65 to 82
- 83 to 100

The EPA also has initiated a survey of pesticides in drinking water, and development of a risk-based strategy for dealing with pesticides in groundwater is under way. Other agencies' activities include U.S. Geological Survey support for studies on groundwater contamination from toxic wastes and various Department of Agriculture programs related to groundwater.

Yet most implementation and enforcement takes place at the state level. Western states traditionally have been concerned with groundwater allocation, and that concern gradually has been spreading to eastern states. But only rather recently has groundwater quality become a prominent issue. Some states—Iowa the outstanding example—have adopted laws much more stringent than the federal programs that guide them. State-level activities include aquifer mapping, description, and classification; development of groundwater quality standards; and development of regulations regarding wells, storage tanks, and nonpoint-source pollution.

Figure 9.9. Percent of Population Dependent on Groundwater for Drinking Water.

Source:
EPA, *National Water Quality Inventory: 1986 Report to Congress* (Washington, DC: EPA, 1987), p. 59.

EPA "Sole-Source" Aquifers

Whidbey Island, WA
Camano Island, WA
Spokane Valley/Rathdrum Prairie, WA/ID
Newberg Area, WA
Cross Valley, WA
Cedar Valley/Renton, WA
North Florence/Dunal, OR
Santa Margarita, CA
Fresno County, CA
Southern Oahu, HI
Missoula Valley, MT
Upper Santa Cruz & Avra Altar Basin, AZ
Edwards, TX
Edwards/Austin Area, TX
Southern Hills System, LA/MS
Chicot, LA
St. Joseph System, IN
Bass Island/Catawba Island, OH
Pleasant City, OH
Buried Valley System, OH
OKI/Miami Buried Valley System, OH
Cattaraugus Creek/Sardinia, NY
Cortland/Homer/Preble System, NY
Clinton Street/Ballpark Valley System, NY
Schenectady/Niskayuna, NY
Kings/Queens Counties, NY
Nassau/Suffolk Counties, NY
Block Island, RI
Seven Valleys, PA
Highlands Aquifer System, NY/NJ
Fifteen Basin System, NY/NJ
Upper Rockaway River, NJ
Ridgewood Area, NY/NJ
Buried Valley System, NJ
N.J. Coastal Plain, NJ
Maryland Piedmont, MD
Prospect Hill, VA
Pawcatuck Basin System, RI/CT
Hunt/Annaquatucket/Pettaquamscutt System, RI
Martha's Vineyard, MA
Nantucket Island, MA
Cape Cod, MA
Monhegan Island, ME

SOLE-SOURCE AQUIFERS

Shown on the map are "sole-source aquifers" designated by the EPA between 1984 and mid-1988. The essential conditions for designation are: (1) the aquifer supplies 50 percent or more of an area's drinking water and (2) aquifer contamination would create a significant public health hazard. Federal financial assistance may be withheld from projects that pose threats to sole-source aquifers. The program's effectiveness is limited, however, because aquifer designation must be triggered by local or state petition and because not all projects are eligible for denial of federal financial assistance. Despite these limitations, sole-source designation may serve as a lever for additional state and local controls.

The EPA also has developed a more comprehensive, three-tiered aquifer classification system. Class I waters are highly vulnerable to contamination. Criteria for this class are similar to, but not the same as, the sole-source criteria. All groundwaters not in Class I, but that are or may be used for drinking water or other beneficial uses, are in Class II. Class III waters are not considered potential sources for drinking water and have only limited beneficial use. The classification is site-specific and is meant to aid the EPA in permitting, Superfund site cleanup, and related decisions.

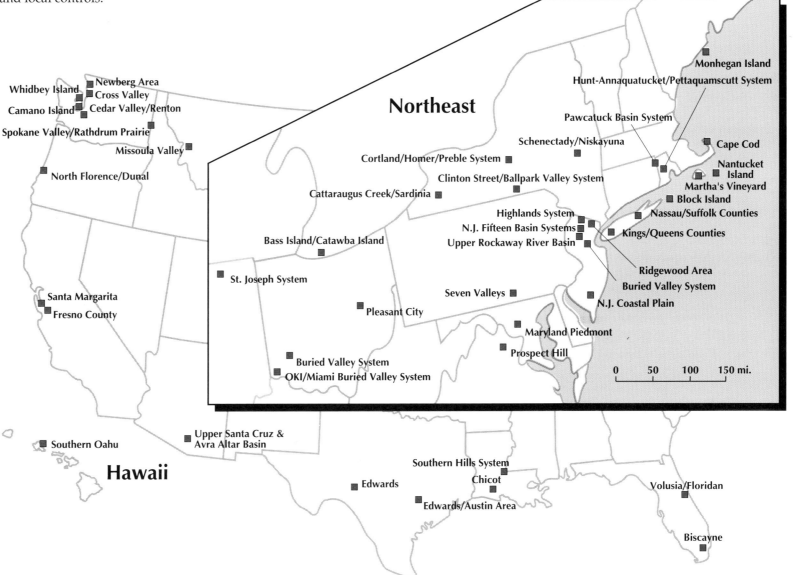

Figure 9.10. Sole-Source Aquifers.

Source: EPA, "Designated Sole Source Aquifers—Nationally" (Washington, DC: EPA, 1988, draft).

WATER QUALITY OF RIVERS AND STREAMS

The Clean Water Act of 1972 decreed that all the nation's surface waters should be in "fishable, swimmable" condition by 1983, and zero discharge of pollutants was to be achieved by 1985. These elusive goals are yet to be met: In 1986, 74 percent of the waters for which states provided data to the EPA were characterized as fishable or swimmable (EPA 1987c).

The accompanying maps portray the condition of rivers and streams (hereafter referred to simply as "rivers") in relation to use categories designated by the states. Most rivers are designated as fishable and/or swimmable, but there are sections designated more stringently for such uses as drinking and food processing as well as a very small proportion of river mileage designated less stringently for such uses as navigation or agriculture. The data are incomplete in that only 40 states provided the EPA with the reports on which this biennial assessment depends. Moreover, there are wide variations in collection and reporting procedures among the states that did cooperate. As indicated in table 9.3, the proportion of river miles for which assessments were completed varies greatly from state to state. In general, the tendency is to concentrate efforts on the more urbanized, industrialized, and heavily used areas. Also, monitoring methodologies vary considerably: Some states have much more extensive networks of monitoring stations than others; and some have used quite sophisticated computer models in making their assessments while others lack such technology. At any rate, considerable professional judgement is exercised in making the final assessments. A further source of state-to-state variability is in the definition of water-use categories such as fishable and swimmable. Although the EPA must approve each state's water-quality standards, there still is considerable scope for variation. In short, the resultant water-quality comparisons are at best crude. Nonetheless, this is the EPA's "standard measure" for water quality.

In total, 74 percent of assessed river miles were found to fully support designated uses. Fecal coliform bacteria were most often cited as a pollutant of concern; and most states also expressed concerns about nutrients, turbidity/suspended solids, biochemical oxygen demand/dissolved oxygen, metals, and toxics. Metals and PCBs were the most commonly reported toxics. The EPA, in attempting cautiously to compare the 1986 results with those obtained in 1984, finds that they are "essentially consistent." An assessment by the Association of State and Interstate Water Pollution Control Administrators (1984), though hampered by data inadequacies and inconsistencies, found that 67 percent of assessed stream miles showed no change over the period. With characteristic optimism, the association concluded that significant progress had been made in controlling point-source pollution—that is, discharges from

Table 9.3. River and Stream Pollution

	Total River Miles	River Miles Assessed	Pollution Sources (relative impacts in percent)[1]					
			Industrial	Municipal	Combined Sewers	Nonpoint Sources	Natural	Other/ Unknown
Alaska	365,000	5,025	85	1	0	12	0	2
Alabama	40,600	12,101	na	na	na	na	na	na
Arkansas	11,438	11,438	na	na	na	na	na	na
Arizona	17,537	1,412	26	10	0	20	44	
California	26,959	9,627	0	16	0	64	0	20
Connecticut	8,400	880	0	40	20	9	0	31
Delaware	579	516	8	6	8	59	19	0
Florida	9,320	6,575	25	29	0	40	2	4
Georgia	20,000	17,000	1	95	0	4	0	0
Idaho	7,310	7,310	2	3	0	78	17	0
Illinois	14,080	3,395	na	na	na	na	na	na
Indiana	na	na	2	56	30	10	0	2
Iowa	18,000	4,365	0	3	0	97	0	0
Kansas	20,600	4,495	7	36	0	25	28	4
Kentucky	40,000	5,683	26	20	0	54	0	0
Louisiana	14,180	2,500	7	26	0	46	17	4
Maine	31,672	31,672	0	100	0	0	0	0
Maryland	9,300	7,440	5	30	0	50	15	0
Massachusetts	10,704	1,676	6	26	16	26	14	12
Michigan	36,350	36,350	na	na	na	na	na	na
Minnesota	na	na	0	42	0	51	0	7
Mississippi	10,274	10,274	5	23	0	72	0	0
Missouri	20,536	20,536	0	1	0	99	0	0
Montana	20,532	19,505	2	3	0	95	0	0
Nebraska	24,000	4,794	1	7	0	92	0	0
New Hampshire	14,544	1,320	12	64	6	18	0	0
New Jersey	6,450	780	25	35	0	35	0	5
New Mexico	3,500	3,500	1	5	0	81	2	11
New York	70,000	3,400	20	40	13	11	0	16
North Carolina	37,359	37,359	12	17	0	71	0	0
Ohio	43,900	6,628	16	36	11	30	0	7
Oregon	90,000	11,855	3	10	0	57	30	0
Pennsylvania	50,000	6,225	7	13	1	71	3	5
Rhode Island	724	724	42	24	0	19	0	15
South Carolina	9,679	2,442	12	60	0	26	0	2
South Dakota	9,937	3,987	4	9	0	34	49	4
Tennessee	19,124	5,748	5	8	0	76	0	11
Texas	80,000	15,942	4	71	0	14	11	0
Vermont	4,863	1,167	11	22	0	50	11	6
Virginia	27,240	4,716	4	34	1	51	10	0
West Virginia	22,819	18,244	4	26	0	64	6	0
Wisconsin	na	na	1	1	0	98	0	0
Wyoming	19,655	19,655	10	4	0	43	43	0

[1] Pollution sources are for those portions of assessed river mileages (see leftmost columns of table) that do not fully support designated uses. River mileages **supporting** designated uses are indicated in figure 9.11.

na indicates that no data or inadequate data were available.

Source: EPA, *National Water Quality Inventory: 1987 Report to Congress* (Washington, DC: EPA, 1987), pp. 19, 21.

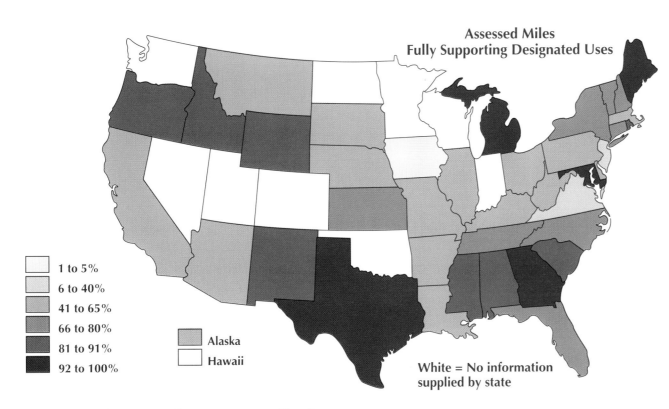

Assessed Miles Fully Supporting Designated Uses

1 to 5%
6 to 40%
41 to 65%
66 to 80%
81 to 91%
92 to 100%

Alaska
Hawaii

White = No information supplied by state

River and Stream Pollution

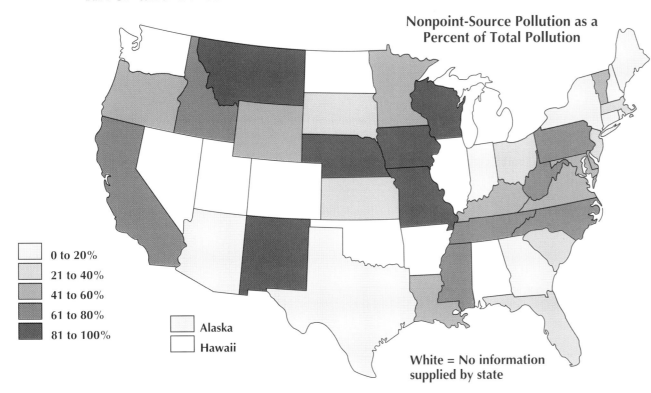

Nonpoint-Source Pollution as a Percent of Total Pollution

0 to 20%
21 to 40%
41 to 60%
61 to 80%
81 to 100%

Alaska
Hawaii

White = No information supplied by state

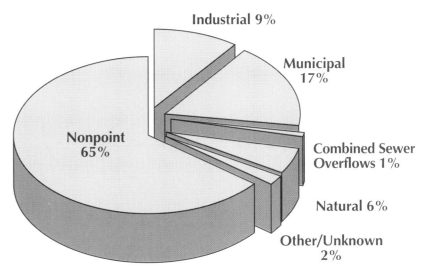

Industrial 9%

Municipal 17%

Combined Sewer Overflows 1%

Nonpoint 65%

Natural 6%

Other/Unknown 2%

Causes for Nonsupport of Designated Uses

such sources as municipal wastewater treatment plants, industrial operations, and combined storm and sanitary sewer system overflows (CSOs).

Nonpoint-source pollution is more difficult to control. Yet it explains an estimated 65 percent of the nonachievement of states' designated uses of assessed waters (see pie chart above). Given the poor quality of the data, the accompanying map must be interpreted with caution. Nonetheless, there seems to be a preponderance of nonpoint-source pollution in several farm-belt states. The major nonpoint sources of pollution are agricultural and urban runoff, construction activities, mining, forestry, land disposal of wastes, and atmospheric deposition. Agriculture is the biggest single source, contributing large quantities of sediment, nitrogen, phosphorous, petroleum, pesticides, and other inorganic chemicals. In the 1970s, the EPA attempted to deal with nonpoint-source pollution by promoting regional land-use planning. Known as "208 planning," after Section 208 of the 1972 Clean Water Act, the program fell far short of early intentions and has been virtually abandoned. Recently, efforts to control nonpoint-source pollution have been reinvigorated—and the Water Quality Act of 1987 requires states to formulate explicit methodologies and time frames for its control.

Figure 9.11. Water Quality of Rivers and Streams.

Source:
EPA, *National Water Quality Inventory: 1986 Report to Congress*, EPA-44/4-87-008 (Washington, DC: EPA, 1987), pp. 19–21.

WATER QUALITY OF LAKES AND RESERVOIRS

Like the assessment for rivers and streams, the assessment of water quality for lakes and reservoirs (hereafter referred to as lakes) is based on reports that states supply to the EPA. The data are plagued by the same limitations and must be interpreted with the same caution.

Seventy-three percent of assessed lake acres were found in 1986 to support their designated uses. In the twenty states that reported on attainment of the Clean Water Act's "fishable, swimmable" goal, an average of 84 percent of lake acres were found to meet the goal. The EPA had requested that states report separately on small lakes (less than 5,000 acres) and large lakes (greater than 5,000 acres). Although most states failed to make this distinction, the EPA believes—based on the information it did receive—that larger lakes are of somewhat better quality than smaller lakes. There is some basis for expecting such a result: Smaller lakes generally have smaller absorptive capacities for the pollutants brought into them through streams and overland flow of water. Another important variable—and one which is not reflected in the assessments—is lake depth: Shallow lakes have less absorptive capacity than deep lakes.

As with rivers and streams, nonpoint-source pollution is cited as the leading cause for nonsupport of designated uses. The Association of State and Interstate Water Pollution Control Administrators (1985) reports that nutrients—mainly nitrogen and phosphorous—are the leading pollutants as measured by number of lake acres affected (59%). Sediment comes in second at 22%, while acidity, salinity, toxics, pathogens, pesticides, and other factors account for much smaller percentages of affected acres. Agriculture is the leading source of pollution. Also significant are urban runoff, modification of drainage and flow regimes, atmospheric deposition, mining, forestry, and land disposal of wastes.

Eutrophication is a natural process whereby water bodies become increasingly rich with such nutrients as nitrogen and phosphorous. When human activities—including urban and agricultural runoff, sewage and septic discharges, industrial emissions, and atmospheric deposition—overenrich lakes with these same nutrients we have a condition known as cultural eutrophication. The abundance of nutrients contributed by such sources as agricultural runoff and septic systems stimulates growth of algae and plants. As this organic matter dies and decomposes, bacterial action consumes large quantities of oxygen. The oxygen depletion affects fish populations, and the weed- and algae-choked waters become undesirable for recreational use.

Eutrophic lakes are those with the greatest organic enrichment. Oligotrophic lakes, by contrast, have low nutrient levels, high dissolved oxygen, and relatively little algae and

Table 9.4. Lake and Reservoir Pollution

	Total Lake Acres	Lake Acres Assessed	Pollution Sources (relative impacts in percent)[1] Industrial	Municipal	Combined Sewers	Nonpoint Sources	Natural	Other/ Unknown
Alaska	12,787,200	27,513	19	0	0	51	0	30
Alabama	505,336	505,336	na	na	na	na	na	na
Arizona	na	na	0	1	0	9	2	88
California	1,397,137	1,279,944	0	0	0	52	48	0
Connecticut	82,900	38,884	0	0	0	32	68	0
Florida	920,320	796,800	8	47	0	43	1	1
Georgia	417,730	417,730	2	96	0	2	0	0
Idaho	362,718	362,718	1	1	0	90	8	0
Illinois	242,359	25,303	10	15	0	75	0	0
Iowa	81,200	73,771	0	0	0	100	0	0
Kansas	na	na	0	0	0	100	0	0
Kentucky	na	na	0	2	0	17	77	4
Louisiana	514,212	467,738	0	0	0	50	0	50
Maine	na	na	0	1	0	88	0	11
Maryland	na	na	2	15	0	65	18	0
Minnesota	na	na	0	1	0	99	0	0
Mississippi	500,000	495,191	0	0	0	100	0	0
Montana	756,450	663,363	na	na	na	na	na	na
Nebraska	198,100	105,840	na	na	na	na	na	na
New Hampshire	na	11	5	0	34	13	37	na
New Jersey	18,923	18,923	0	0	0	100	0	0
New Mexico	5,725	5,725	0	0	0	100	0	0
New York	na	na	2	12	0	75	0	11
North Carolina	na	24	26	0	50	na	0	0
Oregon	500,000	192,000	0	1	0	50	49	0
Rhode Island	na	na	7	39	0	54	0	0
South Carolina	455,000	405,555	45	40	0	15	0	0
South Dakota	na	na	0	0	0	98	2	0
Tennessee	538,603	538,603	0	7	0	89	0	4
Vermont	224,066	224,066	0	6	6	74	4	10
Virginia	na	na	1	1	0	98	0	0
West Virginia	16,158	16,158	0	0	0	100	0	0
Wisconsin	971,000	969,000	0	1	0	90	9	0

[1]Pollution sources are for those portions of assessed lake acres (see leftmost columns of table) that do not fully support designated uses. Lake acres **supporting** designated uses are indicated in figure 9.12.

na indicates that no data or inadequate data were available.

The Great Lakes are excluded.

Source: EPA, *National Water Quality Inventory: 1987 Report to Congress* (Washington, DC: EPA, 1987), pp. 28, 31.

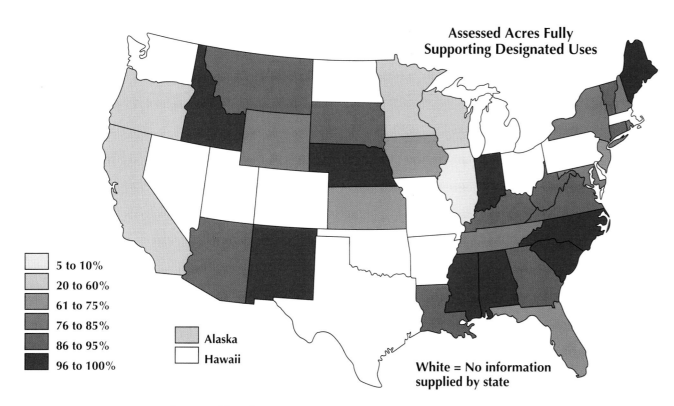

Assessed Acres Fully Supporting Designated Uses

5 to 10%
20 to 60%
61 to 75%
76 to 85%
86 to 95%
96 to 100%

Alaska
Hawaii

White = No information supplied by state

Lake Pollution

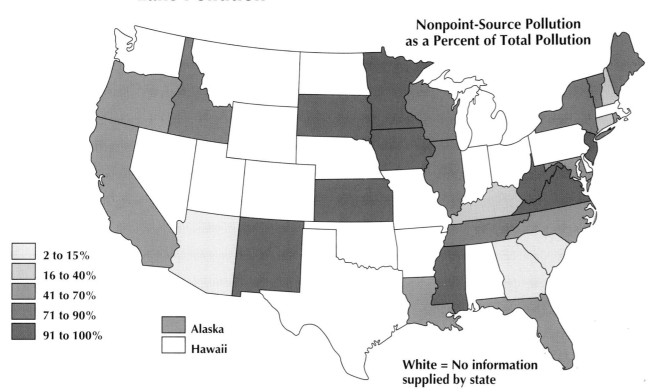

Nonpoint-Source Pollution as a Percent of Total Pollution

2 to 15%
16 to 40%
41 to 70%
71 to 90%
91 to 100%

Alaska
Hawaii

White = No information supplied by state

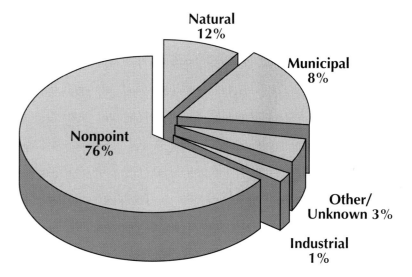

Natural 12%

Municipal 8%

Nonpoint 76%

Other/ Unknown 3%

Industrial 1%

Causes for Nonsupport of Designated Uses

plant growth. Mesotrophic lakes fall somewhere in between in levels of nutrient enrichment and biological productivity. Clearly, eutrophication is a problem (figure 9.14): In the 23 states reporting to EPA on trophic status of lakes, 45 percent of the assessed lakes were reported as eutrophic, 26 percent as mesotrophic, and 12 percent as oligotrophic (status of 17 percent was reported as unknown). Sixty-five percent of the 12,000 lakes assessed in Minnesota were reported to be eutrophic. However, because of the states' tendencies to concentrate assessment efforts on lakes known to have problems, the EPA cautions that the statistics may be biased toward eutrophy.

Some lakes, such as Lake Okeechobee (figure 5.8) and the Great Lakes (figure 9.13), have been the focus of considerable attention. As a result, special initiatives are being taken to clean up these lakes. Other lakes are covered by a variety of state, federal, and local laws and programs. While the Association of State and Interstate Water Pollution Control Administrators reports that progress is being made, considerable obstacles remain to be surmounted. Among them are the problems of atmospheric deposition and its effects on nutrient levels and acidity (see figures 8.9–8.14 and 9.15) and the effects—in many cases poorly understood—of the wide range of toxic contaminants that enter our lakes (see figure 9.13).

Figure 9.12. Water Quality of Lakes and Reservoirs.

Source:
EPA, *National Water Quality Inventory: 1986 Report to Congress,* EPA-440/4-87-008 (Washington, DC: GPO,1987), pp. 28–31.

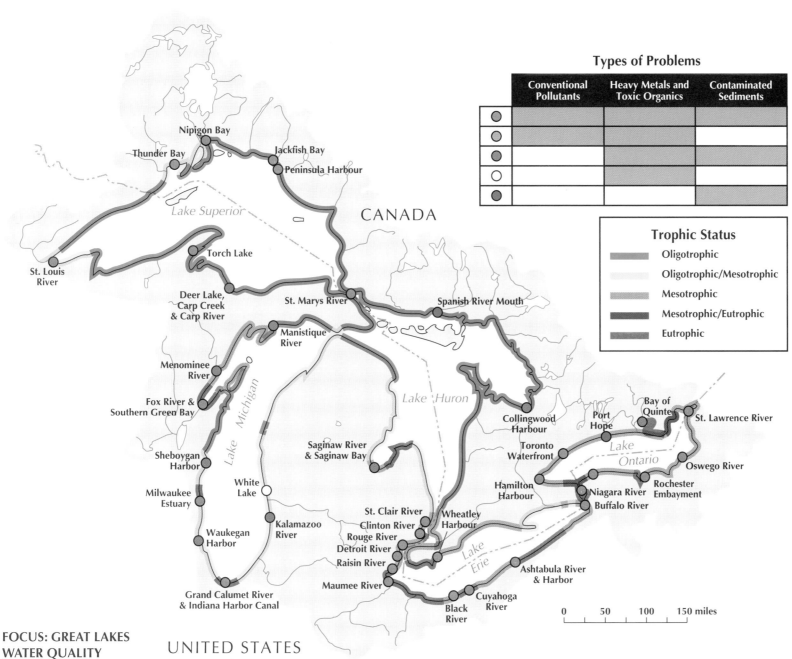

Types of Problems

	Conventional Pollutants	Heavy Metals and Toxic Organics	Contaminated Sediments
◎	▨	▨	▨
◎	▨	▨	
◎		▨	▨
○		▨	
◉			▨

Trophic Status

▬	Oligotrophic
▬	Oligotrophic/Mesotrophic
▬	Mesotrophic
▬	Mesotrophic/Eutrophic
▬	Eutrophic

Figure 9.13. FOCUS: Great Lakes Water Quality.

Source:
Environment Canada, EPA, Brock University, and Northwestern University, *The Great Lakes: An Environmental Atlas and Resource Book* (Chicago and Toronto: Environment Canada, 1987), pp. 34–35.

FOCUS: GREAT LAKES WATER QUALITY

The historic, cultural, economic, and political significance of the Great Lakes rivals their vast physical magnitude. About 37 million people—making up one-quarter of Canada's population and more than one-tenth of the United States' population—live within the Great Lakes' 200,000-square-mile drainage area. The lakes are a key inland transportation route, and along their shores are found huge industrial concentrations. One-quarter of Canada's agricultural production occurs within the Great Lakes Basin. Such intensive development poses enormous threats to the ecological well-being of the world's largest inland freshwater system.

Water quality varies widely among, as well as within, the Great Lakes. Lake Superior is by far the largest and deepest of the five lakes. Its drainage area is also the least populated and industrialized. The largest source of pollutants—local hotspots notwithstanding—is atmospheric deposition. Lake Superior's combination of high assimilative capacity and relatively low pollution input make it oligotrophic—that is, low in ecological productivity and high in dissolved oxygen.

The northern half of Lake Michigan, like Lake Superior, is cold and deep. Its shorelines are for the most part sparsely developed—except in the Green Bay area, which is home to an enormous pulp and paper industry as well as a highly productive fishery. The southern Lake Michigan basin is shallower and thus more vulnerable to pollution. Its western and southern shores are flanked by large urban and industrial complexes, and to the east is found extensive agricultural development. The most concentrated inputs of pollutants occur in the Chicago-Gary, Milwaukee, and Green Bay areas, where eutrophic conditions (overenrichment with nutrients; low dissolved oxygen) prevail.

Northern Lake Huron resembles northern Lake Michigan and Lake Superior: deep, cold waters with relatively few sources of pollution. The southern part of the basin is home to intensive agriculture, the Flint and Saginaw Bay metropolitan areas, and a productive fishery at Saginaw Bay.

Lake Erie is the shallowest and second smallest of the Great Lakes. It also receives the most intensive assaults from human activities. The United States side is heavily urbanized, though there is also a good deal of agriculture, while the Canadian portion of the basin is intensively farmed. Lake Erie's central basin suffers from oxygen depletion during the summer months, and the western section of the lake often is highly eutrophic. In the 1960s, the oxygen depletion, algal blooms, and fish kills had become so severe that many observers were administering Lake Erie's last rites.

Lake Ontario's basin also is quite heavily urbanized and farmed, especially in Canada. Although it is slightly smaller in area than Lake Erie, it is also much deeper. As a result, its overall water quality is much better. Still, there are severe pollution problems in such localities as Hamilton Harbour and the Bay of Quinte.

The connecting rivers between the lower lakes have become major conduits for industrial wastes. Automobile and associated manufacturing operations contribute pollutants to the St. Clair-Detroit River system. The Niagara River is flanked by many active and abandoned hazardous waste sites and receives toxic contaminants from the chemical manufacturing complex in Niagara Falls, New York. The infamous Love Canal (figure 12.5) is but one example of the types of problems experienced in this region.

The United States–Canadian arrangements regarding Great Lakes uses and water quality are often heralded as successful examples of cooperative international resource management. In 1909, the Boundary Waters Treaty was signed, and it created the International Joint Commission (IJC). The IJC, whose authority covers all boundary waters between the two countries, has the ability to approve applications for use, obstruction, and diversion of waters; to study specific problems at the joint request of the two governments; and to arbitrate disputes (the latter power never has been used). A milestone in water-quality management is the Great Lakes Water Quality Agreement of 1972. It established common water-quality objectives, with primary emphasis on reduction of Lake Erie and Ontario phosphorous loadings from municipal wastewater treatment plants. Major new research and monitoring programs also were put into place.

The agreement's first few years brought substantial progress—despite the United States' tardiness in meeting its obligations. Mainly because of upgraded wastewater treatment and limits on phosphorous in detergents, nutrient discharges were lowered and eutrophication became less widespread and severe. At the same time, however, new concerns were being raised. A study of the upper lakes called for phosphorous objectives for Lakes Huron, Michigan, and Superior. The PLUARG (Pollution from Land Use Activities Reference Group) study affirmed that nonpoint pollution from agricultural, urban, and atmospheric sources was indeed significant. Furthermore, attention was being called to a rapidly growing list of toxic contaminants that includes metals, PCBs, mercury, mirex, DDT, dieldrin, aldrin, lindane, dioxin, toxaphene, and volatile organic compounds. The "areas of concern," highlighted on the map, are assessed annually by the IJC. While progress has been made in controlling bacterial pollution and cultural eutrophication, almost all the sites have significant toxics problems.

A key feature of the second Great Lakes Water Quality Agreement, signed in 1978, is its ecosystem perspective, whereby the entire basin is viewed as an interconnected physical, biological, and chemical system. The agreement calls for new basin-wide phosphorous targets (which subsequently have been adopted but not achieved) and confronts toxics issues head-on—in theory calling for zero discharge of persistent toxics. In practice, comprehensive "remedial action plans" have been developed for each of the "areas of concern" shown on the map. In 1985, the governors and premiers of Great Lakes states and provinces signed the Great Lakes Charter, affirming their commitment to regional cooperation. The 1986 Toxic Substances Control Agreement also calls for cooperative efforts and emphasizes environmental and public health over economic concerns. Among the most prominent emerging issues identified by the IJC are persistent toxics, biotechnology, waste management, enforcement and monitoring, corporate policies, institutional arrangements, and public concerns.

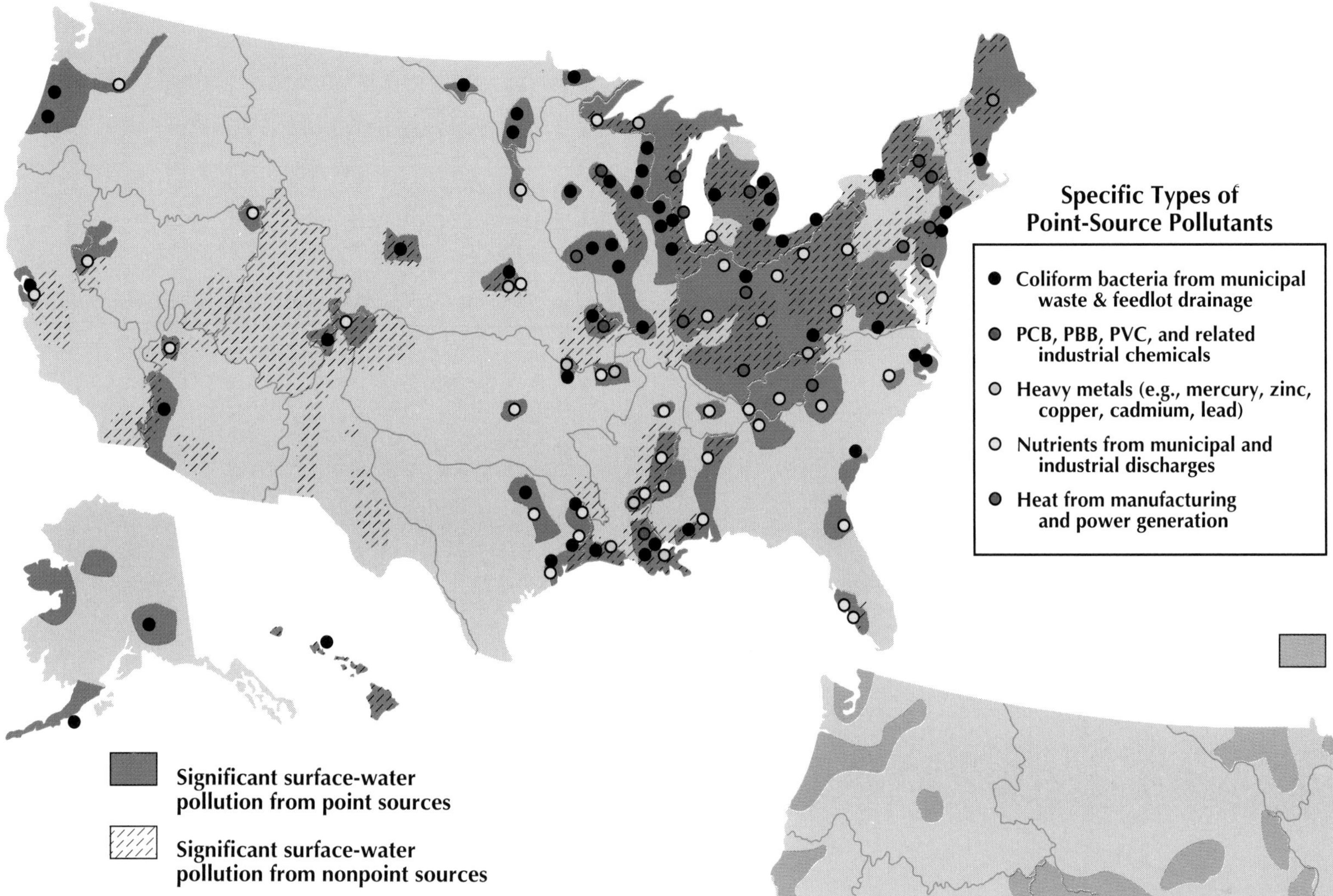

Specific Types of Point-Source Pollutants

- ● Coliform bacteria from municipal waste & feedlot drainage
- ● PCB, PBB, PVC, and related industrial chemicals
- ◒ Heavy metals (e.g., mercury, zinc, copper, cadmium, lead)
- ○ Nutrients from municipal and industrial discharges
- ◐ Heat from manufacturing and power generation

■ Significant surface-water pollution from point sources

▨ Significant surface-water pollution from nonpoint sources

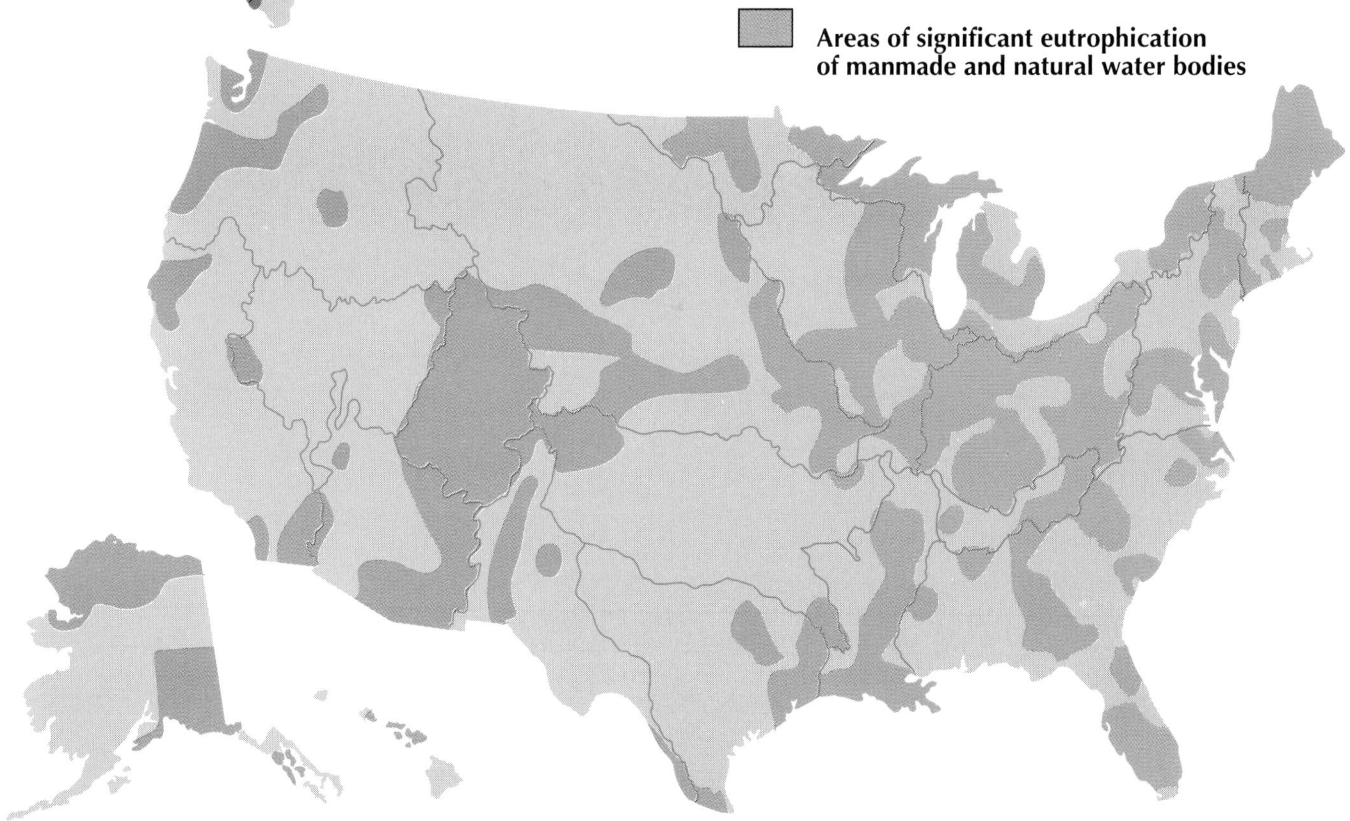

Areas of significant eutrophication of manmade and natural water bodies

Figure 9.14. Surface Water Overview.

Boundaries represent U.S. Geological Survey Water Resource Regions, which are named in figure 9.1.

Source:
U.S. Water Resources Council, *The Nation's Water Resources, 1975–2000*, vol. 1, *Summary* (Washington, DC: GPO, 1979), pp. 61–63.

SURFACE WATER OVERVIEW

The interagency Water Resources Council—created in 1965 and disbanded by President Reagan in 1981—was responsible for periodically assessing the nation's water quantity and quality. Since no comparable effort has succeeded its 1978 assessment, that work continues to serve as a national benchmark.

Figure 9.14 shows areas with significant and widespread pollution problems. Unshaded areas also have serious problems, but they are not so widespread. Point-source discharges from municipal treatment plants, industries, and feedlots contain bacteria, nutrients, metals, and a wide variety of organic and inorganic chemical compounds. Although these sources are regulated by permit, there are many problems with inadequate treatment technologies, malfunctioning facilities, and inadequate enforcement of permit conditions. Agricultural runoff is the leading nonpoint source of pollution, contributing pesticides and other agricultural chemicals. Mine drainage is a major problem in Appalachia, and irrigation return flow is a significant source of dissolved solids over large areas of the West.

Only limited interpretive data are available regarding national and regional trends in surface-water quality. An analysis of 1974–1981 trends using data from two national monitoring networks (Smith, Alexander, and Wolman 1987a, 1987b) reveals that fecal bacteria decreased noticeably. Declines in fecal streptococcus bacteria were especially evident along much of the Gulf Coast and in the central Mississippi and Columbia river basins, while decreases in both fecal streptococcus and coliform bacteria were common in the Arkansas-Red River region and along the Atlantic Coast. Evidence suggests that the widespread declines in fecal bacteria may have resulted from improvements in municipal wastewater treatment.

Decreases in dissolved oxygen deficits (DODs) exceeded increases by a factor of approximately three-to-two. Greatest numbers of decreases occurred in the New England, Middle Atlantic, Ohio, and upper and lower Mississippi regions, while increases were most common in the Southeast and far Northwest. These trends, however, are not particularly pronounced, and there is only weak evidence linking DOD decreases with reductions in biological-oxygen demand produced by treatment of municipal and industrial effluents.

Increases in nitrate concentrations outnumbered decreases by about four-to-one. The greatest numbers of increases occurred east of the Mississippi and in the far Northwest. Major sources of nitrogen include municipal and industrial waste, agricultural runoff, and atmospheric deposition which may be particularly important in the Midwest and Middle Atlantic regions. Overall, it seems that nitrate trends are best explained by trends in nonpoint discharges.

Increases and decreases in total phosphorous were nearly equal. The Great Lakes and upper Mississippi regions had the most frequent decreases, while increases were relatively common in the Southeast. Although nonpoint sources predominate nationally, the decreases in the Great Lakes region probably have resulted, at least in part, from reductions in point-source loads.

Nationally, the numbers of stations with increasing and decreasing concentrations of suspended sediments were nearly equal. Decreases occurred in certain tributaries to the Mississippi, while increases were common in the Arkansas, Red, Columbia, lower Mississippi, and Ohio river basins. Sediment increases were associated with high cropland erosion rates but not with high erosion rates on forest, pasture, or rangeland.

Frequent and widespread increases in chloride concentrations occurred between 1974 and 1981. Greatest numbers of increases were witnessed in the Missouri, Mississippi, Ohio, and Atlantic Coast regions. Decreases were common only in the Great Lakes and lower Colorado regions. While some of the increases may be attributed to increased use of highway salt, overall regional trends were not significantly associated with chloride levels in municipal wastewater and irrigation-return flow.

Decreases in dissolved lead concentrations far exceeded increases. Decreases were most common on the east and west coasts and in tributaries to the Missouri and Mississippi rivers. Increases were concentrated along the Texas-Gulf Coast and the lower Mississippi Basin. The obvious explanation is the sharp decline in the lead content of gasoline. Analysis of dissolved lead concentrations between 1974 and 1985 revealed declines at two-thirds of the sites; half of those were statistically significant. Very widespread declines between 1979 and 1980 apparently correspond with peak declines in leaded gasoline consumption (Alexander and Smith 1988).

Dissolved arsenic concentrations increased at most stations, especially in the Great Lakes, Ohio, and Pacific Northwest regions. Specific sources include fossil fuel combustion, herbicides, detergents, and fertilizers. There is some evidence that atmospheric deposition is the leading contributor.

Trends in dissolved cadmium were rather similar to those for arsenic. Increases were most frequent in the Great Lakes, upper Mississippi, and Texas-Gulf regions, while decreases occurred in a number of basins in the Great Plains region. As with arsenic, there is evidence that atmospheric deposition is a significant explanatory factor. Sources of cadmium include fossil fuel combustion, phosphate fertilizer use, primary metals manufacturing, and solid waste disposal. Concentrations of other trace metals—chromium, iron, manganese, mercury, selenium, and zinc—exhibited few significant trends or clear spatial patterns.

An analysis of pesticide concentrations between 1975 and 1980 (Gilliom et al. 1985) revealed relatively few reportable concentrations. Water and bed-sediment samples from approximately 170 stations were analyzed for eleven chlorinated-hydrocarbon insecticides, seven organophosphate insecticides, and four herbicides. The greatest percentages of detections in water samples were for fairly persistent yet soluble compounds: atrazine, simazine, diazinon, and lindane. For bed-sediment samples, persistent-hydrophobic insecticides had the highest levels of detection: DDE, DDD, dieldrin, chlordane, and DDT. Significant spatial correlations between detection and use on farms were found only for atrazine in water and for DDE, DDD, DDT, and chlordane in bed sediments. Erratic but gradual overall declines were found for organochlorine insecticides in water and bed sediments, but no clear trends were discovered for organophosphate insecticides or herbicides.

FOCUS: THE CHESAPEAKE BAY CLEANUP

With great fanfare, the Chesapeake Bay Agreement was signed in December 1983. It was the capstone to a seven-year study (EPA 1983a) that identified the following major environmental problems: nutrient enrichment; toxic chemical contamination; increasing numbers of areas with low dissolved oxygen; declines in striped bass, submerged aquatic vegetation, and other estuarine life; and substantial population growth and land-use change in the basin. Maryland, Virginia, Pennsylvania, the District of Columbia, and the United States Environmental Protection Agency are the parties to the voluntary agreement. It calls for state and federal actions—cooperative in spirit if mostly separate in implementation—to reduce pollutant loadings, improve habitat, and restore finfish and shellfish populations. A second agreement, signed in 1987, sets specific objectives and timetables for the cleanup program. Specifically it seeks a 40 percent reduction in total nitrogen and phosphorous inputs by the year 2000.

The Chesapeake Bay is the largest estuary in the contiguous United States. It draws on a 64,000-square-mile drainage area that is home to 12 million people. Approximately 59 percent of the basin is covered with forests; 26 percent is crop and pastureland; and 15 percent is in urban and residential use (EPA 1983a). Urbanized land—contributing pollutants in the form of wastewater and runoff—has nearly doubled in area since 1950, and parts of the basin continue to experience very rapid growth. The region's steel, leather, plastics, and chemical industries are major sources of metals and organic compounds. Although the amount of land in agriculture has decreased 24 percent since 1950, remaining lands are being farmed more intensively. Increased adoption of conservation tillage has reduced erosion and runoff, but it is usually accompanied by greater use of herbicides and pesticides (see figure 4.6).

The bay itself is an important commercial shipping route and a key part of the Atlantic Intracoastal Waterway. The estuary is among the world's most productive. It supports a $1-billion-per-year finfish and shellfish industry—this despite recent declines in the harvests of oysters, clams, striped bass, shad, perch, herring, and other species. The bay and associated wetlands also serve as migration routes and wintering grounds for a wide variety of migratory waterfowl. The Chesapeake is highly valued for recreational fishing, sail and powerboating, and simply for its ambience.

Figure 9.15 provides a general overview of the bay's condition; more detailed information is being collected under the Chesapeake Bay Program (see Chesapeake Executive Council 1989). Although it is still too early to comprehensively assess the program's progress, there is little question that the Chesapeake remains an endangered estuary. Phosphorous and nitrogen concentrations tend to be highest in the upper reaches of the bay's mainstem and in its tributaries, where little dilution has yet taken place. Point sources—primarily wastewater treatment plants—are the largest contributors of phosphorous, while nonpoint sources such as agricultural and urban runoff are the greatest sources of nitrogen. The Susquehanna is apparently the major freshwater contributor of these nutrients, though a recent estimate by the Environmental Defense Fund (Fisher et al. 1988) attributes one-quarter of the Bay's nitrogen load to atmospheric deposition.

Eutrophication, the result of overenrichment with nutrients (mainly nitrogen and phosphorous—see figures 9.12 and

Table 9.5. Chesapeake Bay Environmental Quality Classification Scheme

Quality Classification	Level of General Characteristics	Nutrient Enrichment	Total Toxicity Index[1]	Total Nitrogen (mg/L^{-1})	Phosphorous (mg/L^{-1})
Healthy	supports maximum diversity of benthic resources, submerged aquatic vegetation, and fisheries	very low	1	<0.6	<0.8
Fair	moderate resource diversity, reduction of submerged aquatic vegetation, and occasionally high chlorophyll	moderate	1–10	0.6–1.0	0.08–0.14
Fair to Poor	significant reduction in resource diversity, loss of submerged aquatic vegetation, chlorophyll often high, occasional red tide or blue-green algal blooms	high	11–20	1.1–1.8	0.15–0.20
Poor	limited pollution-tolerant resources, massive red tides or blue-green algal blooms	significant	>20	>1.8	>0.20

[1]Toxicity index indicates relative toxicity of trace metals present in bottom sediments.

Source: H. W. Wells, Jr., S. J. Katsanos, and F. H. Flanigan, *Chesapeake Bay: A Framework for Action* (Washington, DC: EPA, 1983), p. 33.

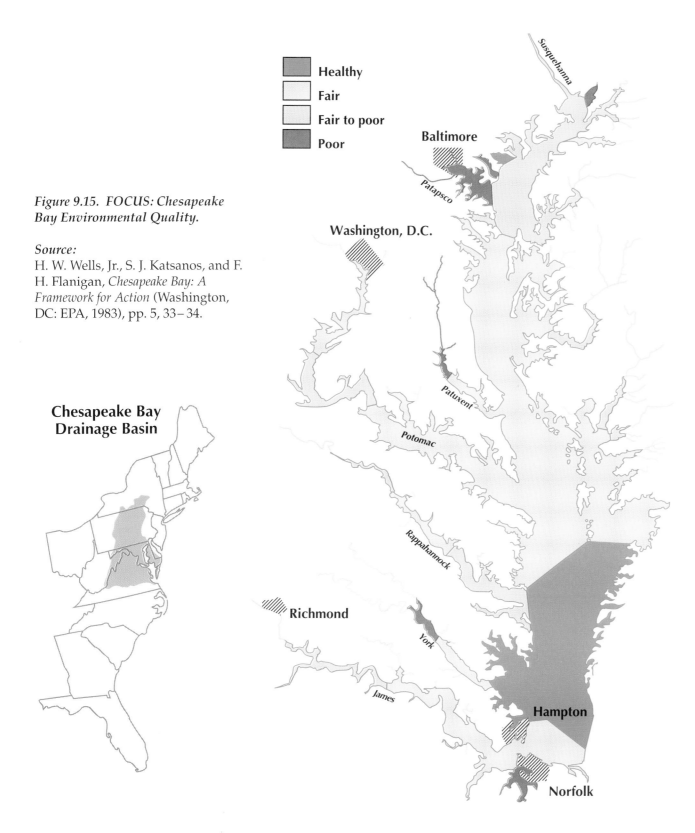

Figure 9.15. FOCUS: Chesapeake Bay Environmental Quality.

Source:
H. W. Wells, Jr., S. J. Katsanos, and F. H. Flanigan, *Chesapeake Bay: A Framework for Action* (Washington, DC: EPA, 1983), pp. 5, 33–34.

Healthy
Fair
Fair to poor
Poor

Baltimore

Susquehanna

Patapsco

Washington, D.C.

Patuxent

Chesapeake Bay Drainage Basin

Potomac

Rappahannock

Richmond

York

James

Hampton

Norfolk

9.14), results in depressed levels of dissolved oxygen in the Chesapeake's bottom waters. The problem is most acute during the summer months. It is most severe in the "deep trough" region which stretches from the Baltimore area south to the Potomac River, and also in a stretch of the Potomac River. Other smaller areas also suffer from severe or moderate oxygen depletion.

Suspended sediments may block out sunlight and reduce photosynthesis. They also absorb or bind nutrients, metals, and organic chemicals. The Susquehanna contributes 40 percent of the sediment load to the bay (but 50 percent of freshwater), the Potomac 33 percent, and the James 16 percent. Turbidity—the total amount of suspended solids in the water column—is highest in the upper portion of the bay and tends to gradually decrease southward. Although the evidence is inconclusive, studies of toxic chemical concentrations in bottom sediments and organisms seem to indicate an increase since the late 1970s. The highest concentrations of several contaminants have been detected in Baltimore Harbor.

Submerged aquatic vegetation (SAV)—important in the aquatic food chain, in controlling shore erosion, in regulating nutrient concentrations and sedimentation, and as habitat—has declined markedly since the 1960s. The losses are attributed principally to human activities, especially cultural eutrophication and sedimentation. There are signs of recent stabilization and limited improvements.

Federal and state improvement projects include finfish and shellfish management, shoreline stabilization, sediment control, wetland restoration, wastewater treatment plant construction and improvements, agricultural conservation programs, improved methods for disposing of dredged materials (Army Corps of Engineers), and a variety of research, education, and training activities. Pennsylvania, a major contributor of agricultural pollutants, is offering financial and technical incentives to encourage farmers to adopt "best management practices"—but it has not been as aggressive in its actions as some of the "downstream states." The District of Columbia banned phosphates, modified its sewage pretreatment program, and is seeking to reduce combined sewer overflows. Virginia is promoting best management practices to reduce urban as well as agricultural runoff and is upgrading sewage treatment. Maryland has put special emphasis on land-use planning. Maryland's Critical Areas Commission reviews and approves local land-use plans for lands adjacent to the bay and its major tributaries. These and other state and federal initiatives are funded by state allocations, federal agency budgets, and special Chesapeake Bay funds provided by the Water Quality Act of 1987. In addition, several private organizations have come to the bay's defense.

MUNICIPAL WASTEWATER TREATMENT

Since 1972 the federal government has subsidized wastewater treatment plant construction to the tune of about $40 billion. The basic goal is to achieve at least secondary treatment at all public facilities. By the EPA's definition, this means 85 percent removal of "conventional" pollutants (solids and organic matter). Primary treatment, by contrast, removes only large solids, whereas tertiary treatment removes additional nitrogen, phosphorous, and other organic chemicals. Although the federal goal has yet to be met, enormous progress has been made since the 1960s. In 1985, however, the basic federal funding share decreased from 75 percent to 55 percent, and during the 1990s it is to be phased out entirely.

Under the Clean Water Act of 1972, the EPA and the states conduct biennial "Needs Surveys" to determine funding needs for meeting the Clean Water Act goals (see EPA 1987a). When and if documented needs for the year 2005 are met (facilities are designed to serve the needs of the projected population in 2005), the "less than secondary" slice of the accompanying pie chart would be virtually eliminated and the portion of the population not served by a collection system would drop to 13.4 percent.

Represented on the map are needs that may qualify for federal assistance. While there does seem to be greater per capita need in the East than in the West, any such spatial generalizations are tempered by the considerable variation in the ways that states documented their needs. Total design-year needs for the United States are $76.2 billion, needs for the 1986 population were $60.3 billion, and the needs that are directly eligible for federal assistance are $36.2 billion.

Given the importance placed on municipal wastewater treatment and also the likelihood that not all identified needs will be addressed (let alone actually arise), it is worthwhile to consider our progress to date. Clearly, pollutant discharges into rivers and streams have decreased since 1972. Yet according to the General Accounting Office (GAO 1986), the available evidence is not methodologically adequate to support any firm conclusions about effects on water quality. Furthermore, questions have been raised—especially by environmental organizations—about the wisdom of handling wastes by first discharging them into water, then later removing them.

Figure 9.16. Municipal Wastewater Treatment.

Source:
EPA, *1986 Needs Survey Report to Congress: Assessment of Needed Publicly Owned Wastewater Treatment Facilities in the United States*, EPA 430/9-87-001 (Washington, DC: GPO, 1987), p. 10.

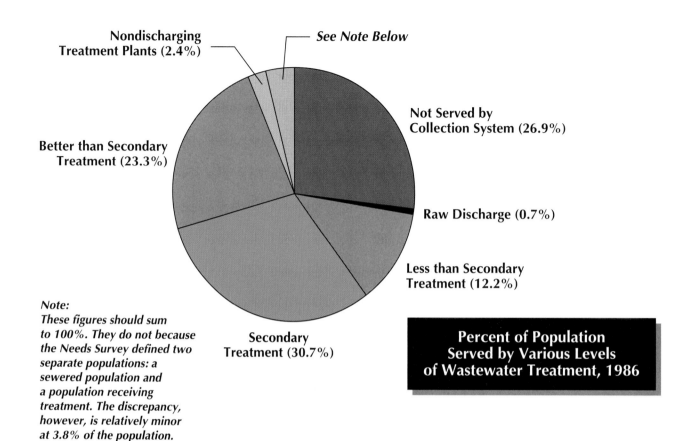

Note:
These figures should sum to 100%. They do not because the Needs Survey defined two separate populations: a sewered population and a population receiving treatment. The discrepancy, however, is relatively minor at 3.8% of the population.

Percent of Population Served by Various Levels of Wastewater Treatment, 1986

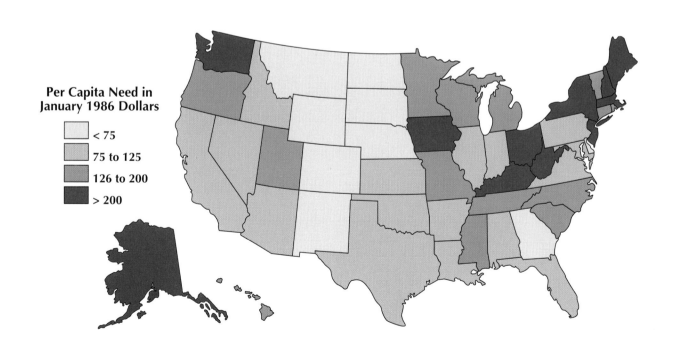

Per Capita Need in January 1986 Dollars

< 75
75 to 125
126 to 200
> 200

Table 9.6. Federal Primary and Secondary Drinking Water Standards

Primary Standards

Contaminant	Health Effects	Milligrams per Liter	Sources
Microbiological			
Total coliforms (coliform bacterial, fecal coliform, streptococcal, and other bacteria)	Not necessarily disease-producing themselves, but coliforms can be indicators of organisms that cause assorted gastroenteric infections, dysentery, hepatitis, typhoid fever, cholera, and others; also interferes with disinfection process	1 per /100 ml	Human/animal fecal matter
Turbidity	Interferes with disinfection	-5 tu (turbidity units)	Erosion, runoff, discharges
Inorganic chemicals			
Arsenic	Dermal/nervous system toxicity effects	0.05	Geological, pesticide residues, industrial waste, smelting
Barium	Circulatory system effects	1	
Cadmium	Kidney effects	0.01	Geological, mining, and smelting
Chromium	Liver/kidney effects	0.05	
Lead	Central/peripheral nervous system damage; kidney effects; highly toxic to infants/pregnant women	0.05	Leaches from lead pipe and lead-based solder pipe joints
Mercury	Central nervous system disorders; kidney effects	0.002	Used in manufacture of paint, paper, vinyl chloride; used in fungicides; geological
Nitrate	Methemoglobinemia (blue-baby syndrome)	10	Fertilizer, sewage, feedlots, geological
Selenium	Gastrointestinal effects	0.01	Geological, mining
Silver	Skin discoloration (Argyria)	0.05	Geological, mining
Fluoride	Skeletal damage	4	Geological, additive to drinking water, toothpaste, foods processed with fluoridated water
Organic chemicals			
Endrin	Nervous system/kidney effects	0.0002	Insecticide used on cotton, small grains, orchards (cancelled)
Lindane	Nervous system/liver effects	0.004	Insecticide used on seed, soil treatments, foliage application, wood protection
Methoxychlor	Nervous system/kidney effects	0.1	Insecticide used on fruit trees, vegetables
2,4-D	Liver/kidney effects	0.1	Herbicide used to control broadleaf weeds in agriculture; used on forests, range, pastures, aquatic environments
2,4,5-TP Silvex	Liver/kidney effects	0.01	Herbicide; cancelled in 1964
Toxaphene	Cancer risk	0.005	Insecticide used on cotton, corn, grain
Benzene	Cancer	0.005	Fuel (leaking tanks); solvent commonly used in manufacture of industrial chemicals, pharmaceuticals, pesticides, paints, plastics
Carbon tetrachloride	Possible cancer	0.005	Common in cleaning agents, industrial wastes from manufacture of coolants
p-Dichlorobenzene	Possible cancer	0.075	Used in insecticides, mothballs, air deodorizers
1,2-Dichloroethane	Possible cancer	0.005	Used in manufacture of insecticides, gasoline
1,1-Dichloroethylene	Liver/kidney effects	0.007	Used in manufacture of plastics, dyes, perfumes, paints, synethetic organic compounds
1,1,1-Trichloroethane	Nervous system effects	0.2	Used in manufacture of food wrappings, synthetic fibers
Trichloroethylene (TCE)	Possible cancer	0.005	Waste from disposal of dry cleaning materials/manufacture of pesticides, paints, waxes, varnishes, paint stripper, metal degreaser
Vinyl chloride	Cancer risk	0.002	Polyvinylchloride pipes (PVC)/solvents used to join them, industrial wastes from manufacture of plastics and synthetic rubber
Total trihalomethanes (TTHM) (chloroform, bromoform, bromodi chloromethane, dibromochloro-methane)	Cancer risk	.10	Primarily formed when surface water containing organic matter is treated with chlorine
Radionuclides			
Gross alpha particle activity	Cancer	15 pCi/l (picocuries per liter)	Radioactive waste, uranium deposits
Gross beta particle activity	Cancer	4 millirems/yr	Radioactive waste, uranium deposits
Radium 226 & 228 (total)	Bone cancer	5 pCi/l	Radioactive waste, geological

Secondary Standards

Contaminant	Criteria/Effects
pH	Water should not be too acidic or too basic; must fall between pH 6.5 and 8.5
Chloride	Taste and corrosion of pipes
Copper	Taste and staining of porcelain
Foaming agents	Aesthetic
Sulfate	Taste and laxative effects
Total dissolved solids (hardness)	Taste and possible relation between low hardness and cardiovascular disease; also an indicator of corrosivity (related to lead levels in water); can damage plumbing and limit effectiveness of soaps and detergents
Zinc	Taste
Fluoride	Dental fluorosis (a brownish discoloration of the teeth)
Color	Aesthetic
Corrosivity	Aesthetic and health-related (corrosive water can leach pipe materials, such as lead, into the drinking water)
Iron	Taste
Manganese	Taste
Odor	Aesthetic

Source:
League of Women Voters Education Fund, *Safety on Tap: A Citizen's Drinking Water Handbook* (Washington, DC: League of Women Voters Education Fund, 1987).

ENFORCEMENT OF THE SAFE DRINKING WATER ACT

Before the 1960s, water treatment generally consisted of bacterial and viral control. In 1962, the U.S. Public Health Service established limits for organic chemicals. The 1974 Safe Drinking Water Act (SDWA) directed the EPA to set national, health-based standards for drinking water. Principal implementation and enforcement rests with states and localities.

Primary standards—or "Maximum Contaminant Levels" (MCLs)—apply to substances capable of threatening human health. The MCL, which is enforceable, is meant to be as low as possible, based on economic feasibility. For carcinogens, the EPA's goal is zero. Nonenforceable secondary standards provide guidelines for taste, odor, and other aesthetic considerations.

While states have the ability to set their own stricter standards, it is the EPA that establishes the national baseline. The agency has moved slowly in implementing new standards for the wide array of synthetic organic, inorganic, volatile organic, and radiological contaminants found in the nation's waters. In response, Congress enacted the SDWA Amendments of 1986 that—among other things—require the EPA to set primary standards for eighty-three additional contaminants by June 1989. The agency is already well behind schedule, although in May 1989 it had proposed new standards for thirty-eight substances.

Although the maps do not differentiate among duration, type, and severity of violation—and although the quality of the data is compromised by differences in recording and reporting procedures—the message remains clear: Enforcement of the Safe Drinking Water Act lags well behind intent of Congress. The National Wildlife Federation (Dean 1988) found that violations in 1987 affected about 40 million people. Formal enforcement actions were brought in only 2.5 percent of the cases where violations were reported. Public notices of the violations, required by the SDWA, were issued in only 6 percent of the cases. The EPA focuses its enforcement activities on "significant noncompliers" (SNCs)—but they account for only 3.9 percent of all violators. Even for the SNCs alone, the EPA's 1989 enforcement target is only 20 percent.

Figure 9.17. Enforcement of the Safe Drinking Water Act.

Sources:
N. L. Dean, *Danger on Tap: The Government's Failure to Enforce the Federal Safe Drinking Water Act* (Washington, DC: National Wildlife Federation, 1988), pp. B-1 to B-14.

Bureau of the Census, *Statistical Abstract of the United States: 1988* (Washington, DC: GPO, 1987).

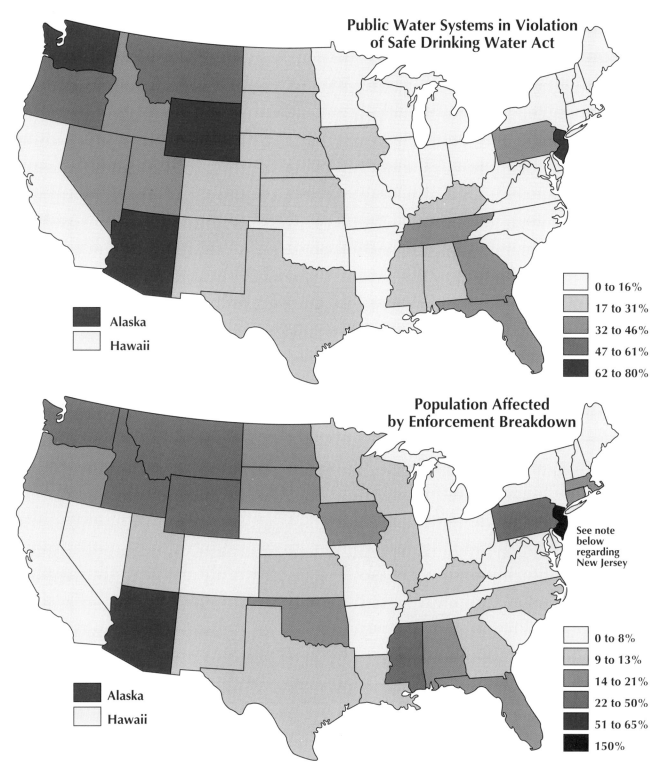

Public Water Systems in Violation of Safe Drinking Water Act

- 0 to 16%
- 17 to 31%
- 32 to 46%
- 47 to 61%
- 62 to 80%

Alaska
Hawaii

Population Affected by Enforcement Breakdown

See note below regarding New Jersey

- 0 to 8%
- 9 to 13%
- 14 to 21%
- 22 to 50%
- 51 to 65%
- 150%

Alaska
Hawaii

The population served by New Jersey community and noncommunity water systems is greater than New Jersey's population since some of these systems serve communities outside the state. This is reflected in a rate that exceeds 100%.

SUMMARY

The federal Clean Water Act, which deals largely with surface water, is administered and enforced principally by the states. The many federal laws and programs that affect groundwater quality also rely heavily on state initiative (figure 9.9). In the West at least, water supply management is to a great degree guided, even determined, by federal policies and actions. Once again, however, specific laws and policies regarding water conservation are principally state and local responsibilities. An analysis by Hrezo et al. (1986) identifies only the Delaware River Basin Commission (New York, Pennsylvania, New Jersey, Delaware) and seven states—Arkansas, California, Connecticut, Delaware, Florida, Minnesota, and New Jersey—as having comprehensive water shortage management plans. Twenty-seven states have drought provisions that represent emergency responses rather than planning efforts.

The Clean Water Act (CWA) relies basically on two types of controls: water quality standards and technology-based controls. Technology-based controls were incorporated directly into the CWA of 1972. For municipal wastewater treatment plants, secondary treatment is the prevailing standard (figure 9.16). Industrial dischargers were to be using "Best Practicable Technology" (BPT) initially by 1977; the Water Quality Act of 1987 extended that deadline to March 31, 1989. BPT is approximately equivalent to the average performance of the best facilities in an industrial category. Ultimately, dischargers are required to use "Best Available Technology Economically Achievable" for toxic pollutants and "Best Conventional Technology Economically Achievable" for conventional pollutants (total suspended pollutants, biochemical oxygen demand, pH, fecal coliform bacteria, oil and grease). The EPA promulgates binding guidelines for various pollutants and industrial categories, with stringent standards applied to new industrial facilities. The initial deadline for adoption of Best Available Technology was 1984; it was extended to March 31, 1989.

As noted in figures 9.11 and 9.12, the Clean Water Act of 1972 established a national "fishable, swimmable" goal for the nation's surface waters. While the states are to maintain consistency with this national goal, they have a good deal of flexibility in setting their own water-quality standards. These standards, which must be approved by the EPA, generally incorporate some combination of narrative criteria (verbal description), numerical criteria (precise concentrations specified), and/or toxicity-based criteria (generally based on lethal doses to organisms). Most states have numerical standards for such conventional pollutants as dissolved oxygen, pH, and temperature. The Water Quality Act of 1987 requires states to adopt criteria for priority toxic pollutants based on a list developed by the EPA.

In its effort to restore waterways that remain substandard, the 1987 act attempts to reinvigorate the water-quality-based approach (as opposed to technology-based controls). In other words, cost or unavailability of specific technologies cannot be the tail that wags the water-quality dog. The states are responsible for ensuring that their technology-based controls are adequate to meet the specific "designated uses" established for their waters. In general, existing water of very high quality is not to be degraded; that is, it is not acceptable to pollute it up to some use-based standard.

Both technology-based and water-quality-based effluent standards are implemented through a national permitting system. Either the state or the EPA issues wastewater discharge permits under the National Pollutant Discharge Elimination System (NPDES). A particular concern is with industrial and commercial wastewater that enters municipal treatment plants. This wastewater may increase the costs and decrease the effectiveness of municipal treatment. Under the EPA's National Pretreatment Program, federal, state, and local governments are developing programs to regulate such wastes. While substantial proportions of the hazardous metals and organic chemicals that they contain are removed by municipal treatment processes, biodegradation, and release to the air, perhaps 10 to 20 percent may be released to surface waters untreated.

The Clean Water Act establishes the rights of citizens to participate in permitting, monitoring, and enforcement. In some parts of the country, these provisions have been used frequently. But free citizen assistance notwithstanding, most water-quality programs are insufficiently staffed to deal with the enormous and complex problems they face.

Along with the Clean Water Act, many other laws, policies, and programs directly affect water quality and quantity. The Safe Drinking Water Act is discussed on page 114. Other major federal laws include the Resource Conservation and Recovery Act, which regulates the generation, transportation, and disposal of hazardous and solid wastes (chapters 11 and 12); the Toxic Substances Control Act, which regulates the manufacture, use, and disposal of chemicals that pose risks to human health and the environment (chapter 12); the "Superfund" legislation, which provides for emergency actions and long-term cleanup of abandoned hazardous waste sites (chapter 12); the Federal Insecticide, Fungicide and Rodenticide Act, which regulates the development, manufacture, use, and sale of pesticides (chapter 12); and the Surface Mining Control and Reclamation Act, which regulates surface mining and provides for restoration of active and abandoned mine sites (chapter 13). Many additional federal statutes less directly affect surface and groundwater, and thousands of state laws, policies, and programs in many cases go well beyond what is required by federal law.

Los Angeles basin from Mt. Wilson Observatory, 1 hour
exposure by Ferdinand Ellerman, 1908.

Kitt Peak National Observatory, Photo File No. 11781

Los Angeles basin from Mt. Wilson Observatory, 5 min.
exposure by John Bedke, 1971.

Kitt Peak National Observatory, Photo File No. 11780

Excess noise and light can be much more than just minor annoyances. Noise, for example, can be very painful: It has long been used as a method of torture. Regular exposure to high levels of noise may induce short-term or long-term hearing loss and contribute to—perhaps even cause—emotional distress and mental disorders. The EPA has estimated that as many as half of all Americans are regularly exposed to noise that interferes with sleep or communications. Noise also interferes with recreational pursuits—witness the recent controversies regarding sight-seeing flights over the Grand Canyon—and may adversely affect wildlife.

Countless local laws and ordinances seek, often with very limited success, to control the discomfort and distress associated with noise. Perhaps the most effective local regulations are indirect ones: the land-use controls, such as zoning and subdivision regulations, that spatially sort people by socioeconomic class. Wealthy suburban neighborhoods, for example, generally are much quieter than poor urban neighborhoods, which, in turn, usually are noisier than higher-income sections of the city.

The state and federal governments also are involved with noise control. Indeed, such centrally produced items as vehicles, airplanes, and appliances are difficult to control effectively at anything less than the federal level. The Noise Pollution Control Act of 1972 directed the EPA to develop noise exposure criteria, regulate major sources of noise, and require noise-related product labeling. In 1977, the EPA released a national noise plan, which, among other things, called for limits on average daily exposure of 65 dB in the short term and 55 dB in the long term (see figure 10.1). The EPA's obligations were further defined by the Quiet Communities Act of 1978, which required the agency to provide financial and technical assistance to states and localities. The Occupational Safety and Health Administration (OSHA) develops and enforces workplace noise standards, while the Federal Aviation Administration regulates aviation noise.

The Departments of Transportation, Defense, and Housing and Urban Development also have noise-related responsibilities.

Federal action to reduce noise has fallen far short of the legislative intent of the early and mid-1970s. Clearly, noise reduction has not been a priority in the 1980s; in fact, the EPA's Office of Noise Abatement was disbanded in 1982. Still, the agency has promulgated noise regulations for trains, railroads, heavy trucks, portable air compressors, and certain other equipment. Enforcement of these regulations, however, has been almost nonexistent. Likewise, only minimal product labeling has occurred. In the workplace, OSHA has set an eight-hour exposure standard of 90 dBA (see figure 10.1). Although 85 dBA is more widely accepted as a minimum safe level, industry concerns thus far have kept the standard at 90. Workplace noise is controlled through equipment engineering and design and use of protective earguards and other devices.

Light pollution has received even less attention than noise. Yet our alteration of normal cycles of daylight and darkness may affect plant photosynthesis and development, interfere with activity patterns of nocturnal animals, and impede sleep and other human activities. The physiological and psychological effects of long summer days and winter nights at high latitudes have been studied, as have human activity patterns in caves and other experimental settings. Research into the various effects of indoor illumination—especially fluorescent lighting—also has been conducted. Yet, except for the protestations of astronomers who wish to maintain dark skies and citizens who demand well-lit highways and public areas, political activity has been minimal.

Not enough information is readily available to produce synoptic national or regional maps of noise or light conditions. Nor would it necessarily be appropriate to try to do so. The approach adopted in this chapter is use of case studies to illustrate two key issues: airport noise (and related local concerns) and conflicts between urban illumination and astronomical observation.

Los Angeles Basin
from Mount Wilson Observatory.
Top: *1908 F. Ellerman.*
Bottom: *1971 J. Bedke.*
Kitt Peak National Observatory Photo File.

Sound Levels and Human Responses*		
Common Sounds	**dB**	**Effect**
Carrier Deck Air Raid Siren	140	Painfully Loud
	130	
Jet Takeoff Auto Horn (3 feet)	120	Maximum Vocal Effort
Pile Driver	110	
Garbage Truck	100	
City Traffic	90	Very Annoying Hearing Damage (8 hours)
Alarm Clock	80	Annoying
Noisy Restaurant Man's Voice (3 feet)	70	Telephone Use Difficult
Air Conditioning Unit (20 feet)	60	Intrusive
Light Traffic (100 feet)	50	Quiet
Bedroom Quiet Office	40	
Library Soft Whisper (15 feet)	30	Very Quiet
Broadcasting Studio	20	
	10	Just Audible
	0	Hearing Begins

*To the ear, each 10 dB increase seems twice as loud.
Note that 70 dB is the point where hearing damage begins.

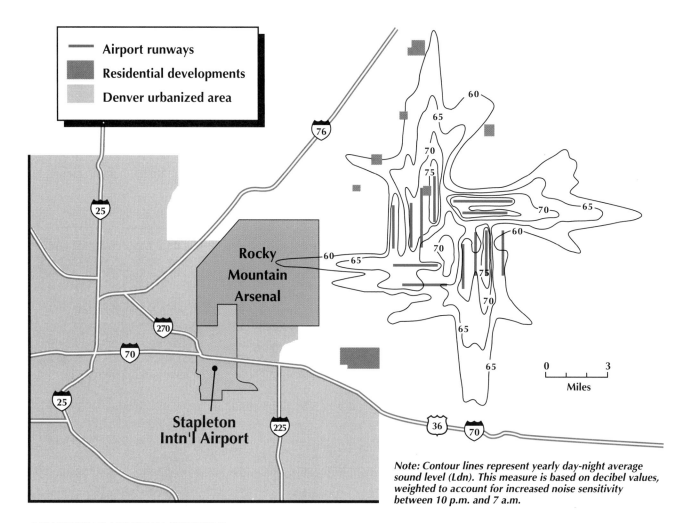

— Airport runways
■ Residential developments
▨ Denver urbanized area

Note: Contour lines represent yearly day-night average sound level (Ldn). This measure is based on decibel values, weighted to account for increased noise sensitivity between 10 p.m. and 7 a.m.

MEASURING NOISE IN DECIBELS

The decibel (dB) is a measure of loudness, which is a function of the frequency (pitch) and intensity (power) of sound. The decibel scale is constructed such that the faintest sound detectable by the human ear is 0 dB. It is a logarithmic scale, meaning that each 10 dB increase corresponds to a tenfold increase in loudness. A 20 dB noise is therefore ten times as loud as a 10 dB noise. Yet to the human ear, the 20 dB noise seems twice as loud. Moreover, loudness is not additive. For example, two pile drivers would not be twice as noisy as one, since there is "masking" of sounds at certain frequencies.

The dBA scale, used to represent noise contours in figure 10.1, assigns greater weight to the sound frequencies to which humans are most sensitive. Leq, or equivalent sound level, is a measure that incorporates variations in sound over a period of time. Ldn, or yearly day-night average sound level, is used in figure 10.2. This measure is weighted to account for increased sensitivity to noise during nighttime hours.

Figure 10.1. Measuring Noise in Decibels.

Source:
EPA, *Noise and Its Measurement*, 1981.

Figure 10.2. FOCUS: Denver's New Airport.

Contours represent noise levels projected for 2020.

Source:
City and County of Denver, *New Denver Airport Environmental Assessment (Draft)*, Exhibit 4.11A, 1988.

FOCUS: DENVER'S NEW AIRPORT

Airports almost invariably act as lightning rods for community concerns about noise and congestion. And since most major jetports are located in or very near densely populated areas, proposals for new or expanded services often face stiff opposition. This is the case not only in United States cities but also in such places as Tokyo, London, and Toronto. Even during the 1950s and 1960s, attempts to site a new jetport in the New York metropolitan area met with failure. Currently, the "Expanded East Coast Plan"—which restructures flight paths for Kennedy, La Guardia, and Newark airports—faces stiff resistance from the many communities that must contend with increased noise. But noise itself is not the only concern; residents are also worried about their property values. Indeed, in response to stiff local opposition to two new airport runways, Dallas-Fort Worth International Airport officials have thought about buying from homeowners the rights to fly over their roofs.

Moreover, recent federal court decisions have affirmed that local governments possess considerable legal latitude for controlling airport noise, and this may lead to more local ordinances that impose restrictions on aircraft size and operation. Already, at least 300 of the nation's airports have some kind of noise-related restrictions in effect.

Against this backdrop, Denver is planning to build a new $2.3 billion airport. Situated 18 miles from downtown Denver, the proposed site would occupy more space than any airport now in operation. Nationally, it is the first such proposal to gain sufficient public approval in some fifteen years. In May 1987, after about fifteen years of studies and controversy over various proposals, citizens in neighboring Adams County approved Denver's annexation of a 45-square-mile plot of land. Fifty-six percent voted in favor; 44 percent against. The proposal enjoys the near-unanimous support of local political and business leaders. But it still faces opposition from citizens concerned about financial, noise, and traffic impacts; and also from United and Continental Airlines, which currently control 85 percent of the Denver market and would be asked (via taxes or fees) to help pay for the new facility.

Noise considerations—along with such factors as economic costs and effects, ground accessibility, air-quality impacts (the County of Denver violates EPA ambient air-quality standards for ozone and carbon monoxide), construction impacts, and social effects—weighed heavily in the analysis of potential sites for a new airport. Of special note is the site alternative that involved expansion of Stapleton Airport into the Rocky Mountain Arsenal. The Arsenal—subject of recent national notoriety because of toxic chemical contamination—would have had to have been "detoxified" to make that option viable.

Noise impacts played prominently in the analysis of alternative runway configurations for the preferred airport site. Figure 10.2 shows noise projections for the year 2020. As noted above, Ldn is a noise measure that takes into account increased sensitivity between the hours of 10:00 P.M. and 7:00 A.M. Noise events occurring during that period are assigned a 10 dBA penalty. The critical values for analytical purposes are Ldn 60 and 65. According to the Federal Aviation Administration's land-use compatibility guidelines, Ldn values above 65 are incompatible with residential uses.

Areas exposed to Ldn 75 or greater are to be contained within airport property. An agreement between Denver and Adams County stipulates that the City and County of Denver may acquire residential development rights—and thereby control or prohibit future development—in areas within the Ldn 65 contour and in certain areas that will be exposed to levels between Ldn 60 and 65. Furthermore, the City and County of Denver have the right to buy out and relocate those residents currently living within the Ldn 60 contours projected for 1995 and 2020 (table 10.1). Additional mitigation measures are to be negotiated among the governments.

In large part, the new Denver airport owes its high chances of success to the availability of a large parcel of sparsely populated land readily accessible to the city. Adams County voters were sufficiently lured by the prospect of commercial and industrial development—perhaps including high-technology enterprises—to approve Denver's annexation of the land. So in an age of powerful local resistance to most such large-scale intrusions, the Denver airport may turn out to be the exception that proves the rule.

Table 10.1. Comparative Noise Impacts

| | Stapleton International Airport | | New Airport | |
	Existing Airport	No Action (1995)	Phase I (1995)	Long Range (2020)
Population				
Ldn 65	14,666	14,389	559	384
Ldn 60	33,341	33,122	675	634
Churches				
Ldn 60	18	19	0	0
Schools				
Ldn 60	8	9	0	0

Denver intends to purchase residences within the 65 Ldn contour.

Source: City and County of Denver, *New Denver Airport: Draft Environmental Impact Assessment, Executive Summary,* 1988.

FOCUS: LIGHT POLLUTION AND OBSERVATORIES

If there is such a thing as an anti-light pollution interest group, its members are astronomers. Their concerns arise basically from the scarcity of sites where the atmosphere is optically suitable for large telescopes. Stable air, minimal water vapor, lack of cloudiness, and freedom from pollution are the necessary conditions for observation of very faint astronomical objects. Few places in the world approach such ideal conditions—and most of those that do are threatened. Moreover—contrary to some thinking—radio and space-based telescopes are not about to replace ground-based optical observations. One threat to dark, clear skies is smog; "light trespass" is another. Light trespass may be defined as the presence of light where it is not wanted or needed, where it disturbs someone. Astronomers are distressed by urban glow because each doubling of the skyglow from urban lights reduces by half the light-gathering ability of telescopes.

The map shows light pollution in California and Arizona, based on 1970 population figures. Areas inside the circles represent exposure to artificial illumination greater than that experienced at Mount Palomar observatory in 1970. In order to avoid this level of light interference, an observatory would have to be placed at least 120 miles away from a population center of

Figure 10.3. FOCUS: Light Pollution and Observatories in the Southwest.

*Note: the units used to define the circles are fractions of **magnitudes.** Magnitudes are units of measurement used to describe the brightness of stars (or in this case urban lights). The lower the magnitude, the greater the brightness. Each unit of magnitude is 2.512 times brighter than the next higher unit of magnitude.*

Source:
M. F. Walker, "Light Pollution in California and Arizona," *Publications of the Astronomical Society of the Pacific* 85 (1973): 508–519.

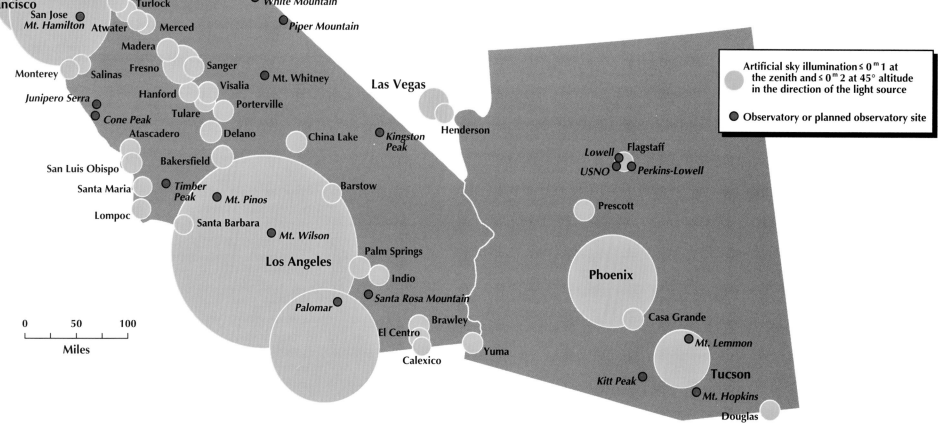

4 million; for a city of 1 million, the minimum distance would be about 70 miles. For smaller settlements of 10,000 to 70,000 population, 10-mile-diameter circles were used to represent regions of excessive artificial illumination. Of course, these numbers were derived in the early 1970s; today's circles would have larger diameters. Moreover, actual skyglow is affected by an area's specific mix of lighting types, as well as by local topographic and atmospheric conditions. Thus the circles are only approximate, meant to define the areas within which it would not be practical to situate an observatory. It can be seen, however, that numerous observatories are already within these regions—many of them having been built during a time when the threat from urban skyglow seemed inconsequential.

A similar study done only for California and based on 1960 census data (Walker 1970)—the "California Site Survey"—used projected 1985 populations to estimate the sizes of the circles for that year. As it turns out, the study's assumptions were much too conservative: Population has increased by about 1 percent per year, while the brightness of outdoor lighting has increased on average 20 percent per year (Hendry 1984)! Our seemingly insatiable demands for more and brighter lighting thus make the current situation considerably more dire than that portrayed on the map.

There are ways to reduce the impact of light. The amount of useful light may be increased—and wasted light decreased—by careful placement of lights, use of shielding to direct the light to where it is needed, use of timers and dimmers, nighttime lighting restrictions or curfews, and consideration to observatory needs in the development of land-use plans. These measures may also help conserve energy. Probably the most effective way of reducing skyglow is to use low-pressure sodium (LPS) lighting. The spectral characteristics of LPS lighting (it is monochromatic) are such that it produces very little glow. Moreover, its operating costs are lower than those for high-pressure sodium or mercury lighting (Crawford 1985). For this reason, some towns and cities have embraced it—at least for certain types of uses. In Europe, LPS is widely accepted. Its major drawback is that it does not permit color differentiation. All light is emitted at one color; that is, in one part of the spectrum. This is the very reason that adverse skyglow is minimized. By contrast, mercury and high-pressure sodium lights emit broadly over the spectrum—and as a result cause much more degradation of the observable sky. Where color is not so important—for example, in parking lots and on highways—LPS lighting may indeed be practical and cost-effective.

In a number of places, astronomers (along with economic factors) have persuaded local governments to adopt outdoor lighting control ordinances. Flagstaff, Arizona, was the first community to do so—in 1958. At 11:00 P.M., when Flagstaff shuts off its illuminated signs, skyglow decreases by 30 percent (Hendry 1984). Flagstaff's original regulations still serve as a model for other municipalities. In 1973, the Arizona legislature passed enabling legislation for city and county lighting ordinances. Scottsdale, Phoenix, and Tucson are among the cities that currently have lighting control ordinances; many counties do as well. In California, San Diego and San Jose are among the cities that have taken action to reduce skyglow. But, as many astronomers are well aware, municipal officials often are reluctant to overhaul familiar practices and procedures.

Most observatories now in operation have suffered to at least some degree from the effects of artificial illumination. A principal effect of skyglow is reduction of a telescope's "effective aperture." The following effective apertures are reported by Crawford (1985).

Observatory	Aperture (inches)	
	Actual	Effective
Kitt Peak (southwest of Tucson)	157	144
Mount Palomar (northeast of San Diego)	200	139
Lick Observatory (near San Jose)	120	68
Mount Wilson (near Los Angeles)	100	45

The Mount Wilson Observatory is now closed, and Palomar's viability is threatened. Eastern observatories, already handicapped by climate, are in many cases seriously impaired not only by skyglow, but also by haze and other forms of pollution. Indeed, Wesleyan University's (Middletown, Connecticut) Van Bleck Observatory has recorded a 20-fold increase in sky brightness. Equipment formerly located at Case Western Reserve University in Cleveland has been relocated to Kitt Peak; Case Western maintains some smaller telescopes for teaching purposes only. Nor are these problems limited to the United States: Israel, East Germany, Czechoslovakia, Spain, Denmark, Sweden, and Great Britain are among the countries grappling with light pollution issues.

Yet, as noted above, there are some encouraging signs. Former Arizona governor Bruce Babbit, for example, has called for a "dark zone" declaration for the entire state. Activist astronomers, individually and through such organizations as the International Dark Sky Association and the American Astronomical Society's Committee on Light Pollution and Radio Interference, are increasingly becoming involved in education and public relations activities. They are developing slide shows, videos, mailings, and press releases, and are working with city councils, schools, and the media. Undoubtedly, they will continue to be vigilant in their efforts to protect the nighttime skies.

Solid waste may be defined and quantified in many ways. Yet regardless of the criteria chosen, the United States almost invariably ranks as the world's largest per capita, as well as total, producer. The Conservation Foundation (1987) estimates that at least 50,000 pounds of waste are produced per person each year, about 26,000 pounds of which are solid waste. But their definition is a very broad one. Solid waste includes not only municipal and industrial wastes (which account for only a small proportion), but also mining wastes, agricultural and silvicultural wastes, demolition debris, and a variety of sludges. Many of these are difficult to quantify, and perhaps some should not be regarded as waste at all. Examples might include crop residues that are incorporated into the soil and forestry residues left to decompose. This chapter focuses on municipal wastes (including wastewater treatment sludge); some of the other types of wastes are discussed in other chapters.

America's municipal waste-generation rate is about 3.6 pounds per person per day (Franklin Associates 1988): by most accounts, the highest in the world. Municipal waste, quite simply, is defined as the material discarded by households, institutions, and commercial establishments. Sludge from municipal wastewater treatment plants generally is not included in this definition; nor is demolition debris. Neither, in theory, are industrial wastes—but in fact they do to varying degrees make their way into the municipal waste stream. Hazardous wastes, defined by the federal Resource Conservation and Recovery Act (RCRA) as "corrosive, ignitable, reactive, or toxic," or capable of posing substantial threats to human health and the environment (however these may be assessed), are to be treated separately from other wastes. Nevertheless, some industrial hazardous wastes—along with most household hazardous wastes—make their way into the municipal waste stream. In short, the definition of municipal waste is not so simple as it might at first seem.

Solid-waste management was a key issue for environmental activists of the early and mid-1970s. Individuals were urged to produce less waste. Recycling programs, most of them local and voluntary, proliferated—but the national recycling rate remained very low. Open dumping and burning of wastes were virtually eliminated; improved sanitary landfill practices were instituted in most areas; and incinerator emissions were reduced. Incinerators that produce useful energy and steam also began to come on line, and the energy crises of the 1970s helped to sustain interest in such technologies into the 1980s.

The RCRA, adopted in 1976, encouraged the development of state solid-waste management plans; provided for research, development, and demonstration projects; and authorized the EPA to develop regulatory criteria for sanitary landfills, call for the closure or upgrading of dumps, and promulgate guidelines for federal procurement of recycled materials. But during the late 1970s and early 1980s, concerns about toxic and hazardous materials seemed to eclipse much of the national concern about "ordinary" solid wastes. Many local recycling initiatives suffered, and states were essentially left on their own to develop RCRA-authorized solid-waste management plans. In 1986, about 10 percent of the municipal solid waste stream was recycled, and energy was recovered from 6 percent (Franklin Associates 1988).

By the mid-1980s, solid-waste issues had reemerged in force. Driven by shortages of landfill space and strong community opposition to siting of new landfills and incineration facilities, many states and communities now require recycling. Ten states have passed returnable beverage container laws, and several states have enacted packaging legislation. The EPA's (1989) "Agenda for Action" calls for 25 percent source reduction/recycling by 1992. The most critical issue in this regard probably will not be lack of will to recycle but rather the assurance of adequate markets for the rapidly increasing volumes of materials. Only very recently have the federal and state governments begun meaningfully to address this issue.

Circle Line Tour Boat Passing Islip Garbage Barge in Bay Ride Flats Section of New York Harbor.
New York Newsday *Photo.*
Ken Sawchuk.

Disposition of Solid Waste Stream

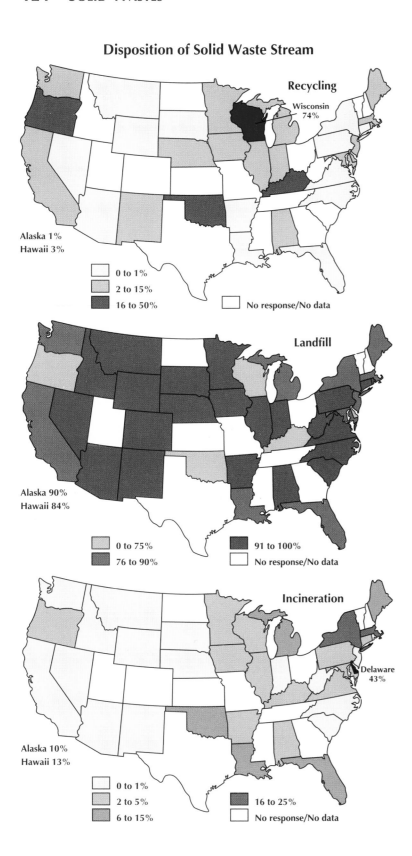

MUNICIPAL SOLID WASTE

As mentioned above, only about 10 percent of municipal solid waste is recycled, and energy is recovered from 6 percent. Nearly all the remainder goes to sanitary landfills—though significant open dumping still does occur in some parts of the country. These figures are in general agreement with those of the Council on State Governments (Brown, Dresser-Gagnon, and Gona 1987)—and this is about the best that can be expected, given their inherent imprecision. That survey puts the national landfill rate at 85 percent and the recycling and incineration rates at 7 and 5 percent, respectively. In response to the council's queries, many of the states indicated that they had plans to recycle and/or incinerate substantial proportions of their municipal wastes.

Figure 11.3 shows that paper and paperboard together constitute the largest share of the municipal discards (35.6 percent in 1986). Other key components include glass (8.4 percent), metals (8.9 percent), plastics (7.3 percent), food wastes (8.9 percent), and yard wastes (20.1 percent). Containers and packaging—mostly made of paper and glass—are the source of 34 percent of the municipal waste; nondurable goods—such as newspapers, books, and magazines—account for 26 percent; and durable goods make up 12 percent. Plastics, and to a lesser degree paper, have shown a general upward trend over the past couple decades. The waste stream of the year 2000 is forecast to be 20 percent larger than that of 1986 (after materials recovery has taken place), with energy recovery from 19 percent of all discarded waste (6.8 percent in 1986). The composition of the waste stream is expected to resemble quite closely its current makeup, although continued proportional growth is forecast for paper and plastics (Franklin Associates 1988).

Currently the recovery rate for paper is between 22 and 28 percent. Glass, which constitutes about 8 percent of the municipal solid waste stream, is recovered at the rate of 10 to 15 percent. The glass industry is expanding its recycling capacity. Iron and steel, which together account for 7 percent of the waste stream, are recovered at rates of 4 to 20 percent. Aluminum—which accounts for only 1 percent of the waste stream, mostly in the form of cans—is a recycling success story. Current recovery is 55 percent, and technology and economic factors could support a higher rate. Only about 1 percent of plastics gets recycled—but the plastics industry is putting a great deal of effort into developing recyclable plastics. Recovery rates for at least some types of plastics probably will rise substantially. Yard and food wastes, though they make up about one-quarter of the waste stream (OTA 1989), generally are not recycled. However, increasing numbers of communities are likely to turn to composting in coming years.

Figure 11.1. Disposition of Municipal Solid Waste Stream.

Note: **Wisconsin** included agricultural, sewage sludge, and other waste streams in its municipal waste calculations.

Source:
R. S. Brown, S. Dresser-Gagnon, and D. Gona, "Solid Waste Programs in the States," *Journal of Resource Management and Technology* 15(3) (1987): 137–138.

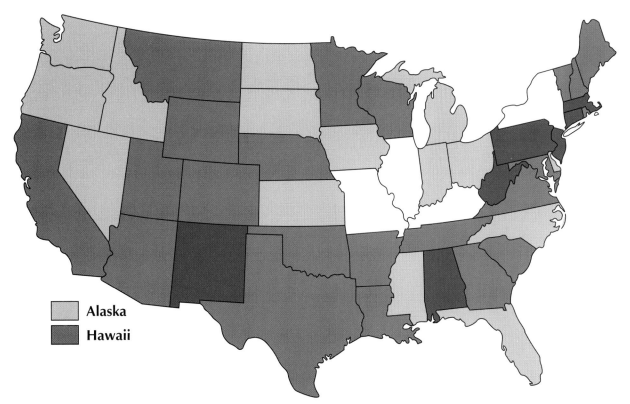

Landfill Capacity Status

☐ No response

▨ No capacity problems

▨ Capacity problems in certain regions or state-wide

▨ Severe statewide capacity problems

☐ Alaska

▨ Hawaii

Figure 11.2. Landfill Capacity Status.

Source:
EPA, *Census of State and Territorial Subtitle D Non-Hazardous Waste Programs*, EPA/530-SW-86-039 (Washington, DC: EPA, 1986).

Figure 11.3. Municipal Waste Stream Composition, 1960–1986.

*Note: Illustration depicts waste stream composition **after** materials recovery.*

Source:
Franklin Associates, Ltd., *Characterization of Muncipal Solid Waste in the United States, 1960 to 2000 (Update 1988)*, EPA/530-SW-88-033 (Washington, DC: EPA, 1988), p. 6.

LANDFILL CAPACITY STATUS

The vast bulk of municipal waste is landfilled. Even if recycling and/or incineration become widespread, ash and other non-recyclable residuals will probably continue to go to landfills. But the required amounts of landfill space could be greatly reduced through composting and resource recovery.

Figure 11.2 indicates that many states face landfill capacity shortages; indeed, in some states and localities the situation is at or near crisis proportions. EPA (1988b) survey results show that 45 percent of municipal solid-waste landfills have five or fewer years of remaining life; only 20 percent have more than 20 years of capacity. In many areas, local resistance has made new or expanded landfills a virtual impossibility.

States and localities have sought to improve landfill management by requiring use of liners, collection and treatment of leachate, control of runoff, venting and/or recovery of methane gas, and restrictions on permitted refuse. Moreover, greater efforts are being made to monitor water and air quality, enforce relevant laws, and provide response plans for such emergencies as fires and equipment failures. The EPA, as of late 1989, is in the process of finalizing minimum national criteria for landfill design and operation, operator certification, restrictions on certain wastes, and education and technical assistance.

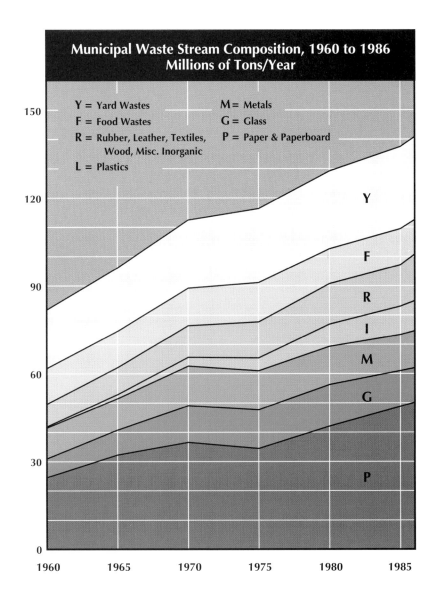

Municipal Waste Stream Composition, 1960 to 1986
Millions of Tons/Year

Y = Yard Wastes
F = Food Wastes
R = Rubber, Leather, Textiles, Wood, Misc. Inorganic
L = Plastics
M = Metals
G = Glass
P = Paper & Paperboard

STATE RECYCLING AND BOTTLE LAWS

Several states have put into place mandatory, comprehensive recycling programs. Oregon's 1983 law is generally considered the first. It requires all communities to provide collection centers for recyclable materials, and those with 4,000 or more residents must collect separated materials at the curbside. Wisconsin's 1984 act is similar: It specifies the number of collection centers that must be provided, based on each community's population. Certain types of landfills also must offer collection services. Wisconsin has established goals for source reduction, recycling, composting, and energy recovery.

Rhode Island's 1986 law was the first to mandate source separation of recyclable materials. Municipalities are responsible for implementing the requirement. Commercial establishments also are required to develop source reduction and separation programs. Rhode Island's initial goal is a minimum recycling rate of 15 percent. Refuse-to-energy plants also have a prominent part in the state's solid waste plans.

New Jersey's 1987 law calls for source separation and also requires that leaves—a substantial component of the municipal waste stream—be composted. Counties are assigned prime responsibility for the act's implementation. The goal is a 25-percent recycling rate. Connecticut passed a recycling and source separation act in 1988. The goal, to be implemented on a regional basis, is 25 percent recycling by 1991. Indeed, after 1991, no "designated recyclable material" is to be accepted at any landfill or waste-to-energy facility. Connecticut also has enacted a packaging act; a task force is seeking ways to reduce packaging waste.

Massachusetts's Solid Waste Act of 1987 provides for five regional recycling programs, each to be serviced by a major "materials recovery facility." The state builds these centers, sets up a statewide marketing cooperative, and provides technical and financial assistance to communities; it is then up to the municipalities to pass their own recycling ordinances and to deliver materials to the regional centers. The goal is 25 percent recycling by 1995. Governor Michael Dukakis, over considerable local opposition, has supported the associated development of refuse-to-energy facilities.

New York State's 1988 law requires municipal-level source separation and recycling "where economically feasible" by 1992. New York will also require that products be labeled to indicate whether they are recyclable, reusable, or made from recycled materials. The goal is ambitious: 50 percent recycling or reduction of waste by 1997. Maryland also passed a recycling act in 1988. Counties with more than 150,000 residents are to develop plans to recycle 20 percent of their waste streams by July 1990; counties with fewer than 150,000 people are to recycle 15 percent (but provisions are made for relaxing these numbers in certain

cases). In counties that do not have an approved recycling plan by 1992, or that have not met their recycling targets by 1994, permits for new construction may—with the state government's endorsement—be withheld.

Florida's 1988 law requires counties and cities with more than 50,000 people to have recycling programs by mid-1989. Special provisions are made for separate collection of construction and demolition debris, tires, lead-acid batteries (through a redemption system), used oil, white goods, and yard wastes. The overall recycling goal is 30 percent by 1994. One aspect of Florida's law points up potential conflicts between recycling and incineration: If a county's recycling goals are proven to have an adverse effect on financial arrangements for waste-to-energy projects, then the state may reduce or alter the goals for that county. Indeed, this kind of threat to recycling programs is precisely one of the reasons that so many environmental organizations oppose incineration.

Pennsylvania's 1988 legislation requires communities with populations greater than 10,000 to begin recycling by September 1990 and those with 5,000 to 10,000 people to begin by September 1991. The law also shifts primary solid-waste planning responsibilities from the communities to the counties. The overall goal is a recycling rate of 25 percent by 1997. Illinois also enacted legislation in 1988. Counties with more than 100,000 people, and also the City of Chicago, are required to develop 20-year waste management plans. Illinois' goal is a 25-percent rate of recycling by 1993.

Statewide recycling programs have taken root in states—including Oregon, Florida, and Wisconsin—that have been especially active in regulating land use and managing growth. They have also flourished in some of the heavily populated northeastern states where landfill space is at a premium. These general trends are likely to continue as additional states enact legislation. The current laws differ considerably in the extent to which they place specific, binding obligations on localities. Most of them have provisions of some sort for technical and financial assistance to localities, as well as various market development activities, including state procurement programs for recycled materials. Most of the programs require—or at least encourage—recycling of paper, glass, metals, and recyclable plastics; some also include yard wastes, major appliances, used oil, and construction and demolition debris.

Beyond the states represented on the map in figure 11.4, many have in place recycling laws and policies that constitute something less than comprehensive programs. In response to a survey by the Council of State Governments (Brown, Dresser-Gagnon, and Gona 1987), nearly three-fourths of responding states reported that they had developed recycling programs. Many of those programs include financial inducements, such as grants, loans,

Table 11.1. Landfills per State	
Alabama	800
Alaska	740
Arizona	185
Arkansas	116
California	720
Colorado	130
Connecticut	188
Delaware	37
Florida	238
Georgia	390
Hawaii	25
Idaho	126
Illinois	275
Indiana	131
Iowa	102
Kansas	463
Kentucky	181
Louisiana	618
Maine	362
Maryland	16
Massachusetts	249
Michigan	257
Minnesota	160
Mississippi	195
Missouri	138
Montana	170
Nebraska	413
Nevada	117
New Hampshire	125
New Jersey	108
New Mexico	214
New York	522
North Carolina	243
North Dakota	139
Ohio	211
Oklahoma	173
Oregon	220
Pennsylvania	1,204
Rhode Island	13
South Carolina	286
South Dakota	357
Tennessee	166
Texas	1,201
Utah	375
Vermont	101
Virginia	264
Washington	260
West Virginia	1,209
Wisconsin	1,033
Wyoming	300

Table 11.1. Landfills per State.

Note: Nationally, 57% of these landfills are for municipal solid waste; 21% industrial waste; 16% demolition debris; 6% other.

Source:
EPA, *Report to Congress: Solid Waste Disposal in the United States,* vol. 2, EPA/530-SW-88-011B (Washington, DC: EPA, 1988), pp. 4–5.

Figure 11.4. State Recycling and Bottle Laws.

Source:
Environmental Action Foundation, "Legislative Summary: Mandatory Statewide Recycling Laws" (Washington, DC, 1989, mimeograph).

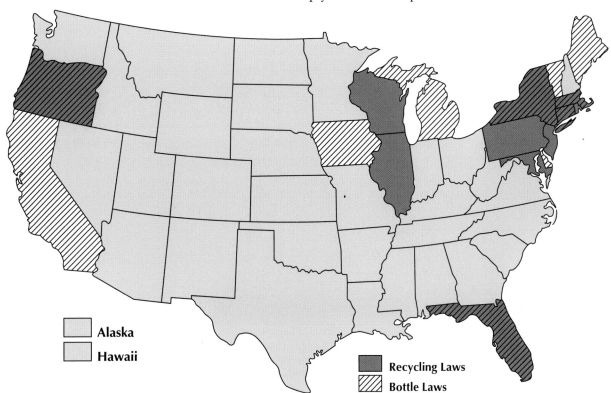

Alaska

Hawaii

Recycling Laws

Bottle Laws

and tax incentives. The State of Washington requires operators of disposal facilities simply to provide "recycling opportunities." A number of states (besides those noted above) have some sort of packaging restrictions—especially on beverage containers. Indeed, container and other packaging restrictions are increasingly being debated in statehouses across the country. Procurement requirements also have been enacted in several states, beyond those noted above (Environmental Defense Fund 1988).

While it is difficult to track all the state-level recycling initiatives, local activities are even more elusive. Countless ordinances, programs, and facilities are coming on line almost daily— but there is no comprehensive, updated compilation of these activities. The Environmental Defense Fund (1988) has reported on a number of local efforts and cites one assessment showing that participation rates average 74 percent for mandatory, weekly programs. Less frequent, voluntary programs have lower participation rates, averaging 31 percent. Among the outstanding success stories reported by the Environmental Defense Fund are several towns in Camden County, New Jersey; Islip, New York (on Long Island); and Hamburg, New York (near Buffalo), with its 98-percent participation rate. In addition to voluntary and mandatory source-separation programs for paper, glass, metal, and/or plastic, some communities simply refuse to accept certain materials—such as news-

papers or yard wastes—at disposal facilities. Community composting facilities, along with programs that shred Christmas trees into mulch, are becoming increasingly common.

Returnable beverage container laws, or "bottle bills" (something of a misnomer, because most such laws apply to metal and plastic containers as well as glass bottles), are essentially state-level phenomena. Although proposals for national legislation have been put forth, they have not—as yet—gotten very far in Congress. Each of the nine states indicated on the map has some sort of mandatory deposit and/or redemption system. As with mandatory recycling legislation, Oregon was the first to pass a bottle bill—in 1972. Vermont followed in 1973, Maine in 1978, and Michigan and Iowa in 1979. Connecticut's law was enacted in 1980; and Massachusetts, Delaware, and New York passed their laws in 1983. Florida adopted a deposit-fee system in 1988. In most cases (Florida, perhaps, an exception), the chief rationale for the laws was litter reduction—not the various virtues of recycling. To that end, the laws have been successful. States with bottle bills report decreases in roadside litter ranging between 15 and 50 percent, with declines in beverage container litter of up to 80 percent (OTA 1989).

In addition to reducing litter, bottle bills have resulted in increased recycling and reuse of materials and savings in landfill space. As noted above, most of the laws apply equally to containers made of glass, metal, or plastic. Florida's new law includes all containers, not just beverage containers. The following recycling data have been compiled by the New York State Department of Environmental Conservation, as reported in Environmental Defense Fund (1988):

	Estimated Recycling Rates (%)		
	Before 1983 Law	1984	1986
Cans	15	59	60
Glass	3	77	80
Plastic	1	33	50

The beverage industry and retail grocers generally oppose returnable container legislation. A key point of contention is the cost incurred in switching from a throwaway system to a returnable system. However, available evidence indicates that at least some of those costs are recovered within a few years. Moreover, there is a net gain in jobs and some energy and resource savings (OTA 1989). Still, bottle bill opponents tend to be well organized and remarkably influential in state legislatures. To the degree that curbside collection of recyclables succeeds, the case for returnable-container legislation becomes all that much harder to put across to legislators and the public.

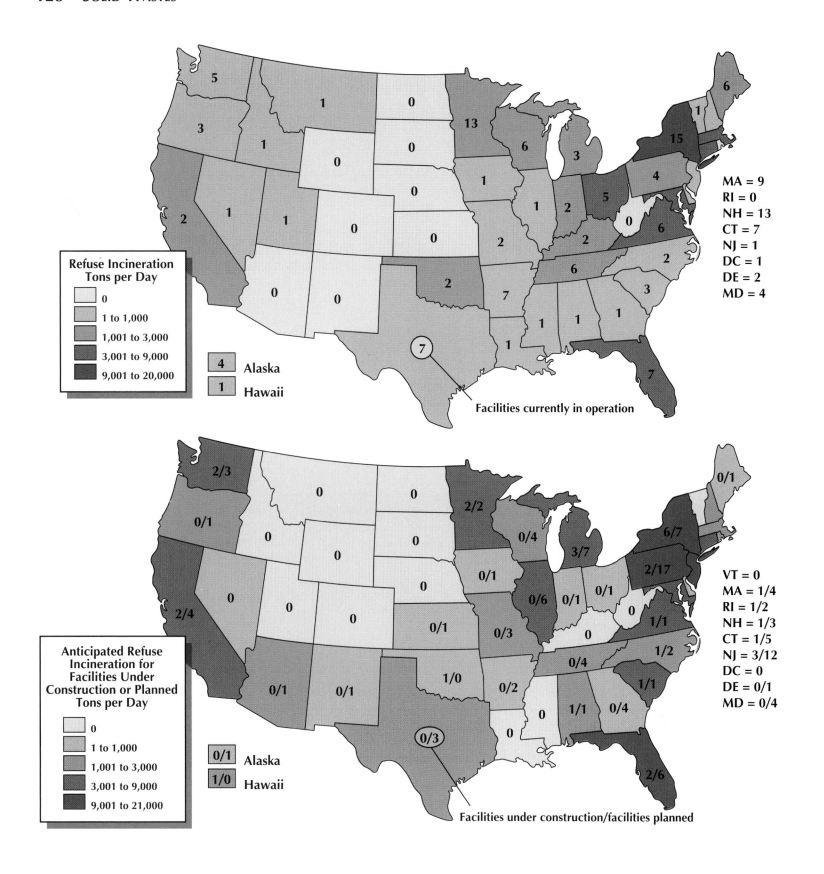

MA = 9
RI = 0
NH = 13
CT = 7
NJ = 1
DC = 1
DE = 2
MD = 4

Refuse Incineration Tons per Day

0
1 to 1,000
1,001 to 3,000
3,001 to 9,000
9,001 to 20,000

4 Alaska
1 Hawaii

Facilities currently in operation

VT = 0
MA = 1/4
RI = 1/2
NH = 1/3
CT = 1/5
NJ = 3/12
DC = 0
DE = 0/1
MD = 0/4

Anticipated Refuse Incineration for Facilities Under Construction or Planned Tons per Day

0
1 to 1,000
1,001 to 3,000
3,001 to 9,000
9,001 to 21,000

0/1 Alaska
1/0 Hawaii

Facilities under construction/facilities planned

Figure 11.5. Refuse Incineration and Refuse-to-Energy Facilities.

Source:
Waste Age, "Waste Age 1988 Refuse Incineration and Refuse-to-Energy Listings," *Waste Age* 19 (11): 195–212.

REFUSE INCINERATION AND REFUSE-TO-ENERGY FACILITIES

For decades, European countries have burned and recovered energy from solid waste. In the United States, a great deal of money was put into incineration research and development during the 1970s, but most of the plants built during that decade eventually failed. The 1980s witnessed a resurgence of these technologies—especially in localities hard-pressed for landfill space. But the controversies associated with incineration also have escalated—in Europe as well as the United States.

Incineration captures part of the energy value of the waste stream, either through mass burning or through the combustion of "refuse-derived fuel" (RDF). In mass burning processes, the waste is sorted to remove explosive and other undesirable materials and to achieve a mix appropriate for combustion conditions. The trash is then burned at very high temperatures. In well-designed furnaces, more than 99.9 percent of chemical compounds—including dioxin—should be destroyed. The heat from this process is used to create steam, which drives a turbine to generate electricity and/or is distributed to buildings as part of a district heating system. Metals may be magnetically removed from the incinerator ash; the rest of the ash usually is landfilled. The refuse-derived fuel process, by contrast, begins by removing large or flammable objects from the incoming trash; then the waste is shredded. Metals are magnetically removed for recycling; other noncombustible materials generally are landfilled. The final product is either finely shredded refuse or compressed pellets or briquets. The RDF is then transported to the site where it is burned—sometimes in conjunction with another fuel—to produce electricity and/or steam.

Incineration reduces the need for landfill space, and insofar as it does not require households to source-separate their trash, it is easier to implement than recycling. Yet critics contend that greater energy as well as material savings can be achieved through recycling. Furthermore, refuse-to-energy projects may actually impede recycling efforts. States and communities may limit their recycling efforts in order to assure sufficient supplies of materials—especially paper—to keep incinerators running. Moreover, air emissions are of concern—particulary the highly toxic dioxins. To the extent that toxins are removed before reaching the smokestack, they end up in the incinerator ash. Thus even though incineration reduces the total volume of material requiring disposal, toxic metals and other chemicals may be concentrated in that waste. The EPA does not currently classify incinerator ash as toxic.

All these environmental concerns have contributed to local opposition to incinerator plans—and have helped make incinerator siting a very treacherous political enterprise. Moreover, financing for incineration projects has become scarcer in recent years. Total debt financing for solid-waste and resource-recovery projects peaked in 1984 at $4.7 billion; by 1987, the figure had dropped to $1.6 billion (Waste Age 1988). According to a survey by Government Advisory Associates (Gould 1988), the number of projects in the advanced planning stages dropped by 12.5 percent between 1986 and 1988, and eight facilities were permanently shut down. Paradoxically, though, the number of facilities in the conceptual stage increased from seventy-five to 139.

The OTA (1989) estimates that 10 to 12 percent (by weight) of municipal solid waste is incinerated and that about one-fourth of that remains in the form of ash. Current incineration capacity, along with anticipated expansions, tends to be concentrated in the northeastern quadrant of the country, Florida, and California. Indeed, Pennsylvania, Florida, Illinois, and California—respectively—are the leaders in debt issues floated for solid-waste and resource-recovery projects.

Of the 1988 existing and advance-planned resource-recovery facilities identified by Governmental Advisory Associates (Gould 1988), 81 percent employ mass burning (down from 74 percent in 1986). Refuse-derived fuel processes account for 18 percent of facilities (down from 24 percent in 1986). Electricity continues to be the primary energy product.

Even though the vast majority of facilities surveyed by Governmental Advisory Associates have some kind of air-pollution control equipment (mostly electrostatic precipitators and baghouse filters), controversies about airborne emissions continue to rage. Among the more common smokestack pollutants are particulates, sulfur dioxide, nitrogen oxides, carbon monoxide, hydrogen chloride, hydrogen fluoride, arsenic, cadmium, chromium, lead, mercury, PCBs, and the much-publicized dioxins and furans. Small amounts of the latter two compounds have proven highly toxic in animal tests. Of course, municipal refuse is highly diverse and contains even more chemicals than those mentioned above. At a 1984 meeting sponsored by the New York Academy of Sciences, participants generally agreed that our technological capabilities for monitoring and controlling sulfur oxides, metals, chlorides, and particulates are adequate—but that PCBs, dioxins, and furans are much more problematic (Neal and Schubel 1987). Debate centers on actual rates of emissions, monitoring, and risks posed by emissions.

Ash management also is an issue. Although metals generally are recovered, the remaining residue usually is landfilled. There are, however, potential uses for the material—in road building, as construction aggregate, for building artificial reefs, and as landfill cover. While not defined by Congress as hazardous waste, the residue does contain small amounts of metals, PCBs, dioxins and furans, and other toxic compounds. EPA regulatory limits apply only to cadmium and lead.

SEWAGE SLUDGE MANAGEMENT

Sludges are generated by industries (mainly iron and steel, chemicals, pulp and paper, and food processing), utilities, and drinking-water and wastewater treatment plants. Municipal wastewater sludge typically contains between 93 and 99.5 percent water, but this content can be reduced by thickening or dewatering processes. Implementation of the wastewater treatment requirements of the 1972 Clean Water Act has more than doubled the annual production of municipal sludge since 1972. Another doubling is expected by the turn of the century (EPA 1984).

Of the approximately 6.9 million dry tons of sludge produced annually, 20 percent is incinerated, 25 percent applied to land (including 6 percent that is distributed and marketed), 6 percent ocean disposed, and 49 percent disposed of in landfills or lagoons (EPA 1988b). Figure 11.6 provides a general indication of how aggressively states are pursuing land application—but only numbers of plants are depicted, not volumes of sludge. Small- and medium-volume treatment plants are more likely than large plants to favor land application, whereas larger plants are more likely to incinerate or distribute and market their sludge.

Sludge—which contains nitrogen, phosphorous, and small amounts of potassium—can act as a fertilizer as well as soil conditioner. Land application occurs primarily on agricultural land, forest land, and reclaimed mine and other lands. Agricultural applications are most common. Federal regulations, as well as various state laws, govern the application of sludge to "food-chain crops": tobacco, crops for human consumption, and feed for animals to be consumed by humans. The primary concern is to limit pathogens, cadmium, and PCBs. Although no specific federal regulations apply to residential use of composted or dried sludge, it is usually recommended that sludge not be applied to vegetable gardens.

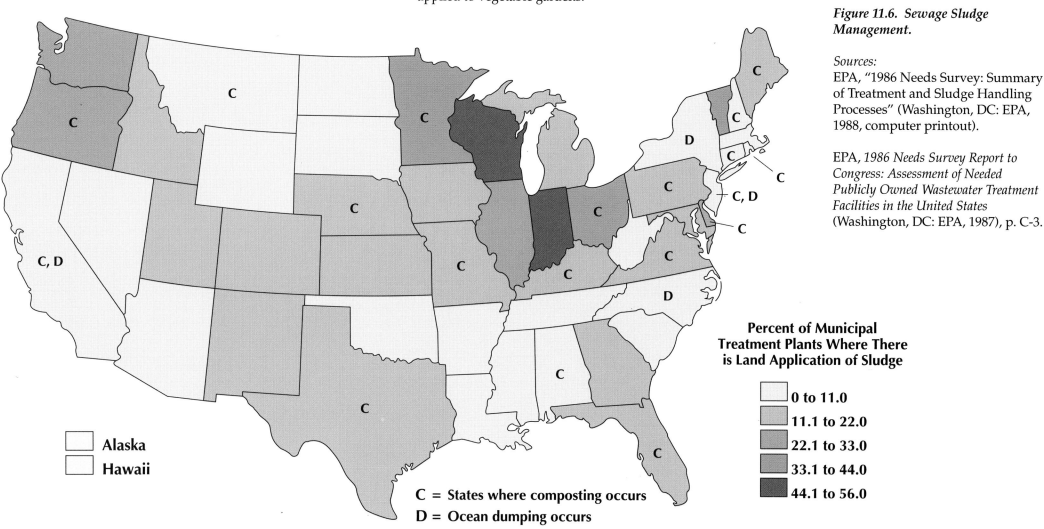

Figure 11.6. Sewage Sludge Management.

Sources:
EPA, "1986 Needs Survey: Summary of Treatment and Sludge Handling Processes" (Washington, DC: EPA, 1988, computer printout).

EPA, *1986 Needs Survey Report to Congress: Assessment of Needed Publicly Owned Wastewater Treatment Facilities in the United States* (Washington, DC: EPA, 1987), p. C-3.

Percent of Municipal Treatment Plants Where There is Land Application of Sludge

- 0 to 11.0
- 11.1 to 22.0
- 22.1 to 33.0
- 33.1 to 44.0
- 44.1 to 56.0

Alaska

Hawaii

C = States where composting occurs
D = Ocean dumping occurs

VOYAGE OF THE ISLIP GARBAGE BARGE

In the spring of 1987, Islip, New York's garbage became comedy material for television talk-show hosts. By summer, it was a point of interest on the Circle Line boat tours around Manhattan. The 3,186-ton cargo of the *Mobro 4000*, guided by the tug *Break of Dawn*, traveled over 6,000 miles in search of a resting place. The trash was rejected by North Carolina, Florida, Alabama, Mississippi, Louisiana, Mexico, Belize, and the Bahamas. Some of the rejections were preemptive: Cuba, for example, sent out gunboats to keep the garbage away. This voyage was the maiden run (and in fact the only run) of what was to be a 10,000-ton-per-day enterprise, employing four barges to haul Islip's refuse to southern destinations. The venture's false start may be attributed to the failure of the partnership that initiated it to secure signed agreements for its ultimate disposal. The *Mobro* returned to New York, amid a flurry of lawsuits and investigations into mob ties, on May 16. The trash was finally unloaded in late August and burned in a Brooklyn incinerator in September.

In the context of the national solid-waste disposal problem, the *Mobro*'s cargo was like a dumpster-load of trash in a sprawling municipal landfill. The same might be said of Philadelphia's ill-fated attempt to dispose of a shipload of incinerator ash: After months of roaming through the Atlantic and Mediterranean, the *Khian Sea*'s 15,000-ton cargo finally "disappeared." But it is the symbolic value—not the physical quantity of trash—that makes such events so powerful. They are at the crest of a groundswell of local discontent about how we deal with trash—discontent that now festers even in the face of rather generous monetary compensations to those who "accept" the waste.

There is a regular exodus of refuse from landfill-short parts of the Northeast. Destinations include landfills in Pennsylvania, Ohio, Kentucky, West Virginia, Michigan, and other states. Though some Pennsylvania communities accept waste from other states, a significant portion of waste from Philadelphia—the state's largest city—is transported out-of-state. Enormous quantities of waste are exported by Long Island communities—to receiving sites as far as 850 miles away. New Jersey sends as much as 60 percent of its municipal waste out-of-state. Although the largest exporters are in the Northeast, they are not the only ones. Missouri, for example, is estimated to transport one-third of its municipal waste out-of-state (OTA 1989). Generally, the waste flows toward the cheaper disposal sites. Still, the costs incurred for this long-range trash transport are enormous; the national price tag has been put at nearly $1 billion per year (Newsday 1989).

Although hazardous-waste transport is regulated by the federal government, there is no comparable control over the interstate commerce in municipal waste. That is left to the states—and some of the major receiving states, including Ohio, are contemplating actions to restrict the influx of trash. Local opposition also has broken out in many receiving communities. Sentiments along the lines of "Don't kill our children with out-of-state trash" are expressed on signs erected by residents in Oakland, Ohio, and many other towns. Trash importation has become a very serious issue in a number of rural West Virginia locales. It appears as if mounting local opposition, along with high transport costs, will make long-range transport of trash an ever less viable option for communities. As the sense of crisis escalates, so too should the impetus to find waste-management alternatives.

Figure 11.7. Voyage of the Islip Garbage Barge, March 22–May 16, 1987.

Sources:
"The Rush to Burn: Solving America's Garbage Crisis," *Newsday*, 1989.

M. Dobbs, "On Garbage Boat, Pride Sustains," *Washington Post*, May 10, 1987: A1, A10.

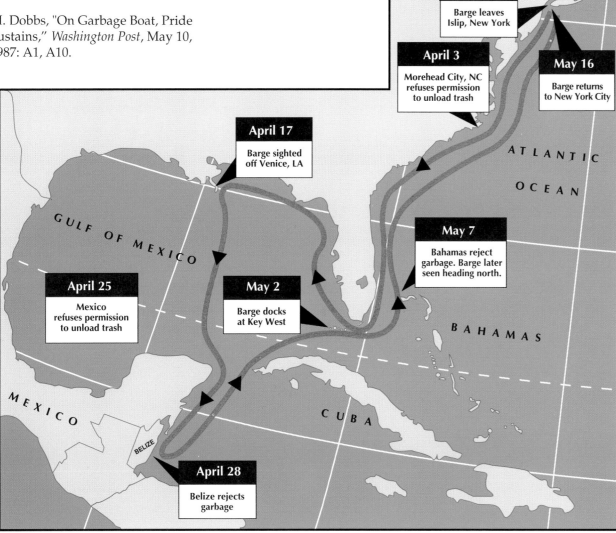

The difference between "ordinary," everyday threats and those that are toxic or hazardous often is just a matter of degree. The Conservation Foundation (1987: 135) confronts this definitional dilemma by describing toxic and hazardous substances as "compounds that can cause serious health and environmental damage, even in small amounts." For our general purposes, this characterization suffices.

By almost any definition, the dimensions of the toxics problem are staggering. More than eight million chemicals are currently registered by the Chemical Abstracts Service—though most of these are not in commercial use. According to the Toxic Substances Control Act (TSCA) Inventory, over 63,000 chemicals were used commercially between 1975 and 1985, with about 1,500 new substances being introduced each year (Conservation Foundation 1987). Potentially toxic chemicals are found in our food, air, and water; they are used in pesticides, drugs, food additives, industrial processes, insulation, packaging, and for many other agricultural, industrial, commercial, residential, and transportation-related purposes.

Not until relatively recently was public debate about toxic and hazardous substances really opened up. Some initial shock waves were sent through a rather complacent populace when Rachel Carson's *Silent Spring* was published in 1962. Her impressionistic account—interpreted as fear-mongering by some—contained a clear and potent message: Pesticides and other chemicals can cause serious, long-term environmental damage. Still, it was not until the early 1970s that toxic and hazardous threats began to be addressed in a major way by Congress and state legislatures. In addition to relevant provisions of federal air and water pollution laws (see chapters 8 and 9), legislation specifically relevant to pesticides and other toxic chemicals was enacted. These laws are described below. During this period DDT was banned (1972), and production of PCBs was initially restricted (1971) and later banned (1976).

The mid- and late 1970s saw an explosion of concern. The dioxin released by a pesticide plant explosion in Seveso, Italy, in 1976; early stirrings about dioxin contamination in Times Beach and elsewhere in Missouri (which really hit the national headlines in the early 1980s); and discovery of toxic chemicals at Love Canal, New York (figure 12.5), all contributed to the alarm. Additional fears were unleashed by the Three Mile Island nuclear accident. The Resource Conservation and Recovery Act of 1976 (RCRA), the Toxic Substances Control Act of 1976 (TSCA), and the "Superfund" law of 1980—each described below—gave the EPA important new powers to regulate the production, use, and disposal of toxic chemicals.

In 1984, more than 2,300 people were killed, and perhaps 500,000 injured, when methyl isocyanate gas escaped from a storage tank at a Union Carbide pesticide plant in Bhopal, India. The world was again shocked in 1986 by the Chernobyl nuclear accident. In the United States, meanwhile, the EPA was responding only very slowly to congressional mandates to regulate pesticides and other chemicals more comprehensively and to clean up abandoned hazardous waste sites. Resultant public apprehension has undoubtedly contributed to recent alarms about illegal dumping of medical wastes in the Atlantic Ocean and use of the pesticide alar in apple production. But, as many risk analysts are quick to point out, public perceptions are skewed by news reports that overreact to some threats yet virtually ignore others that are of equal or greater importance.

Public fear and mistrust are probably nowhere in greater evidence than at the local level—where resistance to the siting of such noxious facilities as landfills and waste incinerators is often fierce. One response to such concerns is the community right-to-know provision added in 1986 to the Superfund law. Under it, facilities must provide information about storage and releases of toxic chemicals to air, land, and water. The initial numbers are staggering—even to the EPA—and bring with them important long-term implications for industrial location, production, and waste-management decisions.

Love Canal, New York.
Top: *1978 infrared photo (red indicates vegetation).*
Bottom: *1988 after remediation.*
J. Goerg, New York State Department of Environmental Conservation.

INDUSTRIAL WASTE GENERATION

Over 99 percent of hazardous wastes are byproducts of basic manufacturing processes, according to the Congressional Budget Office (CBO 1985). The CBO estimates that industries produced 266 million metric tons of hazardous waste in 1983. Chemical and allied-products industries generated almost half this; primary metals industries 18 percent; petroleum and coal-products industries 12 percent; fabricated metal-products industries 10 percent; and rubber and plastics industries 6 percent. Nearly half the waste consisted of nonmetallic inorganic liquids and sludge; liquids and sludges containing metal accounted for about 13 percent; and the rest was composed mainly of various solvents, oily sludges, dusts, solids, liquids, and mixed wastes.

The CBO definition of hazardous waste (the basis for figure 12.1) is a rather broad one—yet its total estimate is remarkably close to those obtained in separate studies by the Chemical Manufacturers Association, EPA, and the Office of Technology Assessment. The General Accounting Office (GAO 1986a) concludes that this is a coincidence: There are too many omissions and uncertainties in all four studies to place a great deal of confidence in the results.

Nonetheless, the CBO results at least allow for a broad comparison among states. Texas, with its large chemical and petroleum-refining complexes, was the biggest generator (13 percent of the national total). Ohio ranked second (7 percent). Other major generators—each contributing about 5 percent—include California, Illinois, Louisiana, New Jersey, Michigan, and Tennessee. The maps reflect the high concentrations of waste-producing industries in the Ohio Valley, Gulf Coast, and northeastern megalopolitan regions. Especially striking are the small eastern states—such as New Jersey and Rhode Island—where relatively large amounts of waste are concentrated in small areas.

About 96 percent of all wastes are managed on-site. The main means of disposal, according to the CBO, are injection into wells or salt caverns (25 percent); discharge into sewage treatment plants, rivers, and streams (22 percent); placement in pits, ponds, or lagoons (19 percent); disposal in lined, hazardous-waste landfills (13 percent); and disposal in unlined sanitary landfills (10 percent). Although individual success stories of waste reduction—the in-plant elimination and/or recycling of wastes—have been widely publicized, overall progress has been slow. Legal and regulatory activity has focused on more measurable and enforceable "end-of-pipe" treatment technologies. Inertia, lack of knowledge, shortage of capital, and traditionally low costs of land disposal have conspired against sustained efforts at waste reduction—despite its economic advantages in many instances.

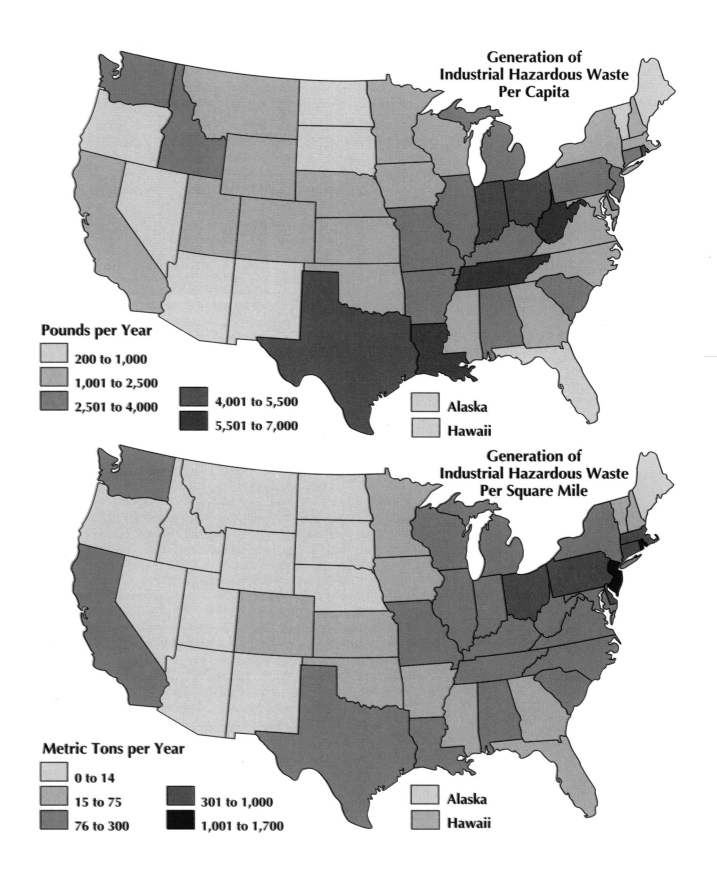

Generation of Industrial Hazardous Waste Per Capita

Pounds per Year

- 200 to 1,000
- 1,001 to 2,500
- 2,501 to 4,000
- 4,001 to 5,500
- 5,501 to 7,000
- Alaska
- Hawaii

Generation of Industrial Hazardous Waste Per Square Mile

Metric Tons per Year

- 0 to 14
- 15 to 75
- 76 to 300
- 301 to 1,000
- 1,001 to 1,700
- Alaska
- Hawaii

INDUSTRIAL EMISSIONS

In 1989—through the Toxics Release Inventory (TRI)—information about facility-specific toxic chemical releases became available for the first time to the general public. The legislative mandate for this disclosure comes from the Emergency Planning and Community Right-to-Know Act of 1986 (also known as Title III of the Superfund Amendments and Reauthorization Act, or SARA), which establishes detailed reporting requirements for specific toxic chemicals. Table 12.1 contains statewide figures on direct releases to air, land, and water—as well as transport to off-site facilities—for some 308 chemicals. In 1987 (the first year of reporting), a total of nearly 20,000 facilities reported releases and transfers in excess of 22.5 billion pounds. Approximately 5 billion pounds of those chemicals were transferred off-site for treatment or disposal.

These numbers are shocking, even to the EPA. Indeed, when they were released to the press in mid-1989, the EPA's spokesperson seemed quite taken aback. Still, the numbers must be treated with caution. To begin with, the TRI is a partial accounting: It does not include releases from landfills, wastewater treatment plants, vehicle emissions, and other sources. There are also uncertainties about the quality and completeness of the data as well as the relative toxicity of the chemicals themselves. The latter will in many cases be revealed only through expensive, time-consuming, detailed local analyses. One chemical—sodium sulfate—accounted for 54 percent of all releases and transfers reported in 1987 (most of it was released to surface waters). In response to arguments that sodium sulfate is not sufficiently toxic, the EPA removed it from the list for 1988. This will significantly change the character of the entire TRI data base.

Since facilities are not required to report the actual timing and rate of chemical releases over the course of the year, it is virtually impossible to develop reasonable estimates of human exposure from the TRI data. Some chemicals may be so diluted or degraded as to pose very little threat; others may be transformed, perhaps through synergistic interactions with other substances, into compounds that pose threats even greater than those from what was initially released. Some chemicals may be particularly harmful to sensitive ecosystems.

Despite these limitations, the TRI data do point to the seriousness of the problems in California and the Gulf Coast, Middle Atlantic, and Great Lakes regions. In fact, figure 12.2 understates the intensity of emissions in some places—particularly when they are averaged over large areas or across large populations, as is the case in such states as Texas and California. Although rural industrial emissions should not be discounted, they tend to pale in comparison with those that occur in some of the nation's more densely industrialized corridors. Overall, air is the medium that receives the greatest quantities of toxic discharge.

Early results for 1988 indicate that toxic releases declined 9 percent from 1988. But EPA officials are quick to caution that these figures may be misleading. Because of the considerable variation in the ways emissions are estimated, the decline may only be a "paper change." Still, it is conceivable that more companies are recycling; shipments that go to recycling centers need not be reported to the EPA.

The TRI data will probably prove most valuable at the individual plant and community level—where they can act as a vehicle for promoting public awareness, raising new questions about toxic exposure, and stimulating more detailed and informative local-level analyses. Although it is too early to gauge the response nationwide, it is already apparent that some community groups are eagerly publicizing and interpreting the new information, some companies are reacting with fear, and other companies are opening new channels of communication with affected communities.

In addition to reporting the TRI data, facilities are required under SARA Title III to report on amounts, locations, properties, and effects of hazardous chemicals used and stored on-site. These annual inventories are submitted to state officials as well as to local emergency planning committees (LEPCs) and fire departments. Like TRI data, this information is to be made available, at the local level, to the public. The LEPCs must develop emergency response plans based on—but not limited to—the presence of 366 "extremely hazardous substances" listed by the EPA. Facilities are also required to notify the public, as well as state and local officials, of accidental releases of certain quantities of any of over 700 hazardous substances.

The EPA's "Acute Hazardous Events Data Base"—compiled shortly after the Bhopal tragedy—documents nearly 7,000 accidents between 1980 and early 1985. These accidents caused 138 deaths, 4,717 injuries, and evacuations of more than 200,000 people. However, the data are incomplete; it is estimated that the actual number of accidents is two and one-half to three times greater than that reported in the data base (Sherman and Silver 1986). An analysis by Cutter and Solecki (1989), which draws on different sources (including data on transportation accidents), reveals that seven states account for a slight majority of documented incidents: California, Illinois, Indiana, Louisiana, Ohio, Texas, and West Virginia. Truck-related transportation accidents prevailed in the western states, while rail accidents and fixed-site releases were predominant in the East. When population, area, and transportation variables are controlled, West Virginia, Alabama, Louisiana, Kentucky, Illinois, Iowa, Idaho, California, Kentucky, Maryland, New Jersey, Rhode Island, and Wyoming emerge as high-risk states.

Figure 12.1. Industrial Hazardous Waste Generation, 1983.

Source:
CBO, *Hazardous Waste Management: Recent Policy Changes and Policy Alternatives* (Washington, DC: CBO, 1985).

To what extent generally is toxic chemical exposure responsible for various types of cancer? Most cancers are caused by cigarette smoking and other "lifestyle factors," and, for a smaller proportion of the population, occupational exposure to hazardous substances is a primary causal factor. But our understanding of the importance of nonoccupational exposure to toxic chemicals is frustrated by insufficient epidemiological studies and the difficulty of sorting out complex and numerous causal and contributory factors. While there is a clear pattern of high cancer-mortality rates in heavily populated and industrialized parts of the country—especially the Northeast—the significance of air and water pollution relative to other factors is unclear.

Using data from an internal EPA data base (the Air Toxics Exposure and Risk Information System), Representative Henry Waxman's office produced a map that depicts high cancer risks from individual facilities. Highest potential risks are in the eastern half of the country, with major risk clusters in the Texas and Louisiana Gulf Coast areas. But the risk estimates are handicapped because the EPA intended the information only for gross comparative purposes, not for estimates of risk from individual facilities. Thus while Waxman's report documents potential cancer threats, it also points to the need for more detailed knowledge about pollutant dispersion, human exposure, and short- and long-term effects.

EPA progress in developing standards for hazardous air pollutants, as required by the Clean Air Act, has been exceedingly slow. Although the Toxic Substances Control Act gives the agency authority to act more quickly under certain circumstances, its actions (or lack thereof) under this law have also come under fire. In 1985, the EPA (1985d) released its "air toxics strategy," which called for stronger EPA control over multiple sources of toxic pollution over small areas (the EPA estimates that vehicles and heating sources account for more than 50 percent of cancer incidence due to air toxics, while heavy industry explains only 20–25 percent), strong state-level programs, more research into local-level exposure and risk, and expanded emergency preparedness and response.

The proposed "Air Toxics Control Act"—introduced to Congress by the Waxman report described above—calls for more detailed congressional direction to the EPA, regulation on an industry-by-industry basis, control of toxic emissions from vehicles, prevention of and response to accidental toxic releases, a Great Lakes protection program, and regulation of "area sources"—small stationary sources—of toxic pollutants. Presidential and congressional proposals for reauthorization of the Clean Air Act also call for new programs to regulate airborne toxic emissions. It is a political issue whose time seems to have come.

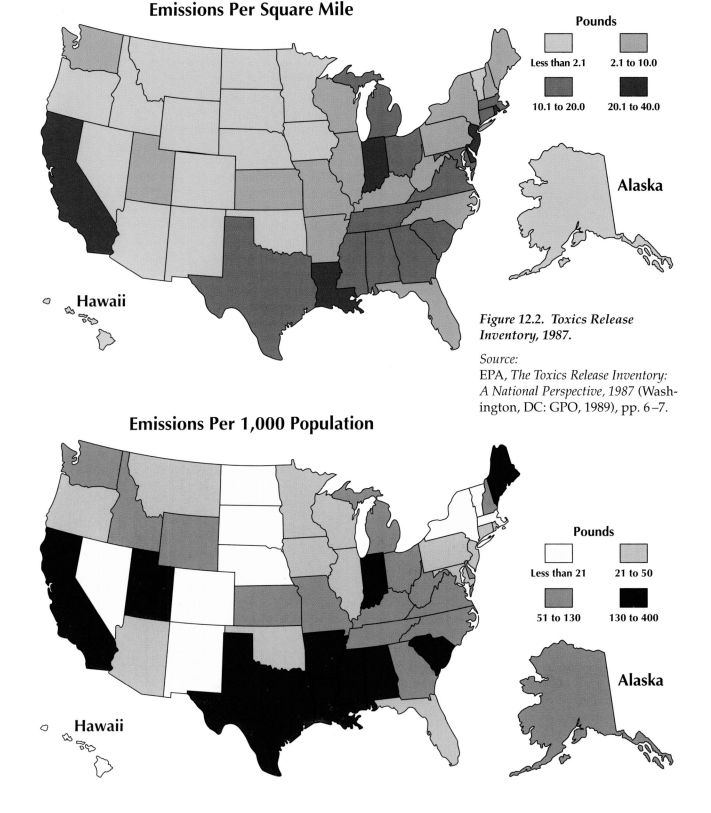

Emissions Per Square Mile

Pounds

Less than 2.1 | 2.1 to 10.0

10.1 to 20.0 | 20.1 to 40.0

Alaska

Hawaii

Figure 12.2. ***Toxics Release Inventory, 1987.***

Source:
EPA, *The Toxics Release Inventory: A National Perspective, 1987* (Washington, DC: GPO, 1989), pp. 6–7.

Emissions Per 1,000 Population

Pounds

Less than 21 | 21 to 50

51 to 130 | 130 to 400

Alaska

Hawaii

Table 12.1. Toxics Release Inventory, 1987

	Number of Facilities	Average Number of Chemicals per Facility	Total TRI Emissions (thousand pounds)	Rank	Percent of State's Emissions to					
					Air	Surface Water	Public Sewers	On-site Landfills	Underground Injection Wells	Off-site Facilities
Alabama	355	4	827,064	4	11.9	64.6	4.0	11.9	0.2	7.6
Alaska	7	8	36,944	41	85.8	14.1	0	0	0	0
Arizona	156	3	126,072	31	13.1	0	7.3	77.0	0	2.5
Arkansas	293	3	374,781	18	14.6	45.7	1.2	29.0	3.5	6.2
California	1,662	4	5,839,808	1	1.4	65.7	4.2	0.8	26.2	1.7
Colorado	172	3	35,331	42	31.2	9.4	8.8	35.5	0	15.1
Connecticut	383	4	86,374	34	30.2	29.2	11.1	2.1	0	27.4
Delaware	53	5	58,819	39	10.3	50.8	27.8	4.4	0	6.8
Florida	419	3	434,686	16	11.5	24.8	9.1	43.9	6.8	3.9
Georgia	636	3	661,731	8	14.1	71.6	7.1	2.3	0	4.9
Hawaii	33	4	5,063	47	21.0	50.2	19.2	4.7	4.3	0.6
Idaho	52	3	73,412	35	5.7	69.1	4.4	20.4	0	0.4
Illinois	1,185	4	468,817	12	21.2	7.1	42.5	2.4	3.0	23.8
Indiana	720	4	731,729	6	15.4	14.5	13.1	33.7	8.7	14.6
Iowa	310	3	71,583	36	54.8	21.4	14.1	1.1	0	8.6
Kansas	184	4	183,391	27	13.5	4.1	3.6	0.6	49.7	28.5
Kentucky	298	5	250,942	22	20.6	30.6	5.4	1.6	10.0	31.8
Louisiana	259	7	1,725,933	3	8.0	45.0	0.1	9.0	32.1	5.9
Maine	83	4	219,561	24	6.7	89.2	2.3	0.9	0	0.9
Maryland	191	4	195,248	25	10.4	57.3	24.5	2.2	0	5.7
Massachusetts	560	3	104,827	33	28.7	2.0	34.5	3.4	0	31.4
Michigan	758	4	742,716	5	15.7	5.1	5.1	0.5	0.9	72.6
Minnesota	301	4	141,498	29	29.7	11.2	49.5	1.2	0	8.4
Mississippi	247	4	656,086	9	8.7	72.2	1.4	2.3	7.1	8.2
Missouri	503	4	292,427	21	17.3	12.4	38.5	19.3	0.3	12.1
Montana	27	5	38,438	40	13.7	2.1	0.1	83.8	0	0.4
Nebraska	139	3	21,150	45	68.1	13.0	5.7	1.7	0	11.5
Nevada	33	3	11,735	46	6.3	0	0.3	92.2	0	1.2
New Hampshire	129	3	65,131	37	19.9	65.1	4.3	1.0	0	9.6
New Jersey	875	4	308,585	20	13.6	17.8	40.0	1.7	0	26.8
New Mexico	32	4	22,528	44	17.0	0	3.3	76.8	0	2.8
New York	765	4	326,075	19	27.4	17.2	20.0	5.4	0	30.0
North Carolina	820	3	441,346	14	21.4	49.2	12.4	6.8	0	10.2
North Dakota	28	3	2,804	50	33.4	14.0	3.4	39.3	0	10.0
Ohio	1,261	4	723,893	7	23.9	9.4	18.1	6.6	9.9	32.1
Oklahoma	193	4	129,781	30	28.1	50.7	1.3	1.9	5.5	12.5
Oregon	217	3	120,605	32	17.4	52.5	11.5	11.6	0	7.0
Pennsylvania	1,027	4	437,634	15	20.0	14.1	9.1	16.2	0	40.5
Rhode Island	166	3	26,623	43	22.3	49.5	11.3	0.3	0	16.7
South Carolina	394	4	518,128	11	12.4	65.8	9.9	1.7	0	10.2
South Dakota	37	2	3,518	49	69.4	0.1	17.6	0	0	12.9
Tennessee	503	4	602,148	10	22.4	32.6	16.1	3.4	20.7	4.8
Texas	999	5	2,799,769	2	8.5	23.6	5.5	29.8	22.5	10.1
Utah	102	4	249,743	23	31.0	0.1	0.8	66.3	0	1.9
Vermont	52	2	4,890	48	28.2	22.8	6.1	3.5	0	39.5
Virginia	399	4	444,050	13	29.8	50.8	12.5	1.6	0	5.3
Washington	306	4	407,079	17	10.0	74.6	1.0	6.2	0	8.3
West Virginia	107	6	170,571	28	20.9	51.2	3.0	6.8	1.0	17.1
Wisconsin	645	3	184,957	26	26.3	9.0	25.0	4.1	0	35.6
Wyoming	27	5	62,597	38	5.0	5.5	0	38.6	49.0	1.8

Table 12.1. Toxics Release Inventory, 1987.

Source:
EPA, *The Toxics Release Inventory: A National Perspective, 1987* (Washington, DC: GPO, 1989), pp. 6–7.

SUPERFUND SITES

At the end of 1980, President Carter signed into law the Comprehensive Environmental Response, Compensation, and Liability Act (CERCLA)—generally referred to as Superfund. It authorizes the EPA, Coast Guard, and other federal agencies to respond to emergencies involving actual or anticipated releases of hazardous substances and also obligates the EPA, states, and polluters to provide for the long-term cleanup of sites on the EPA's National Priorities List (NPL). The initial funding was $1.6 billion, generated largely by a tax on crude oil and selected chemicals. This trust fund has been used to finance cleanup activities (especially emergency cleanups); the EPA then attempts to recover the costs from the parties responsible for the pollution. The Superfund Amendments and Reauthorization Act of 1986 (SARA) increased the fund to $8.5 billion. Moreover, SARA strengthens Superfund's enforcement provisions, emphasizes cleanup methods that reduce the volume and toxicity of waste, imposes stricter cleanup obligations on contaminated federal facilities, and provides for local-level emergency planning, inventories of toxic emissions, and communities' right-to-know (see figure 12.2 and table 12.1).

Figure 12.3 shows density of EPA-listed sites per state; actual numbers for each state are in table 12.2. The list, derived from the EPA's own data plus reports from the states, includes sites

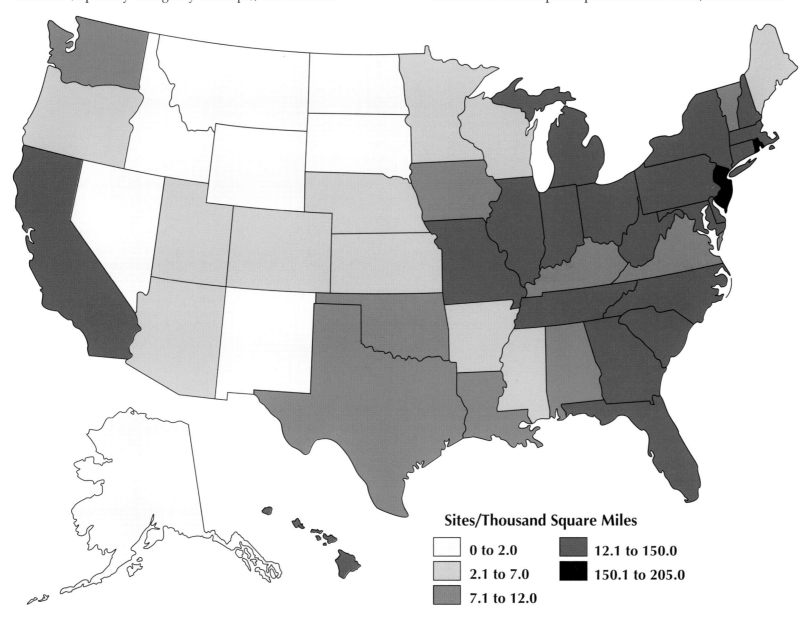

Sites/Thousand Square Miles

☐ 0 to 2.0	▨ 12.1 to 150.0
▨ 2.1 to 7.0	■ 150.1 to 205.0
▨ 7.1 to 12.0	

Figure 12.3. Superfund: Potentially Hazardous Sites.

Source:
EPA, CERCLIS (Washington, DC: EPA, October 5, 1988, computer printout).

where wastes are stored, treated, disposed of, or released. Over 30,000 sites have been inventoried, up sharply from an initial 8,000 in 1980. Industrialized areas of California, Texas, the Great Lakes, Ohio Valley, and Northeast regions, and—to a somewhat lesser extent—the Southeast are strongly represented.

By the General Accounting Office's reckoning (GAO 1987c),

the EPA's list is much too small. The GAO's 1987 estimate ranged between 130,000 and 425,000 sites, while the EPA's inventory at that time was only about 27,000. Why the gross disparity? According to the GAO, the EPA assigns a low priority to site identification, allocating most of its limited funds to cleanup activities. Moreover, states have received little guidance for

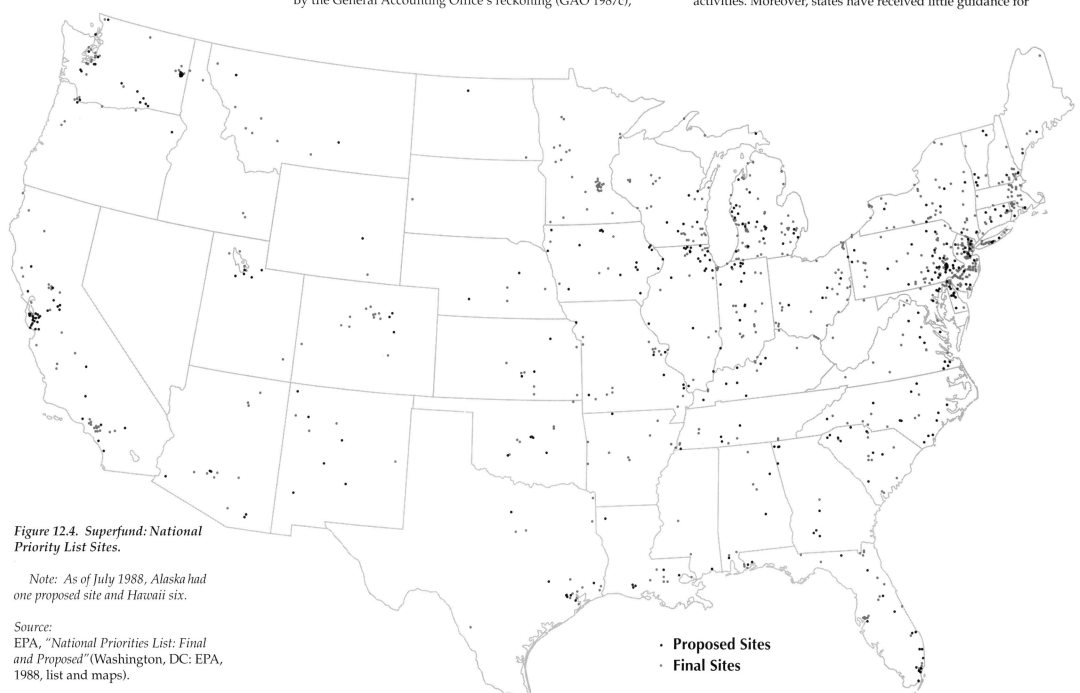

Figure 12.4. Superfund: National Priority List Sites.

Note: *As of July 1988, Alaska had one proposed site and Hawaii six.*

Source:
EPA, *"National Priorities List: Final and Proposed"*(Washington, DC: EPA, 1988, list and maps).

· **Proposed Sites**
· **Final Sites**

developing the lists of sites they report to the EPA. The EPA also has failed to list about 500 sites reported by the states. Four of those sites probably are eligible for the National Priorities List.

Figure 12.4 shows National Priority List sites as of June 1988 (as of March 1989 there were 1,163 sites: 890 final, 273 proposed). These sites are drawn from the larger list, which numbered 30,844 as of March 1989 (EPA 1989b). Most of the sites attained their priority status by scoring highly on the "hazard ranking system." The scores reflect potential harm to humans and the environment from migration of substances via groundwater, surface water, or air; from explosion and fire; and from direct contact at the facility. Of particular importance are the types and quantities of waste present, the degree to which contamination has already occurred (especially groundwater contamination), and the population that lives and works near the site. Once a site is on the list and finalized, it is eligible for long-term cleanup, to be undertaken by the EPA, states, and/or the responsible polluting parties.

Although Superfund began with great promise, its achievements have fallen far short of initial expectations. The program was rocked by scandal early in the Reagan administration—but even since that period, progress has been exceedingly slow. The Office of Technology Assessment (OTA 1988a) characterizes Superfund as "largely ineffective and inefficient" and concludes that it is not working in the way Congress intended it to work. The OTA, while acknowledging that each Superfund site is unique, argues that the program suffers from too much flexibility and lack of central control. The relatively few cleanups that have been undertaken have been compromised by the use of inadequate or inappropriate technologies; the difficulty of attracting, training, and retaining management personnel; and lack of public trust. The costs are very high: They are currently estimated at $10 million per site (Acton 1989) and have ranged between $500,000 and $1 million per acre at fifteen sites studied by the OTA (1988a). Total costs, excluding those for Department of Energy sites, may reach $500 billion over the next fifty years. As of March 1989, remedial work had been completed at only forty-one sites, twenty-six of which had been removed from the NPL (in the past, some such sites have returned to the list for more work). This is from a total of 1,163 sites (EPA 1989b). Even if the process is speeded up substantially, gains may not be readily apparent. The OTA estimated in 1985 that 10,000 sites should be added to the NPL (OTA 1985).

Superfund is but one piece of legislation that deals with toxic and hazardous substances. The Toxic Substances Control Act (TSCA) of 1976 provides for EPA regulation of the production, use, and disposal of chemicals. All new chemicals—excluding food additives, drugs, pesticides, alcohol, and tobacco—are covered, as well as existing chemicals not regulated by other laws. Other major laws include the Federal Insecticide, Fungicide, and Rodenticide Act (see figure 12.8) and the Federal Food, Drug, and Cosmetic Act, which authorizes the EPA and the Food and Drug Administration jointly to set tolerance levels for pesticide residues in food and food products. The Clean Air and Clean Water acts (see chapters 8 and 9) authorize the EPA to regulate hazardous and toxic emissions into air and water, respectively. Toxics in the workplace are regulated by the Occupational Safety and Health Act of 1972. Transport of toxic and hazardous substances is regulated by the Hazardous Materials Transportation Act of 1970, the Federal Railroad Safety Act of 1970, the Ports and Waterways Safety Act of 1972, and the Dangerous Cargo Act of 1952 (which covers water-borne transport).

Perhaps the law that deals most thoroughly with toxic and hazardous threats is the Resource Conservation and Recovery Act (RCRA). RCRA was enacted in 1976 as an amendment to the Solid Waste Disposal Act—but since that time the emphasis has shifted toward hazardous waste. Under Subtitle C of RCRA, the EPA identifies hazardous wastes and regulates their generation, transportation, treatment, storage, and disposal. Each regulated waste is identified and tracked—from "cradle to grave"—by means of a manifest.

Of particular relevance are the 1984 amendments to RCRA, known as the Hazardous and Solid Waste Amendments (HSWA). The HSWA represent a policy shift away from land disposal and toward waste reduction, recycling, and new treatment methods for toxic wastes. Land disposal of certain hazardous wastes is banned—as was the case, for example, for dioxin-containing waste and spent or discarded solvents as of November 1986. Under the HSWA, waste-management facilities must comply with minimum technological requirements. For landfills, this means double liners, leachate-collection systems, and extensive groundwater monitoring. The HSWA also strengthens and expands federal inspection, enforcement, and facility-permitting capabilities; requires regulation of used oil; regulates the use of hazardous waste as fuel; controls hazardous waste export; expands citizen participation opportunities; and puts renewed emphasis on consideration of public health risks. Moreover, the HSWA regulates transportation and disposal of wastes by "small quantity generators": those who produce between 100 kilograms (220 pounds) and 1,000 kilograms (2,200 pounds) of hazardous waste per month. One very significant HSWA provision deals with underground storage tanks. Most tanks that store petroleum or other hazardous substances are to be protected against potential leakage. Operators of all regulated tanks are required to institute leak detection, reporting, and remediation procedures (see also p. 100).

Table 12.2. Potentially Hazardous Superfund Sites	
	Sites/1,000 Square Miles
Alabama	9.9
Alaska	0.3
Arizona	3.8
Arkansas	5.8
California	14.6
Colorado	3.6
Connecticut	95.5
Delaware	89.0
Dist. of Columbia	231.9
Florida	15.0
Georgia	12.4
Hawaii	16.2
Idaho	2.0
Illinois	21.6
Indiana	33.3
Iowa	7.2
Kansas	4.1
Kentucky	11.9
Louisiana	10.5
Maine	3.9
Maryland	26.6
Massachusetts	82.1
Michigan	26.4
Minnesota	4.7
Mississippi	6.7
Missouri	15.6
Montana	1.0
Nebraska	3.7
Nevada	1.2
New Hampshire	15.6
New Jersey	157.1
New Mexico	1.7
New York	29.3
North Carolina	14.4
North Dakota	0.6
Ohio	24.4
Oklahoma	7.8
Oregon	2.7
Pennsylvania	50.8
Rhode Island	201.3
South Carolina	12.2
South Dakota	0.8
Tennessee	16.6
Texas	8.2
Utah	2.2
Vermont	10.4
Virginia	10.9
Washington	9.1
West Virginia	13.3
Wisconsin	6.1
Wyoming	1.1

Table 12.2. Potentially Hazardous Superfund Sites.

Source:
EPA, CERCLIS (Washington, DC: EPA, October 5, 1988, computer printout).

Figure 12.5. FOCUS: Love Canal.

Source:
New York State Department of Health, *Love Canal Emergency Declaration Area: Decision on Habitability* (Albany: New York State Department of Health, 1988), p. 10.

Habitability definitions:

1) "Does not meet habitability criteria": not suitable for residential use without remediation of contaminated soil—but may be used for other purposes (e.g., commercial, industrial) without remediation.

2) "Does not meet habitability criteria, but likelihood of adverse human health consequences is lower than for #1": not presently suitable for unrestricted residential use, but future remediation actions may make area fully habitable.
May currently be used for commercial, industrial, and other non-residential uses without remediation.

3) "Meets all habitability criteria": may be used for residential and/or other purposes.

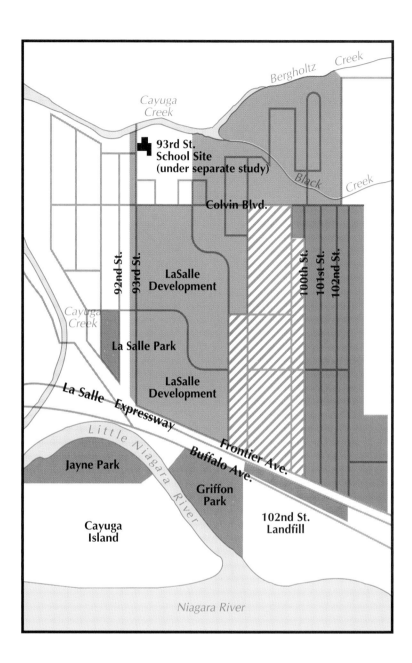

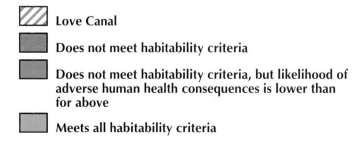

▨ **Love Canal**

■ **Does not meet habitability criteria**

■ **Does not meet habitability criteria, but likelihood of adverse human health consequences is lower than for above**

▨ **Meets all habitability criteria**

FOCUS: LOVE CANAL

Love Canal's widespread notoriety during the late 1970s and early 1980s not only helped spawn the Superfund program; it also gave impetus to a burgeoning NIMBY ("Not In My Back-yard") syndrome. Lois Gibbs—the neighborhood activist who went on to found the national Citizens' Clearinghouse for Hazardous Wastes—virtually represents this transformation in community attitudes. Between 1942 and 1953, Hooker Chemical Company disposed of nearly 44 million pounds of sludges, solvents, fly ash, pesticide residues, and other wastes from its Niagara Falls plant in the rectangular, 16-acre Love Canal tract, a vestige of an aborted 1890s plan to produce cheap hydro power for a model industrial city. In 1953, Hooker reluctantly sold the property, for $1, to the Niagara Falls Board of Education—on the condition that the company be held harmless for any injuries resulting from the chemicals. In 1954, an elementary school was built on the site, and by 1972 the landfill was nearly surrounded by homes whose backyards abutted it.

In the mid-1970s, heavy rain and snowmelt brought chemicals to the surface. But despite the landfill's scarred and blighted appearance, it was used as a children's playground until early 1978. In April 1978, the New York State Commissioner of Health declared Love Canal a threat to human health and the environment and ordered it enclosed with a fence. In August, New York declared a state of emergency, ordered closure of the school, advised evacuation of pregnant women and young children from 239 homes, and then authorized purchase of those homes. Shortly thereafter, President Carter declared a federal state of emergency. The state and federal governments then embarked on a cleanup operation, and several health and epidemiological studies were undertaken.

A second federal emergency was declared in May 1980, paving the way for a voluntary federal-state buyout of an additional 768 families outside the original evacuation zone. This enlarged area—the "Emergency Declaration Area"—consists of the regions shown on the map. The EPA later concluded that this second evacuation—prompted in part by two studies heavily criticized for lack of rigor and validity—was probably unnecessary. After 1978, the canal had been capped with clay, and a leachate treatment facility was constructed. Incineration of dioxin-contaminated soil, yet to take place, will put total cleanup costs over $250 million.

Controversy about Love Canal's resettlement has been almost continuous. In 1988, in the wake of a state study showing generally low levels of chemicals, New York's Commissioner of Health issued his habitability decision, which is represented on the map. It seeks to preserve neighborhoods but carries a proviso about possible noise, odors, and other nuisances—even in "habitable" areas—associated with continuing remedial activities.

DISPOSAL FACILITIES AND TRANSPORTATION

Between 1980 and 1986, only fourteen new commercial hazardous waste-disposal facilities were granted permits for construction and operation; only six of those were actually in operation as of 1986 (New York State Legislative Commission 1987). The 1984 amendments to the Resource Conservation and Recovery Act (RCRA) impose stringent new requirements for the various means of waste disposal (see page 140). They cover types of wastes received, erosion and leak control, monitoring and inspection, and facility closure. New landfills, for example, are to have two liners and two leachate collection systems—and substances are to be banned for land disposal unless specifically approved by the EPA. Incinerators are to meet stringent emission standards for organic hazardous chemicals, hydrogen chloride, and particulates. Additional standards are to be promulgated by the EPA. While the new requirements provide at least some assurance as to a facility's environmental soundness, they also, as of 1987, had resulted in the closing of approximately 1,000 treatment, storage, and disposal facilities—adding to the general sense of crisis regarding hazardous waste management.

Figure 12.6 shows that those states with several facilities already in operation (generally the larger waste-generating states) tend to be making the greatest progress toward siting new ones. The Superfund Amendments and Reauthorization Act of 1986 (SARA—see pages 135–138) requires states to demonstrate adequate waste treatment, storage, or disposal for a twenty-year period by November 1989—or risk losing eligibility for

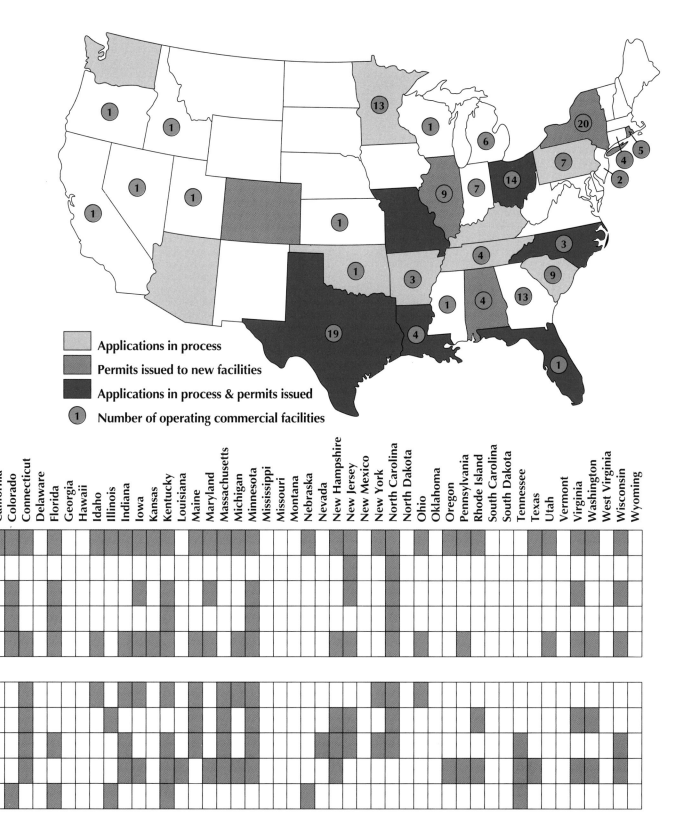

Applications in process

Permits issued to new facilities

Applications in process & permits issued

(1) Number of operating commercial facilities

Superfund monies. Most states are entering into cooperative regional arrangements for waste disposal, but only four states—California, Massachusetts, New Jersey, and North Carolina—expect waste reduction to play prominently in their plans.

In 1986, thirty-six states had siting statutes—up sharply from one in 1972—and thirty-one of those actually had formal siting processes. The New York State Legislative Commission defines a formal process as one that is separate from and goes beyond the basic RCRA requirements. As of 1986, only four of the states with siting processes had actually sited and permitted commercial facilities; and only four of those facilities have actually come into operation. Although ten states have state-wide hazardous-waste-management plans, only two—New Jersey and North Carolina—have "active" strategies for implementing them.

Most states promote the siting of private facilities but do not formally require it. Only a few states actually own or operate their own facilities. In 1987, eleven states had programs for developing new facilities; six actually mandated it. Twenty-four states had specific provisions for state override of local zoning laws. While this is a legally sound course, it is politically treacherous—and many states may be reluctant to follow it.

Figure 12.6 shows the degree to which states engage in various public participation activities. Most states seem principally interested in placating citizens at the municipal and neighborhood levels, the main wellsprings of opposition to facility siting. Of the twenty-one states with siting boards that reviewed applications for new facilities, eleven provided for representation of the community in which the facility is proposed. Even when the "host" community is not specifically represented, board members may at least appear to be sympathetic to or representative of local concerns.

Eleven states provided technical-assistance grants to localities—in most cases to enable them to hire their own technical experts. Whether or not this significantly empowers the communities was not a matter addressed by the survey. Increasingly, communities are offered economic incentives (some say bribes) to facilitate the siting of unwanted facilities. These include direct appropriations from the state; money from the facility developer to hire consultants, expand emergency response capabilities, or offset property tax reductions; and provisions for host communities to impose taxes on the facility's receipts. While public health often is a critical issue, so is maintenance of property values—not only to individuals but also local governments concerned about their tax bases.

Nineteen states had engaged in some type of formal negotiation or mediation; but bargaining undoubtedly also takes place in those states lacking formal provisions. Interestingly, six

states allow local governments—in some sense at least—to make the final siting decisions. While Florida allows for state override and Illinois for state appeal, Colorado, Kentucky, Nebraska, and Tennessee apparently do not permit state preemption.

Overall, the New York State Legislative Commission found that public participation, as they interpret it, does not necessarily lead to greater success in facility siting. However, certain procedures may be effective—most notably, the use of negotiation and the provision of economic incentives. More generally, the probability of success seems to depend heavily on prevailing political climate; local economic, population, and land-use characteristics; and proposed waste-management technology. Landfills and incinerators are apparently more difficult to site than are treatment facilities. Although they have been proposed in nearly equal numbers, the success rate for treatment facilities has been 22 percent, but for both landfills and incinerators, only about 7 percent.

Transportation questions, though not in the national spotlight as often as waste disposal, can provoke outpourings of local concern. Hazardous-materials transport is regulated by several federal agencies. The Department of Transportation (DOT) is the overall lead agency, but significant authority also is exercised by the Federal Highway Administration, Federal Railroad Administration, Federal Aviation Administration, National Highway Traffic Safety Administration, and Coast Guard. The Department of Energy deals with fuels, the Department of Defense with military materials, the Nuclear Regulatory Commission with radioactive materials, the EPA with chemicals and nonnuclear hazardous wastes, and the Federal Emergency Management Agency with coordination and technical assistance for emergency response. The Resource Conservation and Recovery Act imposes procedural and record-keeping obligations on transporters of hazardous materials. States also regulate hazardous-materials transport—some quite extensively, others minimally. Many localities have their own comprehensive emergency-response procedures.

About 90 percent of all accidents reported to the DOT between 1973 and 1983 occurred on highways. Petroleum products—by far the leading hazardous substance transported—accounted for most accidents and injuries. Moreover, most accidents involve handling and loading of materials rather than their actual conveyance. Still, the potential for major transport disasters is very real. The Office of Technology Assessment (OTA 1986b) recently called for better placarding of hazardous materials; national standards for licensing, permitting, and shipment notification; more effective enforcement of legislation; national emergency-response guidelines and training assistance; and better federal data collection and dissemination.

State-Level Household
Hazardous Waste Programs

Alaska

Hawaii

■ Participating States

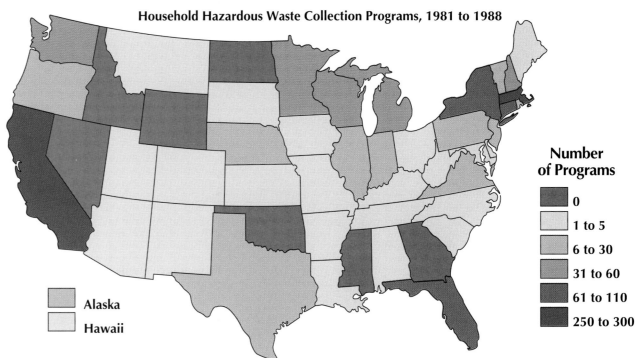

Household Hazardous Waste Collection Programs, 1981 to 1988

**Number
of Programs**

■ 0

□ 1 to 5

■ 6 to 30

■ 31 to 60

■ 61 to 110

■ 250 to 300

Alaska

Hawaii

HOUSEHOLD HAZARDOUS WASTE

Most American homes contain a wide variety of toxic and hazardous substances, many of them potential indoor air pollutants. Without special ventilating systems, tightly insulated and sealed buildings—energy-efficient as they may be—are likely to exacerbate the problem. Among the more publicized indoor pollutants are radon (figures 12.9–12.11), asbestos (figure 12.12), lead (chapter 8), and formaldehyde. The latter is present in foam insulation, wood, carpet and furniture backing, and drapes.

In addition, carbon monoxide is released by heaters, stoves, and fireplaces; nitrogen dioxide is produced by gas and kerosene stoves and heaters (as well as tobacco smoke); and small particles are emitted by stoves, heaters, fireplaces, and tobacco smoking. Moreover, organic chemicals are transferred to the indoor air through vaporization (often when the product is not even in use) of cleaners, polishers, paints, strippers, solvents, wood preservatives, air fresheners, moth repellents, dry-cleaned clothing, drugs and cosmetics, stored fuels, and hobby and automotive products. Furniture, carpets, and drapes may also release organic chemicals to the air. Indeed, the EPA's Total Exposure Assessment Methodology (TEAM) studies reveal that at least a dozen organic contaminants are present in indoor air at concentrations two to five times those of outdoor air—regardless

of whether the setting is rural or urban/industrial. Biological contaminants, such as pollens, molds, fungi, and viruses, may also proliferate and be carried though the air—particularly in commercial buildings with poorly designed or maintained ventilation systems. The federal response to indoor air pollution thus far has been geared largely toward research—with regulations or bans enacted only for a small number of specific chemicals.

The various toxic products used both inside and outside the house eventually will be dispersed, in part through the municipal solid-waste stream. Used motor oil and antifreeze, as well as leftover paints, solvents, insecticides, and cosmetics are examples of what ends up in landfills and sewer systems. All told, however, the toxic/hazardous portion of the municipal waste stream is believed to be quite small (minuscule in comparison with industrial hazardous waste). Various estimates suggest that it is no more than 1 percent by weight (Conn 1989). Yet there is ample cause for concern. Hazardous materials may cause fires, explosions, or other hazards when trash is collected, compacted, transported, landfilled, or incinerated; and they are leached from municipal landfills into groundwater.

States, communities, and local organizations recently have begun to sponsor collection programs. The number of programs,

*Figure 12.7. Household Hazardous
Waste Programs.*

Sources:
Dana Duxbury and Associates, "1981–88 State Level Household Hazardous Waste Laws and Regulation" (Andover, MA: Dana Duxbury and Associates, 1988, photocopied table).

Dana Duxbury & Associates, "The National Listing of Household Hazardous Waste Collection Programs" (Andover, MA: Dana Duxbury & Associates, 1988, photocopied table).

according to the survey on which figure 12.7 is based, rose from two in 1981 to 440 in 1989. Most of them consist of collection days on which householders take their hazardous refuse to a central collection point or—in some cases—put it out for curb-side collection. Enthusiasm often is high, but participation rates generally are quite low, on the order of a fraction of a percent of community households (SCS Engineers 1986). This may, how-ever, result from the infrequency, unpredictability, and incon-venience of collection days; the small quantities of items to be disposed of at any given time, and lack of public awareness as to which materials are potentially hazardous.

Only a few places—among them San Bernardino and Monterey counties (California), Whatcom and Thurston coun-ties (Washington), Ingham County (Michigan), Fairfax County (Virginia), and the City of San Francisco—have attempted permanent collection programs. Florida is the first, and only, state to have sponsored an ongoing collection program, under which counties are required to hold regularly scheduled "amnesty days." Its program also includes model provisions concerning waste minimization and public education.

Unfortunately, household hazardous waste management is constrained by several factors. One is cost. The EPA puts the per-ton cost at about $18,000; this compares with average solid-waste disposal costs of about $20 per ton for the United States, and nearly $40 for the northeastern region (New York State Legislative Commission on Solid Waste Management 1988). Costs per participant have ranged between $30 and $300—and in many cases these figures exclude such hidden costs as those incurred in using on-duty municipal employees.

Liability is another serious issue. Waste collectors may incur liability under the provisions of the Superfund law or under common law. Even though Superfund liability is likely to be relatively small, and in theory recoverable from con-tractors, the entire issue remains murky. The costs of liability coverage are very high, indeed sometimes prohibitive. More-over, innovation may be stifled. Madison, Wisconsin, for example, sponsored a waste exchange where residents took home some of the products discarded by their neighbors—and the one-time project was deemed a success. But because of the potential liability for misidentification and misuse of exchanged products, few municipalities are eager to follow Madison's lead.

The most fruitful course may be reduction of household hazardous waste at the source. Less noxious products could be substituted for the offending ones, and hazardous materials could be acquired only in the quantities needed to do the job at hand. But even if such efforts—limited as they have been thus far—are stepped up, collection programs will still be needed to cope with the inevitable residue of household hazardous waste.

SOME SPECIFIC THREATS

Risks from radon and asbestos are addressed elsewhere in this chapter, and lead is briefly discussed in chapter 8. These and the additional substances considered below are but a few of many that pose significant threats to human health and the environ-ment. Moreover, we say nothing here of the complex, but usually poorly understood, synergistic effects that occur when two or more chemicals act in combination.

PCBs—polychlorinated biphenyls—are a group of synthetic organic compounds. They are responsible for rashes, abdominal pain, and temporary blindness; they may also cause cancer, mis-carriages, and birth defects. Through the 1970s, they were widely used as insulating fluids in electrical transformers and capacitors as well as in the production of plastics, lubricating fluids, inks, and other substances; they were used even for dust control on roads. Although Congress in 1976 ordered the EPA to ban most production and use of PCBs, enormous amounts of the extremely persistent substance remain in the environment. The EPA imposed special disposal requirements in 1980—but PCB threats still loom large from leaking landfills, electrical fires, and other exposure pathways. Indeed, even though individual levels have been declining, PCBs are widespread in humans and wildlife.

Dioxins are a family of chlorinated hydrocarbon compounds, of which one—TCDD—is extremely toxic and persistent. In laboratory tests, even low levels cause cancer, birth defects, and reduced resistance to disease. TCDD unavoidably occurs in the manufacture of the herbicides 2,4,5-T, Silvex, and Agent Orange, which was widely used as a defoliant in Vietnam (all have been removed from the market). TCDD and other dioxins also are released in pulp and paper production and during combustion of municipal wastes—a principal reason for much of the local opposition to municipal solid-waste incinerators (figure 11.5). Trace levels of TCDD are present in the fatty tissue of most Americans; the long-term effects of such exposure are not known.

Toxic metals also provide great cause for concern: among them arsenic, beryllium, cadmium, chromium, copper, lead, mercury, nickel, selenium, and zinc. These metals are produced in certain combustion and smelting processes and are wide-spread in various industrial and agricultural applications as well as a variety of consumer products. One of the exposure pathways for heavy metals—especially cadmium—is uptake by plants where sewage sludge is used as a fertilizer (see figure 11.6). Most of these substances are suspected carcinogens; among the other effects are eye and skin disorders; liver, kidney, and lung damage; nervous-system disorders; and birth defects. As noted in chapter 8, ambient concentrations of lead have declined dramatically in recent years. But the limited evidence regarding exposure to other toxic metals is much less encouraging.

PESTICIDE USE

The pesticides represented in figure 12.8—listed in the caption—account for about half the country's pesticide usage between 1982 and 1985. In terms of absolute quantities applied, Iowa, Illinois, Indiana, Minnesota, and Texas were—in descending order—the top five. The ratios displayed on the map are rather rough approximations. An acre harvested is not necessarily an acre where pesticides were used, and of course actual usage varies greatly depending on specific crops produced, local growing conditions, and regional farming practices. Nonetheless, something of a pattern—if not a very uniform one—emerges. The warmer, wetter parts of the country— particularly in the Southeast—tend to have the highest application rates. Greater applications are needed to control more rapid growth of weeds and proliferation of pests.

A separate analysis by Resources for the Future (Gianessi 1987b) reveals that nationwide approximately 661 million pounds of active ingredients were applied in 1986. Three of them—alachlor, atrazine, and butylate—accounted for about one-third of all applications. The crops accounting for highest-volume pesticide use were field corn and soybeans.

The Federal Insecticide, Fungicide, and Rodenticide Act (FIFRA), initially passed in 1947, was greatly strengthened in 1972. EPA registration requirements were established for all pesticides, and the agency may restrict or prohibit use of new pesticides as well as cancel or suspend use of existing pesticides (see table 12.3)—if the risk to human health or the environment outweighs the pesticide's economic benefit. The EPA also sets requirements for pesticide labeling and application and for farmworker safety.

The Federal Food, Drug, and Cosmetic Act (FFDCA) authorizes the EPA to set tolerance levels (i.e., maximum amounts of residues considered "safe") for pesticides in food and feed crops. The federal Food and Drug Administration and Department of Agriculture are responsible for enforcing the tolerances. The FFDCA also requires that tolerances be established for processed foods, since residues are sometimes concentrated in the processing of food. One portion of the law—the "Delaney Clause"—essentially sets the tolerance level at zero for *any* food additive (or in this case pesticide residue) found to induce cancer in human beings or animals. The EPA is currently reviewing hundreds of pesticides for compliance with the Delaney Clause and—on a priority basis—issuing regulations for their use. Still—depending on how it is interpreted—the Delaney Clause applies to only one-fifth to one-half of total dietary oncogenic (tumor-related) risk from pesticides. Many foods—such as meat, milk, and poultry—escape its provisions.

The Delaney dilemmas aside, the issues of pesticide use and toxicity are daunting. Of the nearly 1.2 billion pounds of pesticides used each year, about 70 percent is for agricultural purposes; 23 percent for forestry, industry, and government programs; and 7 percent for home and garden applications. Most agricultural chemicals are applied to corn, cotton, soybeans, and wheat. Pesticide production has mainly declined in recent years (after rising quite steadily until the mid-1970s), largely due to decreased agricultural production, particularly of the four key crops. Recent retirements of acreage under the Conservation Reserve Program (figure 4.7) will probably contribute to a further downward trend. However, as *total* production of pesticides decreases, their *individual toxicities* may continue to increase. Moreover, herbicide production, while below its 1981 peak, has increased disproportionately since 1960. Increased adoption of conservation tillage will probably keep herbicide use relatively high (see figure 4.6). The U.S. Department of Agriculture (USDA 1989) projected that in 1989 herbicides would account for almost 85 percent of total pesticide use, insecticides 14 percent, and fungicides 2 percent.

Approximately 50,000 pesticides are registered for use in the United States, and they contain some 1,500 active ingredients (i.e., the components that kill or control pests)—most of which are organic compounds. In terms of volumes applied, 60 percent of all herbicides are oncogenic (capable of producing benign or malignant tumors) or potentially oncogenic, while 90 percent of all fungicides and 30 percent of all insecticides fall into this category (National Research Council 1987). The rather limited studies of pesticide residues in human tissue and urine show that exposure is widespread. Residues are present in up to 95 percent of human tissue samples. Levels of most pesticides are, however, declining. Yet even such substances as DDT, heptachlor, and dieldrin—all banned or strictly controlled for some time—are still present in substantial (though declining) amounts.

Animal studies show broadly similar results, with interesting spatial patterns for DDT and dieldrin: They occur in higher levels in birds from the East and West coasts than those in the interior of the country. Toxaphene levels in fish seem to correspond with especially heavy use of the chemical in the southern and midwestern regions. Chlorinated pesticides— such as DDT—are generally widespread in bottom sediments and bottom-dwelling fish, with some particularly high levels in the northeastern Atlantic coastal region and in the Pacific coastal waters of southern California. Pesticides are also widespread in stream sediments, with dieldrin, chlordane, and DDT residues present in almost one-third of sediment samples analyzed by the U.S. Geological Survey (see Conservation Foundation 1987). Groundwater contamination is discussed in chapter 9.

Table 12.3. Pesticides "Removed from Market"

Pesticide	Uses Still Permitted
Aldrin	Some agricultural, moth-proofing, and termiticide uses
Chlordane	Some agricultural and termiticide uses
Compound 1080	Livestock collar retained; rodenticide use under review
DBCP	Hawaiian pineapples
DDT and related compounds	Certain health and disease-control uses
Dieldrin	Some agricultural, moth-proofing, and termiticide uses
Endrin	Use as avicide (bird control)
Ethylene Dibromide	Minor uses and use on citrus for export
Heptachlor	Some agricultural and termiticide uses
Kepone	
Lindane	Certain commercial, residential, agricultural uses
Mercury	Various fungicidal uses
Mirex	
Silvex	
Strychnine	Rodenticide, avicide, and livestock collar uses
2,4,5-T	
Toxaphene	Livestock dip and minor agricultural uses

Sources:
EPA, *Suspended, Cancelled and Restricted Pesticides* (Washington, DC: EPA, 1985).

EPA, *Environmental Progress and Challenges: EPA's Update*, EPA-230-07-88-033 (Washington, DC: EPA, 1988), p. 118.

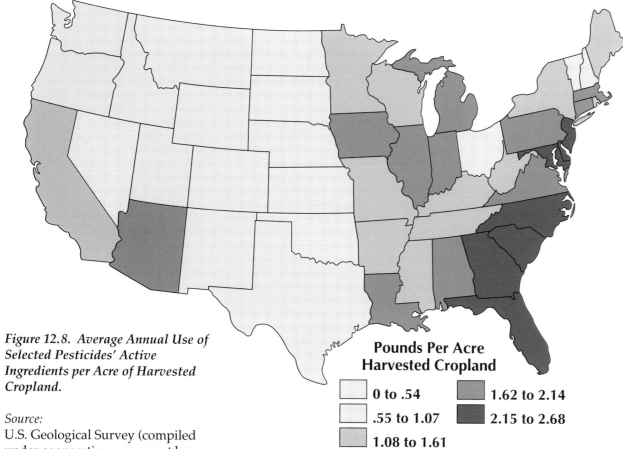

Figure 12.8. Average Annual Use of Selected Pesticides' Active Ingredients per Acre of Harvested Cropland.

Source:
U.S. Geological Survey (compiled under cooperative agreement by Resources for the Future), "Total Use of the 25 Selected Pesticides, Based on Years 1982–85," mimeo, 1989.

The selected pesticides represented on the map are:

Acifluorfen	PCNB
Metolachlor	Carbaryl
Disulfoton	Phorate
Bensulide	Parathion
Metiram	Malathion
Propanil	Diazinon
2,4-D	Methamidophos
Trifluralin	Carbofuran
Cyanazine	Alachlor
Chlorothalonil	Thiobencarb
Vernolate	Atrazine
Methyl parathion	Fluometuron
Ethoprop	

**Pounds Per Acre
Harvested Cropland**

☐ 0 to .54   ▨ 1.62 to 2.14
☐ .55 to 1.07   ▰ 2.15 to 2.68
▨ 1.08 to 1.61

A great deal about pesticide toxicity simply is not known. The 1972 amendments to FIFRA require the EPA to reevaluate the 600 active ingredients previously approved for use. The EPA is also reassessing tolerance levels for the pesticides under review. Many—perhaps most—of these pesticides were inadequately tested by manufacturers when they were initially registered. Indeed, in 1984 the National Academy of Sciences concluded that 84 percent of the active ingredients in use had been inadequately tested for carcinogenicity; 93 percent had not been tested at all for mutagenicity; and 70 percent had not been tested for teratogenicity. Inert ingredients (those that do not kill or control pests)—largely overlooked in the registration and tolerance-setting processes—also may have toxic effects. The EPA's "reregistration" of 600 active ingredients, initially scheduled for completion in 1975, has proceeded exceedingly slowly. Various current estimates put the completion date for the process somewhere in the late 1990s or the early part of the next century.

Direct responsibilities for pesticide regulation are defined principally by FIFRA and FFDCA—and to a lesser extent by various other federal laws. Although direct state authority is limited essentially to enforcement of label restrictions and training of applicators, the 1972 FIFRA amendments allow states to "stretch" their authority. They may restrict or in some cases prohibit pesticide application, monitor residues more vigorously and adopt stricter residue standards than the federal government, implement rigorous worker and community right-to-know procedures, and undertake stringent health-monitoring, accident-response, and other worker-protection programs.

EPA slowness and ineffectiveness have moved some states to enact their own bans on certain pesticides. The states with the most vigorous pesticide-related policies and programs, according to the Fund for Renewable Energy and the Environment (Ridley 1988) are California, Maine, Texas, Connecticut, Hawaii, Maine, Minnesota, New Hampshire, New York, and Wisconsin. The widespread presence of pesticides in groundwater—especially in agricultural regions—has generated a good deal of concern on the part of the states. Notable is Iowa's Groundwater Protection Act of 1987, which provides for extensive monitoring and actions to reduce pesticide and other contamination.

Recently, dramatic news stories have galvanized public concerns about pesticides in food. Apple growers responded to public alarm about the pesticide alar by voluntarily banning its use. Indeed, "alternative" methods of pest control—traditionally downplayed by farmers, the agro-chemical industry, and the federal government—have gained a new measure of respect. Furthermore, the case for reduced chemical dependence in agriculture was recently bestowed with the scientific credibility of a National Research Council (1989) report.

Among the alternative means of pest control are biological controls—such as predators, parasites, and pathogens that weaken or destroy undesirable insects, weeds, and other pests. Various planting techniques—including crop rotation, planting schedules unfavorable to certain pests, and companion planting of certain crops and other plants—also have proven effective. Other techniques include destruction of pest breeding areas, use of genetic controls (such as sterilization by radiation or chemicals), use of sex attractants and hormones to capture or control insects, and breeding of disease-resistant crops.

The concept of integrated pest management (IPM) relies on these alternative methods, in conjunction with minimal, carefully controlled applications of pesticides. Although IPM has been practiced at least since the 1940s, its widespread acceptance has been hampered by lack of necessary basic research, lack of requisite specialized knowledge on the part of farmers, and the vested interests of the agri-chemical industry. Nonetheless, IPM agricultural extension programs reached more than 27 million acres of farmland in 1984, and an additional 3.3 million acres were served by private consultants (Virginia Cooperative Extension Service 1987).

RADON

Radon is a colorless, odorless gas produced by the natural decay of radium-226. It is not the radon gas itself, but rather its "daughters"—further products of the radioactive decay process—that pose threats to human health. Problems can arise in confined spaces, where air movement—and consequently the dispersion of radon gas—is slowed. Radon enters the home through openings in foundations and through water supplies, and as it decays, its daughters adhere to small particulate matter. When these particles are inhaled in sufficient quantities, lung-cancer risks increase significantly. Indeed, various sources put the annual number of radon-induced lung-cancer deaths somewhere between 5,000 and 20,000.

Although radon is second only to cigarette smoking as a cause of lung cancer, its hazardousness was brought to light only recently, when for no apparent reason an employee set off geiger counters at a Pennsylvania nuclear power plant in 1984. The source of the radiation turned out to be radon in his home. Since that time, radon has developed into an important and interesting policy issue: It diverts attention from such issues as corporate and industrial pollution yet puts governments in the uncomfortable position—if only through their provision of information—of directly influencing people's behavior and property values.

Figure 12.9 shows areas where there is at least a reasonable likelihood of encountering high radon levels. Radon is most abundant in soils and rock that contain significant amounts of uranium. Good candidate areas are those with granitic and phosphatic rocks and—of course—uranium-bearing coals and shales. Areas with significant numbers of known occurrences of elevated indoor radon levels are highlighted: the Reading Prong of New Jersey and Pennsylvania, uranium mine tailings in Colorado, and a section of southeastern Massachusetts. However, the actual presence of radon in any area—including those with places characterized by generally high levels—tends to be highly variable. Moreover, the national map is based on limited data and is continually being revised by the EPA.

The EPA has somewhat arbitrarily established a "screening level" of 4 picocuries of radon per liter of air (4 pCi/l) as a

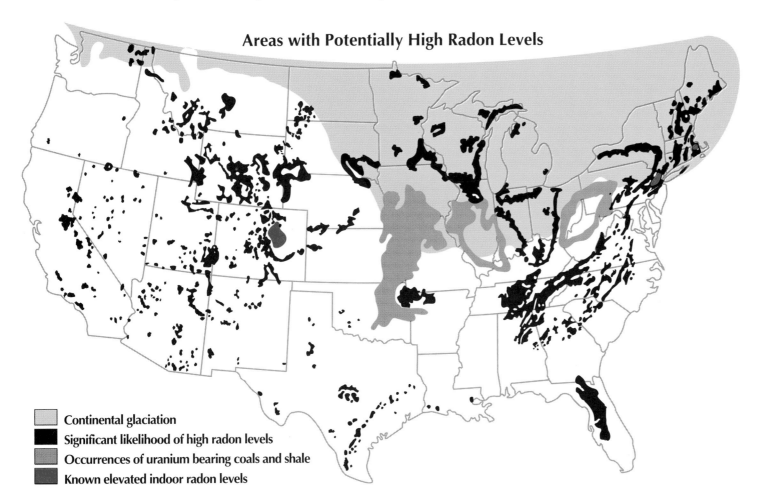

Areas with Potentially High Radon Levels

Continental glaciation
Significant likelihood of high radon levels
Occurrences of uranium bearing coals and shale
Known elevated indoor radon levels

Figure 12.9. Areas with Potentially High Radon Levels.

Source:
EPA, "Areas with Potentially High Radon Levels" (Washington, DC: EPA, 1987, map).

Figure 12.10. Radon Survey Results.

Source:
EPA, "Cumulative State/EPA Indoor State Radon Survey Results" (Washington, DC: EPA, 1988, press release).

Figure 12.11. Status of State Radon Programs.

Source:
EPA, *Summary of State Radon Programs*, EPA 520/1-87-19-1 (Washington, DC: EPA, 1987), p. 14.

threshold for concern. One pCi/l approximately represents the radioactive decay of two radon atoms in 1 quart of air. The lung-cancer risk posed by household exposure to 4 pCi/l of radon (thirteen to fifty lung cancers per 1,000 population) is approximately equal to that of 300 chest x-rays per year. Household test results must, however, be interpreted with caution. Many reported readings are based on charcoal canister tests, which have high margins of error. Testing often is done only once, yet the amounts of radon entering the home may vary enormously through the year, as air flow through the home changes from season to season. Moreover, much of the testing is done in basements, where radon levels are likely to be highest—but where most families spend little time. More accurate and meaningful results can be obtained through yearlong "alpha-track" testing throughout the home. But this is more costly and time-consuming and is usually recommended only after a charcoal canister, basement "screening test" reveals radon levels higher than 4 pCi/l.

Still, the screening results represented in figure 12.10 are cause for concern. Based on its survey of homes in sixteen states, the EPA estimates that in ten of those states, more than 20 percent of homes have radon levels exceeding the threshold value of 4 pCi/l. The EPA—while cautious in making this inference—believes that available evidence points to the distinct possibility of elevated radon levels in all fifty states. Moreover, some analysts contend that radon is the leading water pollutant. It poses little direct threat—but introduces radon into the air through evaporation from showers, cooking, and other activities.

The EPA and states are responding to the radon threat in a number of ways. These include further surveys and evaluations to assess the extent of the problem (1989 survey locations are Alaska, Iowa, Maine, New Mexico, Ohio, Vermont, and various Indian lands); research, training, and demonstration programs for radon mitigation; and public information and assistance activities. Radon levels can be very effectively controlled by sealing cracks in foundations, improving ventilation, and removing radon and its daughters from indoor air. One of the energy-conservation strategies heavily promoted during the energy crises of the 1970s was the tight insulation and sealing of homes and other buildings. If this is not integrated with an efficient air exchange system (and it was not in many cases), radon and other indoor air-pollution problems can be aggravated.

Figure 12.11 provides an overview of state-level activities. The categories, of course, are rather general—and most of the programs are in various evolutionary stages. All states have basic information programs; several states have developed "operational programs." As might be expected, the states where threats loom largest tend to be the most active. In this regard, New Jersey and Pennsylvania (home to the Reading Prong— where elevated radon levels first came to public attention), Colorado (with its uranium mine tailings), and Florida (with its extensive phosphate deposits) clearly stand out.

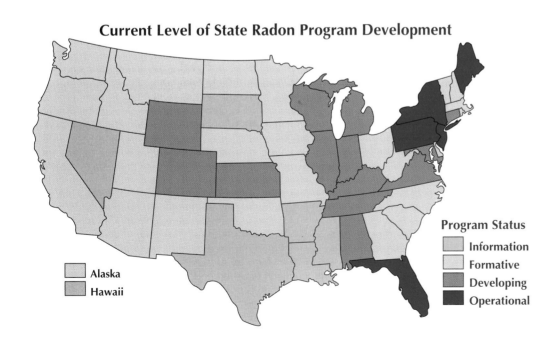

Current Level of State Radon Program Development

Program Status
- Information
- Formative
- Developing
- Operational

Alaska
Hawaii

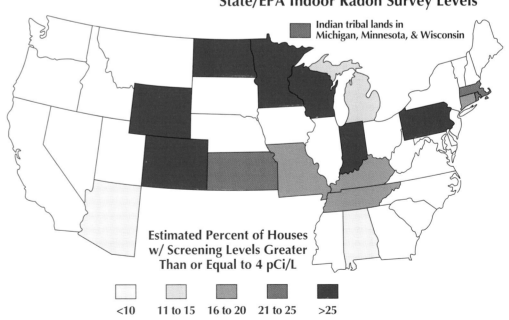

State/EPA Indoor Radon Survey Levels

Indian tribal lands in Michigan, Minnesota, & Wisconsin

Estimated Percent of Houses w/ Screening Levels Greater Than or Equal to 4 pCi/L

<10   11 to 15   16 to 20   21 to 25   >25

ASBESTOS MANAGEMENT

Asbestos—long recognized as a hazard to mining, milling, and manufacturing workers—is associated with lung cancer, meso-thelioma (a cancer of the membrane that lines the chest and abdominal cavities), gastrointestinal cancer, and asbestosis (a disabling, sometimes fatal disease of the lung and pleural tissues for which there is no effective treatment). Asbestos's durability and heat resistance have found wide application in roofing products, insulation, air-conditioning and heating ducts, brakes and gaskets, and many other products. Long-term risks from low-level exposure, though not well understood, are potentially significant—especially when asbestos exposure is combined with cigarette smoking. In mid-1989, the EPA ordered a seven-year phase-out of most asbestos-containing products—but the potential for exposure, especially in buildings, will be with us for many years to come. EPA (1984a) survey results indicate that about 20 percent of all public and commercial buildings have some type of asbestos-containing, friable (prone to crumbling) material. The greatest exposure hazards occur when these materials are damaged or disturbed. Fourteen per-cent of the buildings in the 1984 survey contained damaged material; 9 percent had at least some "significantly damaged" material. Schools are of special concern, because as many as 15 million children—captive in the buildings for lengthy periods—may be exposed.

The first federal program to help schools identify and correct asbestos problems began in 1979. The Asbestos Hazard Emer-gency Response Act (AHERA), passed in 1986 as an extension of an earlier law, requires inspection of public and private schools and development and implementation of management plans. The Occupational Safety and Health Administration (OSHA) admin-isters worker-protection standards for asbestos, while the EPA implements the National Emission Standard for Hazardous Air Pollutants (NESHAP). The NESHAP asbestos regulation, estab-lished in 1973 and amended in 1984 (and again under revision), regulates asbestos removal, transport, and disposal. The EPA provides technical expertise, funds, and information and training centers for asbestos abatement.

Most of the federal programs are administered by the states. Often, as the map shows, their standards exceed federal require-ments. Many states also have their own information, technical-assistance, and funding programs.

Figure 12.12. Asbestos Management.

Source:
National Conference of State Legislatures, "Summary of State Asbestos Programs" (Denver: NCSL, 1989, table).

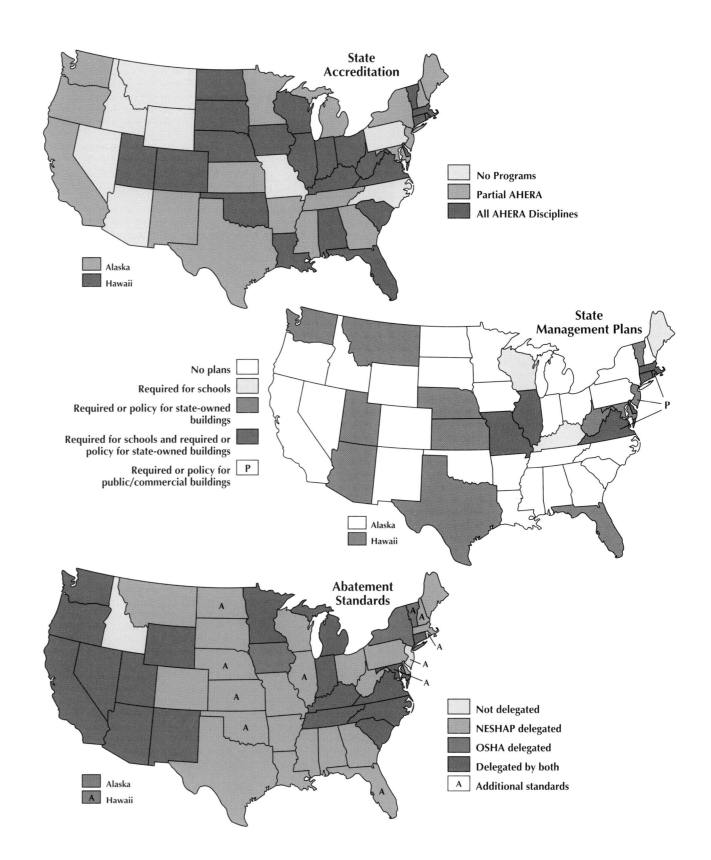

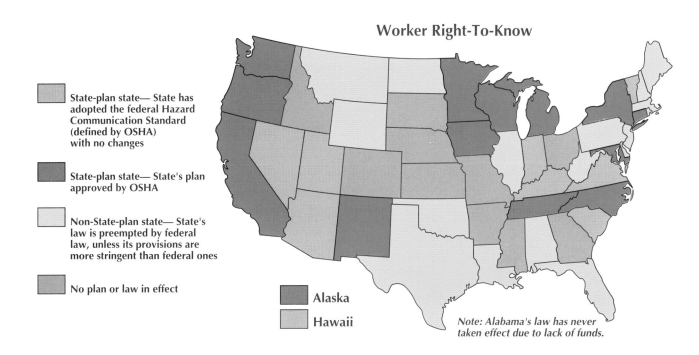

Worker Right-To-Know

State-plan state— State has adopted the federal Hazard Communication Standard (defined by OSHA) with no changes

State-plan state— State's plan approved by OSHA

Non-State-plan state— State's law is preempted by federal law, unless its provisions are more stringent than federal ones

No plan or law in effect

Alaska

Hawaii

Note: Alabama's law has never taken effect due to lack of funds.

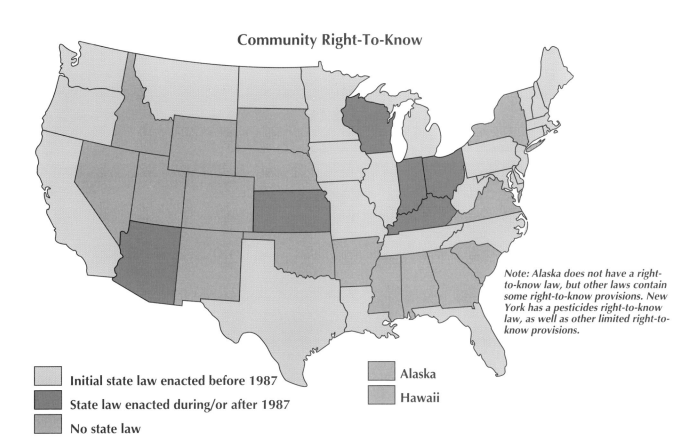

Community Right-To-Know

Note: Alaska does not have a right-to-know law, but other laws contain some right-to-know provisions. New York has a pesticides right-to-know law, as well as other limited right-to-know provisions.

Initial state law enacted before 1987

State law enacted during/or after 1987

No state law

Alaska

Hawaii

WORKER AND COMMUNITY RIGHT-TO-KNOW

The right-to-know concept, legally embodied in the Occupational Safety and Health Act of 1970, authorizes the Occupational Safety and Health Administration (OSHA) to set workplace information, reporting, monitoring, and exposure standards. OSHA's 1983 "Hazard Communication Standard" covers all workplace exposure to hazardous chemicals, that is, those for which there is statistically significant evidence—based on at least one study—of possible acute or chronic health effects. It provides for hazard evaluation, chemical listing, container labeling, employee notification, and training.

The top map in figure 12.13 represents state worker right-to-know provisions. States basically have these options: (1) do nothing (OSHA Standard applies); (2) adopt the OSHA Standard as is or with changes; or (3) adopt their own standards if they are more stringent than OSHA's. State laws may, for example, allow for greater employee rights, provide for emergency response to accidents, or allow fewer exemptions from regulatory requirements. Prior to promulgation of the 1983 federal standard, fifteen states had their own right-to-know laws; now forty have their own laws.

The right-to-know concept was advanced greatly with the 1986 passage of the Superfund Amendments and Reauthorization Act. Title III of that act (figure 12.2) requires local emergency-response plans for chemical accidents, public notification of certain types of accidental chemical releases, compilation and accessibility of information regarding hazardous chemicals used and stored at specific sites (this ties in with the OSHA requirements noted above), and an annual inventory of routine toxic chemical releases. States are responsible for implementing and enforcing Title III.

Many existing state laws (represented on the bottom map) were preempted by the federal law. Although states may require that additional chemicals or facilities be subject to Title III provisions, their own laws must conform with the federal requirements. Besides state laws, some industry-sponsored programs had been in place before Title III—including the Chemical Manufacturers' Association Community Awareness and Emergency Response Program (CAER), after which Title III is in part modeled. Of particular note on the map are the blocks of western and southeastern states that had no community right-to-know provisions prior to enactment of the federal law in late 1986.

Figure 12.13. Worker and Community Right-to-Know.

Source:

Community and Worker Right-To-Know News, 1989: 21–29. By permission of Thompson Publishing Group, 1725 K Street, N.W., Suite 200, Washington, DC 20006, 1-800-424-2959.

The United States, with only 5 percent of the world's population, is responsible for one-third of all energy consumption. Indeed, energy is so cheap and abundant that Americans have been seduced, through much of the country's history, into complacency about its future availability. Large cars, inefficient appliances, and poorly insulated buildings were the norm—at least until recently. In the 1970s our complacency about energy was badly shaken by shortages and price increases. Following the 1974 Arab oil embargo, energy consumption slowed—actually falling in some years during the 1970s—and this is at least partly attributable to higher oil prices.

President Carter's 1977 National Energy Plan, among other things, sought an immediate reduction in dependence on foreign oil, greater use of domestic resources, more conservation, and increased use of renewable energy (solar, wind, hydropower). The Department of Energy was created in 1977, and a much-altered version of Carter's plan was enacted in the form of the 1978 National Energy Act.

The 1979 Iranian revolution started a new round of oil price increases. Carter characterized the resultant energy crisis as the "moral equivalent of war," and in 1979 he set a goal of 20 percent use of renewable energy by the year 2000. Solar energy tax credits were instituted, and many states followed suit in promoting renewable energy. Total energy consumption in the early 1980s approximately equaled that of the early 1970s, and energy consumption per dollar of gross national product had dropped more than 25 percent. At the same time, nuclear energy—largely because of its high capital costs—had fallen into disfavor. In short, the late 1970s and early 1980s seemed to mark the beginning of a new era for renewable energy and energy conservation.

But by the mid-1980s, we were again in an oil "glut"—in part due to conservation's success in reducing demand. The real price of oil fell in the 1980s, and energy consumption and dependence on imported oil in turn crept upward. Federal funding for energy conservation and renewable energy was cut drastically, and residential and business tax credits for solar installations allowed to expire. Reagan administration attempts to open the federal lands and Outer Continental Shelf to greatly expanded leasing were largely thwarted by a combination of economic factors and state, local, and national environmental concerns.

Since 1980, we have had no comprehensive energy plan or policy. Moreover, low prices have provided little stimulus for conservation, exploration, or development of new domestic resources. Our future course, by contrast, could be profoundly influenced by a series of recent revelations. The United States is responsible for about 20 percent of global carbon dioxide emissions—which, in conjunction with other trace gases, threaten to bring about a significant global warming (figure 18.1). Coal combustion is the largest contributor, but oil and natural gas also are significant sources. Concerns about global warming have supplied ammunition to both nuclear- and renewable-energy advocates.

Industrialized countries recently agreed to restrict emissions of chlorofluorocarbons (CFCs), the main culprit in depletion of the earth's ozone layer. Ultimately, this commitment may affect the use and energy efficiency of air conditioners, refrigerators, and other appliances that now use CFCs. Ozone in the lower atmosphere, unlike stratospheric ozone, is regarded as a dangerous pollutant. One way to reduce these ozone levels is through controls on vehicular use (chapter 8)—and this has obvious energy implications. In a related vein, President Bush and Congress have proposed major reductions in sulfur dioxide emissions (chapter 8), most of which come from coal-burning power plants. Finally, evidence is mounting that high-voltage electrical transmission (and even low-voltage fields) are associated with cancer. Thus, even in the absence of any more 1970s-style energy shocks (and there is little assurance that this will in fact be the case), it seems unlikely that energy issues will move far from center stage.

Windmills,
South Point, Big Island, Hawaii.
D. Cuff.

Energy Regions

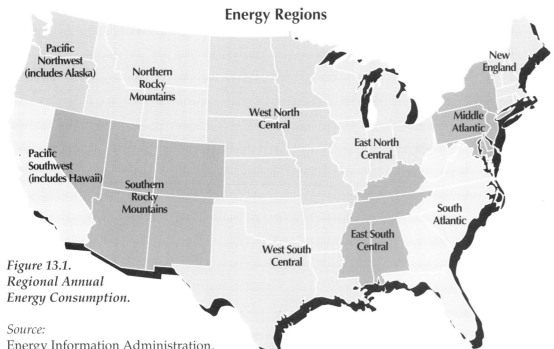

Figure 13.1.
Regional Annual
Energy Consumption.

Source:
Energy Information Administration,
State Energy Data Report:
Consumption Estimates 1960–1986,
DOE/EIA-0214(86) (Washington, DC:
Department of Energy, 1988).

NATIONAL ENERGY CONSUMPTION

Today's heavy dependence on oil,
evident in figure 13.1, is only the
most recent stage in our energy evolution. Preceding it were the wood
era of the 1700s and 1800s and the
coal era of the Industrial Revolution.
In 1986, coal accounted for 23 percent of energy consumption, petroleum 43 percent, and natural gas
23 percent.

The industrial sector consumes
the greatest quantities of energy (36
percent of energy end use in 1986),
with nearly half of it used to
generate process steam. Transportation accounts for 28 percent of
energy end use; cars and trucks
consume about three-quarters of
this. The residential sector of the
energy end-use pie is around 21

percent, and commercial use
accounts for 16 percent. The
greatest single commercial and
residential use is for space heating.
Food production, processing, and
distribution—not directly represented in the above statistics—
consume a rather remarkable one-
sixth of the total U.S. energy
budget. Of course, electrical
generation is an intermediate step
that precedes many end uses—
especially residential, commercial,
and industrial uses. Substantial
amounts of energy included in the
above figures never actually reach
end users because of losses in
generation and transmission. In
1986, electrical generation accounted for about 36 percent of direct

fossil-fuel consumption (Bureau of
the Census 1989).

U.S. dependence on oil peaked
during the 1970s (though total use of
oil was again on the increase by the
mid-1980s). So did its dependence on
imported oil, which approached the
50-percent mark in the mid-1970s.
Most imported oil comes from the
Middle East, and in the early and
late 1970s—when political crises in
that region strengthened the OPEC
(Organization of Petroleum Export-
ing Countries) cartel—world oil
prices increased sharply. The higher
prices brought about energy conservation—particularly during the late
1970s and into the early 1980s. Total
energy consumption, after a temporary drop earlier in the 1970s, fell

Regional Energy Consumption (trillion BTUs)

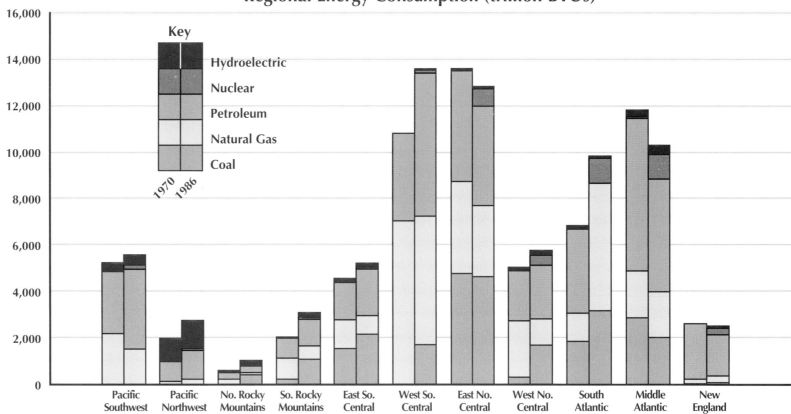

Table 13.1. Nonutility Electrical Generation, 1986		
	Percent from Cogeneration	Percent from Other Sources
Alabama	3.5	<0.1
Alaska	33.6	0.0
Arizona	0.7	<0.1
Arkansas	4.5	<0.1
California	6.1	3.7
Colorado	<0.1	0.2
Connecticut	0.1	0.1
Delaware	4.3	<0.1
Florida	2.9	1.1
Georgia	4.6	0.1
Hawaii	11.1	3.0
Idaho	4.0	2.2
Illinois	0.7	<0.1
Indiana	1.1	3.7
Iowa	1.4	<0.1
Kansas	0.8	0.2
Kentucky	0.0	<0.1
Louisiana	12.2	0.1
Maine	12.9	10.4
Maryland	1.6	0.9
Massachusetts	1.6	2.4
Michigan	4.4	0.2
Minnesota	0.1	3.1
Mississippi	4.3	0.8
Missouri	0.5	<0.1
Montana	0.0	<0.1
Nebraska	<0.1	0.1
Nevada	0.0	0.8
New Hampshire	4.4	5.5
New Jersey	2.3	0.1
New Mexico	<0.1	<0.1
New York	1.7	1.1
North Carolina	4.3	0.1
North Dakota	0.2	<0.1
Ohio	11.5	0.6
Oklahoma	2.3	0.2
Oregon	0.6	1.5
Pennsylvania	1.1	0.8
Rhode Island	5.4	3.2
South Carolina	2.4	0.9
South Dakota	0.0	0.0
Tennessee	3.6	<0.1
Texas	7.0	0.7
Utah	0.0	1.5
Vermont	0.1	1.6
Virginia	5.9	0.2
Washington	0.2	0.3
West Virginia	1.6	0.7
Wisconsin	5.2	1.0
Wyoming	0.6	0.2
United States	3.4	0.9

Source: Edison Electric Institute, *Capacity and Generation of Non-Utility Sources of Energy* (Washington, DC: EEI, 1986), pp. 42–43.

more significantly during this period. Consumption in 1970 was 66.4 quadrillion BTUs (quads). In 1979 it peaked at 78.9 quads, then bottomed out at 70.5 quads in 1983, and by 1987 had risen to 76.0 quads (Bureau of the Census 1989). Furthermore, between the late 1970s and mid-1980s there was a shift away from oil, principally toward coal. This was in part prompted by high oil prices and concerns about our dependence on imported oil.

Between 1970 and 1986, greatest growth in energy use occurred in conjunction with rapid population and/or industrial growth mainly in the southeastern and southwestern parts of the country (figure 13.1). Increased use of coal and petroleum accounted for most of the growth; consumption of natural gas declined in most regions. The most dramatic increases in use of nuclear power took place in the eastern half of the country. Generation of hydropower—long a significant source of energy in the Northwest—increased modestly in several regions, but its overall potential is limited both by physical and political factors. In 1986, hydropower supplied 4.6 percent of all energy consumed.

Because figure 13.1 focuses on commercial energy sources, it does not adequately represent renewable energy sources (hydropower excepted). Not included are data on consumption of wood energy as well as various small quantities of geothermal, waste, wind, photovoltaic, or solar thermal energy—unless the energy was consumed by electric utilities. The Department of Energy estimated that 9 percent of all energy (14 percent of electricity production) was generated from renewable sources in 1984; other estimates top the 10-percent mark (Renewable Energy Institute 1986). Biomass energy—from wood and wood wastes, agricultural crops and residues, and municipal solid waste—supplied 3.0 to 3.5 quads of energy in 1984, according to the Renewable Energy Institute (1986). By the Department of Energy's reckoning, it was 2.5 quads, or 3.4 percent of total energy consumption (Bureau of the Census 1989).

In 1979, President Carter established a goal of 20 percent use of renewable energy by the year 2000. Business and residential purchasers of active solar or wind energy systems were already eligible for federal tax credits; the Energy Security Act of 1980 boosted the income tax credit for homeowners to 40 percent of the first $10,000 spent. The federal government also offered assistance to states, as well as grants and loans to homeowners, for solar and other conservation work. Forty-one states adopted tax incentives that went beyond the federal government's (Sawyer 1986). Solar access for new housing was promoted by legislatures in California, Arizona, and Oregon—as well as in many localities.

During the late 1970s and early 1980s, small and large suppliers of renewable-energy technology entered the marketplace in large numbers. Hydropower enjoyed a resurgence, and use of wood fuels rose 67 percent between 1975 and 1981 (Sawyer 1986). Individuals installed woodstoves, certain industries increased their use of wood, and ethanol (produced from corn) was increasingly used as a gasoline additive.

Research and development funds for renewable energy, which had never really rivaled those for conventional sources, were slashed severely during the Reagan years. The federal energy conservation bank was virtually eliminated, and solar tax credits allowed to expire. State programs, too, were affected by low oil prices, surpluses of electrical generating capacity, and lack of federal direction. Yet several states, most notably California, recently received high marks for their efforts from the Fund for Renewable Energy and the Environment (Ridley 1987).

Conservation, often promoted in conjunction with renewable energy sources, is itself an important "source" of energy: Energy saved is energy gained. The United States, while still highly energy-inefficient by world standards, has made strides since the early 1970s. Between 1973 and 1985, primary energy consumption per unit of gross domestic product has declined an average of 2.2 percent per year (World Resources Institute et al. 1988). Higher energy prices and conservation-related legislation have meant considerably improved energy efficiencies for vehicles, appliances, homes, offices, and industrial operations.

In 1975, the federal Corporate Average Fuel Economy (CAFE) standard was established, and in 1979 a "gas guzzler" tax was imposed on inefficient vehicles. The CAFE standard has now been stagnant for several years at the 1985 level of 27.5 miles per gallon. Under the National Appliance Energy Conservation Act, appliance manufacturers have until 1993 to lower energy consumption by 25 percent. The Public Utility Regulatory Policy Act of 1978 (PURPA) requires utilities to buy electricity from independent producers at fair rates. Greater use of "least-cost" electricity, from a variety of small, mostly renewable sources, is PURPA's objective. It is shared by ten states that had their own comprehensive least-cost provisions and twenty-seven more that were exploring or promoting the concept as of 1987 (Ridley 1988).

Despite resistance from utilities and minimal federal support, PURPA has had some success. One of the successes, really only partly attributable to PURPA, is cogeneration. Industries use excess process heat and steam to generate electricity, which is then used internally and/or sold to utilities. All told, nonutilities accounted for 4.3 percent of the 1986 electrical energy supply—up from 3 percent in 1979. More than three-quarters of all nonutility electricity was produced by cogenerators (Edison Electric Institute 1988).

As indicated in table 13.1, cogeneration was especially important in Alaska, Maine, Hawaii, Louisiana, Texas, California, and New Hampshire.

FOSSIL FUEL, URANIUM, AND GEOTHERMAL RESERVES

Reserves may be defined as known deposits of a resource that can be extracted at a profit under current market conditions using available technology. Resources, by contrast, include all potential deposits of a particular mineral. Part of the total identified resource base will not, under current conditions, be recovered, owing to some combination of inadequate technology, high economic costs, and high risk of failure.

Estimates of the size of the resource base for different fuels varies widely. It is clear, though, that U.S. coal supplies are vast—in terms of both estimated resources and recoverable reserves. By contrast, remaining crude oil (known plus thought to exist) does not greatly exceed that which has already been consumed. Much of the remaining resource is in the Alaskan, Rocky Mountain, and Gulf Coast regions (see figure 7.2). Remaining natural gas—at least that which occurs in conventional reservoirs—is found mostly in the Gulf Coast region. At the 1983 annual production rate, a 60-year supply remained (Cuff and Young 1986). The world's largest deposits of oil shale (known as well as thought to exist) are found in the Rocky and Appalachian mountains. U.S. tar sands potential, concentrated mostly in Utah, is relatively small by world standards. Nuclear fuels, on the other hand, are highly abundant, occurring mostly in the Rocky Mountain region. Potential geothermal (heat) resources are very large, but accessible resources are much smaller (figure 13.3).

Figure 13.2 presents a broad regional overview of energy abundance and scarcity. Clearly, the Mountain states are the richest in energy resources. They contain 75 percent of the nation's low-sulfur coal reserves—and half of those are found in Montana (Cuff and Young 1986). Low-sulfur coal is valued because it burns relatively cleanly, but this is partly offset by the fact that it is mostly subbituminous: its energy value is only about three-quarters that of higher-grade bituminous coal. Thus, more of it is needed, adding to the already-significant costs of transporting it to distant markets. Yet there are several coal-conversion options that could reduce transport costs. They include fluidized bed combustion, gasification, and liquefaction. Support for synthetic liquid and gaseous fuel development, strong in the Carter administration, has withered during the Reagan years. And environmentalists have resisted, because of high energy and water inputs needed to produce the fuel in what is, after all, a rather water-scarce region.

Besides coal, the mountain West is relatively rich in oil shales (from which oil must be extracted at high economic, energy, and water costs), tar sands (like shales, extraction is not generally feasible at present), and uranium-235. Not represented in figure 13.2 are reserves of uranium-238 and thorium, the quantities of which would dwarf those of all other reserves. These fuels may at

some future time be used to power nuclear breeder reactors. Because they produce more fuel than they consume, breeders hold the promise of almost limitless energy.

The West South Central region is also rich in energy resources, principally oil and gas found near the Gulf Coast and in Oklahoma and northern Texas. Texas also has significant tar-sands resources. The West North Central, East North Central, East South Central, South Atlantic, and Middle Atlantic regions all have important coal deposits. In addition, tar-sands are found in Kentucky (East South Central) and oil and gas in North Dakota (West North Central). The coal is concentrated in extensive fields in the Appalachian Mountains and flanking the Mississippi and tributaries—mainly in Illinois, Indiana, Kentucky, Missouri, and Iowa. Other fields of varying dimensions are scattered throughout these regions. Largest reserves are in West Virginia, Kentucky, Pennsylvania, and Ohio. High-sulfur bituminous coals predominate, with over half the nation's high-sulfur coal in Illinois. The Appalachian states contain substantial quantities of low- and medium-sulfur coal, the bulk of it mineable by underground rather than surface methods (see figure 13.2).

Alaska has important oil and gas reserves, and California also is well endowed with oil. Geothermal resources are significant in Alaska and of outstanding importance in California, Oregon, and Hawaii. Modest tar-sands deposits occur in Kentucky (East South Central), Texas (West South Central), and California (Pacific); while uranium oxide occurs in Texas.

Dominating 1987 coal production—most of it bituminous—were Kentucky (18 percent), Wyoming (16 percent), West Virginia (14.9 percent), and Pennsylvania (7.7 percent) (Energy Information Administration 1989a). Western coal production, while less than 50 percent of the national total, has steadily increased since 1973. This trend will probably continue. Because western coal is mostly low-sulfur, much of it can be strip-mined, and western labor is less unionized than eastern labor. Crude oil production is concentrated in Texas (24.9 percent of 1989 production), Alaska (23.4 percent), California (12 percent), Louisiana (5.7 percent), Oklahoma (4.4 percent), and Wyoming (3.8 percent) (Energy Information Administration 1989c). Natural gas production is heavily concentrated in Texas (35.3 percent), Louisiana (29.1 percent), and Oklahoma (11.8 percent) (Energy Information Administration 1989b). Uranium production takes place largely in New Mexico, Texas, and Wyoming—with smaller shares in Arizona, Colorado, Florida, Idaho, Utah, and Washington. Shale oil and tar sands are presently in the developmental stages, and, given the currently low prices of oil, commercial production will probably be nonexistent or small for some time to come. Geothermal production occurs entirely in the western states—in the form of numerous small projects as well as at electric generating plants in California, Utah, and Hawaii.

Figure 13.2. Nonrenewable Energy Reserves.

Source:
D. J. Cuff and W. J. Young, *The United States Energy Atlas,* 2d ed. (New York: Macmillan, 1986), p. 348.

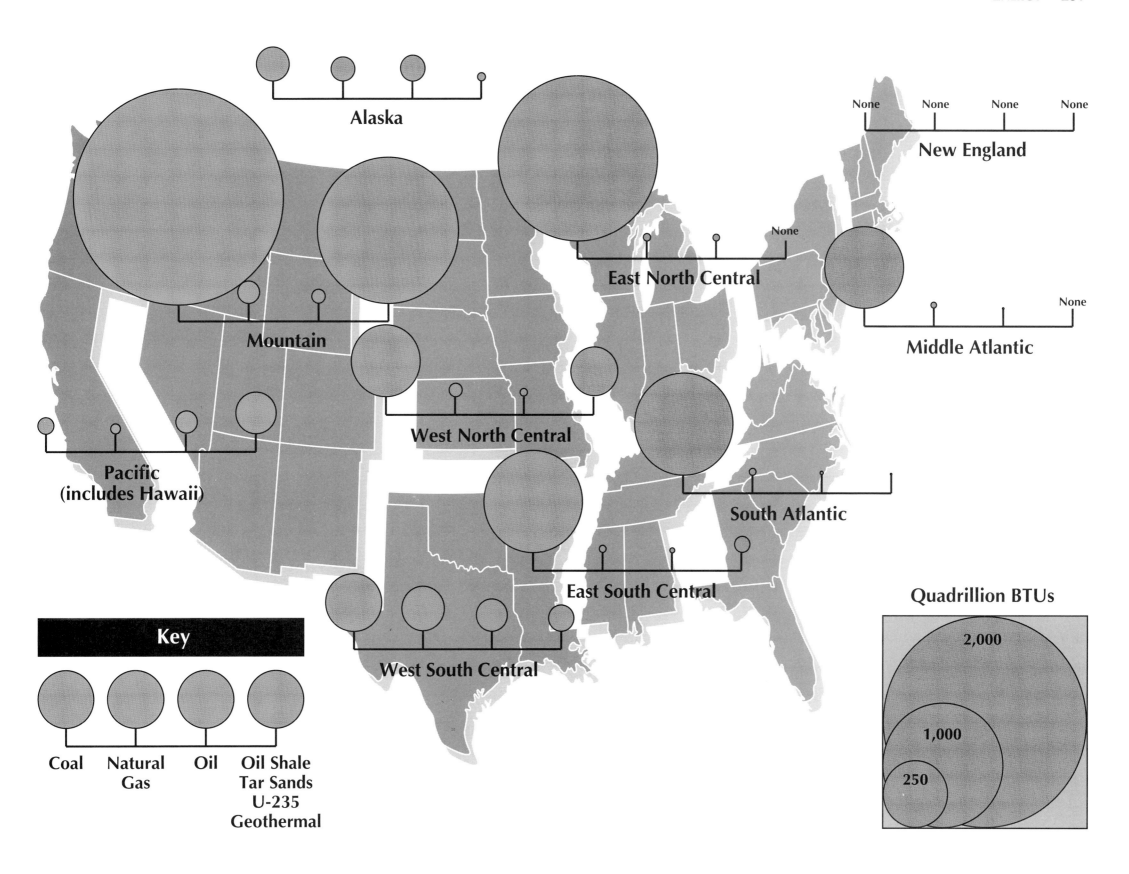

Alaska

New England

None   None   None   None

East North Central

None

Middle Atlantic

None

Mountain

West North Central

Pacific
(includes Hawaii)

South Atlantic

East South Central

Key

West South Central

Coal   Natural   Oil   Oil Shale
        Gas   Tar Sands
                         U-235
                         Geothermal

Quadrillion BTUs

2,000

1,000

250

IN-PLACE GEOTHERMAL SYSTEMS

Figure 13.3 shows total identified heat-in-place in intermediate and high-temperature hydrothermal systems. These are hot springs that create hot water and/or steam that can be used for electricity generation or space heating. Figure 13.3 represents heat available in rocks to a depth of 3 kilometers (9,843 feet). High-temperature heat is found in reservoirs with temperatures averaging over 150°C (300°F); medium temperature heat resides in reservoirs averaging between 90° and 150°C (195° and 300°F). By far, most of the high-temperature heat is in Wyoming and California. Overall, recoverable heat is only about one-tenth that in-place. Not only is recoverability restricted by technology and cost factors, but some resources—most notably Wyoming's large Yellowstone system—are off limits because they are in national parks. Idaho and Oregon have the greatest amounts of intermediate-temperature heat in place. About one-quarter of the in-place heat is accessible at wellhead.

Low-temperature geothermal waters—useful for heating buildings, warming greenhouses, and stimulating fish growth in hatcheries—is very abundant. However, recoverable amounts are quite modest. It is generally assumed that great amounts of heat reside in molten rock chambers—but much of it remains to be identified, much less recovered. Geopressured reservoirs, where heat is found deep beneath the earth's surface (6,000 to 15,000 feet), are abundant in the Texas and Louisiana Gulf Coast regions. Large quantities of energy are in-place, but much smaller amounts are recoverable.

Geothermal resources—while generally considered nonrenewable—have the advantages of relatively low cost, high regional accessibility, and no carbon dioxide emissions. But there is also the possibility of air and water pollution from dissolved salts, minerals, and gases—including such toxics as boron and mercury. Cuff and Young (1986) summarize geothermal occurrences as follows:

	Accessible Resources	Estimated Recoverable Energy
All Hydrothermal Waters	10,837	609
Volcanic	239,155	No Estimates
Geopressured Reservoirs	55,669	130 to 1,347
Total	305,661	739 to 1,956

Units are 10^{18} calories, which is the heat equivalent of 690 barrels of oil, or 3.84 billion BTUs.

Figure 13.3. In-Place Geothermal Systems.

Source:
D. J. Cuff and W. J. Young, *The United States Energy Atlas*, 2d ed. (New York: Macmillan, 1986), pp. 194–195.

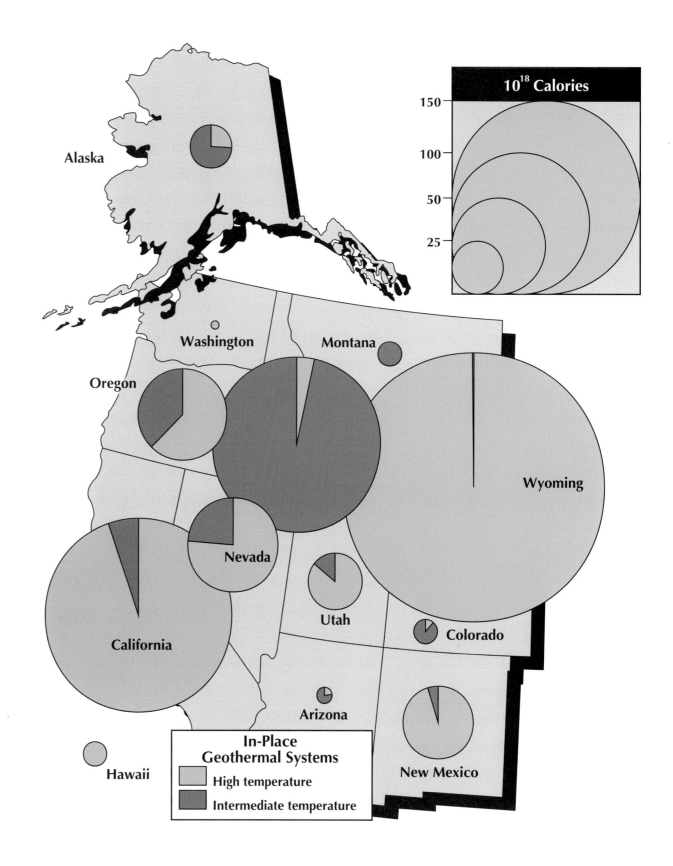

10^{18} Calories

In-Place Geothermal Systems
- High temperature
- Intermediate temperature

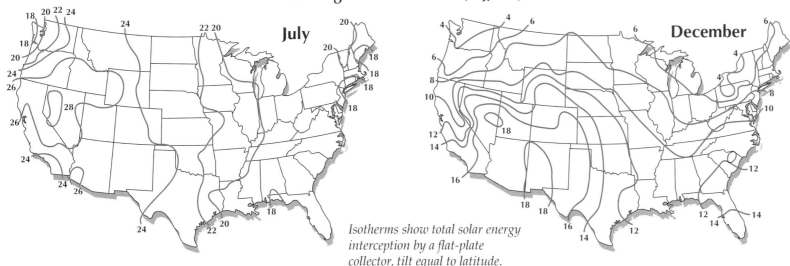

Incoming Solar Radiation (MJ/m²)*

July

December

Isotherms show total solar energy interception by a flat-plate collector, tilt equal to latitude.

Million Joules per square meter (1 Joule equals .2392 calories)

**Million watt hours per square meter per year*

Figure 13.4. Daily Insolation.

Source:
Solar Energy Research Institute, *Solar Radiation Energy Resource Atlas of the United States* (Washington, DC: GPO, 1981), pp. 13–14.

Figure 13.5. Wind Resources.

Source:
D. J. Cuff and W. J. Young, *The United States Energy Atlas*, 2d ed. (New York: Macmillan, 1986), p. 255.

SOLAR AND WIND POWER

The amount of insolation (incoming solar radiation) reaching the earth's surface at a particular place varies with season and climate conditions (mainly cloud cover). By far, the Southwest enjoys the greatest insolation year-round; the Great Lakes states and Northwest get the least. Yet even in the latter areas, solar hot-water heating can satisfy half or more of annual need. Passive solar heating employs building designs that capture and retain solar energy, whereas active systems require a separate collector, storage medium, and system to distribute the heat. Passive systems are generally preferred for new construction; active systems allow retrofitting of existing structures. Potential fuel savings are greatest not in the southern states, but in the northern Great Plains and intermountain West, where both heating needs and insolation are quite high. Besides heating space and water, solar energy can be harnessed to generate electricity. Solar electrical generation holds great potential, but its development has thus far been limited mainly to a few plants in southern California.

Wind power holds greatest promise for those places with consistent winds of at least moderate speed. Figure 13.5 depicts wind regimes at the 50-meter (164-foot) height, a favorable height for large wind machines. The most favorable regimes occur in coastal and mountain regions. Wind farm projects have sprung up across the nation, but the vast bulk of the generating capacity is concentrated in California. If all favorable land areas were saturated with wind machines—a most unlikely prospect given the high initial costs and uncertainties associated with wind—the electrical output would equal about 38 percent of the nation's needed output for 1980 (Cuff and Young 1986).

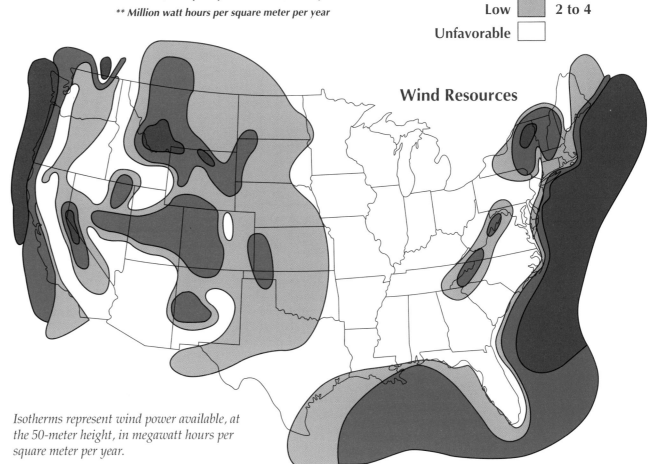

Wind Resources

	MWH/m²/yr**
High	Over 7
Medium	4 to 7
Low	2 to 4
Unfavorable	

Isotherms represent wind power available, at the 50-meter height, in megawatt hours per square meter per year.

SURFACE MINE RECLAMATION

The environmental problems associated with coal are not limited to the sulfur dioxide, carbon dioxide, and particulates that result from its combustion (chapter 8). Large-scale coal mining has been plagued since its inception by questions of regional economic exploitation, labor organization, mine safety, workers' health, and environmental degradation. Underground mining is extremely hazardous. Not only are there risks of cave-ins; explosions can result when a single spark ignites air laden with dust and methane gas. Large numbers of coal miners have suffered from black lung disease—a form of emphysema that is debilitating and often fatal. Despite recent safety regulations (often inadequately enforced), the risks remain high. Moreover, as surface and ground waters pass through mine wastes and abandoned mines, they dissolve sulfuric acid and toxic metals. This phenomenon, known as acid mine drainage, has reached severe proportions in Appalachian coal-mining regions. Another problem, common in Appalachia, is subsidence. Mined-out areas often subside, creating surface depressions and cave-ins. In populated areas, buildings and roads are damaged.

An alternative to underground mining, made practical in recent decades by technological advances, is surface mining—or strip mining. Overlying soil and rock are removed—often in massive quantities—to reach the coal. Although underground mining is still practiced in many areas—including large areas of Appalachia—surface mining is increasingly being favored. Currently, all western coal and about one-half of Appalachian coal are removed by surface methods—in all about 60 percent of U.S. coal. These techniques are cheaper, safer, more efficient, and less labor-intensive. Yet the potential for environmental damage is enormous. Among the effects are scarring of the land, soil erosion, increased flooding, and water pollution.

As of 1978, over a million acres of abandoned surface-mined lands were in need of reclamation (Ridley 1988). Between 1978 and 1986, nearly 2.7 million acres were surface-mined for coal (U.S. Department of the Interior 1987). Several coal states had required some sort of mine reclamation as early as the late 1930s and early 1940s, and additional laws were passed in the 1960s and 1970s. Much of this regulation, however, was ineffective. In the face of growing demand for coal, combined with increased national concern about the environmental effects of surface mining, Congress in 1977 passed the Surface Mining Control and Reclamation Act (SMCRA). The act establishes mining permit requirements that call for detailed reclamation plans, backed by the posting of performance bonds. Mining is prohibited within national parks, forests, wildlife refuges, trails, wild and scenic rivers, recreation areas, and areas on the National Register of Historic Places, as well as within specified distances of dwellings and other buildings, roads, parks, schools, churches, and cemeteries. Furthermore, there is a provision allowing adversely affected individuals to petition to have certain lands designated as unsuitable for mining.

Prime responsibility for implementing the SMCRA rests with the states. States are obligated to enact laws at least as stringent as the SMCRA, to create an agency with sufficient resources to operate the program, to operate the permit system for mining operations, and to provide for enforcement and penalties for violations. States are responsible for deeming certain lands unsuitable for mining—including those where reclamation is not technologically or economically feasible; where mining would adversely affect existing land-use plans, fragile areas, or historic lands; and where mining would interfere with water, food, or fiber supply or imperil life or property on flood-prone or geologically unstable areas. The federal Office of Surface Mining Reclamation and Enforcement regulates mining and reclamation in states that fail to develop their own programs. In addition, the Secretary of the Interior is responsible for regulation on federal lands, which in the West contain 60 percent of federally owned coal reserves. States may, however, enter with the federal government into cooperative agreements that allow them to regulate the mining and reclamation of the federal lands. The bottom map represents the status of state programs as of 1986. Twenty-four states had assumed primacy (i.e., they are responsible for implementing and enforcing the SMCRA), which means that the federal role is limited to oversight and assistance. The federal government had full responsibility in nine states, but most of those did not have active mining operations.

Specific reclamation and protection activities include erosion and sedimentation control, surface-water and groundwater protection, acid and toxic drainage prevention and treatment, mine waste disposal methods that minimize water contamination, proper disposal of spoil (rock that has been removed in mining), removal of highwalls (excavated, exposed rock and soil faces), topsoil replacement, regrading to approximately the original contours of the land, revegetation, restoration and enhancement of wildlife, and removal of unused roads. To ensure successful revegetation, the mine operator is required to maintain new vegetation for at least five years in the East and Midwest and at least ten years in the semiarid West. Indeed, erosion and acid mine drainage are of greatest concern in the humid East, chemical pollution in the Midwest, and wind erosion and revegetation in the West.

The top map shows reclamation activity during the period 1978 to 1986. Although the program receives high praise from the Department of the Interior, the department's statistics do not allow for a rigorous comparison of acres reclaimed with acres needing reclamation. Both the General Accounting Office (GAO) and the National Wildlife Federation have strongly

Surface Coal Mine Reclamation

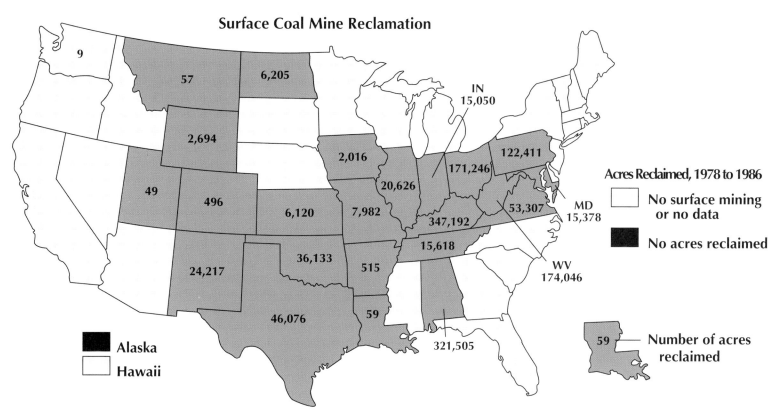

Acres Reclaimed, 1978 to 1986

☐ No surface mining or no data

■ No acres reclaimed

59 — Number of acres reclaimed

■ Alaska
☐ Hawaii

Figure 13.6. Surface Coal Mine Reclamation.

Sources:
U.S. Department of the Interior, Office of Surface Mining Reclamation and Enforcement, *Surface Coal Mining Reclamation: Ten Years of Progress, 1977–1987* (Washington, DC: GPO, 1987).

U.S. Department of the Interior, Office of Surface Mining Reclamation and Enforcement, *OSMRE Annual Report: 1986* (Washington, DC: U.S. Department of the Interior, 1987).

Surface Mine Reclamation: State Program Status

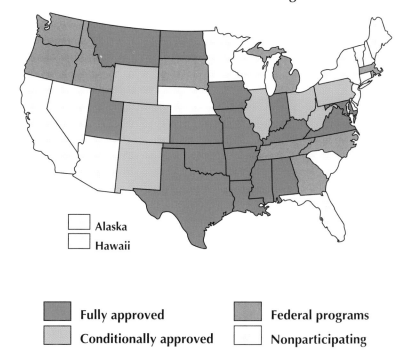

☐ Alaska
☐ Hawaii

■ Fully approved   ■ Federal programs
▨ Conditionally approved ☐ Nonparticipating

criticized the program's administration. The GAO (1987a) found that the states lack comprehensive systems for enforcing the law when mine operators fail to correct violations. The National Wildlife Federation (1985) points to lack of federal enforcement and oversight of state programs, especially in Appalachia and the Midwest. Under the Reagan administration, federal inspection and enforcement staff were cut drastically, and regulations that restricted surface mining on prime farmlands were withdrawn.

In addition to regulating active mining, the SMCRA provides for reclamation of abandoned mine lands (including lands mined underground) by means of a tax on active coal production (comparable to the Superfund program for cleaning up abandoned toxic waste sites; see figures 12.3, 12.4). Emergency response to such incidents as fires, gas leaks, landslides, and subsidence at abandoned mine sites is also supported by these funds. Through 1986, about $1.8 billion had been collected, and more than $1 billion had been awarded to the states. But reclamation is an expensive proposition. Only 33,185 surface-mined acres had been reclaimed; 6,850 of them noncoal acres (the noncoal acres are mostly in the western states). Including refuse piles and areas associated with underground mining, the grand total reclaimed under the federal program (exclusive of separate state programs) was 55,616 acres (U.S. Department of the Interior 1987).

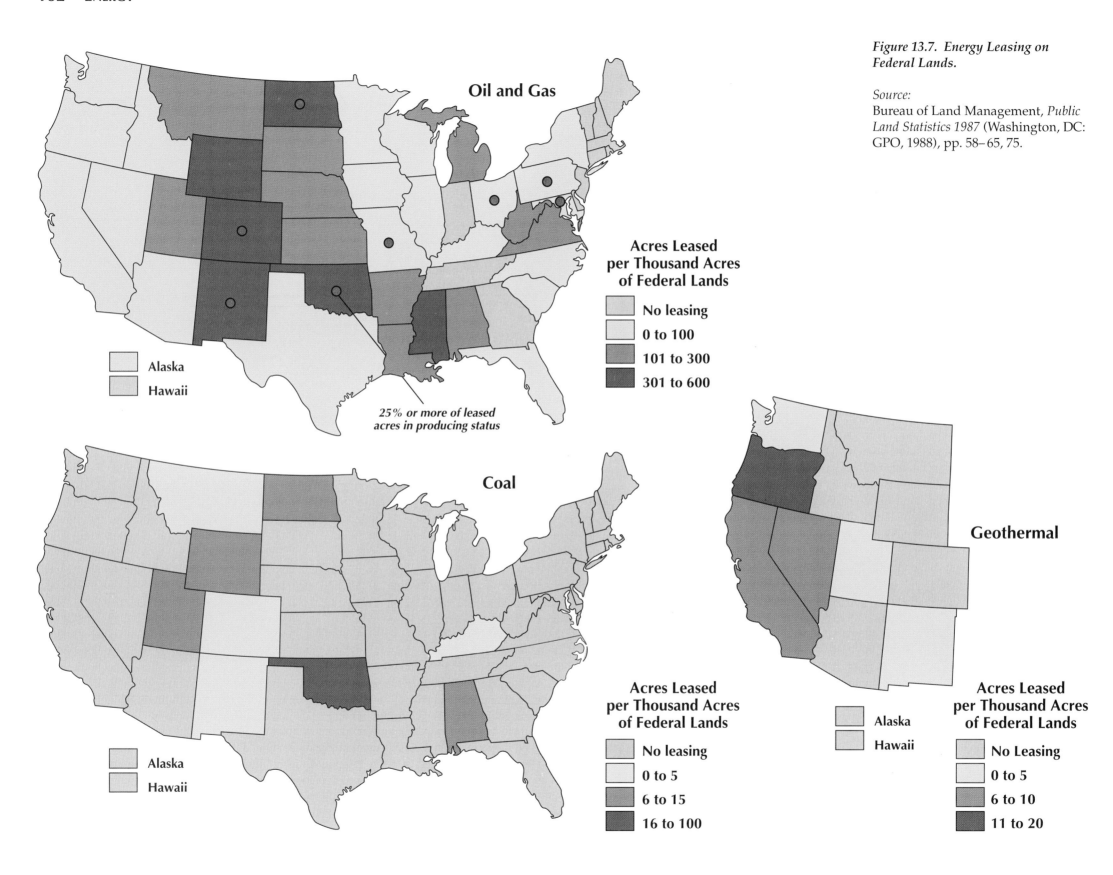

Oil and Gas

Figure 13.7. *Energy Leasing on Federal Lands.*

Source:
Bureau of Land Management, *Public Land Statistics 1987* (Washington, DC: GPO, 1988), pp. 58–65, 75.

Acres Leased per Thousand Acres of Federal Lands

No leasing
0 to 100
101 to 300
301 to 600

Alaska
Hawaii

25% or more of leased acres in producing status

Coal

Acres Leased per Thousand Acres of Federal Lands

Alaska
Hawaii

No leasing
0 to 5
6 to 15
16 to 100

Geothermal

Acres Leased per Thousand Acres of Federal Lands

Alaska
Hawaii

No Leasing
0 to 5
6 to 10
11 to 20

ENERGY LEASING ON THE FEDERAL LANDS

Federally owned lands are quite rich in energy resources. The federal government owns perhaps one-third of the nation's remaining oil, 40 percent of its coal, 80 percent of its oil shale, and large shares of its geothermal and uranium resources (Arrandale 1983). Indeed, the government collects more revenue from energy-related leasing than from any other use of the federal lands, and state and local governments receive royalty shares as well. Yet many of these same energy-rich lands are also highly valued for ecological, aesthetic, and recreational reasons.

The Mineral Leasing Act of 1920 authorizes the Secretary of the Interior to lease energy reserves (except uranium, which is regulated by a separate law) for private production. Leasing did not, however, become a really major enterprise until the 1970s and early 1980s. As of fiscal year 1987, approximately 71 million acres of land were being leased for oil and gas (BLM 1988). Figure 13.7 shows that the greatest oil and gas leasing occurs in the Rocky Mountain and Great Plains states: Not only are high proportions of the federal land base under lease, but—because those states contain large federal landholdings (figure 3.2; table 3.1)—the absolute numbers also are high. Some enormous discoveries have been made in the Western Overthrust Belt, a geologic fault stretching along the Rocky Mountains from Canada to Mexico. The largest discovered fields are in western Wyoming, northeastern Utah, and southeastern Idaho. Within this same region, we find Yellowstone, Glacier, and Grand Teton national parks, as well as federally owned forests, rangelands, and wilderness areas.

Approximately 97 percent of oil and gas leases are for noncompetitive exploration (i.e., there are no known resources, and leasing is either first-come, first-served or based on lotteries). Actual oil and gas production on federal lands accounts for only about 5 percent of total national production (Arrandale 1983). The acreage figures greatly overstate the amount of land occupied by producing wells, since much of the acreage was initially leased for exploration or to gain access to productive areas. Indeed, exploratory and production drilling themselves disrupt fairly small areas of land; the larger concerns are with the pipelines, roads, trails, buildings, debris, waste ponds, litter, and potential for leaks and spills associated with oil and gas development.

The lease restrictions imposed since 1920 by the Department of the Interior have in recent decades become much more onerous, time-consuming, and costly. When James Watt became Secretary of the Interior in 1981, he sought to relax restrictions, reduce the leasing backlog, and allow exploration in national parks, wildlife refuges, and wilderness areas. But his actions provoked intense opposition from environmental organizations and the general public, and they met with strong legal and legis-lative challenges. This, combined with falling energy prices and reduced incentive for frontier exploration and development, prevented the rapid expansion of leasing that Reagan administration officials had at one time anticipated for the 1980s.

Prior to the 1970s, when air-quality laws made low-sulfur coal desirable and technological developments made surface mining cost-effective, western coal production was not very large. Almost all federal coal, of course, is in the West. Conversely, about 60 percent of all western low-sulfur coal lies under federal lands, and another 20 percent is situated such that it cannot be reached without concurrently mining federal deposits (Arrandale 1983). The largest reserves are in the Powder River region of northeast Wyoming and southeast Montana. Leaders in terms of acreage leased are Utah, Wyoming, and Colorado. But as late as 1970, coal production was below the 1945 level—even though leased acreage had expanded enormously in the postwar period. This raised concerns that leaseholders were simply sitting on the resources, waiting for the value of the coal to rise. At the same time, the adverse environmental effects of surface mining, local socio-economic impacts of energy boom and bust cycles, and conflicts with other land uses (such as ecological protection) were becoming increasingly evident. In 1971, the Department of the Interior imposed a two-year leasing moratorium, and in 1973, new prospecting permits were barred and additional leasing limitations imposed. In 1976, over a presidential veto, the Federal Coal Leasing Amendments Act became law. It abolished future preference-right leasing (under which exclusive production leases are awarded to companies that find resources under an exploratory lease—as is still done with oil and gas), required that all leasing be through competitive bidding, and stipulated that the government receive "fair market value." Additional planning and environmental protection requirements are contained in the Federal Land Policy and Management Act of 1976 and the Surface Mining Control and Reclamation Act of 1977 (figure 13.6). During the Carter administration, careful plans were laid for future coal leasing and production—but as with oil and gas, Secretary of the Interior James Watt attempted to accelerate exploration and production. Once again, though environmental concerns and depressed markets conspired against Watt's plans to transfer control of massive shares of the resource to private industry.

The federal government also holds vast oil shale resources in Colorado, Utah, and Wyoming—but despite promotion and subsidies during the Ford and Carter administrations, commercial development of oil shale has yet to take place. The largest acreages of federally owned geothermal resources are in California, with additional resources in Idaho, Nevada, Utah, Oregon, and Idaho.

FOCUS: ALASKAN OIL AND GAS

Alaska's most intense environmental controversies usually involve oil and gas. Recently, debate has raged around the fate of the 19.5-million-acre Arctic National Wildlife Refuge. In 1980, Congress designated 8 million acres of the refuge as wilderness, effectively precluding new resource exploration or development on those lands (see figure 15.4). But beyond this, oil and gas leasing, development, and production are prohibited *anywhere* on the reserve—*until* Congress takes specific action. In 1987, the Department of the Interior presented Congress with several management alternatives for the Arctic Coastal Plain. Its recommendation, however, was that the entire area be open to exploration and development.

The Arctic Coastal Plain is home to grizzly and polar bear, musk-oxen, Dall sheep, wolves, wolverines, moose, snow geese, peregrine falcons, and many other species. But greatest concern is generated by the up to 200,000 caribou that annually migrate across the plain; the coastal area is a major calving ground. While pro-development interests hope to discover "supergiant" oilfields, their opponents see the refuge as the "last great wilderness alternative." The Department of the Interior puts the chance of finding economically recoverable oil at 19 percent (which is actually quite high by industry standards). Estimates of quantity vary widely; the mean is 3.23 million barrels — approximately a 200-day supply of oil.

Congressional deliberations on the refuge's future were abruptly interrupted by the March 24, 1989, Prince William Sound oil spill. About 11.2 million gallons of crude oil were spilled when the tanker *Exxon Valdez* ran aground on a reef. It was the largest tanker spill in North American waters, and while size does not necessarily determine impact, the spill's effects are magnified by the fact that it occurred in a body of water ringed by islands, relatively isolated from the open sea. Thus there was little wind and wave action to disperse the oil, and the region's gravelly beaches virtually precluded removal of oil from the shoreline.

The oil spread to an area of 1,000 square miles and affected 730 miles of coastline—including that of Katmai National Park. Major damage is known to have occurred or likely to occur to herring, salmon, sea otter, diving bird (duck, loon), bald eagle, and bear populations. But it will be many years before damages can be more fully assessed. Exxon has been harshly criticized for the slowness and inadequacy of its response to the spill. Ultimately, President Bush sent Coast Guard Commander Paul Yost and EPA Administrator William Reilly to the scene. But despite Exxon's $1.25 billion cleanup effort, not more than about 15,000 (out of 240,000) barrels of oil were recovered.

The political impacts of the spill loom very large—comparable, according to Secretary of the Interior Lujan, to Three Mile Island's

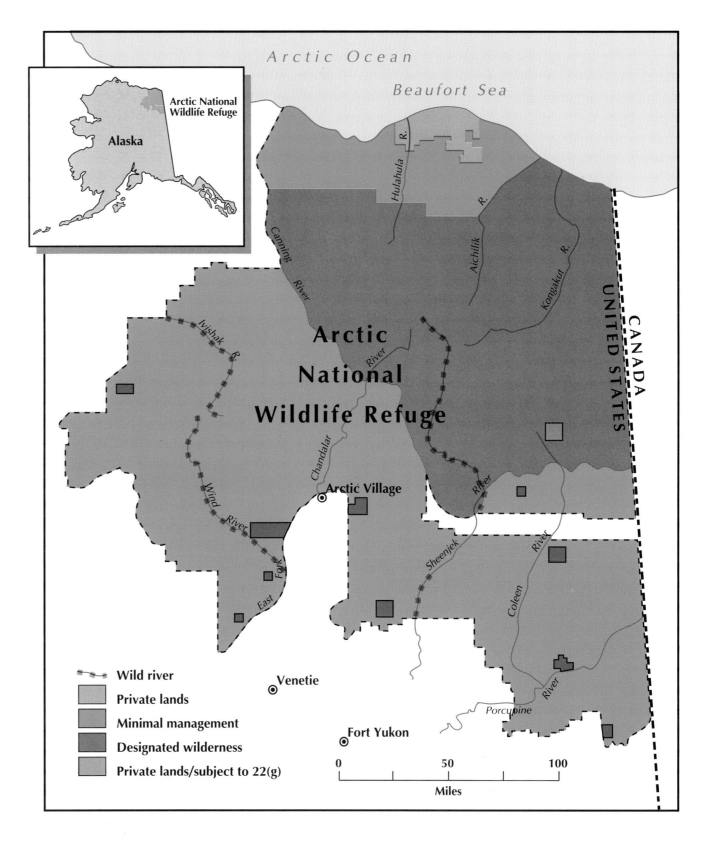

Arctic National Wildlife Refuge

Alaska

Arctic Ocean

Beaufort Sea

CANADA / UNITED STATES

Hulahula R.

Aichilik R.

Kongakut R.

Canning River

Ivishak R.

Arctic National Wildlife Refuge

River

Wind River

East Fork

Chandalar

Arctic Village

Sheenjek River

Coleen River

Venetie

Porcupine River

Fort Yukon

Wild river
Private lands
Minimal management
Designated wilderness
Private lands/subject to 22(g)

0   50   100
Miles

Figure 13.8. FOCUS: Alaskan Oil and Gas.

The first map shows the Department of the Interior's "preferred alternative" for management of the Arctic National Wildlife Refuge. The 1.5-million-acre Arctic Coastal Plain—situated between the Brooks Range to the south and the Beaufort Sea to the north—is at the core of the controversy described in the text. It is represented on the map as the "Minimal Management" area. Along with the remainder of the reserve not privately owned or designated as wilderness, the coastal plain remains in minimal management until Congress makes a determination about its fate. Although minimal management seeks to maintain current conditions, motorized access and limited (no exploratory drilling) oil and gas studies are permitted. These areas may subsequently be designated as wilderness, but the Department of the Interior has made no such recommendations for any refuge lands. Wild rivers are to be managed similarly to minimal management lands—with allowance for guiding and outfitting services and motorized access for "traditional activities" such as hunting, fishing, and trapping.

Sources:
Fish and Wildlife Service, *Arctic National Wildlife Refuge: Final Comprehensive Conservation Plan, Environmental Impact Statement, Wilderness Review, and Wild River Plans* (Anchorage, AK: FWS, 1988).

State of Alaska et al., *State/Federal Natural Resource Damage Assessment Plan for the Exxon Valdez Oil Spill: Public Review* (Juneau, AK: Trustee Council, 1989, draft), p. 10.

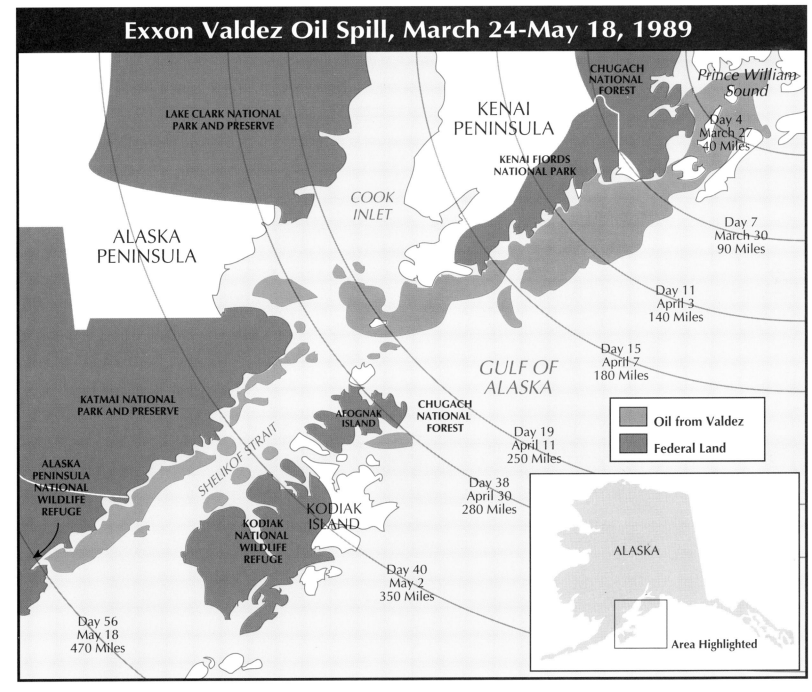

Exxon Valdez Oil Spill, March 24–May 18, 1989

impact on the nuclear industry. Both President Bush and the Congress have called for national oil spill contingency plans, new funds for emergency response, and stricter enforcement against offenders. Bush eased, at least temporarily, his support for oil and gas leasing in the Arctic National Wildlife Refuge (refuge oil would flow, via pipeline, to the port of Valdez). The House Appropriations Committee proposed a one-year ban on drilling off much of the U.S. coast. And the issues were kept in the news by a number of smaller spills in 1989 elsewhere in American waters. But in spite of the national outrage, we continue to move slowly in dealing with environmental threats posed by offshore oil and gas.

NUCLEAR ISSUES

The post-World War II era was a time of heady optimism about our nuclear future—but in many ways, the "atoms for peace" vision has gone sour. No new nuclear power plants have been ordered since 1978, and controversies have marred the construction, licensing, and operation of plants previously committed. Nuclear power generated 18 percent of all electricity and accounted for about 6 percent of all energy needs in 1987 (Bureau of the Census 1989)—a far cry from 1960s projections of 25 percent. Still, the U.S. possesses greater *total* nuclear generating capacity than any other country. Figure 13.9 and table 13.2 show that nuclear power is especially important in New England, New Jersey, Illinois, several South Atlantic states, Minnesota, Nebraska, Arkansas, and Mississippi. The leaders in *total* electricity generated are Illinois, South Carolina, Pennsylvania, California, North Carolina, New York, New Jersey, and Connecticut.

In contrast with fossil fuels, nuclear power does not emit gases to the atmosphere that may contribute to local air pollution, acid deposition, and global warming. Moreover, uranium and thorium ores are abundant (figure 13.2), and uranium mining disrupts less land than coal mining. Why, then, has nuclear power fallen so far short of early expectations? The principal reasons are high capital costs, high costs of electricity generated, low efficiencies (typically on the order of 25 or 30 percent, compared with averages closer to 40 percent for coal-burning plants), safety concerns, shortcomings in plant design and operation, and uncertainties about storage and disposal of radioactive wastes. All these factors were at work even before the Three Mile Island accident took place near Harrisburg, Pennsylvania, in 1979. But that accident, which resulted in a partial meltdown of the core (where the nuclear fuel is contained), shook public confidence much more than prior events. Another major shock came in 1986, with the Chernobyl nuclear accident in the Soviet Union: There were thirty-one deaths, and a cloud of radiation spread over the Ukraine, eastern Europe, and Scandinavia.

Nuclear hazards are not limited to power plant operation. Uranium mining poses high lung cancer risks for miners because they inhale radon gas. Wastes from uranium mining and milling have been left in piles on the ground, buried in municipal landfills, and used in the construction of roads, homes, and other buildings. These problems are concentrated in the Rocky Mountain states, where most uranium mining takes place. Stabilization and sealing of the waste piles, along with cleanup of associated contamination, has been very costly and slow—even though cleanup requirements have been on the books since the 1978 passage of the Uranium Mill Tailings Radiation Control Act.

Figure 13.10 represents other parts of the nuclear fuel cycle:

the processing and production of nuclear fuels and the disposal of nuclear wastes. The controversies now surrounding these military and civilian operations threaten to eclipse even those associated with nuclear power generation. In 1988, the decades-old veil of secrecy surrounding the operation of weapons-related facilities (figure 13.10)—justified on national security grounds—was quite unintentionally lifted. In September, it was revealed that 30 significant "incidents"—including melting of nuclear fuel and extensive radioactive contamination—had taken place at the Savannah River Plant, where until that time nuclear fuels were being produced. The plant's closure, a month before the public revelations, triggered fears about tritium shortages. Tritium decays at a rate of 5.5 percent per year; thus it must be replaced regularly if nuclear warheads are to be kept active. Savannah River was its only producer.

The Savannah River disclosure opened the gates for additional revelations about equipment, training, and management problems at the Hanford complex in Washington state, the Idaho National Engineering Laboratory near Idaho Falls, and the Feed Materials Production Center near Fernald, Ohio, where the Department of Energy (DOE) acknowledged that large numbers of workers and residents had been exposed to uranium waste at the Feed Materials Center. In October 1988, plutonium processing was suspended at Rocky Flats, Colorado. Amid a firestorm of publicity, the DOE conceded that there were serious problems with radioactive and toxic wastes (toxic chemicals are used in production processes) at sixteen sites (all shown in figure 13.10). A recent analysis by the Radioactive Waste Campaign (Coyle et al. 1988) reveals that tritium and other radioactive gases are routinely vented to the atmosphere, and liquid radioactive wastes are routinely released to land and groundwater— sometimes directly into groundwater. The government is charged with failure to adequately isolate and monitor military radioactive waste.

The government now acknowledges health risks from the numerous fires, leaks, and routine releases—even of rather low-level radiation—that have occurred over the years. In January 1989 the DOE and the Pentagon recommended that operations be curtailed at four plants (most likely resulting in closure): Rocky Flats, Hanford, Fernald (Feed Materials), and Dayton (Mound). The overall cleanup will be extraordinarily costly— most estimates range between $90 and $200 billion, but some are even higher.

Meanwhile—in response to the federal government's failure to open its planned permanent repository for high-level military waste near Carlsbad, New Mexico—Idaho Governor Cecil Andrus has barred further shipments of high-level waste from Rocky Flats to Idaho Falls. Carlsbad's stable salt deposits are slated to house vast quantities of military wastes, some of which

Table 13.2
Electrical Generation from Nuclear Plants, 1987

	Percent of Total Generation
Alabama	16.2
Alaska	0.0
Arizona	26.1
Arkansas	31.3
California	23.3
Colorado	0.6
Connecticut	61.9
Delaware	0.0
Florida	16.9
Georgia	17.8
Hawaii	0.0
Idaho	0.0
Illinois	45.7
Indiana	0.0
Iowa	9.9
Kansas	21.0
Kentucky	0.0
Louisiana	24.0
Maine	48.4
Maryland	27.8
Massachusetts	3.3
Michigan	16.5
Minnesota	33.6
Mississippi	34.5
Missouri	11.4
Montana	0.0
Nebraska	41.9
Nevada	0.0
New Hampshire	0.0
New Jersey	57.7
New Mexico	0.0
New York	19.5
North Carolina	61.0
North Dakota	0.0
Ohio	6.3
Oklahoma	0.0
Oregon	10.9
Pennsylvania	24.1
Rhode Island	0.0
South Carolina	61.0
South Dakota	0.0
Tennessee	na
Texas	0.0
Utah	0.0
Vermont	76.3
Virginia	42.5
Washington	6.6
West Virginia	0.0
Wisconsin	25.7
Wyoming	0.0
United States	17.7

Source: Bureau of the Census, *Statistical Abstract of the United States: 1989,*109th ed. (Washington, DC: GPO, 1989), p. 572.

Figure 13.9. Nuclear Power Plant Status, 1988.

Note: Facilities are shown at their approximate locations.

Sources:
Energy Information Administration, *Electric Power Monthly* (Washington, DC: DOE, 1988), p. 16.

Energy Information Administration, *Annual Energy Review 1987*, DOE/ EIA-0384 (87) (Washington, DC: DOE, 1988), p. 212.

will remain radioactive for 240,000 years. But a variety of design, construction, and safety concerns—along with one study showing unusual amounts of moisture seeping into the caverns—forced the DOE in September 1988 to delay indefinitely the facility's opening.

Although military waste accounts for about 97 percent of the volume of high-level nuclear waste, spent fuel from nuclear power plants contains about half the total radiation. The 1983 Nuclear Waste Policy Act requires the DOE to comply with a strict schedule and site-selection criteria for creating a national repository for high-level civilian waste. Congress's initial intent was to create two sites—one in the East, one in the West. In 1986, potential sites were narrowed to three geologically suitable places: Hanford, Washington (basalt lava), Deaf Smith County, Texas (bedded salt), and Yucca Flats, Nevada (volcanic ash). Congress abandoned its own site-selection process in 1987 when it designated Yucca Mountain as the leading candidate for the

waste site. The associated schedule, already set back by at least two years (and possibly indefinitely), calls for studies of the site's geological and hydrological characteristics through 1994, with wastes beginning to arrive around 2003. In the meantime, spent nuclear fuel continues to accumulate in "swimming pools" at nuclear power plants across the country—and, according to one view, should remain there until we learn more about long-term geologic and climate changes that will affect Yucca Mountain or any other "permanent" site.

The Low Level Radioactive Waste Policy Act, passed in 1980 and amended in 1985, requires states to dispose of low-level wastes (LLW) either within their own borders or via a regional compact. Disposal facilities are to be in operation by 1993. Represented in figure 13.10 are the various interstate compacts, as well as the states that have chosen to go it alone. Each unit will have to build a facility—except the Northwest, where the Richland, Washington, site is expected to remain operational after 1992. The

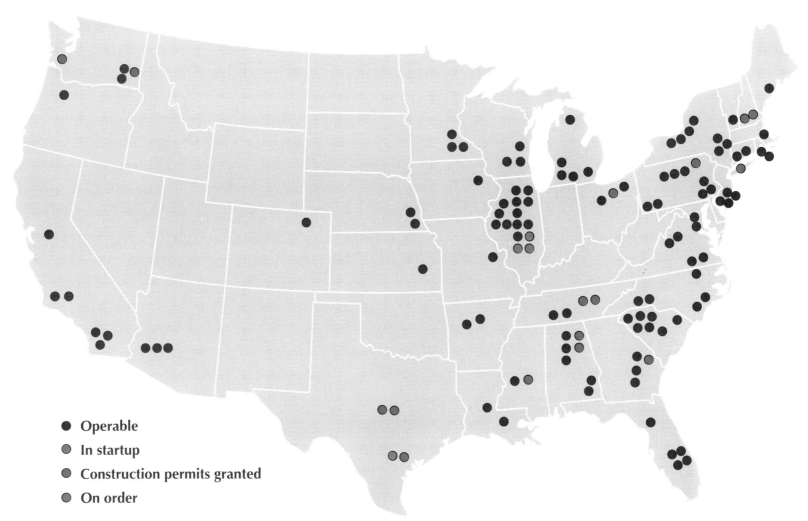

- ● Operable
- ● In startup
- ● Construction permits granted
- ● On order

compact states have had to deal with the politically charged issue of designating a host state for the facility. But the real struggle is just getting under way: the designation of actual sites. As of mid-1989, only Texas, Illinois, and California had made such decisions. Current LLW management consists of disposal at Richland, Washington; Barnwell, South Carolina; and Beatty, Nevada (as noted, only Richland is expected to operate past 1992) and storage of spent fuel in pools at nuclear power plants.

It is evident from figure 13.10 that nuclear materials must be transported over long distances. Uranium mined in the moun-tain states is moved by rail and truck from plant to plant for a series of conversion and enrichment processes and ultimate incorporation into weapons or use in power plants. Spent fuel not stored on-site must be transported to disposal or—for some military fuels—reprocessing sites. Between the fall of 1975 and December 1987, transport accidents numbered 173 (Coyle et al. 1988). Most of the accidents were minor—the majority occurring in DOE parking lots in New Mexico, Tennessee, and Texas. In no case were releases of radioactivity reported. Nevertheless, there is considerable cause for concern: While DOE security proce-dures for the nuclear cargoes themselves are quite rigorous, their provisions for public safety in case of accident are rather less comprehensive.

Figure 13.10. Nuclear Fuel Processing and Waste Disposal.

Sources:
D. Coyle et al., *Deadly Defense: Military Radioactive Landfills* (New York: Radioactive Waste Campaign, 1988).

B. D. Solomon and F. M. Shelley, "Siting Patterns of Nuclear Waste Repositories," *Journal of Geography* (1988): 61.

B. D. Solomon, personal communi-cation, 24 February 1989.

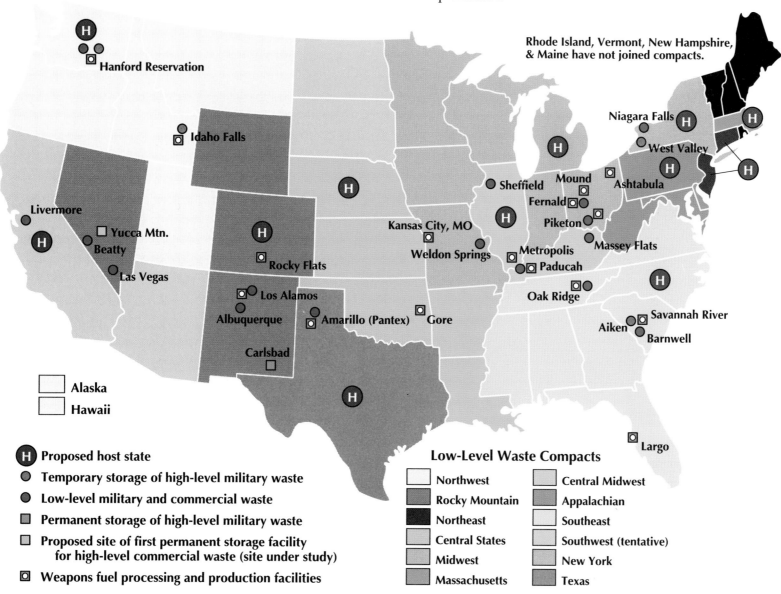

Rhode Island, Vermont, New Hampshire, & Maine have not joined compacts.

Hanford Reservation
Idaho Falls
Livermore
Yucca Mtn.
Beatty
Las Vegas
Rocky Flats
Los Alamos
Albuquerque
Amarillo (Pantex)
Carlsbad
Gore
Kansas City, MO
Weldon Springs
Sheffield
Fernald
Metropolis
Paducah
Oak Ridge
Mound
Piketon
Massey Flats
Ashtabula
West Valley
Niagara Falls
Aiken
Savannah River
Barnwell
Largo

Alaska
Hawaii

H Proposed host state
● Temporary storage of high-level military waste
● Low-level military and commercial waste
▣ Permanent storage of high-level military waste
□ Proposed site of first permanent storage facility for high-level commercial waste (site under study)
◘ Weapons fuel processing and production facilities

Low-Level Waste Compacts

Northwest	Central Midwest
Rocky Mountain	Appalachian
Northeast	Southeast
Central States	Southwest (tentative)
Midwest	New York
Massachusetts	Texas

FOCUS: THE SHOREHAM NUCLEAR PLANT

The Shoreham Generating Station is poised to become the nation's first completed nuclear plant never to go into commercial operation.

At the center of the Shoreham episode is a Nuclear Regulatory Commission (NRC) directive issued in the wake of the 1979 Three Mile Island (TMI) accident. For all nuclear plants, evacuation planning is required within a ten-mile emergency planning zone (EPZ), while protective measures are to be readied for the area between ten and fifty miles from the plant, where possible contamination of water and food would be a major concern.

Shoreham's ten-mile EPZ is shown on the map. Depending on specific accident and weather conditions, sheltering (residents stay inside) or a partial or full evacuation might be advised. Evacuees would follow designated routes and might be asked to report to a "reception center," where they would be checked for radiation before proceeding to their chosen destination or to a "congregate care center."

About 57,000 people reside within the EPZ, while more than 5 million people live between ten and fifty miles from Shoreham. Given the dense highway network on Long Island—overbur-

dened under the best of conditions—and the fact that evacuees might want to move upwind of the plant, toward or even beyond New York City, the possibility of a massive evacuation becomes frightening. As a result, state and local officials have not cooperated in emergency planning. Although Shoreham's advocates argue that the entire island would not need to be evacuated, residents may think otherwise (Social Data Analysts, Inc. 1982; Ziegler and Johnson 1984). At TMI, the number of evacuees from within a fifteen-mile radius was about fifty times the number advised to evacuate. A Long Island survey indicated that 25 to 50 percent of the entire island's population might be expected to evacuate, even in the case of very limited official advisories.

Shoreham, completed in 1985 at a cost of $5.5 billion, is to be sold by its financially strapped owner to New York State for one dollar—thus ensuring that no nuclear power will be produced. Nevertheless, on the assumption that recalcitrant local officials would cooperate in a real emergency, the NRC granted Shoreham a full operating license in 1989. This "realism rule" is likely also to be applied to New Hampshire's Seabrook plant. Although the NRC has yet to concede the struggle, the Shoreham episode is powerful testimony to the potency of local environmental concerns.

Figure 13.11. FOCUS: Evacuation Planning for the Shoreham Nuclear Station.

Source:
Long Island Lighting Company, *Public Emergency Procedures for Zone A: Shoreham Nuclear Power Station* (Hicksville, NY: LILC, 1987, draft), pp. 9, 11.

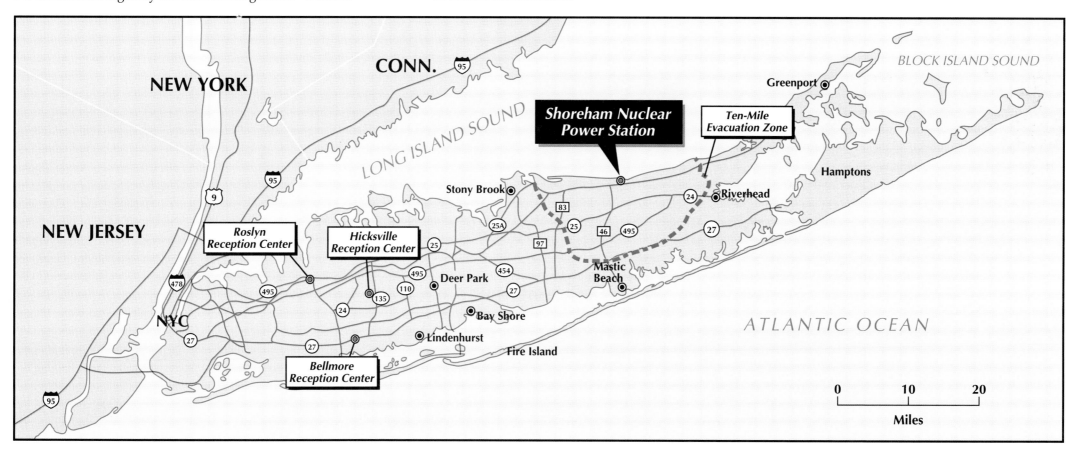

For all practical purposes, minerals are nonrenewable resources. In other words, the time required for their regeneration—usually on the order of tens or hundreds of millions of years—is many orders of magnitude greater than any time frame for human use. As with energy minerals, nonfuel minerals can be conceptualized in terms of resources and reserves. Resources constitute the total amount of minerals available, whether or not locations are actually known. Reserves are those deposits that are recoverable at a profit under current economic conditions, given available technologies. The total resource base for many minerals is enormous—but as a practical matter, recovery of more than a fraction is impossible. This is because of their widespread occurrence in the form of low-grade ores. The mineral is present in combination with other substances—but in low concentrations. High-grade ores, of course, contain relatively high concentrations of minerals-in-question. In the United States, as well as many other countries, high-grade ores containing the most commonly used minerals have been greatly depleted.

Although home to only 5 percent of the world's population, the United States is responsible for about one-third of global mineral consumption. While we are well endowed with a wide variety of minerals, we nonetheless rely heavily on foreign suppliers for a number of key minerals (figure 14.4)—and this raises critical questions about global politics, economics, and shared environmental responsibility. Indeed, as domestic high-grade ores are increasingly depleted, the sense of urgency about future mineral supplies is magnified.

One way to extend supplies is through recycling or reprocessing. It not only saves materials but also conserves energy and water and reduces air and water pollution caused by mining, materials processing, and waste disposal. Although recycling programs are multiplying across the country, recycling rates for most minerals remain low (chapter 11). Some materials—iron and steel scrap, for example—can be easily recovered in milling and manufacturing processes as well as from junked cars, appliances, and other goods. But most materials—and especially those with low market values—are not so readily retrieved, especially from the diverse solid waste stream. As of 1987, old scrap (from discarded products) accounted for about 16 percent of aluminum consumption, 24 percent of copper consumption, 49 percent of lead consumption, 20 percent of silver consumption, and 25 percent of all iron and steel scrap (Bureau of Mines 1988). New scrap, generated in current operations, is much easier to recover—and recovered new scrap indeed does account for substantial proportions of total consumption of many metals. In many plants it was being recovered long before there was significant recycling of old scrap.

In addition to recycling, minerals can be reused—as happens when beverage containers are collected and refilled (figure 11.4). Products can be designed to last longer. Manufacturers can find ways to use smaller quantities of materials in making their products—offering us smaller cars, smaller computers, smaller appliances, and the like. Substitutes can be found for scarce materials: Aluminum can be used instead of copper, optical fibers instead of copper and aluminum wiring, and plastic and aluminum in the place of chromium on cars.

Another way to extend supplies is to mine lower and lower-grade ores. But there are environmental costs: More land usually is disturbed, more energy and water are used, and more water pollution is produced per unit of mineral extracted. Noncoal mining (excluding uranium tailings) already is the single largest source of solid waste, producing about 13,000 pounds per person per year. In recent years, though, domestic mining of a number of minerals—including lead, copper, zinc, iron ore, and nickel—has decreased. But future economic and political trends, uncertain as they are, might very well lead to greater extraction of lower-grade domestic ore—and thus more mine wastes and pollution.

Open-Pit Mine, Arizona.
U.S. Geological Survey.

MINING ACTIVITIES

Figure 14.1 provides an overview of nonfuel mining in the United States. As of 1982, there were 7,500 separate mining and drilling establishments. About 6,000 were for nonmetallic minerals and 1,500 for metallic minerals.

Figure 14.1 indicates that metallic mineral mining, while widespread, is most prevalent in the western states. Mining of nonmetallic minerals is likewise widespread but concentrated in the Southeast and South Central states. The total value of nonfuel mineral production in 1986 was approximately $23.5 billion. About half that value is accounted for by cement (listed as a mineral by the U.S. Bureau of Mines, even though it is a relatively high-value manufactured product), sand, gravel, stone, clay, and lime: low-value minerals that are extracted in enormous quantities. In California, which in 1986 produced 9.7 percent of the total value of U.S. mineral production, cement, sand, and gravel led the list. In Texas, responsible for 7.3 percent, cement and stone were the leaders. Arizona, with 6.6 percent of national production, is an important copper producer, while Florida—at 5.5 percent—produces large amounts of phosphate rock. Iron ore is the leading mineral in Michigan and Minnesota, which each accounted for about 5 percent of 1986 national production. Gold is an important commodity in Nevada,

California, South Dakota, and Montana; copper in New Mexico and Michigan (though Arizona is the leader); magnesium metal in Texas, Washington, and Utah; molybdenum in Colorado, Arizona, Idaho, and New Mexico; and silver in Idaho, Nevada, Montana, and Arizona (U.S. Bureau of Mines Annual 1987). It is evident from figure 14.2 that many of the eastern and southwestern states are relatively mineral-rich in terms of nonfuel mineral production per square mile of area. Figure 14.2 (lower map) also shows the economic importance of mining to the residents of the Rocky Mountain states.

As with coal production, nonfuel mineral production creates significant environmental impacts. The vast bulk of nonfuel minerals are surface-mined, which means that the overlying land is disturbed. These disturbances range from the many small sand and gravel borrow pits to enormous open-pit copper mines. Future supplies of many minerals will have to come from lower-grade ores, since high-grade ores are already largely depleted. Thus, even though production of a number of key minerals has leveled off or declined in recent years, the amount of rock and soil removed per unit of mineral production has in many cases

Figure 14.1. General Mining Activities.

Source:
EPA, *Surface Impoundment Assessment National Report*, EPA 570/9-84-002 (Washington, DC: EPA, 1983), p. 66.

Table 14.1. Mine Waste Generation
(millions of metric tons, 1982)

	Mine Wastes	Tailings	Leaching Wastes	Total
Metals:				
Copper	124	178	200 (dump)	502
Gold	39	24	11 (heap)	74
Iron	102	75		177
Lead	2	9		11
Molybdenum	24	6		30
Silver	20	6	<1 (heap)	26
Uranium	73	na		73
Zinc	1	6		7
Other metals	23	3		26
Subtotal	408	307	211	926
Nonmetals:				
Asbestos	4	2		6
Phosphate	294	109		403
Subtotal	298	111		409
Total	706	418	211	1,335

Source: EPA, *Report to Congress: Wastes from the Extraction and Beneficiation of Metallic Ores, Phosphatic Rock, Asbestos, Overburden from Uranium Mining, and Oil Shale,* EPA/530-SW-85-033 (Washington, DC: EPA, 1985), p. ES-6. Mining and Mineral Production.

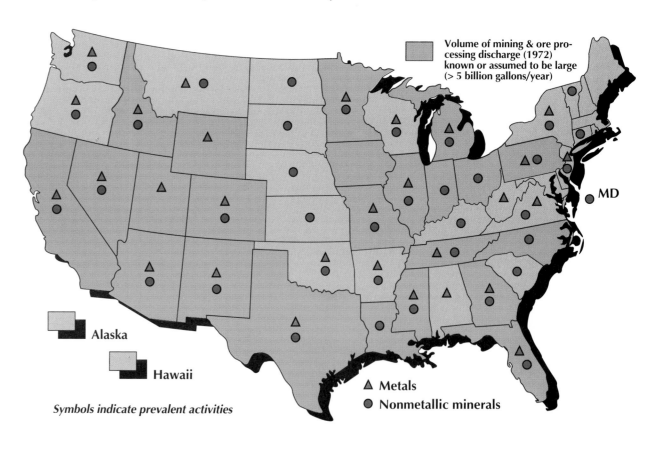

Volume of mining & ore processing discharge (1972) known or assumed to be large (> 5 billion gallons/year)

Alaska

Hawaii

MD

△ Metals
● Nonmetallic minerals

Symbols indicate prevalent activities

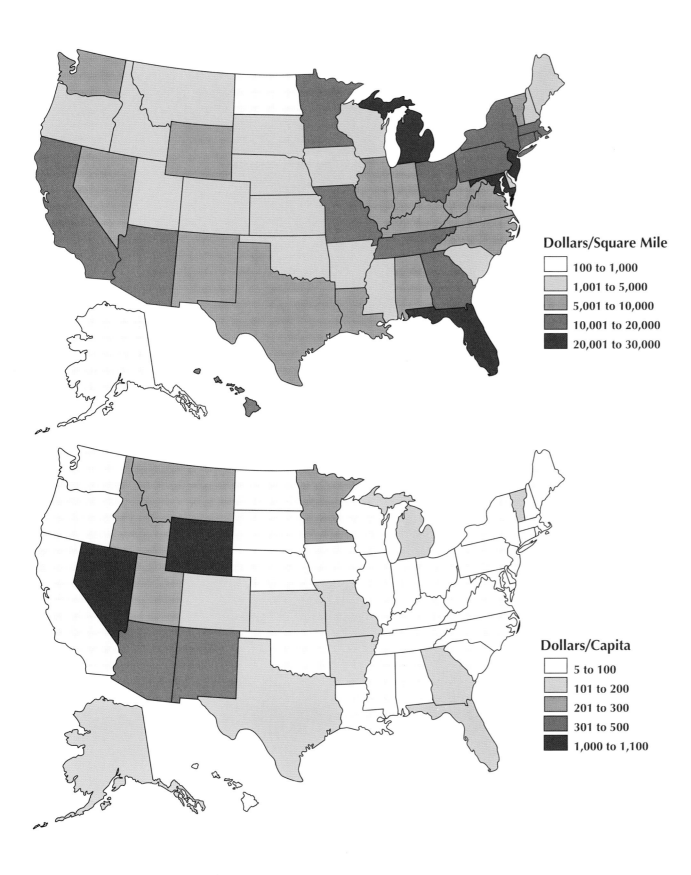

Dollars/Square Mile

- 100 to 1,000
- 1,001 to 5,000
- 5,001 to 10,000
- 10,001 to 20,000
- 20,001 to 30,000

Dollars/Capita

- 5 to 100
- 101 to 200
- 201 to 300
- 301 to 500
- 1,000 to 1,100

increased. In addition to the greater land disruption, more energy is required to extract the desired minerals from lower-grade ores. More water also is likely to be needed. This problem is compounded by the fact that substantial amounts of mineral extraction and processing take place in the water-scarce West. Furthermore, mining usually pollutes the water that is used. Highlighted in figure 14.1 are the states that produce large quantities of polluted mine wastewater.

As noted on page 171, noncoal mining (excluding uranium tailings) produces about 13,000 pounds of solid waste per person per year; it is the largest single source of solid waste. Copper, iron ore, and phosphate mining generate much of the waste, most of it in the form of mine tailings (soil and rock removed to gain access to ores). The tailings generally are deposited in piles or dumped into ponds. Table 14.1 provides a summary of the volumes of waste generated by nonfuel mining. An EPA (1983) nationwide survey revealed that as of 1983 there were 1,754 surface impoundments at 501 separate sites where metals are or were mined, while there were 2,272 surface impoundments at 1,187 nonmetallic mining sites. These impoundments—where liquid wastes are stored, treated, and/or disposed—pose considerable contamination risks to surface and ground waters. Indeed, mining wastes may contain a wide variety of dissolved toxic materials, including arsenic, copper, molybdenum, selenium, and sulfuric acid. Even the more inert materials— sand, clay, and stone—create problems by adding suspended solids to ground and surface waters. But the most hazardous wastes are those from copper, gold, silver, molybdenum, and other metallic mining operations. Unfortunately, the overall scope of the problem is not well understood, since relatively little monitoring occurs. Although some states are now acting quite vigorously to reduce environmental hazards from abandoned and operating mines, federal efforts have lagged. Only a small proportion of federal Abandoned Mined Land Program funds has gone to noncoal mines. Nor does the EPA, as yet, regulate mine wastes as hazardous wastes.

One way to reduce water pollution associated with mining is to recycle the water used. Indeed, this is now required in many cases. But it does not eliminate the ultimate need to dispose of wastes. Threats to ground and surface water can, however, be further reduced by neutralizing acid wastes and using impermeable liners and berms to contain wastes in impoundments.

Figure 14.2. Value of Annual Nonfuel Mineral Production.

Source:
S. D., Smith, *Statistical Summary: Preprint from the 1986 Bureau of Mines Mineral Yearbook* (Washington, DC: GPO, 1987), p. 6.

NONFUEL MINERAL LEASING ON FEDERAL LANDS

The United States government has long encouraged exploitation of the nation's mineral resources. The General Mining Law of 1872 allows prospectors to stake claims on federal lands, and—if the discovery of a valuable mineral can be demonstrated—they can obtain complete private ownership, known as a patent, and thus full rights to all discoveries. This is generally the case for copper, silver, gold, magnesium, uranium, and other "hardrock" minerals. As of the mid-1970s, about 54,000 patents had been issued, and, as of 1988, control of about 3 million acres has been transferred to private interests.

The government has not, in fact, allowed unfettered access to all hardrock mineral lands. Over the years, substantial acreages have been "withdrawn" by the Bureau of Reclamation and other federal agencies, thus precluding their appropriation under the 1872 mining law. Furthermore, designation of wilderness areas under the Wilderness Act of 1964 (figure 15.4)—along with other land designations meant to protect ecological and recreational values—has closed many more acres to mining.

Access to some nonfuel minerals—phosphate, potassium, sodium, sulfur, lead, and zinc—is granted principally through leases. Only small acreages (as of 1987, less than 13,000 acres in total) are leased for other minerals. Leasing for hardrock minerals does occur in a few places; this is provided for by statutes that apply to specific lands. Figure 14.3 shows total nonfuel lease acreages. The vast bulk of New Mexico and Utah's leases are for potassium; Wyoming and Nevada's for sodium; and Missouri's for lead and zinc. All of Montana's leases are for phosphate, as are 82 percent of Idaho's. About three-quarters of California's leases are for sodium.

Many of the nation's most valued mineral resources are concentrated on the federal lands and are accessible only through patents. Those who favor minimal access restrictions argue that more mining of the federal lands—expensive, complex, and fraught with uncertainty as it would be—might enable us to reduce our import dependence for certain strategic minerals (figure 14.4). Indeed, the Carter administration—and especially the Reagan administration—sought to expand the

federal acreages open to mining. The Department of the Interior is still reviewing past mining withdrawals on Bureau of Land Management lands in the western states, and the entire question of how much control the federal government should exert over actual mining practices is still being debated. Some agencies, including the Forest Service, have sought to regulate active mining claims on lands they control. Congress has prohibited establishment of claims in certain national parks and has authorized the Department of the Interior to regulate existing claims. But a more lasting resolution of these issues may have to await a major overhaul of the 1872 law, possibly with much greater provisions for leasing.

Figure 14.3. Nonfuel Mineral Leasing on Federal Lands.

Source:
BLM, *Public Land Statistics 1987* (Washington, DC: GPO, 1988), pp. 68–72.

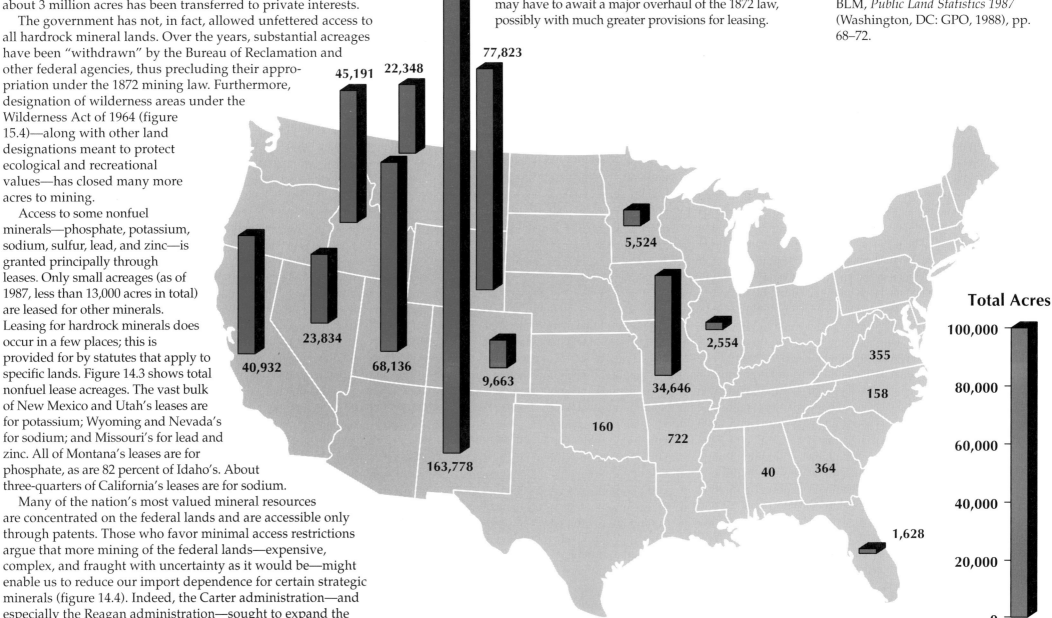

Total Acres

100,000

80,000

60,000

40,000

20,000

0

Figure 14.4. Import Reliance for Key Minerals.

Source:
U.S. Bureau of Mines, *Mineral Commodity Summaries 1988: An Up-to-Date Summary of 87 Nonfuel Mineral Commodities* (Washington, DC: GPO, 1988), p. 2.

IMPORT RELIANCE FOR KEY MINERALS

The United States is amply supplied with many minerals (i.e., supplies should last well beyond the year 2000)—among them boron, magnesium, molybdenum, phosphorous, potash, titanium, and silicon. "Reserve-deficiency" minerals, by contrast, are those for which reserves are significant but not sufficient to meet anticipated industrial needs. Examples include silver, gold, mercury, tungsten, and zinc. Minerals for which we possess "essentially no reserves" include manganese, cobalt, platinum-group metals, chromium, nickel, aluminum, tin, and asbestos.

While some of these minerals are in fact present in the United States, we find it economically, environmentally, or politically advantageous to import them.

Strategic minerals are those used for defense purposes and for which import dependency is either very high or total. Critical minerals also are deemed important for defense—but needs are satisfied from domestic reserves and/or imports from "friendly nations." Among the critical minerals are copper, nickel, and vanadium. Because the definitional boundary between strategic and critical is so fuzzy, the categories often are combined.

The Strategic and Critical Minerals Stockpiling Act of 1979 represents our most recent effort to buffer against future mineral shortages. Its aim is to ensure sufficient availability of resources to see the country through a three-year conventional war. Among the more heavily stockpiled minerals are asbestos, diamonds, manganese, mercury, quartz crystal, silver, talc, tin, and tungsten. Stockpiling goals, however, can shift with the political winds; the Reagan administration, for example, strongly supported a buildup of at least certain stockpiles.

Mineral supplies can also be enhanced through recycling, substitution, and long-term trade arrangements with friendly nations. As noted earlier, there are those who feel that the federal lands can and should supply certain strategic and critical minerals. Other long-term options—all highly contentious—include sea-floor mining, exploitation of Antarctic resources, and reductions in military arsenals.

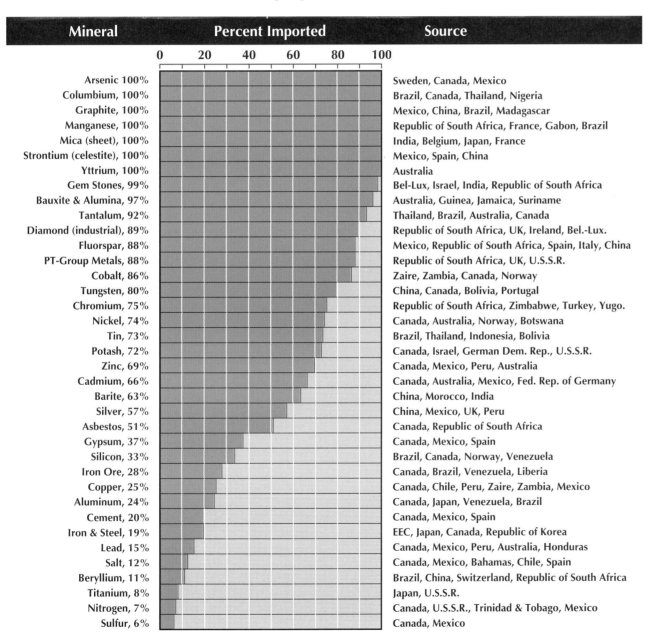

Mineral	Percent Imported	Source
Arsenic, 100%		Sweden, Canada, Mexico
Columbium, 100%		Brazil, Canada, Thailand, Nigeria
Graphite, 100%		Mexico, China, Brazil, Madagascar
Manganese, 100%		Republic of South Africa, France, Gabon, Brazil
Mica (sheet), 100%		India, Belgium, Japan, France
Strontium (celestite), 100%		Mexico, Spain, China
Yttrium, 100%		Australia
Gem Stones, 99%		Bel-Lux, Israel, India, Republic of South Africa
Bauxite & Alumina, 97%		Australia, Guinea, Jamaica, Suriname
Tantalum, 92%		Thailand, Brazil, Australia, Canada
Diamond (industrial), 89%		Republic of South Africa, UK, Ireland, Bel.-Lux.
Fluorspar, 88%		Mexico, Republic of South Africa, Spain, Italy, China
PT-Group Metals, 88%		Republic of South Africa, UK, U.S.S.R.
Cobalt, 86%		Zaire, Zambia, Canada, Norway
Tungsten, 80%		China, Canada, Bolivia, Portugal
Chromium, 75%		Republic of South Africa, Zimbabwe, Turkey, Yugo.
Nickel, 74%		Canada, Australia, Norway, Botswana
Tin, 73%		Brazil, Thailand, Indonesia, Bolivia
Potash, 72%		Canada, Israel, German Dem. Rep., U.S.S.R.
Zinc, 69%		Canada, Mexico, Peru, Australia
Cadmium, 66%		Canada, Australia, Mexico, Fed. Rep. of Germany
Barite, 63%		China, Morocco, India
Silver, 57%		China, Mexico, UK, Peru
Asbestos, 51%		Canada, Republic of South Africa
Gypsum, 37%		Canada, Mexico, Spain
Silicon, 33%		Brazil, Canada, Norway, Venezuela
Iron Ore, 28%		Canada, Brazil, Venezuela, Liberia
Copper, 25%		Canada, Chile, Peru, Zaire, Zambia, Mexico
Aluminum, 24%		Canada, Japan, Venezuela, Brazil
Cement, 20%		Canada, Mexico, Spain
Iron & Steel, 19%		EEC, Japan, Canada, Republic of Korea
Lead, 15%		Canada, Mexico, Peru, Australia, Honduras
Salt, 12%		Canada, Mexico, Bahamas, Chile, Spain
Beryllium, 11%		Brazil, China, Switzerland, Republic of South Africa
Titanium, 8%		Japan, U.S.S.R.
Nitrogen, 7%		Canada, U.S.S.R., Trinidad & Tobago, Mexico
Sulfur, 6%		Canada, Mexico

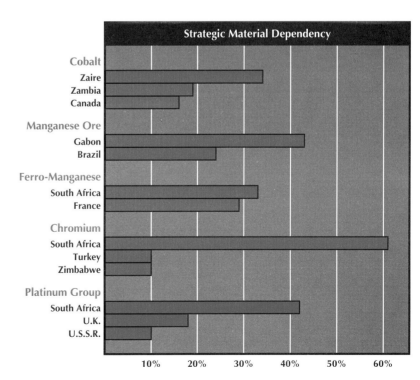

Parks, Recreation, and Wildlife 15

Americans take great pride in their national parks. From its inception in 1872—with the designation of the world's first national park at Yellowstone—the National Park System has become an achievement of remarkable size, ecological and cultural diversity, and scenic beauty. And it is complemented by many thousands of state and local parks, preserves, and recreation areas. But the parks' missions are far from simple: They must contend with competing demands for environmental preservation, recreation, resource extraction, and residential and commercial development.

The initial purpose of national parks was quite simple: scenic preservation. But this was allowed only after Congress was persuaded that the first parks were devoid of significant material resource value (i.e., minerals, water, etc.). In contrast to the notion of scenic preservation was the concept of conservation. The Forest Reserve Act of 1891 and the establishment in 1905 of the Bureau of Forestry (now National Forest Service)—under the initial leadership of Gifford Pinchot—marked the beginnings of a far-reaching federal commitment to "wise use" of the public lands. Renewable resources—especially forests and pastures (chapters 5 and 6)—were not simply to be preserved for posterity but managed so as to ensure sustained yields. Over the years, this evolved into the Forest Service's much-touted "multiple-use" policy: Its lands support resource extraction, recreation, flood control, and more.

During the early part of this century, both the Forest Service and the National Park Service (NPS)—created in 1916—strove to meet growing national demands for recreation. The two agencies were and still are competitors in this regard—but at least since the reign of Franklin Roosevelt, the NPS has been recognized as the nation's premier recreation provider. During the 1950s and 1960s, the NPS launched its "Mission 66" project, which sought to greatly upgrade highway access and visitor facilities for what was by then an extensive system of parks and other areas.

During the 1960s, Mission 66 collided with growing preservationist sentiment. Although the case for preservation had been forcefully made since John Muir founded the Sierra Club in the late 1800s, the cause now garnered much wider popular support. It was enshrined in the 1964 Wilderness Act, which initially set aside 10 million acres of lands. By the 1970s, federal and state land-management agencies were contending with a powerful, increasingly confrontational environmental community. The NPS, for its part, deemphasized highway access, simplified visitor facilities, and limited visitor numbers— especially in fragile backcountry areas. The 1972 National Park System Plan supported comprehensive representation of physiographic and ecological regions.

Meanwhile, as both environmental awareness and leisure time increased, so did the demands placed on the nation's park and recreation resources. Many of the "crown jewels"—the Yosemites, Yellowstones, and Grand Canyons—are quite distant from major cities. Alaska's vast public lands are even much more remote. In response to this imbalance between populations and recreation resources, the Land and Water Conservation Fund (LWCF) was created in 1964. It provides funds to state and local governments for land acquisition—much of it in relative proximity to major urban areas.

LWCF allocations were slashed during the Reagan years—but in 1987 the President's Commission on Americans Outdoors recommended replacing it with a trust fund that would generate $1 billion per year for land acquisition and protection. That recommendation has yet to be implemented—but if it is, it could signal increased support for greenline parks (which combine public and private lands, usually in rural—rather than wild— settings) and land trusts (nonprofit organizations that protect private lands). All this activity—combined with a myriad of local regulations, state plans, and federal laws described elsewhere in this atlas—should ensure lively continuation of the various debates over parks, recreation, and wildlife.

Yellowstone National Park (summer, 1989). R. Mason.

THE NATIONAL PARK SYSTEM

The National Park System is diverse in both composition and purpose. Its parks, recreation areas, lakeshores, seashores, rivers, parkways, monuments, historic areas, and battlefields are meant to serve recreation, education, historic preservation, and ecological protection needs. In terms of acreage, the system is overwhelmingly a western and Alaskan phenomenon—where the vast public landholdings permit creation of large parks. Eastern demands for accessible recreation are, at least partially, satisfied by newer and smaller units—including the many historic areas not shown on figure 15.1.

Of the National Park System units whose principal purpose is outdoor recreation or ecological protection (as opposed to historic protection or education), the most visited in 1987—in descending order—were: Golden Gate National Recreation Area (NRA) near San Francisco; Great Smoky Mountains National Park (NP) in North Carolina and Tennessee; Gateway NRA near New York City; Lake Mead NRA in Nevada and Arizona; Cape Cod National Seashore (NS) in Massachusetts; Gulf Islands NS in Mississippi and Florida; Acadia NP in Maine; Yosemite NP in California; Glen Canyon NRA in Utah and Arizona; Olympic NP in Washington State; Assateague Island NS in Virginia and Maryland; Yellowstone NP in Wyoming, Montana, and Idaho; Delaware Water Gap NRA in Pennsylvania and New Jersey; Rocky Mountain National Park in Colorado; and Point Reyes NS, north of San Francisco (NPS Annual 1988). The Blue Ridge Parkway also was heavily used. These rankings—along with the data in figure 15.2—are less than ideal measures of public interest in particular parks: They do not indicate the nature and purpose of visits, nor do they tell us about specific public concerns. Still, they support the notion that parks easily accessible to large urban areas are among the most highly valued.

Figure 15.2 depicts a rapid increase in overall park use in recent years. Since 1980, however, acquisition activity has almost stood still. A recent study by the National Parks and Conservation Association (NPCA 1988) concludes that the National

Park System lacks potential representation of 42 percent of the ecosystems defined in the 1972 National Park System Plan (NPS 1972). The NPCA calls for the immediate addition of at least forty-six natural areas and forty historic sites, with many more over the long term.

The forty-six natural areas include: Tallgrass Prairie (OK); Jemez Mountains (NM); Florida Keys; Michigan Peninsula; Siskiyou (OR); Great Plains (ND, KS, SD, or WY); Blackrock Desert (NV); Escalante Canyons (UT); Atchafalaya Basin (LA); Currituck Banks (NC); Mojave Desert (CA); Hells Canyon (OR);

Figure 15.1. The National Park System.

Source:
"National Park System Map and Guide" (National Park Service, 1988).

Figure 15.2. Annual Recreation Visits to National Park Service Areas.

Source:
National Park Service, *National Park Statistical Abstract 1987* (Denver: National Park Service, 1988), pp. 37–38.

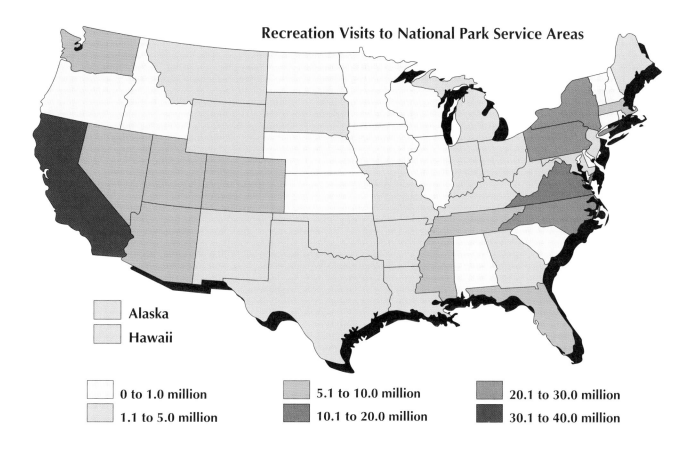

Recreation Visits to National Park Service Areas

Alaska

Hawaii

0 to 1.0 million	
1.1 to 5.0 million	

5.1 to 10.0 million	
10.1 to 20.0 million	

20.1 to 30.0 million	
30.1 to 40.0 million	

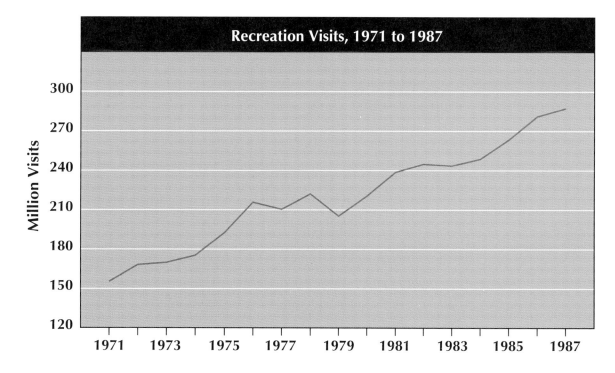

Big Sur (CA); Kauai (HI); Loess Hills (IA, NE); Sonoran Desert/Pinacate (AZ); Lower Altamaha River (GA); San Juan Mountains (CO); Lake Tahoe (NV); Owyhee Canyonlands (OR, ID, NV); Mobile-Tensaw Bottomlands (AL); Nipomo Dunes (CA); Sawtooth Mountains (ID); Arctic Wildlife Refuge (AK); Mt. Edgecombe (AK); Two-Hearted River (MI); City of Rocks (ID); Cobscook Bay (ME); Connecticut River (CT, VT, NH, MA); Machias River (ME); Kings Range/Cape Mendocino (CA); Mississippi River (MN, WI, IA, MO); Montauk (NY); Chesapeake Bay (VA, MD, DE, PA); Amicalola (GA); Oregon Coast, Gauley River (WV); Ruby Mountains or Monitor Valley (NV); Smith River (CA); Nebraska Sandhills (NE); San Rafael Swell (UT); Purgatoire River (CO); Blackwater River (MD); Black River (NC); and Sweetwater Basin (WY).

Expansion of the park system will not necessarily ameliorate problems of overuse. Visitors tend to swarm to the most spectacular and accessible portions of many parks, leaving large areas practically devoid of people. As a consequence, the trail erosion, vegetation damage, litter, and other marks of human use are minimized in some backcountry areas but concentrated in other areas. Is it desirable—to at least some degree—to maintain this pattern, or to try to spread the damage more evenly? Furthermore, to what degree should overall park visitation be limited? Many parks already place limits on total visitation, camping in fragile areas, and other visitor activities.

Park ecosystems can be profoundly affected by human activities and natural processes outside park boundaries. Particular concerns include migration of wildlife, movement of surface and groundwater, and aesthetic issues. Insufficient water flow to the Everglades and overdevelopment at the gateways to Yellowstone and the Great Smoky Mountains national parks are but a couple of the more publicized boundary concerns. While cooperative agreements may be reached with federal agencies that control lands adjacent to parks (though their implementation may be impeded by bureaucratic rivalry or indifference), management of adjacent private lands is much more problematic.

The 1872 Mining Act (figure 14.3) allows mining within park boundaries if there was a claim prior to park designation. It is, however, regulated—and in some cases expressly prohibited. Many park advocates would like to see it banned altogether. A related question is that of the security and rights of inholders (persons who own lands within park boundaries). In this context, how are history and contemporary culture to be treated? And there are even larger questions: How should the spatial and administrative scope of future National Park Service activities be defined? To what extent should its recreation, ecological-protection, and historic-preservation missions be shared with the Forest Service, Fish and Wildlife Service, Bureau of Land Management, and other agencies?

FOCUS: THE 1988 YELLOWSTONE FIRES

Only a couple decades ago, nearly all forest fires—naturally caused as well as human-induced—were seen as our enemy. Smokey the Bear spearheaded a nationwide effort to prevent and control them. But during the 1960s, official attitudes began to change. The environmental movement opened our minds to the concept of wildfires as important ecological processes. Indeed, periodic fires prevent large buildups of debris on the forest floor—buildups that can sustain truly monumental infernos. Moreover, fires vary in intensity and destructive force; one fire might severely char some areas but skip over others entirely. Where old-growth forest is actually destroyed, the process of ecological succession begins again. Some species, such as certain types of lodgepole pine, depend on fires to induce germination of their seeds. Other forest-floor species will reproduce in abundance once they are opened to the light and fertilized by the ashes. The new vegetation patterns created by fire in turn create new animal habitats. The entire process is a dynamic one that seems to work in great, but not entirely predictable, cycles. Ironically, as Matzke and Key (1989) point out, it is fire that has created most of the grand vistas and wildlife habitats so highly valued in our parks and wilderness areas.

In recent decades, Yellowstone and other national parks have sought to restore certain elements of "wildness" that had earlier been sacrificed in the interest of visitor convenience and amusement. Bears, for example, have been weaned of their dependence on garbage dumps that once dotted Yellowstone. In 1972, Yellowstone and several other parks instituted experimental programs that allowed natural fires to run their courses. Yellowstone's initial 340,000-acre program was so successful that in 1976 the "let-burn" acreage was expanded to 1.7 million acres. Soon after, the adjacent Teton Wilderness was brought into the program. Yellowstone's management policy had four basic goals (Yellowstone National Park 1988):

1. To permit as many lightning-caused fires as possible to burn under natural conditions.
2. To prevent wildfire from destroying human life, property, historic and cultural sites, special natural features, or threatened and endangered species.
3. To suppress all man-caused fires (and any natural fires whose suppression is deemed necessary) in as safe, cost-effective, and environmentally sensitive ways as possible.
4. To resort to prescribed burning when and where necessary and practical to reduce hazardous fuels, primarily dead and down trees.

Although the National Park Service's policy had its detractors, its implementation was generally uneventful—until

1988. The extensive fires represented on the map were caused by a rare combination of below-normal precipitation, sustained high winds, and several decades' accumulation of forest-floor debris. An extremely dry June produced about twenty natural fires, eleven of which burned themselves out. Then, in contrast with other dry summers of recent years, the drought persisted through July and especially August—when unusually strong winds fanned the flames. As the fires increased in areal extent, so did the outrage of local businesspeople deprived of their usual summer trade. In late July, the park policy shifted to one of fullest feasible suppression. But by that time, constant media coverage of the fires had severely tarnished the NPS's image. In the ensuing frenzy, politicians were calling for heads to roll, and even President Reagan—previously unaware of the let-burn policy—declared it a bad policy.

By fall, both forest and political fires began to subside. The final Yellowstone toll was 988,975 burned acres, or 44.5% of the park (Yellowstone National Park 1989). For the Greater Yellowstone Area, which includes lands adjacent to the park, the toll was 1.6 million acres (Matzke and Key 1989). The fire-suppression effort within the park alone cost almost $120 million—nearly ten times Yellowstone's annual operating budget. Although tourism had plummeted by late July and August, post-fire curiosity brought record numbers of visitors in October. The 1989 tourist trade has more than recovered, and the fires' effects have become part of the visitors' educational experience.

Yellowstone did not turn into a lifeless moonscape. The burned areas shown on the map vary greatly in type and severity of burn. Of the total of nearly 1 million burned acres, 56.9 percent sustained canopy burns; 37.7 percent sustained surface burns; and 5.4 percent sustained meadow, sage, or grassland burns (Yellowstone National Park 1989). Where canopy burns occurred, the soil was also heated—but generally to a rather limited extent. Even when burning occurred principally at the surface, soil heating was usually low. Up to 15 percent of the areas represented as "burned" may not, in fact, have burned at all. But even where trees were killed, most other plants were not; thus they could regenerate from their roots the following spring.

The outcome of all this is a broad mosaic of open and forested areas. Some areas are blackened severely; in other places, the fires' effects are much more subtle. The spring of 1989 has carpeted many of the more fertile burned areas with wildflowers. The contrast with the blackened forest floor is stunning—and quite a surprise to visitors who expected nothing but devastation. The fires also created new grazing habitat for bison, elk, and antelope. Although many small mammals, birds, and fish were killed during the fires, relatively few large mammals were destroyed. The known toll for

Figure 15.3. FOCUS: The 1988 Yellowstone Fires.

Source:
"Preliminary Survey of Burned Areas: Yellowstone National Park and Adjoining National Forests" (Greater Yellowstone Post-Fire Resource Assessment Team, 1988, map).

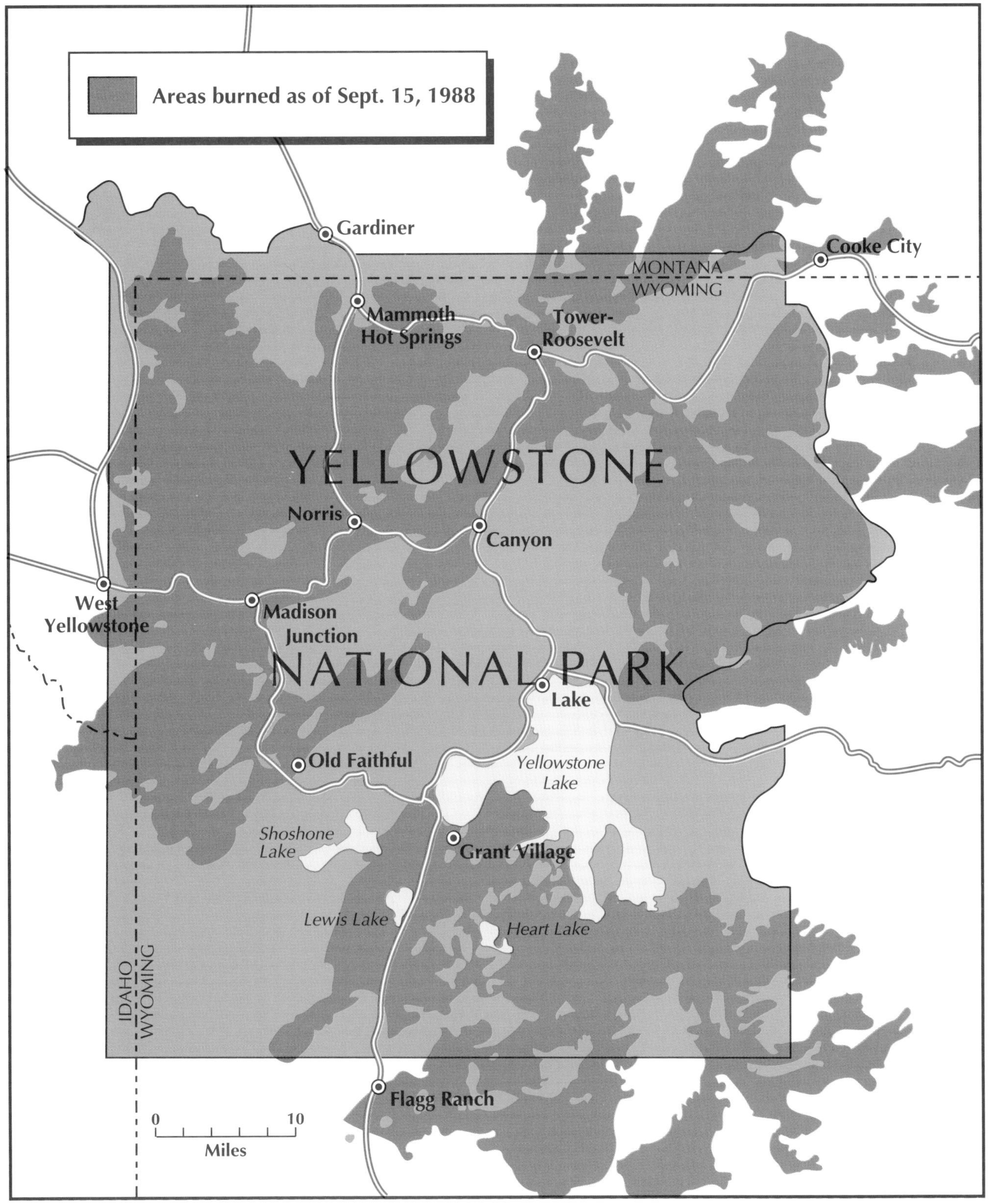

Areas burned as of Sept. 15, 1988

Gardiner

Cooke City

MONTANA
WYOMING

Mammoth
Hot Springs

Tower-
Roosevelt

YELLOWSTONE

Norris

Canyon

West
Yellowstone

Madison
Junction

NATIONAL PARK

Lake

Old Faithful

*Yellowstone
Lake*

*Shoshone
Lake*

Grant Village

Lewis Lake

Heart Lake

IDAHO
WYOMING

Flagg Ranch

0   10

Miles

Yellowstone was 257 elk, four deer, two moose, and nine bison. Not only large mammals, but also scenic and cultural attractions were spared the fires' full destructive effects. Major natural attractions, such as the Upper and Lower Falls and Old Faithful, were unaffected. The historic Old Faithful Inn—with firefighters' help—remained intact.

The 1988 Yellowstone fires were a rare event—but not without historical precedent. Such conflagrations are estimated to affect Yellowstone about every 300 years (Yellowstone National Park 1988). The 1988 fire season was extraordinary not only in Yellowstone but through large areas of the West, especially other parts of Wyoming, Montana, Idaho, and Alaska. These areas, of course, did not get press coverage comparable to Yellowstone's. In response to the unusual conditions—and the extraordinary wrath wrought upon the National Park Service—the let-burn policy was altered. For 1989, at least, the policy was full suppression of all fires. But as the political firestorm continues to die down, a more considered policy is likely to be reinstituted. Indeed, the National Park Service's fire policy may come more closely to resemble that of the U.S. Forest Service. That policy, while similar to the National Park Service's, sets stricter limits for wilderness fires. Once the limits are exceeded, the fires are fought—regardless of their cause.

The 1988 fires provided marvelous opportunities for scientific research and public education. One important lesson is that we cannot control all fires. Indeed, even if we had mounted a full-scale suppression effort from the very beginning of the Yellowstone fires, they still would have gotten ahead of us—particularly in inaccessible, roadless areas. But outside Alaska, at least, such wilderness areas are for the most part limited to relatively small "islands." If we wish to keep them wild, we must manage them—and we do. In some cases, for example, we make amends for our past excesses by helping certain species reestablish themselves. We may also place limits on natural fires, even though we now understand and accept their necessity—or at least we did, before 1988.

The 1988 fires provided an opportunity to try to convey the complexity of these issues to an alarmed public. But the mass media, by and large, chose to ignore subtlety and complexity in favor of grim pictures and battle accounts. As with individual oil spills, beach pollution, and other issues—the media helped the public mistake the trees for the forest. While the National Park Service itself is trying hard to exploit post-fire opportunities for public education, it is probably too late to reach the masses that were horrified, but educated little, during the summer of 1988. This is unfortunate, because one of the consequences of the predicted global warming (figure 18.1) may well be more fire seasons like 1988.

THE NATIONAL WILDERNESS PRESERVATION SYSTEM

The purpose of the Wilderness Act of 1964 is to preserve and protect lands in their natural condition. Timber cutting, motor vehicles (including boats), aircraft landings, and other motorized equipment are for the most part prohibited on designated lands. But certain other activities, such as grazing and mining, have in many cases been allowed to continue. Moreover, mineral exploration is allowed so long as no motorized equipment is used.

Initially, Congress set aside about 9 million acres, to be managed by the U.S. Forest Service, National Park Service (NPS), Fish and Wildlife Service, and Bureau of Land Management (BLM). The system expanded rapidly—reaching 80 million acres by 1980. Before 1975, most eastern lands were excluded because of their extensive history of human use and because of a minimum size requirement of 5,000 acres. The 1975 Eastern Wilderness Areas Act lifted those requirements, adding sixteen new areas (207,000 acres) and providing for the study of more for possible inclusion. The 1980 Alaska Public Interest Lands Act greatly expanded the system, adding 56.4 million acres. In 1984, 8.3 million acres were added in twenty states, and in 1988, 1.7 million acres were added in the State of Washington.

Of the national total of 90.8 million wilderness acres, 42.4 percent are administered by the NPS, 35.8 percent by the National Forest Service, 21.3 percent by the Fish and Wildlife Service, and 0.5 percent by the BLM (Wilderness Society 1989). Bureau of Land Management wilderness holdings are small in comparison to total BLM landholdings because designation of BLM lands was not permitted until 1976. The Wilderness Preservation System, of course, tends to mirror the spatial distribution of public landholdings: It is principally a western and Alaskan phenomenon. Alaska has huge wilderness areas, the largest of them the 8.7-million-acre Wrangell-St. Elias Area. But there are also areas as small as the 5-acre Oregon Islands. Most eastern units are much smaller than 10,000 acres—though there are notable exceptions, particularly in Florida and Georgia.

Visitor use of wilderness areas tripled between 1970 and the mid-1980s. Most recreational use, however, occurs on a small portion of wilderness lands in the lower forty-eight states. It is concentrated in California, North Carolina, and Minnesota. Such heavy visitor use—even from environmentally-conscious

Department of Agriculture

Department of the Interior

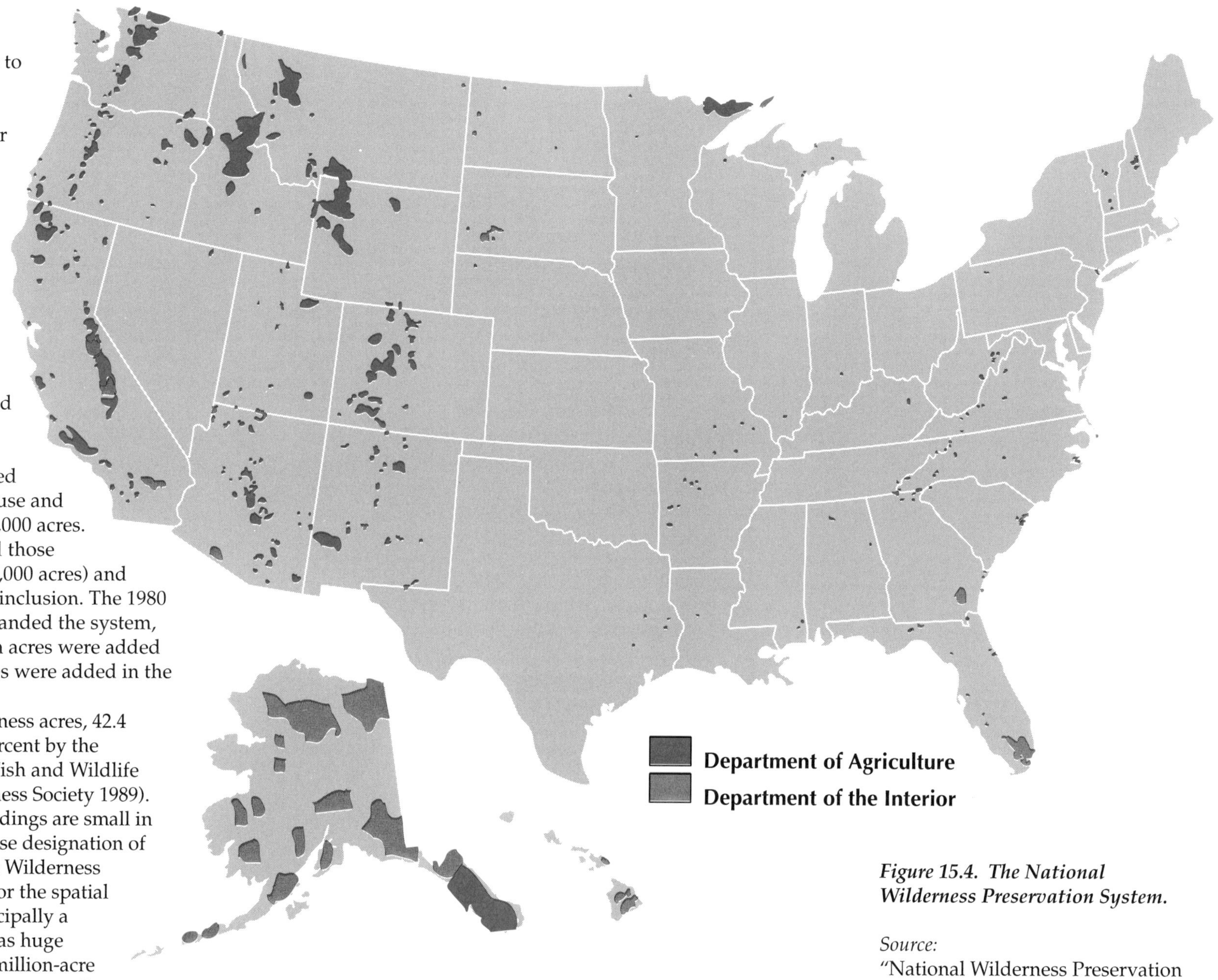

Figure 15.4. The National Wilderness Preservation System.

Source:
"National Wilderness Preservation System" (USGS, 1987, map).

visitors—has significant impacts on areas meant to be largely free of such intrusions. As a result, visitor restrictions have been imposed in many areas.

The management of wilderness areas has always been a contentious issue, pitting timber and mining interests against environmental preservationists. The 1964 Wilderness Act set in motion the complex and lengthy process of reviewing National Forest, Park and Wildlife Refuge lands for possible inclusion in the system. The 1976 Federal Land Policy and Management

Act finally required similar consideration of the vast holdings of the BLM. First, roadless lands over 5,000 acres are inventoried; then the study is narrowed to those areas having appropriate wilderness characteristics. Finally, recommendations for wilderness designation are made to the president and Congress. These various activities have been ongoing—at various rates and in various political climates—over the past 25 years.

During the 1970s, the Forest Service completed two separate studies: RARE (Roadless Area Review and Evaluation) I and II. RARE I, completed in 1973, inventoried 60 million acres of land (the National Forest System currently contains 191 million acres). Wilderness recommendations were made for 12.3 million acres, of which only 45,000 were east of the Rockies. In response to court challenges from environmental organizations, RARE II was undertaken—and more eastern lands were inventoried. The final recommendation (also struck down by the courts) was that 15.4 millions acres (577,000 east of the Mississippi) be declared wilderness, 36 million be maintained as nonwilderness open to multiple uses, and 11 million remain under study. To the chagrin of many environmentalists, the relatively large acreages recommended by the Forest Service for multiple-use management (see pp.1–2, 52, and 177) would be open to possible prospecting, mining, grazing, and timber cutting. Supporters of such activities argue that they need not be intrusive nor inflict long-term damage and that wilderness designation closes access to all but a privileged minority of hikers and campers. Ultimately, the decisions are made by Congress, which has proceeded largely on a state-by-state basis rather than adhering to any general policy.

When James Watt became Secretary of the Interior in 1981, he sought to curtail designation of new wilderness areas and to open existing areas to energy and mineral development. Indeed, the 1964 Wilderness Act provided for continuation of mining claims and leases through 1983. Watt's predecessors, however, had generally sought to restrict leasing as much as possible. Amid a firestorm of controversy and congressional opposition to his plans, Watt sought a compromise. He proposed a moratorium on all mineral leasing until the year 2000—but with broad presidential discretion to allow mining in cases of "urgent national need." His scheme, in fact, would probably have opened large acreages to mining—and would have opened all wilderness lands to development in 2000. The existing law, by contrast, had called for termination of all leasing and claims in 1983, except where Congress decides otherwise. Watt's plans were blocked in Congress, and he finally abandoned them in late 1982. Currently, no *new* leasing or claims are allowed—but existing claims do remain active so long as they meet certain general conditions.

RIVERS AND TRAILS

Four years after the Wilderness Act, Congress sought special protection for rivers and trails. The Wild and Scenic Rivers Act of 1968 initially designated 775 miles on eight rivers: the Clearwater River, Middle Fork in Idaho; Eleven Point River in Missouri; Feather River in California; Rio Grande River in New Mexico; Rogue River in Oregon; Saint Croix River in Minnesota and Wisconsin; Salmon River, Middle Fork in Idaho; and Wolf River in Wisconsin. Another twenty-seven rivers were authorized for study for potential inclusion in the system. By May 1989 the system had grown to 120 rivers or river segments, totaling 9,279 miles—but environmental organizations urge that the pace be stepped up to add at least 1,500 river segments by the year 2000.

Rivers are classified as either wild, scenic, or recreational. As of May 1989, 4,731 miles were designated as wild; 1,629 as scenic; and 2,571 as recreational. All rivers in the system are to be kept free of dams, and future development is prohibited in corridors on each side of the river. Wild rivers are those that are free of impoundments and generally in a primitive condition, with unpolluted water and access principally by trail. Scenic rivers also are free of impoundments and are largely primitive and undeveloped—but accessible in places by road. Recreational rivers are accessible by road or railroad; there may be some shoreline development; and impoundment or diversion may have occurred in the past.

Of the system's 9,279 miles, 8,474 were administered by the federal government (NPS, U.S. Forest Service, BLM, Fish and Wildlife Service), and 805 miles by state and tribal governments. Since most western and Alaskan rivers flow through federal lands, administrative responsibilities are relatively clear cut. In the East—where private ownership of adjacent land is common—much of the planning is undertaken by state and local governments, with federal financial, technical, and legal assistance. Conflicts between governments and landowners are, of course, common. White-water recreation, hydroelectric power generation, and commercial development are among the more contentious of the many competing demands placed on the rivers.

In addition to the federal program, thirty-one states have their own rivers statutes. They vary considerably in scope and strength; in many cases, actual designation of river segments has been minimal. A key reason for the reluctance is resistance from property owners, many of whom view river protection programs as "land grabs"—even when no fee-simple acquisition of land occurs. But the State of Maine, with its many miles of highly valued rivers, is an exception to the rule. Its program protects approximately 1,100 miles of rivers—still only 3 percent of the state total. South Carolina has completed a comprehensive assessment of its rivers, though extensive designation has yet to take place (Olson et al. 1988).

The National Trails System Act of 1968 was predated by several existing long-distance trails—key among them the 2,100-mile-long Appalachian Trail stretching from Georgia to Maine. The trail, built in the 1920s and 1930s mostly by volunteers, is a tribute to the vision and effort of the regional planner, forester, and philosopher Benton MacKaye. He saw it as a physical and spiritual retreat for inhabitants of eastern cities. The Appalachian Trail is now managed by the NPS and the Forest Service, the states through which it passes, and private parties. The Appalachian Trail Conference, established in 1925, continues to coordinate many private, local efforts. Although a great deal of adjacent land has been acquired by governments and conservation organizations, the entire 2,100-mile corridor is not under public control. In some places, the trail's "right of passage" rests upon delicately negotiated—and easily disrupted—cooperative agreements with private property owners. The 2,600-mile Pacific Crest Trail—established shortly after the Appalachian Trail—is in a less precarious situation, since 85 percent of it is on federal lands.

The Appalachian and Pacific Crest trails were designated by the 1968 National Trails System Act, and fourteen more trails were recommended for study. The system was initially designed as one of scenic and recreational trails; Congress added historic trails in 1978. National scenic trails, by law, are to be at least 100 miles long, land-based, limited to nonmotorized use, and both conservation and recreation-oriented. National historic trails, on the other hand, can include waterways, or—where only traces (often inaccessible) of the trail remain—the trail's course can be approximated by markers on nearby highways. To qualify as a national historic trail, the route should have had a major impact on general patterns of American culture (including American Indian culture).

In addition to the national trails, there are those managed by states, local governments, and private individuals; their numbers are indicated on figure 15.6. A good deal of state-level effort—much of it inspired by the national Rails-to-Trails Conservancy—has gone into reclaiming abandoned rail rights-of-way. Some of the state-designated trails may eventually become part of the national network. Trails under study or awaiting possible congressional designation include: the Pacific Northwest Trail in Oregon, Idaho, and Montana; the Desert Trail in Arizona, California, Oregon, Washington, and Idaho; the Dominguez-Escalante Trail in Arizona, New Mexico, Colorado, and Utah; the Indian Nations Trail in Oklahoma; the Old

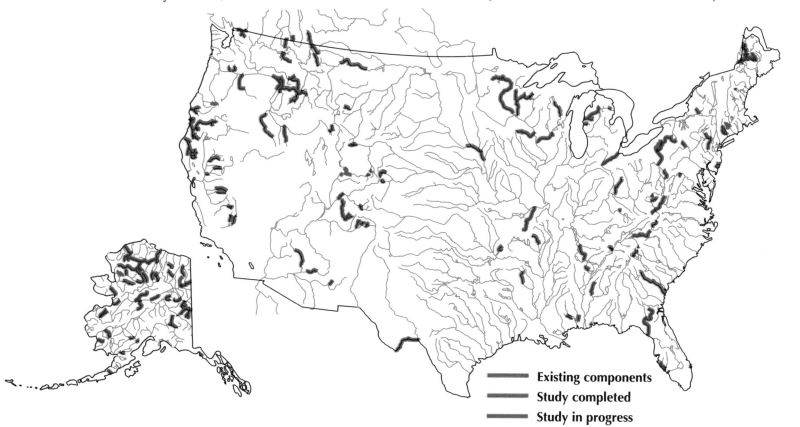

Figure 15.5. Wild and Scenic Rivers.

Source:
"National Wild and Scenic Rivers System" (NPS and National Forest Service, 1988, map).

Existing components

Study completed

Study in progress

Figure 15.6. Scenic and Historic Trails.

Source:
"National Trails System" (National Park, 1988, map).

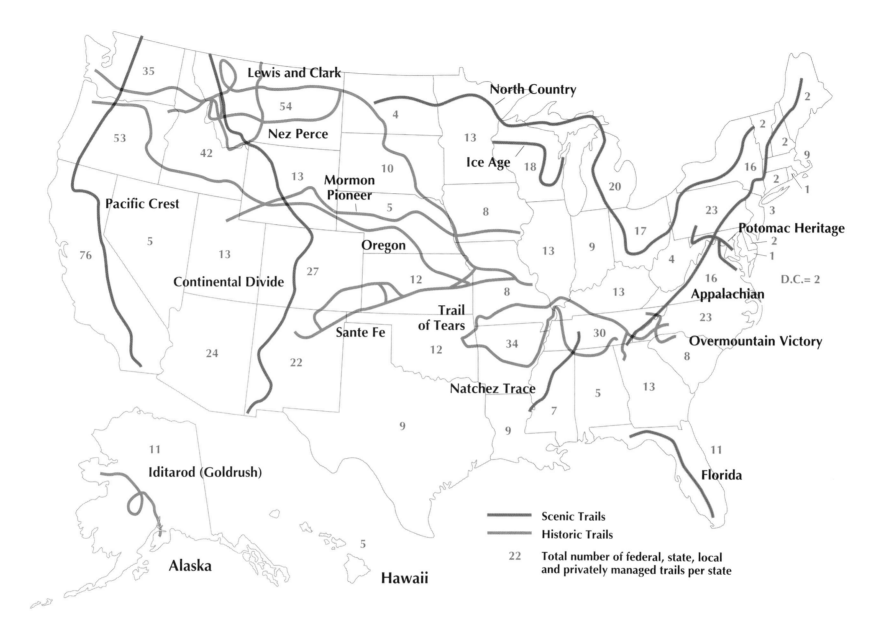

Cattle trails in Texas, Oklahoma, and Kansas; the Bartram Trail in Louisiana, Mississippi, Alabama, Georgia, Florida, South Carolina, and North Carolina; the Daniel Boone Trail in North Carolina, Tennessee, and Kentucky; and the Long Trail in Vermont.

The President's Commission on Americans Outdoors (1987) recently recommended creation of an extensive network of "greenways," which would allow individuals to roam the country by bicycle, horse, or foot. Potential greenways include river and stream courses, abandoned rail lines, utility corridors, wildlife migration routes and flyway corridors, scenic roads and highways, and existing trails, parks, forests, refuges, and recreation areas. The commission also recommended that 2,000 river and stream segments be protected by the year 2000. Metropolitan, as well as more remote wild rivers, are emphasized. The national Wild and Scenic Rivers program is seen as much too concentrated in Alaska, California, and Idaho—with underrepresentation of the nation's midsection. In addition to stepped-up federal efforts, the commission recommended that state and local river and greenway activities be supported by a trust fund providing $1 billion per year in grants. As of late 1989, the fate of that proposal still rested with Congress.

STATE AND LOCAL RECREATION RESOURCES

Because recreation means so many things to so many people, it is impossible ideally to measure its adequacy. If we choose acreage as our measure, we find that state parks and related lands pale in comparison with the federal estate. Indeed, they occupy just one-seventh the acreage held by the National Park Service alone (one-third if Alaska is excluded). Yet they receive more visitors: in 1985, twice as many as the national parks (Myers and Reid 1986). State landholdings are largest in Alaska—which has 7.23 million acres—as well as in Minnesota, New York, Michigan, Florida, Pennsylvania, and Idaho, respectively. Most state-controlled acreage is in parks and forests (New York's 6-million-acre Adirondack Park the largest), with much smaller amounts in natural areas, designated recreation areas, historic areas, and other classifications.

Because of state-to-state differences in availability of federal recreation lands, as well as in state administrative and reporting practices, visitor statistics compiled by the National Association of State Park Directors (1988) must be treated with a good deal of caution. Nonetheless, they reveal a general pattern of highest visitation in the more populous East Coast, West Coast, and Great Lakes states, with the fewest visitors in less-populated, less-accessible states (Maine included). Not surprisingly, the states with highest visitation tend also to have the highest proportions of state and local lands set aside for recreation purposes (figure 15.7). The overwhelming majority of visits are day, as opposed to overnight, visits.

Between 1955 and 1985, the amount of land set aside as state parkland doubled, while visitation more than tripled. Greatest increases in both occurred before 1970; while after 1975, total acreage in state parks actually declined slightly. Lack of funding is a preeminent concern in state park management; a Conservation Foundation survey of state park directors (Myers and Reid 1986) revealed that state parks are even more stressed by budget problems than federal recreation lands. Specific management issues are included, but are by no means limited to facilities development and maintenance, protection of ecologically-sensitive areas, underuse of certain parks, and accommodation of special groups such as the handicapped and the elderly.

The establishment of municipal parks—at least in the older eastern cities—predates the National Park System's 1872 beginnings. Yet city and county parks occupy the smallest areas: County and regional parks account for 0.7 percent of all public recreation land; municipal parks only 0.4 percent (President's Commission on Americans Outdoors 1987). At the same time, they are the most-visited of all U.S. recreation lands (Market Opinion Research 1986). Like national and state recreation lands, local parks suffer from funding shortages. Additional problems include inaccessibility, unsafe conditions, and overcrowding. In many communities, though, new recreation opportunities have been created through the reclamation of abandoned areas, urban waterfronts, canals, and rail rights-of-way. The President's Commission on Americans Outdoors (1987) recently recommended that the ailing Land and Water Conservation Fund—created in 1964 to provide money for federal, state, and local land acquisition—be replaced by a new fund yielding at least $1 billion per year for this same purpose. The commission, seeking to make its recommendations more politically palatable, also recommended increased reliance on visitor fees as a source of funds. As of late 1989, the commission's recommendations were stalled in congressional committee.

Private recreation opportunities range all the way from informal permission to use an individual's land to large commercial enterprises—such as campgrounds, golf courses, and marinas. Without doubt, these opportunities are extremely important—but their precise value is difficult to estimate. Both data and a clear concept of what constitutes private recreation are lacking. Of particular relevance to environmental protection, though, are the growing numbers of land trusts. Land

Figure 15.7. State and Local Recreation Resources.

State and local recreation lands are represented as a percentage of total state land area.

Source:
"1986 Survey of Fifty Statewide Comprehensive Outdoor Recreation Plans" (National Association of State Outdoor Recreation Liaison Officers, 1986, computer printout).

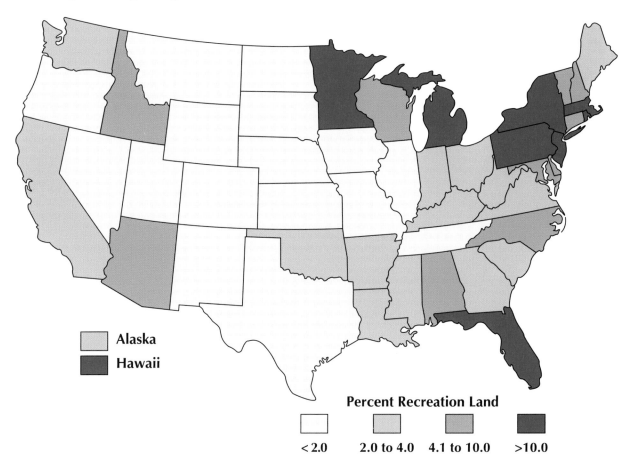

Alaska

Hawaii

Percent Recreation Land

< 2.0   2.0 to 4.0   4.1 to 10.0   >10.0

Table 15.1. Recreation Acres[1]

Per 1,000 Population

Alabama	0.59
Alaska	807.15
Arizona	11.55
Arkansas	1.80
California	1.93
Colorado	8.50
Connecticut	0.08
Delaware	0.16
Florida	0.69
Georgia	0.58
Hawaii	1.41
Idaho	38.43
Illinois	0.10
Indiana	0.16
Iowa	0.19
Kansas	0.47
Kentucky	0.48
Louisiana	0.51
Maine	0.52
Maryland	0.13
Massachusetts	0.21
Michigan	0.87
Minnesota	2.46
Mississippi	1.11
Missouri	0.58
Montana	35.56
Nebraska	0.59
Nevada	71.10
New Hampshire	1.12
New Jersey	0.09
New Mexico	17.70
New York	0.32
North Carolina	0.77
North Dakota	4.52
Ohio	0.10
Oklahoma	0.79
Oregon	12.48
Pennsylvania	0.38
Rhode Island	0.08
South Carolina	0.52
South Dakota	5.03
Tennessee	0.50
Texas	0.27
Utah	22.58
Vermont	1.11
Virginia	0.54
Washington	3.07
West Virginia	0.79
Wisconsin	1.12
Wyoming	66.11

[1]Total of federal, state, and local acres.

Source: "1986 Survey of Fifty Statewide Comprehensive Outdoor Recreation Plans" (National Association of State Outdoor Recreation Liaison Officers, 1986, computer printout).

trusts are private, nonprofit organizations—local, regional, sometimes multistate or national in scale—that seek to protect specific lands for such purposes as ecological preservation, farmland protection, open space provision, and recreation. Lands are acquired through donation or purchase, sometimes to be resold to governments. Land trusts also acquire conservation easements, which place certain restrictions on the use of a parcel of land. The land trust thus has a role as steward, but not owner, of the land. Many land trusts also are active in public education and in arranging land exchanges and management agreements between governments and/or private parties.

Land trusts are principally exurban phenomena, concentrated in the areas adjacent to the large metropolitan populations of the New England, Middle Atlantic, West Coast, and Great Lakes regions. Indeed, in 1988, those four regions were home to 83 percent of local land trusts; New England alone had 45 percent (Land Trust Exchange 1989). Although acreages protected by land trusts pale in comparison with those owned by governments (especially the federal government), the recent growth in land trust activity is impressive. In 1964, there were only ninety-five local land conservation organizations. By 1988, that figure had grown to at least 549 land trusts, with about 2 million acres under their protection (Land Trust Exchange 1989). Additional substantial acreages, not included in the Land Trust Exchange survey, are protected by such national organizations (usually through their local chapters) as the National Audubon Society, the Nature Conservancy, the Trust for Public Land, the American Farmland Trust, the Izaak Walton League, and the National Trust for Historic Preservation. In many instances, the locations of land trust holdings are more important than their size. Land trusts often acquire strategic parcels that are critical links in larger development schemes—or, conversely, that are important elements of government land-protection programs. They also help preserve scenic landscapes—which presently are maintained chiefly through local, regional, and state land-use regulations, in combination with the decisions made by individual landowners.

Some states, such as Maryland and Florida, provide substantial funds to support local land trusts. One of the legislative proposals pursuant to the recommendations of the President's Commission on Americans Outdoors would provide public funds to assist land trusts in their activities. If this becomes a reality, then the importance of land trusts as public-private enterprises could increase substantially. One rather large-scale—indeed, exceptional—example of "public management of private lands" that reaches well beyond the visions of most individual land trusts is New Jersey's Pinelands National Reserve: the subject of the next section.

FOCUS: THE PINELANDS NATIONAL RESERVE

New Jersey's Pinelands National Reserve lies virtually in the heart of the northeastern megalopolis. But its sandy, infertile soils and historic inaccessibility have precluded large-scale farming, industry, or commerce. Instead, over the past three centuries the region's resources have been thoroughly exploited through a series of small-scale enterprises, including lumbering, ironmaking, glassmaking, and berry farming. Beneath the Pine Barrens are vast quantities of extremely pure groundwater. Since precipitation infiltrates rapidly through the overlying sandy soils—allowing for little removal of pollutants—these large aquifers are highly susceptible to contamination. Today, much of the Pinelands region remains sparsely populated—but development pressures from the nearby Philadelphia and New York metropolitan regions have been pushing in from the edges.

The extensive pine and oak forests, along with an unusual array of other plants and animals, give the Pine Barrens a special ecological character. The Pine Barrens are at the very northern fringes of the ranges of some species more common to the South and at the southern limits of the ranges of others more common to the North. Moreover, unique species of plants and animals also are present. The pygmy pines—stunted trees which collectively cover 12,000 acres—are an ecological mystery yet to be fully unraveled. But not just flora, fauna, and groundwater are valued, so are the region's historical assets. The various small-scale industries, the blueberry and cranberry farms, and a rich regional folklore (including the Jersey Devil) are all part of the region's heritage. Furthermore, about 65 percent of the Pinelands is in private ownership—and many of the region's natives, often called "Pineys," are fiercely resistant to new intrusions into their lives by the state and federal governments.

The 1.1-million-acre national reserve—the only such park of its type in the United States—was created in 1978. New Jersey's Pinelands Protection Act defines the actual planning area, which is smaller than the national reserve. The coastal areas shown on the map come under the jurisdiction of the New Jersey Department of Coastal Resources, and they are supposed to be managed in a manner cognizant of planning requirements elsewhere in the Pinelands. Day-to-day planning and management activities are the responsibility of the Pinelands Commission staff. The commission itself, which consists of seven gubernatorial representatives, seven county-appointed representatives, and one federal representative, broadly oversees these activities.

The Pinelands Comprehensive Management Plan, which took effect in 1981, is essentially a zoning scheme. As shown on the map, it divides the Pinelands into a core preservation area where new development is greatly restricted, and an outer protection area, where development is permitted at various

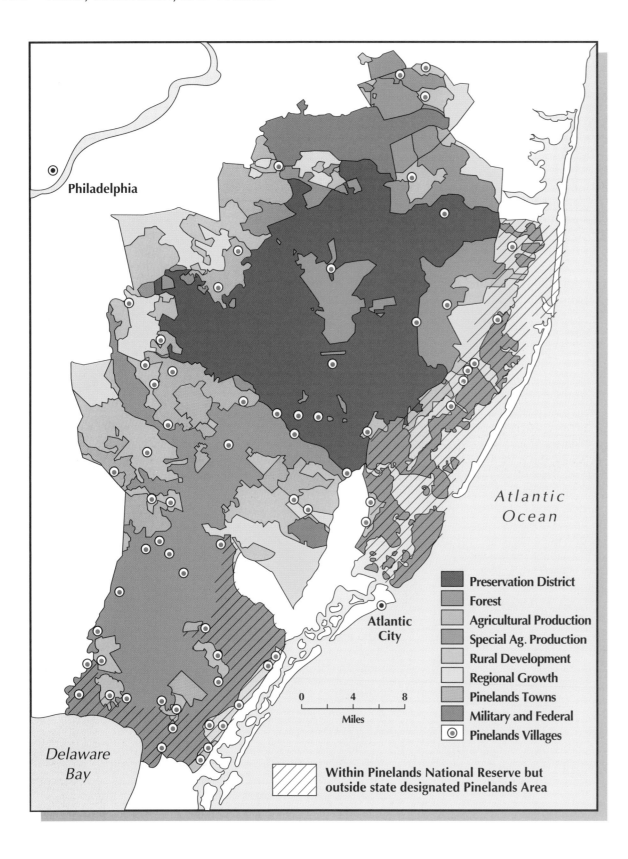

Philadelphia

Atlantic Ocean

Atlantic City

Delaware Bay

0   4   8

Miles

■ Preservation District
■ Forest
□ Agricultural Production
▨ Special Ag. Production
▨ Rural Development
□ Regional Growth
□ Pinelands Towns
■ Military and Federal
◉ Pinelands Villages

▨ Within Pinelands National Reserve but outside state designated Pinelands Area

densities in different zones. This "core-buffer" model addresses some park boundary issues discussed on page 179 and is exemplary of a management approach the United Nations would like to see more widely adopted for biosphere reserves (the Pinelands are one in a global network of these U.N.-designated reserves). The overall zoning scheme rests on the premise that the Pinelands region must accommodate a projected level of future growth. The bulk of that growth is to be directed toward areas best suited for it: the "regional growth" and "rural development" areas. The forestry zones are to support only modest growth, the agricultural areas are to remain in agriculture, and villages and towns are to grow in accordance with certain spatial criteria.

The Pinelands serve as a model for "greenline park planning." This concept, nominally developed in the 1970s, is a means for sustaining ecological, scenic, recreational, and cultural values over relatively large areas. In contrast to traditional park practice, greenline parks include substantial amounts of private land. Management techniques typically include special zoning plans, land trusts, conservation easements, and tax incentives. Greenline proponents speak of the "living landscape": In contrast to conventional national parks, people are allowed, indeed encouraged to a degree, to live there—so long as they engage in such relatively benign pursuits as farming, forestry, fishing, and appropriate tourism.

There is no system of formally-designated greenline parks. But along with the Pinelands, New York State's Adirondack Park—a public-private venture with state, but no federal involvement—is cited as a preeminent greenline example. Although the state Forest Preserve was created in 1885, it was only in 1971 that the Adirondack Park Plan came into being. In many ways, including the conflicts it has generated, it resembles the Pinelands plan. Other greenline examples, which fit the conceptual mold to varying degrees, include Acadia National Park in Maine, the Cape Cod National Seashore in Massachusetts, Gateway National Recreation Area and Fire Island National Seashore in New York, the Upper Delaware Scenic and Recreational River in New York and Pennsylvania, the Chesapeake and Ohio Canal National Historical Park in Maryland, the Cuyahoga Valley National Recreational Area in Ohio, Indiana Dunes National Lakeshore in Indiana, Pictured Rocks National Lakeshore in Michigan, Redwood National Park and the Santa Monica Mountains National Recreation Area in California, Ebey's Landing National Historical Reserve in Washington, and the Columbia River Gorge Scenic Area in Washington and Oregon. If the recent recommendations of the President's Commission on Americans Outdoors are implemented, the greenline list may indeed become considerably longer.

Figure 15.8. FOCUS: The Pinelands National Reserve.

Source:
"New Jersey Pinelands" (New Jersey Pinelands Commission, 1985, map: conceptual representation).

WILDLIFE AND ENDANGERED SPECIES

The issues associated with wildlife conservation are many and complex. They are local and global; they include species whose numbers are abundant—even excessive—as well as those on the verge of extinction; and they deal with species ranging from large trees to fragile alpine wildflowers, from game animals to tiny aquatic organisms.

Globally, about 1.7 million species have been identified—but estimates of the actual total range between 5 and 30 million. The bulk of these are insects. About three-quarters of the world's wild species reside in the tropical zones; most of the rest are found in temperate regions. Although all climatic zones are critical in maintaining life as we know it, it is the tropical rainforests that by far contain the greatest diversity of species. All sorts of products, most now chemically synthesized, were first found in tropical rainforests. Among them are prescription and nonprescription drugs, synthetic fibers, food additives, and insects used as biological pest controls. Vast numbers of agricultural and other domestic plants also trace their ancestry to the huge tropical (as well as other smaller) genetic storehouses—storehouses that in many parts of the world now face severe threats.

But beyond their immediate anthropogenic value, all the world's plants and animals—from the most ordinary to the most exotic—have important ecological functions. Through their respiratory processes, they regulate the balance of atmospheric gases—and ultimately affect global climate. They also decompose wastes, recycle chemical nutrients, remove toxic substances from various parts of ecosystems, and maintain soil fertility. Diverse and abundant species serve humans well, maintaining conditions suitable for sustainable agriculture and renewable-resource economies—and even, over millions of years, creating the fossil fuels upon which we so vitally depend. Species diversity is further valued for a wide variety of aesthetic and recreational reasons—including sightseeing, birding, photography, hunting, trapping, and fishing.

Although the United States lacks extensive tropical rainforests, nearly all other climatic realms are amply represented. This climatic diversity, as well as the country's sheer size, allows for a wide array of plant and animal species. Yet that array is much smaller than it once was, especially before European settlement. At least 500 species have become extinct since 1600: an average of one or two per year. During the Pleistocene period (a period of glaciation when many natural extinctions occurred), fewer than 100 species were known to have been destroyed in North America (Harrington and Fisher 1982). Globally, of course, tropical rainforest extinctions make the rate of extinction much higher than that of the United States; estimates of annual extinctions (fraught with uncertainty as they are) range into the thousands.

The principal reason for loss of species in the United States as elsewhere is loss of habitat. Many species require large, uninterrupted areas for their general sustenance. Humans eliminate habitat through such activities as agriculture, forestry, mining, dredging, filling of wetlands, and commercial and residential development. Habitat also is degraded—even when it is not destroyed—through air and water pollution. Indeed, the effects of pollution may be quite remote from the source, as is the case with damage to high-altitude eastern forests resulting from ozone and other air pollutants (figure 8.13), or with threats to bird populations from pesticides widely dispersed through ecosystems.

Another cause of extinctions is hunting. Although the near-extinction of the Great Plains buffalo is a dramatic case in point, hunting actually is not the reason for most extinctions. Indeed, hunting may play a role in keeping a species' numbers in balance with the available habitat. This becomes a concern—with such species as deer, for example—when humans have created or maintained natural habitat but eliminated or greatly reduced natural predation. In these cases, the debate is not over the management or mismanagement of nature—we are already doing so with or without hunting. Instead, the issues are those of morality, legality, and safety.

Besides hunting, species may be threatened by the incidental or deliberate introduction of nonnative species to an area. This is a concern with biological pest control, since the introduction of a species for the purpose of preying upon a specific pest may inadvertently threaten other, nonpest species. Indeed, in some instances the introduced species proliferates beyond wildest expectations. Yet another threat to species is collection—whether legally sanctioned or outside the law—of rare plants and animals.

How do we deal with species depletion? The chief responses are habitat protection and restoration, regulation of hunting and other activities that threaten species, and establishment of gene banks. Federal efforts to protect wildlife date to the turn of the century, when the Lacey Act made it a federal offense to transport wildlife killed in violation of state laws across state lines. But it was not until 1966 that Congress passed the Endangered Species Preservation Act that established federal agency responsibilities for species conservation. In 1969, and again in 1973, the law was considerably strengthened. It is now known as the Endangered Species Act. The act, administered mainly by the Fish and Wildlife Service, obligates federal agencies to administer programs in ways that improve prospects for species survival. There are federal penalties for export and import of endangered species as well as for destruction of critical habitat and hunting and trapping of protected species. Substantial federal funding (75 percent or more) is available to states for cooperative research and protection programs.

A key element of the Endangered Species Act is the list of Endangered and Threatened Wildlife and Plants. Endangered species are in danger of extinction over all or large areas of their ranges while threatened species are likely to be in that same situation in the foreseeable future. Once a species is listed, the Fish and Wildlife Service is required to prepare recovery plans, leading eventually—it is hoped—to the species' removal from the list. As of March 1989, 874 endangered and 167 threatened species were on the worldwide list. Of those species, 535 (407 endangered; 128 threatened) are found in the United States. Recovery plans have been prepared and approved for 242 species (FWS 1989). As is evident from figure 15.9, the greatest incidence of listed species is generally in the warm, humid parts of the country: Hawaii and the Southeast. California—given its sheer size, long coastline, and climatic and topographic diversity—has the largest number of listed species: eighty-six.

The Endangered Species Act has engendered many controversies, the most famous of them probably the snail darter episode. At the center of it was the act's requirement that federal actions not jeopardize areas designated as critical habitat by the Secretary of the Interior. Work on the Tennessee Valley Authority's Tellico Dam was halted by the tiny snail darter—the subject, for a time, of national media attention. Largely as a response to this, 1978 amendments to the act established an Endangered Species Committee—the "God Committee"—to make decisions about exemptions in certain cases. In fact, the committee has met only infrequently.

A larger issue is that of species listing. New listings fell sharply during the early years of the Reagan administration but picked up in later years. Still, in 1986 the Defenders of Wildlife (Fitzgerald and Meese 1986) identified 3,900 species awaiting decisions about listing. They also pointed to lagging development of recovery plans and shortages of staff and funding.

Habitat preservation for all types of species—endangered or not—is accomplished through the creation of preserves. The first national wildlife refuge, Florida's Pelican Island, was established by Theodore Roosevelt in 1903. Today's refuge system, about 90 million acres in total, is varied and extensive. Although protection of wetlands for migratory waterfowl has been its main emphasis, many other species benefit as well. Indeed, most species on the Endangered Species List occupy habitats in refuges. In addition to the refuges shown in figure 15.10, the system contains waterfowl production areas that are small wetland areas concentrated mostly in the northern Great Plains region; coordination areas that usually are owned by the Bureau of Reclamation or Corps of Engineers but managed by the Fish and Wildlife Service; research centers; and fish hatcheries. Among the key wildlife refuge issues are the question of how much hunting should be permitted, the ethics of

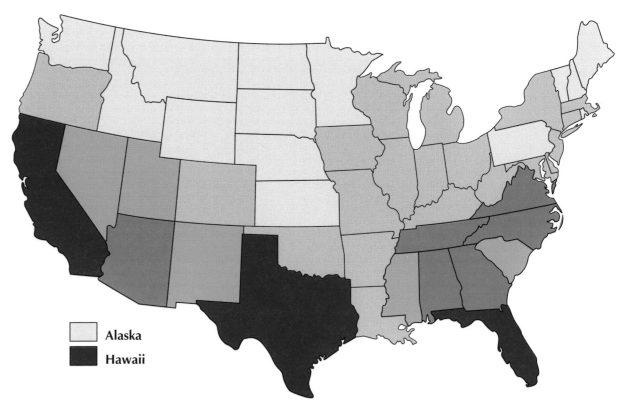

trapping, oil and gas exploration in Louisiana and Alaska (figure 13.7), control of predators that affect grazing, development conflicts, and various types of chemical contamination (California's Kesterson is one example; see figure 4.10).

Wildlife refuges are not the only federal lands that can serve as protected habitats; there are also the national parks, forests, and other federal lands. But it is the states that in most instances have the lead roles in regulating wildlife. Indeed, most states have had hunting and fishing restrictions since the late 1800s. States are engaged in research, planning, species management, habitat acquisition, public information and education, and law enforcement. Principal sources of funding are taxes (including state income-tax checkoffs), fees, and federal payments. Under the 1937 Pittman-Robertson Act, the federal government provides matching grants to states chiefly for the benefit of game animals. The Dingell-Johnson Act, passed in 1950, makes similar grants for fish management. In 1980, Congress passed the Forsythe-Chafee Act, which provides grants for conservation of nongame species of fish and wildlife. These programs provide funds for a variety of activities including research, planning, habitat acquisition, and public education.

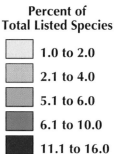

**Percent of
Total Listed Species**

	1.0 to 2.0
	2.1 to 4.0
	5.1 to 6.0
	6.1 to 10.0
	11.1 to 16.0

**Figure 15.9. Occurrence of
Endangered and Threatened Species.**

*Map shows endangered and
threatened species listed in state as
percent of all species listed in ten United
States.*

Source:
Fish and Wildlife Service, 1989,
untitled list.

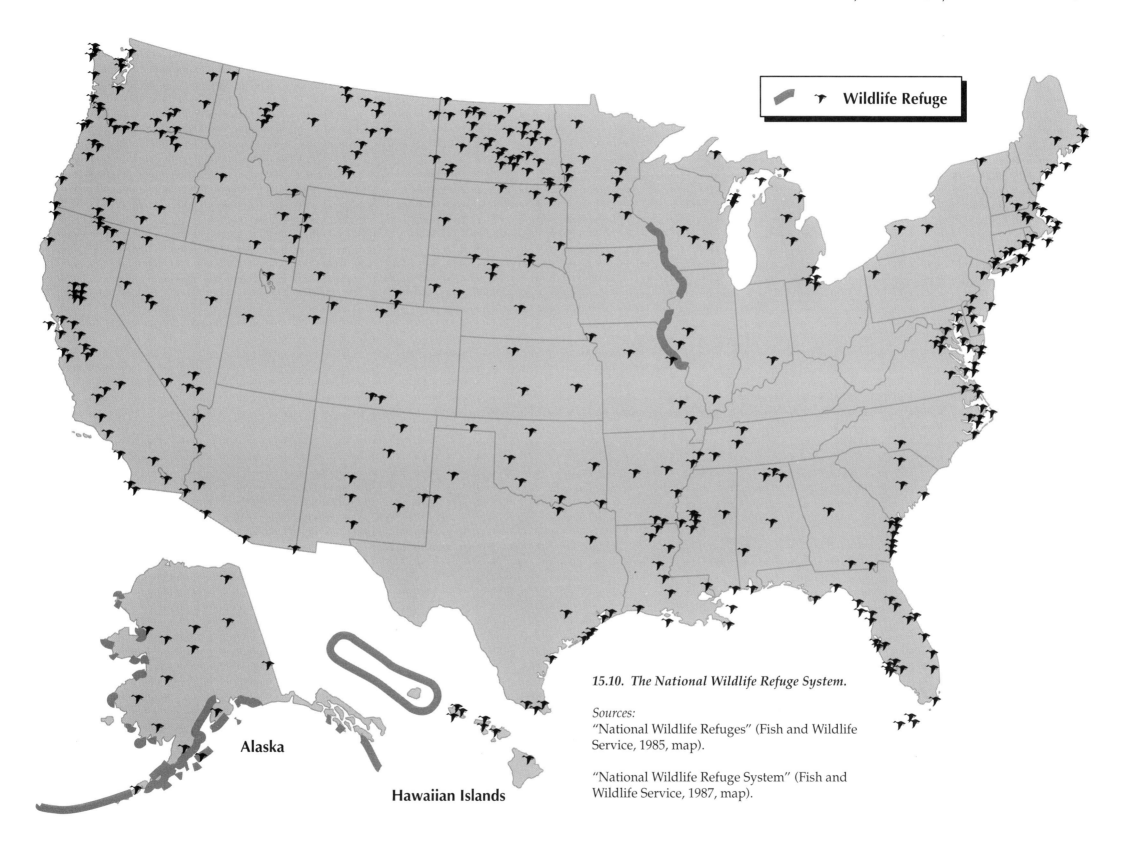

Wildlife Refuge

Alaska

Hawaiian Islands

15.10. The National Wildlife Refuge System.

Sources:
"National Wildlife Refuges" (Fish and Wildlife
Service, 1985, map).

"National Wildlife Refuge System" (Fish and
Wildlife Service, 1987, map).

Earthquakes, volcanoes, fires, severe storms, floods, and related violent events are sculptors of landscapes and agents of ecological change. When they adversely affect us, we see them as hazards. And indeed, hazards are pervasive: Many of the most vulnerable areas are also well suited to agriculture, commerce, housing, recreation, and other human uses.

In the early 1940s, geographer Gilbert White (1945) observed that as expenditures for flood prevention and control increased, so did annual flood-related damage tolls. Reassured by the presence of structural flood controls (dams, levees, diversions), people would move into formerly flood-prone areas. Then, when extraordinary floods did occur—and overwhelm the structural protections—the damages were far greater than those incurred earlier. White and other geographers have argued that land-use planning—not just structural controls—should be used to reduce exposure to flood hazards. This basic argument applies to other hazards as well.

As the nation tools up for the International Decade for Natural Hazard Reduction (the 1990s), we continue to grapple with fundamental issues. We want to know more about physical processes and improve our predictive capabilities. Those capabilities have improved markedly in recent decades—and this has helped reduce death tolls from a number of hazards. In a larger context, we need to know more about the general vulnerability of populations, buildings, and infrastructure. More imponderable, how do hazards—or their chronic threat—affect the mental health of individuals and the social and psychological fabrics of communities? It is important also that we understand the social, political, and economic processes responsible for spatial and socioeconomic variations in hazard vulnerability and damages. How and why, for example, do the effects of some hazards fall most heavily on those least able to cope? Why do annual property damages from most hazards continue to mount?

One concrete response to hazards is to brace for them: to promote public awareness, and to develop warning, emergency-response, and evacuation procedures. Beyond this, mitigation measures may be invoked—including attempts to modify the hazard itself. Examples include structural efforts to control riverine and coastal floods, cloud seeding to control hurricanes, and even injection of liquids into faults to control earthquakes. Conversely, we can reinforce buildings and other structures against hazards, and we can adopt land-use controls aimed at reducing exposure. The latter approach, despite its apparent wisdom in the eyes of many, has really come into its own only rather recently—and reluctantly at that. The outstanding example is the National Flood Insurance Program which obligates participating communities to adopt land-use controls (figure 16.3). All these mitigative responses raise questions about risk versus cost (how, for example, do we assess cost-effectiveness in the face of great uncertainty?) and about how those costs should be borne.

Once disaster occurs, attention turns to recovery and redevelopment. Once again, who should pay? Some losses will be distributed widely through insurance and other programs; others may be completely uncovered. In the aftermath of catastrophe, the urge to help—and its political rewards—often overwhelms any punitive sentiments toward communities and individuals who may have ignored earlier hazard warnings. Reconstruction does provide opportunities for reducing future vulnerability—but governmental regulations that seek to do so often encounter stiff resistance.

The United States' size and physical diversity makes it vulnerable to a great many hazards. They include tornadoes, hurricanes, floods, droughts, hailstorms, snow and ice, heat, lightning, wildfires, ground failures, earthquakes, volcanoes, tsunamis (waves generated by undersea earthquakes), and even biological threats such as viruses and insect infestations. This chapter provides an overview of some of the more widespread hazards, raising broad questions about vulnerability, preparedness, and response.

Mudflow Damage Along Toutle River 25 Miles West-Northwest of Mount St. Helens. U.S. Geological Survey.

TROPICAL CYCLONES

Tropical cyclones form in the low latitudes, deriving moisture and energy from the warm ocean waters. Although they lose strength over cooler ocean waters and over land, they can remain very powerful well outside the tropics. Hurricanes are tropical storms whose sustained winds exceed 75 miles per hour—and in exceptional cases reach as high as 200 miles per hour. But even more destructive than the high wind is the storm surge: a "piling up" of water caused by strong winds and low atmospheric pressures. The surge is intensified when the storm's landfall coincides with high tides. Storm surges are responsible for as much as 90 percent of hurricane-related deaths and damages.

Although Pacific tropical cyclones sometimes affect Hawaii, the most vulnerable parts of the United States are its Gulf and Atlantic coastlines. The main season for North Atlantic tropical cyclones is June to November, and their average annual number—based on 1886–1986 data—is 8.4. The average number of hurricanes is 4.9. Between 1899 and 1986, the U.S. mainland was affected by an average of 3.3 tropical cyclones and 1.8 hurricanes per year (Neumann et al. 1987). Table 16.1 lists the twenty costliest U.S. hurricanes.

A hurricane's energy tends to be concentrated in a relatively small area. Thus the probability of experiencing a hurricane in a given place in a given year is small—even in the highest-probability regions of southern Florida and the Texas Gulf Coast. About three-quarters of the 1985 population residing in Atlantic and Gulf Coast counties have never experienced a major hurricane (winds greater than 110 miles per hour). And the same is true for 87 percent of Florida's rapidly growing coastal population (Godschalk et al. 1989). This inexperience leads most people to underestimate the consequences of truly dangerous storms.

Improved forecasts and warnings have lowered hurricane death tolls in recent decades. But property damages continue to mount—and if coastal populations keep growing as they have been, this trend probably will continue into the next century. Moreover, as congestion increases in many areas, evacuation becomes ever more difficult and time-consuming. It is quite conceivable that some future hurricane—especially if it should strike on short notice in a heavily populated area—could be a major killer.

One response to tropical cyclone threats is to build structures—seawalls, jetties, groins—or to build up beaches in order to hold back storm effects. At best, these measures are only temporary, and they tend to shift undesired impacts to adjacent segments of the coast. Buildings themselves can be elevated, floodproofed, windproofed, and otherwise strengthened—but the costs are high. Such improvements, if not coupled with

additional regulations, may actually encourage new development in vulnerable areas; indeed, the National Flood Insurance Program (figure 16.3) has been blamed for doing just that. Of course, development can be regulated through land-use plans and building codes; this is done to varying degrees by local government and through state coastal zone planning (figure 7.4). When disaster is imminent, the usual response is evacuation. But there are concerns about adequacy of warnings, evacuation routes, emergency procedures, and public willingness to cooperate. One option, suited to built-up areas, is "vertical evacuation": Residents are sheltered in stable, high-rise buildings. Yet another response is to modify hurricane behavior through cloud seeding. Experiments thus far, however, have yielded rather uncertain results.

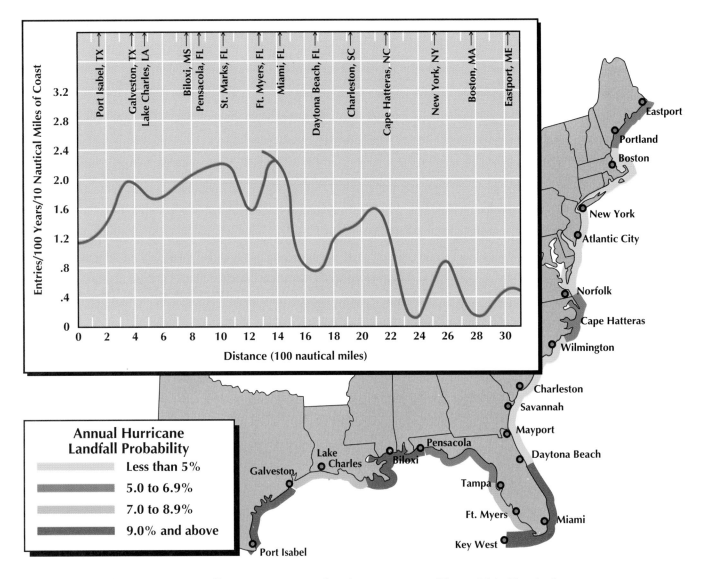

Figure 16.1. Tropical Cyclone Landfall.

Source:
C. J. Neumann et al., *Tropical Cyclones of the North Atlantic Ocean, 1871–1986* (Asheville, NC, and Coral Gables, FL: National Climatic Data Center and National Hurricane Center, 1987), p. 29.

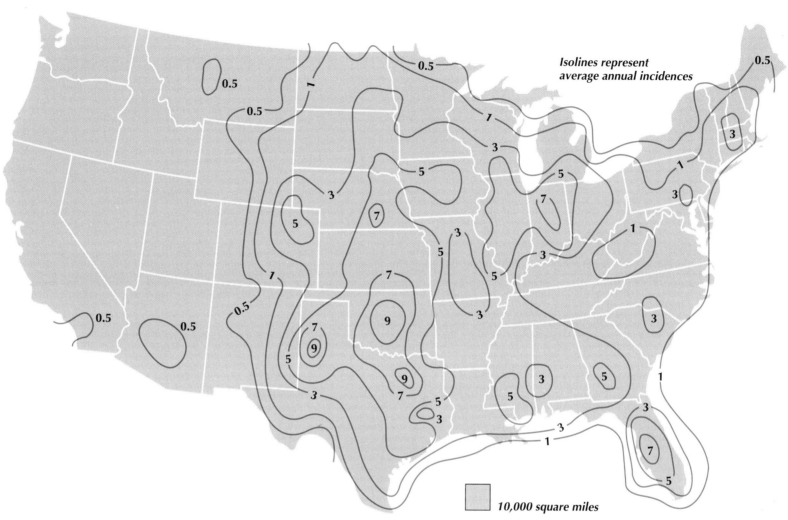

Figure 16.2. Average Annual Tornado Incidence per 10,000 Square Miles, 1953–1980.

Source:
National Weather Service, *Tornado Safety: Surviving Nature's Most Violent Storms* (Washington, DC: GPO, 1982), p. 8.

Isolines represent average annual incidences

10,000 square miles

Table 16.1. Costliest U.S. Hurricanes

		Damage[1] (billion dollars)
1. Hugo (SC)	1989	7.0
2. Betsy (FL/LA)	1965	6.3
3. Agnes (N.E. U.S.)	1972	6.3
4. Camille (MS/AL)	1969	5.1
5. Diana (N.E. U.S.)	1955	4.1
6. New England	1938	3.5
7. Frederic (AL/MS)	1979	3.4
8. Alicia (N. TX)	1983	2.3
9. Carol (N.E. U.S.)	1954	2.3
10. Carla (TX)	1961	1.9
11. Donna (FL/E. U.S.)	1960	1.8
12. Juan (LA)	1985	1.6
13. Celia (S. TX)	1970	1.5
14. Hazel (SC/NC)	1954	1.4
15. Elena (MS/AL/N.W. FL)	1985	1.4
16. FL (Miami)	1926	1.3
17. Dora (N.E. FL)	1964	1.1
18. Eloise (N.W. FL)	1964	1.1
19. Gloria (E. U.S.)	1985	1.0
20. N.E. U.S.	1944	0.9

[1]Adjusted to 1989 dollars.

Source: "The Costliest United States Hurricanes of This Century" (National Hurricane Center, 1989, photocopy).

TORNADOES

Tornadoes are very small but can be incredibly violent. Winds in these rotating columns of air have reached 500 miles per hour. Fortunately, most tornadoes are short-lived, ranging over distances less than 16 miles. Typically, they are associated with the passage of strong cold fronts. The world's best general conditions for tornado development occur in the central United States in the springtime, when advancing polar air masses collide with moisture-laden subtropical air. Atmospheric instability is intensified by long hours of sunlight that heat the lower atmosphere, contributing to the air's buoyancy. Although tornadoes have been recorded in all states, they occur with greatest frequency in a belt—evident on the map—that stretches from Texas to Nebraska. The peak season advances, though rather inconsistently, from south to north through the spring. Under certain conditions, many tornadoes occur over a large area. One such "super outbreak"—in April 1974— spawned 148 tornadoes in thirteen states, causing 315 deaths and over $600 million in damages.

Tornadic winds cause destruction not just by sheer force but also through the impacts of airborne debris that can range in size from sticks to large appliances. While tornado fatalities have decreased in recent decades, property damages keep rising. Our predictive capabilities do continue to improve—especially with recent advances in radar imaging. But tornadoes are very elusive phenomena: National Weather Service warnings (as opposed to watches) rely on actual human or radar sightings. Moreover, local land-use planning holds little promise for reducing potential exposure. The best strategies seem to be improved general forecasts and specific warnings, public eduction about how to brace for a tornado, and—in certain areas—construction of tornado shelters.

FLOODS

Floods occur in all parts of the United States. Coastal flooding is caused mainly by high tides, storm surges (figure 16.1), and tsunamis; while riverine floods are caused by widespread precipitation, snowmelt, or both. Principal areas of riverine flooding are shown on the map. Winter is the peak season for most of the Southeast as well as coastal and west slope areas of California, Washington, and Oregon; early spring is the high season for the northern Great Lakes and New England, lower Mississippi Basin, eastern slopes of Washington and Oregon, and mountains of California and Arizona; and late spring is the peak season for most of the interior mountain West. Flash floods— caused by torrential rains, dam failures, or ice jam breakups—are much briefer and more localized than most riverine floods. Flash-flooding, possible nearly anywhere, is most common and severe in mountain and desert areas of the West.

About 10 million people live in floodplains (areas subject to riverine flooding), and 1986 flood-related property damages totalled $4 billion. While average annual death tolls have fallen (at least over the long term), yearly property damage increments continue to increase. The conventional approach to flood control, as noted earlier, is structural: dams, levees, and diversions. Such measures have encouraged floodplain occupance, on the assumption that the area is free of threat. Then, when natural forces exceed those the structures were designed to guard against, damages are often monumental.

In an attempt to stem mounting losses, the National Flood Insurance Program (NFIP) was initiated in 1968. Without federal assistance, flood insurance would be extremely costly—since those sharing the burden would be those who expect to experience a flood (as opposed, for example, to holders of fire or theft insurance). The NFIP combines insurance subsidies with requirements for state and local floodplain management. The 100-year floodplain (the area with an annual flood probability of one in 100) is subject to stringent development controls. Partly due to the complexity of delineating flood-prone zones, the NFIP got off to a slow start—but community participation picked up rapidly following the 1973 enactment of the Flood Disaster Protection Act. Under that act, property owners in identified flood-hazard areas are ineligible for any kind of federal aid for purchase or development of their property. And communities not participating in the NFIP are ineligible for federal post-disaster assistance. In short, the trade-off for insurance and disaster-recovery benefits is local acceptance of land-use regulations, building codes, and other hazard-reduction measures. The NFIP is expensive. Figure 16.3 shows claims paid over the period 1978–1987. Total payments, after increasing through much of the 1970s, leveled off and then declined (though rather erratically) through the 1980s. Of course, any one

year's payments may be greatly inflated by one or several unusually destructive storms.

Over 40 percent of all payments go to repeat claimants—an indication that flood prevention measures may be inadequate. But the program's weakest—and most criticized—aspect is its treatment of the coastal zone. There the flood hazard is more difficult to map than in riverine settings. It is apparent from figure 16.3 that the largest claims have been in vulnerable coastal states. Indeed, as of 1987, about 72 percent of approximately 2 million NFIP policies were for properties in coastal communities (GAO 1988). The coastal Achilles' heel aside, the high rates of community participation in the NFIP—largely brought about by legislative corrections subsequent to the original 1968 act— would seem to bode well for the long term.

Figure 16.3. National Flood Insurance Program Claims, 1978–1987.

Note: Total U.S. claims 1978–1987 were about $2.7 billion.

Sources:
Federal Emergency Management Agency (1989, computer printout).

W. W. Hays, ed., *Facing Geologic and Hydrologic Hazards: Earth-Science Considerations,* Geological Survey Professional Paper 1240-B (Washington, DC: GPO, 1981), p. B38.

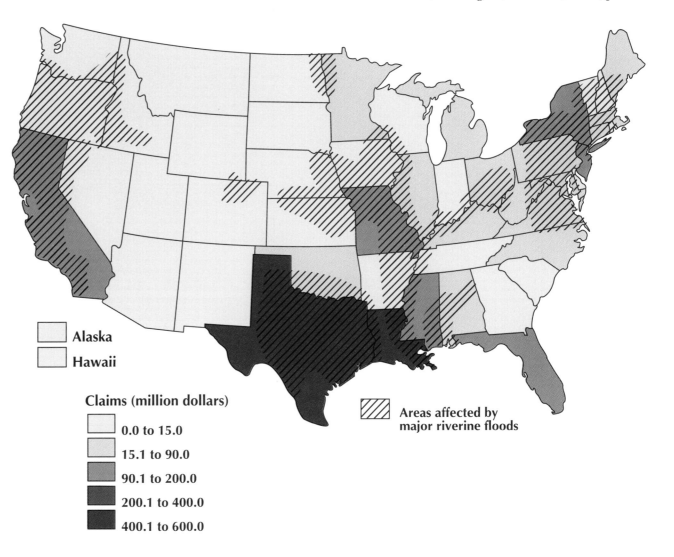

Alaska

Hawaii

Claims (million dollars)

0.0 to 15.0

15.1 to 90.0

90.1 to 200.0

200.1 to 400.0

400.1 to 600.0

Areas affected by major riverine floods

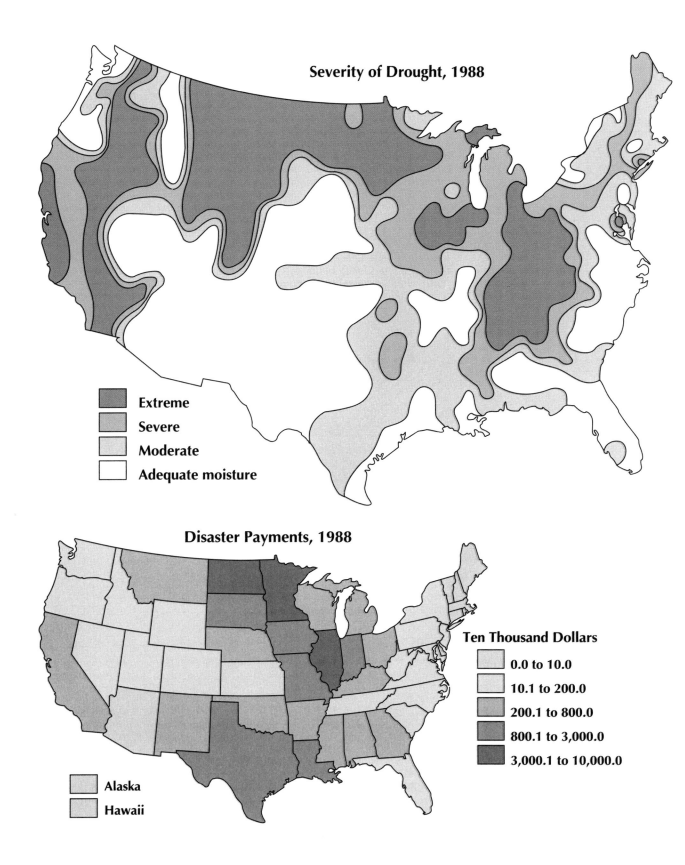

Severity of Drought, 1988

Extreme
Severe
Moderate
Adequate moisture

Disaster Payments, 1988

Ten Thousand Dollars

0.0 to 10.0
10.1 to 200.0
200.1 to 800.0
800.1 to 3,000.0
3,000.1 to 10,000.0

Alaska
Hawaii

FOCUS: THE DROUGHT OF 1988

Only in the 1930s and 1950s were larger areas of the country covered by severe or extreme drought than was the case in 1988. The drought's enormous spatial extent is represented on the top map in figure 16.4, which shows long-term drought conditions as of July 16. In the Northern Great Plains and Midwest, the drought was intensified by its timing: Large precipitation deficits occurred in the spring and critically affected crop growth. In the southern Appalachian region, the drought was a continuation of earlier years' moisture deficits. The hot, dry summer of 1988—perhaps portentous of things to come if significant global warming occurs—has been implicated for high urban ozone levels, wildfires, reduced harvests, and depleted streamflows.

But the drought was considerably quenched by favorable September rainfall and was not as socially or economically devastating as some early accounts would have had it. It did, however, lower corn production 34 percent from 1987, soybeans 21 percent, feed grains 34 percent, and spring wheat 54 percent. Other effects included reductions in range forage production; a record fire season; restricted navigation, transportation, pollutant-absorption capacity, and numbers of fish due to low stream flows; and declines in waterfowl that breed in the northern prairies.

Two key elements of the federal drought response were the June 15 establishment of the Interagency Drought Policy Committee and the August 11 enactment of the Disaster Assistance Act of 1988. The act added about $3.9 billion to the almost $3 billion budgeted under existing programs for drought assistance. On May 31, the U.S. Department of Agriculture had authorized emergency haying and grazing of cover crops on croplands set aside under crop production adjustment programs. On June 21, harvesting of hay was allowed on highly erodible cropland idled under the Conservation Reserve Program (figure 4.7)—with measures prescribed to curb erosion. These and other special exemptions applied to a total of 2,236 counties in forty-three states. The bottom map shows total federal payments made to eligible farmers. As of September 30, 1989, $3.88 billion had been paid, 87 percent of which was for crop-loss reimbursement. Other federal responses included efforts to manage drought impacts on forests, fish, and wildlife, and Army Corps of Engineers dredging activities to keep major rivers navigable.

Figure 16.4. FOCUS: The Drought of 1988.

Sources:
"Disaster Payments System Monthly Payment Report: 19-30-88" (USDA, 1989, computer printout).

National Weather Service and USDA, *Weekly Weather and Crop Bulletin* 75 (29) (1988): 4.

VOLCANIC ACTIVITY

More than three-fourths of the world's volcanoes are concentrated in the "ring of fire" that surrounds the Pacific Basin. But with the exception of those on Alaska's Peninsula and Aleutian Islands, relatively few are found in the United States. Prior to the eruption of Mount St. Helens (figure 16.6), volcanic activity in this century had been limited to Hawaii, Alaska, and the 1914–1917 eruptions of California's Lassen Peak. The California, Oregon, and Washington eruptions shown on the map in figure 16.5 (except Mount St. Helens and Lassen) occurred in the 1700s and 1800s. In no way, however, does this recent lull preclude a return to a much more active regime in the Pacific Northwest.

Principal volcanic hazards are lava flows, avalanches, mudflows, floods, and volcanic ash (tephra) and gases. Lava flows result from nonexplosive eruptions. The lava moves quite slowly and covers relatively small areas—usually not more than a few square miles. Development and movement of lava flows can sometimes be quite accurately predicted. This is true of Hawaii's Kilauea which erupts frequently but gently.

Hot avalanches are composed of freshly erupted fragments of molten or hot solid rock; while mudflows may contain unstable rock from a volcano's flanks. Mudflows and floods may also result from melting of snow and ice or displacement of crater lakes. The effects of these events are generally confined to valley floors and basins, though they can be felt quite far from the volcano itself. Avalanches, flows, and floods occur suddenly and move quickly. In general, their paths are relatively predictable—but foreknowledge of an eruption is prerequisite to predicting the actual event. Because of their high rainfalls and large quantities of snow and ice, the Cascade Mountains of Washington, Oregon, and California are especially susceptible to mudflows. Indeed, large mudflows were created by the recent eruptions of Mount St. Helens (figure 16.6).

Explosive volcanoes send rock fragments (pyroclastic material) and ash into the air. Pyroclastic flows are rapid, avalanche-like movements of hot rocks that are too heavy to remain airborne. Finer material may be carried great distances by the wind; indeed, some very large volcanoes have expulsed great amounts of material that "orbited" the earth long after the eruption. While pyroclastic flows are very rapid and destructive, the impacted areas are relatively modest when compared with the huge areas that may be affected by the ashfall from a big eruption (see figure 16.6). Explosive volcanoes also produce blasts: the high-speed lateral (as opposed to vertical) ejection of hot fragments and gases. Their destructive impacts come more from their searing winds and impacts of rock fragments than from material deposited on the ground.

Substantial areas of the western United States—principally in the Cascade range of California, Oregon, and Washington, as well as the Alaskan Peninsula and Aleutian Islands—are potentially subject to the effects of explosive volcanic eruptions. But as noted above, only Alaska has had numerous eruptions during the past century. In Hawaii, in contrast with Pacific rim locations, lava flows are the chief hazard—and they have occurred with considerable frequency.

Volcanic eruptions cannot be prevented (though some attempts have been made to control their effects). It is possible—though not with minute accuracy—to forecast them, based on earthquake activity and expulsion of gases that typically precede them. But in areas that have been quiet for many decades—or even centuries—monitoring efforts may be inadequate. It is simply too costly to monitor fully all potential sites for future eruptions.

Beyond long- and short-term monitoring and prediction, emergency preparedness is important. Evacuation plans can be keyed to eruption scenarios—including such long-distance hazards as ash deposition. Protective actions might include provision of dust masks and goggles as well as advice to drivers to change air and oil filters frequently. While there is no volcanic counterpart to the National Flood Insurance Program, insurance can help to increase property owners' awareness of the hazard as well as spreading the burden of any losses. Land-use regulations can reduce risks, especially for slow-moving, predictable lava flows. Many individuals living in the shadows of Hawaii's Kilauea have learned to anticipate and react to the volcano's changing moods and activity patterns.

Figure 16.5. Volcanic Activity.

Sources:

T. Simkin et al., *Volcanoes of the World* (Stroudsburg, PA: Hutchinson Ross Publishing Company, 1981), pp. 80–89.

T. Simkin et al., *Volcanoes of the World: 1984 Supplement* (Washington, DC: Smithsonian Institution, 1984), pp. 14–17.

Eruptions from 1760 to Present

- 1 to 5
- 6 to 10
- 11 to 15
- More than 15

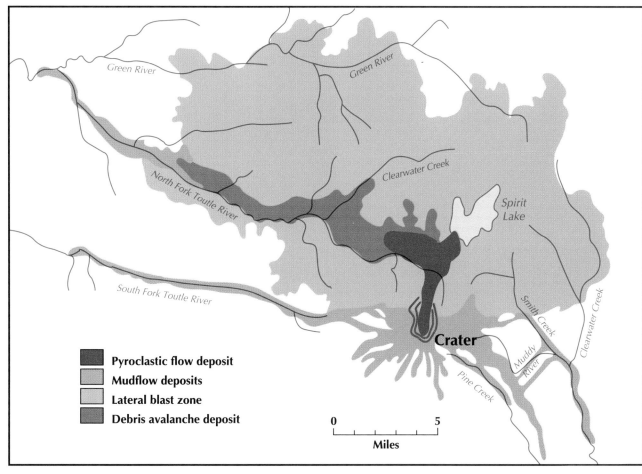

Pyroclastic flow deposit
Mudflow deposits
Lateral blast zone
Debris avalanche deposit

0   5
Miles

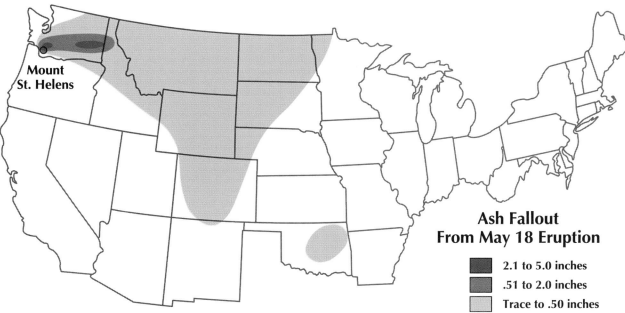

Mount
St. Helens

**Ash Fallout
From May 18 Eruption**

2.1 to 5.0 inches
.51 to 2.0 inches
Trace to .50 inches

FOCUS: MOUNT ST. HELENS

On May 18, 1980, the greatest eruption of historic times in the conterminous United States left sixty dead and at least $1 billion in damages. The Mount St. Helens eruption—and the earthquake that triggered it—caused the north flank of the mountain to collapse. The resultant debris avalanche transported 0.7 cubic miles of material downslope, filling the North Fork Toutle River Valley to an average depth of 150 feet. The accompanying lateral blast—a hot rush of debris, ash, and gases—obliterated everything within an eight-mile radius and flattened trees out to nineteen miles. The pyroclastic flow, composed of volcanic fragments and gases flowing from the lip of the volcano, produced the overlapping, fanlike deposits shown on the top map. Glacier meltwater, combined with ash and avalanche debris, created great mudflows. Sixty-five million cubic yards of material were transported mainly through the Toutle, Cowlitz, and finally Columbia rivers. The eruption also sent a huge column of ash and steam twelve miles into the air, producing fallout over the large area indicated on the map. Travelers were stranded, communities isolated, and crops damaged as far east as Montana.

A 1978 hazard assessment (Crandell and Mullineaux 1978), based on Mount St. Helens' eruptive history, proved generally accurate in its predictions—and very helpful in preparing for the impending threat in 1980. The May 18 eruption also was presaged by more immediate events, including an unusual sequence of earthquakes beginning March 20 and ash eruptions on March 27. Some national forest areas were closed on March 25. Evacuations began on March 27, and on April 3, Governor Dixy Lee Ray declared a state of emergency and sought—not always successfully—to keep all but scientists and property owners out of a "restricted zone" surrounding the volcano (more restrictions were later imposed on property owners). Those efforts were particularly strained by the mountain's remarkable quiescence between mid-April and May 17.

The May 18 eruption jolted the country from its complacency about volcanic hazards. Saarinen and Sell (1985) conclude that most individuals and government agencies prepared for and responded admirably to the unprecedented disaster. But they also found that some agencies functioned much more effectively than others, that a clearer chain of command was needed, that better ways of handling the very difficult issue of access to restricted areas were necessary, and that preparation for the eastern Washington ashfall was inadequate.

Figure 16.6. FOCUS: Mount St. Helens.

Source:
R. I. Tilling, *Eruptions of Mount St. Helens: Past, Present, and Future* (Washington, DC: GPO, undated), pp. 16, 20.

GROUND FAILURE

Ground failure is a widespread but generally underappreciated hazard. It involves landslides, expansive soils, and surface subsidence. Expansive soils, derived from volcanic emissions and clay minerals, shrink and swell with changes in moisture content. The resultant damage to buildings, roads, utilities, and other structures amounts to several billion dollars per year. Expansive soils are abundant through the Great Plains, parts of the Rocky Mountains, and much of the Gulf Coastal Plain, lower Mississippi River Valley, and Pacific coastal regions. Subsidence occurs naturally in areas underlain by limestone and other soluble materials; it is also induced by earthquakes and volcanoes. Substantial areas in the Southeast, Midwest, and South Central regions are vulnerable to natural subsidence through solution, while volcano- and earthquake-related subsidence occurs principally in the lower West Coast states, Alaska, and Hawaii. Human activities—including withdrawal of oil, gas, coal, water, and nonfuel minerals, as well as land development—can cause or accelerate subsidence. Subsidence is responsible for several tens of millions of dollars in losses each year.

Landslides alone cause at least $1 to $2 billion per year in damages and twenty-five to fifty deaths (National Research Council 1985). Direct landslide-related costs include physical damage to property, while indirect costs include loss of tax revenues and loss of agricultural, forest, and industrial productivity. As with other hazards, precise data are unavailable, but it appears that indirect costs substantially exceed direct costs. The most financially devastating landslides have occurred in Alaska, California, and Utah. Although landslides can be very destructive phenomena, they occur mostly in thinly populated areas. As a result, death tolls generally are low.

Figure 16.7 shows areas with medium or high potential for landsliding. Not represented on the map—but relatively abundant—are submarine landslides, which occur in the nation's continental margins. These landslides can affect energy-producing facilities, waste-disposal areas, and military installations. The most vulnerable land areas are the Pacific Coast, Rocky Mountain, northern Great Plains, and Appalachian regions. Landslides, of course, occur on slopes; areas with steepest slopes are the most vulnerable. Detailed local mapping can reveal wide variations in geological susceptibility within the highly generalized areas represented on our map.

Landslides are caused by the gradual erosive action of water, ice, and wind; rapid liquefaction of unstable surface materials by heavy rainfall; removal of supporting material by glaciers, rivers, streams, and road cuts, quarries, pits, and other excavations; overloading from rain, snow, rock fragments, volcanic material, mine wastes, or buildings; and the triggering effects of earth-

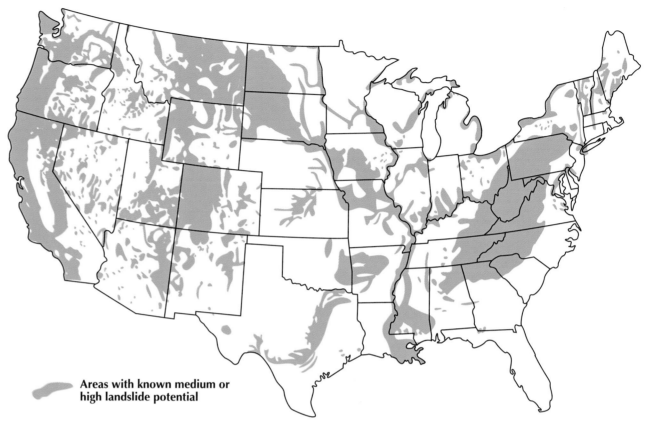

Areas with known medium or high landslide potential

quakes or blasts. Often a combination of these factors is involved. Landslides can almost instantaneously displace vast amounts of material, destroying everything in their paths. When they encounter water, they can create huge waves or build large valley dams.

Landslide damages can be avoided or reduced through land-use regulation, drainage and runoff controls, and careful grading and construction practices. Although the prospects for improved warnings and evacuation are limited, better public education and availability of insurance can help in reducing exposure and sharing the burden of loss. The U.S. Geological Survey (USGS 1982), citing national programs elsewhere, has called for a three-part program of: (1) studies of landslide processes (aimed at prediction), (2) landslide-hazard mapping and risk evaluation (with first priority to major population centers in areas of high landslide incidence), and (3) effective communication of information to the affected public. Top regional priority would go to the West Coast, second and third priority to the Appalachian and Rocky Mountain regions, respectively. The value of such programs has been demonstrated by local experiences: Los Angeles, in particular, has reduced losses on new construction more than 90 percent (National Research Council 1985).

Figure 16.7. Landslide Potential.

Source:
U.S. Geological Survey, *Goals and Tasks of the Landslide Part of a Ground-Failure Hazards Reduction Program,* Circular 880 (Washington, DC: USGS, 1982), pp. 4–5.

Figure 16.8. Seismic Risk Zones.

Sources:
R. A. Ganse and J. B. Nelson, *Catalog of Significant Earthquakes: 2000 BC–1979 (with update, 1980–1987),* Report SE-27 (Boulder, CO: National Geophysical Data Center, 1988).

W. W. Hays, ed., *Facing Geologic and Hydrologic Hazards: Earth-Science Considerations,* Geological Survey Professional Paper 1240-B (Washington, DC: GPO, 1981), p. B5.

President's Office of Emergency Preparedness, *Disaster Preparedness* (Washington, DC: GPO, 1972), p. 75.

Risk zones represent expected damages. They are based on known distribution of damaging earthquakes and their Modified Mercalli (MM) scale intensities, in combination with other geologic evidence. Probable frequency of occurrence was not considered in assigning risk. Risk was not assigned for Alaska and Hawaii.

Minor Damage: *corresponds to intensities V and VI of the MM scale; i.e., most or all people feel earthquake, and there may be slight damage to trees, poles, and structures.*

Moderate Damage: *corresponds to intensity VII of the MM scale; i.e., everyone is affected, and there is some damage to well-built ordinary structures—but considerable damage to poorly built or badly designed structures.*

Major Damage: *corresponds to intensity VIII and higher of the MM scale; i.e., effects ranging from major damage to poorly built structures all the way to virtually total destruction.*

SEISMIC RISK

Earthquakes are sudden movements of the earth, induced by gradual buildup of strain. The more powerful ones are among the world's most destructive hazards. Direct impacts include ground shaking and surface faulting (the differential movement of two sides of a fracture at the earth's surface), while indirect effects include the triggering of ground failures (figure 16.7) and tsunamis (waves, created by undersea earthquakes, that can reach great height in shallow water).

Figure 16.8 shows, in a highly generalized fashion, seismic risk across the conterminous states. Alaska and Hawaii also are seismically active; indeed, very much so—but they are not so well mapped as the other forty-eight states. Not surprisingly, much of California is a high-risk area. So too are parts of the Pacific Northwest, Great Basin, and Rocky Mountain regions. Less appreciated is the seismic potential in some eastern and central areas. The largest recorded U.S. earthquakes, centered at New Madrid, Missouri, occurred in 1811–1812. Although major earthquakes are less common in the East than in the West, the older, colder, more brittle nature of the earth's crust will transmit a given intensity of ground-shaking over a greater distance in the East.

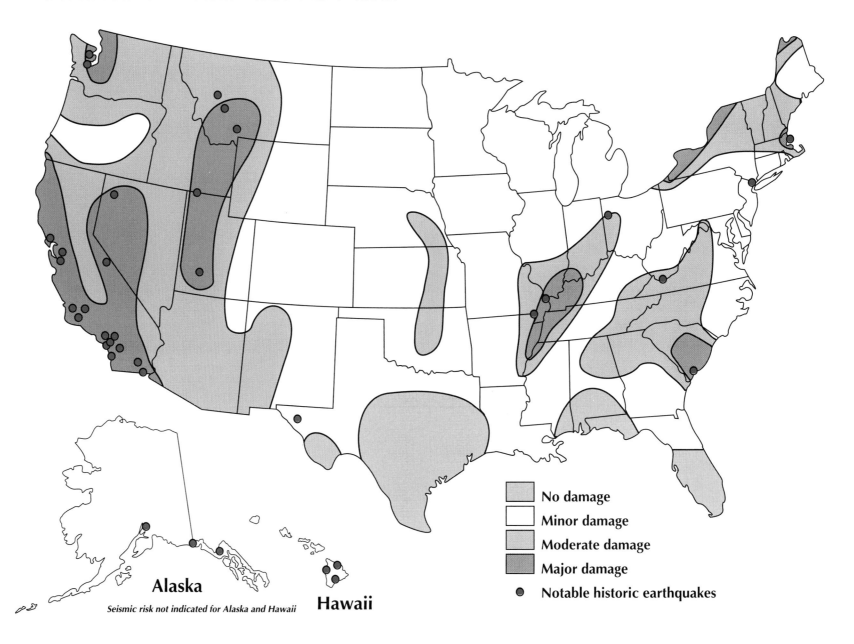

Alaska

Hawaii

Seismic risk not indicated for Alaska and Hawaii

No damage
Minor damage
Moderate damage
Major damage
● Notable historic earthquakes

Earthquake damage potential is determined by many factors, among them the magnitude of the quake, physical characteristics of the soils and rocks that transmit its energy, population density in affected areas, and building, transportation, and other infrastructural characteristics. The greatest earthquake damages—as well as deaths—usually result from structural collapse. Such damage was extensive, for example, in the 1886 Charleston (South Carolina) and 1971 San Fernando (California) earthquakes. The October 1989 Loma Prieta earthquake—centered near Santa Cruz, California—resulted in the collapse of sections of the Oakland Bay Bridge and Nimitz Freeway in the San Francisco area. Earthquake-triggered events such as fires, dam failures (resulting in flooding), landslides, and tsunamis also can take great tolls. Fire was the major culprit associated with the 1906 San Francisco earthquake, while Alaska's 1964 Prince William Sound earthquake triggered surface fault movements, rockslides, snow avalanches, landslides, and tsunamis. Yet even though the Alaska earthquake released about 1,000 times as much energy, it caused about the same amount of property damage and half the number of deaths as the San Fernando quake—which occurred at the edge (as opposed to the center) of a major metropolitan area.

One set of responses to earthquakes is monitoring, mapping, and prediction. Although our predictive capabilities continue to improve, we still do best with rather general predictions of risk. The most promising strategies for reducing deaths and property damages appear to be land-use planning to reduce exposure to risk, and structural and materials standards for new and existing buildings.

Considerable recent progress in earthquake preparedness and response planning notwithstanding, California's potential for disaster remains high. The 1989 earthquake was not the "big one" that many geologists predict. At 6.9 on the Richter scale, it was much smaller in intensity than the 1906 San Francisco quake, which measured 7.9 (each increase of one on the scale results in approximately a thirty-fold increase in energy released from the quake's motion). The U.S. Geological Survey (USGS 1988) warns of a 60 percent chance of an earthquake of magnitude 7.5 to 8.0 along the San Andreas Fault near Los Angeles and a 50 percent chance of one of the same magnitude in the San Francisco Bay area in the next thirty years. But perhaps more startling is the potential for damage in the East. Even a moderate quake—while less probable than in the West—could have enormous consequences. Older buildings, highways, bridges, and water, sewer, and electrical systems—with virtually no modifications to guard specifically against earthquake hazards— are all the more vulnerable. A Charleston-type earthquake (Richter magnitude 7), were it to occur today, could be devastating indeed.

HAZARD LOSSES

A variety of data are available regarding deaths, injuries, and property damages from natural hazards. Ideally, all this information could be drawn together so as to compare damages from different hazards in different places. But, alas, this is not practical; there are too many inconsistencies among the data sets. Different information is collected for different purposes. Thus a given set of statistics, while perhaps internally consistent, may provide only a partial accounting of hazard losses—and a unique partial accounting at that. Inevitably, some figures rely on much more subjective judgments than others. Furthermore, separate sets of statistics for a single type of hazard may have been collected over different time periods—fiscal year and calendar year, for example.

Despite the severe limitations, existing information can be used to develop a general picture of comparative hazard losses. The National Weather Service compiles data on deaths caused by weather events. The twenty-year national normals (i.e., annual deaths averaged over twenty years), through 1987, are as follows: 163 deaths from floods/flash floods, ninety-eight from tornadoes, ninety-seven from lightning, and thirty-three from hurricanes/tropical storms. Twenty-year normals have not yet been established for some hazards, but the 1987 death toll for high wind was fifty-six, for heat forty, and for winter storms thirty (Peters 1988).

Table 16.2 shows outlays for federally declared disasters. Not represented, therefore, are disasters for which no declaration request was made (state governors request declaration by the president) or for which a request was denied. According to one estimate, only 22 percent of all natural disasters receive a federal proclamation (Gordon 1982). The federal outlay, on average, may represent less than 25 percent of the total cost of a disaster (Rubin et al. 1986). Part of the cost is borne by state and local governments, relief agencies, and the insurance industry; but the greatest share (50 to 75 percent) is usually borne by individuals. Red Cross data are summarized in table 16.3. Because of its long-standardized data-collection procedures, the Red Cross is believed to have the best information for comparisons of losses from different disasters (Gordon 1982). Its statistics on injuries may, however, be on the low side. Table 16.4, though highly generalized, provides one view of expected trends in hazard losses. Hurricane and tornado losses are expected to increase greatly as a result of residential encroachment into hazard-prone areas. A smaller increase is forecast for losses due to riverine floods; this reflects the anticipated success of floodplain management programs (figure 16.3). The loss figures are for building costs only; transportation and other infrastructure costs are not included. Total disaster losses are estimated to be two to two and one-half times as high as those reported in table 16.4 (Gordon 1982).

Table 16.2. Federally Declared Disasters, 1965–1985

	Number	Federal Outlay (thousands of current dollars)	Federal Outlay (thousands of 1982 dollars)
Ice and Snow Events	19	151,427	205,511
Hurricanes/Tropical Storms	39	1,173,141	1,947,939
Earthquakes	7	203,881	405,706
Dam and Levee Failures	7	55,764	80,806
Rains, Storms, and Flooding (includes land, mud, and debris flows and slides)	337	1,684,702	2,439,852
High Winds and Waves	2	125,313	120,536
Coastal Storms and Flooding	7	158,261	205,357
Tornadoes	109	441,685	648,352
Drought/Water Shortage	4	1,134	5,344
Totals	531	3,995,308	6,059,403

Source: C. B. Rubin et al., *Summary of Major Natural Disaster Incidents in the U.S.: 1965–85* (Boulder, CO: Natural Hazards Research and Applications Information Center, 1986), p. 10. Based on Federal Emergency Management Agency reports.

Table 16.3. Red Cross Disaster Statistics, 1965–1985

	Number of Events	Persons Killed	Persons Injured	Dwellings Destroyed & Damaged
Hurricanes	39	451	65,719	449,341
Floods	1,514	1,767	39,495	762,371
Windstorms	731	502	14,420	159,032
Tornadoes	891	1,526	35,544	182,750
Other (includes earthquakes)	473	300	3,374	10,344

Notes: Figures are based on fiscal year data (July 1–June 30).

Figures are not strictly comparable, because data are not available for certain characteristics for certain years.

Source: C. B. Rubin et al., *Summary of Major Natural Disaster Incidents in the U.S.: 1965–85* (Boulder, CO: Natural Hazards Research and Applications Information Center, 1986). Data initially from American National Red Cross, *Annual Summaries of Disaster Service Activities.*

Table 16.4. Expected Annual Natural Hazard Losses: 1970 and 2000

	Dollars Per Capita		Annual (million dollars)		Deaths		Housing Units	
	1970	2000	1970	2000	1970	2000	1970	2000
Hurricane	8.36	22.92	1,697.2	5,869.2	99	256	56,406	95,994
Tornado	8.12	20.38	1,656.0	5,219.1	392	920	36,212	52,119
Riverine Flood	13.57	12.40	2,758.3	3,175.3	190	159		
Earthquake	3.83	6.07	781.1	1,553.7	273	400	20,485	22,868
Expansive Soil	3.93	3.89	798.1	997.1				
Landslide	1.82	3.40	370.3	871.2				
Severe Wind	.06	.19	18.0	53.4	5	11	547	748
Tsunami	.07	.16	15.0	40.4	20	44	234	335

Note: All figures are in 1970 dollars.

Source: D. R. Godschalk, D. J. Brower, and T. Beatley, *Catastrophic Coastal Storms: Hazard Mitigation and Development Management* (Durham, NC, and London: Duke University Press, 1989), p. 6. Adapted from W. Petak and A. Atkisson, *Natural Hazard Risk Assessment and Public Policy* (New York: Springer-Verlag, 1982).

The environmentalism of the 1960s and 1970s spawned a great many laws, regulations, and policies—literally forcing the states to adapt, with varying degrees of reluctance, to an intrusive and unfamiliar administrative labyrinth. A principal reason for the strong federal oversight—with its apparent disregard, in many cases, for the country's enormous physical and socioeconomic diversity—was to create a "level playing field." Industry, it was argued, should not flee New York for Louisiana simply because more pollution is allowed there.

In reality, complete uniformity is neither possible nor desirable. States are responsible for much of the implementation and enforcement of federal environmental legislation—and the enthusiasm, competence, and care with which they do so varies considerably from one to another. Many states have their own environmental programs that extend—and sometimes supersede—federal mandates. The importance of state initiative increased enormously under the "new federalism" of the Reagan era—which viewed many federal regulations as excessive and economically counterproductive. In spite of these sentiments, the federal environmental protection infrastructure remained largely intact, but its administration was compromised in various ways. In the early 1980s, agency budgets and staffs—especially the EPA's—were cut. Major new federal initiatives were practically nonexistent.

Thus states were expected to—and indeed did—pick up many of the functions formerly assumed by the federal government. California, followed by eight northeastern states, is developing stringent new air-quality regulations (chapter 8). Concerns about acid deposition have prompted northeastern states to sue the EPA, calling for stricter enforcement of the Clean Air Act in midwestern states. Florida, Vermont, New Jersey, and Oregon have strong state land-use laws. And the list goes on. Key state legislative issues for 1990 include energy efficiency, solid waste management (especially waste reduction and recycling), water quality, land-use management, and environmental impacts of agriculture (Bernau, Pattarozzi, and Rees 1990).

States with the worst problems often have the strongest environmental regulations. That New Jersey, for example, has toxic substances policies undreamed of in Idaho is not surprising. Florida's rapid population growth has been met with laws and programs that would be unpalatable and inappropriate in West Virginia or Nebraska. Revealing as they are, though, state-level summaries tell little about conflicts *within* states. Rural residents in heavily urbanized states, for example, tend to resent environmental controls that interfere with their use of land and resources. California, New York, and Oregon are cases in point.

National environmental groups—such as the Sierra Club and Wilderness Society—have in at least one way benefited from the new federalism: Their memberships surged in the early 1980s. Community-level activism also became much more commonplace through the 1980s. Indeed, it has become increasingly difficult to find places for incinerators, landfills, and other LULUs (Locally Unwanted Land Uses): a phenomenon commonly referred to as the NIMBY (Not in My Backyard) syndrome. In contrast to the largely white, professional, and middle- to upper-class national movements, these local upwellings are more socioeconomically diverse.

Lessons about the environmental movement's socioeconomic homogeneity were not lost on the organizers of Earth Week 1990: They were striving to include broader constituencies in this twentieth anniversary celebration of the original Earth Day. At the same time, general public concern—while remaining strong over the past two decades—has been piqued by beach closings, urban ozone, the Valdez oil spill, and other recent events. The national political picture also has changed—witness EPA Administrator William Reilly, who formerly headed the respected, if relatively conservative, Conservation Foundation. Indeed, as we enter the 1990s, environmental concerns are reemerging on all scales, local to global.

Flathead National Forest, Montana. R. Mason.

STATE EMPLOYMENT PATTERNS

All told, the basic resource activities — agriculture, forestry, fishing, and mining— account for no more than 20 percent of any one state's employment. And of those four, it is mining that usually accounts for the lion's share. With the exception of Kentucky and West Virginia, their relative importance is greater in the West than in the East. In Alaska, Kentucky, Louisiana, Montana, New Mexico, North Dakota, Oklahoma, Texas, West Virginia, and Wyoming, the percentage of workers in all basic resource activities (but principally oil, gas, and other minerals) is at least twice that for the nation as a whole (eleven-

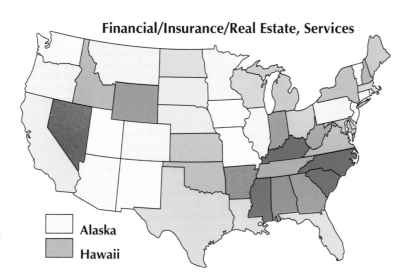

Financial/Insurance/Real Estate, Services

Alaska
Hawaii

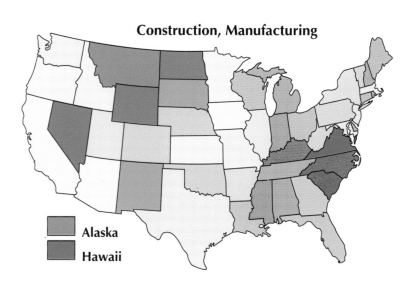

Construction, Manufacturing

Alaska
Hawaii

Importance of Activity to State as Compared to Its Importance to the United States as a Whole

⟨ **Increasing Importance** ⟨   **Same**   ⟩ **Decreasing Importance** ⟩

fold in Wyoming). These ratios are far higher than those for any other industry groups represented on the maps.

The maps show the general importance of manufacturing in much of the East and the relative prominence of transportation, utilities, and trade to the less-populated states in the western half of the country. Fire, insurance, real estate, and services tend to be of least economic importance where manufacturing is highest.

In recent decades, the U.S. economy has undergone a shift away from manufacturing, toward services. In 1950, goods-producing industries and service activities (broadly defined) employed about the same numbers of people. But by 1980, the goods-producing share was 33 percent; services 66 percent (Clark 1985). Furthermore, recent manufacturing growth has been mainly in technology-based industries. Construction and mining, on the other hand, have actually declined.

On balance, long-term economic trends seem to bode quite well for the American environment, with greatest future growth expected in such relatively—but far from entirely—clean areas as communications, services, finance, insurance, and real estate. But from a global perspective, the improvement may be illusory; some of the worst manufacturing impacts are merely being shifted to other parts of the world.

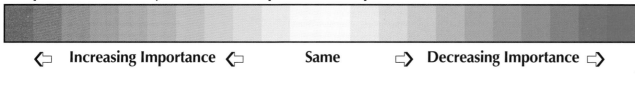

Calculating State Employment Pattern Location Quotients

$$\frac{\text{\# of Employees in a Category in State/Total \# of Employees in State}}{\text{\# of Employees in a Category in U.S./Total \# of Employees in U.S.}}$$

Figure 17.1. State Employment Patterns.

No government employment is represented on these maps.

The maps are scaled so that each is internally consistent. This means that states can be compared with one another on each of the maps but individual states should not be compared between maps.

Source:
Bureau of the Census, *County Business Patterns 1985: United States*, CBP-85-1 (Washington, DC: Department of Commerce, 1987).

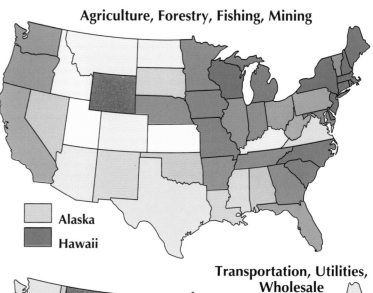

Agriculture, Forestry, Fishing, Mining

Alaska
Hawaii

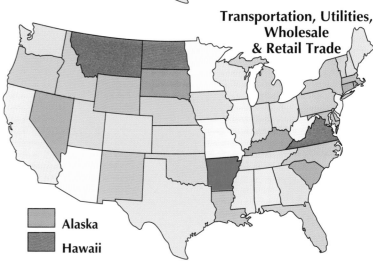

Transportation, Utilities, Wholesale & Retail Trade

Alaska
Hawaii

Pollution Abatement Expenditures/New Capital Expenditures, 1985

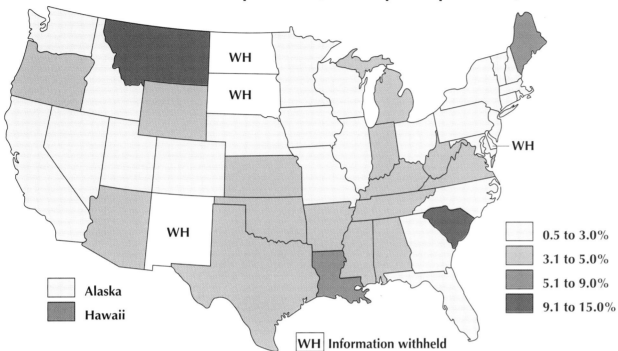

WH
WH
WH
WH
WH

0.5 to 3.0%
3.1 to 5.0%
5.1 to 9.0%
9.1 to 15.0%

Alaska
Hawaii

WH Information withheld

Pollution Abatement Expenditures Per Capita, 1985

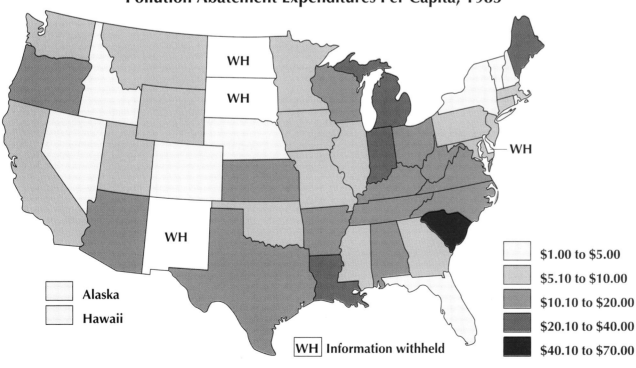

WH
WH
WH
WH

$1.00 to $5.00
$5.10 to $10.00
$10.10 to $20.00
$20.10 to $40.00
$40.10 to $70.00

Alaska
Hawaii

WH Information withheld

POLLUTION-ABATEMENT EXPENDITURES

In 1985, manufacturers with 20 or more employees incurred $2,809.7 million in new capital costs for pollution abatement. Of this, 46 percent was for air; 36 percent for water; and 18 percent for solid waste. Operating costs for pollution abatement, somewhat more evenly distributed across the categories, totaled $11,677.9 million. New capital expenditures were up 29 percent from 1984, but in the early 1970s expenditures increased steadily, peaking at mid-decade. They then declined slowly until 1980—and more rapidly in the early 1980s, rebounding only after 1983. The falloff of the late 1970s and early 1980s clearly was related to economic recession and lower total capital expenditures. But other factors also were involved: Many manufacturers had caught up with backlogged expenditures from earlier in the 1970s; and the eased regulatory climate of the early 1980s (when the largest drops of up to 32 percent occurred) may have prompted some manufacturers to delay new investments.

About 65 percent of all 1985 expenditures were made by four major industry groups: chemical and allied products, transportation equipment, paper and allied products, and petroleum and coal products. Four states—Texas, Michigan, South Carolina, and California—accounted for some 33 percent of total expenditures. The top map offers some evidence—albeit inconclusive—that states making the biggest capital investments in entirely new (rather than replacement) plant and equipment— that is, mostly Sunbelt states—are those whose pollution-abatement expenditures tend to be a greater proportion of all new capital expenditures. The lower map tells a rather similar story. However, states in the Great Lakes core industrial region do pay more, relative to their Sunbelt counterparts, when pollution-abatement costs are computed per capita.

Government and personal-consumption expenditures for pollution control and abatement, like those by industry, stabilized or dropped in the early 1980s but were on the increase by the middle of the decade. The bulk of the early 1980s' government decline is attributed to reduced spending for construction of wastewater treatment plants (figure 9.16). In 1985, business accounted for about two-thirds of expenditures; government 20 percent; and individual consumers the remainder of the $70 billion spent on pollution abatement. This was approximately 1.75 percent of the 1985 gross national product.

Figure 17.2. Pollution Abatement Expenditures.

Sources:
Bureau of the Census, *Pollution Abatement Costs and Expenditures, 1985* (Washington, DC: GPO, 1987), pp. 3–7.

Bureau of the Census, *1986 Annual Survey of Manufactures* (Washington, DC: GPO, 1988), pp. 3.12–3.37.

STATE ENVIRONMENTAL EXPENDITURES

Although all the expenditures represented here were made by state governments, they do include substantial amounts of federal grant monies that were spent by the states. An analysis by the Congressional Budget Office (Sussman 1988)—while not directly comparable with the numbers shown here—reveals that fiscal responsibility has shifted toward the states over the past decade. In the early years of the Reagan administration, in particular, the "new federalist" policies sought to bring about this shift. Between 1982 and 1986, EPA grants for air- and water-quality programs—and especially for hazardous and solid waste programs—declined. At the same time, total state budgets for waste management—and to a lesser extent for air and water programs—increased.

Moreover, the classification scheme used here (air, water, land, materials) is more appropriate to some states' circumstances than others. Still, the maps reveal that per capita expenditures for waste management are quite high in the Northeast; that air-quality budgets are very high not only in California but also in Oregon, Arizona, and Wyoming; that there is no clear pattern for water-quality expenditures; and that land- and water-resource outlays are high in the Rocky Mountain and West Coast regions, where resource-based and recreational activities are important to local and state economies.

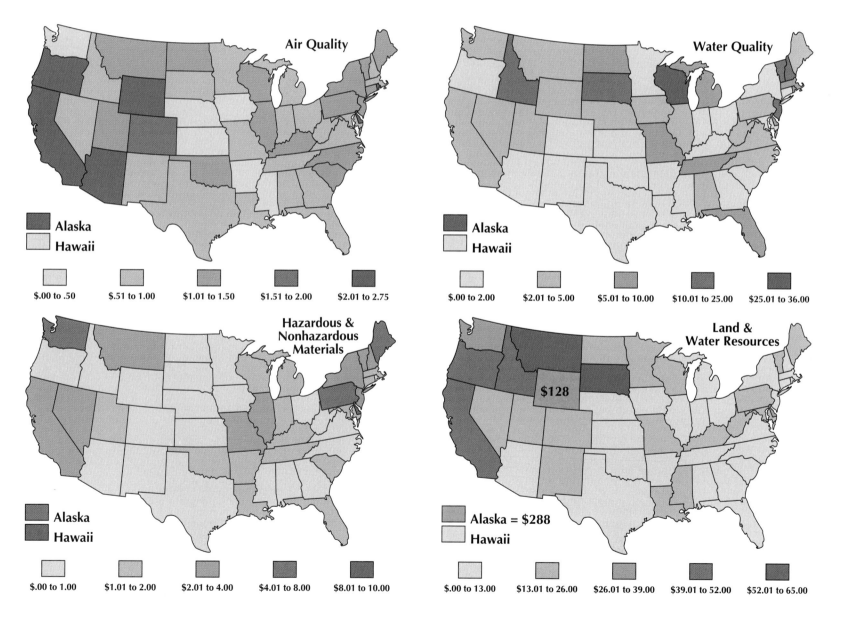

Table 17.1. Per Capita Income, 1987	
	Dollars
Alabama	9,615
Alaska	13,263
Arizona	11,521
Arkansas	9,061
California	13,197
Colorado	12,271
Connecticut	16,094
Delaware	12,785
Florida	12,456
Georgia	11,406
Hawaii	12,290
Idaho	9,159
Illinois	12,437
Indiana	11,078
Iowa	11,198
Kansas	11,520
Kentucky	9,380
Louisiana	8,961
Maine	10,478
Maryland	14,697
Massachusetts	14,398
Michigan	11,973
Minnesota	12,281
Mississippi	8,088
Missouri	11,203
Montana	9,322
Nebraska	11,139
Nevada	12,603
New Hampshire	13,529
New Jersey	15,028
New Mexico	9,434
New York	13,167
North Carolina	10,856
North Dakota	9,641
Ohio	11,323
Oklahoma	9,927
Oregon	11,045
Pennsylvania	11,544
Rhode Island	12,351
South Carolina	9,967
South Dakota	8,910
Tennessee	10,448
Texas	10,645
Utah	9,288
Vermont	11,234
Virginia	13,658
Washington	12,184
West Virginia	8,980
Wisconsin	11,417
Wyoming	9,826

Source: Bureau of the Census (Washington, DC, 1990, news release, CB90-36).

STATE POLITICAL CULTURES

Daniel Elazar's (1984) widely regarded view of American federalism is as follows: the Constitution sets the standard, the Supreme Court sets guidelines, and state governments are left to apply those guidelines in ways consonant with their respective political cultures. It is an apt depiction of much of our environmental-policy administration.

Elazar's political cultures are represented on the map in figure 17.4 and in its caption. Because political culture is a concept that eludes rigorous definition and measurement, its usefulness as an analytic construct is a subject of some debate. Moreover, states are not monolithic entities; many of them have strong representation of multiple political cultures. Indeed, these conflicting cultures are at the root of many land-use and other regulatory conflicts that divide state legislatures along "upstate-downstate" or "rural-urban" lines. Still, it is the dominant political culture— almost by definition—that should guide state policy administration.

Today's mosaic of political cultures is the product of historic settlement and migration patterns—reflecting as they do differing cultures, political ideologies, and the effects of time, external events, and cultural mixing. Clearly evident even today are strong strains of New England's moralistic, communitarian agrarianism; the individualistic, agrarian tendencies of New York, New Jersey, Pennsylvania, Delaware, and Maryland; and the traditionalistic, plantation-centered agrarianism of the South. They are strongly apparent not only in these source regions but also where they were carried westward by migration. In 1980, the U.S. population was approximately equally divided among the states that fall into the three basic categories (Elazar 1984).

To what extent does political culture explain differing levels of environmental commitment? This is difficult to answer, especially given the wide range of environmental issues as well as physical contexts that help define those issues. Yet the moralistic tendencies of New England and the upper Midwest, in particular, seem to be reflected in their political and environmental choices (figures 17.5–17.7). So too do the more individualistic leanings of some of the mountain states. A recent analysis of state land-use laws (Wagendorp 1988) reveals that moralistic states tend to have slightly greater numbers of laws than individualistic states; and that southern, traditionalist states have fewer statutes than northern states.

Figure 17.3. State Environmental Expenditures per Capita, 1986.

Source:
R. S. Brown and L. E. Garner, *Resource Guide to State Environmental Management* (Lexington, KY: Council of State Governments, 1988), pp. 81–92.

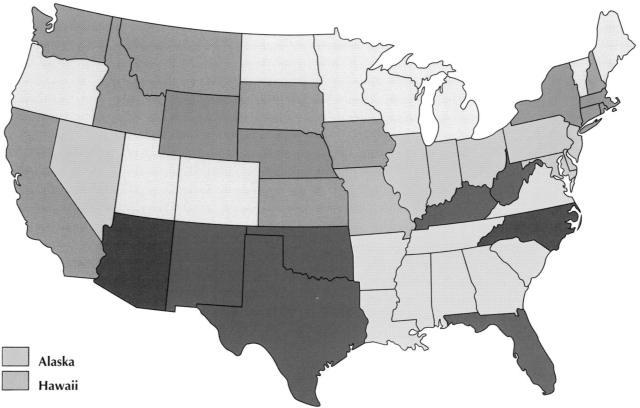

Alaska

Hawaii

Figure 17.4. State Political Cultures.

Source:
D. J. Elazar, *American Federalism: A View from the States,* 3d ed. (New York: Harper and Row, 1984), p. 135.

Individualistic: government responds, in a business-like fashion, to the demands of the political marketplace. Its chief sphere of activity is economic, and it favors economic growth and private initiative. Party loyalty and consistency are highly valued. Corruption, unless egregious, usually is viewed ambivalently.

Moralistic: "good government." Government is a positive force with an obligation to promote the general welfare. Citizen participation is highly valued. Strong party ties are rejected, and there is little tolerance of corruption. Extensive government intervention (especially by local government) in social and economic spheres is accepted, but nongovernment coercion is preferred.

Traditionalistic: a paternalistic, elitist form of government. Family and social ties are important. Government intervenes in private affairs as necessary to maintain traditional patterns. Citizen participation in government is not encouraged.

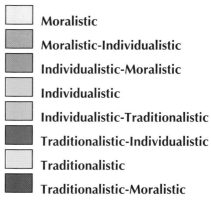

Moralistic

Moralistic-Individualistic

Individualistic-Moralistic

Individualistic

Individualistic-Traditionalistic

Traditionalistic-Individualistic

Traditionalistic

Traditionalistic-Moralistic

The juxtaposition of two culture types indicates either an amalgamation of the two or their separate coexistence—with the first dominant and the second secondary.

NATIONAL ENVIRONMENTAL VOTING RECORDS

Recent congressional environmental votes display clear spatial patterns: they are strongly pro-environment in the Northeast, across the North Central tier of states, and along the West Coast; and relatively weak in the Southeast, southern and central Great Plains, and Rocky Mountain states. Democratic votes are consistently more pro-environment than are Republican votes. Of course, the selection of issues—as well as interpretations about which votes are environmentally correct—determine the results. In making its choices, the League of Conservation Voters tries to represent broadly the environmental community (diverse as it is) as a whole.

In 1983–1984, the Senate voted on extension of Superfund; wastewater-treatment-plant funding; oil and gas drilling restrictions along Florida's Gulf Coast; moratoria on federal coal leasing; various presidential appointments and cabinet policies; funds for the North Dakota's Garrison Diversion water project; maintenance of energy-conservation income tax credits; funds and tax credits for synthetic fuels development; funding for the Clinch River (nuclear) breeder reactor; a Northwest nuclear utility bailout; restrictions on nuclear fuel and technology exports; and a nuclear freeze. Senators Luatenberg (NJ) and Leahy (VT) scored 100 percent; while McClure (ID), Symms (ID), and Wallop (WY) scored 0 percent.

The House in 1983 voted on Superfund funding, victim compensation, and citizen rights to sue EPA and responsible parties; Safe Drinking Water Act Amendments; wilderness designations in Missouri, California, and Oregon; Department of Interior funding; creation of an American Conservation Corps; striped bass conservation; funds for organic farming research and extension programs; water projects in North Carolina, Kentucky, and Florida (the Cross Florida Barge Canal); federal cost-sharing policies for water projects; presidential appointment of former EPA-head Ann Burford to chair the National Advisory Committee on Oceans and Atmosphere (advisory vote); energy-conservation funding; solar- and nuclear-energy research funding; synthetic-fuel-development funding; and billing of utility customers for new power plant construction. Representatives Weiss (NY) and Wolpe (MI) scored 100 percent; while Hansen (ID) and Rudd (AZ) scored 0 percent.

In the 99th Congress (1985–1986), the Senate voted on Clean Water Act enforcement and sanctions; confirmation of Robert Dawson to an Assistant Secretary post in the Army Corps of Engineers; reauthorization of federal pesticide legislation; Superfund funding and victims' compensation; EPA budget authority; funding for development of synthetic fuels; maintenance of automobile fuel-economy standards; Department of the Interior decision-making for offshore oil and gas leasing; funding for road-building in national forests; and a Hawaiian highway that would affect a wilderness area. Senators Leahy (VT), Stafford (VT), and Proxmire (WI) scored 100 percent; while Goldwater (AZ), Symms (ID), McClure (ID), Stennis (MS), and Garn (UT) scored 0.

Because of the low number of key House votes in 1986, the League of Conservation Voters combined its 1985 and 1986 scores. The votes were on water-pollution-control funding; toxic-waste pretreatment requirements for sewage plants; the Superfund "right-to-know" amendment and victims' compensation; reauthorization of federal pesticide legislation; funding for synthetic-fuels development; funding for New York's Westway Interstate Highway; water projects funding and policies; water projects in Oregon and Utah; billboard controls; international family planning aid; creation of an American Conservation Corps; agricultural conservation (the 1985 "farm bill"); establishment of Great Basin National Park; the Columbia River Gorge Protection Act; a nuclear test ban; and sulfur and nitrogen-oxide emission reductions (co-sponsorship; did not reach floor). Representatives Boxer (CA), Waxman (CA), Schroeder (CO), Frank (MA), Markey (MA), Studds (MA), Kostmayer (PA), and Kastenmeier (WI) scored 100 percent; while Kemp (NY) was low scorer at 3 percent.

In the 100th Congress (1987–1988), the Senate voted on Clean Water Act reauthorization; billboard controls; the Appliance Energy Standards Act; energy conservation funding; nuclear waste facility siting and liability; debt relief for the uranium industry; sulfur and nitrogen-oxide emission reductions (signatures on letter to majority and minority leaders; did not reach floor); reauthorization of the Endangered Species Act (co-sponsorship; did not reach floor); and timber cutting in Alaska's Tongass National Forest (co-sponsorship; did not reach floor). Senators Kerry (MA), Chafee (RI), and Leahy (VT) scored 100 percent; while Helms (NC), McClure (ID), Nickles (OK), Symms (ID), and Wallop (WY) scored 0.

During 1987–1988, the House voted on Clean Water Act reauthorization; oil shale sales on public lands; Clean Air Act sanctions; energy conservation funding; Amtrak funding; nuclear liability; nuclear power plant licensing; water projects funding authorization; a Nebraska water project; protection of the Leopard Darter (a threatened species of fish); requirements for shrimp trawlers to use devices to keep sea turtles from drowning in nets; ocean-pollution prevention; clean-air and acid-rain legislation (signatures on letter to Energy and Commerce Committee chairman; no floor vote); and wilderness designation/oil and gas leasing in Arctic National Wildlife Refuge (co-sponsorship; no floor vote). Representatives Aucoin (OR), Evans, L. (IL); Mfume (MD), Morrison, B. (CT), Florio (NJ), and Jontz (IN) scored 100 percent; while Cheney (WY), Herger (CA), Kemp (NY), and Stump (AZ) scored 0. Table 17.2 shows voting patterns for the first session of the 101st Congress.

Table 17.2. 1989 Congressional Votes (101st Congress)		
	Percent Pro-Environment	
	House	Senate
Alabama	54	35
Alaska	20	30
Arizona	28	40
Arkansas	33	85
California	62	70
Colorado	55	50
Connecticut	85	95
Delaware	50	70
Florida	62	65
Georgia	54	80
Hawaii	70	50
Idaho	40	0
Illinois	62	85
Indiana	68	45
Iowa	50	40
Kansas	58	35
Kentucky	41	20
Louisiana	16	10
Maine	90	70
Maryland	69	75
Massachusetts	93	95
Michigan	64	55
Minnesota	59	50
Mississippi	47	10
Missouri	49	25
Montana	45	20
Nebraska	37	60
Nevada	30	80
New Hampshire	70	50
New Jersey	71	90
New Mexico	50	30
New York	69	55
North Carolina	63	40
North Dakota	90	45
Ohio	51	80
Oklahoma	45	20
Oregon	64	45
Pennsylvania	53	75
Rhode Island	95	65
South Carolina	63	55
South Dakota	90	50
Tennessee	49	90
Texas	30	30
Utah	33	15
Vermont	100	90
Virginia	34	45
Washington	79	65
West Virginia	63	70
Wisconsin	61	80
Wyoming	10	0

Source: League of Conservation Voters, *1989 National Environmental Scorecard* (Washington, DC: LCV, 1990).

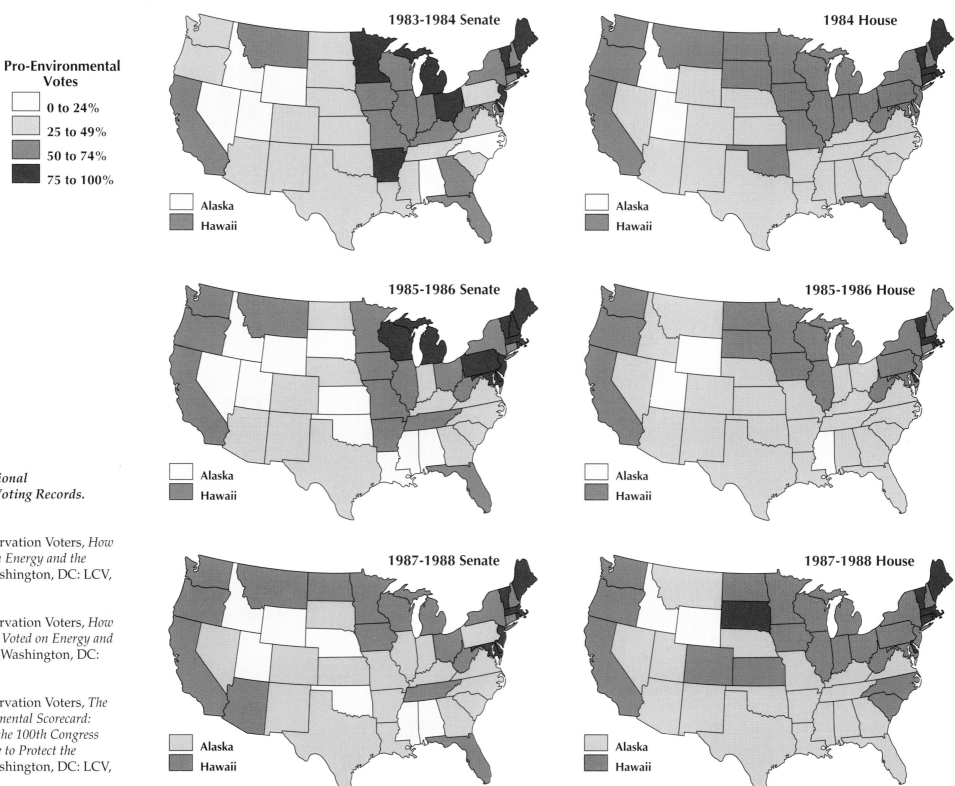

Pro-Environmental Votes

0 to 24%
25 to 49%
50 to 74%
75 to 100%

1983-1984 Senate

Alaska
Hawaii

1984 House

Alaska
Hawaii

1985-1986 Senate

Alaska
Hawaii

1985-1986 House

Alaska
Hawaii

1987-1988 Senate

Alaska
Hawaii

1987-1988 House

Alaska
Hawaii

Figure 17.5. National Environmental Voting Records.

Sources:
League of Conservation Voters, *How Congress Voted on Energy and the Environment* (Washington, DC: LCV, 1985).

League of Conservation Voters, *How the 99th Congress Voted on Energy and the Environment* (Washington, DC: LCV, 1987).

League of Conservation Voters, *The National Environmental Scorecard: How Members of the 100th Congress Voted in the Battle to Protect the Environment* (Washington, DC: LCV, 1988).

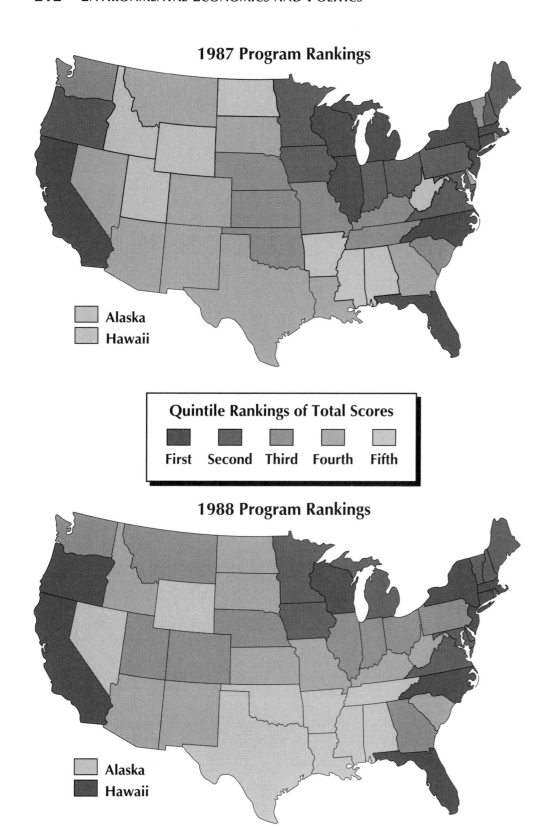

1987 Program Rankings

1988 Program Rankings

Quintile Rankings of Total Scores

First Second Third Fourth Fifth

Alaska
Hawaii

F.R.E.E. Ranking of State Environmental Programs

	1987 Program Rankings							1988 Program Rankings						
	Air	Soil Conservation	Ground Water	Hazardous Waste	Solid Waste	Renewable Energy and Conservation	Total	Surface Water Protection	Reducing Pesticide Contamination	Land Use Planning	Eliminating Indoor Pollution	Highway Safety	Energy Pollution Control	Total
AL	3	3	2	3	3	2	16	4	2	5	4	2	4	21
AK	7	3	3	2	2	1	18	3	2	2	7	2	5	21
AZ	7	3	7	5	2	3	27	4	6	7	4	1	3	25
AR	1	3	2	5	3	4	18	1	3	3	4	2	4	17
CA	10	3	7	9	9	10	48	5	10	8	5	7	9	44
CO	4	6	4	3	4	3	24	5	2	7	5	6	4	29
CT	9	6	9	4	9	7	44	6	8	8	8	6	7	43
DE	1	8	6	3	4	2	24	4	2	6	7	6	7	32
FL	7	4	9	8	6	7	41	5	6	9	9	4	8	41
GA	4	5	7	4	3	3	26	8	2	4	3	4	6	27
HI	4	4	3	2	2	4	19	5	8	7	2	9	7	38
ID	2	1	6	1	2	6	18	4	2	3	5	5	6	25
IL	7	9	5	7	7	6	41	5	4	5	5	6	4	29
IN	6	5	4	6	7	8	36	4	4	6	7	3	4	28
IA	5	10	5	5	7	7	39	8	5	3	6	6	6	34
KS	2	5	8	8	4	2	29	4	3	4	4	4	6	25
KY	7	3	1	6	8	3	28	5	4	3	3	4	4	23
LA	5	3	3	7	2	1	21	2	5	6	2	2	3	20
ME	3	6	7	6	6	8	36	5	7	6	6	4	8	36
MD	3	8	7	6	6	4	34	6	3	8	2	10	6	35
MA	6	4	8	9	6	8	41	5	6	9	9	6	10	45
MI	8	7	8	9	8	3	43	5	6	7	6	6	8	38
MN	5	6	5	9	9	4	38	6	6	7	6	6	7	38
MS	1	3	3	3	2	2	14	4	3	2	3	3	2	17
MO	5	6	6	8	5	1	31	5	2	4	4	5	3	23
MT	2	6	6	6	2	1	23	6	8	4	4	5	2	29
NE	4	6	6	6	6	3	31	8	5	4	2	4	8	31
NV	2	6	6	6	2	1	23	4	3	4	2	2	4	19
NH	6	5	6	6	5	4	32	4	8	8	9	3	6	38
NJ	9	6	7	10	10	5	47	6	5	9	10	7	7	44
NM	1	2	8	5	1	6	23	4	2	4	5	2	5	22
NY	5	5	10	8	8	7	43	5	8	7	9	6	7	42
NC	8	7	8	6	6	7	42	10	5	8	4	5	8	40
ND	1	3	4	2	3	3	16	5	3	4	4	4	6	26
OH	8	8	4	5	5	4	34	5	6	6	5	4	4	30
OK	5	5	5	4	7	3	29	3	2	1	3	5	5	19
OR	6	2	7	5	7	8	35	7	6	10	5	6	8	42
PA	8	6	5	5	3	5	32	4	2	4	8	8	5	31
RI	6	4	6	4	7	3	30	5	6	6	7	5	8	37
SC	6	5	7	5	2	6	31	7	3	5	4	2	3	24
SD	1	8	6	2	2	4	23	6	2	4	3	5	7	27
TN	3	3	4	7	5	7	29	5	2	3	3	2	5	20
TX	7	2	2	5	3	7	26	1	9	3	2	2	2	19
UT	3	4	3	2	1	3	16	5	2	6	5	5	6	29
VT	3	3	5	6	4	7	28	6	6	8	5	4	7	36
VA	8	7	6	2	3	7	33	8	2	5	6	8	5	34
WA	8	1	6	5	5	3	29	4	5	6	6	6	5	32
WV	2	5	2	4	1	1	15	6	4	3	3	5	3	24
WI	9	8	8	7	8	9	49	7	7	7	8	7	9	45
WY	1	3	8	1	2	1	16	6	1	3	2	2	1	15

Note: Highest possible score in each category is 10; highest possible total score is 60.

Figure 17.6. State Environmental Program Ratings.

Sources:
S. Ridley, *The State of the States: 1987* (Washington, DC: Fund for Renewable Energy and the Environment, 1987), pp. 3, 5.

S. Ridley, *The State of the States: 1988* (Washington, DC: Fund for Renewable Energy and the Environment, 1988), pp. 5, 42–43.

STATE ENVIRONMENTAL PROGRAM RATINGS

How are states faring after ten years' experience with the "new federalism" of the 1980s? The maps in figure 17.6 display a general pattern repeated through much of this chapter. The Fund for Renewable Energy and the Environment (FREE), recently renamed Renew America, gives highest marks for environmental programs to the Northeast and North Central states (especially the Northeast), the Middle Atlantic states, the West Coast, and Florida and North Carolina. Most southeastern, southwestern, Great Plains, and Rocky Mountain states appear weak by comparison. The 1989 rankings, not included here, show a similar spatial pattern. They are based on forest management, solid waste recycling, drinking water, food safety, and community growth issues. The rankings for all three years, however, are quite subjective. In figure 17.6 we adopt FREE's practice of summing rankings equally across categories; this assumes—perhaps wrongly—that each category is of equal priority.

There are few regional or state-level surprises in the table's detailed data. California leads in air-pollution control programs and is viewed by FREE as a model for other states. In soil conservation, the farm belt states of the Midwest and Great Plains assume a modest overall lead. Iowa is praised for its comprehensive programs. At the time of the FREE survey, half the states had initiated groundwater protection programs, with New York the leader. More programs have since come on line, in compliance with recent EPA guidelines. Solid and hazardous waste programs are notably minimal in the Rocky Mountain states; while New Jersey is viewed as a clear leader in both categories. California is praised for its encouragement of renewable energy development.

With regard to surface-water protection, the southwestern region—particularly Texas, Oklahoma, and Arkansas—receives especially low marks. North Carolina, by contrast, is the leader. Pesticide control efforts apparently are most vigorous in the New England and West Coast regions but notably deficient in the Southeast, Rocky Mountain, and Great Plains states. California—with its comprehensive registration, monitoring, and drift-control regulations—is the clear leader. Most states regulate land use through zoning and critical-areas regulation, though some have comprehensive land-use plans. Oregon is one and is seen by FREE—with some reservation—as the national leader. Indoor air protection became a key concern only recently. New Jersey, with its smoking restrictions and radon and lead-reduction programs, receives highest marks. Highway safety programs— which affect vehicle fuel economy, hazardous-material transport, and mass transit—are best developed in the congested Middle Atlantic region, particularly Maryland. Massachusetts, with its energy efficiency regulations and tax credits, gets highest marks for energy-pollution control.

MEMBERSHIP IN ENVIRONMENTAL ORGANIZATIONS

Although most Americans see environmental protection as an important national objective, comparatively few articulate their interest through political activism or organizational membership. National groups claim perhaps 7 million members; local and regional activists at most number 25 million (Borrelli 1988). Disproportionately represented in national groups are middle- to upper-income, well-educated whites.

The organizations represented on the maps in figure 17.7 are large, well financed, and have reliable membership data. The Sierra Club, founded by John Muir in 1892, is the oldest. Continuously headquartered in San Francisco, it still draws members heavily from California. The traditional emphasis on preservation of western wildlands has expanded to include such issues as Great Lakes water quality, air toxics, nuclear wastes, and coastal protection. The club is active in Washington as well as through its many state and local chapters. Total 1988 membership was 491,000; the 1987 budget was $18.5 million.

The National Audubon Society, founded in 1905, had a 1988 membership of 550,000 and budget of $32.6 million. It has 510 active local chapters and operates eighty-two wildlife sanctuaries. Principal concerns are preservation of plants, animals, and associated habitats. Somewhat less activist than the Sierra Club, Audubon focuses on such issues as wetlands protection, acid rain, forest-management policy, and global environmental change.

The National Wildlife Federation (NWF), established in 1936, represents a diverse constituency with sporting and other recreational and environmental interests. Its political orientation and demographic profile probably match that of the larger American population more closely than that of any other national environmental organization. Indeed, the map shows a comparatively even distribution of membership rates. The NWF has wide influence, with nearly 5 million members, supporters, and magazine subscribers (2.2 million active members in 1989). Expenditures in 1987 totaled $59.3 million. Recent policy concerns include wetlands, toxic chemicals, air quality, acid rain, groundwater, energy, and public lands and forests.

The Izaak Walton League was established in 1922 in Chicago— and membership today remains greatest in Iowa, Indiana, and Illinois. The local and state chapters, which act with great autonomy, are perhaps the league's greatest strengths. Like the NWF, the league represents the interests of sportsmen as well as other conservationists. Key concerns include outdoor ethics, water quality, wetlands, Chesapeake Bay management, acid rain, range management, and soil conservation. As of 1988, the League had 39,000 members; 1987 expenditures were $1.4 million.

The National Parks and Conservation Association (NPCA), founded in 1919, is dedicated specifically to protection and improvement of the National Park System. The NPCA describes

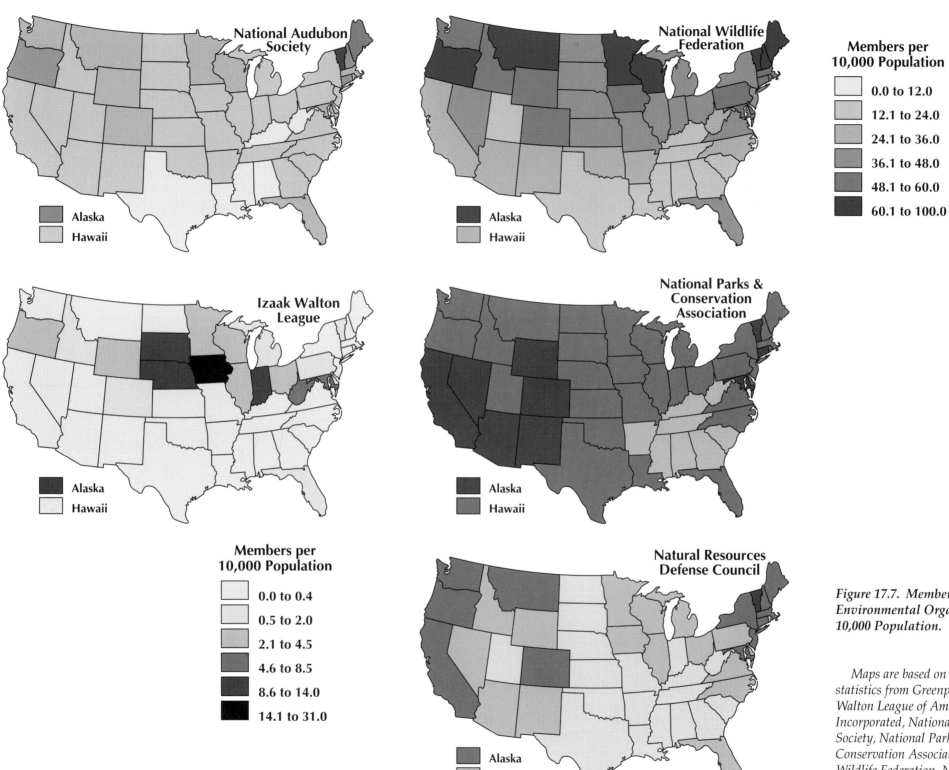

Figure 17.7. Membership in Major Environmental Organizations per 10,000 Population.

Maps are based on membership statistics from Greenpeace, Izaak Walton League of America Incorporated, National Audubon Society, National Parks and Conservation Association, National Wildlife Federation, Natural Resources Defense Council, and Sierra Club.

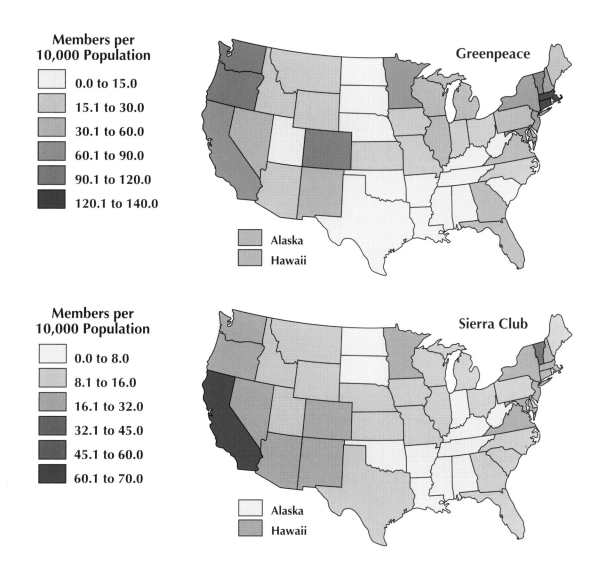

Members per 10,000 Population

- 0.0 to 15.0
- 15.1 to 30.0
- 30.1 to 60.0
- 60.1 to 90.0
- 90.1 to 120.0
- 120.1 to 140.0

Greenpeace

- Alaska
- Hawaii

Members per 10,000 Population

- 0.0 to 8.0
- 8.1 to 16.0
- 16.1 to 32.0
- 32.1 to 45.0
- 45.1 to 60.0
- 60.1 to 70.0

Sierra Club

- Alaska
- Hawaii

itself as conservative-to-moderate; firm yet nonconfrontational. Revenues in 1987 were nearly $3.5 million and membership at least 60,000. Membership is relatively strong in western states with large national parks—including those with relatively low rates of membership in other national organizations.

The Natural Resources Defense Council (NRDC), founded in 1970, is one of a relatively new breed of organizations that operate principally—and very effectively—in the legal arena. In the same category are the Environmental Defense Fund (founded in 1967) and the Sierra Club Legal Defense Fund. Beyond its legal mission, the NRDC devotes much energy to research, advocacy, and education in such areas as air and water quality, toxic and biological hazards, public lands and forests, energy conservation, and nuclear weapons and war. Given its relatively small membership (91,000 members and contributors in 1988), the NRDC is

well financed: 1987 expenditures were $9.2 million. Similarly, the Environmental Defense Fund had 100,000 members and expenses of $7.8 million in 1988.

Greenpeace attracts media attention by climbing smokestacks, staging "die-ins," obstructing nuclear tests and whaling missions, and other dramatic acts. But Greenpeace is also increasingly involved in more conventional research, lobbying, and public education. Key issues—besides oceans and coasts—include toxic chemicals, Great Lakes water quality, and nuclear disarmament. In 1988, Greenpeace had 1.2 million donors (distinct from "members"); 1987 expenses were nearly $22 million.

Other major organizations include Friends of the Earth and Environmental Action—both of which can be described as confrontationist—as well as the somewhat less activist Zero Population Growth, Defenders of Wildlife, and Wilderness Society. The League of Conservation Voters publishes environmental voting records and supports favorable candidates; while the principal thrusts of the Nature Conservancy, Trust for Public Land, and Save the Redwoods League are land acquisition and protection. Among the more moderate, research-oriented organizations are the Conservation Foundation, Union of Concerned Scientists, and Resources for the Future. In recent years, groups from across this spectrum have put forth common environmental agendas (Adams et al. 1985; Maize 1988).

In the early 1970s, most environmental groups enjoyed surges in memberships, and many new groups were formed. Concerns about Reagan administration environmental policies again boosted memberships in the early 1980s. These groups now have considerable financial standing, technical expertise, and political acumen. Relatively new to the scene are the "monkeywrenchers"—those who feel justified in damaging property to protect the earth. The Sea Shepherds, whose director broke with Greenpeace in 1977, and Earth First!, whose director left the Wilderness Society in 1980—often take illegal actions that directly endanger members. Their organizational relationships with the big national groups range from hostility to symbiosis.

Perhaps the most significant phenomenon of the 1980s has been the explosive growth of unaffiliated, single-issue groups. They form in opposition to landfills, power lines, nuclear waste dumps, and other such threats—and, to the dismay of government officials, can be incredibly effective. While many are short-lived, they can permanently raise environmental consciousness. Perhaps the best symbol of this is Lois Gibbs, the Love Canal housewife-turned-activist-turned-founder of the Citizens' Clearinghouse for Toxic Wastes (figure 12.5). Interestingly, perhaps prophetically, these local upwellings are evident not only in the bellwether states of the Northeast, Great Lakes, and West Coast regions—but also in places far removed from the traditional wellsprings of environmentalism.

Greenhouse warming, ozone depletion, tropical deforestation: All are environmental watchwords of the 1990s. The issues are global and demand concerted international responses. Yet those responses must come in the face of great scientific uncertainty and in a world fraught with injustice and inequities. We can only hope that greater understanding of the many threats we face—including the ultimate horror of nuclear war—will help us find the collective will to confront the deep social and political problems that underlie them.

A significant global warming over the next several decades could dramatically affect agricultural productivity and habitability of large areas. Such changes have ample historic precedent. Our climatic history is a series of great ice ages punctuated by relatively brief periods of "interglacial" warming. The difference in this case would be the speed and intensity of the warming and the complexity of the global economy that would be affected.

It is a given that carbon dioxide and other trace gases trap heat in the lower atmosphere. And we know that human activities have added trace gases to the atmosphere: Indeed, carbon-dioxide levels are 25 percent higher than they were in 1860. Much less clear is the role that this might play in bringing about global warming. Even if we agree on its inevitability—and not all climatologists do—the regional and local impacts are much more elusive. Natural ecosystems would be heavily stressed by rapid climate change. Large areas could become unsuitable for farming; while some currently unproductive regions might become arable. Rising sea level—from thermal expansion of ocean waters and melting of polar ice—could flood coastal cities, destroy wetlands, and increase our vulnerability to dangerous coastal storms. While the more developed countries may have the resource, technological, and economic capabilities to adapt, the outlook for the less developed world is considerably more grave.

The depletion of stratospheric ozone is attributed chiefly to emissions of chlorofluorocarbons (CFCs), which are used as coolants, aerosol propellants, solvents, and blowing agents in the production of foam. Also implicated are halons—used in fire extinguishers, refrigeration, and foams—and other chlorine compounds. Though stable in the lower atmosphere, these compounds break down in the stratosphere under the influence of intense ultraviolet radiation. The resultant reactions destroy ozone—which filters out a significant portion of harmful ultraviolet radiation. CFCs also contribute to the greenhouse effect. Signatories to the 1987 Montreal Protocol agreed to freeze halon consumption by 1992 and halve CFC consumption by 1999. The United States and Europe—the leading producers of CFCs—are likely to go further, agreeing to ban CFC production by 2000. But even if all emissions were stopped today, ozone depletion would continue for at least a century, as stable CFCs now in the lower atmosphere gradually diffuse and ascend to the stratosphere.

If CFC emissions were to continue at the 1987 levels—not a far-fetched assumption, because emissions from developing countries may increase dramatically—ozone depletion of anywhere from 3 to nearly 10 percent might be expected over the next century. A 5 percent decrease could cause nearly a million new cases of nonfatal skin cancer annually and about 30,000 cases of potentially fatal cancer. Furthermore, eye cataracts, sunburns, and immune-system deficiencies would increase; photochemical smog and acid deposition would be greater; and terrestrial plants and animals, crops, and aquatic species would be adversely affected. Some U.S. implications of two global threats—greenhouse warming and nuclear war—are presented in this chapter. If we are to deal with these threats concretely, it means changes in politics, economics, production and consumption patterns, and land-use policies in this country and internationally. One utopian framework for "local" action—not by any means the last word on environmental utopias—is "Ecotopia": the subject of the final map (figure 18.3).

*Earth from Space.
NASA.*

GREENHOUSE EFFECT SCENARIOS

Solar energy enters the earth's atmosphere in the form of shortwave, ultraviolet radiation. About half of all incoming energy is absorbed by the earth itself and eventually reradiated to the atmosphere in infrared, longwave form. But part of this reradiated energy is absorbed by atmospheric carbon dioxide and other trace gases, then reradiated back toward earth. This is the "greenhouse effect" that regulates the planet's climate.

Since 1860, atmospheric carbon dioxide has increased by approximately 25 percent—presumably through the release of stored carbon that accompanies fossil-fuel combustion as well as cutting and burning of forests. Although carbon dioxide is the predominant greenhouse gas, other gases also are important. Methane—produced mainly by anaerobic decomposition of organic matter (including that in landfills) and burning of biomass—has approximately doubled in atmospheric concentration over the past century. Nitrous oxides are released from fossil-fuel combustion, agricultural fertilizers, and cutting and burning of forests; while chlorofluorocarbons (CFCs) are used as coolants, solvents, and for various other purposes. These four trace gases account for about 94 percent of anticipated greenhouse warming (Hansen 1988).

If present trends continue, a doubling of atmospheric carbon dioxide (compared with 1900 levels) might be expected sometime between 2030 and 2080. Such a doubling—or an equivalent increase in other trace gases—could increase global surface temperatures between 3° and 5.5°C (5.5° and 10°F). This is equivalent to the warming experienced since the last ice age (18,000 years ago)—but it would occur ten to 100 times faster. Already, much has been made of the fact that the 1980s was the warmest decade of weather-keeping record. Still, this is well within the bounds of natural climatic variability and should not be interpreted as the beginning of a long-term warming.

As a matter of basic principle, more greenhouse gases in the atmosphere can be expected to raise global temperatures. But we cannot discount the considerable uncertainties in our basic physical data as well as projections of future trace-gas emissions. Questions about the rate of absorption of carbon dioxide by green plants and the oceans, as well as complex interactions between the atmosphere and oceans, have yet to be answered with confidence. Negative feedback mechanisms could conceivably reduce the potential for greenhouse warming. For example, the increased cloud cover caused by greater evaporation might reflect more sunlight into space. Conversely, positive feedback processes might accelerate greenhouse warming. Adding to the scientific confusion are uncertainties about possible rates of melting of polar ice. In an even larger context, climate is influenced by sunspot cycles as well as the earth's long-term orbital and rotational variations.

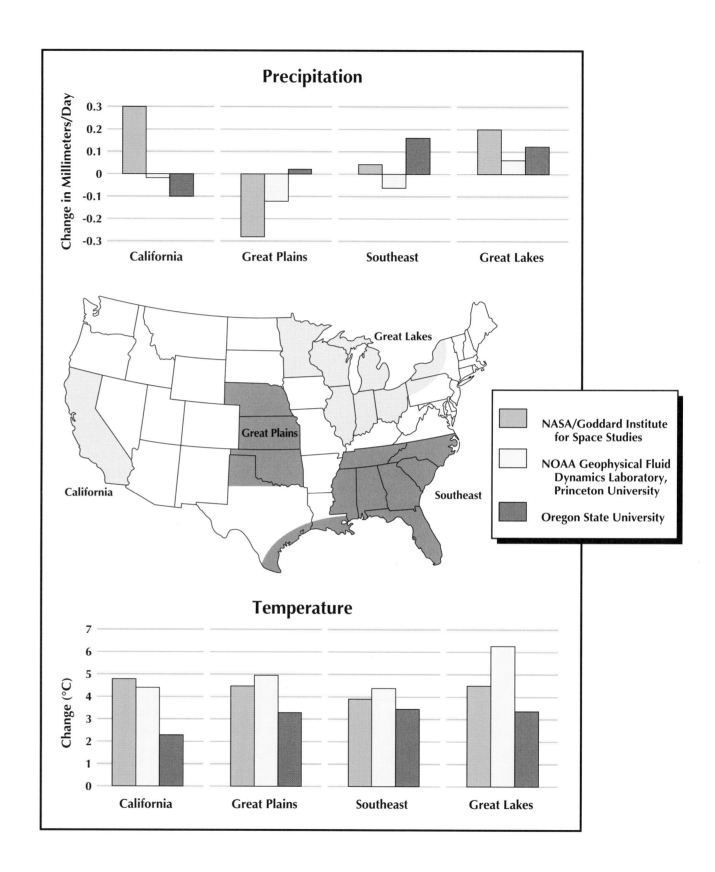

Figure 18.1. Greenhouse Effect Scenarios.

The EPA used three global-scale general circulation models to generate the regional scenarios. Temperature and precipitation changes are those that would accompany a doubling of atmospheric carbon dioxide. The results should be treated as scenarios, not predictions.

Source:
J. B. Smith and D. A. Tirpak, eds., *The Potential Effects of Global Climate Change on the United States: Draft Report to Congress* (Washington, DC: EPA, 1989).

Despite their limitations, global greenhouse models have achieved considerable reliability, inspiring confidence in their predictions. Much more tentative and uncertain, however, are regional and local-level prognoses. Figure 18.1 displays results from the EPA's regional application of several "general circulation models" of ocean-atmosphere interaction (Smith and Tirpak 1989). The results should be treated as scenarios, not predictions.

The California study concentrated on the state's Central Valley (figure 2.1): an oasis of irrigated agriculture and corridor for the transmission of vast quantities of water to both urban and farm users. The scenarios depict greater winter rainfall. Winter runoff from the mountains surrounding the Central Valley would thus be greater, but summer runoff would be lower due to smaller snowpacks. Current water management systems are not designed to store the greater winter runoff and would have to release much of it. Conceivably, this situation could repeat itself through much of the rest of the water-short West.

Rising sea level would mean expansion in volume and higher salinity levels in San Francisco Bay. Wetlands would be inundated and habitats altered. Enormous engineering feats might be required to maintain the Sacramento-San Joaquin Delta Islands, and greater freshwater flows might be needed to repel riverine invasions of saline water. Warmer temperatures would result in higher evaporation rates (and thus greater water demands), increased ozone levels, and greater demand for electricity.

The Southeast has more than 85 percent of the nation's coastal wetlands, supplies 43 percent of the finfish and 70 percent of the shellfish harvest, provides about half the nation's softwood and hardwood timber, and produces tobacco, corn, soybeans, and other crops. Higher temperatures and possible reductions in precipitation could lead to decreased agricultural productivity (especially corn and soybeans), greater need for irrigation, and more pest infestations. Between 10 and 50 percent of farmland might as a result be abandoned. Forest productivity, too—especially in Georgia and Mississippi—could decline significantly. Gulf Coast fisheries would be affected by higher salinity levels and wetlands inundation caused by rising sea level, and much of southern Florida would likely be underwater. Demands for electricity would probably rise sharply.

The Great Lakes Basin not only holds vast amounts of freshwater; it also provides most of the country's corn, 40 percent of its soybeans, and both land- and water-based commercial and recreational opportunities. Despite possible precipitation increases, the greenhouse warming scenarios show lake levels dropping between 1.5 and 12 feet (due to greater evaporation and smaller snowpacks) and reduction in the duration of ice cover by one to three months. While less ice would increase the length of the shipping season, lower lake levels might prompt greater dredging of ports and channels—leaving more contaminated dredge spoils to be disposed. Longer summers—with increased algae growth and longer periods of stratification of lake waters—could lead to greater oxygen depletion and adversely affect fish populations. Lake Erie's shallow basin is especially susceptible (figure 9.13). If on the other hand oxygen levels are maintained, productivity of some fish species might increase. Moreover, agricultural prospects could improve somewhat in Minnesota, Wisconsin, and northern Michigan—but would decline in the Corn Belt. Forests would shift in composition toward hardwoods, savannas, and grasslands (conifers would be eliminated); with overall forest declines expected over a period of 30 to 60 years.

The agricultural productivity of the Great Plains already suffers from soil erosion (figures 4.4), depletion of the Ogallala Aquifer (figure 9.7), and recent drought (figure 16.4). The EPA scenarios show probable decreases in wheat and corn yields, with total acreage reductions between 4 and 22 percent. Irrigation demands could increase, further stressing surface and groundwater supplies. And water quality would be affected by changes in rainfall, runoff, pesticide use, soil erosion, and irrigation flows.

In broad terms, then, greenhouse warming can be expected to shift food crop and forest productivity northward, affect the abundance and health of trees and crops variably, reduce overall biological diversity, eliminate coastal wetlands, and put developed coastal areas at greater risk. One response is to anticipate and prepare for these uncertain consequences. Engineering works—usually at great expense—can perhaps protect coastal areas and ensure adequate water supplies. But, just as with natural hazards, it may be more cost-efficient to prepare in nonstructural ways: through land-use, water resource, energy conservation, and agricultural planning.

We can also attempt to ameliorate the phenomenon. A recent state-level analysis (Machado and Piltz 1988) reveals that Texas is the largest emitter of carbon dioxide; Vermont the smallest. States that rely heavily on coal to generate electricity, as well as those with intense petrochemical development, tend to be the highest emitters per unit value of gross state product. Federal, state, and local governments can reduce carbon emissions by promoting alternative sources of energy, increasing energy efficiency, and improving public transportation. Reforestation also helps offset carbon emissions. Chlorofluorocarbons can be recovered from existing products, and phased out of future products. Methane emissions can be reduced by recovering the gas from landfills, and nitrous oxide by altering fertilizer application practices and stopping deforestation. One of the strongest arguments in favor of such measures—whatever their long-term climatic effects—is their immediate air quality, energy, and land-use benefits.

CLIMATIC EFFECTS OF NUCLEAR WAR

Recent political events notwithstanding, we still have in our possession the nuclear capability to destroy humankind several times over. During the 1980s, as policymakers discussed the prospect of a "survivable nuclear war," the scientific community debated about the kind of world the survivors would inhabit. There is agreement—in broad terms if not in detail—about the immediate devastation that would be wrought by fire, blast (powerful shock waves), early radioactive fallout, and the electromagnetic pulse that would disrupt telecommunications and electric power. But assessing the long-term climatic and ecological effects is a more elusive, entirely hypothetical venture.

According to the widely publicized "nuclear winter" hypothesis, the fires ignited by a nuclear war would loft enough smoke into the air to darken skies over much of the planet. Northern Hemisphere temperatures would plunge by as much as 35°C (63°F), due to reduction of incoming solar radiation. Under these conditions, extinction of humanity becomes a plausible scenario. This grim conclusion comes from the 1983 "TTAPS" model (Turco et al. 1983). But pioneering as it was, that model has severe limitations. It assumes a land-covered earth, and it averages climate change over the entire year.

More recent analyses, including the original authors' own modifications of TTAPS, are more conservative. They take into account the oceans' large heat capacity, relatively rapid removal of smoke from the atmosphere, and the "greenhouse" effect of the smoke—which offsets surface cooling. Represented on the map is the work of climatologists Stephen Schneider and Starley Thompson (1988)—whose calculations indicate that maximum short-term cooling would be 10°C (18°F) in summer; less in other seasons. They call it "nuclear autumn." Although the model's resolution is not fine enough to permit detailed spatial analysis of North America, worthy of note is the expected "patchy," sporadic nature of surface cooling.

The grave importance of nuclear war scenarios is little diminished by the more conservative temperature predictions: An analysis by the international Scientific Committee on Problems of the Environment (Dotto 1986) concludes that a nuclear war's indirect effects could be even more serious than its direct impacts. Even a brief summer cold spell could devastate crops in North America and, at any rate, nuclear war probably would cripple international food trade. Other possible impacts include reduction of stratospheric ozone (by nitrous oxides), injection of chemical pollutants into the atmosphere, and massive damage to ecosystems—especially forests and oceans. Our continued efforts to better understand and predict these effects not only might stimulate efforts to reduce nuclear arsenals, they can also teach us about greenhouse warming and acid deposition.

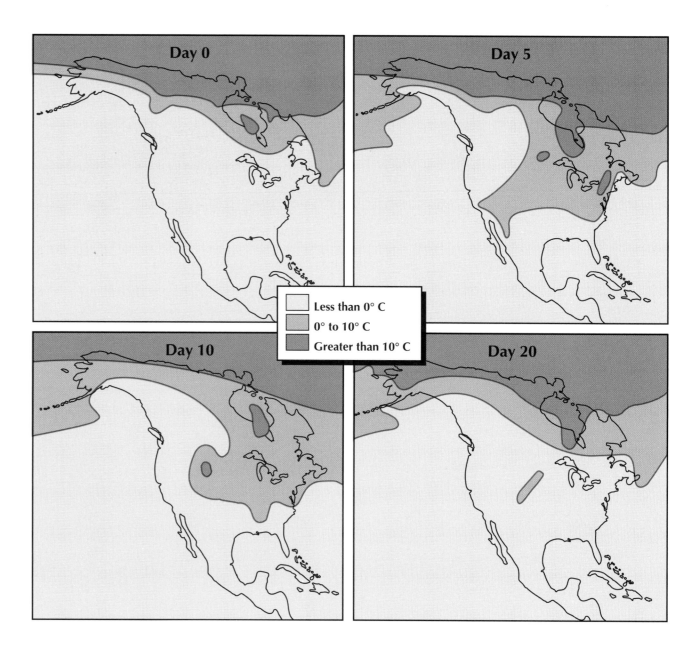

Figure 18.2. Climatic Effects of Nuclear War.

The maps shows average land-surface temperatures initially and at several time intervals after a nuclear exchange. It is based on a July global general circulation model simulation in which 180 Tg (trillion grams) of smoke are injected over NATO and Warsaw Pact regions over a two-day period.

Source:
S. H. Schneider and S. L. Thompson, "Simulating the Climatic Effects of Nuclear War," *Nature* 333 (1988): 223.

ECOTOPIA

The Ecotopian idea was first popularized in Ernest Callenbach's (1975) lively account, set in 1999, of a nation that had freed itself from the rest of the United States through nuclear blackmail. The setting is northern California, Oregon, and Washington; the politics and personal relationships are mellow, peaceful, and environmentally-benign. Its cities—with their mixes of shops, residences, and factories—remind one of Jane Jacobs' (1961) liveable urban places. Motor vehicles are not permitted in Ecotopia, but bicycles are freely available. Materials are recycled, and energy is supplied by direct solar radiation and massive heat exchangers that use sea water. The people are healthy; their air and water are free of toxins.

Several years after Callenbach, Joel Garreau (1981)—in his bestselling *Nine Nations of North America*—wrote of the Ecotopia shown in figure 18.3. His Ecotopia is bounded by the Coastal and Cascade mountain ranges but extends beyond Callenbach's spatial concept to include parts of British Columbia and Alaska. It is a biophysical region blessed with plentiful rainfall and abundant fish, forests, and agricultural lands. Garreau contends that the Ecotopian vision is indeed taking hold in the Pacific Northwest. And there is underlying truth to his hyperbolic account—as evidenced in Oregon's environmentally-progressive politics; California's energy policies; bicycle-friendly Davis, California; the environmentally-active residents of Bellingham, Washington, and Eugene, Oregon; and the other "mini-Ecotopias" throughout the region.

Where it happens first is of little consequence; Ecotopian ideals are achievable virtually anywhere. Indeed, Ectopian concepts have been promoted not just by Callenbach and Garreau, but by various utopian theorists, and recently in the writings of B. F. Schumacher (1973), who advocates locally-based, environmentally-sustainable economies; in Amory Lovins' (1977) renewable, small-scale "soft energy paths"; and in Herman Daly's (1980) steady-state economy. Recently, the "bioregionalist" vision has been advanced—one in which social organization is defined by biophysical boundaries (Sale 1985; Parsons 1985). And there are even fledgling signs that ecological thinking is penetrating traditional political circles. The EPA is cautiously promoting "ecoregional" water resources planning. The bioregion concept has been incorporated to varying degrees in park and natural areas planning (chapter 15). But in the final analysis its greatest advocates may be the citizens who organize to protect their own backyards. If enough of them make the conceptual leap that combines local action with "global thinking"—and, conversely, if Ecotopian visions find enough room for diverse social, political, and economic concerns—then at least one nation's prospects for an environmentally-sustainable future are considerably brightened.

Figure 18.3. Ecotopia.

Source:
J. Garreau, *The Nine Nations of North America* (Boston: Houghton Mifflin Company, 1981).

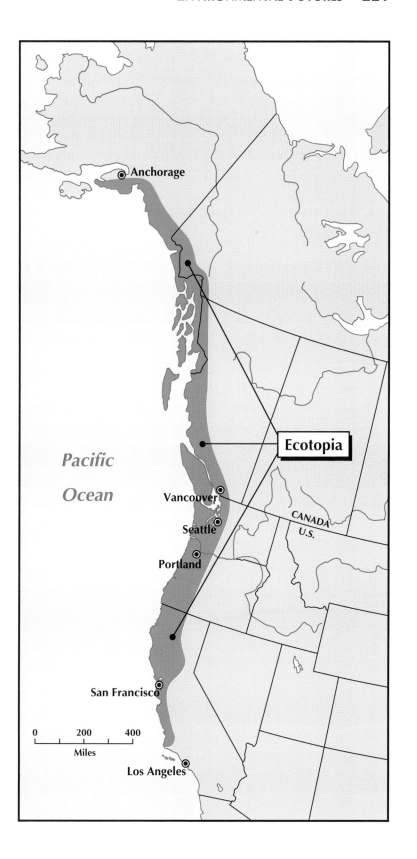

Appendix 1
Measurement Conversion

LINEAR

1 inch (in) = 2.54 centimeters (cm)
1 foot (ft) = 0.305 meter (m)
1 yard (yd) = 0.914 meter (m)
1 mile (mi) = 1.61 kilometers (km)
1 nautical mile = 1.15 miles (mi) = 1.85 kilometers (km)

1 millimeter (mm) = 0.039 inch (in)
1 centimeter (cm) = 0.394 inch (in)
1 meter (m) = 1.09 yards (yd)
1 kilometer (km) = 0.621 mile (mi)

AREA

1 square inch (in^2) = 6.452 square centimeters (cm^2)
1 square foot (ft^2) = 0.0929 square meter (m^2)
1 square yard (yd^2) = 0.836 square meter (m^2)
1 acre (ac) = 43,560 square feet (ft^2) = 0.405 hectares (ha) = 405 square meters (m^2)
1 square mile (mi^2) = 640 acres (ac) = 2.59 square kilometers (km^2)

1 square centimeter (cm^2) = 0.155 square inch (in^2)
1 square meter (m^2) = 10.76 square feet (ft^2) = 1.196 square yards (yd^2)
1 hectare (ha) = 10,000 square meters (m^2) = 2.471 acres (ac)
1 square kilometer (km^2) = 100 hectares (ha) = 0.386 square mile (mi^2) = 247 acres (ac)

VOLUME

1 cubic inch (in^3) = 16.387 cubic centimeters (cm^3)
1 cubic foot (ft^3) = 0.028 cubic meter (m^3)
1 cubic yard (yd^3) = 0.7646 cubic meter (m^3)
1 quart (qt) = 0.946 liter (l)
1 U.S. gallon (gal) = 3.785 liters (l) = 0.83 imperial gallon
1 acre foot = 325,851 U.S. gallons (gal) = 1,234,975 liters (l) = 1,234 cubic meters (m^3)

1 cubic centimeter (cm^3) = 0.061 cubic inch (in^3)
1 cubic meter (m^3) = 35.3 cubic feet (ft^3) = 1.30 cubic yards (yd^3)
1 milliliter (ml) = 0.034 fluid ounce (fl oz)
1 liter (l) = 1.06 quarts (qt) = 0.265 U.S. gallon (gal)

MASS

1 oz (oz) = 28.35 grams (g)
1 pound (lb) = 454 grams (g) = .0454 kilogram (kg)
1 ton = 2000 pounds (lb) = 907.18 kilograms (kg)

1 gram (g) = 0.035 ounce (oz)
1 milligram (mg) = 0.001 gram (g)
1 microgram (µg) = 0.000001 gram (g)
1 kilogram (kg) = 2.205 pounds (lb)
1 metric ton (mt) = 1,000 kilograms (kg) = 1.1 tons (t)

ENERGY AND POWER

1 watt-hour = 3,600 joules (J)
1 British thermal unit (BTU) = 252 calories (cal) = 1,055 joules (J) = 0.293 watt-hour
1 kilowatt-hour (kW-h) = 860 kilocalories (kcal) = 3,413 British thermal units (BTU)
1 quad (Q) = 1 quadrillion kilojoules (kJ) = 2.93 trillion kilowatt-hours (kW-h)

1 calorie (cal) = 4.184 joules (J)
1 kilojoule (kJ) = 0.949 British thermal unit (BTU) = 0.000278 kilowatt-hour (kW-h)
1 kilocalorie (kcal) = 3.97 British thermal units (BTU) = 0.00116 kilowatt-hours (kW-h)

1 barrel (bbl) crude oil = 42 U.S. gallons (gal) = 159 liters (l) = 6,000,000 kilojoules (kJ) = 2,000,000 kilocalories (kcal) = 6,000,000 British thermal units (BTU) = 0.3 kilowatt-hour (kW-h)

TEMPERATURE

Fahrenheit (°F) to Celsius (°C): $°C = \dfrac{(°F-32.0)}{1.80}$

Celsius (°C) to Fahrenheit (°F): $°F = (°C \times 1.80) + 32.0$

Appendix 2
Major U.S. Environmental Legislation

1785 LAND ORDINANCE
Provides for survey of federal lands into 640-acre (one-square-mile) sections. Townships are comprised of 36 sections.

1862 HOMESTEAD ACT
Grants settlers up to 160 acres of land if they live on and farm land for five years.

1862 MORRILL ACT
Grants 13 million acres to states, to be used to raise funds for agricultural and mechanical colleges.

1872 GENERAL MINING LAW
Allows prospectors to stake claims on federal lands and obtain complete ownership if discovery of a valuable mineral can be demonstrated.

1872 YELLOWSTONE PARK ACT
Sets aside Yellowstone as world's first national park.

1891 FOREST RESERVE ACT
Allows President to establish forest reserves (later National Forests) on federal lands.

1897 FOREST MANAGEMENT ACT
Articulates purposes of forest reserves (including water, timber) and authorizes Secretary of Interior to permit timber-cutting on reserves.

1899 RIVERS AND HARBORS APPROPRIATIONS ACT
Prohibits unauthorized discharge of refuse matter into navigable U.S. waters or their tributaries.

1900 LACEY ACT
Makes interstate shipment of wildlife killed in violation of state laws a federal offense.

1902 RECLAMATION (NEWLANDS) ACT
Creates Bureau of Reclamation (Department of Interior), initiates reclamation program, and limits amount of federal water that can be diverted by individual farmers (160 acres of irrigated lands).

1906 ANTIQUITIES ACT
Establishes federal role in historic preservation by creating system of national monuments.

1911 WEEKS ACT
Authorizes purchase of headwater forested lands for inclusion in National Forest System, facilitating creation of eastern national forests.

1916 NATIONAL PARKS ACT
Creates National Park System, and National Park Service as administering agency, for preservation of natural landscapes and associated wildlife, vegetation, and scenery.

1920 FEDERAL WATER POWER ACT
Authorizes Federal Power Commission to issue licenses for hydroelectric power development on federal lands.

1920 MINERAL LEASING ACT
Regulates mining on federal lands and opens unreserved public domain to oil and gas leasing.

1933 TENNESSEE VALLEY AUTHORITY ACT
Creates government corporation to plan for use, conservation, and development of natural resources of Tennessee River Basin area to benefit national social and economic welfare.

1934 TAYLOR GRAZING ACT
Regulates grazing on unreserved federal lands, establishing fee-based system of leasing.

1935 SOIL CONSERVATION ACT
Establishes soil conservation grant and loan programs, and creates Soil Conservation Service, which provides information and technical assistance to farmers.

1936 OMNIBUS FLOOD CONTROL ACT
Institutes national flood prevention program under Army Corps of Engineers and Department of Agriculture.

1937 PITTMAN-ROBERTSON FEDERAL AID IN WILDLIFE RESTORATION ACT
Authorizes excise tax on hunting equipment to provide funds to states for habitat conservation and management of game animals.

1938 FEDERAL FOOD, DRUG AND COSMETIC ACT
As amended, authorizes EPA and Department of Agriculture jointly to set tolerance levels for pesticide residues in foods (raw and processed) and feed crops, and specific labeling requirements for agricultural commodities

1948 WATER POLLUTION CONTROL ACT
(SEE ALSO 1956, 1972, 1977, 1987)
Authorizes federal research, surveys, and investigation regarding water pollution.

1950 DINGELL-JOHNSON ACT
Provides grants to states to assist in fish management.

1954 ATOMIC ENERGY ACT
Atomic Energy Commission created to foster development of commercial nuclear power industry and protect public from dangers of radioactivity.

1955 CLEAN AIR ACT
(SEE ALSO 1967, 1970, 1977)
Authorizes Public Health Service to conduct research and provide support to local agencies dealing with air quality.

1956 FEDERAL WATER POLLUTION CONTROL ACT
(SEE ALSO 1972, 1977, 1987)
Provides for federal enforcement of water-quality standards in cases of pollution of interstate and navigable waters where human health or welfare are endangered. Authorizes federal grants to municipalities for sewage treatment plant construction.

1956 INTERSTATE HIGHWAY ACT
Provides for extensive national network of limited-access highways, with 90 percent of the cost borne by the federal government.

1957 PRICE-ANDERSON ACT
Provides insurance protection for private industry, limiting its liability in case of nuclear power plant accidents.

1960 MULTIPLE USE-SUSTAINED YIELD ACT
Legislative endorsement of national forest multiple-use management policy (i.e., forests are managed for recreation, fish, wildlife, range, and other uses while at same time providing sustained high output of timber).

1964 LAND AND WATER CONSERVATION FUND ACT
Provides funds for local, state, and federal acquisition of lands for parks and open space.

1964 WILDERNESS ACT
Establishes system of wilderness preserves on federal lands, where human impacts are to be kept to absolute minimum.

1965 SOLID WASTE DISPOSAL ACT
(SEE ALSO 1970 RESOURCE RECOVERY ACT)
Precedes RCRA (1976). Initial focus on waste disposal, especially restriction of open burning.

1966 ENDANGERED SPECIES PRESERVATION ACT
(SEE ALSO 1973)

Establishes federal agency responsibilities for species conservation.

1966 NATIONAL HISTORIC PRESERVATION ACT
Authorizes Secretary of Interior to maintain national register of historic districts, sites, structures, and other objects. Provides grant funds for surveys, planning, acquisition, and preservation activities.

1966 NATIONAL WILDLIFE REFUGE SYSTEM ADMINISTRATION ACT
Expands National Wildlife Refuge System and provides for more multiple and public uses of refuges.

1966 WATER QUALITY ACT (AMENDMENTS TO FEDERAL WATER POLLUTION CONTROL ACT)
Expands grants for municipal wastewater treatment plants to $1 billion per year, and requires states to establish standards for all interstate and coastal pollution.

1967 AIR QUALITY ACT (AMENDMENTS TO CLEAN AIR ACT)
Provides for designation of air-quality control regions, setting of air-quality criteria, and issuance of standards for vehicles and stationary sources.

1968 NATIONAL FLOOD INSURANCE ACT
Combines federal flood insurance subsidies with requirements for state and local floodplain management. Amendments tighten requirements and change procedures.

1968 NATIONAL TRAILS SYSTEM ACT
Promotes development of national system of scenic, recreational, and historic trails.

1968 WILD AND SCENIC RIVERS ACT
Creates national system of rivers. Seeks to protect scenic, recreational, geologic, fish and wildlife, historic, cultural, and other values. Designated rivers are to be kept free-flowing, or minimally disturbed.

1969 FEDERAL COAL MINE HEALTH AND SAFETY ACT
Establishes mandatory health and safety standards and provides federal benefits to miners injured by inhalation of coal dust.

1969 NATIONAL ENVIRONMENTAL POLICY ACT (NEPA)
Statement of Congressional concern about environment. Requires "environmental impact statements" for proposals for "major federal action significantly affecting the quality of the human environment." Unanticipated result has been massive volumes of paperwork and much litigation.

1970 CLEAN AIR ACT AMENDMENTS
Sets strict timetable for automotive emission controls, and directs EPA to establish national ambient air quality standards for six pollutants, phase out lead in fuels, and regulate stationary sources and hazardous pollutants.

1970 OCCUPATIONAL SAFETY AND HEALTH ACT (OSHA)
Establishes workplace health and safety standards, with focus on certain toxic and hazardous substances.

1970 RESOURCE RECOVERY ACT
Amends 1965 Solid Waste Disposal Act. Administered by EPA. Provides funds for recycling and requires comprehensive investigation of hazardous waste management.

1971 ALASKA NATIVE CLAIMS SETTLEMENT ACT
Cedes 44 million acres (12 percent of Alaskan land) to native peoples, and makes reparations of $1 billion. In exchange, natives relinquish claims to lands not ceded.

1972 COASTAL ZONE MANAGEMENT ACT
Creates voluntary federal-state partnership, providing funds for states to develop coastal land-use planning programs. 1976 amendments authorize planning and project grants related to economic, social, and environmental impacts of energy developments.

1972 FEDERAL ENVIRONMENTAL PESTICIDE CONTROL ACT
(Renamed FEDERAL INSECTICIDE, FUNGICIDE, AND RODENTICIDE ACT, or FIFRA.)
Replaces FIFRA of 1947. Establishes EPA registration requirements for all pesticides, and authorizes EPA to cancel, suspend, or restrict use of existing or new pesticides. Manufacturers required to submit extensive data to EPA.

1972 FEDERAL WATER POLLUTION CONTROL ACT AMENDMENTS (FWPCA, OR CLEAN WATER ACT)
Sets 1983 goal of "fishable, swimmable" waters and 1985 goal of zero discharge of pollutants. Establishes permit system and associated requirements for municipal and industrial dischargers, calls for dischargers to use "best practical technology currently available" by 1977, and best available technology" by 1983. Expands construction grants program for local sewage treatment plants to $5 billion per year.

1972 MARINE MAMMAL PROTECTION ACT
Imposes moratorium on taking and import of marine mammals and products made from them.

1972 MARINE PROTECTION RESEARCH AND SANCTUARIES ACT
Regulates and/or prohibits ocean dumping and transportation of substances intended for ocean dumping—including sewage sludge, industrial waste, and radioactive waste (this section of the law also is known as the Ocean Dumping Act). Authorizes designation of marine sanctuaries, to be protected for environmental, aesthetic, and recreational purposes.

1972 NOISE CONTROL ACT
Authorizes EPA to regulate noise. Requires research, standard-setting, and product labelling.

1973 ENDANGERED SPECIES ACT
Requires listing of endangered and threatened species, empowers Fish and Wildlife Service to review and approve state and federal agency plans for recovery of endangered species, and provides financial assistance for state programs.

1973 NATIONAL HIGHWAY ACT
Permits cities to use federal highway funds for mass transit projects.

1974 ENERGY REORGANIZATION ACT
Institutes various regulatory and energy conservation measures. Abolishes Atomic Energy Commission, transferring regulation and licensing functions to the new Nuclear Regulatory Commission, and research and development to the Energy Research and Development Administration.

1974 FEDERAL NON-NUCLEAR ENERGY RESEARCH AND DEVELOPMENT ACT
Directs Department of Energy to conduct research emphasizing energy efficiency and conservation and renewable energy sources. In same year, Congress passes Federal Solar Energy Research Development and Demonstration Power Act and Solar Heating and Cooling Demonstration Act. In 1978, Solar Photovoltaic Energy Research Development and Demonstration Act is enacted.

1974 FOREST AND RANGELAND RENEWABLE RESOURCES PLANNING ACT (RPA)
Administered by Forest Service. Requires assessment of all renewable resources every 10 years, and programs for national forest management every five years. Promotes economically-rational commodity production decisions on public lands.

1974 SAFE DRINKING WATER ACT
Authorizes EPA to set standards and monitor for contaminants in drinking water. States and localities assume primary enforcement responsibilities. 1986 amendments expand protection of underground drinking water sources.

1975 EASTERN WILDERNESS ACT
Permits inclusion of eastern lands in National Wilderness Preservation System by lifting requirements that designated lands be at least 5000 acres in size and free of such alterations as roads.

1975 ENERGY POLICY AND CONSERVATION ACT
Establishes mandatory fuel economy standards for new automobiles.

1975 HAZARDOUS MATERIAL TRANSPORTATION ACT
Establishes preeminence of federal statute over state law in case of conflict over hazardous material transport.

1976 FEDERAL LAND POLICY AND MANAGEMENT ACT
Embraces notion of permanent federal ownership of most federal lands, mandates multiple-use management of federal lands, and recognizes environmental concerns. Provides for review of Bureau of Land Management lands for wilderness designation.

1976 NATIONAL FOREST MANAGEMENT ACT
Technically an amendment to the 1974 RPA, but in fact new legislation. Requires plans for national forests and creates mechanisms for resolving conflicts over multiple use. Endorses sustained-yield and even-flow timber management practices.

1976 RESOURCE CONSERVATION AND RECOVERY ACT (RCRA) (SEE ALSO 1984)
Initially oriented toward solid waste management and recycling, emphasis has shifted toward hazardous wastes. Encourages state solid waste management planning, regulates disposal facilities, requires "cradle to grave" tracking of hazardous wastes by EPA, and sets standards for hazardous waste treatment, storage, and disposal.

1976 TOXIC SUBSTANCES CONTROL ACT
Permits EPA to regulate manufacturing, use, and disposal of chemical substances. EPA may require chemical testing (at manufacturer's expense) and has power to ban or restrict chemicals.

1977 CLEAN AIR ACT AMENDMENTS
Creates new standards and compliance procedures, requires stationary sources to use "best available control technology" (BACT), sets ambient standards for several hazardous pollutants, and establishes programs to protect air quality in pristine regions.

1977 CLEAN WATER ACT AMENDMENTS
Expands regulation of toxic substances in water and extends some deadlines from 1972 law.

1977 EARTHQUAKE HAZARDS REDUCTION ACT
Empowers Federal Emergency Management Agency (FEMA) to coordinate federal, state, and local earthquake-related programs. Programs include earthquake prediction, building construction and design, and public education.

1977 SURFACE MINING CONTROL AND RECLAMATION ACT
Establishes permit system and bonding requirements for surface mining, requires reclamation of surface mines (fill mines, return ground to original contour, and restore vegetation and water quality), and prohibits surface mining in national parks, forests, and other federal and state-

designated areas. Primary implementation responsibility is with states.

1978 NATIONAL ENERGY CONSERVATION POLICY ACT
Calls for significant conversion to coal as an industrial energy source, increases natural gas prices (in part through phasing out federal price regulations), imposes a tax on inefficient automobiles ("gas guzzler" tax), provides solar and conservation tax credits for residences, requires utilities to offer basic conservation programs to customers, provides grants for home weatherization and for energy conservation in public buildings, requires the Department of Energy to set appliance efficiency standards, and mandates energy efficiency improvements in federal buildings.
   Other parts of the legislative package include the Public Utility Regulatory Policies Act (PURPA), which promotes industrial cogeneration of steam and electricity and requires utilities to buy electricity from independent producers at fair rates, and the Energy Tax Act, which provides residential and business tax credits for energy conservation.

1978 NATIONAL PARKS AND RECREATION ACT
Makes major additions to the Wild and Scenic Rivers System, National Trails System, and National Wilderness Preservation System.

1978 OUTER CONTINENTAL SHELF LANDS ACT
Declares that industry is liable for oil pollution on outer continental shelf and establishes compensation fund to meet liabilities.

1978 PORT AND TANKER SAFETY ACT
Covers oil and and other dangerous substances transported under U.S. jurisdiction. Regulation, licensing, and inspection under administration of Secretary of Transportation.

1978 PUBLIC RANGELANDS IMPROVEMENT ACT
Seeks to restore rangelands to earlier productivity.

1978 QUIET COMMUNITIES ACT
Extends and amends Noise Control Act of 1972, adding civil penalties for noise pollution, establishing standards for aircraft and commercial products, and developing national noise assessment program.

1978 URANIUM MILL TAILINGS CONTROL ACT
Establishes licensing program and monitoring, management, and remedial requirements for radioactive wastes from uranium mining. Department of Energy has responsibility for inactive sites; mine operators for active sites.

1979 STRATEGIC AND CRITICAL MINERALS STOCKPILING ACT
Recent effort in series of attempts to buffer against mineral shortages by stockpiling enough to see the nation through a three-year conventional war.

1980 ACID PRECIPITATION ACT
Encourages research into causes, sources, and impacts (physical, social, economic) of acid deposition.

1980 ACT TO PREVENT POLLUTION FROM SHIPS
Empowers U.S. government to ensure compliance with established pollution control procedures in the the event of an oil discharge from an American or foreign ship in U.S. waters.

1980 ALASKA NATIONAL INTEREST LANDS CONSERVATION ACT
Classifies huge areas of Alaskan federal domain for preservation, recreation, and resource management. Doubles total acreages of National Park and Wildlife Refuge systems and triples size of National Wilderness Preservation System.

1980 ASBESTOS SCHOOL HAZARD DETECTION AND CONTROL ACT
Establishes federal program for assessment and reduction of risks from asbestos in schools. Financial responsibilities fall mainly upon localities and states.

1980 COMPREHENSIVE ENVIRONMENTAL RESPONSE, COMPENSATION, AND LIABILITY ACT (SUPERFUND) (SEE ALSO 1986)
Establishes $1.6 billion trust fund to finance emergency cleanups of hazardous substances, as well as cleanup of abandoned hazardous waste sites. Authorizes EPA to recover costs from polluters.

1980 ENERGY LEGISLATION:
Series of laws enacted to promote development of new sources of energy. They include the Biomass

Energy and Alcohol Fuels Act, Gasohol Competition Act, Geothermal Energy Act, Magnetic Fusion Energy Engineering Act, Methane Transportation Research Development and Demonstration Act, Ocean Thermal Energy Conversion Act, Renewable Energy Resources Act, Solar Energy and Energy Conservation Act, Wind Energy Systems Act, Wood Residue Utilization Act, and Used Oil Recycling Act.

1980 ENERGY SECURITY ACT
Creates federal Synthetic Fuels Corporation, Solar Energy and Conservation Bank, and other incentives for energy development. Establishes minimum rate for filling Strategic Petroleum Reserve.

1980 FORSYTHE-CHAFEE ACT
Provides grants to states for conservation of nongame species of fish and wildlife.

1980 LOW LEVEL RADIOACTIVE WASTE POLICY ACT
Requires states to dispose of low-level nuclear wastes either within their own borders or by means of regional compacts.

1982 COASTAL BARRIER RESOURCES ACT
Prohibits federal loans, grants, flood insurance payments, and other subsidies for construction work on designated undeveloped portions of barrier islands.

1982 NUCLEAR WASTE POLICY ACT
Sets forth complex procedure for site selection for two facilities capable of isolating high-level radioactive waste for minimum of 10,000 years.

1982 RECLAMATION REFORM ACT
Expands acreage limitation for farms receiving federally subsidized irrigation water from 160 to 960 acres and asserts that additional water use is to be unsubsidized.

1984 RESOURCE CONSERVATION AND RECOVERY ACT AMENDMENTS
Emphasizes waste reduction, recycling, and new treatment methods for toxic materials. Establishes new technological requirements for disposal facilities, adds new regulations, and expands federal role generally.

1985 FOOD SECURITY ACT
Requires farmers to adopt conservation plans for highly erodible lands; establishes a conservation reserve program to remove highly erodible lands from production over the long term; and discourages farmers from converting wetlands to crops. Noncomplying farmers become ineligible for federal subsidy programs.

1986 ASBESTOS HAZARD EMERGENCY RESPONSE ACT
Requires inspection for and abatement of asbestos hazards in schools. Establishes federal standards, training, and certification programs for inspection and abatement.

1986 SUPERFUND AMENDMENTS AND REAUTHORIZATION ACT
Increases cleanup trust fund, established in 1980, to $8.5 billion, imposes new cleanup rules and schedules for Superfund abandoned hazardous waste sites, requires facilities to report routine and accidental toxic chemical releases and inventories, provides for public dissemination of toxics release data, and requires local emergency planning for emergencies involving hazardous substances.

1986 WATER RESOURCES DEVELOPMENT ACT
Seeks to shift financial and management burdens of water resources management away from federal government toward nonfederal interests and gives greater weight to environmental considerations.

1987 NATIONAL APPLIANCE ENERGY CONSERVATION ACT
Requires appliance manufacturers to lower energy consumption 25 percent by 1993.

1987 WATER QUALITY ACT
(AMENDMENTS TO 1977 CLEAN WATER ACT)
Replaces technology-based approach (basis for permits as established under 1972 Clean Water Act) with water-quality approach (i.e., do what is needed to restore waterways that remain polluted). Requires states to develop programs to control nonpoint-source pollution and to implement strategies for reducing discharges of toxic pollutants.

1988 OCEAN DUMPING REFORM ACT OF 1988
Bans ocean dumping of sewage sludge after 1991.

Glossary

ACID DEPOSITION. Precipitation, in either wet or dry form, of acids and acid-forming compounds. Often referred to as "acid rain." Key sources of acids are emissions of sulfur and nitrogen oxides.

ACID MINE DRAINAGE. Acidic runoff from active and abandoned mines, especially coal mines (sulfuric acid). Enters both surface and groundwater.

ACID NEUTRALIZING CAPACITY (ANC). Ability of waters and soils to absorb additional inputs of acidity.

ACTIVE INGREDIENT. Chemical ingredient that is biologically active. May affect humans, fish, wildlife, and vegetation.

ACTIVE SOLAR. Heating system in which air or a liquid is pumped through a solar collector. The captured heat is then stored, used to heat water, or used for space heating.

AEROBIC. Oxygen-consuming organism.

ANAEROBIC. Organism that does not require oxygen for survival.

ANTHRACITE. Coal with high heat value and low sulfur content.

AQUIFER. Underground layer of porous material (rock, gravel, sand) that stores water.

ARABLE. Land capable of producing crops when cultivated.

BARRIER ISLAND. Low narrow ridge, usually parallel to the coast, formed by deposition of sand and usually separated from mainland by sounds, bays, or lagoons.

BIOLOGICAL OXYBEN DEMAND (BOD). Amount of dissolved oxygen required for microorganisms to break down organic materials in a given volume of water over a given period of time (usually five days).

BIOMASS. Total dry weight of all organisms over a specific area; also refers to plant and animal wastes used as fuels.

BIOME. Large regional community with distinctive combination of climate, soil, and vegetation characteristics. Examples include deserts, tropical rainforests, tundra.

BITUMINOUS. Coal with high heat value.

BLAST. Destructive wave of compressed air that accompanies nuclear explosion or volcanic eruption. Volcanic blast usually contains hot rock, ash, and gases.

BRITISH THERMAL UNIT (BTU). Amount of heat required to raise temperature of one pound of water one degree Farenheit.

BUFFERING CAPACITY. Ability of waters or soils to absorb acids into solution without drastically affecting acidity. Determined by amount of buffering agent, such as limestone, that is present.

CAPITAL COSTS. Costs incurred in planning, design, and construction.

CARCINOGEN. Cancer-causing substance.

CHLOROFLUOROCARBONS (CFCs). Organic compounds consisting of carbon, chlorine, and fluorine atoms.

CLEARCUTTING. Cutting of all trees in an area. May result in soil erosion and habitat destruction.

COASTAL PLAIN. Area of low relief bounded seaward by the shore and landward by highlands. Formed by combination of marine and continental processes.

COASTAL ZONE. Coastal waters and adjacent lands. For purposes of state coastal zone planning, refers to those waters and lands specifically designated as the coastal zone.

COGENERATION. Simultaneous production of two useful forms of energy, such as electricity and steam, from the same process.

COMBINED SEWER OVERFLOW. Combined storm and sanitary drainage that exceeds capacity of a wastewater treatment plant. Overflow is discharged directly to surface water. Occurs during periods of heavy rain and runoff.

COMMERICAL TIMBERLAND. Forest land capable of producing more than 20 cubic feet per year of industrial wood in natural stands. Inaccessible areas, as well as areas legally or administratively withdrawn from harvesting, do not qualify.

COMPREHENSIVE PLAN. A plan that combines economic, demographic, and historical analysis with a prescription for an area's future. Usually covers land use, transportation, and recreational and other public facilities.

CONIFER. Needle-bearing tree, usually evergreen, that produces seeds in cones.

CONSERVATION. Philosophy that entails "wise use" of resources, so they are not unnecessarily depleted or degraded, and are available for future use.

CONSERVATION RESERVE PROGRAM (CRP). Component of the 1985 Food Security Act that provides payments to farmers to remove highly erodible croplands from production and put them into grass and tree cover for at least 10 years.

CONSERVATION TILLAGE. Farming practice that involves little or no disturbance of soil. Reduces soil erosion and saves energy, but often entails increased herbicide use.

CONSUMPTIVE USE. Use of water that makes it unavailable for immediate reuse, because of evapotranspiration, seepage, or other losses. Irrigation is a major consumptive use.

CONTINENTAL SHELF. Gently sloping submerged land extending from low-tide line to point where ocean bottom slopes more abruptly (the continental slope).

CRITERIA POLLUTANTS. See list of pollutants under "national ambient air quality standards"

CRITICAL MINERAL. Mineral important for defense and industry, for which U.S. has some domestic supplies or there are friendly nations that can supply the mineral in emergencies.

CRUDE OIL. Raw, liquid hydrocarbon with its various chemical impurities. Converted into various fuels and tar at refineries.

CULTURAL EUTROPHICATION. Overenrichment of an aquatic ecosystem with plant nutrients—mainly nitrates and phosphates—from such human activities as agriculture and municipal sewage treatment.

DECIDUOUS. Trees and shrubs that drop their leaves during part of the year.

DECIBEL (dB). measure of loudness. The decibel scale is logarithmic, which means that each 10 dB increase corresponds to a tenfold increase in loudness.

DIOXINS. Family of over 100 synthetic chlorinated hydrocarbons that are highly toxic at low doses. May cause cancer and birth defects in humans. Principal current use is in herbicides.

DISSOLVED OXYGEN (DO). Amount of oxygen dissolved in a given quantity of water at a specific temperature and atmospheric pressure. Expressed in parts per million. Used as water quality indicator.

DRY DEPOSITION. Atmospheric fallout, without aid of precipitation, of acidic molecules (mainly sulfates and nitrates).

EASEMENT. A legal restriction on what can be done on or with a piece of property.

ENDANGERED SPECIES. Species in imminent danger of becoming extinct.

EPA. United States Environmental Protection Agency. Mission is to control and abate air, water, and other types of environmental pollution. Created in 1970.

EROSION. Chemical, physical, biological, or geological breakdown of soil, and its removal by wind or water.

ESTUARY. Body of water, usually a bay or inlet, partially surrounded by land. Mixing zone for fresh and salt water. Among the most productive of ecosystem types.

EUTROPHIC. Body of water heavily enriched with plant nutrients, principally phosphates and nitrates.

EVAPOTRANSPIRATION. Combined processes of evaporation and transpiration of moisture from the earth's surface to the atmosphere. Transpiration is the transmission of water vapor from the leaves of plants.

EXCLUSIVE ECONOMIC ZONE (EEZ). The 200 miles of coastal waters adjacent to a nation, where—by international convention—that nation has exclusive control over such resources as fish and minerals.

EXPANSIVE SOILS. Soils that shrink and swell with changes in moisture content.

FEDERALISM. System of government that distributes power among central and constituent governments in a manner that seeks to protect existence and authority of both. Guiding principle of U.S. political system.

FLOODPLAIN. Flat, low-lying land adjacent to streams and rivers. Subject to periodic flooding.

FUNGICIDE. Substance used to eliminate or inhibit growth of nonphotosynthetic plants.

GREENHOUSE EFFECT. Gases—including carbon dioxide, methane, and nitrous oxide—intercept heat radiated by the earth and reradiate it toward earth, thus warming the lower atmosphere.

GREENLINE PARK. Relatively large area of land, in combination of public and private ownerships, overseen by local, state, and/or federal governments. Managed for recreational, scenic, environmental, and cultural purposes, with special attention to needs of park residents.

GROIN. Structure extending into water perpendicular to a coastline. Designed to create, expand, or inhibit erosion of beach.

GROSS NATIONAL PRODUCT (GNP). Value of all final goods and services produced in an economy during a year.

GROUND FAILURE. Tendency of land surface to give way or slide under stress from tectonic or other forces.

GROUNDWATER. Subsurface water located in voids in rock and soil.

GULLY EROSION. Removal of soil sufficient to create small channels or ravines.

HARDWOOD. Usually a broad-leaved deciduous tree.

HAZARDOUS SUBSTANCE. Chemical compound that may seriously harm humans or ecosystems, even in small quantities.

HERBICIDE. Chemical used to eradicate or inhibit growth of undesirable plants.

HURRICANE. Intense tropical storm with heavy rains, low central barometric pressure, and sustained winds of at least 75 miles per hour.

IDENTIFIED RESOURCE. Deposits of a resource whose location, grade, quality, and quantity are known

or have been estimated from specific geologic evidence.

INSECTICIDE. Chemical used to eradicate or control insects.

INSTREAM USE. Water use within a stream channel for such purposes as power generation, navigation, and recreation.

INTERATED PEST MANAGEMENT. Combination of chemical (pesticides), biological (predators, parasites, pathogens), and cultivation methods to control pest populations.

ISOHYET. Line connnecting points that receive equal amounts of precipitation.

JETTY. Structure(s) at entrance to a bay or inlet designed to protect shoreline and limit sand deposition in channel.

KÖPPEN. Climate classification system developed in 1918 by Wladimir Köppen. Based on average monthly temperature and precipitation. Has been modified several times.

LAND TRUST. Private, nonprofit organization that acquires land or easements for such purposes as ecological preservation, farmland protection, or provision of open space.

LANDSLIDE. Sudden, large-scale ground failure that results in a destructive flow of rock, soil, water, and other rubble. May be triggered by earthquakes, volcanic eruptions, or heavy rainfall.

LEEWARD. Location facing the direction toward which the wind blows.

LIGNITE. Soft coal with low heat value.

LIQUEFACTION. Loosening of tension between surface rock and/or soil particles that causes those materials to behave like a liquid. Induced by earthquakes or heavy rains.

LONG-RANGE TRANSPORT. Atmospheric transport of pollutants over long distances. Often refers to

transport of sulfur and nitrogen compounds implicated in acid deposition.

MEDITERRANEAN CLIMATE. Climate type marked by hot, dry summers and cool, wet winters. Occurs in areas bordering Mediterranean Sea and west coast areas of continents, centered around 35 degrees latitude.

MEGALOPOLIS. Coalescence of two or more cities along a connecting corridor. Originally reference was to the urbanized corridor connecting Boston and Washington, DC.

MESOTROPHIC. Body of water moderately enriched with nutrients, principally phosphates and nitrates.

MULTIPLE USE. Public land management philosophy that embraces diversity of uses, including timber, recreation, wilderness, and habitat preservation. Guiding concept in national forest management.

MUTAGEN. Substance that produces or accelerates inheritable genetic change.

NATIONAL AMBIENT AIR QUALITY STANDARDS (NAAQS). Maximum allowable concentrations in outside (ambient) air for particulates, sulfur dioxide, carbon monoxide, nitrogen dioxide, ozone, lead.

NONATTAINMENT AREA. Area designated by the EPA for its failure to meet ambient air quality standard.

NATIONAL FLOOD INSURANCE PROGRAM (NFIP). Federal program, initiated in 1968, that combines insurance subsidies with requirements for state and local floodplain management.

NONPOINT SOURCE. Pollution over a large area whose source is not readily identifiable. Examples include agricultural and urban runoff.

NONRENEWABLE. Resource whose supply is finite, or that is replaced on a time scale incommensurate with human time scales.

NUTRIENT. Chemical essential for the growth and reproduction of terrestrial and aquatic plants.

OFFSTREAM USE. Water withdrawn or diverted from ground or surface water sources for such uses as irrigation and public water supply.

OLD-GROWTH FOREST. Uncut forest whose trees may be hundreds or even thousands of years old. Found primarily in limited parts of West Coast region and Alaska.

OLD SCRAP. Scrap metal contained in discarded products.

OLIGOTROPHIC. Body of water with low levels of nutrients, principally phosphates and nitrates.

OPERATING COSTS. Costs incurred in the day-to-day functioning of a process or activity.

ORGANIC COMPOUND. Molecule that contains carbon atoms.

OSHA. U.S. Occupational Safety and Health Administration. Regulates health and safety in the workplace.

OUTER CONTINENTAL SHELF (OCS). The part of the continental shelf beyond the line marking state ownership; these offshore lands are under federal jurisdiction.

OXYGEN-DEPLETING WASTE. Organic material whose decomposition is accomplished by aerobic bacteria.

OZONE LAYER. Layer in stratosphere with relatively high concentrations of ozone. Filters harmful ultraviolet solar radiation.

PASSIVE SOLAR. Heating system which uses direct sunlight for space heating. Generally does not require such equipment as collectors and fans.

PASTURELAND. Lands where native grasses and forbs predominate, as well as lands planted in domesticated grasses and forbs.

PATENT. Document transferring federal lands to private, state, or other ownership.

PERCOLATION. Downward movement of water through soil.

PESTICIDE. Any substance used to kill or restrict populations of organisms undesirable to humans.

pH. Indicates relative acidity or alkalinity of substances on a scale of 0 to 14, based on presence of hydrogen ions. Seven is neutral; lower numbers are more acidic, and higher numbers more alkaline.

PICOCURIE. Measure of radiation equal to one-trillionth of a curie. One curie is the unit quantity of radon that in radioactive equilibrium contains one gram of radon.

POINT SOURCE. Easily identified source of pollution, such as a smokestack, pipe, or drainage ditch.

PRECURSOR. Chemical substance from which another substance is formed.

PRESERVATION. Philosophy whereby valued natural areas are set aside, with human use limited to education, research, and perhaps low-intensity recreation.

PRIMARY SEWAGE TREATMENT. Mechanical process that uses screens and sedimentation tanks to filter and settle solid particles from raw sewage. Removes 30 to 50 percent of solids, producing sludge as a byproduct.

PRIME CROPLAND. Farmland with the best physical and chemical characteristics for producing crops. Usually characterized by low erosiveness, good drainage, lack of stones, and favorable climate conditions.

QUAD. Energy unit equal to one quadrillion British thermal units.

RANGELAND. Land supportive of grazing or browsing animals, such as cattle, sheep, and goats. Vegetation consists mainly of grasses and shrubs.

RECHARGE. Replacement of groundwater through percolation, surface water infiltration, or replenishment from another subsurface source.

RECYCLING. Reincorporation of discarded materials into the production stream. Glass, aluminum, and paper are the main consumer wastes recycled.

REFUSE-DERIVED FUEL. Burnable fuel created from the organic residue of solid waste.

RENEWABLE. Resource that replenishes itself through physical, chemical, or ecological processes. Solar energy, forests, and groundwater are examples. May be depleted through rapid use.

RESERVES. The part of an identified resource that meets specific economic and technological criteria for feasibility of extraction.

RESOURCE. Material extracted from the environment to satisfy human needs or desires.

REUSE. Use of a product, such as glass bottles, again and again.

RICHTER SCALE. Scale that indicates earthquake intensity. Each increase of one is equivalent to a 30-fold increase in energy released by an earthquake's motion.

RILL EROSION. Removal of topsoil by water creating and flowing through series of tiny "valleys."

RUNOFF. Flow of water over the earth's surface.

SEAWALL. Solid barrier used to break waves in effort to protect beaches.

SECONDARY SEWAGE TREATMENT. Second step in sewage treatment, following primary treatment. Aerobic bacteria decompose up to 90 percent of oxygen-demanding wastes. Produces sludge as byproduct.

SELECTIVE CUTTING. Planned, restricted removal of trees of specific ages, sizes, or health, either singly or in groups. Objective is to maintain diverse, uneven stand of trees.

SHEET EROSION. Removal by running water or wind of layers of topsoil.

SKYGLOW. Light from urban areas that obscures the view of the night sky.

SLUDGE. Semisolid byproduct of sewage treatment process.

SMOG. Originally used to describe combination of smoke and fog; now refers to various combinations of pollutants in the atmosphere.

SOFTWOOD. Coniferous tree, usually evergreen.

SOIL CONSERVATION SERVICE (SCS). Agency within U.S. Department of Agriculture that provides farmers with information and technical assistance on soil capabilities and conservation.

SOURCE SEPARATION. Household separation of solid waste into various components, usually paper, glass, metal, and plastic. Separated materials are collected for recycling or reuse.

STORM SURGE. Wind-driven "wall" of water that accompanies landfall of a hurricane or other tropical disturbance.

STRATEGIC MINERAL. Mineral which must be imported, essential for defense and industry.

SUBSIDENCE. Vertical settling of the earth's surface that is induced by natural processes and/or such human activities as underground mining and excessive withdrawal of groundwater.

SUCCESSION. One community of plants and animals replacing another in a given area. May lead to a stable climax community.

SUNBELT. The southern part of the U.S., which has experienced marked population and economic growth over the past two to three decades. Specific definitions vary, but Census Bureau includes North Carolina, South Carolina, Georgia, Florida, Tennessee, Alabama, Mississippi, Arkansas, Louisiana, Oklahoma, Texas, New Mexico, Arizona, southern California, and Hawaii.

SURFACE WATER. Water at earth's surface in form of lakes, reservoirs, streams, rivers, and wetlands.

SUSPENDED SOLIDS. Fine materials carried by water. Contribute to water's cloudiness or turbidity.

SUSTAINED YIELD. Rate at which a resource, especially timber, can be used without exceeding its ability to renew itself.

SYNERGISTIC. Two or more factors interacting to produce effect greater than the sum of the factors working separately. Refers especially to chemical interactions.

SYNTHETIC FUELS (synfuels). Liquid or gaseous fuels produced from coal, oil shale, or other organic materials.

T-VALUE. Maximum amount of soil loss that can be incurred without loss of soil productivity. Expressed as tons/acre/year.

TAILINGS. Residual waste products of mining and mineral processing.

TEMPERATURE INVERSION. Entrapment of layer of cool, dense air under layer of less dense warmer air. Pollutants may be trapped in inversion layer.

TERATOGEN. Substance that causes fetal physical or mental defects.

TERTIARY SEWAGE TREATMENT. Third stage of sewage treatment, following primary and secondary treatment. Uses specialized physical and chemical processes to remove additional nutrients and organic and inorganic chemicals.

THREATENED SPECIES. Species that is still abundant in at least part of its range, but likely to become endangered.

TOLERANCE LEVELS. Legal limits to pesticide, drug, or other chemical concentrations in food products.

TORNADO. Small, extremely violent storm with whirling vortex, visible funnel from cloud to ground, and highly destructive winds.

TOXIC SUBSTANCE. Chemical compound that may seriously harm humans or ecosystems, even in small quantities.

TRANSFER OF DEVELOPMENT RIGHTS. Method of land protection that permits public purchase of the right to develop private land. Development rights may be transferred to other lands considered more suitable for development.

TROPICAL CYCLONE. Large storm system originating in tropics or subtropics, characterized by heavy rains, high potential for destruction, and often-erratic behavior.

TURBIDITY. Measure of the transparency or cloudiness of water based on the amount and type of suspended solids and organisms present.

TSUNAMI. Rapidly-moving ocean wave induced by earthquake activity. Capable of great destruction along coasts. Often referred to mistakenly as a "tidal wave."

UNIDENTIFIED RESOURCE. Resource that is believed but not proven to exist.

VADOSE ZONE (ZONE OF AERATION). Upper part of ground, where varying amounts of moisture are contained in pore spaces of soil and/or rock.

VOLATILE. Readily vaporized at relatively low temperatures.

WASTE REDUCTION. Method of extending resource supplies, conserving energy, and limiting environmental degradation by using resources more efficiently.

WETLAND. Land that retains fresh or salt water all or part of the year. Water-tolerant vegetation rises above water level.

WIND EROSION. Removal of dry, unconsolidated topsoil by wind.

WINDWARD. Location facing direction from which the wind comes.

ZONING. Application of land-use regulations to designated parcels of land. Type and density of development generally are regulated.

Bibliography

COMMON ACRONYMS

BLM   U.S. Bureau of Land Management
CBO   Congressional Budget Office
DOE   U.S. Department of Energy
EPA   U.S. Environmental Protection
       Agency
FWS   U.S. Fish and Wildlife Service
GAO   General Accounting Office
GPO   Government Printing Office
NOAA   National Oceanic and
       Atmospheric Administration
NRDC   Natural Resources Defense
       Council
NPS   National Park Service
NTIS   National Technical Information
       Service
OTA   Office of Technology Assessment
       (U.S. Congress)
SCS   Soil Conservation Service
USDA   U.S. Department of Agriculture
USGS   U.S. Geological Survey

1 INTRODUCTION (INCLUDES PUBLICATIONS OF BROAD SCOPE)

Benner, C. F. 1983. *Conservation and Management of Natural Resources in the United States*. New York: Wiley.

Black, P. E. 1988. *Conservation of Water and Related Land Resources*. 2d ed. Savage, MD: Rowman & Littlefield.

Conservation Foundation. 1987. *State of the Environment: A View Toward the Nineties*. Washington, DC: CF.

Council on Environmental Quality. *Annual Report*. Washington, DC: GPO.

———. 1989. *Environmental Trends*. Washington, DC: GPO.

Council on Environmental Quality and U.S. Department of State. 1980. *The Global 2000 Report to the President*. 3 vol. Washington, DC: GPO.

Cunningham, W. P., and B. W. Saigo. 1990. *Environmental Science: A Global Concern*. Dubuque, IA: Wm. C. Brown.

EPA. 1980. *Environmental Outlook 1980*. EPA-600/8-80-003. Washington, DC: EPA.

———. 1988. *Environmental Progress and Challenges: EPA's Update*. EPA-230-07-88-033. Washington, DC: GPO.

Freedman, W. 1987. *Federal Statutes on Environmental Protection*. New York: Quorum.

Gilpin, A. 1986. *Environmental Planning: A Condensed Encyclopedia*. Park Ridge, NJ: Noyes Publications.

Goldfarb, T. D. 1989. *Taking Sides: Clashing Views on Controversial Environmental Issues*. 3d ed. Guilford, CT: Dushkin.

Hays, S. P. 1959. *Conservation and the Gospel of Efficiency: The Progressive Conservation Movement 1890–1920*. Cambridge, MA: Harvard University Press.

———. 1987. *Beauty, Health, and Permanence: Environmental Politics in the United States: 1955–1985*. New York: Cambridge University Press.

Klee, G. J. 1990. *Conservation of Natural Resources*. Englewood Cliffs, NJ: Prentice-Hall.

Kupchella, C. E., and M. C. Hyland. 1989. *Environmental Science*. 2d ed. Boston: Allyn and Bacon.

Little, D. L., R. E. Dils, and J. Gray. 1982. *Renewable Natural Resources: A Management Handbook for the 1980s*. Boulder, CO: Westview.

Miller, G. T., Jr. 1990. *Living in the Environment*. 6th ed. Belmont, CA: Wadsworth.

Nash, R. F., ed. 1990. *American Environmentalism: Readings in Conservation History*. 3d ed. New York: McGraw-Hill.

Petulla, J. M. 1988. *American Environmental History*. 2d ed. Columbus, OH: Merrill.

Renew America. Annual. *The State of the States*. Washington, DC: Renew America.

Sampson, R. N., and D. Hair, eds. 1990. *Natural Resources for the 21st Century*. Washington, DC: Island Press.

Watson, J. W., and T. O'Riordan, eds. 1976. *The American Environment: Perceptions and Policies*. London: Wiley.

Zelinsky, W. 1973. *The Cultural Geography of the United States*. Englewood Cliffs, NJ: Prentice-Hall.

2 PHYSICAL AND POLITICAL OVERVIEW

Atwood, W. W. 1940. *The Physiographic Provinces of North America*. Boston: Ginn.

Beale, C. L. 1982. "The Population Turnaround in Rural and Small Town America." *Policy Studies Review* 2: 43–54.

Birdsall, S. S., and J. W. Florin. 1985. *Regional Landscapes of the United States and Canada*. 3d ed. New York: Wiley.

Bradshaw, M. 1988. *Regions and Regionalism in the United States*. Jackson, MS: University of Mississippi Press.

Campbell, R. R., and L. Garkovich. 1984. "Turnaround Migration as an Episode of Collective Behavior." *Rural Sociology* 49: 89–105.

Fenneman, N. M. 1928. "Physiographic Divisions of the United States." *Annals of*

the Association of American Geographers 18: 261–353.

Garrison, G. A., et al. 1977. *Vegetation and Environmental Features of Forest and Range Ecosystems*. USDA Agriculture Handbook No. 475. Washington, DC: GPO.

Gastil, R. D. 1975. *Cultural Regions of the United States*. Seattle: University of Washington Press.

Gottmann, J. 1961. *Megalopolis: The Urbanized Northeastern Seaboard of the United States*. Cambridge, MA: MIT Press.

Hammond, E. H. 1964. "Analysis of Properties in Land Form Geography: An Application to Broad-Scale Land Form Mapping." *Annals of the Association of American Geographers* 54: 11–23.

Hunt, C. B. 1974. *Natural Regions of the United States and Canada*. San Francisco: W. H. Freeman.

Jackson, K. T. 1985. *Crabgrass Frontier: The Suburbanization of the United States*. New York: Oxford University Press.

Knox, P. L. 1988. *The United States: A Contemporary Human Geography*. Essex, UK: Longman.

Kuchler, A. W. 1975. *Potential Natural Vegetation of the Conterminous United States*. New York: American Geographical Society.

Lichter, D. T., G. V. Fuguitt, and T. B. Heaton. 1985. "Components of Nonmetropolitan Population Change: The Contribution of Rural Areas." *Rural Sociology* 50: 88–98.

Lobeck, A. K. 1922. *Physiographic Diagram of the United States*. Madison, WI: Wisconsin Geographical Press.

Long, L., and Diana DeAre. 1988. "US Population Redistribution: A Perspective on the Nonmetropolitan Turnaround." *Population and Development Review* 14: 433–449.

O'Hare, W. P. 1988. *The Rise of Poverty in Rural America*. Washington, DC: Population Reference Bureau.

Paterson, J. H. 1989. *North America: A Geography of the United States and Canada*. 8th ed. New York: Oxford University Press.

Pierce, N. and J. Hagstrom. 1983. *The Book of America: Inside the Fifty States Today*. New York: Norton.

Powell, J. W. 1895. *Physiographic Regions of the United States*. New York: American Book Company.

Starsinic, D. E., and R. L. Forstall. 1989. *Patterns of Metropolitan Area and County Population Growth: 1980 to 1987*. Bureau of the Census Current Population Reports, Series P-25, No. 1039. Washington, DC: GPO.

USGS. 1970. *The National Atlas of the United States*. Washington, DC: USGS.

Vankat, J. L. 1979. *The Natural Vegetation of North America: An Introduction*. New York: Wiley.

3 THE AMERICAN LAND

Andrews, R. N. L., ed. 1979. *Land in America: Commodity or Natural Resource?* Lexington, MA: Lexington Books.

Armstrong, R. W., ed. 1983. *Atlas of Hawaii*. 2d ed. Honolulu: University of Hawaii Press.

Arrandale, T. 1983. *The Battle for Natural Resources*. Washington, DC: Congressional Quarterly Inc.

Baldwin, M., et al. 1985. "The Great Public Lands Debate." *American Land Forum* 5(1): 15–22.

Bosselman, F., and Callies, D. 1971. *The Quiet Revolution in Land Use Control*. Prepared for Council on Environmental Quality. Washington, DC: GPO.

Brower, D., and D. Carol, eds. 1987. *Managing Land-Use Conflicts: Case Studies in Special Area Management*. Durham, NC: Duke University Press.

Callies, D. L. 1984. *Regulating Paradise: Land Use Controls in Hawaii*. Honolulu: University of Hawaii Press.

Campbell, F., and J. Wald. 1989. *Areas of Critical Environmental Concern: Promise vs. Reality*. New York: NRDC.

Churchill, W. 1986. "American Indian Lands: The Native Ethic Amid Resource Development." *Environment* 28(6): 12–17, 28–34.

Clawson, M. 1972. *America's Land and Its Uses*. Baltimore: Johns Hopkins.

Clawson, M. 1983. *The Federal Lands Revisited*. Washington, DC: Resources for the Future.

Cooper, G., and G. Daws. 1985. *Land and Power in Hawaii: The Democratic Years*. Honolulu: Benchmark.

Creighton, T. H. 1978. *The Lands of Hawaii: Their Use and Misuse*. Honolulu: University Press of Hawaii.

Culhane, P. C. 1981. *Public Lands Politics*. Baltimore: Resources for the Future.

DeGrove, J. M. 1984. *Land, Growth and Politics*. Chicago: American Planning Association.

de Neufville, J. I., ed. 1981. *The Land Use Policy Debate in the United States*. New York: Plenum.

Fairfax, S. K., and C. E. Yale. 1987. *Federal Lands: A Guide to Planning, Management,*

and State Revenues. Washington, DC: Island Press.

Foss, P. O., ed. 1987. *Federal Lands Policy*. New York: Greenwood Press.

Francis, J. G., and R. Ganzel. 1984. *Western Public Lands: The Management of Natural Resources in a Time of Declining Federalism*. Totowa, NJ: Rowman & Allenheld.

Frey, H. T., and R. W. Hexam. 1982. *Major Uses of Land in the United States*. USDA Agricultural Economic Report No. 535. Washington, DC: GPO.

Geisler, C. C., and F. J. Popper, eds. 1984. *Land Reform, American Style*. Totowa, NJ: Rowman & Allenheld.

Godschalk, D. R. 1987. "Balancing Growth with Critical Area Programs: The Florida and Chesapeake Bay Cases." *Urban Land* 46(3): 16–19.

Healy, R. G., and J. S. Rosenberg. 1979. *Land Use and the States*. 2d ed. Baltimore: Johns Hopkins.

House of Representatives. 1986. *Oversight Hearing on Agricultural Drainage in the San Joaquin Valley, California*. Before a subcommittee of the Committee on Interior and Insular Affairs, No. 99–28. 99th Congress, 1st session.

Jackson, R. J. 1981. *Land Use in America*. New York: Wiley.

King, J. F., ed. 1988. *Sierra*. (Special Issue on U.S. Public Lands). 74(5).

Lewis, J. A. 1980. *Landownership in the United States, 1978*. Information Bulletin No. 435. Washington, DC: USDA.

Linowes, R. R., and D. T. Allensworth, D. T. 1975. *The States and Land-Use Control*. New York: Praeger.

Mandelker, D. R. 1976. *Environmental and Land Controls Legislation*. Indianapolis: Bobbs-Merrill.

Moss, E., ed., for NRDC. 1977. *Land Use Controls in the United States: A Handbook on the Legal Rights of Citizens*. New York: Dial Press/James Wade.

O'Dell, R. 1986. "Alaska: A Frontier Divided." *Environment* 28(7): 10–15, 34–37.

Platt, R. H., and Macinko, G. eds. 1983. *Beyond the Urban Fringe: Land Use Issues of Nonmetropolitan America*. Minneapolis: University of Minnesota Press.

Popper, F. J. 1981a. *The Politics of Land-Use Reform*. Madison, WI: University of Wisconsin Press.

———. 1981b. "Why We Should Care Who Owns the Land: A Background Paper." *American Land Forum* 2(1): 15–19.

———. 1984. "The Timely End of the Sagebrush Rebellion." *The Public Interest* 76: 61–73.

———. 1988. "Understanding American Land Use Regulation Since 1970: A Revisionist Interpretation." *Journal of the American Planning Association* 54: 291-301.

Ridley, S. 1988. *The State of the States: 1988*. Washington, DC: Fund for Renewable Energy and the Environment.

Rosenbaum, N. 1976. *Land Use and the Legislatures: The Politics of State Innovation*. Washington, DC: The Urban Institute.

Short, C. B. 1988. *Ronald Reagan and the Public Lands: America's Conservation Debate, 1979–1984*. College Station, TX: Texas A&M University Press.

SCS. 1981. *Land Resource Regions and Major Land Resource Areas of the United States*. Washington, DC: SCS.

———. 1987. *Basic Statistics: 1982 National Resources Inventory*. Statistical Bulletin No. 756. Ames, IA: Iowa State University Statistical Laboratory.

Watkins, T. H., ed. 1983. "The National Resource Lands of the BLM." *Wilderness*. (Special issue). 47(163).

Wilderness Society. 1989. *Failure in the Desert*. San Francisco: Wilderness Society.

Wolf, P. 1981. *Land in America: Its Value, Use and Control*. New York: Pantheon.

4 AGRICULTURAL LANDS

Batie, S. S. 1983. *Soil Erosion: Crisis in America's Croplands?* Washington, DC: Conservation Foundation.

———. 1985. "Soil Conservation in the 1980s: A Historical Perspective." *Agricultural History* 59: 107–123.

Bills, N. L., and R. E. Heimlich. 1984. *Assessing Erosion on U.S. Cropland: Land Management and Physical Features*. USDA AER-513. Washington, DC: GPO.

Brown, L. R. 1988. "Breakthrough on Soil Erosion." *World Watch* 1(3): 19–25, 42.

Bureau of the Census. 1985. *Graphic Summary of the 1982 Census of Agriculture*. Washington, DC: GPO.

———. 1986. *1984 Farm and Ranch Irrigation Survey*. Washington, DC: Bureau of the Census.

Candee, H., and L. B. King. 1987. *The Broken Promise of Reclamation Reform*. San Francisco: NRDC.

Concern, Inc. 1988. *Farmland: A Community Issue*. Washington, DC: Concern, Inc.

Conservation Technology Information Center. 1988. *1987 National Survey: Conservation Tillage Practices*. West Lafayette, IN.: CTIC.

Cook, K. A. 1987. *American Agriculture at the Crossroads: A Conservation Assessment of the 1985 Food Security Act*. Ankeny, IA: Soil and Water Conservation Society.

Crosson, P. R., and S. Brubaker. 1982. *Resource and Environmental Effects of U.S. Agriculture*. Washington, DC: Resources for the Future.

Crosson, P. R., and A. T. Stout. 1983. *Productivity Effects of Cropland Erosion in the United States*. Washington, DC: Resources for the Future.

Dallavalle, R. S., and L. V. Mayer. 1980. *Soil Conservation in the United States: The Federal Role*. CRS Report 80-144S. Washington, DC: Congressional Research Service.

Doherty, J. C. 1985. "The Urbanizing Countryside." *American Land Forum* 1(1): 49–53.

Editorial Research Reports. 1988. *How the U.S. Got Into Agriculture and Why It Can't Get Out*. Washington, DC: Congressional Quarterly.

Feder, G. L. 1986. "Environmental Influence of Selenium in Waters of the Western United States." In USGS, *United States Geological Survey Yearbook, Fiscal Year 1985*. Washington, DC: GPO.

Frederick, K. D. 1988. "Irrigation Under Stress." *Resources* 91: 1–4.

Furuseth, O. J. 1982. "Agricultural Land Conversion: Background and Issues." *Journal of Geography* 81: 84–93.

Furuseth, O. J. and J. T. Pierce. 1982a. "A Comparative Analysis of Farmland Preservation Programmes in North America." *Canadian Geographer* 26: 191–206.

———. 1982b. *Agricultural Land in an Urban Society*. Washington, DC: Association of American Geographers.

Galston, W.A. 1985. *A Tough Row to Hoe: The 1985 Farm Bill and Beyond*. Lanham, MD: Hamilton Press.

Gersmehl, P. J. 1978. "No Till Farming: The Regional Applicability of a Revolutionary Agricultural Technology." *Geographical Review* 68: 66–79.

Glaser, L. K. 1986. *Provisions of the Food Security Act of 1985*. Agriculture Informa-

tion Bulletin No. 498. Washington, DC: USDA.

Gregor, H. F. 1982. *Industrialization of U.S. Agriculture: An Interpretive Atlas*. Boulder, CO: Westview.

Gustafson, G. C., and N.L. Bills. 1984. *U.S. Cropland, Urbanization, and Landownership Patterns*. USDA. Washington, DC: GPO.

Halbach, D. W., C. F. Runge, and W. E. Larson, eds. 1987. *Making Soil and Water Conservation Work*. Ankeny, IA: Soil and Water Conservation Society of America.

Harlin, J. M., and G. M. Berardi, eds. 1987. *Agricultural Soil Loss: Processes, Policies, and Prospects*. Boulder, CO: Westview.

Held, R. B., and M. Clawson. 1965. *Soil Conservation in Perspective*. Baltimore: Johns Hopkins.

Lee, L. K. 1984. "Land Use and Soil Loss: A 1982 Update." *Journal of Soil and Water Conservation* 39(11): 226–228.

Little, C. E. 1987. *Green Fields Forever: The Conservation Tillage Revolution in America*. Washington, DC: Island Press.

Lockeretz, W. 1987. *Sustaining Agriculture Near Cities*. Ankeny, IA: Soil and Water Conservation Society.

Morgan, R., ed. 1981. *Soil Conservation: Problems and Prospects*. New York: Wiley.

National Research Council. 1986. *Soil Conservation*. 2 vol. Washington, DC: National Academy Press.

Paddock, J., et al. 1987. *Soil and Survival: Land Stewardship and the Future of American Agriculture*. San Francisco: Sierra Club Books.

Phillips, R. E., and S. E. Phillips. 1984. *No-Tillage Agriculture: Principles and Practices*. New York: Van Nostrand Reinhold.

Pierce, J. T., and O. J. Furuseth. 1986. "Constraints to Expanded Food Production: A North American Perspective." *Natural Resources Journal* 26: 15–39.

Risser, J. 1981. "A Renewed Threat of Soil Erosion: It's Worse than the Dust Bowl." *Smithsonian* 11(12): 120–131.

San Joaquin Valley Drainage Program. 1987. *Developing Options: An Overview of Efforts to Solve Agricultural Drainage and Drainage-Related Problems in the San Joaquin Valley*.

Schmude, K. O. 1977. "A Perspective on Prime Farmland." *Journal of Soil and Water Conservation* 32: 240–242.

Schneider, K. 1985. "Crisis at Kesterson." *Amicus Journal* 7(4): 22–27.

Schnepf, M., ed. 1979. *Farmland, Food, and the Future*. Ankeny, Iowa: Soil Conservation Society of America.

———, ed. 1988. *Journal of Soil and Water Conservation*. (Special Issue on the Food Security of 1985). 43(1).

Schroeder, R. A., D. U. Palawski, and J. P. Skorupa. *Reconnaissance Investigation of Water Quality, Bottom Sediment, and Biota Associated with Irrigation Drainage in the Tulare Lake Bed Area, Southern San Joaquin Valley, California, 1986–87*. Water Resources Investigations Report 88-4001. Denver, CO: USGS.

Sheridan, D. 1981. *Desertification of the United States*. Washington, DC: Council on Environmental Quality.

SCS. 1981. *America's Soil and Water: Conditions and Trends*. Washington, DC: SCS.

———. 1987. *Basic Statistics: 1982 National Resource Inventory*. Statistical Bulletin No. 756. Ames, IA: Iowa State University Statistical Laboratory.

Soil Conservation Society of America. 1979. *Soil Conservation Policies: An Assessment*. Ankeny, IA: Soil Conservation Society of America.

Steiner, F. 1987. "Soil Conservation Policy in the United States." *Environmental Management* 11: 209–223.

Swanson, L. E., ed. 1988. *Agriculture and Community Change in the U.S.: The Congressional Research Reports*. Boulder, CO: Westview.

Tanji, K., A. Lauchli, and J. Meyer. 1986. "Selenium in the San Joaquin Valley." *Environment* 28(6): 6–11, 34–39.

Thompson, E. P., Jr. 1984. "Protecting Agricultural Lands." In R. L. Brenneman and S. M. Bates, eds., *Land-Saving Action*. Washington, DC: Island Press.

USDA. Annual. *Yearbook of Agriculture*. Washington, DC: USDA.

———. 1981. *1980 Appraisal: Soil, Water, and Related Resources in the United States*. Parts I and II. Washington, DC: GPO.

———. 1982. *Cropland Outlook and Situation Report*. CUS-2. Washington, DC: USDA.

———. 1985a. *Agricultural Food Policy Review: Commodity Program Perspectives*. Agricultural Economic Report No. 530. Washington, DC: USDA.

———. 1985b. *Cropland Use and Supply: Outlook and Situation Report*. CUS-2. Washington, DC: USDA.

———. 1988. *Agricultural Resources: Cropland, Water, and Conservation Situation and Outlook Report*. AR-12. Washington, DC: GPO.

———. 1989a. *Agricultural Resources: Inputs Situation and Outlook Report*. AR-15. Washington, DC: USDA.

———. 1989b. *Conservation Reserve Program: Progress Report and Preliminary Evaluation of the First Two Years*. Washington, DC: GPO.

USDA, et al. 1981. *National Agricultural Lands Study*. Washington, DC: GPO.

U.S. Department of the Interior, USDA, and EPA. 1979. *Irrigation Water Use and Management*. Washington, DC: GPO.

Urban Land Institute. 1982. "The Agricultural Land Preservation Issue: Recommendations for Balancing Urban and Agricultural Land Needs." *Urban Land* 41(6): 18–26.

Veseth, M. 1979. "Alternative Policies for Preserving Farm and Open Areas: Analysis and Evaluation of Available Options." *American Journal of Economics and Sociology* 38: 97–109.

Ward, J. 1988. *Taxing the Rural Landscape: Improving State and Federal Policies for Prime Farmland*. Washington, DC: NRDC.

5 RANGELANDS AND WETLANDS

Baldwin, M. F. 1987. "Wetlands: Fortifying Federal and Regional Cooperation." *Environment* 29(7): 16–20, 39–43.

Barton, K. 1987. "Federal Wetlands Protection Programs." In M. E. Eno, P .L. DiSilvestro, and W. J. Chandler, eds., *Audubon Wildlife Report 1987*. New York: Academic Press.

Box, T. W., D. D. Dwyer, and F. H. Wagner. 1976. *The Public Range and Its Management: A Report to the President's Council on Environmental Quality*. Logan, UT: Utah State University.

Burke, D. G., et al. 1989. *Protecting Nontidal Wetlands*. Chicago: American Planning Association.

Bureau of Land Management. 1984. *50 Years of Public Land Management: 1934–1984*. Wahington, DC: BLM.

Carter, L. J. 1974. *The Florida Experience: Land and Water Policy in a Growth State*. Baltimore and London: Johns Hopkins.

Conservation Foundation. 1988. *Protecting America's Wetlands*. Washington, DC: Conservation Foundation.

Council on Environmental Quality. 1983. *Our Nation's Wetlands: An Interagency Task Force Report*. Washington, D.C.: GPO.

Cowles, C. D., et al. 1986. State Wetlands Programs: Status and Recommendations. Washington, DC: EPA.

Dana, S., and S. Fairfax. 1980. *Forest and Range Policy*. 2d ed. New York: McGraw-Hill.

EPA. 1988. *America's Wetlands: Our Vital Link between Land and Water*. EPA-87-016. Washington, D.C.: EPA.

Fernald, E. A., and D. J. Patton, eds. 1984. *Water Resources Atlas of Florida*. Tallahassee: Florida State University Institute of Science and Public Affairs.

Florida Governor's Office. 1985a. *Save Our Everglades: Report Card Number 4*. Tallahassee: Governor's Office.

———. 1985b. *Save Our Everglades: Second Anniversary Report Card*. Tallahassee: Governor's Office.

———. 1986. *Save Our Everglades: Report Card Number 6*. Tallahassee: Governor's Office.

———. 1988. *Everglades Status Report*. Tallahassee: Governor's Office.

Forest Service. 1981. *An Assessment of the Forest and Range Land Situation in the United States*. Forest Resource Report No. 22. Washington, DC: GPO.

———. 1984. *America's Renewable Resources: A Supplement to the 1979 Assessment of the Forest and Range Land Situation in the United States*. FS-386. Washington, DC: USDA.

Frayer, W. E., et al. 1983. *Status and Trends of Wetlands and Deepwater Habitats in the Conterminous United States, 1950's to 1970's*. Fort Collins, CO: Colorado State University Department of Forest and Wood Sciences.

Glubiak, P. G., R. H. Nowka, and W. G. Mitsch. 1986. "Federal and State Management of Inland Wetlands: Are States Ready to Assume Control?" *Environmental Management* 10: 145–156.

Heimlich, R. E. 1988. "The Swampbuster Provision: Implementation and Impact." Paper presented at the National Symposium on Protection of Wetlands from Agricultural Impacts, Colorado State University, April 25–29.

Heimlich, R. E., and L. L. Langer. 1986. *Swampbusting: Wetland Conversions and Farm Programs*. USDA Agricultural Economics Report No. 551. Washington, D.C.: GPO.

King, M. L. 1984. "Preserving the Tallgrass." *Sierra* 69(3): 73-76.

Kusler, J. A. 1983. *Our National Wetland Heritage: A Protection Guidebook*. Washington, DC: Environmental Law Institute.

Libecap, G. D. 1986. *Locking Up the Range: Federal Land Control and Grazing*. San Francisco: Pacific Institute for Public Policy Research.

Margheim, G. A. 1988. "Implementing Swampbuster: Two Years of Progress." *Journal of Soil and Water Conservation* 43: 27–29.

Mitsch, W. J., and J. G. Gosselink. 1986. *Wetlands*. New York: Van Nostrand Reinhold.

National Wildlife Federation. 1987. *Status Report of Our Nation's Wetlands*. Washington, DC: NWF.

OTA. 1984. *Wetlands: Their Use and Regulation*. OTA-O-206. Washington, D.C.: GPO.

Pierce, R. 1985. "Shaping a Tallgrass Sanctuary." *National Parks* 59(3–4): 28–29.

Rowley, W. D. 1985. *U.S. Forest Service Grazing and Rangelands: A History*. College Station, TX: Texas A&M University Press.

SCS. 1987. *Basic Statistics: 1982 National Resources Inventory*. Statistical Bulletin No. 756. Ames, IA: Iowa State University Statistical Laboratory.

Shaw, S. P. and C. G. Fredine. 1956. *Wetlands of the United States*. Circular 39. Washington, DC: FWS.

Sprague, H.B., ed. 1974. *Grasslands of the United States: Their Economic and Ecologic Importance*. Ames, IA: Iowa State University Press.

Sullivan, J. 1988. "Bringing Back the Prairie." *Audubon* 90(4): 41–47.

Tiner, R.W., Jr. 1984. *Wetlands of the United States: Current Status and Recent Trends*. FWS. Washington, D.C.: GPO.

———. 1987. *Mid-Atlantic Wetlands: A Disappearing Natural Treasure*. Newton Corner, MA: FWS.

USDA. 1981. *1980 Appraisal: Soil, Water, and Related Resources in the United States*. Parts I and II. Washington, DC: GPO.

Whitfield, E. 1988. "Restoring the Everglades", In W. J. Chandler, ed., *Audubon Wildlife Report 1988/89*. San Diego: Academic Press.

Yates. S. 1982. "Florida's Broken Rain Machine." *Amicus Journal* 4(2): 48–56.

Zinn, J. A., and C. Copeland. 1982. *Wetland Management*. Washington, DC: Congressional Research Service.

6 FORESTS AND FORESTRY

Laycock, G. 1987. "Trashing the Tongass." *Aububon*, 89 (6), 113–127.

Anderson, H. M., et al. 1988. *National Forests: Policies for the Future*. 2 vol. Washington, DC: Wilderness Society.

Birch, T. W., D. G. Lewis, and H. F. Kaiser. 1982. *The Private Forest-Land Owners of the United States*. Resource Bulletin WO-1. Washington, DC: Forest Service.

Clawson, M. 1975. *Forests for Whom and for What?* Baltimore and London: Johns Hopkins.

Dana, S. T., and S. K. Fairfax. 1980. *Forest and Range Policy: Its Development in the United States*. 2d ed. New York: McGraw Hill.

Deacon, R. T., and M. B. Johnson, eds. 1986. *Forestlands: Public and Private*. San Francisco: Pacific Institue for Public Policy.

Ervin, K. 1988. "A Tall Tale of Too Few Trees." *Sierra* 73(6): 34-40.

———. 1989. *Fragile Majesty: The Battle for North America's Last Great Forest*. Seattle: Mountaineer's Books.

Eyre, F. H., ed. 1980. *Forest Cover Types of the United States and Canada*. Washington, DC: Society of American Foresters.

Forest Service. 1981. *An Assessment of the Forest and Range Land Situation in the United States*. Forest Resource Report No. 22. Washington, DC: GPO.

———. 1982. *An Analysis of the Timber Situation in the United States 1952– 2030*. Forest Report No. 23. Washington, DC: GPO.

———. 1984. *America's Renewable Resources: A Supplement to the 1979 Assessment of the Forest and Range Land Situation in the United States*. FS-386. Washington, DC: Forest Service.

———. 1985. *A Recommended Renewable Resources Program: 1985–2030*. FS-400. Washington, DC: Forest Service.

———. Annual. *Report of the Forest Service*. Washington, DC: Forest Service.

Fritz, E. 1983. *Sterile Forest: The Case Against Clearcutting*. Austin, TX: Eakin.

Frome, M. 1984. *The Forest Service*. 2d ed. Boulder, CO: Westview.

Hunt, F. A. 1987. "National Forest Planning: Charting the Future for 191 Million Acres of Trees and Grass." *American Land Forum* 7(3): 18–23.

Irland, L. C. 1982. *Wildlands and Woodlots: The Story of New England's Forests*. Hanover, NH: University Press of New England.

Norse, E. A. 1989. *Ancient Forests of the Pacific Northwest*. Washington, DC: Island Press.

O'Toole, R. 1988. *Reforming the Forest Service*. Washington, DC: Island Press.

Portney, P. R., ed. 1982. *Current Issues in Natural Resource Policy*. Washington, DC: Resources for the Future.

Robinson, G. O. 1975. *The Forest Service*. Baltimore: Johns Hopkins.

Reidel, C. 1978. *The Yankee Forest: A Prospectus*. New Haven, CT: Yale School of Forestry and Environmental Studies.

Steen, H. K. 1976. *The U.S. Forest Service: A History*. Seattle: University of Washington Press.

Vale, T. R. 1988. "Clearcut Logging, Vegetation Dynamics, and Human Wisdom." *Geographical Review* 78: 375–386.

Wilcove, D.S. 1988. *National Forests: Policies for the Future*. 2 vol. Washington, DC: Wilderness Society.

Wilderness Society. 1988. *Ancient Forests: A Threatened Heritage*. Washington, DC: Wilderness Society.

———. 1989. *Old Growth in the Pacific Northwest : A Status Report*. Washington, DC: Wilderness Society.

Wilkinson, C. F., and H. M. Anderson. 1987. *Land and Resource Planning in the National Forests*. Washington, DC: Island Press.

Williams, M. 1989. *Americans and Their Forests: A Historical Account*. New York: Cambridge University Press.

7 COASTAL ZONE MANAGEMENT

Archer, J. H., and J. W. Knecht. 1987. "The U.S. National Coastal Zone Management Program: Problems and Opportunities in the Next Phase." *Coastal Management* 15: 103–120.

Basta, D. J., et al. 1985. *The National Coastal Pollutant Discharge Inventory* (and subsequent reports). Rockville, MD: NOAA.

Blake, G., ed. 1987. *Maritime Boundaries and Ocean Resources*. London and Sydney: Croom Helm.

Brower, D. J., and D. S. Carol. 1984. *Coastal Zone Management as Land Planning*. Washington, DC: National Planning Association.

Chasis, S. 1980. "The Coastal Zone Management Act." *Journal of the American Planning Association* 46: 145–153.

Culliton, T. J., et al. 1989. *Selected Characteristics in Coastal States, 1980–2000*. Rockville, MD: NOAA.

———. 1990. *50 Years of Population Change Along the Nation's Coasts: 1960–2010*. Rockville, MD: NOAA.

Donovan, M. L., and J .P. Tolson. 1987. *Land Use and the Nation's Estuaries*. Rockville, MD: NOAA.

Duedall, I. W., et al., eds. 1988. *Wastes in the Ocean*. New York: Wiley.

EPA. 1987. "Protecting Our Estuaries." *EPA Journal* (Special issue). 13(6).

———. 1989. "Can Our Coasts Survive More Growth?" *EPA Journal*. (Special issue). 15(5).

Galloway, T. D., ed. 1982. *The Newest Federalism: A New Framework for Coastal Issues*. Wakefield, RI: Wilson.

GAO. 1986. *Resource Management: Information on the Coastal Zone Management Program*. GAO/RCED-86-89FS. Washington, DC: GPO.

Godschalk, D. R., and K. Cousins, eds. 1985. "Symposium: Coastal Management: Planning on the Edge." *Journal of the American Planning Association* 51: 263–336.

Gordon, W. R., Jr. 1984. "The Coastal Barrier Resources Act of 1982: An Assessment of Legislative Intent, Process, and Exemption Alternatives." *Coastal Zone Management Journal* 12: 257–286.

Healy, R. G., and J. A. Zinn. 1985. "Environment and Development Conflicts in Coastal Zone Management." *Journal of the American Planning Association* 51: 299–311.

Houck, O. A. 1988. America's Mad Dash to the Sea. *Amicus Journal* 10(3): 21–36.

House of Representatives. 1989. *Coastal Waters in Jeopardy*. House Committee on Merchant Marine and Fisheries. House Document 101-38. 101st Congress.

Hoy, M. and G. Braasch. 1989. Researching the Slough. *Audubon* 91(2): 99–105.

Jackson, T. C. and D. Reische. 1981. *Coast Alert: Scientists Speak Out*. San Francisco: Friends of the Earth.

Kaufman, W., and O. H. Pilkey, Jr. 1983. *The Beaches Are Moving: The Drowning of America's Shoreline*. Durham, NC: Duke University Press.

Lins, H. F. 1980. *Patterns and Trends of Land-Use and Land Cover on Atlantic and Gulf Coast Barrier Islands*. USGS Professional Paper 1156. Washington, DC: GPO.

Mayer, G. F., ed. 1982. *Ecological Stress and the New York Bight*. Columbia, SC: Estuarine Research Foundation.

Mead, W. J., et al. 1983. *Offshore Lands: Oil and Gas Leasing and Conservation on the Outer Continental Shelf*. San Francisco: Pacific Research Institute for Public Policy.

Menzie, C. A. 1983. "Environmental Concerns about Offshore Drilling: Muddy Issues." *Oceanus* 26(3): 32-38.

Millemann, B. 1986. *And Two If By Sea: Fighting the Attack on America's Coasts*. Washington, DC: Coast Alliance.

Minerals Management Service. Annual. *Federal Offshore Statistics: Leasing, Exploration, Production, & Revenues*. Washington, DC: GPO.

———. 1986. *Managing Oil and Gas Operations on the Outer Continental Shelf*. Washington, DC: GPO.

———. 1987a. *Leasing Energy Resources on the Outer Continental Shelf*. Washington, DC: GPO.

———. 1987b. *Outer Continental Shelf Oil & Gas 5-Year Leasing Program, Mid-1987 to Mid-1992: Proposed Final*. Washington, DC: MMS.

Mitchell, J. K. 1986. "Coastal Management since 1980." In E. M. Borgese and N. Ginsburg, *Ocean Yearbook 6*. Chicago: University of Chicago Press.

NOAA. Series. *A National Atlas: Health and Use of Coastal Waters, United States of America*. Folio maps. Rockville, MD: NOAA.

———. 1987a. *Biennial Report to the Congress on Coastal Zone Management: Fiscal Years 1984 and 1986*. Rockville, MD: NOAA.

———. 1987b. *Strategic Assessment: Fact Sheets*. Rockville, MD: NOAA.

National Research Council. 1985. *Oil in the Sea*. Washington, DC: National Academy Press.

NRDC. 1989. *Ebb Tide for Pollution: Actions for Cleaning Up Coastal Waters*. New York: NRDC.

OTA. 1986. *Ocean Incineration: Its Role in Managing Hazardous Wastes*. OTA-O-313. Washington, DC: GPO.

———. 1987. *Wastes in Marine Environments*. OTA-O-334. Washington, DC: GPO.

Pait, A. S., et al. 1989. *Agricultural Pesticide Use in Estuarine Drainage Areas: A Preliminary Summary for Selected Pesticides*. Rockville, MD: NOAA.

Payton, B. M. 1985. "Ocean Dumping in the New York Bight." *Environment* 27(9): 26-32.

Pilkey, O. H., Jr., and W. H. Neal. 1983. *The Beaches are Moving*. Durham, NC: Duke University Press.

Platt, R. H. 1985. Congress and the Coast. *Environment* 27: 12–17, 34–40.

———. 1987. "Coastal Wetland Management: The Advance Designation Approach." *Environment* 29(9): 16–20, 38–43.

Platt, R. H., G. Macinko, and K. Hammond. 1983. "Federal Environmental Management: Some Land-use Legacies of the 1970s." In J. House, ed., *United States Public Policy: A Geographical View*. Oxford: Clarendon.

Platt, R. H., S. G. Pelczarski, and B. K. R. Burbank, eds. 1987. *Cities on the Beach: Management Issues of Developed Coastal Barriers*. Chicago: University of Chicago, Department of Geography Research Paper No. 224.

Ricketts, P. J. 1986. "National Policy and Management Responses to the Hazard of Coastal Erosion in Britain and the United States." *Applied Geography* 6: 197—221.

Swanson, R. L., and M. Devine. 1982. "Ocean Dumping Policy." *Environment* 24(5): 14-20.

Swanson, R. L., and C. J. Sinderman. 1979. *Oxygen Depletion and Associated Benthic Mortalities in the New York Bight, 1976*. Professional Paper 11. Washington, DC: NOAA.

U.S. Department of the Interior. 1987. *Report to Congress: Coastal Barrier Resources System*. Draft. Washington, DC: USDOI.

U.S. Department of the Interior, Heritage Conservation and Recreation Service. 1978. *Report of the Barrier Island Work Group*. Washington, DC: GPO.

Warsh, C., et al. 1988. *Strategic Assessment of Near Coastal Waters: Northeast Case Study*. Rockville, MD: NOAA.

Wells, J. T., and C. H. Peterson. No date. *Atlantic & Gulf Coastal Barriers*. Baton Rouge, LA: Louisiana State University.

Wolf, W.A., ed. 1985. "Symposium on Coastal Zone Management." *Natural Resources Journal*. (Special issue). 25(1).

8 AIR QUALITY AND ACID DEPOSITION

Borman, F. H. 1985. "Air Pollution and Forests: An Ecosystem Perspective." *BioScience* 35: 434–441.

Churchill, W. 1986. "American Indian Lands: The Native Ethic Amid Resource Development." *Environment* 28(6): 12–17, 28–34.

Council on Environmental Quality. 1978. *Environmental Quality: The Ninth Annual Report*. Washington, DC: GPO.

Council on Environmental Quality. 1987. *Environmental Quality: The Sixteenth Annual Report*. Washington, DC: GPO.

Cowling, E.B. 1982. "Acid Precipitation in Historical Perspective." *Environmental Science & Technology* 16: 110A-123A.

Crandall, R.W. 1983. *Controlling Industrial Pollution: The Economics and Politics of Clean Air*. Washington, DC: Brookings Institution.

DOE. 1981. *Acid Rain Information Book: Final Report*. DOE/EP-0018. Springfield, VA: NTIS.

EPA. *Annual. National Air Quality Emissions and Trends Report*. EPA-450/4-89-001. Washington, DC: GPO.

———. 1978. *National Air Quality, Monitoring, and Emissions Trends Report, 1977*. EPA-450/ 2-78-052. Research Triangle Park, NC: EPA.

———. 1979. *Protecting Visibility*. Research Triangle Park, NC: EPA.

———. 1980. *Acid Rain*. EPA-699/9-79-036. Washington, DC: EPA.

———. 1986. *National Air Pollutant Emission Estimates 1940–1984*. Research Triangle Park, NC: EPA.

———. 1988. *Ozone and Carbon Monoxide Summary Report: Areas Proposed for Nonattainment per Mitchell-Conte Amendment*. Research Triangle Park, NC: EPA.

Flynn, J. 1989. "Ohio River Basin: Packhorse of the East." *Amicus Journal* 11(1): 36–38.

Glass, N. R., et al. 1982. "Effects of Acid Precipitation." *Environmental Science & Technology* 16: 162A-169A.

Gordon, S. 1973. *Black Mesa: The Angel of Death*. New York: John Day.

Hartwell, T. D., et al. *1984. Study of Carbon Monoxide Exposure of Residents of Washington, D.C. and Denver, Colorado*. Research Triangle Park, NC: EPA.

Hinrichsen, D. 1988. "Parks in Peril." *Amicus Journal* 10(1): 3–5.

House of Representatives. 1986. *Acid Deposition Control Act of 1986*. Hearings before a subcommittee of the Committee on Energy and Commerce on H.R. 4567. 99th Congress, 2d session.

Irving, P. M. 1989. *Acidic Deposition: State of Science and Technology*. Washington, DC: National Acid Precipitation Assessment Program.

Johnson, A. H. 1986. "Acid Deposition: Trends, Relationships, and Effects." *Environment* 28(4): 6-11, 34-43.

Johnson, A. H., and T. G. Siccama. 1983. "Acid Deposition and Forest Decline." *Environmental Science & Technology* 17: 294A–305A.

Jones, C. O. 1988. *Clean Air: The Policies and Politics of Pollution Control*. Pittsburgh: University of Pittsburgh Press.

Kahan, A. M. 1986. *Acid Rain: Reign of Controversy*. Golden, CO: Fulcrum.

Kneese, A. V. and F. L. Brown. 1981. *The Southwest Under Stress: National Resource Development in a Regional Setting*. Baltimore: Johns Hopkins.

LaBastille, A. 1981. "Acid Rain: How Great a Menace?" *National Geographic* 160: 652–681.

Likens, G. E., et al. 1979. "Acid Rain." *Scientific American* 241(4): 43–51.

Luoma, J. R. 1984. *Troubled Skies, Troubled Waters: The Story of Acid Rain*. New York: Penguin.

MacKenzie, J. J., and M. T. El-Ashry. 1990. *Air Pollution's Toll on Forests and Crops*. New Haven, CT: Yale University Press.

McLaughlin, S. B. 1985. "Effects of Air Pollution on Forests." *Journal of the Air Pollution Control Association* 35: 512–534.

Malm, W., et al. 1989. *National Park Service Report on the Winter Haze Intensive Tracer Experiment*. Fort Collins, CO: NPS.

Mello, R. A. 1987. *Last Stand of the Red Spruce*. Washington, DC: Island Press.

Mohnen, V. A. 1988. "The Challenge of Acid Rain." *Scientific American* 259(2): 30–38.

National Atmospheric Deposition Program. Annual. *NADP/NTN Annual Data Summary*. Fort Collins, CO: Colorado State University Natural Resource Ecology Laboratory.

———. No date. *Distribution of Surface Waters Sensitive to Acidic Precipitation: A State-Level Atlas*. Fort Collins, CO: Colorado State University Natural Resource Ecology Laboratory.

National Research Council. 1983. *Acid Deposition: Atmospheric Processes in Eastern North America*. Washington, DC: National Academy Press.

———. 1986. *Acid Deposition: Long-Term Trends*. Washington, DC: National Academy Press.

Olsen, A. R. 1988. *1986 Wet Deposition Temporal and Spatial Patterns in North America*. Richland, WA: Pacific Northwest Laboratory.

Omernik, J. M., and G. E. Griffith. 1986. "Total Alkalinity of Surface Waters: A Map of the Upper Midwest Region of the United States." *Environmental Management* 10: 829–839.

Omernik, J. M., and A. J. Kinney. 1985. "Total Alkalinity of Surface Waters: A Map of the New England and New York Region." Corvallis, OR: EPA.

Omernik, J. M., and C. F. Powers. 1985. "Total Alkalinity of Surface Waters: A National Map." *Annals of the Association of American Geographers* 73: 133–136.

OTA. 1985. *Acid Rain and Transported Pollutants: Implications for Public Policy*. OTA-O-205. New York: UNIPUB.

———. 1988. *Urban Ozone and the Clean Air Act: Problems and Proposals for Change*. Springfield, VA: NTIS.

Park, C. C. 1987. Acid Rain: Rhetoric and Reality. London: Methuen.

Postel, S. 1984. *Air Pollution, Acid Rain, and the Future of Forests*. Worldwatch Paper 58. Washington, D.C.: Worldwatch.

Raufer, R. K., and S. L. Feldman. 1987. *Acid Rain and Emissions Trading*. Totowa, NJ: Rowman & Littlefield.

Reed, P. D. 1986. "When Is An Area That Is In Attainment Not An Attainment Area?" *Environmental Law Reporter* 16: 10041–10048.

Regens, J. L., and R. W. Rycroft. 1988. *The Acid Rain Controversy*. Pittsburgh: University of Pittsburgh Press.

Renew America. 1989. *The State of the States 1989*. Washington, DC: Renew America.

Rhodes, S. L., and P. Middleton. 1983. "The Complex Challenge of Controlling Acid Rain." *Environment* 25(4): 6–9, 31–38.

Roth, P. 1985. *The American West's Acid Rain Test*. Washington, DC: Worldwatch.

Rudzitis, G., and J. Schwartz. 1982. "The Plight of the Parklands." *Environment* 24(8): 6–11, 33–38.

Russell, D. 1988. "L.A. Air." *Amicus Journal* 10(3): 10–20.

Scheiman, D. A. 1986. "Facing Facts." *Amicus Journal* 7(4): 4–9.

Scholle, S. R. 1983. "Acid Deposition and the Materials Damage Question." *Environment* 25(8): 25–32.

Schrenck, H. H., et al. 1949. *Air Pollution in Donora, Pa.: Epidemiology of the Unusual Smog Episode of October 1948. Preliminary Report*. Public Health Bulletin No. 306. Washington, DC: U.S. Public Health Service.

Schroeder, P., and A. R. Kiester. 1989. "The Forest Response Program: National Research on Forest Decline and Air Pollution." *Journal of Forestry* 87(1): 27–32.

Schwartz, S. E. 1989. "Acid Deposition: Unraveling a Regional Phenomenon." *Science* 243: 753–761.

Smith, R. A., and R. B. Alexander. 1986. "Correlations Between Stream Sulphate and Regional SO_2 Emissions." *Nature* 322: 722–724.

Streets, D. G., D. A. Knudson, and J. D. Shannon. 1983. "Selected Strategies to Reduce Acidic Deposition in the U.S." *Environmental Science & Technology* 17: 474A–485A.

Tomlinson, G. H., II, ed. 1990. *Effects of Acid Deposition on the Forests of Europe and North America*. Boca Raton, FL: CRC Press.

Trijonis, J. J. 1982. "Existing and Natural Background Levels of Visibility and Fine Particles in the Rural East." *Atmospheric Environment* 16: 2431–2445.

Trijonis, J. J. and D. Shapland. 1979. *Existing Visibility Levels in the U.S.: Visibility in the Suburban/Nonurban Areas During 1974–76*. Research Triangle Park, NC: EPA.

Turk, J. T. 1983. *An Evaluation of Trends in the Acidity of Precipitation and the Related Acidification of Surface Water in North America*. USGS Water Supply Paper 2249. Washington, DC: GPO.

Wallace, L. A., et al. 1987. *The Total Exposure Assessment Methodology (Team) Study*. Washington, DC: EPA.

Wetstone, G. S., and S. A. Foster. 1983. "Acid Precipitation: What is it Doing to Our Forests?" *Environment* 25(4): 10–12, 38–40.

White, J. C., ed. 19877. *Acid Rain: The Relationship Between Sources and Receptors*. Amsterdam: Elsevier.

Woodman, J. N. and E. B. Cowling. 1987. "Airborne Chemicals and Forest Health." *Environmental Science and Technology* 21: 120–126.

Yanarella, E. J., and R. H. Thara, eds. 1985. *The Acid Rain Debate: Scientific, Economic, and Political Dimensions*. Boulder, CO: Westview.

9 WATER USE AND QUALITY

Alexander, R. B., and R. A. Smith. 1988. "Trends in Lead Concentrations in Major U.S. Rivers and Their Relation to Historical Changes in Gasoline-Lead Consumption." *Water Resources Bulletin* 24: 557–569.

Aller, L., et al. 1985. *DRASTIC—A Standardized System for Evaluating Ground-Water Pollution Potential Using Hydrogeologic Settings*. EPA 600/2-85-018. Washington, DC: EPA.

Anderson, T. L., ed. 1986. *Water Rights: Scarce Resource Allocation, Bureaucracy, and the Environment*. San Francisco: Pacific Institute for Public Policy.

Ashworth, W. 1986. *The Late, Great Lakes: An Environmental History*. New York: Alfred A. Knopf.

Association of State and Interstate Water Pollution Control Administrators. 1984. *America's Clean Water: The States' Evaluation of Progress 1972–1982*. Washington, DC: ASIWPCA.

———. 1985. *America's Clean Water: The State's Nonpoint Source* Assessment. Washington, DC: ASIWPCA.

Bocking, R. C. 1972. *Canada's Water: For Sale?* Toronto: James Lewis & Samuel.

Burns, N. M. 1985. *Erie: The Lake that Survived*. Totowa, NJ: Rowman and Allenheld.

Calabrese, E. J., C. E. Gilbert, and H. Pastides, eds. 1989. *Safe Drinking Water Act: Amendments, Regulations, and Standards*. Chelsea, MI: Lewis.

Caldwell, L. K., ed. 1988. *Perspectives on Ecosystem Management for the Great Lakes*. Albany: State University of New York Press.

Candee, H., and L. King. 1987. *The Broken Promise of Reclamation Reform*. New York: NRDC.

Canter, L. W., R. C. Knox, and D. M. Fairchild. 1987. *Groundwater Quality Protection*. Chelsea, MI: Lewis.

Carothers, A. 1988. "A Desert of Waters: Toxic Pollution and the Great Lakes." *Greenpeace* 13(4): 10–15.

Chelimsky, E. 1988. "Fighting Groundwater Contamination: State Activities to Date and the Need for More Information from EPA." Statement Before Senate Subcommittee, May 17, 1988. GAO/T-PEMD-88-7. Washington, DC: GAO.

Chesapeake Bay Program. 1987. *The State of the Chesapeake Bay: Second Annual Monitoring Report*. Annapolis, MD: CBP.

———. 1988. *Monitoring the Status of the Chesapeake Bay: The Estuarine Perspective*. Annapolis, MD: CBP.

Chesapeake Executive Council. 1987. *Second Annual Progress Report under the Chesapeake Bay Agreement*. Annapolis, MD: CBP.

———. 1989. *The First Progress Report Under the 1987 Chesapeake Bay Agreement*. Annapolis, MD: CBP.

Conacher, D., and Associates. 1988. *Troubled Waters on Tap*. Washington, DC: Center for the Study of Responsive Law.

Concern, Inc. 1986. *Drinking Water: A Community Action Guide*. Washington, DC: Concern, Inc.

———. 1988. *Groundwater: A Community Action Guide*. Washington, DC: Concern, Inc.

Conservation Foundation. 1984. *America's Water: Current Trends and Emerging Issues*. Washington, DC: CF.

———. 1987a. *Groundwater Protection*. Washington, DC: CF.

———. 1987b. *State of the Environment: A View Toward the Nineties*. Washington, DC: CF.

Conservation Foundation and Institute for Research on Public Policy. 1989. *Great Lakes, Great Legacy?* Washington, DC: CF.

Council on Environmental Quality. 1981. *Contamination of Ground Water by Toxic Organic Chemicals*. Washington, DC: GPO.

"Cumulative Effects on Landscape Systems of Wetlands." 1988. *Environmental Management*. (Special issue). 12(5): 561–771.

Dean, N. L. 1988. *Danger on Tap: The Government's Failure to Enforce the Federal Safe Drinking Water Act*. Washington, DC: National Wildlife Federation.

D'Elia, C. F. 1987. "Nutrient Enrichment of the Chesapeake Bay: Too Much of a Good Thing." *Environment* 29(2): 6–11, 30–33.

D'Itri, F. M., and L. G. Wolfson, eds. 1987. *Rural Groundwater Contamination*. Chelsea, MI: Lewis.

Edwards, M. D. 1987. *Plan for the Design, Development, Implementation, and Operation of the National Water Information System*. Open-file Report No. 87–29. Denver: USGS.

El-Ashry, M .T., and D. C. Gibbons, eds. 1988. *Water and Arid Lands of the Western United States*. New York: Cambridge University Press.

Environment Canada, EPA, Brock University, and Northwestern University. 1987. *The Great Lakes: An Environmental Atlas and Resource Book*. Chicago and Toronto: EPA and Environment Canada.

EPA. 1983a. *Chesapeake Bay Program: Findings and Recommendations*. Washington, DC: EPA.

———. 1983b. *Results of the Nationwide Urban Runoff Program*. Washington, DC: EPA.

——— 1983c. *Surface Impoundment Assessment National Report*. EPA 570/9-84-002. Washington, DC: EPA.

———. 1984a. *Ground-Water Protection Strategy*. Washington, DC: EPA.

———. 1984b. *National Statistical Assessment of Rural Water Conditions*. EPA 570/9-84-004. Washington, DC: EPA.

———. 1984c. *Report to Congress: Nonpoint Source Pollution in the U.S.* Washington, DC: EPA.

———. 1987a. 1986 *Needs Survey Report to Congress: Assessment of Needed Publicly Owned Wastewater Treatment Facilities in the United States*. EPA 430/9-87-001. Washington, DC: GPO.

———. 1987b. *Agricultural Chemicals in Ground Water: Proposed Strategy*. Washington, DC: EPA.

———. 1987c. *National Water Quality Inventory: 1986 Report to Congress*. EPA-440/4-87-008. Washington,DC: EPA.

———. 1987d. *Wellhead Protection: A Decision-Makers' Guide*. EPA 440/6-87-009. Washington, DC: EPA.

———. 1988. *Musts for USTs: A Summary of the New Regulations for Underground Storage Tank Systems*. EPA/530/UST-88/008. Washington, DC: EPA.

———. 1989. *Fact Sheet: Drinking Water Regulations Under the Safe Drinking Water Act*. Washington, DC: EPA.

Evans, M. S., ed. 1988. *Toxic Contaminants and Ecosystem Health: A Great Lakes Focus*. New York: Wiley.

Fairchild, D. M., ed. 1987. *Ground Water Quality and Agricultural Practices*. Chelsea, MI: Lewis.

Fisher, D., et al. 1988. *Polluted Coastal Waters: The Role of Acid Rain*. New York: Environmental Defense Fund.

Folk-Williams, J., et al. 1982–1985. *Water in the West*. 3 vol. Washington, DC: Island Press.

Foreman, R. L. 1981. *Indian Water Rights: A Public Policy and Administrative Mess*. Danville, IL: Interstate Printers and Publishers.

Fradkin, P. L. 1981. *A River No More: The Colorado River and the West*. New York: Alfred A. Knopf.

Franco, D. A., and R. G. Wetel. 1983. *To Quench Our Thirst: The Present and Future Status of Freshwater Resources of the United States*. Ann Arbor: University of Michigan Press.

GAO. 1979. *Colorado River Basin Water Problems: How to Reduce Their Impact*. CED-79–11. Washington, DC: GAO.

———. 1986. *The Nation's Water: Key Unanswered Questions About the Quality of Rivers and Streams*. GAO/PEMD-86-6. Washington, DC: GAO.

———. 1988. *Groundwater Standards: States Need More Information from EPA*. GAO/PEMD-88-6. Washington, DC: GAO.

Geraghty, J. J., et al. 1973. *Water Atlas of the United States*. Port Washington, NY: Water Information Center.

Gianessi, L .P., and H. M. Peskin. 1986. *The RFF Environmental Data Inventory*. Washington, DC: Resources for the Future.

Gilliom, R. J., R. B. Alexander, and R. A. Smith. 1985. *Pesticides in the Nation's Rivers, 1975–1980*. USGS Water Supply Paper 2271. Washington, DC: GPO.

Gordon, W. 1984. *A Citizen's Handbook on Groundwater Protection*. New York: NRDC.

Gottlieb, R. 1988. *A Life of Its Own: The Politics and Power of Water*. Orlando, FL: Harcourt Brace Jovanovich.

Great Lakes Basin Commission. 1976. *Great Lakes Basin Commission Framework Study*. Ann Arbor, MI: GLBC.

Hathaway, J. 1988. "The Delaney Clause and Carcinogenic Pesticides." *Environment* 30(9): 4–5.

Henderson, T. R., J. Truaberman, and T. Gallagher. 1984. *Groundwater: Strategies for State Action*. Washington, DC: Environmental Law Institute.

High Country News. 1987. *Western Water Made Simple*. Washington, DC: Island Press.

Hileman, B. 1988. "The Great Lakes Cleanup Effort." *Chemical & Engineering News* 66(6): 22–39.

Hirsch, R. M., W. M. Alley, and W. G. Wilber. 1988. *Concepts for a National Water Quality Assessment Program*. USGS Circular 1021. Washington, DC: GPO.

Holden, P. W. 1986. *Pesticides and Groundwater Quality: Issues and Problems in Four States*. Washington, DC: National Academy Press.

Howe, C. W., and K. W. Easter. 1971. *Interbasin Transfers of Water*. Baltimore: Johns Hopkins.

Hrezo, M. S., P. G. Bridgeman, and W. R. Walker. 1986. "Integrating Drought Planning Into Water Resources Management." *Natural Resources Journal* 26: 141–167.

Hunt, C. E. 1988. *Down by the River: The Impact of Federal Water Projects and Policies on Biological Diversity*. Washington, DC: Island Press.

McPhee, J. 1970. *Encounters with the Archdruid*. New York: Farrar, Straus and Giroux.

International Joint Commission. Annual. *Report on Great Lakes Water Quality*. Windsor, ON: IJC.

———. 1986. *Reports Issued Under the 1972 and 1978 Great Lakes Water Quality Agreements: A Bibliography-May 1986*. Windsor, ON: IJC.

Irwin, R. J., and D. Lagerroos, eds. 1988. *Sweet Water, Bitter Rain: Toxic Air Pollution in the Great Lakes Basin*. Madison, WI: Sierra Club.

Jaffe, M., and F. Dinovo. 1987. *Local Groundwater Protection*. Chicago: American Planning Association.

Krupnick, A. J. 1985. "The Chesapeake Bay Cleanup." *Resources* 79: 1–5.

Kusler, J. A. 1985. "Roles Along the Rivers." *Environment* 27(7): 18–20, 37–44.

Landman, J. 1987. *A Citizen's Handbook on Water Quality Standards*. New York: NRDC.

League of Women Voters Education Fund. 1987. *Safety on Tap: A Citizen's Drinking Water Handbook*. Washington, DC: LWV.

Lee, L. K., and E. G. Nielsen. 1987. "The Extent and Costs of Groundwater Con-

tamination by Agriculture." *Journal of Soil and Water Conservation* 42: 243–248.

Maass, A. 1951. *Muddy Waters: The Army Engineers and the Nation's Rivers*. Cambridge, MA: Harvard University Press.

Mendeloff, J. M. 1988. *The Dilemma of Toxic Substance Regulation*. Cambridge, MA: MIT Press.

Miller, T. O., G. D. Weatherford, and J. E. Thorson. 1986. *The Salty Colorado*. Washington, DC, and Napa, CA: The Conservation Foundation and John Muir Institute.

National Academy of Sciences. 1989. *Drinking Water and Health*. 9 vol. Washington, DC: National Academy Press.

National Research Council. 1986. *Ground Water Quality Protection: State and Local Strategies*. Washington, DC: National Academy Press.

National Research Council and Royal Society of Canada. 1985. *The Great Lakes Water Quality Agreement: An Evolving Instrument for Ecosystem Management*. Washington, DC: National Academy Press.

Nielsen, E. G., and L. K. Lee. *The Magnitude and Costs of Groundwater Contamination from Agricultural Chemicals*. Agriculture Economic Report No. 576. Washington, DC: USDA.

Nriagu, J. O., and M. S. Simmons, eds. 1984. *Toxic Contaminants in the Great Lakes*. New York: Wiley.

Officer, C. B. "Chesapeake Bay Anoxia." *Science* 223: 22–27.

Oppenheimer, T. 1988. "Humpty Dumpty." *Amicus Journal* 10(1): 14–23.

OTA. 1984. *Protecting the Nation's Groundwater from Contamination*. 2 vol. OTA-0-233. Washington, DC: GPO.

Page, G.W., ed. 1987. *Planning for Groundwater Protection*. Orlando, FL: Academic Press.

Patrick, R., E. Ford, and J. Quarles. 1987. *Groundwater Contamination in the United States*. 2d ed. Philadelphia: University of Pennsylvania Press.

Peterson, D. F., and A .B. Crawford, eds. 1978. *Values and Choices in the Development of the Colorado River Basin*. Tucson: University of Arizona Press.

Petsch, H. E., Jr. 1985. *Inventory of Interbasin Transfers of Water in the Western United States*. Denver, CO: USGS.

Price, B. 1990. *Water Reclamation: Here, Now . . . and How*. Lancaster, PA: Technomic.

Reisner, M. 1986. *Cadillac Desert: The American West and Its Disappearing Water*. New York: Viking.

Reisner, M., and S. Bates. 1989. *Overtapped Oasis: Reform or Revolution for Western Water*. Washington, DC: Island Press.

Renew America. 1989. *State of the States, 1989*. Washington, DC: Renew America.

Rice, R. G. 1985. *Safe Drinking Water: The Impact of Chemicals on a Limited Resource*. Alexandria, VA: Drinking Water Research Foundation.

Sierra Club Legal Defense Fund. 1989. *The Poisoned Well: New Strategies for Groundwater Protection*. Washington, DC: Island Press.

Skogerboe, G. V., ed. 1982. *Water and Energy Development in an Arid Environment: The Colorado River Basin*. Oxford: Pergamon.

Sloggett, G., and C. Dickason. 1986. *Ground-Water Mining in the United States*. USDA. Washington, DC: GPO.

Smith, R. A., R .B. Alexander, and M. G. Wolman. 1987a. *Analysis and Interpretation of Water Quality Trends in Major U.S. Rivers, 1974–81*. USGS Water Supply Paper 2307. Reston, VA: GPO.

———. 1987b. "Water-Quality Trends in the Nation's Rivers." *Science* 235: 1607–1615.

Solley, W. B., C. F. Merk, and R. R. Pierce. 1988. *Estimated Use of Water in the United States in 1985*. USGS Circular 1004. Washington, DC: GPO.

Sun, R. J., ed. 1986. *Regional Aquifer-System Analysis Program of the U.S. Geological Survey: Summary of Projects, 1978–84*. USGS Circular 1002. Washington, DC: GPO.

USGS. Annual. *National Water Summary*. Water-Supply Paper. Washington, DC: GPO.

U.S. Water Resources Council. 1978. *The Nation's Water Resources, 1975–2000*. 4 vol. Washington, DC: GPO.

Walton, S. 1982. "Chesapeake Bay: Threats to Ecological Stability." *Bioscience* 32: 843–844.

Ward, C. H., W. Giger, and P. L. McCarty. 1985. *Ground Water Quality*. New York: Wiley.

Weatherford, G., and L. Brown, eds. 1986. *New Courses for the Colorado River*. Albuquerque: University of New Mexico Press.

Wells, H. W., Jr., S. J. Katsanos, and F. H. Flanigan. 1983. *Chesapeake Bay: A Framework for Action*. Washington, DC: EPA.

Welsh, F. 1985. *How to Create a Water Crisis*. Boulder, CO: Johnson.

White, G. F. 1969. *Strategies of American Water Management*. Ann Arbor, MI: University of Michigan Press.

Worster, D. 1985. *Rivers of Empire: Water, Aridity, and the Growth of the American West*. New York: Pantheon.

10 NOISE AND LIGHT POLLUTION

Bragdon, C. R. 1980. *Municipal Noise Legislation*. Atlanta: Fairmont Press.

Crawford, D. L. 1985. *Light Pollution: The Adverse Impact of Urban Sky Glow on Astronomy and on the Environment*. Tucson, AZ: Kitt Peak National Observatory.

Denver City and County. 1988. *New Denver Airport Environmental Assessment*. (Draft). Denver, CO: Denver City and County.

EPA. 1977. *Toward a National Strategy for Noise Control*. Washington, DC: GPO.

Fletcher, J. L., and R. G. Busnel, eds. 1978. *Effects of Noise on Wildlife*. New York: Academic Press.

Harvey, M. W., J. W. Frazier, and M. Matulionis. 1979. "Cognition of a Hazardous Environment: Reaction to Buffalo Airport Noise." *Economic Geography* 55: 263–286.

Hendry, A. 1984. "Light Pollution: A Status Report." *Sky & Telescope* 67: 504–507.

Kryter, K.D. 1985. *The Effects of Noise*. 2d ed. Orlando, FL: Academic Press.

Milne, A. 1979. *Noise Pollution: Impact and Countermeasures*. New York: David and Charles.

National Academy of Sciences. 1981. *Effects on Human Health from Long-Term Exposure to Noise*. Washington, DC: National Academy Press.

New York Times. May 19, 1988. "Groundbreaking Set for New Denver Airport": A-22.

———. July 31, 1988. "How Denver Managed to Sell a New Airport": E-4.

Sullivan, W. 1984. "Endangered Night Skies." *CoEvolution Quarterly* 43: 12–15.

Walker, M. F. 1970. "The California Site Survey." *Publications of the Astronomical Society of the Pacific* 82: 672–698.

———. 1973. "Light Pollution in California and Arizona." *Publications of the Astronomical Society of the Pacific* 85: 508–519.

Walker, M. F. 1977. "The Effects of Urban Lighting on the Brightness of the Night Sky." *Publications of the Astronomical Society of the Pacific* 89: 405–409.

Walton, S. 1980. "Noise Pollution: Environmental Battle of the 1980s." *BioScience* 30: 205–207.

11 SOLID WASTES

Allan, T., B. Platt, and D. Morris. 1989. *Beyond 25 Percent: Materials Recovery Comes of Age*. Washington, DC: Institute for Local Self-Reliance.

Blumberg, L., and R. Gottlieb. 1989. *War on Waste: Can America Win Its Battle With Garbage?* Washington, DC: Island Press.

Brown, R. S., S. Dresser-Gagnon, and D. Gona. 1987. "Solid Waste Programs in the States." *Journal of Resource Management and Technology* 15(3): 132–144.

Chandler, W. U. 1983. *Materials Recycling: The Virture of Necessity*. Worldwatch Paper 56. Washington, DC: Worldwatch.

Concern, Inc. 1988. *Waste: Choices for Communities*. Washington, DC: Concern, Inc.

Conservation Foundation. 1987. *State of the Environment: A View Toward the Nineties*. Washington, DC: CF.

Cowen, W. T. 1987. "Massachusetts Fiddles as Capacity 'Burns' Away." *Waste Age* 18(12): 118–124, 181.

Environmental Action Foundation. 1989. *Legislative Summary: Mandatory Statewide Recycling Laws*. Washington, DC: EAF.

Environmental Defense Fund. 1985. *To Burn or Not to Burn*. New York: EDF.

Environmental Defense Fund. 1988. *Coming Full Circle: Successful Recycling Today*. New York: EDF.

EPA. 1984. *Environmental Regulations and Technology: Use and Disposal of Municipal Wastewater Sludge*. EPA 625/10-84-003. Washington, DC: EPA.

———. 1986a. *Census of State and Territorial Subtitle D Non-Hazardous Waste Programs*. EPA/530-SW-86-039. Washington, DC: EPA.

EPA. 1986b. *Subtitle D Study: Phase I Report*. EPA/530-SW-86-054. Washington, DC: EPA.

———. 1988a. *Evaluation of Scientific Issues Related to Municipal Waste Combustion*. Washington, DC: EPA.

———. 1988b. *Report to Congress: Solid Waste Disposal in the United States*. 2 vol. EPA/ 530-SW-88-011/011B. Washington, DC: EPA.

———. 1989. *The Solid Waste Dilemma: An Agenda for Action*. EPA/530-SW-89-019. Washington, DC: EPA.

Franklin Associates, Ltd. 1986. *Characterization of Municipal Solid Waste in the United States, 1960 to 2000*. Washington, DC: EPA.

———. for EPA. 1988. *Characterization of Municipal Solid Waste in the United States, 1960–2000*. (Update 1988). EPA/530-SW-88-033. Washington, DC: EPA.

Goldoftas, B. 1987. "Recycling: Cutting the Waste in Trash." *Technology Review* 90: 28–35ff.

Gould, R. N. 1988. "Refuse-to-Energy is Not Dead." *Waste Age* 19(11): 61–66.

———, ed. 1990. *1990–91 Resource Recovery Yearbook: Directory & Guide*. New York: Governmental Advisory Associates.

Graff, G. 1988. "The Looming Crisis in Plastics Waste Disposal." *Issues in Science and Technology* 4: 105–110.

Hershkowitz, A. 1987. "Burning Trash: How It Could Work." *Technology Review* 90: 27–34.

Hilton, B. 1987. "Rhode Island Chooses the Fast Lane." *Waste Age* 18(11): 165–168.

Hurst, K., and P. Relis. 1987. *The Next Frontier: Solid Waste Source Reduction*. Santa Barbara: Community Environmental Council.

Institute for Local Self-Reliance. 1986. *Environmental Review of Waste Incineration*. Washington, DC: ILSR.

Mattheis, A. 1987a. "New Jersey Lays Down the Law." *Waste Age* 18(6): 59–60.

———. 1987b. "New Lease on Life for Connecticut Landfills?" *Waste Age* 18(8): 81–85.

———. 1987c. " 'Opportunity' to Recycle Knocks in Oregon." *Waste Age* 18: 33–37.

———. 1988. "Are New York's Recycling Plans Realistic?" *Waste Age* 19(1): 63–68.

Neal, H. A., and J. R. Schubel. 1987. *Solid Waste Management and the Environment: The Mounting Garbage and Trash Crisis*. Englewood Cliffs, NJ: Prentice-Hall.

Newsday. 1989. *Rush to Burn: Solving America's Garbage Crisis?* Washington, DC: Island Press.

OTA. 1989. *Facing America's Trash: What Next for Municipal Solid Waste?* OTA-O-424. Washington, DC: GPO.

Pollack, C. 1987. *Mining Urban Wastes: The Potential for Recycling*. Washington, DC: Worldwatch.

Relis, P., and A. Dominski. 1987. *Beyond the Crisis: Integrated Waste Management*. Santa Barbara, CA: Community Environmental Council.

Robinson, W. D. 1986. *The Solid Waste Handbook: A Practical Guide*. New York: Wiley.

Selke, S. E. 1990. *Packaging and the Environment*. Lancaster, PA: Technomic.

"Waste Age 1988 Refuse Incineration and Refuse-to-Energy Listings." 1988. *Waste Age* 19(11): 195–212.

Wilson, G. B., and D. Dalmat. 1983. "Sewage Sludge Composting in U.S.A." *BioCycle* 24(5): 20–23.

12 TOXIC AND HAZARDOUS THREATS

Acton, J. P. 1989. *Understanding Superfund: A Progress Report*. Santa Monica, CA: Rand Corporation.

American Cancer Society. Annual. *Cancer Facts & Figures*. New York: ACS.

Andrews, R. N. L. 1987. "Local Planners and Hazardous Materials." *Journal of the American Planning Association* 53: 3–5.

Asbestos Abatement Regulatory Service. *State and Local Laws and Regulations*. Revised bimonthly. Washington, DC: AARS.

Association of State and Territorial Solid Waste Management Officials. 1987. *State Programs for Hazardous Waste Site Assessments and Remedial Actions*. Washington, DC: ASTSWMO.

Barnes, D. 1983. "An Overview of Dioxin." *EPA Journal* 9(3): 16–19.

Battelle Columbus Division, et al. 1988. *Assessing Asbestos Exposure in Public Buildings*. EPA 560/5-88-002. Washington, DC: EPA.

Bezdicek, D. F., ed. 1984. *Organic Farming: Current Technology and Its Role in Sustainable Agriculture*. Madison, WI: American Society of Agronomy.

Bond, D. H. 1984. "At-Sea Incineration of Hazardous Wastes." *Environmental Science and Technology* 18(5): 148A–152A.

Borrelli, P. 1982. "Not in My Backyard: The Legacy of Love Canal." *Amicus Journal* 4(2): 42–47.

Bosso, C. J. 1988. *Pesticides & Politics: The Life Cycle of a Public Issue*. Pittsburgh: University of Pittsburgh Press.

Bottrell, D. 1979. *Integrated Pest Management*. Washington, DC: Council on Environmental Quality.

Braun, S. L., L. M. Nido, and M. Dies, Jr. 1988. "Asbestos in Schools: The New AHERA Regulations." *Inquiry & Analysis* January: 1–5.

Brenner, D. J. 1989. *Radon: Risk and Remedy*. Salt Lake City: W. H. Freeman.

Brown, M. 1979. *Laying Waste: The Poisoning of America by Toxic Wastes*. New York: Pantheon.

Brown, M. H. 1987. *The Toxic Cloud*. New York: Harper & Row.

———. 1988. "Love Canal Revisited." *Amicus Journal* 10(3): 37–44.

———. 1989. "A Toxic Ghost Town." *Atlantic* 263(1): 23–28.

Bureau of National Affairs. 1987. *Pesticides: State and Federal Regulation*. Washington, DC: Bureau of National Affairs.

Cannon, J. A. 1986. "The Regulation of Toxic Air Pollutants: A Critical Review." *Journal of the Air Pollution Control Association* 36: 562–573.

Carson, R. 1962. *Silent Spring*. Boston: Houghton-Mifflin.

Cassel, S. 1988. "Managing Household Hazardous Waste: A Framework for Action." *Environmental Impact Assessment Review* 8: 307–322.

CBO. 1985. *Hazardous Waste Management: Recent Policy Changes and Policy Alternatives*. Washington, DC: CBO.

———. 1990. *Federal Liabilities Under Hazardous Waste Laws*. Washington, DC: GPO.

Christian, J. J. 1983. "Love Canal's Unhealthy Voles." *Natural History* 92(10): 8–16.

Cohen, S. 1984. "Defusing the Toxic Time Bomb: Federal Hazardous Waste Programs." In N. J. Vig and M. E. Kraft, eds., *Environmental Policy in the 1980s*. Washington, DC: Congressional Quarterly Press.

Colten, C. E. 1990. "Historical Hazards: The Geography of Relict Industrial Wastes." *Professional Geographer* 42(2): 143–156.

Concern, Inc. 1988. *Household Waste: Issues and Opportunities*. Washington, DC: Concern, Inc.

———. 1988. *Pesticides: A Community Action Guide*. Washington, DC: Concern, Inc.

Condron, M. M., and D. C. Sipher. 1987. *Hazardous Waste Facility Siting: A National Survey*. Albany, NY: New York State Legislative Commission on Toxic Substances and Hazardous Wastes.

Conn, W. D. 1989. "Managing Household Hazardous Waste." *Journal of the American Planning Association* 55: 192–203.

Conservation Foundation. 1987. *State of the Environment: A View Toward the Nineties*. Washington, DC: CF.

Consumer Product Safety Commission. 1988. *The Inside Story: A Guide to Indoor Air Quality*. Washington, DC: CPSC.

Cross, F. B. 1989. *Environmentally Induced Cancer and the Law: Risks, Regulation, and Victim Compensation*. Westport, CT: Greenwood Press.

Crosson, P. R., and S. Brubaker. 1982. *Resource and Environmental Effects of U.S. Agriculture*. Washington, DC: Resources for the Future.

Cutter, S. L. 1987. "Airborne Toxic Releases: Are Communities Prepared?" *Environment* 29(6): 12–17, 28–31.

Cutter, S. L., and W .D. Solecki. 1989. "The National Pattern of Airborne Toxic Releases." *Professional Geographer* 41: 149–161.

Dahlsten, D. L. 1983. "Pesticides in an Era of Integrated Pest Management." *Environment* 25(10): 14–54.

Dowling, M. 1985. "Defining and Classifying Hazardous Waste." *Environment* 27(3): 18–20, 36–41.

Doyle, P., and L. Morandi. 1988. "State Radon Programs: The Role of Legislation." *State Legislative Report* 13(10). Denver: National Conference of State Legislatures.

Environ Corporation. 1983. *Approaches to the Assessment of Health Impacts of Groundwater Contaminants*. Washington, DC: OTA.

EPA. 1981. *Asbestos in Schools*. EPA 560/5-81-002. Washington, DC: EPA.

———. 1984a. *Asbestos in Buildings: A National Survey of Asbestos-containing Friable Materials*. EPA 560/5-84-006. Washington, DC: EPA.

———. 1984b. *National Survey of Hazardous Waste Generators and Treatment Storage and Disposal Facilities Regulated Under RCRA in 1981*. Washington, DC: EPA.

———. 1985a. *Acute Hazardous Event Data Base*. EPA 560-5-85-029. Washington, DC: EPA.

———. 1985b. *The Air Toxics Problem in the United States: An Analysis of Cancer Risks for Selected Pollutants*. Washington, DC: EPA.

———. 1985c. *Report to Congress on Injection of Hazardous Waste*. Washington, DC: EPA.

———. 1985d. *A Strategy to Reduce Risks to Public Health from Air Toxics*. Washington, DC: EPA.

———. 1986a. *Airborne Asbestos Health Assessment Update*. EPA/600/8-84/003F. Washington, DC: EPA.

———. 1986b. *Asbestos Fact Book*. A-107/86-002. Washington, DC: EPA.

———. 1986c. *Indoor Radon Fact Sheets*. Washington, DC: EPA.

———. 1986d. *National Priorities List Fact Book*, June 1986. Washington, DC: GPO.

———. 1986e. *Pesticides Fact Book*. EPA-107/86-003. Washington, DC: EPA.

———. 1986f. *RCRA Orientation Manual*. EPA 530-SW-86-001. Washington, DC: GPO.

———. 1986g. *Report to Congress on the Discharge of Hazardous Wastes to Publicly Owned Treatment Works*. EPA/530-SW-86-004. Washington, DC: EPA.

———. 1986h. *Superfund: A Six Year Perspective*. Washington, DC: EPA.

———. 1987a. *Indoor Air Facts*. Washington, DC: EPA.

———. 1987b. "The New Superfund." *EPA Journal*. (Special issue). 13(1).

———. 1987c. *Summary of State Radon Programs*. EPA 520/1-87-19. Washington, DC: EPA.

———. 1988a. *Chemicals in Your Community: A Guide to the Emergency Planning and Community Right-to-Know Act*. Washington, DC: EPA.

———. 1988b. *EPA Study of Asbestos-Containing Materials in Public Buildings: A Report to Congress*. Washington, DC: EPA.

———. 1988c. *National Dioxin Study: Report to Congress*. PB88-192687CBT. Springfield, VA: NTIS.

———. 1989a. *Report to Congress on Indoor Air Quality*. EPA/400-1-89. Washington, DC: EPA.

———. 1989b. *Superfund Progress Report*. Washington, DC: EPA.

———. 1989c. *The Toxics-Release Inventory: A National Perspective*. EPA 560/4-89-005. Washington, DC: GPO.

EPA and U.S. Consumer Product Safety Commission. 1988. *The Inside Story: A Guide to Indoor Air Quality*. EPA/400/1-88/004. Washington, DC: EPA.

EPA and U.S. Department of Health and Human Services. 1986. *A Citizen's Guide to Radon: What It Is and What to Do About It*. OPA-86-004. Washington, DC: EPA.

Epstein, S. S., et al. 1982. *Hazardous Waste in America*. San Francisco: Sierra Club Books.

Ferrey, S. 1987. "Toxic Shell Game." *Amicus Journal* 9(3): 7–9.

GAO. 1986a. *Hazardous Waste: EPA Has Made Limited Progress in Determining the Wastes to Be Regulated*. GAO/RCED-87-27. Washington, DC: GPO.

———. 1986b. *Nonagricultural Pesticides: Risks and Regulation*. GAO/RCED-86-97. Washington, DC: GPO.

———. 1986c. *Pesticides: EPA's Formidable Task to Assess and Regulate Their Risks*. GAO/ RCED-86-125. Washington, DC: GPO.

———. 1986d. *Pesticides: Need to Enhance FDA's Ability to Protect the Public from Illegal Residues*. GAO/RCED-87-7. Washington, DC: GPO.

———. 1987a. *Air Pollution: States Assigned a Major Role in EPA's Air Toxics Strategy*. GAO/RCED-87-76. Washington, DC: GPO.

———. 1987b. *Hazardous Waste: Uncertainties of Existing Data*. GAO/PEMD-87-11BR. Washington, DC: GPO.

———. 1987c. *Superfund: Extent of Nation's Potential Hazardous Waste Problem Still Unknown*. GAO/RCED-88-44. Washington, DC: GPO.

———. 1988a. *Hazardous Waste: New Approach Needed to Manage the Resource Conservation and Recovery Act*. GAO/RCED-88-115. Washington, DC: GPO.

———. 1988b. *Indoor Radon: Limited Federal Response to Reduce Contamination in Housing*. GAO/RCED-88-103. Washington, DC: GPO.

Gerusky, T. M., and A. J. Hazle. 1987. "Radon: Reports from the States." *Environment* 29(1): 12–17, 35–39.

Gianessi, L. P. 1987a. "Lack of Data Stymies Informed Decisions on Agricultural Pesticides." *Resources* 89: 1–5.

———. 1987b. *Use of Selected Soluble Pesticides in Agricultural Crop Production by State*. Washington, DC: Resources for the Future.

Gibbs, L. 1982. *The Love Canal: My Story*. Albany, NY: State University of New York Press.

Gilliom, R. J., R. B. Alexander, and R. A. Smith. 1985. *Pesticides in the Nation's Rivers, 1975–1980*. USGS Water Supply Paper 2271. Washington, DC: GPO.

Glick, B. J. 1982. "The Spatial Organization of Cancer Mortality." *Annals, Association of American Geographers* 72: 471–481.

Glickman, T. S. 1988. "Hazardous Materials Routing—Risk Management or Mismanagement?" *Resources* 93: 11–13

Goldman, B. A., J. A. Hulme, and C. Johnson. 1985. *Hazardous Waste Management: Reducing the Risk*. Washington, DC: Island Press.

Gordon, W., and J. Bloom. 1985. *Deeper Problems: Limits to Underground Injection as a Hazardous Waste Disposal Method*. Washington, DC: NRDC.

Gough, M. 1986. *Dioxin, Agent Orange: The Facts*. New York: Plenum.

———. 1989. "Estimating Cancer Mortality." *Environmental Science and Technology* 23(8): 925–930.

———. 1990. "Environmental Exposures and Cancer Risks." *Resources* 98: 9–12.

Greenberg, M. R., ed. 1985. "Cancer Atlases: Uses and Limitations." *The Environmentalist* 35: 189–190.

———. 1987. *Public Health and the Environment*. New York: Guilford.

Greenberg, M. R., and R. F. Anderson. 1984. *Hazardous Waste Siting: The Credibility Gap*. New Brunswick, NJ: Rutgers University Center for Urban Policy Research.

Hadden, S. G. 1986. *Read the Label: Reducing Risk by Providing Information*. Boulder, CO: Westview.

Hirschorn, J. S. 1988. "Cutting Production of Hazardous Waste." *Technology Review* 91(3): 52–61.

Hohenemser, C., et al. 1983. "The Nature of Technological Hazard." *Science* 220: 378–384.

Holleb, A. I., ed. 1986. *The American Cancer Society Cancer Book*. New York: Doubleday.

House of Representatives. 1989. "Statement of the Honorable Henry A. Waxman, Chairman, Subcommittee on Health and the Environment, Committee on Energy and Commerce, on the Introduction of the Air Toxics Control Act of 1989."

Huisingh, D., et al. 1986. *Proven Profits from Pollution Prevention: Case Studies in Resource Conservation and Waste Reduction*. Washington, DC: Institute for Local Self Reliance.

Kolata, G. B. 1980. "Love Canal: False Alarm Caused by Botched Study." *Science* 208: 1239–1242.

Kupchella, C. E. 1987. *Dimensions of Cancer*. Belmont, CA: Wadsworth.

Lake, R. W., ed. 1987. *Resolving Locational Conflict*. New Brunswick, NJ: Rutgers University Center for Urban Policy Research.

Landy, M. 1986. "Cleaning Up Superfund." *The Public Interest* 85: 58–71.

Lautenburg, F. R., and D. Durenberger. 1989. *Lautenburg-Durenberger Report on Superfund Implementation*. Washington, DC: Senate Subcommittee on Superfund, Ocean and Water.

Lawless, E. W. 1977. *Technology and Social Shock*. New Brunswick, NJ: Rutgers University Press.

Lester, J. P. 1988. "Superfund Implementation: Exploring Environmental Gridlock." *Environmental Impact Assessment Review* 8: 159–174.

Lester, J. P., et al. 1983. "Hazardous Wastes, Politics, and Public Policy: A Comparative State Analysis." *Western Political Quarterly* 36: 258–285.

Levine, A. G. 1982. *Love Canal: Science, Politics and People*. Boston: Lexington.

Levinson, H. 1990. "Wasting Away:

Policies to Reduce Trash Toxicity and Quantity." *Environment* 32(2): 10–15, 31–36.

McCarthy, J. 1986. *Superfund: How Many Sites: How Much Money?* Washington, DC: Congressional Research Service.

McGlashan, N. D., and J. R. Blunden. 1983. *Geographical Aspects of Health*. London: Academic Press.

Machado, S., and S. Ridley. 1988. *Eliminating Indoor Pollution: Focus Paper 4*. Washington, DC: Renew America.

Marco, G. J., R. M. Hollingworth, and W. Durham. 1987. *Silent Spring Revisited*. Washington, DC: American Chemical Society.

Mattheis, A. 1987. "Collecting Household Toxics: Is It Worth the Effort?" *Waste Age* 18(2): 76–85.

———. 1988. "Household Toxics Programs Are Here to Stay." *Waste Age* 19(4): 99–104.

May, T. W., and G. L. McKinney. 1981. "Cadmium, Lead, Mercury, Arsenic, and Selenium Concentrations of Freshwater Fish, 1976–1977." *Pesticide Monitoring Journal* 15: 14–38.

Miller, R., et al. 1986. "The Regulation of Toxic Air Pollutants: Critical Review Discussion Papers." *Journal of the Air Pollution Control Association* 36: 986–996.

Morehouse, W., and M. A. Subramaniam. 1986. *The Bhopal Tragedy: What Really Happened and What It Means for American Workers and Communities at Risk*. New York: Council on International Affairs.

Mott, L. 1984. *Pesticides in Food: What the Public Needs to Know*. San Francisco, CA: NRDC.

Muri, W., and J. Underwood. 1987. *Promoting Hazardous Waste Reduction*. New York: Inform, Inc.

National Academy of Engineering, ed. 1986. *Hazards: Technology and Fairness*. Washington, DC: National Academy Press.

National Cancer Institute. 1987–1988. *Atlas of U.S. Cancer Mortality*. Bethesda, MD: National Institutes of Health.

National Research Council. 1985. *Reducing Hazardous Waste Generation*. Washington, DC: National Academy Press.

———. 1987. *Regulating Pesticides in Food: The Delaney Paradox*. Washington, DC: National Academy Press.

———. 1989. *Alternative Agriculture*. Washington, DC: National Academy Press.

Nazaroff, W. W., and A. V. Nero, Jr. 1988. *Radon and its Decay Products in Indoor Air*. New York: Wiley.

Nelkin, D. M., and M. S. Brown. 1984. *Workers at Risk: Voices from the Workplace*. Chicago: University of Chicago Press.

New York State Department of Health. 1981. *Love Canal: A Special Report to the Governor and Legislature*. Albany: NYSDOH.

———. 1988. *Love Canal Emergency Declaration Area: Decision on Habitability*. Albany: NYSDOH.

New York State Legislative Commission on Solid Waste Management. 1988. *Household Hazardous Waste: An Overview*. Albany: New York State Senate.

New York State Legislative Commission on Toxic Substances and Hazardous Wastes. 1987. *Hazardous Waste Facility Siting: A National Survey, June 1987*. Albany: New York State Legislature.

New York State Office of Public Health. 1978. *Love Canal: Public Health Time Bomb*. Albany: NYSOPH.

Nicholls, G. P., D. A. Deieso, and D. Nash. 1987. "Radon: Report from the States." *Environment* 29(2): 12–15, 34–38.

Nickell, N., and S. Ridley. 1988. *Reducing Pesticide Contamination: Focus Paper 2*. Washington, DC: Renew America.

OTA. 1983. *Technologies and Management Strategies for Hazardous Waste Control*. OTA-M-196. Washington, DC: GPO.

———. 1985. *Superfund Strategy*. OTA-ITE-253. Washington, DC: GPO.

———. 1986a. *Serious Reduction of Hazardous Waste*. OTA-ITE-318. Washington, DC: GPO.

———. 1986b. *Transportation of Hazardous Materials: State and Local Activities*. OTA-SET-301. Washington, DC: GPO.

———. 1987. *From Pollution to Prevention: A Progress Report on Waste Reduction*. OTA-ITE-347. Washington, DC: GPO.

———. 1988a. *Are We Cleaning Up? 10 Superfund Case Studies*. OTA-ITE-362. Washington, DC: GPO.

———. 1988b. *Issues in Medical Waste Management: Background Paper*. OTA-BP-O-49. Washington, DC: GPO.

———. 1990. *Coming Clean: Superfund Problems Can Be Solved*. PB90-178823CBT. Springfield, VA: NTIS.

Pimentel, D., and J. H. Perkins, eds. 1980. *Pest Control: Cultural and Environmental Aspects*. Boulder, CO: Westview.

Purin, G., et al. 1987. *Alternatives to Landfilling Household Toxics*. Sacramento, CA: Golden Empire Health Planning Center.

Redfield, S. E. 1984–1985. "Chemical Trespass?—An Overview of Statutory and Regulatory Efforts to Control Pesticide Drift." *Kentucky Law Journal* 73: 855–918.

Regenstein, L. 1982. *America the Poisoned*. Washington, DC: Acropolis.

Reilly, W. K. 1989. *A Management Review of the Superfund Program*. Washington, DC: EPA.

Research Triangle Institute. 1986. *1986 National Screening Survey of Hazardous Waste Treatment, Storage, Disposal, and Recycling Facilities*. Research Triangle Park, NC: EPA.

Ridley, S. 1988. *The State of the States 1988*. Washington, DC: Fund for Renewable Energy and the Environment.

Riggan, W. B., et al. 1987. *U.S. Cancer Mortality Rates and Trends, 1950–1979*. EPA/600/1-83/015. Washington, DC: GPO.

Robertson, D. K., et al. 1987. "Liquid Household Hazardous Wastes in the United States: Identification, Disposal, and Management Plan." *Environmental Management* 11: 735–742.

Royston, M. G. 1979. *Pollution Prevention Pays*. New York: Pergamon.

Schwartz, A., and R. Frank. 1987. "Poisons in Your Home: A Disposal Dilemma." *Audubon* 89(3): 12–16.

Scott, R. M. 1989. *Chemical Hazards in the Workplace*. Chelsea, IL: Lewis.

SCS Engineers. 1986. *A Survey of Household Hazardous Wastes and Related Collection Programs*. EPA/530-SW-86-038. Washington, DC: EPA.

Scully, J., ed. 1986. "Hazardous Wastes." *Environment*. (Special issue). 28(3).

Segel, E., et al. 1985. *The Toxic Substances Dilemma: A Plan for Citizen Action*. Washington, DC: National Wildlife Federation.

Senate. 1988. *Environmental Issues Related to the Use of Pesticides*. Hearing before Committee on Environment and Public Works. 100th Congress

———. 1989. *Government Regulation of Pesticides in Food: The Need for Administrative and Regulatory Reform*. Committee on Environment and Public Works. S. Prt. 101–55. 101st Congress, lst Session.

Sexton, K. 1986. "Indoor Air Quality: An Overview of Policy and Regulatory Issues." *Science, Technology, and Human Values* 11: 53–67.

Sheiman, D. A. 1989. *A Who's Who of American Toxic Air Polluters: A Guide to More Than 1500 Factories in 46 States Emitting Cancer-Causing Chemicals*. New York: NRDC.

Sheiman, D. A., and K. Silver. 1986. *A State By State Analysis of EPA's Acute Hazardous Events Data Base*. Washington, DC: National Campaign Against Toxic Hazards and NRDC.

Sheldon, L. S., et al. 1988. *Indoor Air Quality in Public Buildings*. Research Triangle Park, NC: EPA.

State and Territorial Air Pollution Program Administrators and Association of Local Air Pollution Control Officials. 1984. *Toxic Air Pollutants: State and Local Regulatory Strategies: A Survey*. Washington, DC: STAPPA and ALAPCO.

Technical Review Committee. 1988. *Love Canal Emergency Declaration Area Habitability Study Final Report*. Volumes I-V. Albany, NY: New York State Department of Health.

Thompson Publishing Group. 1987. *Community Right-to-Know Manual: The Guide to SARA Title III*. (Periodically updated). Washington, DC: Thompson.

Trost, C. 1984. *The Chemical Industry and Its Threat to America*. New York: Times Books.

Tschirley, F. H. 1986. "Dioxin." *Scientific American* 254: 29–35.

USDA. 1989. *Agricultural Resources: Inputs Situation and Outlook*. AR-15. Washington, DC: USDA.

U.S. Public Health Service. *Annual Report on Carcinogens*. Research Triangle Park, NC: Department of Health and Human Services.

Virginia Cooperative Extension Service. 1987. *The National Evaluation of Extension's Integrated Pest Management (IPM) Programs*. Blacksburg, VA: VCES.

Whittaker, J., et al. 1982. "Risk-Based Zoning for Toxic Gas Pipelines." *Risk Analysis* 2: 163–169.

Williams, M., and D. Duxbury. 1987. "Managing Household Hazardous Wastes." *EPA Journal* 13(3): 11–13.

Williams, N. M., et al. 1988. *Pesticides in Ground Water Data Base: 1988 Interim Report*. Washington, DC: EPA.

Wilson, B. 1987. *The Politics of Asbestos*. New York: Dolphin Books.

Ziegler, D. J., J. H. Johnson, Jr., and S. D. Brunn. 1983. *Technological Hazards*. Washington, DC: Association of American Geographers.

13 ENERGY

Ahearne, J. F. 1989. "Will Nuclear Power Recover in a Greenhouse?" *Resources* 94: 14–17.

Alaska, State of, et al. 1989. *State/Federal Natural Resource Damage Assessment Plan for the Exxon Valdez Oil Spill*. Public Review Draft. Juneau, AK: Trustee Council.

Alford, P. N., and A. N. Dravo. 1986. *Hot Stuff: Issues in the Management of High-Level Radioactive Waste*. Washington, DC: National League of Cities.

American Council for an Energy Efficient Economy. 1988. *Energy Efficiency: A New Agenda*. Washington, DC: ACEEE.

American Physical Society. 1985. *Radionuclide Release from Severe Accidents at Nuclear Power Plants*. New York: APS.

Arrandale, T. 1983. *The Battle for Natural Resources*. Washington, DC: Congressional Quarterly Inc.

Bartlett, D. L., and J. B. Steele. 1985. *Forevermore: Nuclear Waste in America*. New York: W. W. Norton.

Blackburn, J. O. 1987. *The Renewable Energy Alternative: How the United States and the World Can Prosper Without Nuclear Energy or Coal*. Durham, NC: Duke University Press.

BLM. 1988. *Public Lands Statistics 1987*. Washington, DC: GPO.

Borrelli, P. 1987. "Oilscam." *Amicus Journal* 9(4): 21–25.

Bureau of the Census. 1989. *1989 Statistical Abstract of the United States*. 109th ed. Washington, DC: GPO.

Calzonetti, F. J., and B. D. Solomon, eds. 1985. *Geographical Dimensions of Energy*. Dordrecht: D. Reidel.

Campbell, J. L. 1988. *Collapse of an Industry: Nuclear Power and the Contradictions of U.S. Policy*. Ithaca, NY: Cornell University Press.

Carter, L. J. 1987. *Nuclear Imperatives and Public Trust: Dealing with Radioactive Waste*. Washington, DC: Resources for the Future.

Chandler, W. U., H. S. Geller, and M. Ledbetter. 1988. *Energy Efficiency: A New Agenda*. Washington, DC: American Council for An Energy-Efficient Economy.

Church, A. M., and R. D. Norton. 1981. "Issues in Emergency Preparedness for Radiological Transportation Accidents." *Natural Resources Journal* 21: 757–771.

Clough, N. K., P. C. Patton, and A. C. Christiansen, eds. 1987. *Arctic National Wildlife Refuge, Alaska: Coastal Plain Resource Assessment*. Washington, DC: FWS, USGS, and BLM.

Cogan, D., and S. Williams. 1983. *Generating Energy Alternatives: Conservation, Load Management, and Renewable Energy at America's Electric Utilities*. Washington, DC: Investor Responsibility Center.

Congressional Quarterly Editors. 1985. *Energy and Environment: The Unfinished Business*. Washington, DC: Congressional Quarterly.

Coyle, D., et al. 1988. *Deadly Defense: Military Radioactive Landfills*. New York: Radioactive Waste Campaign.

Crane, L. T. 1984. *Residential Energy Conservation*. Washington, DC: Congressional Research Service.

Cuff, D. J., and W. J. Young. 1986. *The United States Energy Atlas*. 2d ed. New York: Macmillan.

Deudney, D., and C. Flavin. 1983. *Renewable Energy: The Power to Choose*. New York: W. W. Norton.

DOE. 1980. *Geothermal Energy and Our Environment*. Washington, DC: DOE.

———. 1983. *Nuclear Plant Cancellations: Causes, Costs, Consequences*. DOE/EIA-0392. Washington, DC: GPO.

———. 1987a. *Integrated Data Base for 1987: Spent Fuel and Radioactive Waste Inventories, Projections, and Characteristics*. DOE/RW-0006. Washington, DC: GPO.

———. 1987b. *Recommendations for Management of Greater-Than-Class-C Low Level Radioactive Waste*. DOE/NE-0077. Springfield, VA: NTIS.

———. 1987c. *The 1986 State-by-State Assessment of the Low-Level Radioactive Waste Received at Commercial Disposal Sites*. DOE/LLW 66T. Washington, DC: DOE.

Edison Electric Institute. 1988. *1986 Capacity and Generation of Non-Utility Sources of Energy*. Washington, DC: EEI.

Energy Information Administration. Annual. *Annual Energy Review*. DOE/EIA-0384. Washington, DC: EIA.

———. 1989a. *Coal Data: A Reference*. DOE/EIA-0064(87). Washington, DC: EIA.

———. 1989b. *Natural Gas Annual*. DOE/EIA-0. Washington, DC: EIA.

———. 1989c. *Petroleum Supply Annual*. DOE/EIA-0340. Washington, DC: EIA.

Federal Emergency Management Agency. 1988. *Post-Exercise Assessment: Shoreham Nuclear Power Station*. New York: FEMA.

Flavin, C. 1989. "Ten Years of Fallout." *World Watch* 2(2): 30–37.

FWS. 1988a. *Arctic National Wildlife Refuge Final Comprehensive Conservation Plan, Environmental Impact Statement, Wilderness Review, and Wild River Plans*. Anchorage, AK: FWS.

———. 1988b. *Comparison of Actual and Predicted Impacts of TAPS and Prudhoe Bay Oilfields on the North Slope of Alaska*. Fairbanks, AK: FWS.

GAO. 1986a. *Nuclear Energy: Environmental Issues at DOE's Nuclear Defense Facilities*. GAO/RCED-86-192. Washington, DC: GPO.

———. 1986b. *Nuclear Wastes: Unresolved Issues Concerning Hanford's Waste Management Practices*. Washington, DC: GPO.

———. 1986c. *Surface Mining: Interior Department and States Could Improve Inspection Programs*. GAO/RCED-87-40. Washington, DC: GPO.

———. 1987a. *Surface Mining: State and Federal Use of Alternative Enforcement Techniques*. GAO/RCED-87-160. Washington, DC: GPO.

———. 1987b. *Surface Mining: State Management of Abandoned Mine Land Funds*. GAO/RCED-87-57. Washington, DC: GPO.

Gever, J., et al. 1986. *Beyond Oil: The Threat to Food and Fuel in the Coming Decades*. Cambridge, MA: Ballinger.

Gordon, D. 1989. "Concern for Fuel Efficiency is Here—Again." *Nucleus* 11(3): 1, 4.

Harrowsmith. 1987. "The Danger Spreads: Mounting Evidence that Radioactive Releases all Over the Country Have Lethal Effects." *Harrowsmith* May/June.

House, J. W. 1983. "Energy Problems and Policies." In J. W. House, ed., *United States Public Policy: A Geographical View*. Oxford: Clarendon.

Johnson, C., D. May, and C. Pring. 1984. *Still Stripping the Law on Coal*. New York: NRDC.

Johnson, J. H., Jr. 1985. "A Model of Evacuation-Decision Making in a Nuclear Reactor Emergency." *Geographical Review* 75: 405–418.

Kasperson, R. E., ed. 1983. *Equity Issues in Radioactive Waste Management*. Cambridge: Oelgeschlager, Gunn, & Hain.

Kirby, A. M. 1988. "High-Level Nuclear Waste Transportation: Political Implications of the Weakest Link in the Nuclear Fuel Cycle." *Environment and Planning C: Government and Policy* 6: 311–322.

League of Women Voters Education Fund. 1982. *A Nuclear Power Primer: Issues for Citizens*. Washington, DC: LWV.

———. 1985. *The Nuclear Waste Primer: A Handbook for Citizens*. New York: Nick Lyons Books.

Lovins, A. B. 1977. *Soft Energy Paths: Toward a Durable Peace*. Cambridge, MA: Ballinger.

Lovins, A. B., and L. H. Lovins. 1982. *Brittle Power: Energy Strategy for National Security*. Andover, MA: Brick House.

Lovins, A.B., et al. 1989. *Least-Cost Energy: Solving the CO2 Problem*. 2d ed. Andover, MA: Brick House.

Macinko, G. 1983. "The Surface Mining

Control and Reclamation Act (1977)." In J. W. House, ed., *United States Public Policy: A Geographical View*. Oxford: Clarendon Press.

Markowitz, P. 1985. *The Least-Cost Alternative to New Power Plant Construction: A Strategy for Ensuring Utility Investments in Conservation and Renewable Energy Resources*. Washington, DC: Public Citizen.

Marshall, E. 1986. "Nuclear Waste Program Faces Political Burial." *Science* 233: 835–836.

Melosi, M. V. 1987. "Energy and Environment in the United States: The Era of Fossil Fuels." *Environmental Review* 11(3): 167–188.

Moskovitz, D. H. 1989. "Cutting the Nation's Electric Bill." *Issues in Science and Technology* 5(3): 88–93.

Murauskas, G. T., and F. M. Shelley. 1986. "Local Political Responses to Nuclear Waste Disposal." *Cities* 3: 157–162.

National Academy of Sciences. 1979. *Energy in Transition*. San Francisco: W. H. Freeman.

National Research Council. 1980. *Effects on Populations of Exposure to Low Levels of Ionizing Radiation: 1980*. Washington, DC: National Academy Press.

———. 1981. *Coal Mining and Ground-Water Resources in the United States*. Washington, DC: National Academy Press.

———. 1984. *Social and Economic Aspects of Radioactive Waste Disposal: Considerations for Institutional Management*. Washington, DC: National Academy Press.

National Wildlife Federation. 1985. *Failed Oversight: A Report on the Failure of the Office of Surface Mining to Enforce the Federal Surface Mining and Control Reclamation Act*. Washington, DC: NWF.

Nuclear Regulatory Commission and Federal Emergency Management Agency. 1988. *Criteria for Preparation and Evaluation of Radiological Emergency Response Plans and Preparedness in Support of Nuclear Power Plants*. NUREG-0654/FEMA-REP-1. Washington, DC: NRC and FEMA.

Openshaw, S. 1986. *Nuclear Power: Siting and Safety*. London: Routledge and Kegan Paul.

OTA. 1983. *Industrial and Commercial Cogeneration*. OTA-E-192. Springfield, VA: NTIS.

———. 1984a. *Environmental Protection in the Federal Coal Leasing Program*. OTA-E-237. Washington, DC: GPO.

OTA. 1984b. *Nuclear Power in an Age of Uncertainty*. Washington, DC: GPO.

———. 1985. *Managing the Nation's Commercial High-Level Radioactive Waste*. Washington, DC: GPO.

———. 1986. *Western Surface Mine Permitting and Reclamation*. OTA-E-280. Washington, DC: GPO.

———. 1988. *An Evaluation of Options for Managing Greater-Than-Class-C Low-Level Radioactive Waste: Background Paper*. OTA-BP-O-50. Washington, DC: GPO.

———. 1989. *Oil Production in the Arctic National Wildlife Refuge: The Technology & the Alaskan Oil Context*. OTA-E-395. Washington, DC: GPO.

Pasqualetti, M. J., and K. D. Pijawka. 1984. *Nuclear Power: Assessing and Managing Hazardous Technology*. Boulder, CO: Westview.

President's Commission on the Accident at Three Mile Island. 1979. *Report of the President's Commission on the Accident at Three Mile Island*. Washington, DC: GPO.

Prochaska, J. R. 1986. "Low-level Radioactive Waste Disposal Compacts." *Virginia Journal of Natural Resources Law* 5: 383–411.

Pryde, P. R. 1983. *Nonconventional Energy Resources*. New York: Wiley.

Renewable Energy Institute. 1986. *Annual Renewable Energy Review: Progress Through 1984*. Washington, DC: REI.

Resnikoff, M. 1983. *The Next Nuclear Gamble: Transportation and Storage of Nuclear Waste*. Washington, DC: Council on Economic Priorities.

———. 1987. *Living Without Landfills*. New York: Radioactive Waste Campaign.

Ridley, S. 1987. *The State of the States 1987*. Washington, DC: Fund for Renewable Energy and the Environment.

———. 1988. *The State of the States 1988*. Washington, DC: Fund for Renewable Energy and the Environment.

Rogers, R. 1987. "Alaskan Perspectives: On Jobs, Royalties, Conservation, and Survival." *Amicus Journal* 9(4): 26–27.

St. Aubin, K., ed. 1987. *1977–1987: The Abandoned Mine Land Program*. Springfield, VA: Association of Abandoned Mined Land Programs.

Sant, R. 1979. *The Least-Cost Energy Strategy: Minimizing Consumer Costs Through Competition*. Pittsburgh: Carnegie Mellon University Press.

Sawyer, S. W. 1986. *Renewable Energy: Progress, Prospects*. Washington, DC: Association of American Geographers.

Sills, D. L., C. P. Wolf, and V. B. Shelanski, eds. 1982. *Accident at Three Mile Island: The Human Dimensions*. Boulder, CO: Westview.

Slesin, L. 1987. "Power Lines and Cancer: The Evidence Grows." *Technology Review* 90(7): 53–59.

Social Data Analysts, Inc. 1982. *Attitudes Toward Evacuation: Reactions of Long Island Residents to a Possible Accident at the Shoreham Nuclear Power Plant*. Setauket, NY: Social Data Analysts.

Solomon, B. D., and F .M. Shelley. 1988. "Siting Patterns of Nuclear Waste Repositories." *Journal of Geography* 87(2): 59–71.

Speer, L., et al. 1988. *Oil in the Arctic: The Environmental Record of Oil Development on Alaska'a North Slope*. New York: NRDC.

———. 1989. "Oil Development and the Arctic National Wildlife Refuge." *Environment* 31(4): 42–43.

Stobaugh, R., and D. Yergin. 1983. *Energy Future*. New York: Random House.

Union of Concerned Scientists. 1985. *Safety Second: A Critical Evaluation of the NRC's First Decade*. Washington, DC: UCS.

U.S. Department of the Interior. Annual. *OSMRE Annual Report*. Washington, DC: DOI.

———. 1987. *Surface Coal Mining Reclamation: 10 Years of Progress, 1977–1987*. Washington, DC: GPO.

Van Til, J. 1981. *Living with Energy Shortfall: A Future for American Towns and Cities*. Boulder, CO: Westview.

Walker, D. A., et al. 1987. "Cumulative Impacts of Oil Fields on Northern Alaskan Landscapes." *Science* 238: 757–761.

Watkins, T. H. 1988. *Vanishing Arctic: Alaska's National Wildlife Refuge*. New York: Aperature.

World Resources Institute and Institute for International Development. 1988. *World Resources 1988–1989*. New York: Basic Books.

Ziegler, D. J., and J. H. Johnson, Jr. 1984. "Evacuation Behavior in Response to Nuclear Power Plant Accidents." *Professional Geographer* 36: 207–215.

Ziegler, D. J., J. H. Johnson, Jr., and S. D. Brunn. 1983. *Technological Hazards*. Washington, DC: Association of American Geographers.

14 NON-ENERGY MINERALS

Bureau of Mines. Annual. *Minerals Yearbook*. Washington, DC: GPO.

Bureau of Mines. 1988. *Mineral Commodity Summaries 1988*. Washington, DC: GPO.

Cameron, E. N. 1986. *At the Crossroads: The Mineral Problems of the United States*. New York: Wiley.

Clark, J. P., and F. R. Field, III. 1985. "How Critical Are Critical Materials?" *Technology Review* 88(6): 38–46.

Council on Economics and National Security. 1981. *Strategic Minerals: A Resource Crisis*. Washington, DC: CENS.

EPA. 1983. *Surface Impoundment Assessment National Report*. EPA 570/9-84-002. Washington, DC: EPA.

———. 1985. *Report to Congress: Wastes from the Extraction and Beneficiation of Metallic Ores, Phosphate Rock, Asbestos, Overburden from Uranium Mining, and Oil Shale*. EPA/530-SW-85-033. Washington, DC: EPA.

GAO. 1987. *Federal Land Management: Nonfederal Land and Mineral Rights Could Impact Future Wilderness Areas*. GAO/RCED-87-131. Washington, DC: GPO.

Johnson, W., and J. Paone. 1982. *Land Utilization and Reclamation in the Mining Industry, 1930–1980*. Information Circular 8862. Washington, DC: Bureau of Mines.

Leontief, W., et al. 1983. *The Future of Nonfuel Minerals in the U.S. and World Economy*. Lexington, MA: Lexington Books.

Leshy, J. D. 1987. *The Mining Law: A Study in Perpetual Motion*. Washington, DC: Resources for the Future.

OTA. 1985. *Strategic Materials: Technologies to Reduce U.S. Import Vulnerability*. Washington, DC: GPO.

Olen, P .M., et al. 1985. "Mining and Wilderness: Incompatible Uses or Justifiable Compromise." *Environment* 27(3): 13–18.

15 PARKS, RECREATION, AND WILDLIFE

Allin, C. 1982. *The Politics of Wilderness Preservation*. Westport, CT: Greenwood Press.

Baden, J., and D. Leal, eds. 1989. *The Yellowstone Primer: Land and Resource Management in the Greater Yellowstone Ecosystem*. San Francisco: Pacific Research Institute for Public Policy.

Bartlett, R. A. 1985. *Yellowstone: A Wilderness Besieged*. Tucson: University of Arizona Press.

Berger, J., and J. W. Sinton. 1985. *Water, Earth, and Fire: Land Use and Environmental Planning in the New Jersey Pine Barrens*. Baltimore: Johns Hopkins.

Blockstein, D. E. 1989. "Toward a Federal Plan for Biodiversity." *Issues in Science and Technology* 5(4): 63–67.

Brenneman, R. L., and S. M. Bates, eds. 1984. *Land-Saving Action*. Washington, DC: Island Press.

Carey, A., and S. Carey. 1989. *Yellowstone's

Red Summer*. Flagstaff, AZ: Northland.

Chandler, W. J., ed. 1989 (and other years). *Audubon Wildlife Report 1989/90*. New York: Academic Press.

Chase, A. 1986. *Playing God in Yellowstone: Destruction of America's First National Park*. New York: Atlantic Monthly Press.

———. 1987. "How to Save Our National Parks." *Atlantic Monthly* 260(1): 35–44.

Collins, B. R., and E. W. B. Russell, eds. 1988. *Protecting the New Jersey Pinelands: A New Direction in Land-Use Management*. New Brunswick, NJ: Rutgers University Press.

Connally, E., ed. 1982. *National Parks in Crisis*. Washington, DC: National Parks and Conservation Association.

Conservation Foundation. 1972. *National Parks for the Future*. Washington, DC: CF.

———. 1985. *National Parks for a New Generation*. Washington, DC: CF.

———. 1987. *State of the Environment: A View Toward the Nineties*. Washington, DC: CF.

Corbett, M. R.,ed. 1983. *Greenline Parks: Land Conservation Trends for the Eighties and Beyond*. Washington, DC: National Parks and Conservation Association.

Coyle, K. J. 1988. *The American Rivers Guide to Wild and Scenic River Designation*. Washington, DC: American Rivers.

Davis, J. S. 1986. "The National Trails System Act and the Use of Protective Federal Zoning." *Harvard Environmental Law Review* 10: 189–255.

Davis, T. 1986. "Managing to Keep Rivers Wild." *Technology Review* 89: 26–33.

DiSilvestro, R. L. *The Endangered Kingdom: The Struggle to Save America's Wildlife*. New York: Wiley.

Dunlap, T. 1988. *Saving America's Wildlife*. Princeton, NJ: Princeton University Press.

Echeverria, J. D., and J. Fosburgh. *American Rivers Outstanding Rivers List*. Washington, DC: American Rivers.

FWS. Monthly. "Endangered Species Technical Bulletin." Washington, DC: FWS.

Fitzgerald, J., and G. M. Meese. 1986. *Saving Endangered Species: Amending and Implementing the Endangered Species Act*. Washington, DC: Defenders of Wildlife.

Foresta, R. A. 1984. *America's National Parks and Their Keepers*. Washington, DC: Resources for the Future.

———. 1987. "Transformation of the Appalachian Trail." *Geographical Review* 77: 76–85.

Gallagher, T. J., and A. F. Gasbarro. 1989. "The Battles for Alaska: Planning in America's Last Wilderness." *Journal of the American Planning Association* 55: 433–444.

GAO. 1987. *Parks and Recreation: Limited Progress Made in Documenting and Mitigating Threats to the Parks.* GAO/ RCED-87-36. Washington, DC: GPO.

Greater Yellowstone Post-Fire Resource Assessment Committee. 1988. *Preliminary Burned Area Survey of Yellowstone National Park and Adjoining National Forests: Project Summary.* Mimeo.

Harrington, W., and A. C. Fisher. 1982. "Endangered Species." In P. R. Portney, ed., *Current Issues in Natural Resource Policy.* Washington, DC: Resources for the Future.

Hartzog, G. B., Jr. 1988. *Battling for the National Parks.* Mt. Kisco, NY: Moyer Bell.

Hunt, C. E., and V. Huser. 1988. *Down by the River: The Impact of Federal Water Projects and Policies on Biological Diversity.* Washington, DC: Island Press.

Jeffery, D. 1989. "Yellowstone: The Great Fires of 1988." *National Geographic* 175: 255–273.

Kusler, J. 1985. *Public/Private Parks and Management of Private Lands for Park Protection.* Madison, WI: University of Wisconsin Institute for Environmental Studies.

Land Trust Exchange. 1989. *1989 National Directory of Conservation Land Trusts.* Alexandria, VA: LTE.

Little, C. E. 1975. *Green-Line Parks: An Approach to Preserving Recreational Landscapes in Urban Areas.* Washington, DC: GPO.

Mackintosh, G., ed. 1989. *Preserving Communities and Corridors.* Washington, DC: Defenders of Wildlife.

Martin, W. D. 1986. *Trends in State Park Operations in the United States, 1975-1985: A Report to the National Association of State Park Directors.* Bloomington, IN: Indiana University, Leisure Research Institute.

Mason, R. J. 1991. *Environmental Conflict and Accommodation: Planning for the Pinelands National Reserve.* Philadelphia: Temple University Press.

Matzke, G., and D. Key. 1989. "Wildfire in the West's Woods: Fire Policy in the Wake of the Fires of 1988." *Focus* 39(2): 1–2, 18.

Mitchell, J. G. 1978. "The Re-Greening of America." *Audubon* 80: 29–52.

Myers, J. P., et al. 1987. "Conservation Strategy for Migratory Species." *American Scientist* 75: 19–26.

Myers, P., and S. N. Green. 1989. *State Parks in a New Era.* 3 vol. Washington, DC: Conservation Foundation.

Myers, P., and A. C. Reid. 1986. *State Parks in a New Era.* Washington, DC: Conservation Foundation.

Nash, R. 1982. *Wilderness and the American Mind.* 3d ed. New Haven: Yale University Press.

National Association of State Outdoor Recreation Liaison Officers. 1986. *1986 Survey of 50 Statewide Comprehensive Outdoor Recreation Plans* (SCORPS). Mimeo.

National Association of State Park Directors. 1988. *Annual Information Exchange: April 1988.* Mimeo.

National Parks and Conservation Association. 1988. *Investing in Park Futures: The National Park System Plan.* Washington, DC: NPCA.

NPS. Annual. *National Park Statistical Abstract.* Denver: NPS.

———. 1972. *Part Two of the National Park System Plan: Nature.* Washington, DC: GPO.

———. 1986. *National Trails Assessment.* Washington, DC: NPS.

———. 1987. *Summary: Status of the Wild and Scenic Rivers Program.* Washington, DC: NPS.

New Jersey Pinelands Commission. 1980. *Comprehensive Management Plan for the Pinelands National Reserve and Pinelands Area.* New Lisbon, NJ: NJPC.

OTA. 1987. *Technologies to Maintain Biological Diversity.* Washington, DC: GPO.

O'Gara, G. 1989. "Beyond the Burn." *Sierra* 74(1): 40–51.

Olson, W. K. 1988. *Natural Rivers and the Public Trust.* Washington, DC: American Rivers, BLM, NPS, and Forest Service.

Outdoor Recreation Resources Review Commission. 1962. *Outdoor Recreation for America.* Washington, DC: GPO.

President's Commission on American Outdoors. 1987. *Americans Outdoors: The Legacy, the Challenge.* Washington, DC: Island Press.

Pye, S. J. 1982. *Fire in America: A Cultural History of Rural and Wildland Fire.* Princeton, NJ: Princeton University Press.

Rails-to-Trails Conservancy. 1989. *Converting Rails to Trails.* Washington, DC: RTTC.

Reed, N., and D. Drabelle. 1984. *The United States Fish and Wildlife Service.* Boulder, CO: Westview.

Romme, W. H., and D. G. Despain. 1989. "The Yellowstone Fires." *Scientific American* 261(5): 37–46.

Runte, A. 1979. *National Parks: The American Experience.* Lincoln, NE: University of Nebraska Press.

Sax, J. 1980. *Mountains Without Handrails: Reflections on the National Parks.* Ann Arbor, MI: University of Michigan Press.

Schiff, S. D. 1986. "The Pine Barrens: Vast, Vital, Vulnerable." *Amicus Journal* 7(4): 28–33.

Simon, D. J., ed. 1988. *Our Common Lands: Defending the National Parks.* Washington, DC: Island Press.

Simpson, R. W. 1989. *The Fires of '88: Yellowstone Park & Montana in Flames.* Helena, MT: American Geographic Publishing.

Stone, C. D. 1975. *Should Trees Have Standing? Toward Legal Rights for Natural Objects.* Los Altos, CA: William Kaufmann.

Stone, R. D. 1989. "National Parks and Adjacent Lands." *Conservation Foundation Letter* 1–8.

Stottlemyer, R., et al. 1987. Special Section: "External Threats to Ecosystems of US National Parks." *Environmental Management* 11: 87–119.

Tober, J. A. 1989. *Wildlife and the Public Interest: Nonprofit Organizations and Federal Wildlife Policy.* New York: Praeger.

Wilderness Society. 1988. *Ten Most Endangered National Parks.* Washington, DC: Wilderness Society.

———. 1989. "The National Wilderness Preservation System." Map. Washington, DC: Wilderness Society.

Williams, T. 1989. "Sifting Ashes in Yellowstone." *Audubon* 91(6): 30–43.

Wolf, P. 1981. *Land in America: Its Value, Use and Control.* New York: Pantheon Books.

Wright, H., and A. W. Bailey. 1982. *Fire Ecology: United States and Southern Canada.* New York: Wiley.

Wuerthner, G. 1988. *Yellowstone and the Fires of Change.* Salt Lake City: Haggis House.

Yellowstone National Park. 1988. *The Yellowstone Fires: A Primer on the 1988 Fire Season.* West Yellowstone, MT: YNP.

———. 1989. *Yellowstone Fires 1988: A Special Supplement to Yellowstone Today.* West Yellowstone, MT: YNP.

16 NATURAL HAZARDS

Advisory Board on the Built Environment. 1983. *Multiple Hazard Mitigation.* Washington, DC: National Academy Press.

Advisory Committee on the International Decade for Natural Hazard Reduction. 1987. *Confronting Natural Disasters: An International Decade for Natural Hazard Reduction.* Washington, DC: National Academy Press.

———. 1989. *Reducing Disasters' Toll: The United States Decade for Natural Disaster Reduction.* Washington, DC: National Academy Press.

Alesch, D. J., and W. J. Petak. 1986. *The Politics and Economics of Earthquake Hazard Mitigation.* Boulder, CO: University of Colorado Institute of Behavioral Science.

Algermissen, S. T., et al. 1982. *Probabilistic Estimates of Maximum Acceleration and Velocity in Rock in the Contiguous United States.* Open-File Report 82-1033. Denver, CO: USGS.

Arnell, N. W. 1984. "Flood Hazard Management in the United States and the National Flood Insurance Program." *Geoforum* 15: 525–542.

Atkinson, W. 1989. *The Next New Madrid Earthquake.* Carbondale and Edwardsville, IL: Southern Illinois University Press.

Baker, E. J. 1979. "Geographical Variations in Hurricane Risks and Legislative Response." *Coastal Zone Management Journal* 5: 263–283.

Burby, R. J., and S. P. French. 1981. "Coping with Floods: The Land Use Management Paradox." *Journal of the American Planning Association* 47: 289–300.

Burton, I., R. W. Kates, and G. F. White. 1976. *The Environment as Hazard.* New York: Oxford University Press.

Coffman, J. L., C. A. von Hake, and C. W. Stover, eds. 1982. *Earthquake History of the United States.* NOAA and USGS Publication 41–1. Washington, DC: GPO.

Comfort, L. K. 1988. *Managing Disaster: Strategies and Policy Perspectives.* Durham, NC: Duke University Press.

Committee on Disasters and the Mass Media. 1980. *Disasters and the Mass Media.* Washington, DC: National Academy Press.

Committee on Ground Failure Hazards. 1985. *Reducing Losses from Landsliding in the United States.* Washington, DC: National Academy Press.

Crandall, D. R., and D. R. Mullineaux. 1978. *Potential Hazards from Future Eruptions of Mount St. Helens Volcano.* USGS Bulletin 1383-C. Washington, DC: GPO.

Drabek, T. E. 1986. *Human System Responses to Disaster: An Inventory of Sociological Findings.* New York: Springer-Verlag.

Earthquake Engineering Research Institute. 1986. *Reducing Earthquake Hazards: Lessons Learned from Earthquakes.* El Cerrito, CA: EERI.

Fitzsimmons, A. R. 1984. *Natural Hazards and Land Use Planning: An Annotated Bibliography.* Boulder, CO: Natural Hazards Research and Applications Information Center.

Foster, H. D. 1980. *Disaster Planning: The Preservation of Life and Property.* New York: Springer-Verlag.

Foxworthy, B. L., and M. Hill. 1982. *Volcanic Eruptions of 1980 at Mount St. Helens: The First 100 Days.* USGS Professional Paper 1249. Washington, DC: GPO.

Friesema, H. P., et al. 1979. *Aftermath: Communities After Natural Disasters.* Beverly Hills, CA: Sage.

Fujita, T. T. 1987. *U.S. Tornadoes. Part I: 70-Year Statistics.* Chicago: University of Chicago, Department of Geophysical Sciences.

Ganse, R. A., and J. B. Nelson. 1981. *Catalog of Significant Earthquakes: 2000 BC–1979* (with update, 1980–1987). Report SE-27. Boulder, CO: National Geophysical Data Center.

GAO. 1988. *Statistics on the National Flood Insurance Program.* GAO/RCED-88-155FS. Washington, DC: GPO.

Godschalk, D. R., D. J. Brower, and T. Beatley. 1989. *Catastrophic Coastal Storms.* Durham, NC: Duke University Press.

Gordon, P. D. 1982. *Special Statistical Summary: Deaths, Injuries, and Property Loss by Type of Disaster, 1970–1980.* Washington, DC: Federal Emergency Management Agency.

Greene, M. R., et al. 1981. "The March 1980 Eruptions of Mt. St. Helens: Citizen Perceptions of Volcano Threat." *Disasters* 5: 49–66.

Haas, J. E., R. W. Kates, and M. Bowden, eds. 1977. *Reconstruction Following Disaster.* Cambridge, MA: MIT Press.

Harris, S. L. 1980. *Fire & Ice: The Cascade Volcanoes.* Seattle: The Mountaineers.

Hays, W. W., ed. 1981. *Facing Geologic and Hydrologic Hazards: Earth-Science Considerations.* USGS Professional Paper 1240-B. Washington, DC: GPO.

Hebert, P. J., G. Taylor, and R. A. Case. 1984. *Hurricane Experience Levels of Coastal County Populations: Texas to Maine.* Miami, FL: National Hurricane Center.

Keller, S. A. C., ed. 1987. *Mount St. Helens: Five Years Later.* Cheney, WA: Eastern Washington University Press.

Kimball, V., and K. Hutton. 1981. *Earthquake Ready.* Culver City, CA: Peace Press.

Kusler, J. A. 1982. *Regulation of Flood Hazard Areas to Reduce Flood Losses.* Washington, DC: U.S. Water Resources Council.

Lipman, P. W., and D. R. Mullineaux, eds. 1981. *The 1980 Eruptions of Mount St. Helens.* USGS Professional Paper 1250. Washington, DC: GPO.

May, P. J., and W. Williams. 1986. *Disaster Policy Implementation: Managing Programs under Shared Governance.* New York: Plenum.

Mitchell, J. K. 1974. "Natural Hazards Research." In I. R. Manners and M. W. Mikesell, eds., *Perspectives on Environment.* Washington, DC: Association of American Geographers.

———. 1984. "Hazard Perception Studies: Convergent Concerns and Divergent Approaches During the Past Decade." In T. F. Saarinen, D. Seamon, and J. L. Sell, eds., *Environmental Perception and Behavior: An Inventory and Prospect.* Chicago: University of Chicago, Department of Geography.

———. 1989. "Confronting Natural Disasters: An International Decade for Natural Hazards Reduction." *Environment* 30(2): 25–29.

National Research Council. 1983. *Multiple Hazard Mitigation.* Washington, DC: National Academy Press.

———. 1985. *Reducing Losses from Landsliding in the United States.* Washington, DC: National Academy Press.

Neumann, C. J., et al. 1987. *Tropical Cyclones of the North Atlantic Ocean, 1871–1976.* Asheville, NC: National Climatic Data Center.

Petak, W. J., and A. A. Atkisson. 1982. *Natural Hazard Risk Assessment and Public Policy.* New York: Springer-Verlag.

Peters, B. E. 1988. *Natural Hazard Deaths in 1987 in the United States: A Summary.* Fort Worth, TX: National Weather Service.

Platt, R. H., G. Macinko, and K. Hammond. 1983. "Federal Environmental Management: Some Land-use Legacies of the 1970s." In J. W. House, ed., *United States Public Policy: A Geographical View.* Oxford: Clarendon Press.

President's Interagency Drought Policy Committee. 1988. *The Drought of 1988: Final Report.* Washington, DC: PIDPC.

President's Office of Emergency Preparedness. 1972. *Disaster Preparedness.* Washington, DC: GPO.

Radbruch-Hall, D. H., et al. 1982. *Landslide Overview Map of the Conterminous United States.* USGS Professional Paper 1183. Washington, DC: GPO.

Ritchie, D. *Superquake! Why Earthquakes Occur and When the Big One Will Hit Southern California.* New York: Crown.

Rosenfeld, C. L. 1980. "Observations on

the Mount St. Helens Eruption." *American Scientist* 68: 494–509.

Rossi, P., J. Wright, and E. Weber-Burdin. 1982. *Natural Hazards and Public Choice: The State and Local Politics of Hazard Mitigation.* New York: Academic Press.

Rubin, C., et al. 1986. *Summary of Major Natural Disaster Incidents in the U.S.: 1965 to 1985.* Washington, DC: Federal Emergency Management Agency.

Saarinen, T. F., and J .L. Sell. 1985. *Warning and Response to the Mount St. Helens Eruption.* Albany, NY: State University of New York Press.

Schuster, R. L., and R. W. Fleming. 1986. "Economic Losses and Fatalities Due to Landslides." *Bulletin of the Association of Engineering Geologists* 23: 11–28.

Simkin, T., et al. 1981. *Volcanoes of the World.* Stroudsburg, PA: Hutchinson Ross.

Simpson, R. H., and M. B. Lawrence. 1971. *Atlantic Hurricane Frequencies Along the U.S. Coastline.* NOAA TM NWS SR-58. Springfield, VA: NTIS.

Thompson, S. A., and G. F. White. 1985. "A National Floodplain Map." *Journal of Soil and Water Conservation* 40: 417–419.

Tilling, R. I. No date. *Eruptions of Mount St. Helens: Past, Present, and Future.* USGS. Washington, DC: GPO.

———. 1982. *Volcanoes.* Washington, DC: USGS.

Trenberth, K. E., G. W. Branstator, and P. A. Arkin. 1988. "Origins of the 1988 North American Drought." *Science* 242: 1640–1645.

USGS. 1982. *Goals and Tasks of the Landslide Part of a Ground-Failure Hazards Reduction Program.* Circular 880. Washington, DC: GPO.

———. 1988. *Probabilities of Large Earthquakes Occurring in California on the San Andreas Fault.* Open-file report 88-0398. Denver: USGS.

Warrick, R. A., et al. 1981. *Four Communities Under Ash: After Mount St. Helens.* Monograph 34. Boulder, CO: University of Colorado Institute of Behavioral Science.

White, G. F. 1945. *Human Adjustment to Floods: A Geographical Approach to the Flood Problem in the United States.* Chicago: University of Chicago, Department of Geography.

———, ed. 1974. *Natural Hazards: Local, National, Global.* New York: Oxford University Press.

White, G. F., et al. 1976. *Natural Hazard Management in Coastal Areas.* Washington, DC: NOAA.

Whittow, J. 1979. *Disasters: The Anatomy of*

Environmental Hazards. Athens, GA: University of Georgia Press.

Wilhite, D. A., and W. Easterling, eds. 1987. *Planning for Drought: Toward a Reduction of Societal Vulnerability.* Boulder, CO: Westview.

Wright, J. D., et al. 1979. *After the Clean-Up: Long-Range Effects of Natural Disasters.* Beverly Hills, CA: Sage.

Wright, J. D., and P. H. Rossi, eds. 1981. *Social Science and Natural Hazards.* Cambridge, MA: Abt Books.

17 ENVIRONMENTAL ECONOMICS AND POLITICS

Abbey, E. 1975. *The Monkey Wrench Gang.* New York: Avon.

Adams, J. H., et al. 1985. *An Environmental Agenda for the Future.* Washington, DC: Island Press.

Andrews, R. N. L. 1980. "Class Politics or Democratic Reform: Environmentalism and American Political Institutions." *Natural Resources Journal* 20: 221–241.

Albrecht, S. L. 1972. "Environment Social Movements and Counter-Movements: An Overview and an Illustration." *Journal of Voluntary Action Research* 1(4): 2–11.

Bernau, D., C. Pattarozzi, and M. N. Rees. 1990. *State Issues 1990: A Survey of Priority Issues for State Legislatures.* Denver: National Conference of State Legislatures.

BNA Editorial Staff. 1988. *U.S. Environmental Laws: 1988 Edition.* Washington, DC: Bureau of National Affairs.

Borrelli, P., ed. 1988. *Crossroads: Environmental Priorities for the Future.* Washington, DC: Island Press.

Brown, R. S., and L .E. Garner. 1988. *Resource Guide to State Environmental Management.* Lexington, KY: Council of State Governments.

Clark, D. 1985. *Post-Industrial America: A Geographical Perspective.* New York: Methuen.

Commoner, B. 1987. "A Reporter at Large: The Environment." *New Yorker* June 15: 46–71.

Conservation Foundation. 1987a. *State-by-State Environmental Data Summaries.* Washington, DC: CF.

———. 1987b. *State of the Environment: A View Toward the Nineties.* Washington, DC: CF.

Cook, B. J. 1988. *Bureaucratic Politics and Regulatory Reform: The EPA and Emissions Trading.* Westport, CT: Greenwood.

Council of State Governments Staff. 1988. *Book of the States, 1988–89.* Lexington, KY: Council of State Governments.

Ehrlich, E. M., T. J. Lutton, and J. B. Thomasian. 1985. *Environmental Regulations and Economic Efficiency.* Washington, DC: CBO.

Elazar, D. J. 1984. *American Federalism: A View From the States.* 3d ed. New York: Harper & Row.

EPA. 1987. *Unfinished Business: A Comparative Assessment of Environmental Problems: Overview Report.* EPA/230/2-87/025a. Washington, DC: EPA.

———. 1988. *Future Risk: Research Strategies for the 1990s.* SAB-EC-88-040. Washington, DC: EPA.

———. 1989a. "Protecting the Earth: Are Our Institutions Up to It?" *EPA Journal.* (Secial issue). 15(4).

———. 1989b. "Who Needs the Feds: Environmental Success Stories from Grassroots America." *EPA Journal.* (Special issue). 15(6).

———. 1990. "Earth Day." *EPA Journal.* (Special issue). 16(1).

Farber, K. D., and G. L. Rutledge. 1986. "Pollution Abatement and Control Expenditures." *Survey of Current Business* 66(7): 94–105.

Friends of the Earth, et al. 1982. *Ronald Reagan & the American Environment.* San Francisco: Brick House.

Fulton, W. 1986. "Silicon Strips." *Planning* 52(5): 8–12.

Herbers, J. 1987. "Take Me Home, Country Roads." *Planning* 53(11): 4–8.

Hoffmann, G. W., ed. 1981. *Federalism and Regional Development: Case Studies on the Experience in the United States and the Federal Republic of Germany.* Austin, TX: University of Texas Press.

House, J. W., ed. 1983. *United States Public Policy: A Geographical View.* Oxford: Clarendon Press.

Jessup, D. H. 1988. *Guide to State Environmental Programs.* Washington, DC: Bureau of National Affairs.

Kamieniecki, S., R. O'Brien, and M. Clarke. 1986. *Controversies in Environmental Policy.* Albany, NY: State University of New York Press.

King, J. F., ed. 1988. "Election 88." *Sierra.* (Special issue). 73(6).

Knox, P. L., et al. 1988. *The United States: A Contemporary Human Geography.* Essex, UK: Longman.

Kraft, M. E., and N. J. Vig. 1984. "Environmental Policy in the Reagan Presidency."

Political Science Quarterly 99: 415–439.

Lake, R. W., ed. 1987. *Resolving Locational Conflict.* New Brunswick, NJ: Rutgers University Center for Urban Policy Research.

Lamm, R., and T. Barron. 1988. "The Environmental Agenda for the Next Administration." *Environment* 30(4): 12–15, 30–35.

League of Conservation Voters. 1989 and other years. *National Environmental Scorecard.* Washington, DC: LCV.

Magder, R. 1990. *America in the 21st Century: Environmental Concerns.* Washington, DC: Population Reference Bureau.

Maize, K. P., ed. 1988. *Blueprint for the Environment.* Salt Lake City: Howe Brothers.

Milbrath, L. W. 1984. *Environmentalists: Vanguard for a New Society.* Albany, NY: State University of New York Press.

Mitchell, R. C. 1980. "How 'Soft,' 'Deep,' or 'Left'? Present Constituencies in the Environmental Movement for Certain World Views." *Natural Resources Journal* 20: 345–358.

Morrison, D. E., and R. E. Dunlap. 1986. "Environmentalism and Elitism: A Conceptual and Empirical Analysis." *Environmental Management* 10: 581–589.

National Parks and Conservation Association. 1988. *National Parks and Conservation Association: Five-Year Plan.* Washington, DC: NPCA.

O'Hare, M. 1977. "Not on My Block, You Don't." *Public Policy* 25: 407–458.

O'Hare, M., L. Bacow, and D. Sanderson. 1983. *Facility Siting and Public Opposition.* New York: Van Nostrand.

Paehilke, R. C. 1989. *Environmentalism and the Future of Progressive Politics.* New Haven, CT: Yale University Press.

Petulla, J. 1987. *Environmental Protection in the United States: Industry, Agencies, Environmentalists.* San Francisco: San Francisco Study Center.

Pierce, N., and J. Hagstrom. 1983. *The Book of America: Inside the Fifty States Today.* New York: Norton.

Portney, P. R. 1988. "Reforming Environmental Regulation: Three Modest Proposals." *Issues in Science and Technology* 5(2): 74–81.

———. 1990. "Taking the Measure of Environmental Regulation." *Resources* 99: 2–4.

Renew America. 1989. *The State of the States: 1989.* Washington, DC: Renew America.

Ridley, S. 1987, 1988. *The State of the States.* Washington, DC: Fund for Renewable Energy and the Environment.

Rosenbaum, W. A. 1977. *The Politics of Environmental Concern.* 2d ed. New York: Holt, Rinehart, and Winston.

Schnaiberg, A. 1977. "Politics, Participation and Pollution: The 'Environmental Movement'." In J. Walton and D. E. Carns, *Cities in Change: Studies on the Urban Condition.* 2d ed. Boston: Allyn and Bacon.

Schwab, R. M. 1988. "Environmental Federalism." *Resources* 92: 6–9.

Seley, J. *The Politics of Public Facility Planning.* Lexington, MA: Lexington Books.

Siegel, L. 1984. "High-Tech Pollution." *Sierra* 69(6): 58–64.

Sills, D. L. 1975. "The Environmental Movement and Its Critics." *Human Ecology* 3: 1–41.

Speth, J. G. 1988. *Environmental Pollution: A Long-Term Perspective.* Washington, DC: World Resources Institute.

Stavins, R. N. 1989. "Harnessing Market Forces to Protect the Environment." *Environment* 31(1): 5–7, 28–35.

Sussman, F. E. 1988. *Environmental Federalism: Allocating Responsibilities for Environmental Protection.* Washington, DC: CBO.

Tucker, W. 1982. *Progress and Privilege: America in the Age of Environmentalism.* New York: Anchor/Doubleday.

Udall, S. L. 1988. *The Quiet Crisis and the Next Generation.* Layton, UT: Gibbs-Smith.

Vig, N. J., and M. E. Kraft. 1984. *Environmental Policy in the 1980s: Reagan's New Agenda.* Washington, DC: Congressional Quarterly, Inc.

Wagendorp, J. 1988. "Conservation Land-Use Programs and Political Cultures in the United States: A Pilot Study." Paper presented at meeting of the Association of American Geographers, Phoenix, April 6–10.

Wenner, L. M. 1982. *The Environmental Decade in Court.* Bloomington, IN: Indiana University Press.

18 ENVIRONMENTAL FUTURES

Abrahamson, D. E., ed. 1989. *The Challenge of Global Warming.* Washington, DC: Island Press.

Barth, M. C., and J. G. Titus, eds. 1984. *Greenhouse Effect and Sea Level Rise.* New York: Van Nostrand Reinhold.

Beardsley, T. 1989. "Not So Hot: New Studies Question Estimates of Global Warming." *Scientific American* 261(5): 17–18.

Benedick, R. E. 1989. "The Ozone Protocol: A New Global Diplomacy." *Conservation Foundation Letter* 4: 1–8.

Bennett, J. O., et al. 1984. "Foreseeable Effects of Nuclear Detonations on a Local Environment: Boulder County, CO." *Environmental Conservation* 11: 155–165.

Berg, P., ed. 1975. *Reinhabiting a Separate Country: A Bioregional Anthology of Northern California.* San Francisco: Planet Drum Foundation.

Berner, R. A., and A. C. Lasaga. 1989. "Modeling the Geochemical Carbon Cycle." *Scientific American* 260(3): 74–81.

Bolin, B., et al. 1986. *The Greenhouse Effect: Climatic Change and Ecosystems.* SCOPE 29. Chichester, UK: Wiley.

Bunge, W. 1988. *The Nuclear War Atlas.* Oxford and New York: Basil Blackwell.

Callenbach, E. 1975. *Ecotopia: The Notebooks and Reports of William Weston.* Berkeley, CA: Banyan Tree.

———. 1981. *Ecotopia Emerging.* Berkeley, CA: Banyan Tree.

Crutzen, P. 1985. "The Global Environment After Nuclear War." *Environment* 27(8): 6–11, 34–37.

Crutzen, P., and J. Birks. 1982. "The Atmosphere After a Nuclear War: Twilight at Noon." *Ambio* 11: 114–125.

Daly, H. E. 1977. *Steady-State Economics: The Economics of Biophysical Equilibrium and Moral Growth.* San Francisco: W. H. Freeman.

———, ed. 1980. *Economics, Ecology, and Ethics.* San Francisco: W. H. Freeman.

Devall, B., and G. Sessions. 1985. *Deep Ecology: Living as if Nature Mattered.* Layton, UT: Gibbs M. Smith.

Dotto, L. 1986. *Planet Earth in Jeopardy: Environmental Consequences of Nuclear War.* Chichester, UK: Wiley.

Dudek, D. J. 1988. *Offsetting New CO_2 Emissions.* New York: Environmental Defense Fund.

Ehrlich, P., et al. 1984. *The Cold and the Dark: The World After Nuclear War.* New York: W. W. Norton.

———. 1983. "Long-term Biological Consequences of Nuclear War." *Science* 222: 1293–1300.

Ember, L. R., et al. 1986. "Tending the Global Commons." *Chemical and Engineering News* 64(47): 14–64.

"The Environmental Consequences of Nuclear War: A New Scientific Consensus from SCOPE and the United Nations." 1988. *Environment.* (Special issue). 30(5).

EPA. 1983. *Can We Delay a Global Warming?* Washington, DC: GPO.

————. 1989. "The Greenhouse Effect: How It Can Change Our Lives." *EPA Journal*. (Special issue). 15(1).

————. 1990. "The Greenhouse Effect: What Can We Do About It?" *EPA Journal*. (Special issue). 16(2).

Fiske, S. T., et al. 1983. "Images of Nuclear War." *Journal of Social Issues*. (Special issue). 39: 1–97.

Gallant, A. L. 1989. *Regionalization as a Tool for Managing Environmental Resources*. EPA/600/3-89/060. Corvallis, OR: NSI Technology Services Corporation and EPA.

Garreau, J. 1981. *The Nine Nations of North America*. Boston: Houghton Mifflin.

Graedel, T. E. 1989. "Regional and Global Impacts on the Biosphere." *Environment* 31(1): 8–13, 36–41.

Graedel, T. E., and P. J. Crutzen. 1989. "The Changing Atmosphere." *Scientific American* 261(3): 58–68.

Hansen, J. E. 1988. "The Greenhouse Effect: Impacts on Current Global Temperature and Regional Heat Waves." Statement to House of Representatives Subcommittee, July 7.

Harwell, M. A. 1984. *Nuclear Winter: The Human and Environmental Consequences of Nuclear War*. Bedford, MA: Springer Verlag.

Harwell, M. A., and T. C. Hutchinson. 1985. *Environmental Consequences of Nuclear War*. Volume II. Ecological and Agricultural Effects. New York: Wiley.

Harwell, M. A., and C. C. Harwell. 1987. "Updating the 'Nuclear Winter' Debate." *Bulletin of the Atomic Scientists* 43(8): 42–44.

Hewitt, K. 1983. "Place Annihilation: Area Bombing and the Fate of Urban Places." *Annals, Association of American Geographers* 73: 257–284.

Hoffman, J. S., and M. J. Gibbs. 1988. *Future Concentrations of Stratospheric Chlorine and Bromine*. EPA/400/1-88/005. Washington, DC: EPA.

Houghton, R. A., and G. M. Woodwell. 1989. "Global Climatic Change." *Scientific American* 260(4): 36–44.

Hughes, R. M. 1989. "Ecoregional Biological Criteria." In EPA, *Water Quality Standards for the 21st Century*. Washington, DC: EPA.

Hughes, R. M., and D. P. Larse. 1988. "Ecoregions: An Approach to Surface Water Protection." *Journal of the Water Pollution Control Federation* 57: 912–915.

Jacobs, J. 1961. *The Death and Life of Great American Cities*. New York: Random House.

Jacobson, J. L. 1989. "Swept Away." *World Watch* 2(1): 20–26.

Jager, J. 1988. "Anticipating Climatic Change: Priorities for Action." *Environment* 30(7): 13–15, 30–33.

Katz, A. M. 1982. *Life After Nuclear War: The Economic and Social Impacts of Nuclear Attacks on the United States*. Cambridge, MA: Ballinger.

Leaning, J., and L. Keyes, eds. 1983. *The Counterfeit Ark: Crisis Relocation for Nuclear War*. Cambridge, MA: Ballinger.

Lovins, A. B. 1977. *Soft Energy Paths: Toward a Durable Peace*. New York: Harper & Row.

Lyman, F., et al. 1990. *The Greenhouse Trap: What We're Doing to the Atmosphere and How We Can Slow Global Warming*. Washington, DC: World Resources Institute.

MacCracken, M. C., and F. M. Luther, eds. 1985a. *Detecting the Climatic Effects of Increasing Carbon Dioxide*. DOE/ER-0237. Springfield, VA: NTIS.

————, eds. 1985b. *Projecting the Climatic Effects of Increasing Carbon Dioxide*. Springfield, VA: NTIS.

Machado, S., and R. Piltz. 1988. *Reducing the Rate of Global Warming: The States' Role*. Washington, DC: Renew America.

MacKenzie, J. J. 1988. *Breathing Easier: Taking Action on Climate Change, Air Pollution, and Energy Insecurity*. Washington, DC: World Resources Institute.

Malone, T. F., and R. Corell. 1989. "Mission to Planet Earth Revisited: An Update on Studies of Global Climate Change." *Environment* 31(3): 6–11, 31–35.

Mason, R. J., W. D. Solecki, and E .L. Lotstein. 1987. "Comments on 'On "Bioregionalism" and "Watershed Consciousness."'" *Professional Geographer* 39: 67–68.

Mintzer, I. M., and W. R. Moomaw. 1990. *Escaping the Heat Trap: Probing the Prospects for a Stable Environment*. Washington, DC: World Resources Institute.

Mintzer, I. M., W. R. Moomaw, and A. S. Miller. 1990. *Protecting the Ozone Shield: Strategies for Phasing Out CFCs During the 1990s*. Washington, DC: World Resources Institute.

National Research Council. 1983. *Changing Climate*. Washington, DC: National Academy Press.

————. 1985. *The Effects on the Atmosphere of a Major Nuclear Exchange*. Washington, DC: National Academy Press.

————. 1989a. *Global Environmental Change*. Washington, DC: National Academy Press.

————. 1989b. *Ozone Depletion, Greenhouse Gases, and Climate Change*. Washington, DC: National Academy Press.

OTA. 1979. *The Effects of Nuclear War*. Washington, DC: GPO.

Omernik, J. M. 1987. "Ecoregions of the Conterminous United States." *Annals of the Association of American Geographers* 77: 118–125.

Parsons, J. J. 1985. "On 'Bioregionalism' and 'Watershed Consciousness.'" *Professional Geographer* 37: 1–6.

Pepper, D. 1984. *The Roots of Modern Environmentalism*. London: Croom Helm.

Pepper, D., and A. Jenkins, eds. 1985. *The Geography of Peace and War*. Oxford: Basil Blackwell.

Pittock, A B., et al. 1985. *Environmental Consequences of Nuclear War, Volume 1: Physical and Atmospheric Effects*. New York: Wiley.

Platt, R. H. 1984. "The Planner and Nuclear Crisis Relocation." *Journal of the American Planning Association* 50: 259–260.

Roan, S. 1989. *Ozone Crisis: The 15-Year Evolution of a Sudden Global Emergency*. New York: Wiley.

Rosenberg, N. J., et al., eds. 1989. *Greenhouse Warming: Abatement and Adaptation*. Washington, DC: Resources for the Future.

Sagan, C. 1983. "Nuclear Winter: Global Consequences of Multiple Nuclear Explosions." *Science* 222: 1283–1292.

————. 1985. "Nuclear Winter: A Report from the World Scientific Community." *Environment* 27(8): 12–15, 38–39.

Sale, K. 1985. *Dwellers in the Land: The Bioregional Vision*. San Francisco: Sierra Club Books.

Schneider, S. H. 1989a. "The Changing Climate." *Scientific American* 261(3): 70–79.

————. 1989b. *Global Warming: Are We Entering the Greenhouse Century?* San Francisco: Sierra Club Books.

————. 1989c. "The Greenhouse Effect: Science and Policy." *Science* 243: 771–781.

Schneider, S. H., and S. L. Thompson. 1988. "Simulating the Climatic Effects of Nuclear War." *Nature* 333: 221–227.

Schumacher, E. F. 1973. *Small is Beautiful: A Study of Economics as if People Mattered*. London: Sphere Books.

Sedjo, R. A. 1989. "Forests: A Tool to Moderate Global Warming?" *Environment* 31(1): 14–20.

Seidel, S., and D. Keyes. 1983. *Can We Delay a Greenhouse Warming?* Washington, DC: EPA.

Sessions, G. 1987. "The Deep Ecology Movement: A Review." *Environmental Review* 11: 105–126.

Shea, C. P. 1989. "Mending the Earth's Shield." *World Watch* 2(1): 27–34.

Smith, J. B., and D. A. Tirpak. 1989. *The Potential Effects of Global Climate Change on the United States: Draft Report to Congress*. Washington, DC: EPA.

Thompson, S. L., and S. H. Schneider. 1986. "Nuclear Winter Reappraised." *Foreign Affairs* 64: 981–1005.

Titus, J. G., ed. 1986. *Greenhouse Effect, Sea Level Rise and Coastal Wetlands*. EPA-230-05-86-013. Washington, DC: EPA.

Tonn, B. E. 1986. "500-Year Planning: A Speculative Provocation." *Journal of the American Planning Association* 52: 185–193.

Trexel, M. C., and W. R. Moomaw. *Reforesting America: Combatting Global Warming?* Washington, DC: World Resources Institute.

Turco, R., et al. 1987. "Nuclear Winter Revisited." *Amicus Journal* 9(1): 4–6.

Walljasper, J. 1989. "Can Green Politics Take Root in the U.S.?" *Utne Reader* 35: 140–143.

Ward, J., R. Hardt, and T. Kuhnle. 1989. *Farming in the Greenhouse: What Global Warming Means for American Agriculture*. New York: NRDC.

Index